The
Hump

BURMA ROAD

Kunming

CHINA

YUNNAN

king

R Mekong

Kengtung

Hanoi

Haiphong

iang Rai

iang Mai

HAINAN

INDO-CHINA

R Mekong

Phitsanulok

SIAM
(THAILAND)

R Mekong

goda

BANGKOK

BURMA 1942: The Japanese Invasion

BURMA 1942:
The Japanese Invasion

Both sides tell the Story
of a Savage Jungle War

Ian Lyall Grant and Kazuo Tamayama

THE ZAMPI PRESS
Chichester, West Sussex

First published in 1999 by The Zampi Press,
6, St Martin's Square, Chichester,
West Sussex, PO19 1NT.

British Library Cataloguing in Publication Data
Lyall Grant, Ian, 1915-
Burma 1942: The Japanese Invasion: both sides tell the story of a savage jungle war.
1. World War, 1939-1945-Campaigns-Burma
I. Title II. Tamayama, Kazuo
940.5'425
ISBN 0-9521083-1-3

Designed, typeset and produced by Articulate, Emsworth, Hampshire.
Printed and bound by in the UK by The Cromwell Press, Trowbridge, Wiltshire.
Book jacket design by Diana Mead.
Maps by The Map Studio, Romsey, Hampshire.
Index by Michael Forder BA Nottingham, Weymouth, Dorset.

This book is dedicated to those gallant soldiers and airmen of many nationalities who gave their lives for their beliefs in the First Burma Campaign in 1941/42.

CONTENTS

PART ONE
The Struggle to Hold Rangoon

PART TWO
The Long Retreat

LIST OF MAPS

APPENDICES

ILLUSTRATIONS

PART ONE

ACKNOWLEDGEMENTS

Many people have been kind enough to help me in this attempt to produce a balanced and truthful account of the First Burma Campaign. Of course my co-author, Dr Kazuo Tamayama, has been the chief contributor. His widespread research among Japanese records and his many Japanese contacts have provided the information from 'the other side of the hill' which is essential to an objective account. His swift answers to the many queries I have raised and his shrewd comments have helped immensely with the narrative.

On the British side, among those who have helped me (and most of whom were present in this campaign though sadly not all still survive), I am particularly grateful to George Aitchison, Charles Couborough, Major Dicky Day, Major Nigel Elsworth, Lieutenant-Colonel Patric Emerson, Antony Foucar, Major Alan Fradgley, John Fuller, Lieutenant-Colonel Robert Grant, Major Roy Hudson, Squadron-Leader Tony Jutsum, Professor Desmond Kelly, Major Bruce Kinloch, Eustace Lord, Leon Lubett, Lieutenant-Colonel Dick McCaig, Colonel Richard Mace, Lieutenant-Colonel Charles MacFetridge, Brigadier John Randle, Major-General Jim Robertson, Colonel Charles Searle MD, Major 'Plug' Smith, Major-General Dennis Swan, Brigadier Charles Swift, Lieutenant-Colonel Peter Tyrrwhit-Drake, Brigadier W.H. Wilberforce and Sir Eric Yarrow.

Britain has a wonderful store of historical records and, with hardly any exceptions, they are very well-organised and controlled by staff who go out of their way to help the diligent enquirer. The Public Record Office at Kew, that treasure-house of official records, the Imperial War Museum, the National Army Museum and the Liddell-Hart Centre for Military Archives at King's College London gave me much help and I am greatly indebted to them for permission to quote from some of their records. A number of Army regimental museums also gave me significant help for which I am very grateful, notably the Queen's Own Hussars Regimental Museum at Warwick, the Tank Museum at Bovington, the Royal Inniskilling Fusiliers Museum at Enniskillen, the Cameronians (Scottish Rifles) at the Low Park Museum at Hamilton and the Gurkha Museum at Winchester.

Among a number of libraries who took much trouble to obtain books for me the West Sussex County Library and the marvellous old Prince Consort's Library at Aldershot were particularly helpful.

On the Japanese side, Dr Tamayama had many books in his own collection but has asked me to acknowledge the great help he received from the Library of the War History Department at the Japanese Ministry of Defence and the National Congress Library, both in Tokyo.

Japanese veterans' associations are very well organised and he is deeply indebted to the many survivors of the Burma campaigns who have helped him, notably Mr Satoru Inazawa and Mr Toshihiro Matsumura, (both 112 R), Mr Kenji Niina and Mr Sadao Nakata, (both 143 R), Mr Koji Kawamata (214 R), Mr Kazuo Imai (215 R), Mr Ichiro Tamogami (33 Div Engrs) Major-General Renichi Misawa (33 Mtn Arty), Mr Toshiaki Ishigami (18 Hy Fd Arty), Mr Shuichiro Yoshino (11 B), Major-General Saitaro Ushiyama (18 D), Dr Kenji Sudo (MD), Mr Yoshito Yasuda (5 Air D) and to Mr Takeo Harada, son of Colonel Harada (215 R), for some interesting photographs. To these I must add Mr Takuo Isobe (215 R) for his gift of the 215 Regimental History and a number of photographs, Mr Yoshishige Matsuda (214 R) for his gift of the 214 Regimental History and Mr Kiyomichi Takemoto (154 R) for the gift of many books about the Burma War which have proved most helpful. *(R = Regiment. D = Division. MD = Medical Corps B = Hygiene.)*

Finally I join with my co-author in expressing our deep gratitude to our long-suffering wives, Jenny and Sazanami, for their forbearance over the past three years while their husbands were absorbed for long hours in the production of this book.

Ian Lyall Grant
Chichester, 1998.

The co-authors at work.

FOREWORD

by Field Marshal Lord Carver, GCB, CBE, DSO, MC

Major-General Ian Lyall Grant, with the co-operation of Dr Kazuo Tamayama, has, in this book, written what must henceforth be regarded as the most authoritative account of an unfortunate campaign, in which he served himself as a 26-year old Major in the Bengal Sappers of the Indian Army. There have been other accounts, but none which have benefited so much both from the detailed representation of the Japanese action and from the author's personal experience. The story of this short, disastrous campaign, lasting from January to May 1942, is beset by controversy: from the strategic decisions which led, first, to Burma being left virtually defenceless, and then to a succession of *ad hoc* panic measures to try and save it; to the performance of the Burmese, Indian, Gurkha and British soldiers who fought against great odds in a vain attempt to implement those decisions; and then to withdraw, in conditions of great hardship, to India.

The authors deal fairly with these controversies and make clear that the British forces were unprepared and ill-equipped in every way for the tasks they were called upon to perform, in contrast to their Japanese opponents, whose military capability, in every sense, had been grossly underestimated. They also make clear that, although there were failures at every level, the sweeping allegations, made at the time and since, of a general lack of fighting spirit were, with the exception of the Burmese troops, unjustified. Major-General Lyall Grant's story, admirably supplemented by excellent sketch maps, records many instances of great heroism, endurance and imaginative action by British, Indian, Gurkha and some Burmese soldiers. Many of the same soldiers demonstrated those qualities again when they reconquered Burma three years later.

This book makes an important contribution to the history of the Second World War.

Michael Carver
FM

INTRODUCTION

In his dispatch of 14 July 1942 General Sir Archibald Wavell summed up the First Burma Campaign with his accustomed brevity:

"The loss of Burma has been from a strategical point of view our most serious reverse of the Japanese war. It has deprived our Chinese allies of a flow of munitions to continue their long resistance; it has made the establishment of air bases within effective range of Japan a matter of extreme difficulty; it has exposed India to a serious threat of invasion; and it has had a disastrous effect on British prestige in the East. The reasons for this reverse merit some examination."

In 1943 a tremendous and successful effort was put into learning and applying the lessons learnt in 1942, but it was not the time to examine the reasons for Burma's loss and the victories of later years soon overshadowed the earlier defeats. So it is not surprising that there are still some myths about why Burma fell in 1942. Hence the aim of this book, using the many sources from both sides now available, is to tell for the first time the true story. It is a highly dramatic tale and full of surprises; for the British were unprepared for a war in Burma and totally ignorant about their adversary. It is a harrowing tale, for this immensely long retreat, under a blazing sun and punctuated by a series of savage battles, was one of the most physically arduous campaigns of World War II. It is also a melancholy tale, for Burma could have been successfully defended if Winston Churchill had given its defence the higher priority that his Army advisers wished. The failure to defend Burma against invasion was not only, as soon became apparent, a major strategic error, but also a dereliction of Imperial duty whose memory even eventual victory could not efface.

Historically there were many unique features. It was the longest retreat that British forces had ever made, or are ever likely to make. It was the first time that the British had fought with the Chinese against a foreign foe. For three months the British fought without a line of communication and for two months without any air support. It was the opening phase in what was to become the longest campaign of World War II, and it was a significant part of the only war in which the British have ever fought against the Japanese, their allies in World War I.

Everyone who has fought in a war knows that few people really know what happens. Even at battalion headquarters, and certainly at higher levels the truth of the fighting is already distorted. As General Sir Ian Hamilton wrote in 1908.

"On the actual day of battle naked truths may be picked up for the asking; by the following morning they have already begun to get into their uniforms."

Hence to attempt to write a true campaign history more than fifty years after the event has its problems. This is particularly true of 1942 in Burma where many of the records written at the time were destroyed. Those written later are inevitably massaged towards a suitable record for posterity. There is, however, one way that an objective history can be achieved and that is by comparing the accounts of the same incidents from the two sides. For the Burma war this is particularly difficult as few Britons can read Japanese, a language which for Westerners might as well be written in code. As a result many of the versions of this campaign that have been written are wildly inaccurate.

I have been very lucky in having the enthusiastic help and support of my co-author Dr Kazuo Tamayama. His untiring research, not only into such Japanese archives as exist but also into the profusion of Japanese books and personal accounts of the campaign that have now emerged, has been fundamental in giving an objective account of what really happened. His advice on many points has been most helpful, and many new facts have emerged which make it possible for the first time to tell the true story of some of the battles. However, this book is written from the British point of view and, having tried to be completely objective, I take full responsibility for the opinions expressed and for the judgements made in choosing between conflicting accounts. And, of course, it is one of the privileges of an author, aided by the benefit of hindsight, to criticise his betters.

This book explains why the British, who had fought many jungle wars, were ill-equipped and totally unprepared for the conditions of this one, while the Japanese, who had never fought in the jungle, used the conditions successfully. Eastern culture is different from Western and the Japanese belief that, under any circumstances, death was preferable to surrender not only made them a very formidable foe, but also led to both sides waging a notably savage war. War is a dreadful business and I have not concealed atrocities where I know of them. Contrary to the rumours spread by deserters and those far from the battle front, there were not many. The worst atrocities were undoubtedly those committed against stragglers and refugees by Burmese paramilitary forces and dacoits.

Retreats, unlike advances, are not glamorous affairs. They are often a prelude to victory but when victory is finally achieved, there is a natural feeling that any retreats suffered en route are best forgotten. However, they are an inevitable part of war, particularly for democracies who commonly fail to prepare adequately for their own defence. There is much to be learned from an honest account of them. Moreover they are great teachers and those who take part in them are made sharply aware of their own deficiencies, and what must be done to remedy them. In 1942 in Burma the British, despite many defeats, did rather better in the face of a brilliant advance than is generally realised. By the end of the campaign they had learned their lesson well.

We now have a highly professional Army and none of our present soldiers have been faced with the problem of leading untrained men into battle with inadequate support and against a first-class enemy. It is to be hoped that they will never have to, but it would be rash to bank on it. If such an eventuality should arise, however, they may find, although conditions have greatly altered, that some of the experiences described in this book are of interest.

The Struggle to Hold Rangoon

Chapters 1 - 13, Maps 1 - 16

CHAPTER ONE

Japan's Amazing Gamble

In December 1941, Japan, with one half of its army engaged in an all-out struggle to subjugate China and one quarter facing the Russians in Manchuria, decided to attack America, Britain and Holland. To understand how a major power like Japan came to take this extraordinary national gamble, which for six months was stunningly successful, it is necessary to take a quick glance at the history of modern Japan.

Japan Emerges from Seclusion to Become a World Power

After three hundred years of isolation from the rest of the world Japan, ruled by war lords and still on a medieval economy, was forced by a US fleet in 1854 to conclude a Treaty of Amity and Commerce with America and to open its ports to free trade with foreigners. In Japan a civil war followed and resulted in the restoration of the power of the monarchy in 1868. The Emperor Meiji and his advisers soon observed that industrial power was the basis of the ascendancy of the Western powers. They also noted that in international circles it was not only accepted but customary that developed nations should acquire empires. Accordingly it was decided that Japan would modernise itself on Western lines. Experts from many countries were invited, and well paid, to come to Japan and impart their knowledge. At the same time specially selected Japanese were sent abroad to all the major countries to learn as much as possible about Western skills.

Britain at that time was the still unchallenged leader in naval matters and so the Japanese navy was modelled on British lines while Germany was chosen as the role model for the army. As Japanese industry developed it became apparent that Japan was woefully short of raw materials. There were two solutions to this, one of which was trade, and so in 1871 Japan signed a Treaty of Amity with China. Another solution was empire, so in 1875, profiting from its own experience, it used its new fleet to force a Treaty of Amity on the unwilling Koreans and established itself in Okinawa to the south and various islands to the north. These moves led to trouble. A rebellion in Korea brought friction with China and in 1894 war broke out between Japan and China. Japan won and China yielded both Taiwan and Korea.

Towards the end of the nineteenth century China was in a disorganised state and foreign powers took advantage of this by establishing trading spheres of interest, Russia in the north, Britain in the Yangtse basin in the centre, Japan opposite Taiwan and the French in the south. In 1899 a major Chinese rebellion (the Boxer Rebellion) against the Government for permitting this foreign infiltration nearly succeeded but was put down with the help of the foreigners, Japan and Russia taking a leading part.

However, as Russia continued to expand its empire, tension rose between Britain and Russia in the Middle East. Japan was also feeling threatened by Russian expansionism based on the new Trans-Siberian railway. Britain was popular in Japan both because of its help in building up the navy and because it was the first country to abandon the unequal privileges obtained in Japan by foreigners under the early treaties. So in 1902 an Anglo-Japanese Alliance was formed. Now insulated from outside interference by the Royal Navy, Japan attacked and defeated the Russian Eastern fleet and launched a land attack to capture the Russian Pacific naval base at Port Arthur. The Russians thereupon dispatched their Baltic fleet around South Africa to join the battle but on arrival it was totally destroyed by the Japanese fleet, whose main battleships had been built at Barrow-in-Furness. Meanwhile the Japanese army defeated the Russian army in the East and Russia sued for peace. Three points are of relevance to later times. Firstly, the Japanese attacked Russia without declaring war, an act praised in the contemporary edition of *The Times* as an admirable method of obtaining surprise. Secondly, Russian prisoners of war were very well treated and Japan received world-wide praise for its humanity. Thirdly, a team of British Army observers watched all the operations and were deeply impressed with the Japanese army, particularly their infantry. Their views were widely publicised by their leader, Lieutenant-General Sir Ian Hamilton.

In World War I Japan loyally supported Britain, using her Navy to assist in curtailing the activities of German raiders in the Pacific and Indian Oceans. Britain was at full stretch in defending its Atlantic lifelines and was much relieved that Japanese support ensured the security of the British Empire in the Far East. Japan, however, had not abandoned her wish for an empire. The rest of the world being preoccupied with the war in Europe, Japan tried to clear up its relations with China in a secret treaty. Some of their proposals were acceptable but others went beyond what a sovereign nation could agree. China made the proposals public and as a result of an outcry in Japan as well as in China, and a remonstrance from Britain and America, the more objectionable proposals were dropped. Although Japan made some useful gains, the affair left a legacy of distrust in China and public opinion in the United States was alienated.

World War I had a profound effect on international relations. While the European belligerents became impoverished, the two major countries who had been involved on a much lesser scale, Japan and the United States, became relatively more influential. In the West the huge number of war casualties, and the dreadful conditions in which most of the war had been fought, had led to a revulsion against the traditional concept of the balance of power to maintain international stability. It was naively maintained that all international disputes could in future be settled by reason and arbitration, so disarmament was the way forward. The popularity of this view was by no means lessened by its obvious economy.

At the Conference of Paris in 1919, Japan was proud to be ranked fourth among the Allies after the United States, Britain and France. However, China was also included in the Council of Ten and this led to trouble for Japan. Japan was awarded a mandate to govern the ex-German colonies in the Marianas, Caroline and Marshall Islands but its request to take over Tsingtao and the German sphere of influence in North China was (not surprisingly) contested by China who could not see why one ally should yield territory to another. Agreement not being reached, the Chinese delegation retired prematurely from the conference.

Another Japanese aim in Paris had been to obtain a formal statement condemning racial discrimination. This view, if sincerely held,[1] would now seem unexceptionable, and indeed admirable, but was then opposed by Britain (largely on the promptings of Australia and New Zealand who feared mass immigration) and by the United States public who, despite President Wilson's ideals, were fearful of mass immigration from Eastern nations to their Pacific coast. The result was unfortunate as it, not unnaturally, fuelled a 'them' and 'us' feeling in Japan which helped to inspire an 'Asia for the Asians' movement.

Before the 1921 Washington Conference a British Imperial Conference was held in London. At this Conference a debate on the Anglo-Japanese Treaty, due for renewal in 1923, was held. Canadian opposition to renewal contrasted with strong support from Australia and New Zealand. The British were reluctant to give up the Treaty but they were aware (as indeed the venue of the coming conference indicated) that world leadership was passing to the United States. From Washington the British Ambassador warned Lord Curzon, the Foreign Secretary, that the American people thought of Japan in the same way as many British thought of Germany in 1913, as the inevitable enemy of the next war, and viewed a British association with Japan as we should have viewed an American association with Germany at that time. These were strong words and indicated that Britain must choose between the United States and Japan. The result of this

---

1. Japan's aim seems to have been to have its own status acknowledged, for the Japanese by no means regarded the Koreans, Taiwanese and Chinese as equals.

American pressure was a diplomatic fudge at the Conference where it was agreed to set up a Four Power Pact (including France) under which these powers agreed to respect each others' rights and to consult in the case of any crisis. Under cover of this the British did not renew the Anglo-Japanese Treaty when it came up for review in 1923. Japan was not deceived. Faced with the choice of siding with Japan or the United States, Britain had chosen the latter. Relations with Britain were never to be the same again. Under British sponsorship Japan had been admitted into the club of world powers; now she felt that she was being elbowed out. As Admiral of the Fleet Lord Chatfield was to comment later, "we had weakened most gravely our Imperial strategic position. We had turned a proved friend ... into a potential and powerful foe."[2]

Japanese dismay was enhanced by the important naval agreement at this Conference. Before World War I Britain had maintained a Navy larger than any two other navies put together. Now a more humble role, in line with Britain's reduced circumstances, was agreed. In future the ratio for capital ships was to be:

    United States 5
    Britain 5
    Japan 3
    France 1.75
    Italy 1.75

This ratio did not please Japan who felt that 3.5 would have been fairer in view of her large merchant navy. However, she gained a prohibition on the fortifying of any Pacific island and on the setting up of a major naval base in either Hong Kong or the Philippines and this was some consolation.

In the 1930s there were still powerful figures in Britain who considered that the security of the Empire would best be assured by seeking a rapprochement with Japan. President Roosevelt, aware of this, authorised his delegate to the Second London Naval Conference in 1936 to warn any British pro-Japanese faction that 'if Great Britain is even suspected of preferring to play with Japan to playing with us' he would 'approach public sentiment' in the dominions to make them 'understand clearly that their future security is linked with us.'[3] This threat to subvert the British dominions may have been bluff but it is an indication of the tensions which were to exist in Anglo-US relations throughout the war in the Far East.

The Army's Pressure for Overseas Expansion

Japan by no means shared the current lack of enthusiasm in the West for the establishment of new empires and moreover did not observe any marked keenness by those who already had them, to give them up. The Japanese population was increasing sharply and further expansion both to obtain raw materials and to provide opportunities for her energetic people seemed desirable. Western nations, alarmed by a flow of cheap goods from Japan, started imposing tariffs to protect their own industries, Britain being no exception. A contemporary observer in Tokyo noted that there was "a strong temptation to cast the samurai sword into the mercantile scales that seemed unfairly weighted against Japan."[4]

This was no idle comment for since World War I the political power of the Army had been steadily increasing. An Imperial Decree in 1890 had initiated universal compulsory education at primary school level. The decree ordained a curriculum that included a strong element of respect for superiors, of patriotism in war and of unswerving loyalty to the Emperor. In every school a small shrine was built containing a photograph of the Emperor and a scroll of the Imperial Decree. Pupils were ordered to stop and bow in front of the shrine when they came to school and in this way a deep respect for the Emperor was fostered. In 1925 a scheme for a degree of military training was introduced into secondary schools. The discipline and patriotism that these systems engendered was exploited by the Army during the two years' national service. Imperial ex-Servicemen Associations were set up throughout the country and all who had done national service were members. Those who had done well in their training gained prestige in their local communities. These Associations were influential in guiding public opinion.

During the 1920s Baron Kijuro Shidehara was Minister of Foreign Affairs. It was his firm belief that it would be greatly to Japan's advantage to maintain friendly relations with China. If China were equally open to trade with all countries, Japan with its low costs and long cultural relationship would be assured of a dominant place in China's trade. This wise view came under increasing pressure from the growing nationalist party. In 1929 the Great Depression hit the many small peasant farmers in Japan very hard and near-starvation was widespread. This made the Army increasingly restive and insubordinate for this frugal and hard-working class provided the bulk of their recruits. Politically motivated secret societies were common and unpopular politicians were not infrequently assassinated. At the end of 1931 Baron Shidehara was swept from office and this marked a turning point in Japan's relations with China.

In September 1931 the Kwantung Army, which garrisoned the southern part of the Chinese province of Manchuria, arranged secretly for a short section of rail on the South Manchurian Railway to be demolished and claimed that this was

---

2. Elphick, Peter, *Far Eastern File*, p.20.
3. The quotation is from Callahan, Raymond, *Burma 1941-1945*, p.15.
4. Chamberlin, W.H., *Japan Over Asia*, p.20.

sabotage by anti-Japanese bandits. Without any authorisation from the govern-ment in Tokyo, they declared that in order to safeguard Japanese interests it was necessary to take over Mukden and the whole of Manchuria, which they pro-ceeded to do. This high-handed action was known in Japan as the 'Manchurian Incident'. In 1932 Japan severed Manchuria from China and made it a separate country, called Manchukuo, with the exiled last emperor of China as head of state.

The League of Nations protested strongly at these actions, as did the United States, but the Japanese ignored them. When in 1932 the League increased its pressure, Japan resigned from the League. Two years later Japan attended a Naval conference in London intended to up-date the Washington Conference of 1921. Japan, however, now felt that the Western nations were ganging up on her, so she abrogated the previous agreement and refused to be tied by any further naval restrictions.

The military faction in Japan was now steadily gaining in influence as their proclaimed 'Imperial Mission' in North-East Asia brought more jobs and oppor-tunities and steadily reduced the poverty caused by the 'Great Depression' of 1929/30. An ever-increasing share of the national budget was now being allotted to the Armed Forces and the country was running more and more deeply into debt. A courageous Minister of Finance attempted to curb the military expendi-ture. But in 1936 there was an attempted coup by a number of young officers in Tokyo. With the soldiers under their command they seized the Army Ministry and Police Headquarters. They murdered the brave Minister of Finance and another cabinet minister, attempted to murder the Prime Minister but killed his brother-in-law by mistake, and killed the Director of Military Training against whom they had a grudge. After three days the uprising collapsed largely due to the determi-nation of the Emperor to make no concessions. Those concerned were arrested and court-martialled. Thirteen young officers, all from well-known families, and four civilians were sentenced to death and executed.[5]

1936 was a year of some importance for in that year Japan also made an Anti-Comintern pact with Germany, the pact being joined the following year by Italy. This was a logical step for Japan which was strongly opposed to both commu-nism and to a USSR which had inherited all the expansionist ideas of the old Russia.

The Fatal Decision

In 1937 there took place an incident which was to decide the fate of both China and Japan for many years. As a result of the expansion following the 'Manchurian Incident', Japan had obtained the right to deploy small forces in North China to protect Japanese interests. At the Marco Polo bridge just outside Peking Japanese and Chinese troops were face to face. An incident occurred or was fabricated, firing broke out and the fighting got out of hand. A cease-fire was arranged but it did not hold. Fighting spread to Shanghai and before long became general. It is uncertain who was behind the original incident. The Chinese communists wanted a war for their own purposes as much as the more extreme members of the Japanese army.

In Japan many members of the government, and indeed officers in the army and navy, were appalled at this reckless move. But there was a surge of nationalist feeling in the country to support the war and the government were assured by the military faction that it would soon be over. China would accept a compromise peace recognising the 'independent' status of Manchukuo and giving Japan extensive rights in China. Prince Konoye and his government, though with misgivings, therefore decided to back the Army and general mobilisation was ordered. Wiser heads in Tokyo were in no doubt about the magnitude of the task so lightly undertaken by the Army, so a War Cabinet and an Imperial General Headquarters were set up to co-ordinate the war effort.

With hindsight it is obvious that the decision to invade China, quite apart from the moral factor, was a disastrous misjudgement. The events of the previous few years had roused a strong nationalist feeling in China and although militarily they were to prove no match for the Japanese, they were in no mood to give in. Japan, however, gained widespread early successes. They soon captured all the main Chinese ports even as far as Canton, 1500 miles south of Peking. Advancing inland they captured the nationalist capital of Nanking. Thinking to terrorise the Chinese into submission they sacked this city, killing some forty thousand civilians and prisoners of war.[6] This disgraceful act not only did nothing to persuade the Chinese to accept Japanese domination but did much to turn sentiment in the rest of the world against Japan.

The Western powers, and particularly the United States, strongly resented this unprovoked aggression which they saw as a Japanese attempt to get the resources and trade of China for itself. Except for the Axis powers, foreign reaction was uniformly hostile but, as the European powers were now preoccupied with the Italian invasion of Ethiopia, the Spanish Civil War and the rapidly increasing threat of Germany, their protests carried little weight. Similarly, although President Roosevelt made some ominous remarks about putting aggressor nations in 'quarantine', in fact no talk of sanctions followed. Nevertheless as the war dragged on

---

5. There is a story, which appears to be apocryphal, that they were not executed but exiled to countries in S.E. Asia with orders to assume a new identity and help Japan if opportunity offered.
6. This is the figure given in *Rising Sun*, Time-Life Books Inc., 1977, a book produced by a team of researchers and journalists. Much higher figures are often quoted but without giving a source.

into 1938 there were misgivings in Japan not only in civil but also in some military circles that Japan had embarked on a war which she could not win.

The Japanese had reasoned that the superiority of their own equipment and the acute shortage of Chinese equipment would before long oblige China to sue for peace. But Chiang Kai-shek and his forces had retired into the mountainous region around Chungking, some 1500 miles deeper into China than Nanking. Here the United States were supplying them with modern equipment. Although the Japanese had deployed 850,000 troops, victory seemed as far away as ever. The American supplies were the crucial factor. The Japanese estimate was that in July 1940 China was receiving the following tonnages monthly:

Via Russia . . . . .500 tons
Via Hong Kong . . . . . . .6,000 tons
Via French Indo-China 15,000 tons
Via Rangoon . . . . .10,000 tons

By the end of the year they had managed to close all the supply routes except the

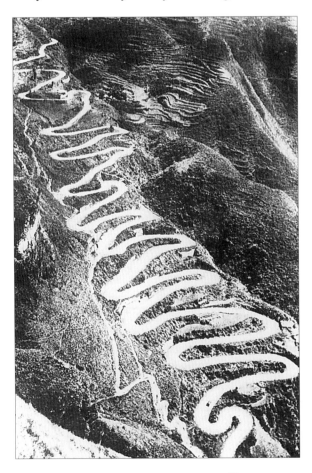

A spectacular section of the 1400-mile 'Burma Road' between Lashio and Chungking, completed in 1938. HMSO.

Burma one, but the supplies along this route were now estimated to have risen to 15,000 tons a month. Burma had suddenly become a very important country to Japan.

The Dilemma of Japanese Strategy

In 1939 there was another ominous occurrence when the Kwantung army was involved in a clash with the Soviets at Nomonhan on the border of Manchukuo and Outer Mongolia. Fighting went on for several months and the Russians, led by an up-and-coming young General called Zhukov, had markedly the best of it. However, both sides were content to bring the fighting to an end when the war in Europe erupted.[7]

Among Japanese military strategists there were two factions. The 'Northerners' believed that the main danger to Japan lay from Russia in the north-west and any further expansion should be devoted to strengthening Japan's position there. The 'Southerners' believed that a golden future lay for Japan in the mineral, oil and rice-rich countries of South-East Asia.

In 1940 the collapse of France and Holland, and Britain's defeat on the continent, made the European colonies in SE Asia, now only weakly protected, look very tempting. The views of the 'Southerners' were greatly strengthened. But the same events had induced the United States to start a major re-armament programme, to abrogate their 1911 Trade Treaty with Japan and to place a limited embargo on the export of certain strategic materials. This was alarming and there was clearly no time to be lost. Although no final decision for a southern advance was taken, the Japanese moved stealthily into Indo-China with the aim both of closing the supply route to the Chinese through Saigon and of preparing suitably sited airfields to support a possible invasion across the Gulf of Siam. German pressure on Vichy France ensured compliance in Indo-China with Japanese wishes.

The hand of the 'Southerners' was further strengthened by an extraordinary chance. In November 1940 the German raider *'Atlantis'* intercepted the Blue Funnel liner *'Automedon'* off the Nicobar Islands. The latter refused to halt and broadcast a 'raider attack' SOS, whereupon the *Atlantis* opened fire at point-blank range with two six-inch guns aimed at the *Automedon's* bridge. The captain was killed and a German boarding party seized the bridge and broke open the safe. There they found a Top Secret paper from the British Chiefs of Staff describing in detail the weakness of British forces in the Far East and the impossibility of increasing them at present. The paper soon reached the German Naval

---

7. The Japanese officers who were captured in this struggle were court-martialled on their return and some were forced to commit suicide before the verdict was delivered.

Attaché in Tokyo who, after referring to Berlin, handed it over to the Japanese, who could scarcely believe their luck.

Talks took place in Berlin in March 1941 between the German and Japanese foreign ministers. In these Herr Ribbentrop tried to convince the Japanese that Britain was all but finished and would soon be given the coup-de-grace. He advised Japan to attack Singapore as soon as possible but to avoid getting into conflict with the United States. He hinted strongly that Germany had some problems with Russia. On the way home Mr Matsuoka had talks with Stalin in Moscow and, with his eye on Japan's advance to the south, concluded a mutual non-aggression pact between Japan and Russia.

In June 1941 Germany, without informing Japan, invaded Russia in 'Operation Barbarossa' and had huge initial successes. It looked as though Russia would be defeated and in Japan this strengthened the hand of the 'Northerners'. If Russia collapsed there would be a good chance for expansion in the north. Matsuoka was discredited and left the government. However the 'Southerners' continued to press their case and at an Imperial Conference in July, although the northern view was favoured, no final decision was taken and further advances into Indo-China were agreed. Then in August came a bombshell. The United States froze all Japanese assets. The British and Dutch governments followed suit. This effectively cut off the supply of oil and scrap iron[8] to Japan. Oil in particular was Japan's Achilles' heel. By the end of 1941 Japan would have about twelve month's supply left in storage. After that time she would be forced to withdraw from China. In Japan this tipped the scale decisively in favour of the 'Southerners', for the oil in the Dutch East Indies was now vital to prevent an ignominious retreat from empire.

Unless America could be persuaded to modify her stand, there seemed to be only one choice now, apart from capitulation. This was to drive south into SE Asia while Russia and Britain were still preoccupied in the great struggle with Germany and before the United States was fully re-armed. Such a move would be impossible in the face of a hostile American fleet and therefore a pre-emptive attack on the US Pacific Fleet would be necessary. As American steel production was some ten times as great as that of Japan, to challenge America as well as China, Britain and possibly Russia was a staggering risk. The Japanese, however, gambled that Germany would defeat Russia and Britain, and that America, faced with a powerful German empire in Europe and a powerful Japanese empire in Asia, would be prepared to compromise.

At an Imperial Conference in September the proposal for a southern attack, to the dismay of the military faction, was not agreed by the Emperor. Prince Konoye was given six weeks to try and effect a diplomatic settlement with the US. He found that no agreement was possible that did not include the withdrawal of Japanese troops from China. This was impossible for the military faction to accept. Konoye resigned and was replaced by the War Minister, General Hideki Tojo. Now General Tojo was not the most senior officer in the Army and was never in the position of being a dictator.[9] Like the leaders of the Japanese Navy, he personally doubted the wisdom of the southern plan but was subject to strong pressure from the hierarchy in the Army to take action while there was enough oil left to do it. So the decision was taken and preparations for a southern thrust went ahead. In mid-October the Japanese government presented their conclusion to the Emperor at another Imperial Conference as the constitution required. To their dismay he still did not agree. Speaking directly, rather than through the Lord Chancellor as custom decreed, he strongly advised another attempt at negotiation with the Americans.[10]

Consequently the Japanese put another set of proposals to the United States. America, after consultation with Britain, China and the Dutch government, sent back a stark reply requesting, among other things, the withdrawal of all Japanese military, naval, air and police forces from China and Indo-China, and the recognition of the Nationalist government at Chungking as the only government of China. To the Japanese this was a clear ultimatum. Oil stocks were running down and action could not be delayed. Preliminary moves for hostilities had already been taken and Japanese merchant ships had been recalled to home waters. Tojo and his cabinet now returned to the Emperor. This time the Emperor remained silent when the war plan was presented and, after an embarassing pause, the cabinet retired. The die was cast and the incredible gamble was on.

On the 29th of November the American Secretary of State, Cordell Hull, warned the American Chiefs of Staff and the Allied Governments that war with Japan was imminent. There was no reason for anyone to be taken by surprise. But they were.

8. Scrap iron was essential for Japan's steel industry.
9. General Sugiyama, the Army Chief of Staff, General Hata, C-in-C China, and General Count Terauchi, C-in-C Southern Area, were all senior to him.
10. General P.S. Wang, Chiang Kai-shek's Head of Intelligence, was to claim in April 1942 that he had obtained copies of the minutes of this meeting and forwarded them to Washington and London. Burchett, W.G., *Bombs Over Burma*, 1944, p.189.

CHAPTER TWO

Burma's Fatal Weakness

The View from London

Since World War II the general opinion has been that in 1941, Britain, facing Germany and Italy without its French ally, was quite simply unable to spare the resources required to defend its Far Eastern possessions against a Japanese attack. Hence the rapid defeats suffered by the British in Hong Kong, Malaya and Burma. Of course there is much truth in this view. In Britain a pre-war mood of pacifism, derived from the horrors of World War I, had received political support. Britain's armed forces and their equipment had been allowed to fall below the level necessary to protect itself and its overseas possessions even with France's help. But was the best use made of the little that was available?

It had been an accepted feature of British strategy between the wars that the two vital parts of the Empire to be defended were Britain and Singapore. The defence of both these bastions was planned and controlled directly from London. A large proportion of the small pre-war allotment of defence funds had gone into the construction of a huge naval base at Singapore, the idea being that a substantial fleet would proceed there if there was any likelihood of a threat from the East, meaning of course, Japan. This fleet, which in an emergency would most probably be supported by the US Pacific Fleet, would be quite strong enough to deter the Japanese, the only major power in the East, from threatening Burma, Malaya or Australia.

The weakness of this theory had always been that it was most unlikely that Britain would be involved in a war in the Far East unless she was also engaged in a war in Europe. After World War I the Royal Navy had been drastically reduced and, unless helped by the navies of such allies as France and Italy, had by the late thirties no prospect whatever of being able to spare a substantial fleet for the Far East while still protecting Britain's vital oceanic life-lines. In 1940 the loss of the French fleet and the switch of the Italian fleet from ally to enemy completely destroyed the "main fleet to Singapore" strategy and it was clear to many that defence of the eastern rim of the British Empire must depend primarily on air and ground forces.

In 1940, Britain, facing the prospect of a German invasion, did all she could to avoid provoking Japan, including agreeing to close the 'Burma Road'[1] for three months during the monsoon (no great concession as at this period it was barely usable, as the Japanese well knew). By 1940 both the British and the Americans had broken the Japanese diplomatic code. As a result the Allies, by intercepting radio traffic, were fully aware of the content of Japanese diplomatic negotiations with the Germans and Russians and knew much about the possible Japanese strategic moves overseas. As war drew nearer this knowledge became ever more valuable. Churchill was under immense pressure dealing with operations in the Atlantic and Middle East as well as all the problems of industry and of the Home Front. He was therefore content to agree that America should take the lead in negotiations with the Japanese.

The Prime Minister, anxious always to attack the main enemy, Germany, became deeply involved in the plans to defeat the small German force which formed the core of the Axis army in North Africa, an operation which he regarded as being of top priority after the defence of Britain. In this view he did not have the support of the General Staff in the War Office who thought that the defence of Singapore was more important. Although he knew through decoded signals that Germany was pressing Japan to attack Singapore, he was also aware that there was a powerful moderate party in Japan.[2] He found it difficult to believe that the Japanese would be so unwise as to start a war with Britain and the Netherlands while still embroiled in China and subject to the latent threat of Russia. If they did embark on such a "mad enterprise" it was highly probable that the United States would come in and this would ensure beyond any doubt that the war would be won and Britain's long and bitter struggle would be crowned with success. No doubt another factor was that both he and some of his advisers underrated the quality of the Japanese armed forces. In a Most Secret directive dated 28 April 1941 he wrote:

"Directive by the Prime Minister and Minister of Defence

Japan is unlikely to enter the war unless the Germans make a successful invasion of Great Britain, and even a major disaster like the loss of the Middle East would not necessarily make her come in … It is very unlikely, moreover, that Japan will enter the war either if the United States have come in, or if Japan thinks they would come in consequent upon a declaration of war. Finally it may be taken as almost certain that the entry of Japan into the war would be followed by the immediate entry of the United States on our side.

---

1. The supply route to China via Rangoon.
2. Churchill, Winston, *The Second World War*, Vol. 3, pp.161-172.

These conditions are to be accepted by the Service Departments as a guide for all plans and actions ... There is no need at the present time to make any further dispositions for the defence of Malaya and Singapore beyond those modest arrangements which are in progress..."[3]

This directive, which was issued without any discussion with the Chiefs of Staff,[4] switched the priorities of the Middle East and Far East and was not altered before the Japanese attack. It effectively prevented any preparations for war being made in Burma.

The View from Singapore.

At a Singapore Defence Conference in October 1940[5] the defence of Burma, which was under the command of the Commander-in-Chief Far East, was considered. It was decided that a minimum of 566 aircraft were required for the defence of Malaya and Burma, the distribution between each area depending on circumstances. In addition to these, a fighter squadron was required permanently for the defence of Rangoon and suitable maritime aircraft should be provided for the defence of the Andaman and Nicobar Islands covering the approaches to Rangoon. Recommendations were also made for a substantial increase to the land forces in Burma. The conclusions of that part of the report referring to Burma were:

"a. The military garrison of Burma is at present based on internal security requirements alone. Hitherto, the defence of the country from external aggression has rested on the defences of Malaya and Indo-China.

b. With the forces at present available, the most that can be done is to hold the northern part of Tenasserim[6] and Rangoon. The vital installations in the Rangoon area, the oilfields and the vital installations in eastern India are entirely unprotected from air attack.

c. We stress the need for the provision of additional forces, particularly Air Forces, anti-aircraft defences, adequate local Naval defence and artillery to support the land forces."

The Chiefs of Staff in London considered this report but did not agree it. The Chiefs decided that 336 aircraft would be sufficient for Malaya and Burma. In the event even this reduced figure was not achieved. There were only 158 serviceable aircraft available in Malaya when the attack came and 18 low-performance fighters in Burma. Insufficient weight seems to have been given to the large distances involved in the Far East which restricted the capability of British fighters designed for the short range requirements of the defence of Britain. The Air Staff seem also to have underestimated the quality of the Japanese Air Force.

The First Anglo-American Summit

In June 1941 the war took a dramatic turn. Germany launched Operation Barbarossa, her massive invasion of Russia. For Britain it was absolutely vital that Russia should not collapse and so from July 1941 many aircraft, tanks and vital supplies such as rubber were sent, at great cost to the Navy, straight from British factories to Murmansk. Similar supplies, some of which had previously been earmarked for Britain, were sent from America. In July Japan called up one million men, many of them reservists, and took over all the military bases in Indo-China. In August Churchill and Roosevelt had their first summit meeting on board HMS *Prince of Wales* in a Newfoundland harbour. They discussed the British strategy that the sea lanes must be kept open, that massive bombing would defeat Germany and that the Germans should only be attacked on land where their forces were small enough to give a chance of success, for instance in the Middle East. The Americans agreed with the first proposition, were divided on the second and did not agree on the importance of the third. They thought that the Far East was more important than the Middle East.

A main aim of the conference for the British was to discuss the growing threat of Japan. They hoped to get the Americans to issue a firm warning to Japan that if they tried any further expansion to the south, they would risk war with the United States. They believed that this would effectively deter the Japanese and thus avoid the necessity of strengthening the Far East. The British thought that this course of action had been agreed, but in fact the Americans were not yet ready for war and were disinclined at this stage to issue what was virtually an ultimatum. They resolved for the moment to continue negotiations.

The View from Thailand

For the Japanese the attitude of Thailand was critical. To invade Malaya and Burma they would need the use of the port of Bangkok and the Thai railways. The Thai army was far from negligible and their soldiers were tough. If heavy casualties were to be avoided it was vital that the early landings across the beaches in southern Thailand should be unopposed.

The Thai people, however, were fiercely proud of never having been

3. WO 106-2620.

4. Kennedy, Major-General Sir John, *The Business of War,* p.108.

5. Prasad, Bisheshwar, *The Retreat from Burma*, 1941-42, p.425.

6. Tenasserim was the name given to that part of Burma from Moulmein to Victoria Point at the southernmost tip.

colonised and were determined to maintain their independence. Although there were many British in the country, for the major part of their trade was with the British Empire, the British were not seen as a threat and were generally popular. The Japanese take-over of Manchukuo and now French Indo-China, however, had alarmed the Thais. Trade with Japan was increasing and more Japanese were entering Thailand. The interests of some employees of Japanese firms (who were in fact army officers in disguise) seemed to be more geographical than commercial and the arrogance of some Japanese was not endearing. Since 1940 it had been clear to the Thai government that if the British and Japanese clashed they would be faced with a very difficult decision.

On the one hand they had no illusions that they could stand up for long against the powerful and modern Japanese forces and they had no wish for a war to be fought in their country if it could be avoided. However, in 1940-41 it looked as though the Axis powers were going to win the war. If they sided with the British, as most Thais wished, were the British strong enough to protect them from invasion? It seemed unlikely. The Dutch and French had been defeated by Germany and all Britain's efforts seemed to be devoted to its own survival. Tentative contacts with the British in Singapore in July 1941 only confirmed this view. If they sided with the Japanese would they suffer from a British attack? Again, in view of current British weakness, particularly in the air, it seemed unlikely. To side with which country would be most profitable? Japan had recognised the great strategic importance of Thailand and had used her powerful position in Indo-China to mediate in a dispute between the Thais and Cambodia. As a result Thailand had acquired a large slice of disputed territory there, though not as much as she had hoped for. The Thais had other boundary disputes with Burma and Malaya. It looked possible, and was strongly hinted by the Japanese, that these might also be settled in Thailand's favour (as they were in 1943). The Thai prime minister, Pibul[7], gave a secret verbal promise to the Japanese in October 1940 to support them if they embarked on an invasion of Malaya or Burma.

However, Pibul seems to have been quite ready to forget this promise if circumstances changed and in fact the Thai government asked both the British and Americans in October 1941 for guarantees of effective support if they were invaded. Neither country could give them. On 25 November Pibul asked if the British and Americans would give a public warning to Japan that an invasion of Thailand would result in a declaration of war by their two countries. Churchill favoured this course but Roosevelt was unable to agree, as under the American Constitution he had no authority to do so. So the Thai government continued to sit on the fence to the very end. This drove the Japanese planners to distraction as they made unsuccessful efforts to obtain agreement to a 'right of passage'

General Count Terauchi, C-in-C Southern Area, visiting Yenangyaung in November 1942. General Sakurai has his back to the camera.

through Thai territory, on which their whole operational plan depended. Finally the *C-in-C Southern Area*, General Count Terauchi, took the decision for the invasion fleet to sail and land in Thailand with or without permission.

The Thai Cabinet knew that this fleet was on its way and in the late afternoon of 7 December received a formal request for non-resistance and transit facilities from the Japanese Ambassador supported by some military staff officers. The Cabinet decided not to resist but, before this decision could be promulgated, Pibul, whose signature as commander-in-chief was constitutionally essential, disappeared on a 'tour of inspection' and could not be contacted. It was not until the next morning, after the invasion had landed, that he returned to Bangkok and, to the great relief of the Japanese, the decision was broadcast. An informed view is that he had been much impressed by the arrival of the two British capital ships and thought that even now the British might achieve a dramatic success. He, therefore, 'disappeared' until it was clear whether or not the British would succeed in intercepting and destroying the approaching convoy.[8]

The View from India

At the end of June, General Wavell had been transferred from the Middle East to be Commander-in-Chief in India. Surveying his parish in July he saw at once that the Japanese threat was increasing. The Japanese were now firmly established in Indo-China, the essential launch pad for action against Malaya, and were building new airfields there. Their bombers had the range from Indo-China to reach Rangoon and from Thailand to reach some of India's most vital targets near Calcutta, such as the huge steelworks and ammunition factories at Tatanagar. India had no modern aircraft and virtually no air defences. He therefore asked the Chiefs of Staff to remedy this deficiency and queried whether it

---

7. Two of Pibul's children were at school in Britain. Gilchrist, Sir Andrew, *Malaya 1941*.
8. Gilchrist, Sir Andrew, *Malaya 1941*, p.49

General Sir Archibald Wavell, Theatre Commander for Burma from 12 December 1941. IWM.

was wise to continue sending so many fighter aircraft (250 Hurricanes a month)[9] to Russia when they were vitally necessary for the defence of India and the Far East. The Chiefs of Staff thought much the same but the War Cabinet were not prepared to change their views although they got no thanks from Stalin for their decision. Nor were they prepared to divert aircraft from Britain or the Middle East.

Another aspect of India's defence concerned Wavell much more directly. This was the realisation that India had no responsibility for the defence of Burma although Burma's security was of vital interest to India. The command arrangement was that the Commander-in-Chief Far East, with Headquarters at Singapore, was responsible for the defence of both Malaya and Burma and answerable directly to the Chiefs of Staff in London. That this was thoroughly unsound had been pointed out by three successive Commanders-in-Chief in India. The defence of Burma, and particularly its air defence, was an integral part of the defence of north-east India and the important steel and armament factories around Calcutta. Far East Command in Singapore were short of everything and could spare nothing for the defence of Burma, to them a low priority and one to which they gave little attention. As Wavell was to comment in his Despatch:

> "Except as a subsidiary air base, Burma hardly entered into the strategical plans of the Far East Command, which was concerned with the defence of Hong Kong and Malaya; whereas for India Burma was a vital bulwark."

The two Headquarters at Singapore and Rangoon, therefore, not only had very different problems but were 1100 miles apart. Although the War Office was responsible for the administration of Burma, in practice many of the units in Burma were based on India and administered from there. Moreover, there was a substantial Indian population in Burma for which India was ultimately responsible. There was much experience to show that to divorce operational from administrative control was always unwise. Finally, and most importantly, the only place from which help could reach Burma quickly if she were to be attacked was India.

In 1940 Lieutenant-General T.J. Hutton, the Chief of the General Staff in

India, had visited the War Office and raised this issue, but unsuccessfully. Wavell personally pressed the point on a visit to London in September 1941 but to no avail. On his return he visited Burma and Singapore and discussed the problem with the Governor of Burma and the GOC Burma Army, Lieutenant-General D.K. McCleod, and with Air Chief Marshal Sir Robert Brooke-Popham, the Commander-in-Chief (C-in-C) in the Far East. The first two agreed with him but the latter felt (though it is difficult now to see why) that a change would complicate the problems of supply to China. Wavell, who saw clearly the vital importance of the issue, sent these views to London on 11 November 1941 and pressed his point again. This time the Chiefs of Staff agreed but the Defence Committee delayed a decision. It was not until 12 December, four days after the Japanese attack, that the Prime Minister gave his consent. The delay in making this essential decision was to have disastrous consequences.

The View from Burma

Burma was ethnically and geographically a part of South-East Asia and in the nineteenth century its relations with India had been stormy. After a number of Burmese incursions into India, the East India Company had in 1824 sent an expedition to Rangoon which, after two years' fighting, signed a peace treaty under which Tenasserim and part of the Arakan were ceded to the Company. Sixty years later, after a number of provocations, Lord Dufferin, the Viceroy of India, sent another expedition to Rangoon which duly captured Mandalay and deposed King Thibaw. After much doubt and hesitation Burma was, with Royal assent, then included in the British Empire and annexed to India. Henceforth it was ruled as a province of India.

The Burmese naturally disliked this arrangement. Their roots were in South-East Asia, not India, and their religion was a different one.[10] As their own experience of running a modern state developed, they naturally wished to run their own affairs with a view, of course, to eventual independence. Accordingly, in 1937, the administration of Burma was split off from India, and Burma was made responsible to a new Burma Office in London. Henceforth all communications from the government of India to the government of Burma had to be sent via their respective offices in Whitehall. This brilliant piece of bureaucracy did little to ease co-operation between the two countries.

At the same time the Burmese were given increased power in the government of their country. One result of this was a heightening of interest in political matters and a growth of nationalism. Some of the brightest of the young educated

9. Kennedy, Sir John, *The Business of War,* p.178.
10. Except for the Karens, who were mainly Christian.

Burmese began to advocate independence. The Japanese were quick to take advantage of this movement as we shall see. Meanwhile the British were well aware of this potential internal security problem. To deal with this there were two regular British battalions in Burma, the 1st Battalion, the Gloucestershire Regiment (1st Glosters) and the 2nd Battalion, the King's Own Yorkshire Light Infantry (2nd KOYLI), stationed respectively near Rangoon and Mandalay,

Burma had its own small army. The officers for this Burma Army were provided by officers on secondment from the British and Indian Armies. However, Burma had long been considered a military backwater. A posting to Burma was considered to be agreeable to those interested in field sports and a pleasant life but of no value to those interested in furthering their careers. Consequently few ambitious army officers chose to go there. The appointment of the General Officer Commanding was traditionally a final posting for a worthy Indian Army officer about to retire. However, in spite of being repeatedly informed by Whitehall between 1938 and late 1941 that it was very unlikely that war would ever come to Burma, there were those in Burma who saw clearly what might happen and did their best to do something about it. Agreement was obtained to expand the four Burma Rifles battalions to eight and a Burmese Sapper and Miner Company was raised, while in response to political pressure recruitment was widened to include the Burmans from Central Burma. These lowlanders, who formed the bulk of the population, were not considered to be as loyal or reliable as the hillmen previously enlisted, and so it was to prove. Officers and instructors for these new units were found from the old Burma Rifles battalions and by milking the two British battalions. In November 1940 service in the Burma Auxiliary Force (similar to the Territorial Army) was made obligatory for all European British subjects of military age and this provided a valuable pool of experienced and able young men with knowledge of the country and its language.

In addition to the Army there was also a strong force of military police under civil control, the Burma Military Police, and part of these were later split off to form units in what was called the Burma Frontier Force. These latter units were largely composed of Indians and Gurkhas who were domiciled in Burma. The military police had a good reputation in peacetime and the Burma Frontier Force units were a useful source of intelligence, as well as providing a helpful outpost screen on many occasions. But they were not trained, nor naturally of much use, for formal fighting against a major enemy.

In March 1941 the Chiefs of Staff had ordered India to send the 13th Indian Infantry Brigade (13 Brigade) to Burma. The following July it was decided to organise the units in Burma into a field force and the 1st Burma Division (1 Burdiv), commanded by Major-General J. Bruce Scott, was established with the

1st and 2nd Burma Brigades and 13 Brigade under command. It was reinforced by the 27th Indian Mountain Artillery Regiment (2nd, 12th and 23rd Indian Mountain Batteries), the 1st Burma Field Company and 56 Madras Sapper and Miner Field Company (56 Field Company) from India, together with some essential administrative units. A second Indian infantry brigade, the 16th, was sent to Burma on Wavell's initiative at the end of November and this was held in reserve under Burma Army Headquarters. No more reinforcements were received before the Japanese war started a week later.

Making the Country Ready for War

The fundamental changes required to make a democratic country ready for a total war, however, could only be imposed from the top by the Burmese government after widespread discussion. This was not made any easier by the British Government policy of avoiding provocation to the Japanese and assuring everyone that there would be no war in Burma. However, radical measures were essential. The railways needed to be militarised, as did the inland water transport and the labour in the docks. A Movement Control staff needed to be established to control movement on rail, road, sea and river. It was vital to set up an adequate Intelligence organisation to include the small current civil one. The Burmese Military Police needed to come under Army command. An Air Raid Precaution system and an Air Observer Corps needed to be established. To many people in Burma, however, with war officially declared unlikely, to surrender control of the commercial systems, which they had managed for many years, to some unknown military authority was unpalatable to say the least. Unfortunately the Burma Army Headquarters in Rangoon, in effect the Burma War Office, was very small and in fact no larger than a normal second class district headquarters in India. It had neither the know-how nor the staff capacity to effect these changes. General Wavell saw clearly that these adjustments were essential, would take time and needed to be done well before operations started. But there was nothing he could do until Burma was placed under C-in-C India's command.

The Threat Increases

Meanwhile in Singapore, the increasing menace of Japan was being studied. When war became imminent the C-in-C Far East informed Lieutenant-General McLeod that "he was to protect the airfields in Tenasserim in order to maintain the Imperial air route to Singapore and to safeguard the 'Burma Road' and communications with China." This meant covering, with one division, a front longer than that of France with Belgium, Germany, Switzerland and Italy. The best routes for vehicles from Thailand to Burma (see Map 3) were tracks from the Thai railway which led into the southern Shan States from Chiang Rai in the north and further south from Chiang Mai. In the south there was a more direct but more rugged route, much of it a footpath, from Raheng to Miyawadi and over the Dawna Range to Moulmein. Further south still a possible but rather longer route lay through the Three Pagodas Pass. McLeod estimated the probable strength of a Japanese attack as two divisions, supported by eight bomber squadrons and four fighter squadrons. This turned out to be remarkably accurate, though rather alarming for RAF Burma which consisted of one squadron of obsolescent 'Buffalo' fighters. However he thought, not so accurately but in accordance with standard British military thinking at the time, that the main attack would come along the roads of the two northern routes and only a brigade would be used on the direct approach via Raheng. He decided to hold the line of the Salween and deployed HQ 1 Burdiv and two brigades to cover the two northern routes and 2 Bur Brigade to cover the southern ones. 16 Brigade was held in reserve.

On 8 December the war with Japan started and by the 11th the British strategy for the defence of the Far East was in ruins. The Royal Navy had suffered a shattering set-back by the sinking of HMS *Prince of Wales* and *Repulse*, and the naval base at Singapore, which lay at the heart of the strategy, was now useless. The RAF had been overwhelmed in northern Malaya and were never to regain the initiative. It was obvious that whatever the outcome of the ground fighting in the Malayan peninsula, GHQ Far East in Singapore could no longer control any operations in Burma. On the 12th the War Cabinet agreed at long last to place Burma under the command of the C-in-C India.

Wavell Takes Command

General Wavell was now informed by the Prime Minister that he would get the 18th British Division and the 17th Indian Division as reinforcements for Burma, plus four squadrons of fighters and later six bomber squadrons. Wavell at once sent no less than 61 staff and specialist technical officers to boost up AHQ Burma. Among these were Major-General E.N. Goddard, to take charge of administration, a Deputy Chief Engineer, a Director of Movements, a Director of Transportation and an Embarkation Commandant. On the 21st Wavell visited Rangoon, being already aware that most of the promised reinforcements were unlikely to materialise as they were being diverted to Malaya. However, he still hoped to get two East African brigades from Kenya as well as part of 17 Division.

The next day Wavell cabled the CIGS, stressing the importance of Burma for both India and China in the war against Japan and giving his appreciation of the situation. He said:

"Burma is essential base for operations against Japan, it is only route for supplies to China, it is integral part of defence of Eastern India, where large proportion of munitions factories are sited. Its security is, therefore, absolutely vital to prosecution of War against Japan."[11]

He added that Burma was far from secure and required immediately a second division plus two bomber squadrons and two modern fighter squadrons, the provision of the aircraft being particularly urgent.

From secret intelligence he was informed that an immediate assault on Burma was not imminent and so he decided to replace Lieutenant-General McLeod with Lieutenant-General T.J. Hutton, who was the Chief of the General Staff at GHQ India. Hutton, a British Army Gunner officer, was a brilliant and experienced staff officer and Wavell felt he was well suited to the task of getting Burma organised on to a war footing.

From Rangoon Wavell flew to Chungking to confer with Generalissimo Chiang Kai-shek. His aim was to persuade the Generalissimo to deploy one American Volunteer Group (AVG) squadron of fighters to defend Rangoon and to ask for the release to the Burma Army of some urgently needed lease-lend war material which was piling up in Rangoon docks and could not be quickly moved to Chungking. He also wanted to discuss assistance from the Chinese Army. Unfortunately the interview did not go well. Chiang Kai-shek, who knew better than Wavell how his troops could compete with the Japanese, was not prepared to send anything less than a large force into Burma to ensure that it would not be defeated. Wavell, who realised that the British would have to provide most of its administrative support, asked for a smaller force, which offended the Generalissimo. Wavell was unwilling to discuss world strategy as he had, of course, no authority to do so and this also caused offence. Nevertheless a few days later the Generalissmo[12] authorised one of his two AVG squadrons to be used alternately for the defence of Rangoon and also released to the British some urgently needed war material from the Rangoon docks.

The Second Anglo-American Summit

Real progress was at last being made in Burma when it was suddenly disrupted by a fatal decision on the other side of the world. On 12 of December, Winston Churchill had sailed to America in HMS *Duke of York* for a second

11.Prasad, Bisheshwar, *The Retreat from Burma*, p.454.
12. There may have been some confusion over nomenclature, Chinese 'armies' were equivalent to British divisions. See Appendix 5.

Far left: Lieutenant-General T.J. Hutton, Army Commander in Burma from 27 December 1941 to 5 March 1942. HMSO.

Generalissimo Chiang Kai-shek, Head of State and C-in-C of the Chinese armed forces.

major Anglo-American conference to review the war. He did not return to Britain until 15 January 1942. General Sir John Dill, although no longer CIGS (for General Sir Alan Brooke had taken over at the beginning of December), had accompanied the Prime Minister together with the other two Chiefs of Staff. The major achievements of the conference were the decisions to defeat Germany first and to establish the Combined (British and US) Chiefs of Staff Committee. But the organisation for defeating the Japanese had also been discussed. It was obvious that the naval war in the Pacific would be an American responsibility as the war in China would be a Chinese one. There remained a gap and President Roosevelt and General Marshall hatched up a proposal for a combined American-British-Dutch-Australian (ABDA) Command to be set up with its headquarters on the island of Surabaya (but later changed to Lembang, near Bandoeng, in Java). Its responsibilities would cover all land, sea and air operations from inclusive Burma on the left flank to inclusive the Philippines on the right. They further proposed that the Supreme Commander of this huge area should be General Wavell, with an American deputy. Flattering though it was to have a British commander chosen by the Americans, Winston Churchill hesitated to accept this plan as he could see some of its weaknesses but, the importance of Anglo-American co-operation being so great, he finally did so.

In this way, two great American leaders, working with the best of intentions from a global map on the other side of the world, dealt a fatal blow to one of their main aims, the defence of the 'Burma Road' to China.

When Wavell first got the news on the 30th of December he at once recommended that the defence of Burma should remain the responsibility of the C-in-C India, a view endorsed by the Governor of Burma who said that "since India assumed direct responsibility the situation here has been positively dynamic." But his plea was refused on the grounds that it would harm relations with the

Chinese. This ignored the fact that China's main interest was that Burma should be defended as efficiently as possible. General Wavell was later to comment:[13]

"I think that this decision was a serious error from the military point of view. From my headquarters in Java, 2000 miles distant from Rangoon and concerned as I was with an immense area and many international problems, it was impossible for me to give as close attention to the problems of Burma as was desirable; nor had I any reinforcements at my disposal to aid Burma. They must come almost entirely from India. Moreover, administration of the forces in Burma had necessarily to be conducted from India; and it is always wrong to separate operational and administrative responsibility... During the five weeks that Burma remained under ABDA Command, I was only able to pay two hurried visits and, owing to faulty signal communications, messages and reports from Burma sometimes took several days to reach me in Java. It was during these five weeks that the fate of Burma was decided."

13. Supplement to *The London Gazette*, 11 March 1948.

CHAPTER THREE

Japanese Preparations
and Tenasserim Attacked

While the British in Burma struggled to prepare for war, the Japanese were earning the fruits of eighteen months' shrewd and detailed planning. Contrary to what is sometimes believed, the Japanese troops used in Malaya and Burma had no previous experience or training in jungle warfare. However a team of Japanese staff officers had done all they could to learn about the conditions in which they would have to fight in a drive to the south. Their first move was in July 1940 when two general staff officers for each country, using false names, were sent for two months to Hong Kong, Malaya, Indonesia, Burma and the Philippines. Their task was mainly to assess local conditions and to contact possible allies among the local population. They were followed by others, also with false identities, who studied the terrain and logistic problems.

To collate the basic knowledge required for fighting in the 'southern area' a small planning staff had been assembled in Taiwan at the end of 1940 and given the task of finding out as much of military interest as they could about these five countries.[1] They were dedicated and experienced officers and they devoted themselves to collecting information of every sort from travellers, businessmen, bankers, merchant seamen and, of course, spies. There were many Japanese expatriates living in these countries who were required, as a matter of course, to report through their Consul any matters of interest to an invading army. Prominent among these in Burma were a Dr Suzuki in Rangoon, who had many leading Burmese among his patients, and a well-known and much respected Japanese Buddhist monk called Nagai. Apart from the obvious matters of climate, topography, resources, local customs, enemy forces, communications, ports and airfields, much interest was taken in clothing, in medical precautions against disease for both men and horses, and in matters of hygiene. Copies of all available maps were obtained and reproduced, some with the place names overprinted in Japanese and all with a Japanese version of the map information panel. This was particularly easy in Burma for the country had been fully mapped by the highly professional Survey of India and there was complete coverage at quarter-inch scale and almost complete at one-inch scale. Such maps could be purchased freely, and were. In September 1941 many coloured copies of these maps for the

A view in central Japan in 1946. Much of Japan resembled parts of Burma.

whole of Burma, enlarged to the standard Japanese scale of 1:50,000, were printed in Japan.

By mid-summer this information had been collated and the weapons, clothing
and equipment suitable for operations in the southern regions had been decided.
Now troop trials of the equipment and of the technique of landing operations
were carried out, first in an exercise from China to Kyushu, the southernmost
island of mainland Japan, and then another to the coast of southern China. From
these exercises it was learnt how many men and horses could be crammed into
a ship and how to keep them fit on a voyage of several days in bad weather. The
techniques of climbing down rope ladders into landing craft, firing grenade dischargers, machine guns and light guns from the boats and jumping overboard
with weapons into the surf were practised and the best methods recorded. Finally
a remarkable booklet was prepared for issue to each man when he embarked.
This gave an excellent summary of all that had been learnt about war and campaigning in the tropics. A similar document would have been invaluable to
British troops and to those Indian troops who could read English. As it was they
were given no briefing before landing in Burma and were mostly entirely ignorant of the problems they would have to face. (See Appendix 9.)

The Burma Independence Army (BIA)

Colonel Suzuki (no relation to the Dr Suzuki mentioned above) was the senior
of the original pair of staff officers sent to Burma and on his return he set up a

1. Masanobu, Tsuji, *Singapore, The Japanese Version*, p.22

group called M-Kikan whose aim was to win over Burmese to the Japanese side by forming a Burma Independence Army (BIA). Suzuki was a charismatic character and a great enthusiast, just the man to raise a private army. After a clandestine visit to Burma in 1940 he had realised the possibilities of using the young idealists of a political party dedicated to Burmese independence and whose members called themselves the Thakins. This party had three factions. One faction believed in making progress by democratic means and without outside help. Another would accept outside help but not from the Fascist Asian countries (a thinly-veiled reference to Japan), while the third was prepared to adopt any means likely to help the cause. Three Thakins from the third group, of whom a young man called Aung San was the leader, had already left Burma secretly to try and get help from China for their independence movement. With the help of the Japanese military police, Suzuki located these men in Amoy in south China and persuaded them that Japan was a better ally than China. With the support of General Headquarters in Tokyo, he arranged for twenty-seven of their friends to be smuggled out of Burma secretly on Japanese cargo ships and to receive military training in Hainan. They called themselves the 'Thirty Comrades'. Meanwhile Suzuki arranged for four small Japanese businesses, in reality cells of M-Kikan, to be established in four Thai towns. These were Chiang Mai, Raheng, Kanchanaburi and Ranong, the latter a small town on the other side of the river from Victoria Point. These were well placed on the main strategic routes into Burma.[2] (See Maps 2 & 3.)

The original aim of the BIA was to enter Burma and foment independently an armed insurrection. However, as plans matured for a Japanese invasion, this aim was changed and the BIA role became to support the Japanese expeditionary force. The majority of the 'Thirty Comrades' entered Thailand in late December and the BIA was formally established in Bangkok on 28 December 1941 with 78 Japanese officers and NCOs and 200 Burmese. After Thailand entered the war, rifles and light machine guns were imported through Bangkok and the BIA were armed. Each area had a Japanese commander and some Japanese NCOs but the BIA appointed their own officers, Aung San becoming a major-general. They were to play an auxiliary but significant part in the invasion.[3]

The Japanese Plan

The Japanese plan was for the *25th Army* of three divisions, the *5th, 18th* and the *Imperial Guards*, to invade Malaya and when a good measure of success had been achieved, for the *15th Army* of two divisions, the *33rd* and the *55th*, to invade Burma. A sixth division, the *56th*, was to be held in reserve in Japan until shipping was available. The initial aim for *15th Army* was to prevent interference

Lieutenant-General Shojiro Iida,
Commander of the
Japanese 15th Army. HMSO.

from Burma with the *25th Army's* line of communication, to capture the Tenasserim airfields and to
keep the peace in Thailand. If the attack on Malaya
went well, *55 Division* would then invade Burma
from Raheng and capture Moulmein. They would
be followed by *33 Division* who would seize the
crossings over the River Salween in the vicinity of
Pa-an. Both divisions would then advance and capture Rangoon. It was not, at this stage, planned to
capture the whole of Burma, mainly because of the shortage of shipping. The
order for *15th Army* to complete the conquest of the whole country would be
issued later.

The commander of *15th Army* was Lieutenant-General Shojiro Iida, aged 54.
He had originally been appointed to command *25th Army* for the invasion of
Malaya but this command was later given to General Yamashita. Iida had the reputation of being a serious soldier and a tough commander. He came of a distinguished military family. His father had commanded the *4th Regiment* of the
Imperial Guards Division with much distinction in the Russo-Japanese war and
had later commanded the division. He had been rewarded for his services with a
baronetcy. General Shojiro Iida had also commanded the *Imperial Guards*
Division in the fighting in China and it was from this command that he had been
appointed army commander.

The *33rd Division* came from a mountainous region north-west of Tokyo. It
had been mobilised and sent to China in 1939 and had seen much fighting there
and was now a first-class battle-hardened division. As in all the old divisions,
each battalion had four rifle companies and an MMG company. In contrast, the
55th Division came from Shikoku, the smallest of the four islands of mainland
Japan. Like all divisions raised in and after 1940, it only had three rifle companies and an MMG company in each battalion. (See Appendix 7 for organisation
and numbering of Japanese units.) Together with *56 Division*, it had been raised
in the summer of 1940 in cadre form. As a result of the Emperor's provisional
agreement in September 1941 that preparations could be started for an expansion
of the war, it was mobilised, reservists were called up and it was brought up to
full strength in early October. Training was at once started for landing across

2. Izumiya, Tatsuro, *The Minami Organ.*
3. *ibid.*

beaches. About two-thirds of the division were soldiers of two or more years' service and the remainder were young conscripts with nearly a year's training. They had a great advantage over similar new divisions in the Indian Army for officers and men had the same background and spoke the same language. They had been to the same or similar schools and received the same military indoctrination while, thanks to the fighting in China, many officers and soldiers were battle-experienced. Another important feature of both divisions was that their rifle companies started the campaign with a strength of more than 200 men as against their normal strength of 180. This was to allow for casualties and attrition.

The Army Air Force

Japanese air forces were divided into the Army Air Force and the Navy Air Force and were under the command of their respective Services. The Army Air Force for Malaya, Burma and Indonesia was under the command of General Count Terauchi at HQ Southern Area and he had a Deputy Chief of Staff, Lieutenant-General Sakaguchi, in charge of air operations. To retain flexibility, air forces were not allotted to formations and General Iida had none under his command. The air forces were divided into two divisions. It was the 5th Air Division which mostly operated in Burma and the 3rd Air Division in Malaya, but in the big raids on Rangoon on 23 and 25 December bombers from both air divisions took part. The 5th Air Division had two groups, 10th Dan and 4th Dan. 10th Dan had 37 fighters, 28 light bombers, nine long-range reconnaissance aircraft and 24 transport aircraft. 4th Dan, which had 24 fighters, 28 light bombers and 28 heavy bombers, was transferred from the Philippines by 22 January.

The Move to Thailand

On 13 November 1941, *Headquarters 55 Division* and *112 Regiment*[4] embarked in Shikoku and on the 26th reached Haiphong in Indo-China. They stayed in north Indo-China to avoid giving away their intention of moving south. On 8 December the two formations moved to Saigon by train, then to Phnom Penh by truck and finally in small parties by train to Bangkok where they assembled at the end of December. *143 Regimental Group* embarked separately and reached southern Indo-China on 27 November, remaining at sea off Saigon. It later joined up with the main Malayan invasion fleet and split off from them to land further north in Thailand on 8 December. *144 Regimental Group* was left behind in Japan. It was to sail in the opposite direction and capture the lightly defended American outpost of Guam in the Marianas Islands. Later it went on to Rabaul in the Bismarck Archipelago and it was not until January 1944 that it rejoined its division in Burma at Akyab.

33 Division came by sea from China but did not reach Bangkok until 10 January. It also had only two regiments; 213 Regiment and two mountain gun battalions had been left in China for lack of shipping. Shortly after it reached Thailand, *33 Division* moved up by rail and truck to the Raheng area.

The Capture of Victoria Point (Map 2)

143 Regiment was to be the first formation to enter Burma. The task of this group was to land in the Kra Isthmus, protect the Bangkok-Singapore railway line which here ran close to the Burmese frontier and then seize the airfield in Burma at Victoria Point. To ensure co-ordination they were placed under command of *25th Army* for the actual landings. They went ashore on four beaches, landing a battalion group on three of them and a company group on the fourth. These beaches were in Thailand between Chumphon and Prachuab. Unfortunately for them, their landing, difficult enough in the wind and rain of the north-east monsoon, was opposed. Although an agreement was signed between the Japanese Ambassador and the Thai Premier at 9.30am on the 8th, permitting Japanese forces to pass through Thailand, the news took some time to percolate through to some areas. The Thai standing orders to the army and police were for any invasion to be resisted. At Prachuab, the Thais resisted the Japanese and hard fighting continued until mid-day on the 9th. The Japanese lost two company commanders and 49 soldiers killed there, while another 28 men were killed on the other beaches. These substantial casualties were hushed up as the official Japanese line was that the Japanese troops were being welcomed into Thailand.

On the 10th, probably as a result of the news of Pearl Harbour, the sinking of HMS *Prince of Wales* and *Repulse* and the early successes in Malaya, the attitude of the Thai government (but not the Thai people) changed. Negotiations on a Thai-Japan Treaty of Mutual Assistance started, was tentatively agreed on the 11th and officially signed on the 21st. On 25 January Thailand, under Japanese pressure, declared war on Britain and the United States.

On 11 and 12 December Colonel Uno, the Regimental Commander of *143 Regiment,* and *2/143 Battalion*[5] moved in vehicles to Kra Buri on the Kra River, which formed the boundary with Burma (see Map 2). They had brought with them some folding boats and Colonel Uno and one company embarked in these while the rest of the battalion group crossed the river to Marang and made their way south along the river bank. It was to take them three days of very rough going through the jungle to reach Maliwun. On the 14th, the boats being well in the lead, Colonel Uno landed his company at Maliwun where they were provid-

---

4. A Japanese infantry regiment was equivalent to (though larger than) a British infantry brigade.
5. For the numbering of Japanese battalions and companies see Appendix 7.

ed with vehicles by the BIA and drove the 20 miles to Victoria Point. There was no opposition. Victoria Point had been guarded by a platoon of Burma Frontier Force police who, obeying their instructions, had demolished certain vital targets and retired by boat the day before. An Indian doctor from the local clinic stayed until the 14th when he decided to leave by boat with some of his staff. They were intercepted by a party of the M-Kikan[6] from Ranong who, recognising the doctor, allowed them to escape. Mr Naiff, the Sub-Divisional Officer, and Mr Achard, Inspector of Police, both Anglo-Indians, bravely stayed at their posts, their orders to retire not having been received because of the destruction of the wireless station. They were taken prisoner by the Japanese and handed over, with the administration of the area, to the M-Kikan. Their fate is uncertain. The Governor's report, written after the campaign was over, states that it was understood that they were taken as prisoners to Bangkok, but it was rumoured at the time, and widely believed, that they were thrown into the local jail and allowed to die of thirst.

Meanwhile the British had launched their first land offensive. A year before, GHQ Singapore had considered the problem of an attack on Malaya. A plan was made for a raiding party from Burma to cross into Thailand and to destroy two large steel bridges on the Bangkok-Singapore railway just south of Prachuab. This was a highly important operation, for the railway was the supply line for the forces invading Malaya and, as mentioned above, the Japanese had sent a considerable force to protect it. The task was allotted to BFF2 Battalion of the Military Police. The headquarter company was British and Indian but the majority of the soldiers were Gurkhas. They had assembled near the frontier some months before and done many reconnaissances in the frontier area. Almost certainly the Japanese knew of this. The force was organised into three columns. At dusk on 12 December they crossed the Maw Daung Pass into Thailand. The first column ran into the Japanese near Prachuab and lost 15 killed before withdrawing. The other two joined together and, under the command of Captain E.J. Stephenson, pressed on; but they got lost, the Thai maps being highly inaccurate and misleading. Eventually, much exhausted, they reached the railway but could find no bridges. After an abortive 12-hour search and increasing sightings of Japanese they decided to pull out and returned to Burma on the 16th. In the absence of sufficient aircraft to destroy these targets from the air, this plan was sound but it needed highly trained troops and surprise. Even with these it would have taken luck to succeed in the face of the Japanese precautions.

Meanwhile, a party of about one hundred men from Victoria Point, led by Lieutenant Furutuki, had moved up the coast by boat and occupied Bokpyin. When this was verified, the Officer Commanding the Mergui garrison ordered one of the BFF2 companies under Major S.W.A. Love to go down to the south

3/112 Battalion Group, led by elephants, force their way through the virgin jungle of the Tenasserim range en route to Tavoy.

and restore the situation. A boatload of mortar and other ammunition sent forward for him unfortunately failed to arrive, but despite this Love decided to attack. The Japanese were well dug-in on a small hill covering a strongly-built police station and court house and, although the attackers closed to hand grenade range, the attack was beaten off. Sadly Love, who was an able and forceful leader, was killed and his second-in-command wounded and so the force, with little ammunition left, decided to withdraw. A second force of one company from the 2nd Burma Rifles was sent from Mergui to renew the attack, which it did on 28 December, supported by a small gun on a Naval motorboat. This attack was successful. Lieutenant Furutuki was killed and, having run out of ammunition, the Japanese retired overland to Victoria Point.

On 20 December, two Buffalo fighters from Mergui, led by Flying Officer P. M. Bingham Wallis RAF, were ordered to attack targets of opportunity in the Chumphon-Victoria Point area. At Victoria Point the two pilots reported having thoroughly strafed the barracks which "was full of Japanese troops".[7] It was in fact a very successful sortie. They achieved complete surprise and the Japanese record that 29 soldiers were killed.

2/143 Battalion left Victoria Point on 23 January and crossed back into Thailand, eventually reaching Moulmein on 27 February. The other two battalions of 143 Regiment had already moved up through Bangkok to Raheng where 55 Division was concentrating.

6. Not officially the BIA until 28 December 1941.
7. Shore, Christopher, and Cull, Brian, *Bloody Shambles*, Vol.1, p.241.

The Loss of Tavoy

Meanwhile *3/112 Battalion Group*, totalling some 1500 men and commanded by Major Oki, left Bangkok on 3 January to attack Tavoy. Their plan was a typically daring one. They went first by train to Kanchanaburi (where they were helped by the local BIA team) and then in small motor-boats up the notorious River Kwai to Wanpo. From here they set out to force their way over the steep and jungle-covered Tenasserim Range which here divides Thailand from Burma. There were no maps and no paths but an advance party had reconnoitred a difficult but possible route. Each soldier had to carry seven days' rations plus either 120 rounds of ammunition or a mountain artillery shell (14lbs) in addition to his normal kit. To carry heavy weapons and more ammunition local oxen were used to supplement the Japanese horses. Several elephants supplied by the Thai army were in the lead (elephants have a remarkably good cross-country performance) and were followed by the engineers to clear a path. It was very hard going particularly for the horses and oxen of which several were lost, while hosts of leeches harassed the men. They could only make about two miles a day through the dense jungle and in spite of killing some oxen and dumping their loads, began to run out of food. However, on14 January they crossed the crest of the range and the going became easier. On the 15th they emerged from the forest onto a grassy plain and saw before them the village of Myitta, whence a motor road led over another but smaller range to Tavoy, 34 miles away.

Tavoy was an important town of some 30,000 inhabitants. It was defended by the 6th Burma Rifles (6 Burif), one of the new battalions, and they were reinforced on the evening of the attack by two companies of the 3rd Burma Rifles (3 Burif) who arrived by boat from Mergui. The 6 Burif had an outpost of two platoons in Myitta and a two-company position astride the road on the crest of a ridge behind them, supported by a third company. On the 16th the outpost fired at the advancing Japanese and then retired, leaving the Japanese to occupy Myitta where they spent the night and rested the next day. In the evening, after dark, they continued their advance along the road. According to the Japanese, about two hours later they bumped the British position. Their advanced scouts were fired on and three Japanese soldiers were killed. So the Japanese sprayed the British position with MMG fire and got a mountain gun into action which fired five shells. On this the Burma Rifles retreated and the Japanese occupied the village. The Burma Rifles had been prey to many exaggerated rumours and the three forward companies, instead of retreating to the next position at Wagon as planned, melted away into the forest and made for Moulmein, about 200 miles away to the north. On the 18th the Japanese continued their advance in daylight along the road, but using branches of trees for concealment of both men and horses. They took cover twice when British planes appeared but were apparently unobserved and bivouacked for the night close to Tavoy to prepare for the next day's attack.

In Tavoy the CO of 6 Burif was now left with only one of his own companies, two 3 Burif companies, a detachment from the Kokine Battalion of the BFF and a detachment from the Tenasserim Battalion of the Burma Auxiliary Force (BAF). About 9am on the 19th, the Japanese attacked the airfield and the BFF police put up a spirited defence. An attack on one of the companies in the main perimeter was also held for a time and the Japanese admit to a number of casualties. But as officer casualties mounted, Lieutenant-Colonel Cotton judged correctly that his men would not hold for long and, soon after mid-day, decided to evacuate the town. The necessary demolitions were carried out with admirable coolness by the BAF detachment as the defence crumbled, a rumour of large Japanese reinforcements having caused most of the remaining Burma Rifles to make for the forest and head for home.[8] The remnants of the force under Colonel Cotton then withdrew up the road and were picked up some twenty miles to the north by the 4th/12th Frontier Force Regiment (4th/12th FFR) who had been sent down in support from Moulmein.

At 3pm the Japanese occupied Tavoy. Their total casualties in the whole operation had been 23 killed and 40 wounded. A BIA detachment under Captain Kawashima had followed the Japanese and this party now set up an autonomous administration and started recruiting volunteers for the BIA. They claim that within two weeks the town was back to normal.

This small action has been described in some detail because it had a disproportionate effect on the Burmese troops. The Burma Rifles concerned had suffered a serious loss of morale from which they never fully recovered and this affected other units also. The image had been created of strong forces of Japanese being able to appear suddenly out of impassable jungle and it would long be a bogey. But one must recognise that the Burmese troops were subject to much psychological pressure. There was a strong pro-independence (and thus anti-British and pro-Japanese) movement among the politically-minded in Burma. This grew with each Japanese success and British failure. Anyone identified with the losing side would clearly be in trouble if the invasion succeeded. Worse, their families would be friendless and at grave risk. The pressure for those domiciled in Burma to desert and go home was growing.

The Evacuation of Mergui

After capturing Tavoy *3/112 Battalion* marched north along the coast road to

---

8. Of the two companies from 3 Burif only 30 Chins, well led by Subedar Sima Zam, were seen again in this campaign.

Moulmein, which fell the day before they arrived. Mergui was now cut off. It was defended originally by the 2nd Burma Rifles Battalion (2 Burif) and the two companies of 3 Burif, but the latter had been sent to Tavoy. On the 19th, AHQ in Rangoon, seeing that there was now no point in holding Mergui, ordered the garrison and non-Burmese civilians to withdraw to Rangoon by sea. Considerable stocks of rubber and tungsten had already been evacuated. Withdrawal took place on the 20th and 22nd, the power station and other installations having been demolished. Both Victoria Point and Mergui had been bombed by the Japanese, the latter quite heavily, but at neither place was there any actual contact with the enemy.

An integral part of these preparatory Japanese moves was the formation and use of Colonel Suzuki's Burma Independence Army. In Tenasserim the BIA followed the Japanese into Victoria Point, Mergui and Tavoy, took over control, recruited more members and thus allowed the Japanese to rejoin their main forces.

The Battle in the Air

The Japanese had rightly foreseen that air forces would play a major part in the campaign and, taking advantage of the long range of their aircraft, they transferred a powerful air force from Manchuria to Thailand. As the British had expected, it was not long before this was used against Burma. The first raids on Rangoon were actually made by the *3rd Air Division* supporting the invasion of Malaya. The first assault came on 23 December when 87 bombers escorted by 34 Type 97 fighters[9] attacked both Rangoon and the airfield at Mingaladon 15miles away. The target in Rangoon was not the docks or the oil refinery, which the Japanese naturally wished to capture intact, but the town itself. The aim was to terrorise the population and encourage dock labourers and other essential workers to flee. As there were few shelters and many people came out into the streets to see what was happening, casualties were high. A major exodus started, the

Burmese retiring to their villages, and the Indians, who formed the bulk of the dock labourers, starting off on the long trek to India. This was the

The bombing of Rangoon on Christmas Day 1941.

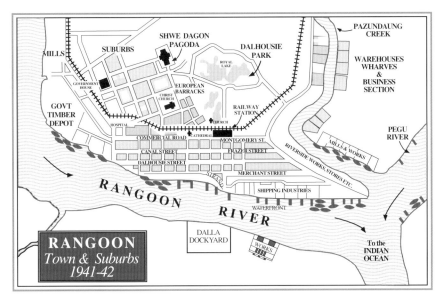

beginning of a severe problem for the authorities. On the 25th, Christmas Day, a raid by 67 bombers increased the number of evacuees. The escort this time was increased to 32 Type 97 fighters and 25 Oscars. There were still no anti-aircraft guns in Burma and the defence depended on 18 RAF Brewster Buffaloes, no match for the Oscars, and the 21 Tomahawks of the American AVG squadron. The Tomahawks were good fighters and about the equal of Hurricane IIs. There was an efficient Observer Corps organisation and this, together with the single radar set which was still at Moulmein, gave adequate warning of both these raids. In the two raids ten heavy bombers and five fighters were shot down, for the loss of four Tomahawks and six Buffaloes. The size of these heavy bomber losses was an unpleasant shock for the Japanese.

On 31 December some help arrived from India in the shape of the 8th Heavy and the 3rd Indian Light Anti-Aircraft Batteries. They were very welcome since the RAF and AVG had only 29 aircraft left to face more than 150 Japanese. On 4 January a force of 21 Japanese fighters was successfully driven off and a lull followed with only occasional night raids. For the moment the allied air forces had deterred the Japanese raiders. It was a most valuable achievement which allowed several troopships to land their desperately needed reinforcements without interference.

9. In this campaign the Japanese used two types of fighter, the older Type 97 whose performance was inferior to that of a Hurricane, and the new Type 1, the 'Oscar'. The Oscar, which was the Army version of the better known Navy 'Zero', was more manoeuvrable than a Hurricane but it was also more vulnerable. Where it did score was in having a much greater range.

CHAPTER FOUR

Fiasco at the Frontier

When General Hutton assumed command in Burma, he brought with him from India the very capable Brigadier 'Taffy' Davies to be his Chief of Staff. In early January they prepared an 'appreciation'[1] of the task which faced him. It was to prove to be substantially accurate. Faced with the hundreds of miles of frontier with Thailand the only possible plan seemed to be to guard the main routes crossing the great Salween River (see Map 3). These were, from north to south, one motorable track from Chiang Rai in north Thailand which led into Burma through the Shan States. Another did the same thing further south from the Thai railhead at Chiang Mai but there was a stretch of more than 50 miles near the Salween crossing which was only suitable for pack animals. Although these two routes lead to the centre of Burma, they were long and passed through many miles of hilly country. Further south still there was a route from the Thai railway at Phitsanulok leading to Raheng and then over the Dawna Range to Kawkereik and Rangoon. Some 40 miles of this was only a pack-track through hilly forests. Finally there was an easy but longer route from the railway at Kanchanaburi through the Three Pagodas Pass to Moulmein, although most of this was only a mule path (see Map 3).

It was clear that Rangoon was the key to the defence of Burma. Not only was it the largest city, main port and centre of industry, it was a communication centre for road, rail and water transport. As long as Rangoon was held and the sea approaches were secure, reinforcements could continue to reach Burma. Moreover the great strategic importance of Burma to the Allies was that it now contained the only major supply route to China. It was vital to keep China in the war, for half the Japanese Army was tied down there. Rangoon was the vital southern terminal of this supply route, known as the 'Burma Road'[2]. Unfortunately, the Burma Road ran north from Rangoon and for some 700 miles was roughly parallel to the frontiers of Thailand and Indo-China. Any of the main trans-border tracks might be used to cut the road. It was plainly impossible with the tiny forces available to be strong everywhere, or indeed, anywhere. A choice had to be made. Hutton decided, correctly and perhaps helped by secret intelligence, that the main Japanese attack would be aimed at Rangoon and, in spite of

56

the poor approach, was likely to come via Raheng. In the north he would keep only a small part of his force, based on Toungoo and with patrols forward to the Salween, and hope to get Chinese support to stop any incursion there. The long strip of Tenasserim to the south could not be defended and the small garrisons there should hold out as long as possible and then be withdrawn.

To implement these decisions, Hutton ordered 16 Brigade from Mandalay to move (via Rangoon) to Kawkareik, covering the route into Burma via Raheng. On 9 January 1942 Major-General Smyth VC arrived in Rangoon with Headquarters 17th Indian Infantry Division (17 Division) and was sent forward to Moulmein to take charge of the 2nd Burmese Brigade (2 Bur Brigade, already in Moulmein) and 16 Brigade on its arrival.

Major General J.G. Smyth, VC, MC.

'Jackie' Smyth was one of the stars of the Indian Army. He had won his VC with the Sikhs in France in World War I and had later earned an MC on the North-West Frontier of India. He had been chosen in 1923 to attend the two-year course at the Staff College at Camberley, which took only four or five students from the Indian Army on each course, and had been selected to stay on to do a three-year tour there as an instructor.[3] Lord Gort VC had been Commandant of the Staff College during his time and they had kept in touch. When, in the late Thirties, war with Germany seemed imminent, Lord Gort had promised Smyth a command if he was in a position to arrange it. In the summer of 1939 Smyth had just finished commanding his battalion, the 15th Sikhs. He took the gamble of retiring from the Indian Army and returning to the UK on retirement leave. The gamble paid off. Lord Gort was made Commander-in-Chief of the British Expeditionary Force and in due course Smyth was given command of a front-line Territorial Army brigade which soon crossed the Channel to France. After a successful period of command culminating in Dunkirk, however, General Auchinleck insisted on his return to India and promised him the command of one of the new Indian Army divisions then forming. A spell in Quetta followed until in October 1941 he was appointed to command the 18th Indian Division (later re-numbered as the 19th), one of these new divisions. Two months later he was summoned to Delhi for a long interview with General Wavell and was offered command of the17th Indian Division, shortly to go to Burma. Aged 48, he was

---

1. The Army term for a logical study.
2. Strictly speaking, the term 'Burma Road' applied to the sector between the railhead at Lashio and Chungking, the Chinese wartime capital. This was about three times as long as the stretch from Rangoon to Mandalay and had been constructed by the Chinese in 1938-40, a remarkable feat. Strategically the whole route from Rangoon to Chungking was referred to as the Burma Road.
3. His successor as instructor was a Colonel William Slim.

not only outstandingly brave and a highly trained officer but had a lively and out-going personality.[4] He already had command experience in World War II and seemed an excellent choice for what was clearly going to be a difficult campaign.

Most unfortunately, however, Smyth was not completely fit. He had been a noted athlete in his youth and had always prided himself on his fitness. But in Quetta in the summer of 1941 he had had a bout of malaria and, more seriously, suffered an anal fissure, an injury often extremely painful. He also suffered from what was diagnosed as dyspepsia at the time but was later thought to have been a mild heart attack. He was operated on for the anal fissure in the local hospital. When he was offered command of 18 Division he took medical advice and, being assured that he should soon recover, accepted the post, knowing that the division was not expected to go overseas to Iraq for another six months. When in Delhi for his unexpected interview with Wavell he was not feeling well but put it down to influenza of which there was then a local epidemic. At this interview Smyth was in a difficult position. To refuse command of a division about to go into action, the peak of a professional soldier's ambition, was not only painful but might be misconstrued, even for a VC. From subsequent actions it is clear that he kept quiet and hoped for the best. It was an unfortunate decision. After the interview he retired to his bed for seven days, laid low as he thought by influenza, and his staff preceded him to Burma.

The Build-up Continues

On 16 January, the 46th Indian Infantry Brigade (46 Brigade) arrived by sea at Rangoon and was sent up to the Bilin River, also to come under command of 17 Division. Smyth now had three infantry brigades under command and three Sapper and Miner field companies, the 1st Burma, 24th Bombay and 60th Madras. But he had no field artillery and the only supporting guns were provided by the 5th and 12th (Indian) Mountain Batteries and a section of four Bofors guns provided by the 3rd Indian LAA Battery. His area of responsibility stretched from Mergui in the south to Papun in the north, a distance of about 400 miles.

Hutton's redistribution of his forces took some time to implement and was not helped by the Japanese air force which during this period bombed Martaban, Kyondo and Moulmein, the latter several times (see Map 5). Nor was the deployment easy even without this interference. Although there was a direct rail link from Rangoon to Martaban, a town opposite Moulmein on the north bank of the Salween, it was only a metre-gauge railway mostly single line and with a limited capacity.[5] There was no through road because the only bridge over the River Sittang was the railway one. There was a metalled road much of the way, but for 15 miles either side of the Sittang bridge there was only a dusty track, impassable in wet weather. As a result, most vehicles had to go to the forward area by rail, although three ferries across the Sittang river were able to take a limited number. Ferries again had to be used at Martaban to cross the Salween estuary to Moulmein, with another two ferry crossings for those going on to Kawkereik. The latter two were ferries made from country boats and they could handle about one vehicle an hour. This was a rather imperfect line of communication for a force dependent on vehicles.

The Action at Kawkareik

The unit which, since early December, had been covering the approach across the frontier from Raheng was the 4th Battalion of the Burma Rifles (4 Burif), commanded by Lieutenant-Colonel Abernethy. This was a battalion of 2 Bur Brigade, whose headquarters was in Moulmein, some eighty miles away. 4 Burif was deployed covering those main tracks across the densely forested Dawna Range which led to Kawkareik, a small town set back from the frontier. The battalion had suffered many malaria casualties and its strength was only about two-thirds of what it should have been. Smyth had been ordered to hold the frontier as long as possible so he decided to strengthen this cover by sending 16 Brigade (Brigadier J.K. 'Jonah' Jones) to Kawkareik to relieve 4 Burif. However, both because of 4 Burif's knowledge of the country and to speed up the move, he ordered 4 Burif to stay on the frontier and come under command of 16 Brigade. To compensate for this the 4th/12th Frontier Force Regiment (4th/12th FFR) was switched from 16 Brigade to 2 Bur Brigade in Moulmein.

16 Brigade was also ordered to send a company to cover the approach to Moulmein over the Three Pagodas Pass eighty miles south of Kawkareik and this task was allotted to a company of the 1st Battalion of the 7th Gurkha Rifles (1st/7th Gurkhas). A company from the 1st Royal Battalion of the 9th Jat Regiment (1st/9th R Jats) was detailed to escort a section of mountain guns going by road to Kawkareik via Kya-in (see Map 5). This latter group was however recalled before it had gone far. As a result, this Jat company, like the Gurkha company, took no part in the battles at either Kawkareik or Moulmein.

Having made these arrangements, Smyth moved his headquarters back to Kyaikto, mid-way between the Bilin and Sittang rivers. From the 8th to the 15th, 16 Brigade moved by steamer up the Gyaing river to Kyondo and thence by truck to Kawkareik and the frontier. The trucks, of which there were not very

4. He had published a novel and had a sharp sense of humour. His description in *Before the Dawn* of how his Territorial Army brigade was nearly sent to Finland to "fall upon" the Russians is a gem of military writing.
5. All the railways in Burma were metre gauge.

many as it was a marching brigade, took the long route via Metheraw to the ferry over the Haungtharaw river at Kya-in.

The Japanese Advance to Kawkereik

The Japanese were also busy deploying their troops. *The Imperial Guards Division* had entered Thailand by road from Cambodia on 9 December and had moved into Bangkok to assert the Japanese presence. They stayed in Bangkok until *55 Division* arrived and then, leaving a battalion there in an internal security role (for there had been a number of anti-Japanese incidents), they moved south to join *25 Army* in the invasion of Malaya.

55 Division, which was to lead the Japanese advance into Burma, moved with *112 Regiment* (less the battalion which had gone to Tavoy) to Bangkok by road and rail from Saigon at the end of December. At the same time *143 Regiment*, which had landed earlier over the Kra Isthmus beaches, returned to its division with two battalions, its third battalion having gone to Victoria Point. On 28 December, an advance party of a platoon of infantry and a party of the BIA, led by the CO of *2/112 Battalion*, started for Mae Sot, a Thai village close to the Burmese border, to plan the advance across the frontier and the crossing of the Dawna Range to Kawkareik. *55 Division* then followed them to Phitsanulok by

rail whence the divisional transport company shuttled them to Raheng. From Raheng it was about forty miles to Mae Sot. Between these two places were two ranges of hills, two to three thousand feet high and covered with dense tropical forest, genuine jungle as the word is commonly understood. Across these hills was a narrow and steep path, impassable for vehicles, so a strong force of Japanese and Thai sappers, supported by infantry working parties, were set to work to produce a motorable track.[6]

Japanese troops marching towards the Burmese frontier from Raheng.

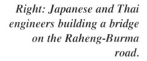

*Above: Lieutenant-General
Yiroshi Takeuchi
Commander of
55 Infantry Division.]*

*Right: Japanese and Thai
engineers building a bridge
on the Raheng-Burma
road.*

It being impossible at this stage to get trucks to the border, the Japanese planned to carry out the first phase of their campaign without vehicles other than those they could pick up. In addition to their own horses they procured locally some elephants and a large number of oxen to be used as pack animals or to drag sledges. In spite of this assistance, soldiers were required to carry heavy loads of food and ammunition and the bicycle company to carry their machines as well as their weapons. Many soldiers' diaries complain of the toughness of this approach march through the jungle: "our hardships baffle description" is a typical statement, and it took four long days to reach Mae Sot. *112 Regiment*, less *3/112 Battalion*, arrived in the middle of January and were followed by most of *143 Regiment* (less *3/143 Battalion* which was still in Tenasserim) and *HQ 55 Division*, which arrived by 19 January.

With BIA help, the advance party had discovered that in addition to the motorable track to Kawkareik from Miyawadi, a village on the Burmese side of the Thoungyin river which formed the frontier, there were also two other passes over the Dawna Range in this district (see Map 4). To the north of the road was the Kyawku pass, leading through Nabu to Pa-an on the Salween. At Mepale a path led from this route back on to the main track. South of the road was the Kwingale pass which, like the main track, led to the small town of Kawkareik. The commander of *55 Division*, Lieutenant-General Takeuchi, decided to

---

6. British engineers had advised the Thai government about a possible alignment for a road a few years before and this route was adopted.

advance along the road and the southern track and sent only a patrol towards Mepale and the northern pass. *112 Regiment* with its second battalion took the road and sent its first battalion to cross the frontier at Yebu, a few miles north, and to join the main track some miles further on. *55 Divisional Reconnaissance Regiment*[7] crossed the frontier at Palu, a few miles further south and took the forest track which led via the Kwingale pass to Myohaung, a village close to Kawkareik. *143 Regiment*, which had only reached Mae Sot on the 19th, was in reserve to follow whichever track proved most advantageous. *HQ 55 Division* followed along the road.

The British Defence

Brigadier J.K. Jones, formerly of the 1st Gurkhas and now commander of 16 Brigade, was aged 50 but was credited with being fitter than many younger men. To meet the expected Japanese thrust he had established a small administrative base in Kawkareik under his staff captain, set up his tactical headquarters beside the road forward at milestone 22, about six miles north of the town, and was busy deploying his freshly-arrived brigade. The road from Kawkereik to the frontier, 38 miles away, was a very steep and rough one, climbing about 3000 feet in ten miles and with very dense jungle on either side. On the eastern side of the range it descended equally steeply and nine miles from the frontier at Miyawadi emerged into flat country. On 20 January, 4 Burif had two companies covering the northern tracks, one at Nabu and one between Mepale and Tichara (see Map 4). Their HQ and one company were at milestone 18[8] and their fourth company was in reserve at 'Misty Hollow' awaiting relief by a company of the 1st/7th Gurkhas. Misty Hollow was a small plateau where vehicles and mules could harbour off the road about four miles west of the crest of the range. The 1st/7th Gurkhas had one company and battalion HQ in the main position at milestone 36 and one company, 'D' Company, about two miles short of Miyawadi, with a platoon in Miyawadi itself. Their third company had first gone to Kwingale but on the 20th was on its way to Misty Hollow. The1st/9th R Jats had one company deployed forward at the Kwingale pass covering the tracks leading to Kawkareik from the south while its HQ and two companies were in reserve near Kawkareik. The 1st (and only) Company of Burma Sappers was deployed preparing demolitions to the road between milestones 38 and 49.

No-one except 4 Burif had had any time to learn anything about their surroundings, but fortunately HQ 16 Brigade had the assistance not only of Mr Maurice Maybury, the very helpful British Sub-Divisional Officer (SDO) of the Burma Civil Service at Kawkareik, but also of an experienced forest officer who worked for the big firm of Steel Brothers extracting teak from the forest. The latter's name was Raymond Hall and he had lived for some years in a forest bungalow at Mepale. He was widely known in the district and much respected by the Burmese. Since the war started his many contacts had been a major source of information about the activities across the border. When 16 Brigade arrived he was taken on as the brigade Intelligence Officer. Another person who had proved invaluable was the Indian postmaster at Miyawadi. Although highly alarmed at his exposed position in the village, from which nearly all the inhabitants had fled because of shooting across the river by the Thai police, he continued to monitor the activity on the airfield at Mae Sot and to report by telephone when any aircraft arrived or took off. This not only gave early warning to Kawkareik and Moulmein but enabled the RAF to make some effective raids.[9]

With the brigade so widely dispersed, communications were of vital importance. Unfortunately the two Indian Army battalions had no wireless sets[10] and so a small Indian signal section from divisional HQ had been detached to 16 Brigade.[11] Their sets worked sporadically but suffered from battery trouble as there was only one charging set. Cable was laid between brigade and the two Indian battalion HQs but to begin with all units on the road tapped in to the telegraph line from Miyawadi to Moulmein.

It is clear that the leading 'D' Company of the 1st/7th Gurkhas near Miyawadi was very isolated and must have felt distinctly lonely facing what was already known to be a considerable build-up of Japanese troops across the river. Lieutenant-Colonel Abernethy, whose 4 Burif had been holding the position previously, had protested hotly that to hold so far forward was militarily unsound. He had been overruled by General Smyth who considered that a military presence bolstered morale in the area and aided the flow of information from across the frontier.

The Japanese Attack

The first Japanese attack in the frontier area was by the Japanese Air Force which on 12 January bombed Kyondo, sinking a steamer and putting the landing stage out of action. This was followed the next day by a raid on Sukhli and Misty

7. This reconnaissance 'regiment' had two mounted infantry companies and one MMG company. (See Appendix 7.)

8. The milestones were numbered from Kyondo. Kawkareik was milestone 16.

9. The RAF destroyed two light bombers on the Miyawadi airstrip on 10 January. The postmaster stuck to his post until the end and managed to escape through the forest to Martaban.

10. Sets which had been satisfactory in the Middle East were found to be inadequate in Burma because of rapid fungus growth and the severe effect of screening by trees. *(British Army Signals in the Second World War.)*

11. This signal section had two British officers, two British NCOs and 12 Indian signallers under a Havildar.

Hollow. Raids on these two places became almost daily occurrences, culminating in a series of raids on Sukhli on the the 20th. The troops were concealed and well dug-in and casualties were surprisingly few.

The main attack started at 0500 on 20 January. The platoon in Miyawadi was surprised in the dark. Some men were killed and the rest made their way back to their company, two miles further back, on whom the main attack now fell. D Company remained in touch with battalion HQ until 0930 when the telephone line was cut. Their last report said that they were surrounded and short of ammunition. Colonel White, the battalion commander, together with the brigade Intelligence Officer, went forward with the company of Gurkhas from Kwingale and a platoon each of the R Jats and 4 Burif to restore the situation. They met the advancing Japanese at the foot of the hills and in the skirmish that followed had a number of casualties, the invaluable Raymond Hall being killed. It was an unfortunate loss of a very good man. Colonel White was also missing and the force retired to a covering position at Thingannyinaung. Brigadier Jones now put Abernethy in command of both battalions until White turned up at Sukhli that evening with the covering force. There was no news of the Gurkha 'D' Company near Miyawadi and everyone feared that it had been lost, so Jones ordered a withdrawal to the main position at milestone 36 and instructed the Burma Sappers to blow all the road demolitions between Thingannyinaung and Sukhli. He also ordered the two Burif companies from milestone 18 and Misty Hollow to join the Gurkhas in the main position at milestone 36, while the Gurkha company from Thingannyinaung was ordered to march to milestone 18 and come under command of HQ 4 Burif. Why he chose to mix up the two battalions like this is unclear.

In fact 'D' Company, commanded by Captain Eric Holdaway, was not lost and held out for several hours. Finally, when it was clear that they were not going to be relieved, he and his company abandoned their two trucks, broke out of their encirclement and, with all their personal weapons and mules, made their way north-west through the forest.[12] In these first two clashes *2/112 Battalion* had lost 20 killed and about 50 wounded and their advance became much more cautious.[13]

On the Palu-Kwingale track the story was very different. A Jat patrol encountered the mounted infantry of the enemy *55 Reconnaissance Regiment* making its way up from Palu. The patrol opened fire and claimed to have inflicted casualties before retiring in its truck to Ale Mekane and reporting the advance. After dark that evening this Japanese battalion attacked the Jat company in its position near Kwingale. In the confusion of a night attack the company commander misread the situation and ordered the company to disperse back down the track to

Kawkareik. This was serious as it exposed 16 Brigade's right flank. By dawn on the 21st neither the main position at milestone 36 nor the 4 Burif company on the north flank at Mepale had been attacked. The Japanese, however, were advancing unopposed on the southern flank. So Brigadier Jones deployed the two reserve companies of the Jats to cover each of the two tracks from Kwingale where they emerged from the hills at Tadangu and Myohaung. He also ordered that the main demolition of the road at about milestone 37 should be blown at dawn on the 21st and this was duly done by Lieutenant Eustace Lord and his Burma Sappers. This demolition, which blew the road away where it crossed the face of a rocky precipice, was expected to cause the enemy considerable delay. The Japanese, however, had no trucks at this stage and diversions could eventually be found for pack animals, so the demolitions, though tiresome later, were only a temporary hindrance to their advance.

The night of the 20th/21st had been an unhappy one. All troops in Burma took some time to learn how to handle night attacks in the forest. Rumours of Japanese on all sides were rife. Throughout the night there was much indiscriminate shooting at shadows by nearly all units. Colonel Abernethy commented (not referring to his Burmese troops) that "the effect of the Jungle on these young soldiers was most marked as they, including British and Indian officers, actually showed me enemy moving in the jungle which was nothing more than the effect of light and shade on trees and undergrowth. There were no enemy in the vicinity."

The Decision to Withdraw

The order to the 1st R Jats company to disperse from Kwingale had had an unfortunate effect on the whole battalion and wild rumours abounded. The 1st R Jat War Diary frankly records that the CO acted in an indecisive manner and this feeling rapidly spread through the ranks. Jones had little faith that their reserve companies would hold if seriously attacked. Soon after midnight he had therefore advised Maybury, the SDO, to evacuate civilians from Kawkereik and to destroy all government property of use to the enemy. He had also asked the SDO to go to Kyondo and arrange for boats to be collected on the river there and bullock-carts on the far bank. Jones then reported the situation to HQ 17 Division. Smyth, who had never wished to hold so far forward, obtained Hutton's permission for a withdrawal if 16 Brigade were in danger of being cut off.

Brigadier Jones now moved his own HQ to Hlaingwa, three miles west of

---

12. Holdaway and his company reached the Salween, floated down it in sampans and rejoined their battalion successfully at Martaban.
13. The Commander of *112 Regiment* was later censured for his slow advance.

Kawkareik, and the administrative units to milestone 7 about six miles further west. That morning Kawkareik, now fortunately deserted, was the target for a heavy air raid and the telephone terminal was destroyed.

Later in the morning news came in that the Jat company at Myohaung had encountered the enemy and the company commander had been killed. It was clear that the Japanese advance on the southern flank was continuing so Brigadier Jones decided that he could wait no longer. He had already isssued a warning order and at 1800 hours on the 21st, using the discretion he had been granted, he ordered a withdrawal from the main position that night. The only road back to Moulmein involved crossing a wide river at Kya-in by a locally-manned ferry and, as it could only take one vehicle at a a time, this was a very slow process. He therefore ordered unnecessary kit to be jettisoned and surplus vehicles burnt. This move, though logical, did nothing for morale. At 2000 hours the convoy left for the primitive civilian ferry some ten miles away. Then disaster struck. The first vehicle to cross was an ammunition truck, heavily overloaded as such trucks often were. In the dark it attempted on the far bank to drive off the ferry before the latter was properly secured. This tilted the ferry which filled with water and sank, as did the truck. There was now no way of getting any vehicles back or of avoiding much loss of equipment.

A Chaotic Withdrawal

The plan was for the withdrawal to start at midnight on the 21/22nd. The Jats would hold a lay-back position a mile north of Kawkareik and trucks would be sent up to milestone 23 to pick up the troops marching down from the main posi-tion. HQ 4 Burif and its Gurkha company would allow the main force to pass through and then join in behind them. The main force would take up a covering position at milestone 13 and the Jats would pass through in their turn and estab-lish a bridgehead at Kyondo.To conform with this, Abernethy sent off a mounted runner to try and contact his northern two companies and tell them to rendezvous at Zathabyin near Moulmein.

The main body of the 1st/7th Gurkhas and one company of 4 Burif duly retired down the main track. Unfortunately, wild rumours from the police that the Japanese were already approaching Kawkareik from the south and using poison gas induced the Jat CO at 2200 hours to order a rather disorderly withdrawal of his battalion to Kawkareik. The move was hastened by the premature ignition of some trucks carrying ammunition which made a lot of noise and sounded like an attack. So when the Gurkhas reached milestone 18 in vehicles, having marched the first ten miles, there was no sign of the Jats or anyone else. Communications had now entirely broken down and neither the Brigadier nor Brigade Major could be contacted. The 1st/7th Gurkhas took charge of the stores dumped there and, together with the Burma Sappers, set about destroying as much as they could of the vehicles and equipment. They then drove on through Kawkareik to milestone 13. About 0430 hours on the 22nd, the HQ 4 Burif column sent its mules on ahead and followed down the road in trucks. Unfortunately the Jats, now in Kawkareik, thought that the last troops had already passed through. The mules were mistaken for enemy and received a hot reception. The mules came streaming back up the road and fled into the forest discarding their loads, the following drivers assuring Colonel Abernethy that the enemy were now in the town. Though not fully convinced, Abernethy knew that this was possible so turned his vehicles round and drove back a few miles up the road. There was no sign of any enemy. He then burnt his trucks and led his force west across country towards Kyondo. Meanwhile, in Kawkareik, the Jats were sure they were under attack and crowded onto vehicles to withdraw. The Jat war diary comments acidly that "no clear picture can be painted of this [*occasion*] as it was nothing short of a panic."

Brigadier Jones had ordered the 1st/7th Gurkhas to hold a lay-back position at milestone 13 through which the Jats were to withdraw and had gone forward with his Brigade Major to meet them. He had ordered his own headquarters back to milestone 7 and the administrative units to Kyondo. In his absence a panic arose in Brigade Headquarters apparently sparked off by the sound of exploding ammunition in some of the burning trucks in Kawkareik and the battle with the mules. Believing that Kawkareik had fallen, the Staff Captain and most of Brigade HQ retired in some disorder to Kyondo. Here they encountered the SDO who had spent the day organising transport for a withdrawal and evacuating the police and other government servants to Moulmein. The Staff Captain spoke on the phone to General Smyth in Moulmein and gave him a very inaccurate account of the situation indicating that the Japanese were in Kawkareik and the brigade and brigadier lost. He was given permission to withdraw and with the SDO's help sent the administrative units off to Moulmein, having destroyed all the HQ vehicles and wireless sets and thrown mortars and LMGs into the river. The SDO, understanding that his withdrawal arrangements were no longer required, followed him.

With daylight, order was restored. By mid-day on the 22nd everyone (except Colonel Abernethy's force) had reached Kyondo where the ferry was damaged by another air raid. There was no sign of the SDO and no knowledge of his arrangements. Unwisely, many mules were turned loose when they could have been swum across the river. Unwisely, because mules were very useful to the Japanese as replacements for their horse casualties, which had been heavy on the march to Mae Sot. Jemadar Jug Lal of the Jats succeeded in recovering many of the machine guns and mortars that had been cast into the river. Eventually the whole force crossed the Haungtharaw River and marched south of the Gyaing River to Kawbein, which they reached on the evening of the 23rd (see Map 5). Early on the morning of the 24th they were picked up by steamer and ferried to Martaban. Abernethy, meanwhile, marched across country on the north bank of the Gyaing, being hospitably received and buying food in the villages. One of his northern companies joined him at the rendezvous, Zathabyin, where they were picked up by boat and reached Martaban on the 25th.[14] The Japanese entered Kawkareik on the 23rd and the next day were visited by five Blenheims of the RAF. Unfortunately the bombers missed the most prominent building in the town, which was housing *HQ 55 Division*.

This hasty withdrawal was a deplorable start to the campaign. *55 Division* had never been in action before although many of its officers and men were battle experienced. It was not a very strong division. In this part of the advance it had only four infantry battalions and, like all the divisions raised in 1941, these had three rifle companies each instead of the normal four.[15] The terrain gave great advantages to the defence if it were properly used and the commander of *112 Regiment* had been rattled by the early resistance. Yet out of the whole brigade only one company of the 1st/7th Gurkhas had fought seriously with the Japanese.

Hutton wanted to sack Brigadier Jones but Smyth saw that the failure lay elsewhere and did not agree. His decision was justified as Jones did very well later in the campaign and won a DSO. Steps were taken, however, to replace the CO of the Jats. Wavell was to sum up the episode tersely and accurately in his Despatch:[16]

> "It is quite clear that the enemy were allowed to gain cheap initial successes through bad handling of local commanders, lack of training and in some instances lack of fighting spirit on the part of our troops. It was an unfortunate beginning to the campaign and had serious results in raising the morale of the enemy and depressing that of our own troops."

This action showed for the first time in Burma, but not for the last, that the greatest weakness of raw troops fighting in this theatre was a psychological one. Their total ignorance of what to expect made some young soldiers nervous before a shot was fired. Others were affected by the abundant rumours about the savagery and allegedly superhuman capabilities of the enemy. Many had had no time to overcome the natural feeling of fear that most people feel at first when entering a dense forest full of wild beasts, especially at night. They had yet to learn, as the Japanese already had, that the dark and the forest were to be welcomed as friends and not feared as enemies.

The fundamental reason for the fiasco at Kawkereik was the lack of preparation and training, before the war started, for fighting in this theatre: it was no fault of 16 Brigade that they had had neither the time nor the opportunity for such training.

14. The northern company of 4 Burif had successful encounters with two enemy patrols near Mepale and maintained its position covering the Nabu track. No orders reached them but on the 23rd, realising something was amiss, they withdrew successfully via Nabu to the Salween and thence by boat to Martaban.
15. Their rifle companies, however, had a strength at this time of more than 200 men each.
16. Supplement to *The London Gazette*, 5 March 1948, p.1671.

CHAPTER FIVE

Moulmein Falls

Between 23 and 29t January, the Japanese made a determined attempt to achieve air superiority, and there was much air fighting by day over Rangoon. In this week, 17 Japanese aircraft were shot down and ten badly damaged[1] for the loss of two AVG and ten RAF planes. For the moment the Japanese acknowledged defeat and returned to sporadic night attacks on Rangoon and attacks on the British ground forces. There were now no British fighters left. However, the good news was that three squadrons of Hurricanes arrived from Egypt at the end of January,[2] but the bad news was that some of these were the obsolescent Mark 1s and the spares support was quite inadequate. As a result, never more than 30 were serviceable at any one time and this number steadily dwindled. There were also two Lysander squadrons for army co-operation, one RAF and one Indian Air Force, and these were used on occasion as light bombers. In early February a light bomber Blenheim squadron arrived. This could only provide an average of six aircraft for action on any one day.

Wavell's instructions were that the Japanese must be fought as far forward as possible. There were sound strategic reasons for this. There were two good airfields at Mudon and Moulmein and it was highly desirable to hold these so as to keep the enemy air force as far as possible from Rangoon, the entry point for reinforcements and supplies. The railway used for supplying China ran up the west side of the Sittang valley for 200 miles, so to allow the Japanese to reach this river would mean that the rail link would inevitably be cut. Chinese confidence in the British determination to defend Burma was essential if they were to deploy their

A Curtiss P-40 'Tomahawk' of the AVG with its distinctive war-paint.

troops to help. Moulmein and Tenasserim had long been in British possession and the Karens, who formed the bulk of the inhabitants, were very loyal. It would be disgraceful to abandon them without a fight. But compelling as these reasons were, they made it very difficult for Smyth, the man in charge of the tactical battle. Thus, while Hutton loyally tried to carry out Wavell's orders, he found himself in continual dispute with Smyth, who knew that if his untrained troops were widely dispersed in 'penny packets' they were likely to be defeated in detail.

Moulmein was the third largest town in Burma with a population approaching 100,000. It had been under British influence and protection since 1826 and the inhabitants got on well with the British.[3] It was highly undesirable to abandon either them or the British and Indian businesses there. But Moulmein was on the far bank of the mighty Salween River, here about a mile-and-a-half wide. To fight a defensive battle against a superior enemy with such a barrier at your back and no British-manned boats or ferries was not a highly recommended military manoeuvre. In a telegram on 22 January, General Wavell, from his HQ in Java, stressed to Hutton the need for defending Moulmein so, as far as he and Smyth were concerned, it had to be done. For its defence Smyth had allotted the 2nd Burma Brigade (2 Bur Brigade), consisting of 3 Burif (less two companies), 7 and 8 Burifs and the 4th/12th FFR. Supporting them were 12 Mountain Battery (four guns), a troop of the 3rd Indian Light Anti-Aircraft Battery (four Bofors guns) and a platoon (about 50 men) of 60 Field Company, Madras Sappers and Miners, plus supply and medical units.

General Wavell, with an inadequate staff and poor communications, was immersed in a welter of international problems at his improvised HQ near Bandoeng in Java. Nevertheless he now paid one of the only two visits that he was able to make to Burma during his time at ABDACOM. Aeroplanes in those days were slow and far from comfortable. After a tiring ten-hour flight on the night of 24/25 January he landed at Rangoon for a conference with Hutton and confirmed Hutton's view that Moulmein should be held as long as possible but not to the bitter end. The following night he flew back to Bandoeng.

There had been several air attacks that week both on Moulmein town and airfield. One had set a large part of the town on fire and was only contained by the Sappers blowing up a number of houses in its path. As a result, most of the

---

1. These figures are from Japanese records.
2. The Hurricanes were fitted with long range tanks and made hops of about three hours, flying in formation with a Blenheim bomber as navigator. There were nine hops from Iraq to Rangoon. Cotton, M.C., *Hurricanes Over Burma*, p.122.
3. When the Japanese captured Moulmein, they did not trust the BIA, who had little support in the town, to set up an effective administration there, as they had at Tavoy. So a military administration was set up and the BIA withdrew to Mudon. Izumiya, Tatsuro, *The Minami Organ*.

Burmese had naturally fled to the countryside. Under arrangements made by Colonel Pelly, the able and co-operative District Comissioner, and the staff of 2 Bur Brigade, British (and Indian where requested) women and children were already being evacuated from Moulmein and sent back by rail. Now a start was made with backloading surplus stores.

Although the air attacks caused few casualties, they undoubtedly had an unsettling effect on the morale of the Burmese. Major (later Brigadier) Hugh Wilberforce, who commanded 5 Mountain Battery, was in Moulmein during one raid:

> "A squadron of enemy fighter planes appeared overhead. One by one they peeled off and strafed the airfield at low level. There were only two old Buffalo fighter planes on the field and their pilots would have been fully justified in taking cover. Instead these two brave men ran to their planes and took off, determined to give battle; we could see them bare-headed in their cockpits urging their planes on like jockeys riding a finish. They never reached more than tree-top height before both were shot into the ground."

Their courageous action was much admired by the Army but was deplored by the more experienced members of the RAF; they considered that to try and take off in such conditions was suicidal and a waste of valuable pilots.

On 28 January Hutton and Smyth visited Moulmein and it was agreed that plans should be made for a withdrawal if the attack could not be held. It was also

RNZAF pilots of 67 Squadron RAF at Mingaladon with one of their Brewster 'Buffalo' aircraft. Shores and Cull.

agreed that Brigadier R.G. Ekin, from 46 Brigade, should take over operational command of 2 Bur Brigade from Brigadier Bourke if the Japanese mounted an attack. This highly irregular arrangement was justified on the grounds of the heavy responsibilities of the local commander in respect of the control and evacuation of the the civil population. Although Smyth was to report to Hutton that Brigadier Bourke was stout in figure and stout in heart, there may also have been some doubt about his tactical ability to fight the battle and effect a withdrawal in the face of the enemy. It says much for the characters of the two brigadiers that, awkward as the arrangement was, in fact they got on very well.[4]

One or two of the District Commissioners in frontier areas had foreseen the role that a resistance organisation might play if war came. At this meeting in Moulmein it was agreed that a guerrilla organisation should be established in Karenni, the province north of Moulmein which was the homeland of the Karens. Many of the hill tribes, and notably the Christian Karens, remained staunchly loyal to the British throughout the war. Unfortunately the Karen homeland was quickly lost. An exceptional officer from the 1st Burma Rifles, Major Hugh Seagrim, who was deeply attached to the Karens and spoke their language fluently, was allotted some rifles and volunteered to stay behind and organise a resistance movement in Karenni. The idea was excellent but unfortunately the British retreated so far and so fast that he could not be supported. If it had been possible to hold Rangoon his actions against the Japanese line of communication might have had a decisive effect.[5]

The Japanese Approach Moulmein

55 Division, after crossing the Dawna Range, had concentrated west of Kawkareik. They collected what was useful of the abandoned British equipment, which was not much but included several trucks, and their sappers improvised a new ferry at Kya-in from sampans. On 26 January, General Iida of *15th Army* ordered them to capture Moulmein and at the same time instructed *33 Division* to concentrate in an area east of the Salween with a view to advancing on Pa-an and crossing the river there. (See Map 5.)

---

4. Captain Edwards-Stuart of the 4th/12th FFR commented that it was "a most unjustifiable slur on Brigadier Bourke who had previously conducted the defence most capably." NAM, 1977-11-232, *With the 4th Sikhs in Burma.*

5. In early 1943 the RAF started the "moonlight war" and the vital wireless equipment was parachuted to Seagrim. The Japanese were acutely aware of the danger his activities posed to their line of communication and, indeed, of the encouragement they gave to disillusioned Burmese nationalists in Rangoon. So they sent a task force to look for him which took savage reprisals against the Karens. To stop this Seagrim, a man of rare character, gave himself up, was tried by court-martial and in 1944 was executed. When the tide of war turned in mid-1944, it became possible to re-activate the Karen resistance and their guerrilla units were then highly successful.

On 28 January, *55 Division* ordered *1/143 Battalion* to advance from Kyondo down the north bank of the Gyaing River and occupy Kado at its junction with the Salween. *HQ 143 Regiment*, with *2/143 Battalion* and *143/3 Company* under command, was to advance south of the Gyaing towards Moulmein. They would protect the right flank while the rest of *55 Division* crossed the Haungtharaw River at Kya-in and followed the road south towards Metheraw. Before reaching there, *112 Regiment* (less *3/112 Battalion*) and *HQ 55 Division* took another road leading west to Moulmein through Winpot. The *Reconnaissance Regiment* went on to Metheraw before turning west for Mudon, about 15 miles from Moulmein, with the aim of attacking Moulmein from the south (see Map 5).

Meanwhile the 4th/12th FFR had reached Moulmein about 12 January and been sent down to the end of the railway at Ye, about 100 miles to the south. The next day they were recalled to Moulmein. A week later they were sent down to Ye again to support the Tavoy garrison but when that place fell they returned to Moulmein, a detachment of 60 Field Company demolishing three bridges on the railway between Ye and Mudon. On 26 January a motorised company patrol under Captain 'Sam' Manekshaw,[6] driving up into the low forest-covered hills east of Mudon, was ambushed by the Japanese of the *Reconnaissance Regiment*. After a sharp skirmish, the patrol managed, with some difficulty, to extricate itself and withdrew to a position in the woods north of Mudon. There it was joined by the rest of the battalion (less one company) on the 28th. On the 29th the battalion was ordered back to Moulmein but left 'D' Company at Mudon to assist the withdrawal of 'C' Company of the 1st/7th Gurkhas. This was the company which had been covering the approach through the Three Pagodas Pass (Map 3) and with whom contact had been made the day before. However, that night 'D' Company was heavily attacked and cut off from Moulmein. It withdrew to the south and both it and the Gurkhas succeeded in making their way across country to the Salween, crossing it in sampans and rejoining their units a week later at Kyaikto. This left the 4th/12th FFR with only three companies in Moulmein on which *55 Division* was now closing in.

The Battle at Moulmein

In Moulmein (see Map 6), Brigadier Bourke had deployed his two-and-a-half Burma Rifles battalions on an 11 mile perimeter south and east of the town, making the maximum use of the River Salween to the north and west and the Ataran River to part of the east. A separate Burma FF police unit guarded the airfield which was ouside the perimeter but within the range of 12 Mountain Battery. A long ridge ('the Ridge') with Pagodas on it ran north and south for the length of

A Japanese 75mm mountain gun, the only artillery weapon used by the Japanese before the capture of Rangoon. IWM.

the town and was the dominating tactical feature. Brigade HQ was on the southern end of the Ridge and the 4th/12th FFR, which was in brigade reserve, also held a position there. As later experience showed, such long perimeters could not be held against the Japanese tactics of infiltration at night.

The 8th Burma Rifles (8 Burif) was recruited from Sikhs and Punjabi Muslims domiciled in Burma. It was rightly considered the most reliable of 2 Bur Brigade's Burma Rifle battalions and was allotted the defence of the southern sector of the perimeter. The eastern sector was held by 3 Burif (less two companies) and the western and northern river-banks by 7 Burif. Although 3 Burif had been apparently strengthened by the arrival of 30 Chins from Tavoy, the exaggerated rumours disseminated by some of these men had an unsettling effect on the battalion.

The Japanese had only three infantry battalions for the attack as the one which had captured Tavoy had not yet arrived, and *1/143 Battalion* (less one company) was still on the north side of the Gyaing River. They also had, however, the *Reconnaissance Regiment* and five companies of mountain artillery, each company having only two guns because of the difficulty of ammunition supply. These mountain guns had more than twice the range of the British ones but fired a smaller shell (14lbs compared with 20lbs). Their plan was for an attack from the south by the *Reconnaissance Regiment*, from the south-east by *112 Regiment* (less *3 Battalion*) and from the east by *2/143 Battalion*. Soon after 0700 hrs on 30 January, four British trucks full of Japanese soldiers appeared coming up the main road from the south and whether by design or by mistake attempted to drive

---

6. The adjutant of the 4th/12th FFR was Captain 'Turk' Rahman. In one of the wars between India and Pakistan in the 1960s he was C-in-C of the Pakistan Army and his friend Captain Manekshaw was C-in-C of the Indian Army!

through the wire barrier at the perimeter.[7] An alert Sikh sentry opened fire with an LMG and other posts joined in. The Japanese hastily sprang out of their vehicles and dispersed, but lost more than a dozen men killed. A general attack on the southern sector then developed but was held, 12 Mountain Battery providing effective support. On the eastern sector, however, *2/143 Battalion* succeeded in crossing the River Ataran at Hmyawlin and *112 Regiment* (less one battalion) crossed further south near the airfield (see Map 6).

Brigadier Ekin, who had only been informed that morning by the Divisional Commander of his new role, had crossed from Martaban to take command around noon on the 30th, when the battle had already started. Getting the impression at once that 3 Burif were badly rattled, and no doubt judging that such a large area could never be defended, he ordered a withdrawal to a shortened line using the Ridge as the eastern perimeter. Meanwhile he deployed his reserve of the 4th/12th FFR to hold the centre of the Ridge and moved his headquarters, which had been on the south end, to a more central position. On the airfield the small BFF garrison fought well and held up the Japanese for some hours before being finally driven back. After dark they dispersed and most reached Martaban successfully, having inflicted some casualties.[8] The 8 Burif held their positions throughout the day but in the northern sector 7 Burif began to disintegrate and after dark the Japanese began attacking the Ridge itself, where they were firmly held by the 4th/12th FFR. At 2300 hrs Ekin shortened the perimeter again to hold a box covering the Ridge and the main jetties. This box was rectangular and about four thousand yards from north to south and one thousand from east to west. Sporadic firing continued all night but, although some Japanese accounts speak of severe fighting, no serious attack developed and casualties on both sides seem to have been few.

Early on the 31st, *143/3 Company*, which had been removed from its battalion at Kado and was in reserve with *HQ 143 Regiment*, was sent along the bank of the estuary to enter Moulmein from the north. A company from 7 Burif, who were holding that sector, were taken by surprise and fled towards the main jetties. The Japanese then overran the unarmed gunners of the LAA battery, the four guns being lost although two breech blocks were saved.[9] Ekin was therefore obliged to pull back his northern perimeter. The CO of 8 Burif in the south informing him that his men were now getting very exhausted, Ekin judged that the town could not be held much longer. Moreover if the enemy gunners moved, as they could now do, to a position from which they could fire on the river crossing, the ferries would almost certainly cease to operate. He therefore gave Smyth his views and was given permission to withdraw when he considered it necessary.[10] Hearing that many Burmese soldiers were already streaming down to the riverside, he decided that delay would increase the casualties without any material advantage and, at 8am, ordered his troops to contract the box to a bridgehead round the main jetties. Major Dick Ward RE had organised fifteen ferries which were being held in readiness in Martaban. These were now ordered to steam across and five of them to berth at each of the three main jetties.

The Withdrawal from Moulmein

The steamers had Burmese civilian crews who for some days had been far from happy with their lot. Whenever an air raid warning was given they insisted on moving their vessels into mid-stream. Now an armed guard of Sappers from 1 Burma Field Company had been put on each vessel to boost their confidence and ensure compliance. Each unit had orders which jetty to use and the wounded and the medical units were the first to leave. Officers had been detailed to control the embarkation which, after some trouble with Burmese stragglers, went well, the covering troops, mainly of the 4th/12th FFR, holding back the enemy and counter-attacking when necessary. There were a number of acts of gallantry in the desperate circumstances as the enemy closed in on the jetties. Major John Hume of 12 Mountain Battery distinguished himself by leading a party to recover two mountain guns which had been surrounded, thus saving all four of his guns. Second Lieutenant Mehr Dass attempted a similar feat with the Bofors guns and managed to drag one to the quayside but it proved impossible to load it onto the ferry. He went ashore again to collect some of his men and was captured. The last boat to leave from Mission Street Jetty carried Brigade HQ and, among others, the Sappers of 60 Field Company who had just blown up the power station and telephone exchange. As a last party of troops were embarking, the enemy appeared on the quay and the Sappers were ordered ashore to drive them off. They succeeded, although their leader, Captain Jardine, was killed. Meanwhile the steamer left and the last parties holding the bridgehead were perforce abandoned. Fortunately the Japanese had only one gun in a position to fire on the steamers, all but one of which arrived safely.

For those left behind there was nothing to do except try and avoid capture. Fortunately the Japanese, too, were exhausted and more than happy after their

---

7. This was *55 Division's Reconnaissance Regiment* in trucks captured at Mudon. They had also captured three trucks at Kawkareik but these had been destroyed in a 'friendly fire' Japanese air attack.

8. A Japanese account says that the company commander of *112/5 Company* was killed at the airfield.

9. The Japanese claim to have got one of these Bofors into action and to have shot down one British fighter plane.

10. The telephone to Kyaikto continued to work right up to the end.

arduous advance to take advantage of some captured dumps of food. One of the most remarkable of many escapes was organised by Jemadar Malligarjunan of 60 Field Company. When Jardine was killed he took charge of his party and concealed them under the Mission Street jetty. The Japanese set up a mortar on the jetty but his party were undetected. Colonel Taylor, the CO of 3 Burif, with two of his officers, had received no orders to retire and had also been left behind and had taken refuge under the same jetty. After dark, hearing some odd sounds coming from an adjacent yard, he went to investigate.

"Peeping round a wall I was staggered to find the Sappers industriously building a petrol-barrel raft with their Jemadar giving instructions in loud whispers. Having completed the raft, they launched it, but the Jemadar, apparently not being satisfied, had the raft pulled ashore and taken to pieces to replace a leaking barrel. It was then re-launched, but still the Jemadar was not happy about it and had it rebuilt a second time. Then he smiled his satisfaction, came up to me, and saluting smartly said "Raft taiyar hai, Sahib" (The raft is ready, Sir). We climbed aboard but, as we dared not use paddles, the Jemadar and his men stripped and gently slid the raft into the water and guided it to safety. By keeping calm and cool in the face of the enemy, he saved me, two other officers and all his men from capture."

Retrospect

British records, necessarily approximate, give a total for this operation of 617 men killed or missing, the majority believed to have been Burmese troops who had deserted. In the fighting at Moulmein, the 4th/12th FFR only lost four soldiers and three followers killed. The Japanese claim to have killed 225 men and taken 148 prisoners of war. In view of the small number of casualties in the 4th/12th FFR the Japanese figures for British killed seem to be greatly inflated. Colonel Oharazawa, the commander of *112 Regiment*, reported repeated charges and heavy fighting but seems to have been prone to exaggeration. He was a nervous man who relied heavily on alcohol and was shortly to be relieved of his command.

Japanese casualties in *2/143 Battalion* were given as 14 killed and in the *Reconnaissance Regiment* as 20 killed and 11 wounded, but no figures are recorded for the two battalions of *112 Regiment*.

The Japanese claim to have captured at Moulmein one (unserviceable) Blenheim bomber, seven 'armoured cars', four Bofors guns, some vehicles, mules, equipment and dumps of military stores.[11] They also discovered a cache of 5000 drums of aviation spirit in the rubber plantation near the aerodrome. This was a most valuable find enabling them to use the airfield as soon as they could fly in bombs, which they quickly did. Of course, it was important to puncture these drums as the Japanese attack became imminent but, in the absence of a joint Army/RAF headquarters and with all the other pressing problems, it was probably a task not even considered.

The capture of Moulmein completed the first aim of the Japanese invasion. They had so far used only one inexperienced division but had quickly achieved their goal. Nevertheless, General Iida was not too well pleased with the performance of *55 Division*. He was not deceived by Colonel Oharazawa's report and noted in his diary that this division never advanced until the enemy retreated.

The most serious disadvantage for the British was the loss of the airfield which gave the Japanese fighters a base closer to Rangoon and forced the RAF back to Mingaladon. But the truth was that although it was deemed politically and strategically necessary to fight at Moulmein, on the far shore of a huge river, it was tactically unsound. The lack of British boats or ferries, and the certainty that the crews of the Burmese boats would sooner or later desert, made an early withdrawal inevitable. The result was a gain in morale for the Japanese and a loss of valuable equipment.

The evacuation in broad daylight was skilfully conducted and, in spite of the fact that the RAF were unable to give any support, the casualties, mostly deserters, were by no means excessive for such a hazardous operation. A lengthy defence would have been disastrous as the garrison could and would have been cut off by a thrust across the Salween further north. Nevertheless, both sides were inexperienced and, if the rest of the Burma Rifles had been as good as 8 Burif, the Japanese might have been made to pay more dearly for their success. It had become clear that the Burmese units, though very useful in a reconnaissance role or in irregular fighting, could not be trusted to hold their positions in a set-piece battle and were therefore a danger to the other units involved.[12] General Smyth saw this clearly and asked that the Burmese units should be converted to a guerrilla role. There were political difficulties, however, and Hutton, although he sympathised, judged it far too late to make such a radical change.

---

11. *Memoir of 112 Regiment*, p.56.

12. Letter, dated 3 June 1942, from Major-General Bruce Scott to Lieutenant-General Hutton: "I very much regret that our own experience in Burdiv has been that the indigenous races of Burma enlisted in the Burma Rifles are almost all equally unreliable and should never be used for any other than reconnaissance and intelligence duties." *Hutton Papers*.

CHAPTER SIX

The Japanese Force the Salween
at Martaban and Pa-an

February 1942 was to be a disastrous month for the British in South-East Asia. The great tragedy of Singapore was fast approaching its climax. At the beginning of the month, however, things did not look too bad in Burma. The Japanese had captured Tenasserim, which no-one had thought it would be possible to hold anyway, but they had not yet crossed the Salween. Fate, however, had some nasty blows in store for the British leaders.

Misfortunes of the Senior Commanders

General Hutton was anxious to bring 1 Burdiv down to the south to reinforce 17 Division which was trying to cover a 160-mile front on the Salween from Martaban to Papun. However, there were rumours of enemy forces concentrating in Thailand at Chiang Mai, and further north at Chiang Rai, so they could not be moved at present.[1] His problem would be solved if the Chinese forces were to move into the Shan States. He therefore arranged to confer with General Chiang Kai-shek near the Burma-China border and on 2 February flew up to Lashio for the meeting. He travelled in an army co-operation aircraft, a Lysander, with his ADC in a second one. The flight was delayed by refuelling difficulties but the pilot decided to press on to Lashio and land there in the dark. Unfortunately only primitive navigation aids were available and he got lost. Running out of fuel, he decided to attempt a forced landing in a clearing in the forest. The plane crashed and the unconscious pilot was trapped. Hutton, badly bruised but otherwise unhurt, managed to scramble out and tried to free the pilot. A fire started and Hutton continued his efforts in the intervals of trying to beat out the flames with his khaki greatcoat.

Meanwhile the pilot of the second aircraft, also out of fuel, decided to try and land beside the first to give help. But realising the danger he first flew up to 2000 feet and invited his passenger to jump out with his parachute, not a very attractive manoeuvre in the dark for the ADC, who had scarcely ever flown before. However, he did what he was told and landed safely in a tree, while the pilot crash-landed his aircraft near the first one, destroying it but fortunately not himself. With these reinforcements Hutton was able to drag the first pilot, still uncon-

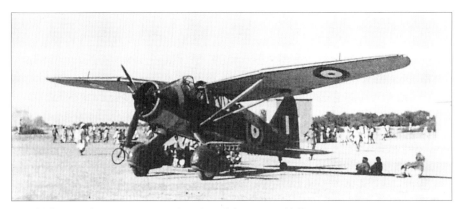

A British Lysander army co-operation aircraft in Burma 1942.

scious but badly burned, from the wreckage. Some villagers soon appeared and the unconscious pilot was taken to hospital where he died a few days later. Hutton, although badly bruised, managed to retrieve some of his kit and, borrowing his ADC's greatcoat, hitched a lift to Lashio. The next day he held successful talks with the Generalissimo before flying back to Rangoon to meet Wavell.[2]

After a ten-hour night flight from Bandoeng, Wavell arrived at Rangoon on the 5th, and on the 6th went up with Hutton to Kyaikto to visit HQ 17 Division, where he got the impression that things were going relatively well. 48 Indian Infantry Brigade (48 Brigade) had arrived in Rangoon on 31 January. If the Japanese could be held, British strength could be built up faster than the enemy's. He impressed on everybody that the Japanese were not supermen, key points must be firmly held and that attack was the best means of defence. The line of the Salween should be watched and powerful fighting patrols used to dominate the 'no man's land' between the two armies. That night Wavell flew back the 2000 miles to Java but not before he had made a decision of profound importance. Impressed by the open country west of the Sittang river he ordered the experienced 7th Armoured Brigade, which was on its way from the Middle East to Malaya, to be diverted to Rangoon.

Smyth had made a good impression, but he did not reveal to Wavell that he was becoming increasingly unfit. He was still suffering from his anal fissure, a malady which can be very painful and which he had hoped was on the mend. But Burma was much hotter than northern India at this time of year and the rigours

1. In fact there were hardly any Japanese there but this was the start of the build-up of three Thai divisions, combined with a deliberate Japanese deception plan aimed at keeping the Chinese in north Burma.
2. *Hutton Papers*. (Liddell Hart Centre for Military Archives, King's College, London.)

of campaigning were unhelpful. The wound had not healed and was septic. Perhaps Hutton had noticed something, for on the next day, 7 February, Smyth was visited by the senior medical officer from AHQ, the DDMS, and this officer recommended that Smyth should be examined by a medical board. The following day, the 8th, Smyth wrote a confidential letter to Hutton explaining his trouble and saying:[3]

"…The wound only stopped bleeding ten days ago and is still discharging. I didn't feel too grand yesterday and your DDMS insisted that ADMS should have a look at me. He finds nothing *organically* wrong with me that a few months' comparative rest wouldn't put right. I should hate to go sick - its a thing I've never done in the whole of my service. I feel if I could have a month off ... and swop jobs with someone in a more sedentary job in India for a few months I should be absolutely OK for a command in the field again (if required)… Meanwhile I shall carry on here perfectly happily as long as you like. So sorry."

On the 11th, Smyth's ADMS and another surgeon examined Smyth under medical board procedure. They found nothing organically wrong and Smyth was emphatic that he was perfectly capable of carrying on. According to a letter written after the war, they concluded that it was essential for Smyth to have two months complete rest at the earliest opportunity and meanwhile started a course of injections of iron arsenate every four days.[4] The Board, however, did not say that Smyth should be medically down-graded and seems to have declared him fit to do his job. Its proceedings were, of course, forwarded to Army HQ and Hutton, beyond alerting the Military Secretary in India of a possible future problem, took no further action. It was not a good prelude to a period of severe fighting.

On 11 February Brigadier 'Punch' Cowan reported to Smyth. He had been sent over from India to replace Brigadier Jones after 16 Brigade's poor showing at Kawkareik. Cowan is recorded as having said after the war that he found the divisional commander in a "very nervous and jittery state; not at all the Smyth I knew".[5] Two days later Smyth sent Cowan back to General Hutton both to explain the division's plans and to ask for approval for Cowan to stay at HQ 17 Divison as Brigadier General Staff. This was an unusual appointment in a division but justified by its isolation. Hutton agreed, Jones was reprieved, and Cowan, who had never commanded a brigade, became in effect second-in-command of 17 Division.

Meanwhile, on 10 February, Wavell, returning from a last visit to Singapore and not seeing too well in the dark with his one eye, fell several feet off a dock

Right: Major-General J.G. 'Jackie' Smyth, VC, GOC, 17th Indian Infantry Division.

Far Right: Major-General D.C.T. 'Punch' Cowan, Smyth's successor as GOC 17th Indian Infantry Division.

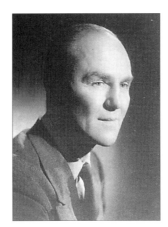

on to some rocks. He treated this lightly in a signal to the Prime Minister reporting on his visit:

'…While returning from Singapore I fell from quay in dark and have broken two small bones in back. Damage not serious but I shall be in hospital for a few days, and somewhat crippled for two or three weeks probably.'[6]

Such an injury, however, is inevitably very painful and not helped by the need for flying long distances in military aircraft or bumping in military cars over bad roads. He was in bed for nearly a week and on the 20th was still unfit to travel.[7] Wavell, at 59, was an outstandingly robust man, both physically and mentally. The clarity of his thought was unaffected and he continued to run crisply the first of the great inter-Allied commands of the war. Nevertheless this accident could scarcely have come at a more inopportune time as the following two weeks saw the loss of Singapore, the desperate but hopeless fight to hold the Dutch East Indies[8] and the crucial battles which decided the fate of Burma.

17 Division's Plan

With the arrival of 48 Brigade, General Smyth had most of a division, although still woefully short in artillery. His personal view remained that it was

---

3. *ibid*. Smyth, letter to Hutton, 8 February 1942.
4. Mackenzie, Col. K.P., RAMC, letter to Smyth dated 28 September 1955.
5. Draper, Alfred, *Dawns Like Thunder*, p.72.
6. Kirby, S.W., *The War Against Japan*, Vol.4, p.88.
7. Pownall, Lt-Gen. Sir H., *Chief of Staff*, Vol.2, pp.87,89.
8. The Japanese conquest of the Dutch East Indies was completed on 8 March.

very unwise to hold so far forward and to spread his forces so widely that they inevitably ran the risk of being defeated in detail. His preference was to withdraw to the Bilin and fight a delaying battle there, before withdrawing to the Sittang for the final defence of Rangoon. This view was shared[9] by Brigadier 'Taffy' Davies, Hutton's Chief of Staff, but Wavell, hoping always to reinforce Burma, had ordered a forward strategy, backed by offensive action. Hutton, therefore, ordered Smyth to contest the line of the Salween and hold firmly the key points such as Martaban, and the likely crossing-points at Pa-an and Papun, together with back-up positions at Thaton and Bilin. So, at the beginning of February, Smyth had ordered 16 Brigade, with its headquarters at Thaton (Map 8), to be responsible for the southern half of the Salween front,while 46 Brigade watched the northern half. 48 Brigade was in reserve near Bilin with the role of dealing with any coastal landings and 2 Bur Brigade was in Kyaikto with responsibility for local defence of this area and the Sittang Bridge.

Evidence that the enemy were preparing to cross the Salween began to accumulate, and on 5 February Smyth switched 16 and 46 Brigades, so that 46 Brigade now became responsible for the southern half of the front. At the same time he reduced the frontage allotted to each brigade by sending 2 Burif (less a company) to Papun in an independent role. This move took some days to complete and involved some switching of battalions between brigades, always an

Colonel Harada, Commander of 215 Infantry Regiment, discussing the route to Pa-an with the headman of Dawlan village.

unsettling factor as mutual trust is not established overnight. Nor did it give units much time to prepare for the imminent Japanese assault.

The Japanese Plan

General Iida's plan was for *55 Division* to cross the Salween, capture Martaban and advance astride the road and railway on Thaton and Bilin. Amphibious operations along the coast were specifically ruled out as being too hazardous in the face of expected British naval intervention. Meanwhile, the formidable *33 Division* had crossed the frontier at Miyawadi, marched up the Kawkareik road to milestone 24 and then struck across country, via Nabu and Dawlan, to the forest near Pa-an. They were ordered to cross the Salween in the area of Pa-an, destroy any enemy in the area and move north-east of *55 Division* towards the Sittang River. No wheeled transport had yet reached Kawkareik from Thailand and so ammunition and supplies were scarce and needed to be conserved. As much use as possible was to be made of captured mules and vehicles and supplemented by local bullock-carts.

A *33 Divisional* order issued at this time is of interest. It gave instructions that the foolish behaviour in China must on no account be repeated and in particular:

"a. Soldiers are not allowed to go into civilian houses alone.

b. Rape, pillage and arson are strictly prohibited.

c. Goods obtained from local people must be paid for.

d. When a company purchases goods from local people, there must be an officer or staff-sergeant in charge and for this cash will be made available."

This was a wise precaution as the Japanese were relying on a large measure of Burmese support, which indeed with the help of the BIA they often got, many personal accounts contrasting their welcome in Burma with that in China, where they were feared and hated.

The Action at Martaban

46 Brigade, commanded by Brigadier Ekin, was one of the three original brigades in 17 Division (the other two having been despatched to Singapore) and had been equipped for fighting in Iraq, where it was to be trained. Now it was to have its baptism of fire under very different circumstances. Brigade HQ was established at Thaton, as was the brigade reserve, the 2nd Battalion, the King's Own Yorkshire Light Infantry (2nd KOYLI) less one company. At Martaban were the 3rd/7th Gurkhas with one company of the 2nd KOYLI under command. At Kuzeik, the ferry terminal opposite Pa-an, the 7th/10th Baluch Regiment

---

9. Private letter to General Kirby, 4 February 1956.

(7th/10th Baluch) were taking over from the 1st/7th Gurkhas, while at Duyinzeik, on the road from the Pa-an ferry to Thaton, the 5th/17th Dogra Regiment (5th/17th Dogras) were taking up a position on both sides of the Donthami river. Supporting troops, based at Thaton less detachments, were the 12th Mountain Battery and 60 Field Company of the Madras Sappers.

The disadvantage of trying to hold such a wide front, as Smyth had foreseen, was that the Japanese could produce numerical superiority at any point that they chose and, in fact, they now had one division (of two regiments) facing a battalion at Martaban and another division (also of two regiments) facing a battalion at Pa-an. Lieutenant-Colonel Stevenson of the 3rd/7th Gurkhas, commanding the garrison at Martaban, had reason to feel rather isolated. He had no artillery, brigade HQ was 38 miles away, and the road and rail behind him, which ran roughly parallel to the Salween, were very vulnerable. Martaban was at the end of a long narrow ridge round which the Salween took a sharp turn (see Map 7). The road and railway ran north up the west side of the ridge and a short seven-mile road ran up the east side. One or two footpaths over the ridge joined the two roads.

During the first week of February a number of Japanese patrols had attempted to cross by boat from Moulmein and had been driven off while Martaban was repeatedly shelled and bombed. On 8 February the RAF retaliated by bombing Moulmein and Kado. That night the Japanese assault began. *143 Regiment* moved north up the river in boats from Moulmein and Kado. They landed on the west bank of the Salween at Hmawbi, 11 miles upstream from Martaban, and headed west towards the Martaban-Thaton road where they established a road-block eight miles north of Martaban. They cut the telephone wires and, as radio contact could not be established with brigade, the British garrison was now cut off.

Stevenson was not yet aware of the strength of the Japanese advance. A patrol sent up the main road to find the break in the telephone cable (which might have been the result of sabotage or bombing) ran into the road-block, and Captain Stourton and all the members of the patrol except one were killed. A 3rd/7th Gurkha reconnaissance patrol up the east road encountered a small party of Japanese who were, in fact, a flank guard covering the force crossing the road further north. Stevenson sent off two Gurkha companies under 2nd-Lieutenant Carver to deal with them. They came on a road-block and, after a brisk action and a bayonet charge, cleared it, killing several enemy and capturing a number of weapons including an infantry gun and two grenade-dischargers.

That evening Lieutenant-Colonel Stevenson, accompanied by Major Haughton of the 2nd KOYLI, saw to the west large numbers of men moving across country from the river and realised that he was cut off by a strong force.[10]

He was now faced with the classical dilemma of a retreat. His last orders were to hold Martaban firmly and he was not to know that his brigade had made determined but unsuccessful efforts to tell him to withdraw.[11] To disobey orders in such a situation can easily be misinterpreted. However, Stevenson rightly judged that there was no point in staying, and indeed to do so would only lead to an unnecessary defeat. He therefore decided to break out that night. His plan was to move up the east road to its end and then, having destroyed his vehicles and the captured weapons, to head north across country, finally turning west to hit the Thaton road. 'D' Company was left to cover the main road three miles from Martaban, with orders to cross the ridge and follow the main party. The plan succeeded but the march was a very arduous one with little food or water. Inevitably there were stragglers and twenty of them were taken prisoner. 'D' Company had a very difficult time but most of them eventually got through. By the second evening the exhausted battalion, and the company of the 2nd KOYLI, had reached the road and were able to get in touch with HQ 46 Brigade, who provided transport to Thaton. Total casualties in the 3rd/7th Gurkhas were 80 (killed, wounded and missing).[12]

The Battle at Kuzeik (Pa-an)

Meanwhile, *33 Division* was also forcing a crossing further north. The first contact had taken place at the beginning of February (see Map 7). At that time the 1st/7th Gurkhas were in a position on the west bank of the Salween. They were covering the ferry crossing from Pa-an (pronounced Pa-arn) and had established a platoon standing patrol on the east bank. A party of the the BIA were in Pa-an but lay low. On 1 February a Japanese reconnaissance party, which had been investigating crossing places further north, entered Pa-an and, before departing, replaced the Union Jack on a prominent building with the Japanese flag. On the 3rd the spearhead of *215 Regiment*, led by their mounted infantry platoon, entered the town. The Gurkhas were ready and a sharp action followed. Medium machine guns joined in from across the river (here only about 800 yards wide) and finally, as the enemy build-up increased, the patrol withdrew across the river in a motor-boat. The Japanese had 12 killed including two officers. The Japanese retaliated with an air strike and shelling on the main Gurkha position and continued to assemble in the forest near Pa-an where they suffered another

10. It was part of *112 Regiment* which had crossed from the island of Bilugyun.
11. In attempting to get through to him an armoured car and two carriers had been lost at the roadblock and the liaison officer had been killed. (The armoured car was one of the handful of antiquated vehicles possessed by the 1st Armoured Car Company, BAF.)
12. Lt-Col. H.R. Stevenson, personal account 18 February 1942

26 casualties in two successful attacks by the RAF.[13]

On 8 February the 7th/10th Baluch relieved the 1st/7th Gurkhas at Kuzeik. The orders to their CO, Lieutenant-Colonel 'Jerry' Dyer, were to deny the ferry crossing at Pa-an and, by vigorous patrolling for ten miles to the north and five miles to the south, to identify and delay any enemy crossings so that the Brigade reserve battalions (the 5th/17th Dogras and the 2nd KOYLI) could counter-attack and drive them into the river. Accordingly a two-platoon patrol base was established at Myainggale south of Kuzeik and another to the north. The main position was a half-saucer of open rice fields about 600 yards long adjoining the river on its east flank and the Duyinzeik road on the south. The edges of the saucer were steep and thickly wooded (see Map 8).

Because of the heavy patrolling commitment there had been little time to develop the position beyond the digging of simple slit trenches and in any case there was no barbed wire available. Various false alarms of Japanese infiltration kept the battalion on their toes and the Japanese did their best to add to the confusion by ostentatiously moving boats and bullock carts to the north of Pa-an to simulate a crossing somewhere there.

Apart from having no barbed wire (many defence stores were virtually non-existent in Burma in 1942) a serious weakness of the Baluch position was that it had no artillery support. Consequently, on the 8th, Brigadier Ekin decided to add to the garrison a section of two mountain guns from 5 Mountain Battery in Thaton. There was no time for them to march to Kuzeik so they were lifted in two 30cwt trucks and went round with their detachment by road. Although they fired some shells into Pa-an on the 9th they were to be of no use in the coming battle because the actual crossing place was outside their range and the main position was too shallow for them to be used to give defensive fire on the perimeter.

The Japanese Attack

Unknown to the 7th/10th Baluch, the enemy *215 Regiment* (less its *3rd Battalion*) was concentrated in the forest close to Pa-an and was busy collecting information about the British positions. *214 Regiment* was also concentrating in the same area and preparing to cross the river at Kawku about eight miles to the north. On the night of 10/11 February, *2/215 Battalion* crossed the river to Pagat, four miles south of Pa-an. They crossed in small boats[14] rowed by local Burmese, the divisional engineers constructing two rafts, towed by motor-boats, for the horses. Here the river was only about 800 yards wide. *215/7 Company*, which crossed first, attacked the patrol base in Myainggale and were soon joined by *215/8 Company*.[15] Together they succeeded in overrunning the base, its commander, Subedar Mehr Khan, and many men being killed. They were fortunate

in their timing, observation posts on the river having been withdrawn in anticipation of a pending relief. 'A' Company had just left, leaving one platoon behind.
A platoon from 'B' Company, under Subedar Mehr Khan, had only just arrived.
The rest of 'B' Company were on their way out from the main position to take
over when they found themselves engaged with most of *2/215 Battalion*. After a
brisk fight they managed, with some difficulty, to extricate themselves and to
return to the main position. On the following night, *1/215 Battalion* also crossed
the river in the same way and at the same place. The plan was for *2/215 Battalion*
(less *5 Company* which, together with *3* and *4 Companies* from *1/215 Battalion*,
was in regimental reserve) to attack the main position from the south-west, while
1/215 Battalion came up on their left flank and formed a road-block astride the
Duyinzeik road on the probable line of reinforcement or retreat.

Meanwhile the Japanese Air Force had not been idle. The Baluch position was
bombed and machine-gunned by a large force on the 9th and the attack was
repeated on the 10th and 11th. There were only about thirty-five casualties but
much kit and some ammunition was destroyed.

After dark on the 11th, *2/215 Battalion* moved forward for the assault. It was
a very dark night and the going was rough so it was not until about 0200, just as
the moon came up, that they were in a position to attack. They had decided on a
silent attack with the bayonet. Soldiers were forbidden to load their rifles and
only the MMGs, which were on the western flank, and some of the LMG gunners were allowed to fire. Their bayonets were coated with mud to prevent their
shine being seen. This was a type of attack in which the Japanese specialised. It
was much esteemed in the Japanese army, partly because it had overtones of the
samurai warriors of the past. In training, great emphasis was placed on bayonet
drill and on fieldcraft (at which the Japanese were exceptionally good). It was
nothing new to *215 Regiment* who had often carried out such attacks in China.
There was no artillery preparation, and their plan was to get as close as possible
in the dark and then charge in with bayonets and grenades, hoping to catch most
of the garrison asleep. However, the 7th/10th Baluch were alert and fired parachute flares from their mortars. Surprise was not achieved, so the Japanese
employed the technique of advancing by short rushes and lying down, and in this
way closed up on the position.

The British Defence

The 7th/10th Baluch were dug in in a shallow semi-circle, facing west and with

13. *Memoir of 215 Regiment.*
14. Nearly every house in the riverside villages in Burma had a boat.
15. At this stage many Japanese companies were more than 200 strong, with the aim of providing
immediate replacements for casualties.

their backs to the river. To the south and south-west, where the main attack came, was 'C' Company commanded by Captain Siri Kanth Korla, a pre-war regular officer. Beyond them to the west was 'B' Company, with only one platoon and a section of MMGs, commanded by Second-Lieutenant John Randle, aged 20 and with five month's service. Beyond him to the west and north was 'D' Company, with two platoons under Second-Lieutenant 'Jake' Jervis. 'A' Company with one platoon and a section of MMGs under Captain Bill Cayley covered the river front to the east. Battalion HQ and the guns were near the track along the river bank to the ferry. On the 11th the telephone wire back to Brigade HQ via Duyinzeik was cut and, despite continuous efforts, no contact could be made by wireless. There was an eerie feeling in the Baluch position and everyone was aware that an attack was imminent. Two-hour officer watches were organised at battalion headquarters and sure enough at about 0200 hrs the first shots were fired. The Japanese closed in and savage hand-to-hand fighting took place on 'C' Company's front. Captain Korla personally led a series of counter-attacks. He and his company of Dogra Brahmins held out for nearly four hours and all the survivors were loud in his praise. The fighting had quickly spread to the small 'B' Company who made good use of the MMGs that they had been allotted. Colonel Dyer, the CO, left his HQ with the adjutant to see the position for himself but they soon found themselves pinned down by fire, partly from their own troops, and did not return to battalion HQ until dawn.[16] After about four hours of confused struggle, the Japanese began to get the upper hand. Finally 'C' and 'B' companies were overrun and the attack surged onto 'A' and 'D' Companies. The CO, who had gone forward again, was seriously wounded when a Japanese bullet, fired at short range, shattered his jaw. He was helped by Second-Lieutenant Coubrough to a sheltered position near the river bank and could take no further part in the battle.

The End of the Action

At *HQ 215 Regiment*, just before dawn, there had still been uncertainty as to how the battle was going and they feared that in daylight the superior British firepower might turn the scales. Accordingly, *2/215 Battalion's* infantry gun company, which was with *HQ 215 Regiment*, was ordered to join the fray in an infantry role.[17] Leaving a small party with the guns, the rest of the *Gun Company* moved round the west side of the Baluch position at first light and attacked south down the river bank, overrunning battalion HQ and the guns, and killing everyone they came across, including the wounded Colonel Dyer, who refused to surrender. By 0800 it was all over and the Japanese were mopping up. There being no more organised resistance, the survivors fought their way north in small parties, aiming at Duyinzeik.[18]

According to the Japanese, the British dead, including those killed at Miyainggale, numbered 289 officers and men. Five officers, three VCOs and 65 men of the Baluch managed to fight their way out and when the several platoon patrols who had been out of the camp all came in the battalion mustered about 200 officers and men. Six officers, including the Regimental Medical Officer, and 229 men were taken prisoner. Most of the prisoners had fought their way out, but surrendered when they found themselves surrounded by *1/215 Battalion*, who had reached the road to Duyinzeik at about 0300 hours. Both mountain guns and a number of MMGs and mortars were lost. The Japanese claim to have had only 17 men killed and 33 wounded.

Captain Siri Kanth Korla (who had been taken prisoner but escaped) was awarded an immediate DSO, a rare distinction. It had been a very desperate fight for a 'green' and unsupported battalion up against a much more powerful and experienced Japanese foe. The 7th/10th Baluch had fought it out with exemplary courage and this was not to be forgotten in 17 Division. There was, however, in British eyes at the time, a very ugly side to this action. The survivors were convinced that many of the wounded had been either shot or bayoneted to death, as indeed the figures seemed to indicate since few of the prisoners were wounded.[19] The Japanese had learnt in China to fight a kill-or-be-killed war and this savage pattern, since the Japanese would never surrender, was increasingly to become the custom for both sides in the Burma war.

Captain Bruce Toothill's Story

One of the Baluch parties which tried to fight its way out from the Kuzeik position on the 12th included the Subedar-Major, and was led by Captain Bruce Toothill, who had been with battalion HQ. They went through the forest and succeeded in striking the Duyinzeik road about three miles west of the river, but all at once found themselves surrounded by a horde of yelling Japanese. Toothill rushed behind a tree and tried to shoot his way through with his revolver but was hit three times, the last shot through the mouth knocking out his teeth, damaging his gums and breaking his jaw. The Subedar-Major tried to throw a grenade and was bayoneted to death. Toothill felt so badly injured that he made signs to a

16. Inexperienced troops being attacked in the forest at night for the first time nearly always blazed away at shadows and often at each other.

17. Story of Lieutenant Tadashi Suzuki, who was in the *215 Regimental Gun Company* at the time.

18. I am indebted to John Randle and Charles Coubrough for much of this account of the battle. Coubrough was at battalion HQ until the end and managed to avoid being 'mopped up'. He escaped the following night but was picked up by a Japanese patrol near the Donthami river two days later.

19. It is only fair to add that in a purely bayonet attack the proportion of killed to wounded is necessarily high.

Japanese soldier standing over him to finish him off but the soldier refused. Curiously, in the light of other incidents, he was well treated. Carried by other prisoners on a stretcher improvised out of bamboo, signal wire and bamboo matting, he was taken to the Japanese company HQ and given a heap of straw to lie on for the night. Thence he was carried by his men back to Pa-an where he joined the other officer prisoners and with them went down the river to Moulmein. There his broken leg and face were attended to and he was deposited in the jail, but given a bed, mattress, pillow and blanket. Though he had a very hard time, eating and drinking being difficult and painful, he was not ill-treated or interrogated (perhaps because he couldn't talk) as many others were. It would seem that his courageous resistance won the respect of his captors. He ended up in Rangoon jail and survived the war.[20]

The Failure to Counter-attack

HQ 46 Brigade, who were at Thaton, had only taken over the southern half of the forward area on 9 February from 16 Brigade. They were required to watch about 40 miles of the River Salween and do their best, following Wavell's instructions repeated by Hutton, to identify and counter-attack any enemy attempt to cross it. However, without armour or motorised infantry, to react quickly enough to an enemy crossing was clearly going to be difficult. On the 9th they took over from 16 Brigade command of both the 3rd/7th Gurkhas who, together with a company of 2nd KOYLI, were cut off in Martaban and the 7th/10th Baluch. 46 Brigade's third battalion, the 5th/17th Dogras, was at Duyinzeik where the road from Pa-an to Thaton crossed the Donthami river by a rickety ferry. This battalion was deployed on both sides of the river with the result that it could move in either direction, but in neither quickly. All four towns occupied by the brigade were bombed between the 8th and 11th, some several times.

46 Brigade's first concern was Martaban, which was being surrounded. On the 9th, Divisional Headquarters ordered its evacuation but a strong armoured patrol failed to get through with the message, many of them being killed. In fact Lieutenant-Colonel Stevenson decided on his own initiative to break out that night and his force was to reach Thaton on the afternoon of the 11th, but as far as Brigade knew on the 10th, and most of the 11th, they were either holding out or had been overwhelmed. When the news came in on the 11th that there had been a substantial enemy crossing south of Pa-an the lack of reality in the plan was exposed. Brigadier Ekin, fearing that the Martaban road might now be undefended, hesitated to commit his reserve battalion to Kuzeik as had been planned. His decision was reinforced by a wireless message received in Brigade Headquarters at 1400 hours on the 11th, which purported to come from the

7th/10th Baluch, and said that they had successfully repelled the force which had crossed the river. In fact this signal appears to have been sent by the sophisticated signallers of *33 Division* who had picked up the style of the British messages which were mainly being sent in clear.

Lieutenant-Colonel Dyer had sent a written message to the Dogras in the evening of the 11th, saying that he expected to be attacked that night and asking for their support. This information was presumably passed on to 46 Brigade. As a result Ekin ordered the Dogras to advance to Kuzeik but whether he did it that night, as he remembered later, or next morning as the Dogras say in their war diary, is not clear.[21] What happened next is also uncertain. The Dogras record that a patrol, size unspecified, that night made contact with the enemy and suffered a few casualties. The Japanese flank guard, a platoon of *215/2 Company* commanded by Second-Lieutenant Kiuchi, say that they were attacked by a company and repulsed it, losing one man killed and two badly wounded. What is certain, is that it took several hours to get the other half of the Dogras across the river on the morning of the 12th and the battalion did not leave Duyinzeik until 1100 hours. It was far too late. They had hardly made contact with the Japanese when they were recalled.

Comparison of the British and Japanese Forces

So far the British forces had been unable to hold the Japanese attacks. The reason was not far to seek. The Japanese were of one nationality, spoke one language and had been motivated from early days to believe that the highest honour was to die for their Emperor. Many officers and NCOs were battle-experienced and their organisation and training was well suited to warfare in a country with few communications. A Japanese division was superficially very similar to a British division but the hardiness and versatility of their soldiers enabled them to increase the "teeth" at the expense of the "tail". So a Japanese rifle company, normally about 150 strong but at this stage of the campaign often 200 or more, was about twice the strength of a similar British company.

In contrast, the British/Indian Army spoke a variety of languages and most of the officers and men had to learn Urdu, the common *lingua franca*. At this stage many young officers spoke it imperfectly. The rapid sixfold expansion of the Indian Army found it at the end of 1941 at its weakest. The majority of officers had only just emerged from officer cadet training units and in many of the last units formed, such as those in Burma, some 85% of the men were recruits with

---

20. Toothill, Captain H.B., *Personal Account*, IWM 77/153/1.
21. The 5th/17th Dogras were by no means well enough trained to make a night advance and attack on the Japanese.

only a few months' basic training. Many of these lads (*'jawans'* was the Indian Army term) had never moved far from their villages before taking their first journey to their training depots. To pitchfork these men into battle overseas against a first-class enemy, and with only rudimentary artillery and air support, was asking too much.

The battle at Kuzeik was the first attempt by the British to stand their ground against a major Japanese attack, albeit in a hastily-prepared position. Without wire or artillery support and against first-class opposition it was doomed to failure. Nevertheless it was a courageous and gallant effort and the lessons learned would not be forgotten.

CHAPTER SEVEN

The Battle at the Bilin River

General Hutton was finding it increasingly difficult for one man to carry out his wide range of responsibilities. His position could scarcely have been more complicated. Burma was on its way to independence and had its own parliament and Prime Minister. Although Defence and Foreign Affairs were subjects reserved to the Governor, Home Affairs and Finance were matters for parliament. Wavell was nominally his Theatre Commander but he was 2000 miles away and so swamped with problems in his vast international command that it was impossible for him to give the time to Burma that it needed. Consequently many of the responsibilities of a theatre commander, such as liaison with the Chinese, with the Americans concerned with China and with the Burmese government, fell on Hutton. For all British and Indian Army administrative problems, such as reinforcements, personnel matters, equipment and supplies, he had to deal with GHQ India, 1500 miles away to the west. At the same time he was Chief of the General Staff at the Burmese War Office, and this produced a multitude of administrative problems for the Burma Army as well as involving him in major political discussions with the Governor and senior Ministers. As Army Commander he was responsible for liaison with the Royal Navy and the RAF, neither of whom were under his command, and for planning ahead the campaign to defend Burma, while he was also obliged to control the fighting and virtually act as corps commander. It is not surprising, therefore, that on 13 February he asked General Wavell to appoint a proper corps commander and also a high level liaison team to deal with the Chinese. Both these requests were absolutely vital and if Wavell had still been in India would surely have been answered positively and promptly. As it was there was no reply. They coincided with the fall of Singapore and the Supreme Commander, who was in hospital, had other matters to deal with.

The Withdrawal to the Bilin River

Following General Wavell's last instructions, General Hutton now emphasised to Smyth the importance of holding the 'Thaton-Duyinzeik line' before falling back to the Bilin River and added that he should not withdraw without reference to AHQ. This turned out to be a mistake. The British had yet to learn the fundamental lesson that Japanese tactics were different from those taught in the West. They did not advance along roads as Western staff colleges believed that all first-class armies must.

On 13 February, *215 Regiment* opened an artillery and mortar bombardment on the 5th/17th Dogras, who had now been reinforced in Duyinzeik by the 1st/7th Gurkhas, but did not follow it up. This was strange, and Smyth and Ekin became increasingly uneasy. It looked very much as though the Japanese were moving round 46 Brigade's northern flank, which, indeed, was exactly what they were doing. General Smyth had always been in favour of fighting initially on the Bilin river before falling back to the main position on the Sittang. He now felt that there was no time to be lost if he was to reach the Bilin before the Japanese and he could wait no longer. He therefore ordered a withdrawal and informed General Hutton of his reasons. For this action, which was absolutely correct, he was later reprimanded by General Hutton who was determined to stick to Wavell's strategy.

The 2nd KOYLI formed the rear-guard at Thaton and covered two bridge demolitions by 60 Field Company south of the town. They were supposed to be evacuated by train but when, after several hours, no train had appeared, they set off on foot. Apparently no-one informed the railway personnel and, several hours late, the train appeared and steamed happily through the front line and on to Thaton. The town appeared deserted and the only people around were two Yorkshiremen who had been consoling themselves in a nearby contractor's store and had been left behind when their battalion moved. Having loaded some valuable stores, mostly liquid, from the contractor's store, these two accompanied the train back to Bilin, narrowly escaping a very warm reception as they reached the front line.

Although the Bilin river was not in itself much of an obstacle and could be forded in many places, the gap between its estuary and the forested hills to the north formed a bottleneck for the road and railway. This tended to confine any enemy advance to a relatively narrow front so there was a fair chance of fighting a divisional defensive battle there (see Map 9). Although he knew that he was facing two Japanese divisions, General Smyth, no doubt aware of the dangers of encirclement, decided to defend the position in depth. To cover the 15-mile front, he deployed only one brigade, Brigadier Jones's 16 Brigade, reinforced by the 2nd KOYLI and the 5th/17th Dogras. The latter were to provide an outpost screen east of the river to cover the road and rail bridges south of Bilin. He also allotted to 16 Brigade all his artillery, that is 5 and 12 Mountain Batteries and two World War I 18-pounders of the Burma Auxiliary Force (BAF) being used in an anti-tank role, as well as three ancient armoured cars of the 1st Armoured Car

Company, BAF. This was quite a responsibility for the brigadier whom Cowan had only the week before been sent out to replace.

Smyth's plan was for 16 Brigade to hold the line of the river and for 46 Brigade to fall back through them to Kyaikto. 48 Brigade remained in reserve at Kyaikto and were told to be prepared to hold a position on the Thebyu river covering Kyaikto if necessary. Because of the unwise policy of attempting a stand on the 'Thaton-Duyinzeik line', however, there was very little time to implement this plan. For, as Smyth knew, the Japanese were on the move.

The Japanese Approach

The Japanese were in a hurry. Not only were they aware that the British were being reinforced through Rangoon but their supplies were limited. *214 Regiment*, who had not yet been engaged, were in the lead. They had entered Burma on 1 February and crossed the Salween on the night of 12/13 February at Kawku, some eight miles north of Pa-an. From there they advanced through the forest on a good path up the valley of the Kyakat Chaung and by the evening of the 14th the leading elements had reached Kwingale, about seven miles north of Bilin town and three miles east of the river (see Map 9). That night (14th/15th) they sent a composite company forward to cross the bamboo bridge (marked on the map) across the Bilin at Ahonwa, about six miles north of Bilin town, and occupied a small hill on the west side of the river. On the 15th, *1/214 Battalion* crossed the same bridge and extended the position to a hill west of Paya and about a mile further south.

33 Division's other regiment, *215*, after their success at Kuzeik, avoided Duyinzeik and advanced north-west by cross-country paths through Tonbo and the Pabein Reserved Forest. They were aiming to cross the Bilin at Yinon, two miles north of Ahonwa. The flank guard of *2/215 Battalion*, who were in the lead, had a clash early on the 17th with British forces retreating from Thaton and there were losses on both sides. Later on the same day, *1/215 Battalion*, who were moving up the road, contacted the 17th Dogra screen covering the Bilin bridges and drove them back over the river in some disorder. After dark, *2/215 Battalion* sent a strong fighting patrol across the river into Bilin village and engaged 8 Burif. These feints accomplished, both battalions then moved on north towards Yinon.

HQ 55 Division advanced north from Martaban behind *143 Regiment*. *112 Regiment* had been left behind in Moulmein to maintain order while a military government was being established in this large and important city. *2/143 Battalion*, advancing astride the road and railway, occupied Thaton on the 17th. *143 Regiment* then turned west and crossed the estuary of the Bilin by ferry to

Lieutenant-General Seizo Sakurai,
Commander of 33 Infantry Division.

Zokali and headed north for the railway with the aim of outflanking the British position on the Bilin. Their leading elements reached Taungzon on the afternoon of 19 February.

General Sakurai of *33 Division* now proposed that while *214 Regiment* engaged the British frontally, *215 Regiment* should move quickly round behind the British and trap them. General Iida did not agree. He thought the plan too risky. He confided to his diary that the characters of his two divisions were utterly different. *33 Division* was too agressive and *55 Division* was too cautious. He would need to be careful. General Sakurai at *33 Division*, however, felt that a very good opportunity was being lost.

The British Plan

While 16 Brigade was being deployed in the Bilin position on the 16th, General Hutton arived at Kyaikto to see General Smyth and visited some of the unit's there. Before leaving, he explained the importance of gaining time for the arrival of reinforcements who were expected shortly and stressed that there was to be no withdrawal from the Bilin line without his specific permission.

From Bilin a road led up the west bank of the Bilin River to Yinon. Brigadier Jones's plan (see Map 10) was for one company of 2nd KOYLI to go to Yinon to watch a shallow ford there while the rest of the battalion established themselves in the area of Danyingon. On their right would be 8 Burif (less one company) holding the area of Bilin town, and further south the 1st R Jats covering the two bridges and extending to Hninpale. The Dogras would remain as an outpost screen and the 1st/7th Gurkhas were in reserve near Brigade HQ in the Bilin Rubber Estate. In fact the battle would divide itself into two halves. The northern sector was from Yinon to Chaungbya and the southern from Bilin to Hninpale. For clarity, the action in each sector is described separately although they took place simultaneously.

The Action in the Northern Sector

When the 2nd KOYLI moved out towards Danyingon on the morning of 16 February, they surprised a party of Japanese in the village. This was a platoon advance guard. Although the enemy fled, losing a number of men killed including their platoon commander,[1] it soon became apparent that there was a considerable hostile force already on the west bank of the river in this area. It was, in fact, *1/214 Battalion*. The KOYLI company destined for Yinon was sent on ahead with an escort of the only three Bren gun carriers that the battalion possessed and duly reached its destination safely. Meanwhile the British made several attempts to clear Danyingon village but met stiff opposition and suffered substantial casualties, as did the Japanese. Eventually they fell back on a position protecting the road and containing the village from the west and south.

Brigadier Jones decided to use his reserve to assist the 2nd KOYLI and that evening, at 9pm, the 1st/7th Gurkhas were ordered to prepare for a dawn attack the next morning, the 17th, to restore the situation at Danyingon-Paya. Now the 1st/7th Gurkhas, like the Dogras, had left Duyinzeik at 0100 hours on the 15th and reached Hninpale at 0100 hours on the 16th after a gruelling 32-mile cross-country march in which they had narrowly avoided encountering *215 Regiment*. They had only reached the Bilin Rubber Estate at 1300 hours on the 16th and were pretty exhausted. Nevertheless they moved out at midnight and, well supported by 5 Mountain Battery (which had also moved up during the night) and their own mortars, attacked with great determination early on the 17th. However, they were up against a first-class battalion well dug in and, after several attempts and mounting casualties, were forced to call off the attack. Gurkha casualties were not light. Major Burke and 18 Gurkhas were killed and Captain Rae and 25 Gurkhas were wounded, while 30 Gurkhas were missing. The British were to learn the hard way that to attack experienced and well dug-in Japanese troops was a very formidable task.

General Smyth now ordered 48 Brigade to send forward the 1st/4th Gurkhas in trucks to come under the command of 16 Brigade and make another attack on Danyingon. Supported by 5 Mountain Battery and the mortars of all three battalions, they attacked late that afternoon through the forest south of the village, while one company assaulted Point 318, a small hill to the west. The hill was not defended and proved a most useful OP for the guns and the RAF as it gave a good view of both sides of the river. But the attack through the forest failed, one company losing its way and the other being driven back with some loss. While this attack was taking place, the Japanese, who had now been reinforced with a second battalion, established a road-block about two miles further north. Two bren-gun carriers from the 2nd KOYLI, and three wheeled carriers from the 1st/7th Gurkhas, went up to investigate but were driven back by mortar and automatic fire. That night, Colonel Harada, commander of *215 Regiment*, crossed the river and discussed with Colonel Sakuma of *214 Regiment* their plans for the

1. Account of Mr Koji Kawamata.

advance to the Sittang, which General Iida had ordered for 20 February. He was accompanied by two companies of *1/215 Battalion*, presumably because *214 Regiment* felt under pressure.

On 18 February another attempt was made to clear the road-block in the northern sector. This time the carriers were supported by two armoured cars and a platoon of the 2nd KOYLI. After a two-hour struggle, in which the Japanese had heavy losses attempting close-quarter attacks,[2] Major Haughton was killed by a mortar bomb and the British were forced to abandon any attempt to reach the company in Yinon, which was now isolated. Fortunately the Japanese, although they were aware of this company's position, took no action as they did not wish to give away their own concentration on the east bank of the river. During the day the RAF gave some welcome help, Blenheim bombers making two effective raids on Japanese positions on both banks. This seems to have deterred the Japanese from carrying out an attack planned for that afternoon.

The Japanese account[3] of this action is of interest. *2/214 Battalion*, with a regimental 75mm gun, had crossed the river on the 17th and took up a position on the right of their first battalion. It was they who had put in the road-block. They were impressed at meeting British soldiers for the first time. They 'struggled against repeated attacks by the British who were supported by armour and airplanes'. They mistook either the armoured cars or the carriers for tanks. Their account states: "7 Company immobilised a tank when it stopped at the barricade by throwing a grenade through a loop-hole. However two tanks came shooting continuously into our positions and while we were coping with this another tank came and towed the first one away." There were, of course, no tanks in Burma on either side at this stage although on both sides they would shortly appear.

General Iida commented in a book that he wrote after the war:[4]

"Around Bilin we received strong and firm resistance by troops from British mainland, King's Own Yorkshire, who fought fiercely."

But he added that the Japanese gained confidence that they could beat them.

Writing of this incident many years later, the editor of the official history of *214 Regiment* wrote:

"Soldiers of *214 Regiment*, who had been fighting against the Chinese army, were for the first time attacked by aeroplanes and fought against an army with modern equipment… Repeated training in close quarter attack on tanks and armoured cars proved fully effective and so they did not find them too frightening. What really surprised them was the vast amount of shelling and the amount of British small arms fire. This was something they had never experienced or imagined. The Japanese army stressed saving ammunition. Even the artillery tried to hit its target with only one shell. In contrast the British fired a barrage which was like ploughing the land with shells... The Japanese did not know how to deal with the British who advanced in the jungle shooting continuously in every direction. Japanese weapons were inferior and their ammunition supply limited. From this first experience the Japanese realised that the only way to win was to attack the flanks or back of the British, where they could not develop their full strength, and to attack at night."

46 Brigade now arranged for a fighter aircraft to drop a message on the afternoon of the 18th to the isolated company of 2nd KOYLI at Yinon, ordering them to withdraw at once to Thebyuchaung. The message fell on a sandbank in the river and was duly retrieved, the company setting off at once through the forested hills. On the way they noticed that some of the tracks had been marked.[5] They bivouacked that night and while marching along a village track on the 19th, they bumped into a strong Japanese patrol. After a short fight, in which they inflicted some casualties and themselves lost two men killed, they reached Thebyuchaung that evening. They were lucky. The patrol was an advance party for the main body of *215 Regiment* who crossed the river at Yinon on the night of the 19th, some 26 hours behind them, and advanced towards Alugyi which was only four miles north-east of Thebyuchaung. This route had presumably been chosen when General Sakurai believed that he would be ordered to block the British retreat. That night, the 18th, 16 Brigade was subjected to a series of probing attacks by *214 Regiment* using tracer ammunition and fire crackers, apparently fired out of mortars. As usual, all three battalions responded to this with enthusiasm, thus disclosing their positions. They had fought very well but there was still much to learn.

Action in the Southern Sector

Meanwhile on the southern sector of the front, the Dogras, as already recounted, had been driven across the river on the afternoon of the 17th by *1/215 Battalion*, and *143 Regiment* had started to make its presence felt. The Dogras had retired in some disorder, losing many of their weapons and were sent back

---

2. *ibid.*

3. *Memoir of 214 Regiment.*

4. Iida, Shojiro, *Senjin Yawa.*

5. This had been done by parties from the BIA to mark the route to the Sittang bridge.

to Kyaikto to re-equip. General Smyth now realised that six battalions were too much for one brigade HQ to handle, so he ordered forward Brigadier Hugh-Jones and HQ 48 Brigade together with the 2nd/5th R Gurkhas. Hugh-Jones was to take command of the southern sector which would now comprise the 1st R Jats, the 8th Burif and the 2nd/5th R Gurkhas. Brigadier Jones still commanded the three battalions in the northern sector and moved his 16 Brigade HQ further north to be nearer them. Smyth also moved the 1st/3rd Gurkhas forward to Alugale, where they could both cover the tracks coming in from the north and the roadbridge at Thebyuchaung. Brigidier Ekin and a reduced 46 Brigade remained at Kyaikto. Kyaikto was also where Divisional HQ and the 4th/12th FFR, which was in divisional reserve, were located. Each forward brigade now commanded only one of its original battalions and whether it was wise to mix up the battalions like this is doubtful. Units fight best with people that they know. But it was perhaps inevitable in view of Smyth's original decision to defend the Bilin line with only one brigade.

The new CO of the Jats, to replace the one who had failed at Kawkareik, had just taken over command on the 16th. He was Lieutenant-Colonel B. R. Godley and was a very different character from his predecessor. He had been briefed by General Hutton to restore the battalion's morale and was determined to ensure that the 1st Royal Jats retrieved their reputation. The Jats were holding a position in the southern sector astride the road and railway. They were dug in on the bank of the river, here about 150 yards wide, between south of Bilin and Hninpale with three companies forward and one in reserve.

At 1700 hours on the 17th, the Dogras and one 8 Burif company (who had been on the east bank) having all crossed the Bilin river, the CO of the Royal Jats, to whom the decision had been delegated, ordered 24 Field Company to blow the road and railway bridges, which they duly did. Later that afternoon two Japanese engineer officers in an ambulance arrived at the demolished road bridge and made a detailed examination. In view of the Red Cross prominently displayed on the vehicle, a captured British ambulance, the second-lieutenant commanding the company overlooking the bridge forebore to open fire. The British had much to learn about such artful Japanese ruses.

That night (17/18 February) Japanese patrols were active and there was firing along much of the front. Bilin village was held weakly by 8 Burif, who were covering a two-mile front, and they were pushed out of the village. The Jats reported that their left flank was uncovered so the 2nd/5th R Gurkhas were ordered to send a company to support 8 Burif. In the morning, on information that there were Japanese moving through the gap, the Gurkhas advanced to the river between 8 Burif and the Jats without meeting any opposition and left two companies in position there. Meanwhile the Jats had sent back a company to replace the Gurkhas in brigade reserve. A report now being received that there had been enemy landings on the coast to the south, the 2nd/5th R Gurkhas were ordered to send a company to patrol along the road through Taungale to Tangzun. They were also ordered to send a company back to brigade reserve to free the Jat company to return to its battalion.

That night (18/19 February) the Gurkha companies on the river bank were both attacked by patrols. On one front, some mounted Japanese drove a herd of cattle towards the British. The Gurkhas, as Hindus reluctant to shoot the cows, allowed them to come quite close before they realised what was afoot. However, directly the enemy opened fire, the Gurkhas returned it and drove them off, several cows being killed. Casualties in both companies, at two killed and five wounded, were light. The Jats were to suffer worse casualties in an unfortunate 'friendly fire' incident. Their company which had been in brigade reserve, while returning to its battalion in the dark, fired on the Gurkha reserve company under the impression that they were Japanese. Before order was restored the Jats had lost five killed, eight wounded and two missing. The Gurkhas, who were dug in, had only one man wounded. Unfortunately, Colonel Godley was not informed that the 'enemy' were Gurkhas and believed that Japanese patrols were penetrating behind his position.

The Jats had another drama that night. Like the Gurkhas, they had also been attacked by small parties of the enemy and had had one or two casualties. But in one sector, several men had retreated without orders. Colonel Godley had the men brought before him the next morning and, in the presence of the Subedar-major and two other VCOs, personally chastised them with a bamboo cane. This firm but highly irregular action was accepted as reasonable by all ranks and the soldiers concerned soon proved that the incident had merely been an aberration.

In the very early hours of the morning of the 19th, a report came in that the Japanese were outflanking 48 Brigade from the south having possibly come by sea. In fact this was the leading troops of *55 Division*, that is *143 Regiment*, who had crossed the Bilin estuary to Zokali. So 'B' company of the 2nd/5th was sent off in the dark down the road to Taungale and Taungzun. There was a screen of Burma military police and Burma FF units spread out to the south with the task of reporting any enemy landings from the sea. The Gurkhas went through Taungale to Zohtak where they found that the police post had been deserted. They then returned to the rail crossing near Taungale and advanced to Taungzun along the railway. As they approached the railway station there the leading platoon was shot up from the jungle, losing two men killed. They returned the fire with interest and the enemy dispersed. A carrier patrol of the 2nd/5th now went on along the road to Pauktaw, just short of Taungzan, where there was a Burma FF detachment. The latter reported that a Japanese force was approaching from the estuary to the south. Both parties withdrew to Brigade HQ after brushing aside some BIA south of Taungale and leaving a platoon road-block on the Taungale road just south of the main road.

Brigadier Hugh-Jones now decided to try and clear this flank, so at dawn on the 19th he sent off 'A' company of the 2nd/5th R Gurkhas to pick up the platoon road-block and patrol the Taungale/Taungzun road. They had not gone far when at Taungale they met a series of Japanese road-blocks in the village. However, by a series of hooks on either side of the road and the liberal use of Tommy guns and LMGs, they succeeded in clearing the route through the middle of the village. This successful action took most of the day and to clear the village completely before dark was impossible, for there were still many Japanese in the fringes, so the company was withdrawn. In the southern sector the fighting had been relatively light but it was clear that the enemy encirclement was getting difficult to hold.

The Withdrawal to Kyaikto

Late on the 18th, General Smyth played his last card by committing his final effective reserve to the battle. The 4th/12th FFR (less a company watching the coast approaches to Kyaikto) had been in divisional reserve. It now went forward in trucks to Alugale, then marched in the dark north-east across country to Paingdawe and from there struck east towards Kazaing which they reached soon after mid-day. Their orders were to create a diversion by attacking the enemy out-flanking 16 Brigade to the north. They were not to become heavily involved and after the action were to come into 16 Brigade reserve. Unfortunately, wireless communication with brigade HQ could not be established so no artillery support was available. Nevertheless in the afternoon two companies assaulted and captured a wooded hill on 16 Brigade's left flank, driving the Japanese off at the point of the bayonet. Mortaring and enemy counter-attacks caused mounting casualties and so the battalion was withdrawn into reserve at Chaungbaya. Casualties were 12 killed, 40 wounded and three missing.

General Hutton, who was adhering loyally to General Wavell's clearly expressed policy, had given strict orders that Smyth was not to retire from the Bilin line without his express permission. Because of his many other responsibilities, however, Hutton could not give the battle his full attention so whether it was wise to give Smyth such a rigid order is very doubtful. General Smyth was now in the sort of quandary which often arises in a retreat. He had already retired once (quite correctly) without orders and been reprimanded for it. To do it again was to take a grave risk of being relieved and branded as a 'runner'. On the 18th, having visited his two brigades on the Bilin, he wrote to General Hutton that he was committing his last reserve and that "there appeared to be a grave risk of not being able to disengage the troops unless a further withdrawal was ordered."[6] Kirby's Official History considers that Smyth should have insisted on retiring that night, as he wished, and risked the consequences. Had he done so, his troops would have been less exhausted for the arduous retreat to the Sittang but, of course, no time would have been gained *vis-a-vis* the Japanese who would have started their follow-up a day earlier. As it was, Hutton came to Kyaikto on the morning of the 19th and, after discussing the situation, authorised Smyth to withdraw at his own discretion.

General Smyth now recalled that in a similar situation at Dunkirk, when he had been one of the two brigade commanders concerned, his divisional commander had ordered two brigadiers to liaise and decide between themselves how to co-ordinate their withdrawal. It had worked very well, so he now issued a framework for the withdrawal that night and ordered the commanders of 16 and 48 Brigades to form a joint HQ and decide the details. The plan was for 16 Brigade to retire first. They would be followed by 48 Brigade as rear guard. During the move 48 Brigade would be reconstituted with its original battalions, the 1st/3rd, 1st/4th and 2nd/5th Gurkhas. All other units would come under command of 16 Brigade who would march on through Kyaikto and harbour in the Boyagyi rubber estate three miles to the north-west. When all troops had passed through Thebyuchaung, 48 Brigade would blow the road and rail bridges over the Thebyu river and march and ferry in MT back to Kyaikto.

16 Brigade sent its transport and wounded men back at 0200 on the 20th, and the troops started off at 0430. There was no Japanese interference, apart from some bombing of their positions after they had left, and after a rest and meal at the Bilin rubber estate, where they sorted out the new grouping, they marched on through Kyaikto to the Boyagyi rubber estate, arriving there after dark. HQ 17 Division had arranged for a 'tactical' train to go to Mayangon station and this was used on the 20th to evacuate stores and unit equipment dumped by the forward units at Thebyuchaung.

Things did not go quite so well with 48 Brigade. On the 19th, the 1st R Jats were having some trouble with Japanese being reported on all sides and the Gurkhas fighting a battle at Taungale behind them. When at 0300 hours on the 20th a carrier arrived with an order for the CO to report at once to Brigade HQ, he declined to go on the grounds that he could not leave his battalion at such a

---

6. This phrase was quoted in Lt-Gen. Hutton's *Report on Operations in Burma* in the Supplement to *The London Gazette* of 5 March 1948.

moment. It was a serious misjudgement, for he knew that withdrawal was in the air and he had an excellent second-in-command who could have taken over or represented him.[7] Like many others, his radio only worked intermittently; the only message he received was garbled but seemed to refer to RAF bombing. Colonel Godley, in view of the battalion's reputation at Kawkareik, was naturally somewhat sensitive about withdrawing without direct orders but, as he was clearly getting isolated, he withdrew his battalion before dawn from the river bank into a defensive box in the forest north of Taungale. It was just as well he did as the positions he had abandoned were shortly afterwards effectively bombed by the RAF; indeed one of the positions he still occupied was machine-gunned, fortunately without causing any casualties.

Colonel Godley's actions, however, were not appreciated by the 2nd/5th R Gurkhas who were forming the rearguard. No-one knew where he was and their withdrawal, and that of 48 Brigade, was delayed for several vital hours before they could contact him. At about 1000 hours a wireless message did get through ordering him to withdraw to Brigade HQ by 1130. In fact, the 1st R Jats did not pass through the rearguard at the cross-roads south-west of Bilin until 1500 hours. This delay might have had the most serious consequences if the Japanese had decided to encircle the two brigades. Even so, it was a poor start to what was to become the race for the Sittang. The efficient Japanese signallers had intercepted a message in clear ordering the withdrawal, and *215 Regiment* were already well on their way to the Sittang bridge.[8]

48 Brigade's withdrawal was not interfered with, apart from some bombing in Thebyuchaung where the 1st/3rd Gurkhas held a lay-back position. Half the 1st/9th R Jats were picked up in trucks and lifted to the Boyagi Rubber Estate, west of Kyaikto. The other half reached Kyaikto at 10.30 pm. The 2nd/5th R Gurkhas got in at 0200 on the 21st, followed by 8 Burif and the 1st/3rd Gurkhas about an hour later.

Before leaving Thebyuchaung soon after 7 pm, the 1st/3rd Gurkhas had some contact with both enemy divisions, for the road was inclusive to *33 Division* and the railway to *55 Division*. In the first incident, a flank guard on the railway had a prolonged skirmish with what appeared to be a mixed force of Japanese and Burmese who were clearly advancing through the forest up the railway line. In the second, a map case belonging to Brigadier Hugh-Jones having somehow been left beside the road a few miles south of Thebyuchaung, the Brigadier and his BM decided to recover it. They went back in two Gurkha carriers but ran into a Japanese patrol. After a brisk fight they managed to withdraw unscathed, thanks to some skilful driving. In the third incident, a patrol had gone north to try to recover three wounded men of the 2nd KOYLI who had been left in the care of a village headman. To their surprise they saw a large force of Japanese marching north-west from Alugyi. Unfortunately the patrol was ambushed on its return and the battalion, having covered the blowing of the road and rail bridges, left without them. So this invaluable information was not discovered until the survivors managed to rejoin their unit at the Sittang, when it was too late.[9]

The 5th and 12th Mountain Batteries were the only source of artillery support in the Bilin fighting. They both did very well, particularly the 5th Mountain Battery whose close defensive fire support in the northern sector, where the heaviest fighting took place, was an unpleasant surprise for the Japanese. The 15th and 28th Mountain Batteries had also now arrived at Kyaikto. Unfortunately the ship carrying their mules also carried a miscellany of small administrative units and General Hutton, feeling these would be more hindrance than help, had turned it back. As a result the two batteries had to transport their guns in vehicles and were roadbound. Thus 28 Mountain Regiment supporting 17 Division now had two pack batteries (5 and 12) and two truck-borne batteries (15 and 28).

At this stage the Sappers in 17 Division consisted of only two field companies, 24 and 60.[10] 60 Field Company had blown one road and one rail bridge south of Thaton and a reinforced-concrete rail bridge ten miles north of it. 24 Field Company, having demolished the road and rail bridges over the Bilin, the latter under the noses of the Japanese engineers sent to prevent the demolition,[11] went back to Kyaikto and prepared for demolition the bridges over the Kadat Chaung, which at this season was almost dry. To give 17 Division a third field company, the Malerkotla Field Company from 1 Burdiv had been temporarily transferred to 17 Division at Kyaikto. They prepared the road and rail bridges over the Thebyu Chaung for demolition and on the 20th blew them behind the rearguard.

So ended the Battle of the Bilin. General Smyth's 17 Division had held up the Japanese advance for four precious days. The RAF had given excellent close support which the Army had been able to see and appreciate. The Infantry, some of them in action for the first time, had done very well and all the battalions (except one) had fought with distinction. Japanese infantry killed are given as 25 in *214 Regiment*, including the CO of *2 Battalion*, and 14 in *215 Regiment*. The casualties in *143 Regiment* are not known.

7. Major B.C.H. Gerty.
8. Who sent this message has never been disclosed but it must have been one of the three formation HQ; one account, which is probably correct, says firmly that it was HQ 17 Division.
9. *Reconstituted War Diary*, WO/172 956.
10. The remainder of 1 Burma Field Company, which had suffered from many desertions, had been recalled to come under Army HQ in Rangoon.
11. From *History of 33 Engineer Battalion*.

Smyth's two brigades had been opposed by two Japanese divisions but in fact only two and a half enemy regiments had been engaged. From *55 Division*, *112 Regiment* was still dealing with Moulmein-Martaban and had not been present. More sinisterly, *215 Regiment*, less two companies which had been deployed to help *214 Regiment* in its fight with 16 Brigade and less a company which had probed the British position south of Bilin, was being held in reserve on the east bank of the Bilin river. General Sakurai had wished to use it in conjunction with *143 Regiment* to surround the two British brigades but General Iida did not agree. He had other plans. On the same night that the British began their retreat, *215 Regiment* started its advance and crossed the Bilin at Yinon. Before dawn its leading elements passed through Alugyi village only four miles north-east of Thebyuchaung. That evening their main body had caught up the British rearguard and for a short time were marching along a forest track only a few miles to the north of it. Where they were going would soon become all too clear.

CHAPTER EIGHT

The Seeds of Disaster are Sown

The story of the defeat of the 17th Indian Division at the Sittang River is a terrible one, and losses were very heavy. There are many different accounts of what happened. This is not surprising as it was the key battle of the 1942 campaign and destroyed the last hope of holding Rangoon, and therefore Burma. It was nothing short of a disaster and one for which the troops were in no way to blame. Ill chance played a big part but some of the senior commanders must take the main share of the responsibility.

The reason for the defeat is simply explained. There was only one bridge over the wide Sittang estuary. This was the railway bridge, 550 yards long, a true bottleneck. No proper bridgehead defence had been established and the Japanese seized the key feature commanding the bridge before the bulk of 17 Division reached it. To prevent its capture the bridge was demolished with three-quarters of 17 Division still on the wrong side. This is the story of how this desperate action came to be taken.

General Hutton loyally supported General Wavell's strategy of holding up the Japanese for as long and as far away from Rangoon as possible, so that sufficient reinforcements could be brought in to defeat them. He knew that the 7th Armoured Brigade, originally destined for Malaya, had been diverted by Wavell and, after a pause in Ceylon, was on its way to Burma. The 1st Cameronians (and a pioneer battalion) were due to arrive from India on the same day, 21 February. There was hope that the experienced 7th Australian Division, en route to Australia from the Middle East, would be diverted to Rangoon. If there was to be any chance of defeating the Japanese, he must get these units into Burma in time to support the last defensive position before Rangoon. This position was the Sittang River. He wished, therefore, to cause the maximum delay at the Bilin, but he was realistic enough to see that, without another division, 17 Division was unlikely to be able to hold for long the two Japanese divisions opposing them. Hence he had also to plan for the possible need to evacuate Rangoon and to carry on the war in North Burma.

Now Rangoon was by far the largest city in Burma with about half-a-million inhabitants, nearly half of whom were non-Burmese. It was the centre of government and housed the Burmese Parliament.[1] It was the only major port, it was the hub of all communications by road, rail and water, and it contained virtually all the major industries. The task of evacuating the 12,000 British and 185,000 Indian civilians was a huge one and beyond the capacity of the small Burma Civil Service. Law and order were beginning to break down. The head of the Burma Railways was being difficult and on 20 February refused to run any more trains to Mandalay. With the Governor's help he was dispatched to run the railways in northern Burma and Colonel Biddulph was put in charge of the railways in the south. It was vital to get the Chinese to enter Burma from the north and one of their conditions for advancing was that they would be supplied with food, petrol and medical services. All these problems faced Hutton and his small staff apart from fighting the battle. It is quite clear that he badly needed the corps commander for which he had asked on 14 February. The harvest was being reaped of that fatal decision in Washington which had split operational and administrative control. Had Wavell still been in India, a corps commander would surely have been supplied in time. As it was, India could take no action without a direct order from ABDACOM in Java and ABDACOM had other things on its mind.

The Withdrawal from the Bilin to Kyaikto

Meanwhile, a very critical situation was developing for 17 Division. Smyth does not yet seem to have fully appreciated its urgency. 48 Brigade were the rearguard in the withdrawal from the Bilin. On the 20th they passed through the 1st/3rd Gurkhas at Thebyuchaung about 7pm and received a message from Smyth which said:

> "You know best the condition of your troops and the local situation. I leave you therefore a free hand to harbour for the night wherever you wish. I think, however, you should make a big effort to get west of the Thebuchaung River before dark if you can. I have sent you some MT to assist. The sooner you get into Kyaikto the better I shall be pleased, as we have still unlocated parties of Japanese in the coastal area and there may of course be other parties working round the flanks. When we do get you right back, I hope very much to be able to give you a little rest."[2]

While this message shows admirable solicitude for the tough time the soldiers were having, it betrays an astonishing ignorance of the true position and of the potential danger of envelopment. At the very time that this message was received in Thebuchaung, *215 Regiment* was marching through a village in the forest four miles to the north (see Map 11).

The distance between the road and rail bridges over the Bilin river to the similar bridges in Kyaikto was 19 miles. 16 Brigade made a clean break from the Bilin at first light on the 20th and, passing through the 4th/12th FFR's lay-back position at Chaungbaya, reached the road at the Bilin rubber estate. Here they had a meal while the 4th/12th marched through, reaching Kyaikto in the late evening and returning into divisional reserve. 16 Brigade dropped the 1st/4th Gurkhas here to rejoin 48 Brigade and then marched on towards Kyaikto. After 12 miles they were picked up in MT sent from Kyaikto and ferried to the Boyagyi rubber estate about four miles west of that town. The 8 Burif now switched to 16 Brigade to replace the 1st/4th Gurkhas. They did not reach Kyaikto until after midnight.

48 Brigade had lost three or four hours owing to the delay caused by the Jats. Their rearguard battalion, the 2nd/5th R Gurkhas,[3] did not reach Kyaikto until 0200 hours on the 21st. In the dark, the exhausted units were allotted areas in the town, which was protected by 46 Brigade, and promptly lay down and fell asleep. They did not get much rest. About an hour before first light Japanese patrols[4] fired a few bursts of tracer into the camp from the west and south, accompanied by much yelling, and one or two units, not on the perimeter, started firing back. Units which had arrived in the dark were not dug-in and had no idea who was where. A general *feu-de-joie* followed in which most units joined until it became light. Regrettably there were some casualties, many of them among those who were trying to stop the firing, and a valuable couple of hours was wasted.

This action by one or more 'jitter' patrols was a standard Japanese tactic designed to make the enemy disclose his positions and rob him of sleep. It worked well against inexperienced troops, but those who had encountered it before soon learnt to hold their fire until they could see a definite target. It became a standing order that firing inside the perimeter was forbidden, and in this area only the bayonet should be used. Most commanders recognised quickly what was happening on this occasion but curiously General Smyth was not one of them. He recorded in a book after the war that his headquarters had been the probable objective of a Japanese attack.[5]

---

1. Burma was on its way to independence and only Defence and Foreign Affairs were the prerogative of the Governor.
2. Kirby, S.W., *The War Against Japan*, Vol.2, p.64.
3. The 2nd/5th R Gurkhas were delayed two miles west of Thebyuchaung while they had a meal and loaded some of their kit, dumped there on the way forward, on the tactical train waiting at Mayangon station. The 1st/3rd Gurkhas passed them at this time and reached Kyaikto at 10pm.
4. Probably from *1/143 Battalion*.
5. Smyth, Brigadier Sir John, *Before the Dawn*, pp.180,181.

In order to ensure efficient control of the line of communication, General Hutton had in February established a 'Line of Communication Area' (L of C Area) and put Major-General Victor Wakeley in charge. His responsibility covered the L of C from Rangoon to the Sittang bridge for the defence of which he was able to call on 2 Bur Brigade. Brigadier Bourke of 2 Bur Brigade, however, was responsible for guarding a 50-mile front and all he could spare for the defence of the bridge was 3 Burif, now about 200 strong.

Brigadier Ekin of 46 Brigade had been for some days responsible for the defence of Kyaikto and the area back to the Sittang bridge. He was far from happy with the situation. He knew that no proper bridgehead had been formed at the Sittang. The one company of the 2nd Duke of Wellington's Regiment (2nd Duke's) was on the west bank, and the only unit on the east bank was the weak 3 Burif, who had been the first to make for the ferries at Moulmein. Moreover he was very suspicious of the apparent lack of Japanese follow-up along the road. This indicated to him not that the Japanese were being sluggish, but that they were out-flanking the British as they had done at Thaton. On the 20th, therefore, he went to divisional headquarters and suggested to General Smyth that his brigade, which was relatively fresh, should go back early on the 21st and form a secure bridgehead at the Sittang.[6] Smyth did not agree. He thought that the tentative Japanese follow-up was the result of the casualties inflicted in the successful fighting on the Bilin.[7]

Smyth was sticking to the standard staff college solution of withdrawing through a lay-back and the lay-back troops then becoming the rearguard. But the Japanese were not advancing in a standard staff college manner. Unorthodox measures were required and Ekin was certainly right that a strong group should have gone back to the bridgehead as early as possible on the 21st. Later that day, strongly supported by the other two brigadiers, he suggested that all vehicles, other than those absolutely essential, should at once be sent back over the bridge. This proposal was also turned down on the grounds of the traffic congestion that it would cause at the bridge, but Smyth may also have known that the decking of the bridge had not yet been completed.

On this day the 2nd Duke of Wellington's Regiment (less the one company at the Sittang bridge) was sent up from Rangoon by train to join 17 Division at Kyaikto. They were accompanied by a message saying that they "should be sent back to guard the bridgehead as early as possible".[8] They were allotted to 46 Brigade. Two important signals were also received by HQ 17 Division on the 20th. One was from General Hutton, and General Smyth recorded:

"On the evening of the 20th the Army Commander asked my concurrence to further withdrawal behind the Sittang river. I wired concurrence but explained that brigades could go no further without a certain amount of rest."

It would seem from this that General Hutton was urging Smyth not to delay further withdrawal. Another message came from the Army Commander's chief-of-staff, Brigadier Davies. It said that there were reliable reports of Japanese parachute troops having been seen in Thailand and it would be wise to take precautions against a drop, aimed at capturing the bridge intact, in the open country west of the Sittang bridge.[10] This message was to have a significant impact on the coming battle.

It is relevant here to consider the position of the divisional engineers who were to play a critical part in the unfolding drama. On 18 February, the Malerkotla Field Company arrived at Kyaikto having been temporarily transferred from 2 Burdiv. So, on 19 February, the CRE, Colonel A.E. 'Tuffet' Armitage, had three field companies and 18 Artisan Works Company (who were mostly unarmed) under command. On that day he was ordered to send 60 Field Company back across the Sittang by train to build a bridge over the Waw canal. This would enable the 7th Armoured Brigade, due on the 21st, to reach the Sittang. On the 20th, presumably on orders from HQ 17 Division, he ordered 24 Field Company to go back by road over the Sittang river, collect all the sampans and local boats in the area and take them over to the west bank. 18 Artisan Works Company was also sent back the same evening by train with the task of improving the jetties for the three motorised ferries.

1 Burma Auxiliary Force Artisan Works Company, who were not under command of 17 Division, had been working for a week on the formidable task of bolting down sleepers on each side of the railway line on the Sittang bridge so that vehicles could drive over it.[11] This was not an easy task on such a long and narrow bridge with occasional trains still passing through. They had just finished, and 24 Field Company was the first unit to drive its vehicles back over the

6. Brigadier Cowan was also present.

7. Smyth, Brigadier Sir John, *Report on Operations*, dated 26 February 1942, para 1(h).

8. Bisheshwar, Prasad, *The Retreat from Burma, 1941-42*, p.160.

9. Smyth, Brigadier Sir John, *Report on Operations*, para 3(a).

10. The *1st Parachute Regiment*, allotted to *15 Army*, was in a ship sunk by an explosion in the South China Sea on 3 January. Although there were few casualties and the men went on to Bangkok, all its parachutes were lost. The *2nd Parachute Regiment*, allotted to *25 Army*, dropped on the Palembang oilfields on 14 February.

11. A commonly used Japanese PR photograph, which shows neat planking on the bridge, was taken much later.

bridge, the OC, Major 'Plug' Smith, driving the first lorry himself.[12] This left the Malerkotla Field Company as the only divisional Sappers on the east bank of the Sittang. On the evening of the 20th they took over responsibility for the demolitions in Kyaikto.

From Kyaikto there were two routes leading to the Sittang bridge. The railway ran through forest close to the river estuary and was therefore vulnerable to a force moving up the coast in boats. The 'road', after running across paddy fields for a couple of miles, was just a trace cut through the forest on the alignment of a proposed road. It was about 40 yards wide and the trees and brushwood that had been cleared were stacked along each side. It was very uneven and inches deep in dust. Vehicles snaked and bumped their way along it raising a cloud of white dust visible in the air from miles away. Some three to five miles north-west of Kyaikto lay the Boyagyi rubber estate which stretched between the road and the railway. By either route it was about 16 miles with very little water from Kyaikto to the Sittang bridge.

The Plan for Withdrawal to the Sittang

At a conference at 0900 on the 21st, Smyth outlined his plan for the next stage of the withdrawal. Briefly, the whole division would withdraw along the trace. The 4th/12th FFR would be in the lead and would leave at 1000 hours in MT with the task of strengthening the bridgehead. They were expected to reach the bridge around 1300 hours. Their CO, Lieutenant-Colonel Edward, had already left by jeep at 0900 to plan the bridgehead defence.[13] They would be followed by Advanced Divisional HQ,[14] the Malerkotla Sappers (less firing parties) and divisional troops. These would spend the night in the Mokpalin Quarry area about five miles short of the bridge. 4 Burif would march along the railway as a flank guard to the south and the Burma Military Police unit, BFF2, would cover the tracks to the north. 48 Brigade was to be the leading brigade, but on the 21st their first battalion would only go as far as the Mokpalin quarries, the second as far as Inkabo-auk and their third to Sanigsaw. These places were some seven and ten miles short of the bridge. 16 Brigade, nearly all of which had spent the night in the Boyagyi rubber estate four miles west of Kyaikto, would stay where it was and prepare to move early on the 22nd. 46 Brigade, which had not been engaged at the Bilin and was forming the covering force at Kyaikto, would now become the rearguard. On the 21st, supported by 28 Mountain Artillery Regiment (less a battery), it would hold the line of the Kadat Chaung with its HQ and guns in the north-east corner of the Boyagyi estate. Each formation would be accompanied by its own transport. No-one would cross the Sittang on the 21st and the whole division would cross the river on the 22nd.

This was an astonishing plan in view of the danger, indeed likelihood, of a Japanese outflanking movement both north and south. It showed a complete lack of any sense of urgency in getting across the Sittang. It was apparently influenced by the desire to rest the troops, who were certainly very exhausted by their four days of fighting at the Bilin river. But the result was that, on this vital day, the leading troops would only march 11 miles, and half the division would scarcely move at all. Brigadier Ekin was horrified. He saw clearly that a terrible risk was being taken.

Although it is easy with hindsight, that invaluable ally of the historian, to see that Smyth was making a serious mistake, it is less easy to see why he did so. He had been in Kyaikto for a week and was well aware of the local geography. He was a very competent officer and had earlier been conscious of the need to get quickly across the Sittang. To send the whole division and its transport along a very bad track was bound to be a slow form of movement even if the enemy did not interfere. Surely at least one brigade should have gone back to the river on the 21st? All troops were marching, so why not send one brigade along the railway?[15] This route had the added advantage of having water at the two railway stations and of carrying the telegraph line to which the signallers could tap in telephones. If Smyth believed that the bridge would not be ready to take vehicles until the evening of the 21st (which is nowhere mentioned), this only emphasised the need to have a strong bridgehead garrison and to get vehicles ready to cross the bridge the instant it was ready. Certainly it was hot, and much of his force were emotionally and physically exhausted, hungry and short of sleep. But it was his task to drive them on to safety.

The answer must surely be that his illness had affected his judgement. No doubt the strain of conducting the four-day battle at the Bilin and the successful withdrawal after it, combined with lack of sleep, had aggravated his sickness. This is borne out by a remark he made in a letter to Brigadier Hugh-Jones in India three months later.[16] He wrote: "In Burma I became extremely unwell although I hope you and the other brigadiers never noticed it." There can be no

12. Unfortunately 24 Field Company's War Diary for February and March was destroyed during the retreat. It is impossible to be certain whether their vehicles (and those of 60 Field Company which they were looking after) crossed on the night of the 20th or the 21st but private accounts make it clear that the bridge was not fit to take vehicles until dark on the 21st. (See also note 31 in Chapter 9.)

13. He reached the bridge at around 1030 hours. *Letter to Colonel Foucar*.

14. Rear Divisional HQ had gone back on the 20th.

15. On the 22nd, 4 Burif marched back as a flank guard along the railway from the Boyagyi rubber estate and reached Mokpalin in seven hours without hindrance.

16. *Hutton Papers*. Letter dated 20 May 1942. By May, Smyth was a very sick man and could hardly walk. He was diagnosed as having had a mild heart attack at Quetta the previous year. However, he made a full recovery.

doubt that if he was really ill, as he seems to have been, it was also his duty to hand over command. He had an able deputy at hand and many thousands of men were relying on his judgement for their lives.

Withdrawal from Kyaikto

Two battalion commanders who had particularly distinguished themselves at the Bilin were Lieutenant-Colonel W.D.A. 'Joe' Lentaigne of the 1st/4th Gurkhas and Lieutenant-Colonel R.T. 'Ronnie' Cameron of the 2nd/5th R Gurkhas. Both battalions were in 48 Brigade which was going to lead the move back. Lentaigne, knowing time was short, had got his men a meal of tea and dry biscuits and was ready to move. Cameron, whose battalion was to be the leading one, had arranged a more substantial meal which took a little time to prepare and consume. Only ten minutes' notice was given of the start time and so Lentaigne's battalion was switched to the lead. This switch was to make a profound difference to the fortunes of each battalion.

About 0800 on the 21st, the 3rd/7th Gurkhas crossed the road bridge in Kyaikto and a firing party from the Malerkotla Sappers demolished it behind them. The rail bridge in Kyaikto over the Kadat Chaung, almost dry at this season, had already been blown.[17] The CO of the 4th/12th FFR, Lieutenant-Colonel W.D. Edward, left in a jeep at 0900 to recce the bridgehead and reached the bridge in a little under two hours. 48 Brigade started off at 1100, and the rearguard of 46 Brigade moved to its new positions at about 1430 hours. During the morning, Japanese bombers had bombed the town intermittently but apart from starting some fires (which were deliberately increased by the Sappers) had done little damage. They had also bombed the marching columns and one fighter was shot down by small arms fire and its pilot, Lieutenant Yamamoto, killed.[18] However, there was no sign of any enemy follow-up along the road and no information from the Burma FF units which formed a screen from Kyaikto up to the range of hills some ten miles to the north-west. If the orders had been to go hard for the bridge there was still, just, time for the whole division to reach the bridge before midnight. But this was not the order, and Ekin's 46 Brigade had been told to cover the withdrawal by holding the line of the Kadat Chaung, which ran from the north through Kyaikto, until the next morning.

'Friendly Fire' on 21 February

Now a most unlucky event was to occur which weakened and slowed down the division and could scarcely have come at a more unfortunate moment. In the morning, seven Japanese aircraft appeared and started bombing the retreating column, but to everyone's delight were chased off by three RAF Hurricanes.

Delight turned to dismay when the Hurricanes came down to tree-top level and machine-gunned the column causing casualties and chaos. An ambulance under tow with another truck became a particular target and all the wounded were killed.[19] Worse was to come. Either these pilots, or the pilot of some other RAF reconnaissance plane, reported a column of several hundred enemy vehicles, with its head at Inwa, on the short road leading north out of Kyaikto to Kinmun.[20] Unfortunately whoever made the report was mistaken. There were no Japanese vehicles on this road. Nor were there any Japanese vehicles on this day west of the Bilin River. It is easy to become disoriented when flying over a carpet of forest and particularly when engaged in combat. What was seen must have been the retreating 17 Division on the Kyaikto-Sittang road.

Later on in Burma this report would have been received with scepticism. It was unknown for the Japanese, highly conscious of concealment, to expose themselves to air attack in this way.[21] It was also very unlikely that they could have got across the demolished road bridges quite so quickly, and anyway they had few vehicles at this stage.[22] However, HQ 17 Division swallowed this report and unwisely decided to ask the RAF for a strike on what they felt was a most important target. Air Vice-Marshal Stevenson had visited HQ 17 Division a few days previously. He and Smyth had got on well, Smyth making a point of praising the help of his RAF liaison officer. Stevenson was determined to do his best for the Army and ordered a maximum strike. AHQ had given Air HQ a bombline of a north-south line two miles west of Kyaikto. Somebody blundered somewhere and at the briefing for the pilots the target was given as on the Kyaikto-Mokpalin road, which was the wrong side of the bombline, instead of the Kyaikto-Kinmun road or the Kyaikto-Bilin road. Consequently, after suffering the enemy air attack in the morning, the marching columns and the troops in the Boyagyi rubber estate were delighted at the arrival at about 1500 hours of five Blenheims from Magwe, supported by Hurricanes and AVG Tomahawks.[23] A minute or two later they were not so pleased as this force, often at tree-top height, proceeded to bomb and strafe them relentlessly until dusk.[24] Major Bruce

17. Major E.R.B. Hudson, TD, RE. Paper to *RE Journal*.
18. *Memoir of 33 Mountain Artillery Regiment*, p.113.
19. Captain Vic Ashwell, 1st/3rd GR, *Personal Account*.
20. Another account says the column was reported on the Bilin-Kyaikto road.
21. In fact Japanese vehicles were at this time forbidden to move in daylight and even General Iida, obeying his own orders, was on one occasion obliged to ride on his horse four miles in the heat of the day rather than use his car. *Iida's Personal Diary*.
22. The first Japanese vehicle to cross the border from Thailand reached Moulmein on 20 February. The only vehicles that they had forward at this time were those that they had captured.
23. It was the maximum strike force that the RAF could mount, see Appendix 4.
24. The Hurricanes with their eight high-speed machine guns were devastating in a ground attack role.

Kinloch of the 1st/3rd Gurkhas has written a graphic description of these devastating attacks:

> "Streams of tracer bullets from the multi-gunned fighters scythed through the branches with a high-pitched snarl which merged into a continuous ear-splitting crescendo of sound as the planes screamed over again and again just skimming the tree tops, strafing and bombing without a moment's respite. The earth heaved and shuddered under the thud of bombs. The screams of injured mules mingled with the groans and cries of sorely wounded and dying men. An ambulance was burning fiercely, the occupants dead and the Sikh driver cut in half…"

After a few attacks the Army assumed that they must be planes captured by the Japanese and fired back. After more attacks they didn't care whose they were. Several units claimed to have shot down one or two planes and in fact two Blenheims are recorded as having been shot down by ground fire (the crews were saved) and many fighters returned to their base riddled with bullet holes. Casualties from these attacks were never officially estimated as they were swallowed up in the losses over the next two days, but there is no doubt that they were heavy. Many vehicles were destroyed, while the mules that were not killed bolted into the forest, the vital equipment that they carried, particularly wireless sets and mortars, being lost. These repeated attacks inevitably caused some lowering of morale as well as a most serious delay. Soldiers took cover during the attacks and took some time to get started again, while some vehicles which were still runners got stuck trying to get round the bomb craters. It was by far the worst 'friendly fire' incident of the entire Burma war.

Many RAF books refer obliquely to this occasion. The diary entry of a Canadian RAF pilot, who was flying a Hurricane on that day, is quoted in a book privately circulated in Canada:

> "Just heard that the troops and trucks that we strafed yesterday were British, not Japs… That strafing killed about one hundred and sixty game British soldiers, maybe some guys we knew. We all feel terrible about it."

AVM Stevenson was unwise enough to attempt to cover up this incident in his dispatch after the campaign. "After an exhaustive enquiry," he wrote, "I have failed to reach a firm conclusion that our aircraft did, in fact, bomb our own troops at this time and place." In a letter to General Hutton commenting on the latter's dispatch, he wrote:

"It is possible but uncertain that the Japanese used captured British aircraft, or more likely that JA 97 medium bombers were mistaken for Blenheims as plan silhouettes are almost exactly similar. An enemy column was attacked in great force by us between Kyaikto and Bilin [on the 21st]. This attack did not commence until after 1600 hours and the bomb-line for this attack was laid down by AHQ as two miles to the west of Kyaikto".[25]

It was a pity he took this line. Of course, everyone knew they were Allied planes, the AVG fighters with their sharks' jaws painted on the nose being unique, and the pilots made no secret of the mistake. The Army was very grateful to the RAF for keeping the superior Japanese air force away and for their heroic support on many occasions. They were well aware that occasional mistakes were inevitable, particularly in this densely forested countryside and when everyone was so inexperienced. It would have been far better for inter-Service relations to have acknowledged the mistake and identified the cause, so that procedures could be developed to ensure that such incidents never happened again.

Even without this horrific attack it had been a very hot and trying march for divisional troops and 48 Brigade. The whole cleared area was ankle deep in dust. The brushwood heaped along the sides hindered taking cover in the forest. The troops marched with a file on each side with the vehicles ploughing a serpentine course along the middle and throwing up clouds of choking white dust. They duly reached their limited destinations but many hours behind schedule.

The Position at Dusk on 21 February

Unfortunately the 4th/12th FFR had been badly hit by the morning air attack and suffered some 50 casualties. Many of their vehicles were destroyed. This delayed them so much that they did not reach the bridge until it was getting dark. They were to find that the main part of 3 Burif were on Buddha Hill[26] near the bridge (see Map 12). Colonel 'Donnie' Edward had planned for his battalion to take over 'Buddha' and 'Pagoda' hills while the 3 Burif moved to 'Bungalow Hill'. However, this was impracticable in the scrub jungle in the dark, so he left 3 Burif where they were and deployed his exhausted battalion for the night between them and the bridge. He planned to re-adjust the layout at first light.

25. *Hutton Papers*, Letter dated 29 June 1942. This comment about the bomb-line, which was quite correct, makes it absolutely clear that the staff error responsible for the faulty briefing was not in Army HQ.
26. Called by the British 'Buddha Hill' and more accurately by the Japanese 'Hill 135', the spot height marked on the map.

HQ 17 Division had been told by Army HQ on 14 February that they would be responsible for the demolition of the Sittang bridge.[27] Having reached their destination of the Mokpalin Quarries, they now woke up to their responsibilities and at 1900 hours on the 21st the CRE informed Major Richard Orgill[28] that the Malerkotla Sappers were to prepare the bridge for demolition and to have it ready by 1800 hours the next day. This was the first Orgill had heard of it, and it was a bombshell for the exhausted company. However, Orgill at once called an 'O' Group and ordered the company to march to the bridge in the dark and start work. Why this vital task was handled in this haphazard manner at the last moment is unclear but it would appear that both Smyth and his CRE believed that charges had already been fixed on the bridge and all the Sappers would have to do was to detonate them. Unfortunately they were mistaken.

In the evening of the 21st, Brigadiers Ekin and Jones, both still in the Boyagyi rubber estate with 46 Brigade covering the rear, discussed whether they should press on during the night, as they both wished to do, but came to the conclusion that this would cause chaos to the spread-out 48 Brigade ahead of them. They decided, however, to leave as early as possible the next morning, sending the vehicles off at 0530 hours to be followed closely by 16 and then 46 Brigade. They agreed that the two brigades would march without any gaps so that they could support each other if there was trouble. Orders were issued accordingly. At 0100 hours, a signal arrived from Divisional HQ, who seem at last to have realised the extreme urgency, that they should move as early as possible. However, it was decided that it was too late to change the orders and to attempt to do so in the dark would only cause chaos.

One other important factor in the events of this day was that General Hutton, having authorised, and by implication encouraged, the withdrawal from Kyaikto to the Sittang on the 20th, heard that General Chiang Kai-shek was going to land at Lashio on his way back from India. Realising that, if Rangoon were to be saved, it was vital to speed up the advance of the Chinese troops from the north, he flew up to Lashio on the 21st to confer with the Generalissimo. He was out of luck. Chiang's plane circled Lashio but, because of a report of Japanese aircraft in the vicinity, did not land and flew on to Chungking, so Hutton flew back to Rangoon empty-handed on the 22nd. There he was to find that, in his absence, a desperate crisis had developed.

---

27. WO 172/369.
28. Richard Orgill was a tough and adventurous officer who, three years earlier, had led a team in an assault on Tirich Mir, one of the highest mountains in the Hindu Kush.

CHAPTER NINE

The Disaster at the Sittang Bridge

L ate in the evening of 21 February, an ominous piece of news reached General Smyth at the Mokpalin Quarries. The news came from BFF2 who had formed the screen north of Kyaikto. That afternoon they had encountered large Japanese forces advancing west and had fallen back towards the Sittang, some miles north of the bridge. Accordingly, Smyth ordered the 1st/4th Gurkhas to cross the river to the west bank at 0415 hours on the 22nd, followed by HQ 48 Brigade and Divisional HQ. 12 Mountain Battery (less a section) with their mules and two guns were to cross the river by ferry. The Malerkotla Sappers were ordered to prepare the bridge for demolition and an 'Immediate' coded message was sent to 16 and 46 Brigades urging them to start as soon as possible.

It was a dark and moonless night. The 1st/4th Gurkhas[1] were crossing by the catwalk cantilevered out on the upstream side of the bridge when one of the last of the Divisional HQ vehicles (which were driving over the bridge without lights) veered off the track and got jammed across the narrow bridge. This was a disaster as the truck[2], because of the girders, could not be tipped over the side. It took more than two hours for the Sappers, personally directed by the CRE, to clear it and meanwhile a long queue of vehicles built up waiting to cross, including most of the transport of 16 and 46 Brigades which had now arrived. In those two hours practically all the divisional transport could have crossed. It had become light, and the trucks had started moving again, when at about 8am the situation took a new and unwelcome turn. From the north-east came the ominous and unmistakeable sound of machine-gun fire.

The First Japanese Attack on the Bridge on 22 February

Dawn, on that never-to-be-forgotten day, 22 February, found 17 Division extended over 14 miles between the Boyagyi rubber estate and the west bank of the Sittang. As a result of being caught by the enemy while so widely dispersed, and because of the unfortunate 'friendly fire' air attack which destroyed most of the wireless sets, Divisional HQ lost all control and there were three quite sepa-

---

1. Less 'C' Company, who were further back in the column.
2. It was a truck from HQRE.

rate actions on this day. One was on the east bank of the Sittang in the bridge-head, one on the east bank near Mokpalin and one was further east still on the Kyaikto road. In each case the pattern becomes clearer if the actions of the Japanese, who held the initiative, are considered first.

Both *33* and *55 Divisions* had started their advance from the Bilin on the night of the 20 February, but their roles were very different. General Iida's plan was that *55 Division*, with *143 Regiment*, was to advance along the railway and pro-tect the left flank of the advance. They would be followed by a newly-arrived engineer battalion tasked with repairing the rail bridges. *33 Division* was to advance across country as fast as possible and seize the Sittang bridge. Members of the BIA had already been sent ahead to choose and mark the routes.

General Sakurai's plan for *33 Division* was that *215 Regiment*, which had not been fully engaged at the Bilin, would go hell-for-leather for the bridge and cap-ture it before it could be demolished. They were to cross the Bilin at Yinon on the night of the 19th/20th and march through the forest on village paths via Melan, Alugyi, Ngapyawdaw and Kinmun to Pyinkadogon, about three miles east of the bridge (see Map 11). It was this force, marching from Alugyi to the north-east, which the 1st/3rd Gurkha patrol had seen north of Thebyuchaung on the evening of the 20th. *214 Regiment* (less *3 Battalion*) had had a hard fight at the Bilin and would start a few hours later. *3/214 Battalion*, which had been in divisional reserve at the Bilin, would take a more northerly route than *215* as far as Ngapyawdaw and then a more southerly one through Winkalaw, hitting the Kyaikto-Mokpalin trace south-west of Meyongale. Its aim was to form a road-block and delay 17 Division until the bridge had been captured.

1/215 Battalion, supported by *33/9 Mountain Artillery Company* and *33/1 Engineer Company*, reached Pyinkadogon early on the morning of the 22nd. Major Mugita, its commander, decided not to wait for his *4 Company* or for *2/215 Battalion*, who were following, and at 0800 launched an attack on Sittang vil-lage.[3] They met unexpected resistance and were shot up by a force which includ-ed armoured cars, so the leading *1 Company* commander, Lieutenant Hashimoto, decided to occupy instead Hill 135, which the British called 'Buddha Hill', and which overlooked the village and the bridge (see Map 12). There was only light resistance (from 3 Burif) and they reached the top.

His right-hand platoon, accompanied by an engineer party led by Lieutenant Tamogami, first attacked the armoured cars and carriers with grenades and anti-tank mines. They then attempted to rush past 'Pagoda Hill' and seize the bridge with the aim of removing the demolition charges. On the way, they overran an advanced dressing station (ADS) which was in a wooden house beside the road on the north of the hill. Here they captured three doctors from HQ 17 Division including Colonel K.P. Mackenzie RAMC, the ADMS, and 24 other medical personnel.[4]

However, the 4th/12th FFR held firm on the top of 'Pagoda Hill' and 'D' Company of the 2nd Duke's was sent across the bridge to reinforce them. Two companies of the 4th/12th FFR, together with 'D' Company of the 2nd Duke's, then counter-attacked to restore the situation. They drove the Japanese off all of 'Pagoda Hill' and attacked 'Buddha Hill'. A Japanese account of their attack on the bridge records that they got almost to the end of the bridge but then encountered a line of Indian soldiers advancing and firing automatic weapons from the hip and were driven back, several men being killed, and the attack was abandoned.[5] Meanwhile, the Japanese were strongly reinforced on 'Buddha Hill' by *2* and *3 Companies* and a platoon of MMGs on either flank. They were unable to capture 'Pagoda Hill' but succeeded in holding 'Buddha Hill' in the face of determined British attacks in which Captain "Sam" Manekshaw of the 4th/12th FFR took a prominent part before being severely wounded.[6] Casualties in the 4th/12th FFR were 11 killed and 40 wounded. This ended the first Japanese attempt to capture the bridge. 'D' Company of the Duke's now moved south and dug in on 'Bungalow Hill' while the remainder of 3 Burif took up a position in the centre of the bridgehead.

The Second Japanese Attack on the Bridge on 22 February

General Smyth, whose Tactical HQ was only about 200 yards from the bridge, now put Brigadier Hugh-Jones in command of all the bridgehead troops. About 1230 Brigadier Hugh-Jones[7] moved his tactical HQ across the river and into the bridgehead. Shortly afterwards heavy shelling started on 'Pagoda' and 'Buddha Hills'. Casualties began to mount seriously. Hugh-Jones therefore withdrew the bridgehead troops back across the river and decided to hold the position by fire

3. The Japanese used Japanese Standard Time in official documents. This was necessary for the co-ordination of their widespread operations. Local and personal accounts generally use local time, which in Burma was $2^1/_2$ hours different. Hopefully the correct adjustments have been made in the narrative.

4. Colonel Mackenzie and his team ended up in Rangoon jail where they spent the next three-and-a-half years. Colonel Mackenzie was the senior regular officer taken prisoner in Burma, the next senior being Lieutenant-Colonel Power of the Dogras, captured the following day. Although Brigadier Hobson was also captured later he was an able and experienced businessman who had been given an emergency commission as a brigadier in order to liaise with the Chinese. Sadly Hobson, who had conducted himself admirably in prison, was killed on the day of his release in 1945 in a 'friendly fire' air attack.

5. Account of Mr Yoshizo Abe.

6. He led his company with much determination and won an immediate MC.

7. It is confusing that two brigadiers had rather similar names. Brigadier Hugh-Jones commanded 48 Brigade and Brigadier Jones commanded 16 Brigade. Where confusion is likely Brigadier Jones' name is prefixed with his nickname 'Jonah'.

The east end of the Sittang Bridge. A Japanese warrant officer reached close to this point in the first attack.

from the west bank. Major Orgill was told to stand by for a hasty demolition of the bridge should it prove necessary.

The Japanese now made a second attempt to reach the bridge. A platoon of *3 Company*, accompanied by a platoon of engineers, advanced towards the bridge with the same aim as before, but were held up by the heavy shelling. Mr Tsuyoshi Endo, who was in *3 Company*, said that the shells exploded in the trees, it was impossible to move and their casualties mounted. When the shelling stopped, they started to move towards the bridge but encountered two platoons of the 1st/3rd Gurkhas attacking from the south, and could make no progress. At about 1530 General Smyth ordered the bridgehead to be re-established. Accordingly, two companies of the 1st/4th Gurkhas,[8] supported by ''D' Company of the 2nd Duke's, crossed the bridge and, against light opposition, re-occupied 'Pagoda Hill'. The 2nd Duke's then moved to their old position on 'Bungalow Hill', 3 Burif and 'B' Company (less a platoon) of the 1st/3rd Gurkhas held the centre, and the 4th/12th FFR set up an inner perimeter.

The Japanese account of this fighting sums up by saying that it was very lucky for the Japanese that Hill 135 (Buddha Hill), "which is an essential guard for the bridge", was not properly defended.[9] Unquestionably, the British failure to establish an effective bridgehead before the arrival of the Japanese, and the consequent inability to use the road, was a disastrous handicap and led to a very confused situation. This was aggravated throughout the 22nd by the complete lack of communication between the British forces at the bridge and those at Mokpalin. The air attacks on the 21st had destroyed many of the wireless sets and no radio communication was established. The telegraph line along the railway and over the bridge was unusable, probably because it had been cut by shell-fire. As a result there was no co-ordination of the fighting.

That afternoon, General Smyth received a telephone call from General Hutton calling him to a meeting at 1100 hours the next morning at milestone 53, between Waw and Pegu on the Pegu road, about 25 miles from the bridge. So in the

Colonel Haranda studying the west bank through binoculars. The lack of concealment suggests that this is a posed photograph after the battle.

evening he returned to his Main HQ which was at Laya, about five miles from the river, leaving Brigadier 'Punch' Cowan at the bridge. Later that evening he relieved Cowan with Lieut-Colonel Simpson, the GSO1 of the Division. Brigadier Hugh-Jones was now fully responsible for the defence of the bridge and his orders were clear. It was vital that the bridge did not fall intact into Japanese hands.

While all this action was going on, the Malerkotla Sappers were desperately trying to get the bridge ready for demolition. It had been thought that all the preliminary work had been done. In fact wooden boxes to hold the explosive had been fitted on three spans but the explosive had been removed a few days previously[10] and placed in a cache at the end of the bridge, together with the detonators and detonating fuse. The latter was of an antiquated and unreliable pattern.[11] Orgill and his Sappers had to work non-stop through the night and the next day to ensure an effective demolition. But by 6pm on the 22nd he was able to report that two spans of the 11-span bridge were ready for demolition and a third was as ready as the lack of suitable material allowed. Although the bridge had been under sporadic fire, the Malerkotlas had had scarcely any casualties.

Another Sapper activity was to have a profound effect on the battle. 24 Field Company had spent the 21st collecting all the boats and sampans they could find from villages up and down the river and had taken them to the west bank, south

---

8. 'C' Company of the 1st/4th Gurkhas had come up the river bank during the morning, entered the bridgehead and rejoined its battalion.

9. This account, and the comment at the end of it, comes from *Memoir of 215 Regiment*. There is a slight input from *Memoir of 33 Division Engineers*.

10. Presumably to prevent sabotage or premature demolition of the bridge by air attack. Commercial gelignite, which was virtually the only explosive available in Burma at that time, would explode if hit by a rifle bullet or shell splinter.

11. Fuse, Instantaneous, Detonating (FID). 'Cordtex', a much more efficient commercial product, was used in the second half of the campaign.

of the bridge. The company had then been sent back to assist 60 Field Company in strengthening for the Stuart tanks the bridges on the track between Waw and the Sittang. On the morning of the 22nd, after the Japanese attack had started, General Smyth ordered his CRE[12] to destroy the three hundred boats that had been collected to prevent them falling into enemy hands. Accordingly, 18 Artisan Works Company were duly ordered to destroy all the boats that morning with pickaxes and they did so. Unfortunately, the three motor ferries, which had been on the east bank when the attack started, had been captured by the Japanese. General Smyth's decision (for it must have been his) to destroy the boats was to turn out to be a most unfortunate one.

The Fighting on the Kyaikto Road on 22 February

The Japanese were well aware that troops marching along a road, particularly if accompanied by trucks, were very vulnerable to an attack from the surrounding forest. *3/214 Battalion*, using village paths, had marched westward through the forest, and planned to intercept the retreating British forces south-west of Meyongale. When they struck the road, they encountered a "British column with armoured cars and light tanks" (*sic*, presumably carriers). *214/12 Company*, who were in the lead, established a road-block with an infantry section and two MMGs but were attacked almost at once and could not set up any barricades. The other three companies soon joined in and attacked the British column from the flank, causing much confusion. *12 Company* had the hardest time and they suffered many casualties. After some fierce close-quarter fighting the British "retreated" (*sic*) towards the Sittang, leaving behind many vehicles and weapons. *214 Regiment* withdrew and rendezvoused at Mokpalin quarries, about three miles to the west.[13] *2/214 Battalion*, following up along the 'road', came up with the British rearguard, suffered a few casualties in a skirmish and sheered off to march through the forest parallel to the trace.

On the British side, directly after the transport of the two brigades had cleared the Boyagyi rubber estate at 0500 hours, 16 Brigade marched off followed by 46 Brigade. Both the brigadiers had decided to keep their brigades closed up without gaps between units or brigades so that in the event of trouble units could help each other. However, things were not to work out so tidily. The Duke of Wellington's Regiment had only arrived in Burma from India on the 14th and had been sent by AHQ up to Kyaikto, where they arrived on the 20th, leaving one company, which had been sent ahead, at the Sittang. At Kyaikto they had come under command of 46 Brigade and deployed one company, with 4 Burif guarding the railway to the south of the town. This company had been ordered to leave 4 Burif, who were to withdraw along the railway, and to return to its own battalion as they marched off from Boyagyi. Unfortunately they got lost and missed the rendezvous. Returning to the railway they found a large body of Japanese marching along the line ahead of them. They therefore took to the forest, eventually crossed the Sittang by ferry six miles north of the bridge, and joined up with their battalion at Pegu on the 26th. This company took no part in the action at the Sittang.

Brigadier 'Jonah' Jones and 16 Brigade made steady progress, setting fire to many of the damaged vehicles abandoned after the previous day's air attack. When they reached the Mokpalin quarries, however, the sound of LMG and mortar fire could be heard from the rear and they realised that 46 Brigade was in action. Brigadier Jones therefore decided to picquet the road forward. This technique, well understood in the Indian Army as a similar method was commonly used on the North-West Frontier, involved one battalion putting out small groups of soldiers in the forest on either side of the road. These groups acted as flank guards while the column passed through and they then joined the tail of the column while another battalion repeated the performance at the front. It was a slow process but it prevented surprise and the Brigade reached Mokpalin unscathed in the afternoon. Here 'Jonah' Jones assumed command of all the troops assembled there.

It was ironic that Ekin, who had pressed hard for a more speedy withdrawal, should be the one whose brigade would suffer most from Smyth's leisurely plan. For 46 Brigade was to run into severe trouble. About two hours after leaving the Boyagyi rubber estate, he was obliged to halt his column to wait for the third company of the 2nd Duke's who had missed the rendezvous. It did not appear, however, and the march was resumed. A gap of about a mile had now opened up between the two brigades. About 0930 hours the head of the column was stopped by fire from both sides of the road.

This was *3/214 Battalion's* ambush. The whole column now came under fire from the forest. Colonel Stevenson of the 3rd/7tth Gurkhas ordered two companies to move round the south side of the block. The first, 'D' Company under Captain Harris, was to hold a position on the far side while the second was to put in an immediate attack on the block from the south.[14] The attack failed and Stevenson was wounded. A confused fight followed for an hour or so. The

12. There is no record of General Smyth giving this order but it is inconceivable that the CRE, who was part of Divisional HQ, would take such action without a direct order. Smyth's Tactical HQ was at this time close to the bridge. It is significant that neither Smyth nor Cowan subsequently mentioned this incident as they surely would have done if the CRE had acted on his own.
13. From *Memoir of 214 Regiment*.
14. After some time, when it appeared that the block would not be broken, 'D' Company of the 3rd/7th Gurkhas resumed its march, skirted Mokpalin to the south and reached the river bank. It then made its way to the bridge and crossed it. *WO 172/966*.

Japanese mortared and fired at the column from the forest and the troops fired back, but the Japanese were very good at concealment and fieldcraft, and targets were hard to pick out. The column became dispersed and there were many casualties.

Ekin now decided that drastic measures were required. Summoning the three COs, he gathered a mixed force of some five hundred men who, led by Brigade HQ, advanced through the forest to the west of the road with the aim of clearing the road-block and enabling the rest of the column to advance along the road. To an extent this succeeded, for *3/214 Battalion* had also suffered substantial casualties[15] and withdrew to their rendezvous. Hence, at least some of the remaining parts of the three battalions were able to continue their march along the road and reached Mokpalin safely. But Ekin's column found the going very difficult in the thick forest and the column split up into small parties. His party spent the night in the forest between the road and the railway with Japanese on all sides and finally reached the Mokpalin railway station on the 23rd. His brigade major, Major Guy Burton, "who had shown outstanding qualities of courage and energy throughout the day",[16] took his party north and crossed the Sittang several miles north of the bridge. Colonel Owen of the 2nd Duke's took his small group to the river south of the bridge. They swam the river successfully but Owen was treacherously murdered by a Burmese in a village on the west bank, where the unarmed party were resting after their crossing. Most of Colonel Stevenson's party reached Mokpalin, but Stevenson and a few others went further north and, many days later and much weakened, joined 2 Bur Brigade at Toungoo.

No official record of 46 Brigade's casualties in this ambush exist but the war diary of the 1st/9th R Jats (written after the campaign and by no means always accurate) states that 46 Brigade had "close on 1000 casualties". Certainly on 24 February, only 798 men of this brigade would muster on the west bank of the Sittang although some small parties managed to rejoin their units later.

The Fighting at Mokpalin on 22 February

The Japanese recount that, in the morning of the 22nd, *215 Regiment's* second battalion, *2/215*, reached Pyinkadogon and, leaving *8 Company* in reserve, were ordered to attack the British in the area of Mokpalin railway station. They moved off through the forest in single file but the soldiers were very tired and advanced slowly. The leading unit reached a white road with many vehicles and British soldiers resting around them. Before they could choose a suitable position they were detected and firing started. As they slowly arrived they came under severe fire. Co-ordination between their units was impossible while the heavy fighting continued. A few soldiers actually reached the road and fired from beneath British vehicles. In the afternoon, the reserve *8 Company*, which had initially been ordered to advance on the left flank of the battalion, was switched to the right flank (*i.e.* north) of the other companies and reached the railway line, repulsing a British attack. Its aim was to relieve the pressure on *1/215 Battalion* holding 'Buddha Hill', and it was to cause a lot of trouble.

At about sunset a Regimental gun came up and fired several shells into the Mokpalin station area. After dark all quietened down in the *5* and *6 Company* sectors but the British continued to shell the hill occupied by *7 Company* throughout the night. At 0200 hours on the 23rd, Colonel Harada ordered *2/215 Battalion* (less *6* and *8 Companies*) to withdraw to Pyinkadogon and they reached there at dawn carrying 20 stretchers. At the same time he ordered *1/215 Battalion* to continue to hold Hill 135 ('Buddha Hill') so they sent back their wounded and dug-in as deeply as they could.[17]

The British side of the story is that, early on the 22nd, the 2nd/5th R Gurkhas were approaching the river from the east. Just as they reached the village of Mokpalin, they suddenly came under fire from Japanese in the forest north of the track. Colonel Cameron at once organised an attack and, using 'blitz'[18] tactics for the first time, cleared and picqueted the road through the village. From a small hill opposite the railway station, he saw that another small hill overlooked the road further north so he continued the advance and captured it. From this hill, which became known as 'OP Hill', he perceived that 'Buddha Hill' dominated the road and bridge and appeared to be held by the Japanese. Although he had only one mortar, the others having been destroyed by the air attack the day before, and no guns having yet arrived, he decided on an immediate two company attack on 'Buddha Hill' before the Japanese had become established. The Japanese, however, were now holding this hill in strength with *1/215 Battalion*. Resistance, supported by MMGs, was fierce, the attack failed and there were many casualties.

The 1st/3rd Gurkhas and two mountain batteries had now arrived and the two colonels conferred on 'OP Hill'. They agreed that the 2nd/5th R Gurkhas would hold a firm base in Mokpalin while the 1st/3rd Gurkhas would attack both 'Pagoda' and 'Buddha' hills supported by a preliminary bombardment by 28 Mountain Artillery Regiment. Unfortunately, being completely out of touch with the troops on the west bank, they did not know that 'Pagoda Hill' was held by

---

15. *214 Regiment* recorded 41 men killed and about a hundred wounded in this action. *Memoir of 214 Regiment*.

16. Brigadier Ekin's 3rd Report, written about a year later. *Hutton Papers*.

17. This account is from *Memoir of 215 Regiment*.

18. A technique of advancing with automatic weapons and firing from the hip at anything that can be seen, or any possible place for concealment.

the 4th/12th FFR. After 25 minutes' preliminary bombardment by the ten mountain guns, part of which fell on HQ 48 Brigade and the unfortunate 4th/12th FFR,
who were all consequently withdrawn across the river by Brigadier Hugh-Jones,
a company attack went in on each feature.

These attacks were pressed home with determination. The two leading platoons of 'B' Company of the 1st/3rd Gurkhas, aiming at 'Pagoda Hill', veered too
far to the left but succeeded in reaching the top of 'Pagoda Hill' in time to block
the second Japanese advance towards the bridge. 'C' Company, under Lieutenant
Fay, fought their way to the top of the ridge on the south-east corner of 'Buddha
Hill' close to the large stone statue of Buddha but were held up by Japanese dug
in on the reverse slope and supported by MMGs. The Japanese resisted stubbornly and Fay was wounded.

Colonel Ballinger now committed his reserve, 'D' Company, under Captain
Peter Stephens. They attacked 'Buddha Hill' on the left of 'C' Company and also
fought their way up to the crest. Stephens had been wounded in this attack but he
took command of both companies and organised a second attack to push the
Japanese off the feature. He gallantly led this attack himself, firing an LMG from
the hip, but was met with a hail of fire. Stephens was killed outright and the attack
stalled.

Unable to make out from his HQ on 'OP Hill' how things were going, the CO,
Colonel Ballinger, went forward with a reconnaissance party, picking up on the
way the reserve platoon of 'B' Company as an escort. They suddenly came upon
the leading element of *215/8 Company* who held up their hands in surrender. It
was a ruse. As the British came closer, the Japanese threw themselves on the
ground and concealed LMGs opened fire. Colonel Ballinger and most of his
escort were killed.

When this news came in, Major Bradford, the second-in-command of the battalion, took a carrier to Mokpalin railway station to see if Colonel Cameron and
the 2nd/5th could give any help. However, Brigadier 'Jonah' Jones and his 16
Brigade had arrived during the afternoon and taken up positions between
Mokpalin and the river. 'Jonah' Jones had now assumed command of all the
troops in the area and, telling Bradford that no troops could be spared to renew
the attack, ordered the 1st/3rd to pull back and hold 'OP Hill' at all costs.

215/8 Company was now active in the forest and scrub north of 'OP' Hill and
it was difficult to execute these moves. The two companies of the 1st/3rd Gurkhas
which had attacked 'Buddha Hill' were now isolated. They were running out of
ammunition, food and water. Although they had managed to get most of their
wounded back, efforts to resupply them failed, as did subsequent attempts to get
an order through to them to withdraw. Nevertheless, under their Gurkha subedars,

they decided to hold on for the night. Unknown to Brigadier 'Jonah' Jones in Mokpalin the bridgehead had now been re-established. At this stage it would have been possible, if they had abandoned their vehicles, for most of the troops on the east bank to have reached the bridge on foot along the edge of the river west of the railway line, although they were, of course, unaware of this. (See Note 14.)

Darkness was now approaching and only remnants of 46 Brigade had so far come in and it was known that they had been ambushed and dispersed. Brigadier 'Jonah' Jones, therefore, arranged a perimeter camp (or 'box" as it would later be called) for the night. It was not easy. On the road from Mokpalin to the bridge was a solid line of vehicles parked nose-to-tail and often double-banked. Only those in the Mokpalin area could be protected. The 2nd/5th R Gurkhas held the east side of the road, across the road and railway to the south were the 8th Burif, on their right along a flood protection bank were the 2nd KOYLI, on some high ground to their right the 1st/9th R Jats, and holding 'OP Hill' were the 1st/3rd Gurkhas (less three companies) reinforced by two platoons of the 2nd/5th R Gurkhas. The 1st/7th Gurkhas and two companies of the Duke of Wellington's Regiment were in reserve near the railway station. Some other parties from 46 Brigade were also in the perimeter stiffening up the block across the road to the south. During the night, 'Jonah' Jones planned another attack to be made on 'Buddha' and 'Pagoda' hills, this time by the 1st/7th Gurkhas, soon after first light on the 23rd. It would be supported by virtually the whole of the divisional artillery, all still on the east bank. This comprised 5 Field Battery, BAF (4 x 18-pdrs) and 15 and 28 Mountain Batteries plus one section of 12 Mountain Battery. It was to be a noisy night.

The British Action on the West Bank of the Sittang on 23 November.

The night of 22/23 February was a very tense one. The British forces were now split into two, rather than three, separate groups. Brigadier Hugh-Jones was out of touch with those at Mokpalin and had no reliable news about the position there. He was very conscious of his responsibility for preventing this vital bridge from falling into Japanese hands. He believed that if the enemy captured the bridge intact they might reach Rangoon before it could be defended. He had learned from Lieutenant Macrae commanding 'B' Company of the 1st/3rd Gurkhas, who had now joined the bridge garrison, that the rest of 48 Brigade was under attack near Mokpalin railway station, but the only news of the other two brigades was from Captain Harris (see note 14), who believed that 46 Brigade had been lost, and from stragglers who said, as stragglers often do, that both brigades had been overrun. The position being held in the bridgehead was by no means a strong one. Above all, all the commanders of the bridgehead troops, British and Indian, had expressed doubts about whether they could hold their positions against a serious enemy attack as their troops were becoming desperately tired. His orders were that the two companies of the 1st/4th Gurkhas were to return to the west bank for their anti-parachutist role at first light so a dawn attack, which was probable, might be disastrous.[19]

In fact there were the best part of two companies of the 1st/3rd Gurkhas only about 600 yards away, but Hugh-Jones refused a request from Captain Bishop[20] of the 1st/3rd to take out a patrol from 'B' Company to try and contact them. He felt that Bishop, who was still lame after an accident in Rangoon, was not fit enough to undertake such a dangerous task. Nor did he feel that it was wise in the very confused situation to send out any other patrols to contact in the dark the troops on the east bank. At 0200 hours he summoned Major Richard Orgill and asked him if he could guarantee to demolish the bridge if the Japanese held the east bank and could fire directly on the bridge. Orgill said he could not guarantee it, as he could not be certain that the fire would not disrupt the firing circuits, but he would do his best.[21] The Malerkotla Sappers had prepared three of the big spans for demolition, numbers 4, 5 and 6 from the east bank, but there had not been enough material to make a complete cut of number 4. All three spans were within 300 yards of the enemy side of the river.

Brigadier Hugh-Jones was now getting very tired and worried. At about 0330 the Japanese manged to get an MMG into a position so that it could fire bursts directly down the bridge, and all efforts to dislodge it failed. Half-an-hour later there was a great deal of small arms fire and shelling from the south. Most of this fire was British but the Japanese had now switched their mountain guns onto targets around Mokpalin station and *215/8 Company* was probing the south-east face of the bridgehead.

By the early morning, the bridgehead garrison were short of ammunition and exhausted by lack of sleep and lack of food. At about 0415 hours on the 23rd, Hugh-Jones held a conference on the west bank. At this conference Hugh-Jones decided that he could no longer be certain of holding the bridge throughout the next day. The bridge could not *for certain* be blown in daylight and therefore it must be blown before dawn. He told a staff officer to ring up Divisional HQ and ask for General Smyth's formal approval. This officer got through to Brigadier Cowan and explained the position.[22] In 1955, General Cowan described the occasion as he then remembered it in a letter to General Smyth:[23]

"Hugh-Jones had a conference with Lentaigne and Edwardes (*sic*), and it was their considered opinion that the bridge should be blown because they did not consider the troops would 'stand up' to a Jap attack of any intensity. Furthermore they considered that all officers and other ranks who could get over the bridge had already done so. All this information was given to me over the telephone by an officer deputed by Hugh-Jones, as the latter had gone forward to arrange for evacuation of the bridgehead troops."

Smyth, woken up by Cowan, thought about the problem for five minutes and then spoke to Hugh-Jones and authorised the demolition. Accordingly, at 0500, Hugh-Jones ordered the bridgehead troops to withdraw across the bridge and told Major Richard Orgill to demolish it when the last troops were over. Colonel W.D. 'Donnie' Edward of the 4th/12th FFR was in charge of the withdrawal and at 0520 he gave the order to fire.

The charges on all three spans were connected with detonating cord so that they would explode simultaneously. Orgill passed on the order to Lieutenant Bashir Ahmad Khan of the Malerkotla Sappers who lit the reserve safety fuse, returned to his foxhole on the west bank and pressed the exploder for the electrical circuit. There was a huge explosion and an immediate hush fell on the battlefield. Two spans fell into the river but the third, for which there had not been enough explosive, was damaged but did not fall. Under the circumstances it was a very successful demolition.[24]

At some time during the night a radio message from Brigadier 'Punch' Cowan had got through to Brigadier 'Jonah' Jones on the east bank. Fearing all codes had been destroyed, it was sent uncoded in morse and said rather enigmatically "Friends waiting to welcome you at the east gate".[25] There was no answer. Shortly after the demolition, Cowan arrived at the bridge. As he was talking to Hugh-Jones, Subedar Maya Singh of the 1 R Jats appeared from across the river[26] with a message from Brigadier 'Jonah' Jones. The message, which was apparently an

19. These where the reasons for his decision which Hugh-Jones gave in a private letter to General Smyth while recuperating from dysentery in Simla on 15 May 1942. IWM, Smyth Papers.

20. Bishop had been adjutant of the 1st/3rd Gurkhas and was on his way from hospital in Rangoon, after an accident, to rejoin his battalion.

21. Orgill to Kirby, 1 December 1955. *Hutton Papers*, 3/1-6.

22. The identity of the staff officer is unknown and there is no record of this conversation.

23. Letter dated 8 October 1955. *Hutton Papers*.

24. Both. Lieutenant Bashir Ahmad Khan and Lieutenant Roy Hudson wrote detailed accounts of this demolition.

25. Colonel Foucar's account of the 1942 operations, p.90.

26. Subedar Maya Singh had volunteered to swim the river but by chance had found a boat in a riverside house.

The demolished Sittang Bridg, looking south-west. Two spans are down and one is damaged. Note the open country on the west bank.

answer to Cowan's signal, said that he was going to withdraw to the river and fight his way north between the railway and the river bank, planning to reach the bridge about 4pm. On seeing this message, which clearly indicated that the bridge had been blown prematurely, Hugh-Jones collapsed and fell down the embankment on which they were standing. Cowan now put Colonel Lentaigne temporarily in command of all troops on the west bank until Hugh-Jones recovered.

British Action on the East Bank on 23 February

The British forces on the east bank had had a noisy and confused night. 28 Mountain Regiment kept up harassing fire on the hill occupied by *215/7 Company*, while the Japanese mountain guns retaliated by firing on Mokpalin from both the north and south. A number of vehicles were set on fire and exploding ammunition added to the hubbub. Brigadier 'Jonah' Jones's HQ had come in for some accurate shelling and mortaring and he was obliged to move it. After dark on the 22nd, a group of cyclists came along the railway and dismounted just short of the 2nd KOYLI position. Identified as Japanese, they were shot up and 20 bicycles were recovered in the morning. This was a reconnaissance unit of *55 Division*. Japanese patrols from *3/214 Battalion* and *143 Regiment* were active during the night from the south-east to the south-west of the perimeter but were successfully rebuffed. Suddenly, as it was getting light, came the sound of a gigantic explosion, and all firing ceased.

Sadly, the Japanese were as surprised as everyone else, as up to that time they had thought that they were getting the worst of the fighting. Now they knew that, although they had failed to capture the bridge, they had won the battle. They were dead tired and getting very short of ammunition, so they decided to rest and put in an attack by *2/215 Battalion* (less two companies) down the road on Mokpalin after dark. There had been no plan to attack the bridge that morning.

For the British, the demolition was a fearful blow. The force on the east bank included nearly all the fighting troops in 17 Division. There were two British battalions, two Indian battalions and four Gurkha battalions, together with more than half of the divisional Gunners then in Burma. Unfortunately there were no Sappers, who could have been helpful in this situation. Everyone realised that they were cut off and some felt that they had been abandoned.[27] The two companies of the 1st/3rd Gurkhas who had attacked 'Buddha Hill' the day before were out of ammunition, food and water and out of touch with their battalion. Under their Gurkha Subedars they had gallantly clung to their position on the hill throughout the night. They decided now to withdraw and rejoin their battalion. Unfortunately they encountered *214/8 Company* which had penetrated into the forest behind them. In the confused fighting which followed they were forced to disperse in small parties. Some managed to rejoin their unit, some reached the river bank and succeeded later in crossing the river and some did the same north of Sittang village, but many went north-east and were captured by the Japanese.

Brigadier 'Jonah' Jones, who had been planning an attack up the river bank to the bridge, now decided that the best course would be for all units to hold their present positions during the day and to cross the river that night. This would give time for arrangements to be made to get the wounded across. He therefore ordered units to collect what flotation material they could find from the vehicles, local houses and bamboo clumps in the forest, and prepare for an improvised crossing of the river, here about 1100 yards wide. These orders were given out about 0930 hours. When the withdrawal started, the 1st/3rd Gurkhas and the 2nd Duke's were to cover the northern sector, the 2nd/5th R Gurkhas and the 1st/7th Gurkhas were to cover the east and the 2nd KOYLI and 8 Burif were to cover the south. Building of rafts, and such evacuation of the wounded as was possible, was to start at once.

During the morning, more individuals and scattered parties from 46 Brigade turned up to join those who had come in the evening before. One of these parties was Brigadier Ekin's. He joined 'Jonah' Jones but, having no staff, although senior, he wisely did not interfere with Jones's command. He had, though, had several encounters with the enemy during the night and was aware that there

---

27. One war diary says bitterly (and inaccurately): "HQ 17 Div had withdrawn 15 miles to Waw, having resigned itself to the loss of the whole of 17 Div (less Div HQ)."

were strong Japanese forces approaching from the south-east and therefore time was short. On visiting his units he observed that there was much confusion. Many men, not being able to find their units, had already begun to move towards the river. He discussed this with Jones and both agreed that an earlier withdrawal was advisable. It was a wise decision. 'Jonah' Jones then called an 'O' Group from available units and set 1400 hours as the time of withdrawal. The scrub jungle gave some concealment to a move to the north-west and west, while an anti-flooding embankment gave some protection to those going west across the paddy fields to the south.

Around mid-day, morale was not increased when some RAF Blenheims bombed the British position round Mokpalin. The raid straddled the position, not killing many people but destroying and setting fire to many vehicles and increasing the number of wounded who were already a serious problem. A Japanese reconnaissance plane flew over unscathed at low level but was unwise enough to make a second run. It was duly shot down, which cheered everyone up, and the pilot was killed.[28] The Mokpalin area was also bombed by the Japanese during the morning but accounts differ on the extent of the attack.

During the afternoon large numbers of men from the Mokpalin area reached the river over a wide front. Orders had been given to carry as many things that would float as possible. These included petrol cans, seat cushions, water containers (pakhals) and wooden poles. Sporadic Japanese shelling had set fire to some vehicles on the road and, seeing that this gave some cover to the withdrawal, the 2nd/5th Gurkhas set fire to the remainder. There was a narrow beach along the edge of the river and activity on it was mostly concealed from the enemy by scrub, or the cliff on the bank of the river. In the afternoon the tide was going out and the river becoming shallower but there was quite a strong current, particularly in the deepest part near the west bank. For strong swimmers the crossing was slow but not too difficult, in spite of occasional mortar and MMG fire. For less good swimmers it was a desperate gamble. Unfortunately there were many non-swimmers, notably among the Gurkhas from the mountains of Nepal, where opportunities for swimming are rare. Not all of these could be persuaded to take the risk of making a first attempt aided by dubious flotation material, and too many of those who did try were drowned.

It was not long before the surface of the river was dotted with hundreds of swimmers and makeshift rafts. Of course, nearly everyone trying to cross had to abandon their weapons and these were thrown into the river. There were some houses along the river bank and these were ransacked for material. The wounded had first priority and they filled the few substantial rafts. Officers, among whom Lieutenant-Colonel Cameron of the 2nd/5th and Major Faithfull of the 2nd

Duke's were prominent, did their best to encourage everyone else to make an effort to get across. There were countless acts of heroism by those who could swim and did their utmost to help the non-swimmers but, in spite of all these efforts, many drowned and many could not face the crossing.

In these desperate circumstances, officers in particular, most of whom could swim, were faced with a severe moral problem. None wished to abandon their men, but the order, correctly, was for all to cross the river who could. Lieutenant-Colonel Henry Power of the Dogras, few of whom could swim being hillmen like the Gurkhas, solved the problem by detailing certain key officers and men to cross first and organising the other officers to help as many of the remainder as possible to follow them. He, himself, took charge of a rear party who would be the last to leave. In the end not everyone got away. Power was captured and spent the next three and a half years in Rangoon Jail.

Some of the troops on the southern perimeter had not received news of the earlier time for the withdrawal. The 2nd KOYLI and the 8th Burif came under some pressure from *143 Regiment*. However, they held their covering positions successfully, in spite of mounting casualties, until it was obvious that orders had gone astray, whereupon they withdrew to the river bank. The wounded were carried or dragged in blankets. The tubby figure of Lieutenant-Colonel Keagan of the 2nd KOYLI was prominent walking calmly about and encouraging his soldiers in their preparations for the crossing. Many men could swim with some form of assistance. Doors, wooden cupboards, thatch and anything that would float were put to good use. Sadly while supervising this, Keagan was mortally wounded by a mortar bomb. He was carried on to a raft but did not survive.[29]

To the north, the 1st/3rd Gurkhas on 'OP Hill' had also not heard of the revised time of withdrawal, the officer sent to tell them having been wounded en route. A visit to Mokpalin about 5pm disclosing that everyone had left, Major Bradford led the garrison of 'OP Hill' west through the forest and reached the river without incident, about six hundred yards south of the bridge. The possibility of crossing the bridge by the fallen girders looking attractive, Captain Bruce Kinloch of the 1st/3rd Gurkhas made a solo reconnaissance of the end of the bridge, which was unguarded, and proceeded up Pagoda Hill. Here, to mutual surprise, he met, face-to-face round a large tree, a Japanese officer whose men were holding a covering position. Quickly throwing a grenade, Kinloch dodged back down the hill, fortunately untouched by a fusillade of enemy bullets. It still looked, however, as though it might be possible to establish a small bridgehead at the end of the hill

28. Unfortunately that morning, too, in a separate incident, a Hurricane was shot down by British ground fire somewhere in the bridge area.

29. Officially six officers and 200 other ranks of 2 KOYLI got across the river, but when the number of wounded and sick had been deducted the battalion strength was only about 80 all ranks.

to cover the use of the bridge, so Kinloch, his Gurkhas being completely exhausted, led two platoons of the 2nd Duke's up the river bank in an attempt to achieve this. Unfortunately the Japanese had anticipated him. Kinloch's men reached the end of the bridge satisfactorily but when they tried to move up the hill, they received a hot reception and were driven back with some casualties.

Some of the British soldiers in this party now swam the river, as did Kinloch and two other officers. Kinloch's party succeeded in finding a large and only slightly damaged sampan which would take about 15 men. They paddled this back across the river and loaded it with their battalion doctor and as many wounded as it would take. Kinloch then took it over to the west bank and, helped by Captain John Hedley of 4 Burif, who had crossed the river further south with the help of a wooden cupboard, brought it over again for a second load, this time staying on the east bank himself while Hedley took the boat back. Major Bradford then decided to lead the remainder of the 1st/3rd Gurkhas south down the beach to a place where more boats could be seen on the other side, the bootless Kinloch being left to dispatch the last of the wounded on the third trip. After an agonising wait, Hedley and the boat duly re-appeared through the early morning mist of the 24th and Kinloch was able to dispatch the last group of wounded men and accompany them himself. They were the last to cross.

Another fine effort was by Major Robinson of the 2nd Duke's. He had stayed with those of his men who couldn't swim and his party was increased by many unattached Indian and Gurkha soldiers. Robinson felt that it was still best to make use of the bridge if possible, so together with Corporal Fox and Lance-Corporal Roebuck he swam the river and by great good luck found some rope on the far bank. With this they rigged up a life-line between the western fallen girder and the east bank. It was a brilliant move. With this aid some 300 British, Indian and Gurkha non-swimmers were, that night, helped across the river.

As the sun came up on the 24th the mist began to clear and Kinloch, back on the west bank, witnessed a tragic scene on the eastern side. Large numbers of Japanese emerged from the forest and surrounded the remnants of his battalion. There was a brief fight before they surrendered. Major Bradford handed over his pistol to a Japanese officer, but Subedar Major Gagan Sing Thapa refused to do so and, having fired at the Japanese officer, shot himself through the heart. The Japanese officer then shot and mortally wounded Bradford before himself being shot through the head by a Gurkha corporal.

There seemed to be no British troops on the west bank near the bridge so those who had crossed made their way north-west to the road, the seriously wounded in bullock-carts commandeered from a nearby village. For the remainder, marching across the paddy fields (for the west bank, unlike the east, was open country) mostly naked under a burning sun was no joke and the sharp rice stubble was very painful to bare feet.[30] The 1st/4th Gurkhas were covering the withdrawal with a company at Nyaungkashe railway station, about two miles from the bridge, and their main body at Laya railway station, about three miles further back. Here they gave every-one hot tea and blankets and moved them on to Waw as trains became available. At Waw, hot meals were available as well as some clothing. As soon as possible they were moved on to Pegu to be re-equipped and re-organised. Half the Division had been lost and it was no longer possible to hold the line of the Sittang. Unless pow-erful reinforcements arrived, Rangoon, and therefore Burma, was doomed.

Losses

The Japanese were thoroughly exhausted by their rapid march and the fight-ing and were obliged to pause while stragglers caught up and supplies and ammunition were replenished. Their infantry regimental histories record that *215 Regiment* at the bridge lost 29 men killed and about 60 wounded. *214 Regiment* on the Kyaikto road lost 41 killed and about 100 wounded. *143 Regiment* who were only lightly engaged lost four killed and eight wounded. These figures do not include gunners and engineers. They claim that the British left 1300 dead[31] and they took 1100 prisoners of whom 120 were from Britain.

No accurate figures exist of the British losses as the actual strengths of the units before the battle are not known. The best estimate is that slightly more than half the Infantry in 17 Division were lost. On 24 February the all ranks Infantry strength of 17 Division's three brigades was:

     16 Brigade 1170
     46 Brigade 798
     48 Brigade 1516

As most of the survivors had had to swim the river, there were heavy losses in rifles, in mortars and in the vital LMGs and Tommy guns.

The Japanese claim to have captured a lot of heavy equipment including 8 field guns, eight mountain guns,[32] seven Bofors, eighy carriers, 300 vehicles and 139 horses and mules. These figures seem to be exaggerated, but not by much. All the guns seem to have been successfully rendered unserviceable as there is no Japanese record of their being used later on. Many of the vehicles had been

---

30. Kinloch's party, fearing that the Japanese might have crossed to the west bank, marched in bare feet across the fields all the way to Waw, reaching it late at night on the 24th. The unlucky Kinloch, leading the party though half asleep, trod on a poisonous snake and was bitten. Fortunately first aid by another officer was effective and he managed to keep going.
31. Claims of dead bodies counted were seldom accurate. These presumably included many who drowned as well as those who were killed in the RAF and AVG air attack on the 21st.
32. British official figures are four 18-pdr field guns and ten mountain guns.

The Sittang Bridge in 1944, still unrepaired. North is to the right in the picture. IWM

burnt and were beyond repair. The animals, however, were particularly useful to the enemy as their losses of horses had been high.

Retrospect

The controversy about this bridge demolition has never died. We know now that *1/215 Battalion* had no plan to attack the bridge on the morning of the 23rd and *2/215 Battalion*, most of which had been withdrawn to Pyinkadogon, did not intend to attack Mokpalin until the evening. It was therefore not necessary to demolish the bridge on the morning of the 23rd. However, Hugh-Jones had no idea what the Japanese were planning. He had been given the simple aim of ensuring at all costs that the bridge did not fall into Japanese hands intact and he had been ordered to guard against a parachute attack. From what he knew it looked probable that the bridge might be captured if it were not blown before dawn. So he decided it must be done and, on the limited information that he had, it was the right decision. But it was one that he should never have had to make. Tragically, he could never forget the terrible results of his decision for several thousand men and, after the war, he took his own life.[33]

With hindsight it was unfortunate that General Smyth, with his whole division in a most critical position, chose to remove himself and his chief-of-staff to Laya railway station five miles from the battle[34] and hand over full responsibility to a subordinate not fully in the picture. If he had been at the bridge, or gone there when the crisis arose, he might well have accepted the risk to the demolition circuits and the risk of a parachute attack. But this can only be conjecture.

Much later, the Commander-in-Chief of the Pakistani Army, Lieutenant-General Attiqur Rahman, MC, who, as a young officer was one of the last to withdraw from the bridgehead with the 4th/12th FFR, was to write:[35]

"The confusion in the command level in this area was really very great. [*On the 22nd*] Hugh-Jones, our Brigade Commander… brought his tactical HQ to the east side of the Sittang bridge and soon realised that either we had to leave that end or we had to fight off even our own troops in that dense area. In fact he told the two battalions to go back to recce out some positions on the west bank and I remember going back with the Adjutant of the 1st/4th Gurkhas and we ran into Jacky Smythe (*sic*) who was waving a pistol at us as he thought we were running away from the other side of the bridge. It took us some time to convince him but he was in a roaring temper … it was quite wrong of Jacky Smythe to command when he was so ill. Everyone knows that he was a very brave soldier but unless a divisional commander, especially in the jungle, is 100 per cent fit, I think it is very unfair on his troops."

This eye-witness account hardly gives the impression of a divisional commander coolly appreciating the desperate situation and deciding the best method of saving his division.

What does seem clear is that the decision that was not made was far worse than the decision that was made. During the day of the 22nd it was becoming obvious that the Japanese were firmly entrenched on 'Buddha Hill' and were unlikely to be shifted. In addition to the attacks from the west, two unsuccessful attacks had been made on 'Buddha Hill' from the south. This must have been known on the west bank as a company of the 1st/3rd Gurkhas had joined the bridge garrison after the second attack. Since the road curled round 'Buddha Hill', there was, therefore, virtually no chance now of withdrawing any more of the vehicles or guns over the river. This being the case, it was vital to get as many men across the bridge as possible. Shortly before 5pm on the 22nd, Captain Harris and 'D' Company of the 3rd/7th Gurkhas came up the edge of the river and in over the bridge, using the same route as 'C' Company of the 1st/4th

33. As did Richard Orgill, but not as far as is known for the same reason.
34. Apparently against General Cowan's advice. Draper, Alfred, *Dawns Like Thunder*, p.108.
35. Letter to Ronald Lewin dated 20 July 1981. IWM, MISC 66, Item 1022.

Gurkhas in the morning. This showed how a withdrawal form the west bank could be effected. This was the plan for the 23rd which 'Jonah' Jones had made independently. It was the only possible one and should surely also have been made by Smyth on the 22nd. Wireless and telephone communication had failed, but in this desperate situation surely several small patrols, or a boat, or an air drop could have been organised to try and get a message through to Brigadier 'Jonah' Jones on the east bank? If this had been done, the bulk of the 17 Division might have crossed the bridge successfully on the night of the 22nd/23rd.

Smyth always maintained that the cardinal errors which led to the catastrophe were that General Hutton, following General Wavell's policy, obliged him, firstly, to try and hold impossibly isolated positions at Kawkareik, Moulmein, Martaban and Pa-an and, secondly, to stay too long in the Bilin position.[36] As a result the troops suffered unnecessary casualties and were thoroughly exhausted before they started their retreat to what should have been the main position behind the Sittang. In this line he was loyally supported by Brigadier Cowan and his staff. However, in 1955 General Cowan wrote in a private letter to Smyth:

"I think that it would have been wise to send Ekin's brigade back to the bridge the day before we commenced our withdrawal. You will remember Ekin pressed for this. It meant taking a chance at Div HQ till the 16th and 48th Brigades joined us. However, that is being wise after the event."

Smyth commented that this would have been taking too big a risk as he did not know at the time whether the two brigades would be closely followed up by the enemy.

General Wavell had no doubts about what had gone wrong and later summed up the situation with his usual terse clarity:

"The battle of the Sittang bridgehead on February 22nd and 23rd really sealed the fate of Rangoon and lower Burma. From reports of this operation which I have studied I have no doubt that the withdrawal from the Bilin river to west of the Sittang was badly mismanaged by the headquarters of the 17th Indian Division, and that the disaster which resulted in the loss of almost two complete brigades ought never to have occurred."

---

36. There are several accounts that the decking of the Sittang bridge to take vehicles was not completed until the evening of the 21st. If this is so, an earlier retreat to the Sittang would have run into problems with the vehicles as the ferries had a low capacity.

CHAPTER TEN

Wavell Tries to Save Rangoon

Reorganisation after the Sittang Disaster

W hen General Hutton flew back on 22 February from his abortive attempt to meet the Generalissimo at Lashio, he found that the military situation had taken a serious turn for the worse. Rangoon was now threatened and some vital decisions had to be taken. Without perhaps realising quite how serious was the position of 17 Division, he called Smyth back twenty miles to a conference at milestone 53 at 1100 hours on the 23rd. Apart from his own staff this meeting was also attended by the commanders of 7th Armoured Brigade, who had just arrived, 2 Bur Brigade and an *ad hoc* 'Pegu Force'. Smyth, who received on the 22nd the message to attend the conference, would certainly have been justified on the 23rd in staying with the battle and sending Cowan back to deputise for him. What actually happened, however, was that Smyth himself attended the conference. An observer was even to note that he seemed to be the most cheerful person present.

No-one else was very cheerful. The whole strategy of holding off the Japanese long enough to send in reinforcements through Rangoon was now in tatters. The race had only just been lost. 7th Armoured Brigade had landed on the 21st and had unloaded their tanks with commendable speed. The bridges on the road to the Sittang were ready for tanks as far as Abya (see Map 13). Two fresh British battalions, the 1st Cameronians and the 1st West Yorkshire Regiment, had also arrived. If 17 Division had got across the Sittang virtually intact, even without its transport and heavy equipment, there would have been a chance of holding up the Japanese longer and disrupting their strategy. Now, however, there were not enough troops to attempt to hold the line of the Sittang, and Pegu was the next place at which it might be possible to make a stand.

However, the Japanese, too, were worried. They were getting very short of ammunition and were much concerned about the British tanks and the possible arrival of Chinese on their northern flank. In fact there was perhaps, even at this late stage, a chance of holding Rangoon. The Australian Government had asked for the recall of two of the three experienced Australian divisions which had been fighting in the Middle East. They were on their way back when Singapore fell and with it a fourth Australian division, sadly inexperienced, was lost. The importance of holding Burma and its vital supply line to China had now become clear to both the British and Americans. Wavell had asked that both experienced Australian divisions should be diverted to Burma. It seemed likely that only one could get there in time, so Churchill, supported by a personal message from President Roosevelt, asked Prime Minister Curtin if he would agree to the leading one, the 7th Australian Division, being diverted to Rangoon. When Curtin refused, Churchill diverted the convoy so that it could reach Rangoon by the 26 or 27 February and repeated his request, supported by powerful arguments. Curtin again refused and the convoy was ordered back on to its original course.[1]

This refusal caused some ill-feeling between the two leaders, especially as Curtin had already referred to the failure to provide adequate defences for Singapore as an "inexcusable betrayal". It is difficult, however, not to sympathise with Curtin. The defence of Australia had been based on British assurances that Singapore would be firmly held. On this basis, Australia (and New Zealand) had sent their main forces many thousands of miles away to fight under British direction. They had done well but suffered considerable losses in Greece, Crete and Malaya. In all these places it was apparent that very inadequate air support had been provided. Now it looked as though Australia itself might be threatened, even invaded. Curtin was doubtful whether Churchill regarded this eventuality quite as seriously as the Australians. Moreover, he felt (as Wavell probably did too) that from the Far East "we saw the trend of the Pacific situation more clearly" than people in London.

Certainly on paper it seems that if the experienced Australian 7th Division had landed while the Japanese were still held on the Sittang, the Japanese might have been prevented from capturing Rangoon and then, as Chinese strength built up, soundly defeated. But it would have been a very close-run thing. The Australian convoy, on a routine movement, had not been tactically loaded[2] and to marry troops with their equipment would have taken a couple of days. Moreover the Australian Infantry, battle-experienced as they were, would have taken a few days to adjust to the very different conditions and tactics of a forest war.

On the morning of the 23rd, General Hutton was still hoping that the Australians would be coming. Meanwhile it was vital to get what remained of 17 Division operational again. In the withdrawal from Kyaikto to the Sittang almost the whole of two brigades had been lost (although small numbers continued to find their way back) with virtually all their equipment. 46 Brigade's losses had been particularly high and so it was disbanded, the remnants of the units going to 16 and 48 Brigades. A third Indian brigade was due to land shortly and this would give 17 Division three brigades again. Meanwhile every effort was made to get the troops re-equipped although they would remain woefully short of automatic weapons for the rest of the campaign.

On the 26th General Smyth submitted a six-page written report[3] to General Hutton on the Bilin and Sittang battles. In his conclusion he wrote that:

"The troops undoubtedly fought well and inflicted severe casualties on the Japanese throughout this period of intensive fighting; they would, however, have done much better, inflicted far higher casualties and retained their own cohesion had they been trained in this form of warfare."

In his report, Smyth specifically commended Brigadiers Jones (16 Brigade) and Cowan (Brigadier General Staff), Lieutenant Colonels Ballinger (killed) (1st/3th Gurkhas), Lentaigne (1st/4th Gutkhas), Cameron (2nd/5th R Gurkhas), Edward (4th/12th FFR), White (1st/7th Gurkhas) and Keegan (killed) (2nd KOYLI) and Brigade-Majors Burton and Somerville. He also praised Lieutenant-Colonel Thompson (A/Q), Captains Kean and Bird (liaison officers) and the work of the Royal Engineers (*sic*, in fact Indian and Burmese Engineers) under the CRE, Lieutenant-Colonel Armitage. This is rather ambiguous as far as Armitage is concerned. Colonel Armitage was a sick man and had already been in hospital in Rangoon with a kidney complaint. He had looked very ill at the Sittang bridge and was now evacuated sick to India. He was replaced by Major R.S.B.Ward RE who had been OC of the 1st Burma Field Company. Another change was of the GSO1, Lieutenant-Colonel Simpson, who, although he was to be awarded an OBE at the end of the campaign, was replaced by Major Guy Burton. Although Brigadier Hugh-Jones is omitted from the list of those commended, Smyth never blamed him then or later for his recommendation about the bridge and always took full responsibility for the fatal decision himself.

Changes in the Command

On the 25th General Smyth had also sent a personal letter to General Hutton in which he asked for two month's leave as soon as he could be spared. He felt very much in need of a rest and felt also that the troops would perhaps do better under new management, particularly as there was, in 'Punch' Cowan, a really efficient substitute ready to step into his shoes. On receipt of this letter Hutton, on the 26th, sent a Most Immediate signal to the Military Secretary at GHQ in India saying that, although Smyth appeared well and cheerful and the medical

1. Churchill, Winston, *The Second World War*, Vol.4, p.145.
2. *ibid*, p.144.
3. *Hutton Papers*, 2/1-21.

authorities had pronounced him fit, he could only assume that he had lost confidence in his ability to command and should be relieved. He asked for approval to replace him with Cowan and to send Smyth back to India forthwith.[4]

Another important change was in the air. After the early reverses and retreats in Burma there were inevitably those in Whitehall and GHQ India who sought a scapegoat, and on 18 February the Viceroy, presumably advised by the Commander-in-Chief, General Hartley, cabled London that he was sure that the reason that the troops in Burma were "not fighting with sufficient relish" (a silly phrase) was due to the lack of drive and inspiration from the top. Churchill at once referred this cable to Wavell for his opinion, adding that he was prepared to send out General Alexander at once. Wavell did not at first agree and was reluctant to make a change, but on the 20th he received an appreciation from Hutton, written on the 18th, which gave an objective view of the situation. In his appreciation, Hutton was looking ahead at the problem of Rangoon and taking a realistic view. He said (correctly) that he could not be certain of holding the position on the Bilin River. If he failed to do so he thought, also correctly, that the enemy might somewhere cross the Sittang, much less of an obstacle than the Salween, without great difficulty and would then be able to close the main road and rail route to the north which lay close to it. The evacuation of Rangoon might then become an imminent necessity. Wavell also received a signal saying that, in accordance with this appreciation, preliminary steps were being taken for the evacuation of Rangoon and that the Syriam oil refineries had been closed down. Meanwhile, Air Vice-Marshal Stevenson, who was not under Hutton's command, cabled that he was taking steps to move the RAF to Magwe and Akyab, with their main base in Eastern India. Wavell, quite out of touch with the real position, could not see any reason for these drastic actions which he thought unnecessarily defeatist and so cabled his agreement to a change of command.[5]

On the 22nd, therefore, Hutton on his return from Lashio found a private message waiting for him which said that, in view of projected reinforcements (a sweetener based on the possible arrival of an Australian division), General Alexander was coming out to replace him in command and he would remain as his Chief of Staff. The same day, the Chiefs of Staff ordered that ABDACOM should close down and operational command in Burma should revert to the Commander-in-Chief in India. Alexander, who was commanding Southern Command in Britain, had a high reputation with the public at this time. He was an unusually brave and cool man and had commanded the rearguard with distinction at Dunkirk. A handsome aristocrat, he was a great favourite of Winston Churchill's and the latter no doubt felt that by sending out such a figure he would be seen to be doing all that was possible to save the situation. But in fact it was an empty gesture for, except that his leadership might give greater inspiration to the British troops, Alexander could do nothing that Hutton could not do equally well or better. More troops and aircraft were all that could save Burma.

Hutton was an exceptionally able man with a fine record. Like Alexander, he had fought for several years in France in World War I, being wounded three times and earning an MC and bar and four mentions in despatches. After the war he had mainly held important staff jobs. However, many people who met him in Burma felt that although he was very clever and able, he lacked that certain charisma which a commander needs to inspire confidence. An experienced war correspondent, James Hodson, who arrived in Rangoon on 27 February, had no difficulty in getting an interview with Hutton, who indeed later asked him to lunch. Hodson found him cool and relaxed and commented:

> "Hutton looked as much like a university professor as a general. He sat at a roll-top desk, looked at us over his spectacles and, answering a tele-phone from time to time, talked of the military situation. It is grim."[6]

It is very doubtful, however, if anyone else who had been in Hutton's shoes would have done any better or indeed as well. As Wavell was to admit later, Hutton had an exceptionally difficult problem, more difficult perhaps than Wavell, two thousand miles away, realised at the time. Kirby's Official History[7] is notably fair to Hutton:

> "Hutton, who was at one and the same time acting as Chief of the General Staff of a Burma War Office trying to organise the country for defence, and as both an army and a corps commander trying to conduct operations with an inadequate staff, cannot be held responsible that major strategical decisions were not always taken in time... Having the courage of his convictions, he informed his superiors of the facts as he saw them, and set about taking the preparatory steps necessary to ensure a smooth evacuation and the demolition of the port [Rangoon]... The authorities in London and India, blaming the local commander for a course of events for which they themselves were largely responsible, decided to swap horses in mid-stream. Burma... was to suffer the added complication of a change in local command at the most critical stage of the campaign. We see first

4. *Hutton Papers, Personal Signal for MS (India) from Hutton*, 26 February 1942, 1030hrs.
5. The Governor of Burma, Sir Reginald Dorman-Smith, as his telegrams to the Secretary of State for Burma show, was an enthusiastic supporter of Hutton and in no way concerned in this change.
6. Hodson, J.L., *War in the Sun*, p.327.
7. Kirby, S.W., *The War Against Japan*, Vol.2, p.103.

Wavell in charge, then Wavell and Hartley, then Hartley alone and then a few days later Wavell once again; we see Hutton superseded by Alexander. In such circumstances it was almost impossible for any plan or policy to remain consistent."

Success in the Air

The first action in the highly dramatic events of the next two weeks was an important success by the RAF and AVG. The Japanese capture of Moulmein had given them two airfields, well stocked with petrol and within easy range of Rangoon. Fortunately, however, the vital radar set stationed there, the only one in Burma, had been evacuated safely to Mingaladon where it was efficiently operated. Consequently, when the Japanese air force on the 25 and 26 February made a determined effort to knock out the Allied air force, they were successfully intercepted by the Allied fighters. The Japanese force consisted of 47 fighters and 12 light bombers. Early on the 25th, the 4th Dan had flown into Moulmein and the 10th Dan into Mudon from Thailand. On the next two days they were met by 44 RAF Hurricanes and AVG Tomahawks, still based either on the main airfield at Mingaladon or on satellite strips cut in the paddy fields nearby. At the same time Blenheim bombers from Magwe attacked the enemy airfields at Moulmein and Mudon. In the confused fighting on these two days the Japanese claim that they only lost three fighters and two light bombers in the air although a number were damaged not only in the air but also in landing on the bombed airfields. They claim to have shot down one Blenheim and one Hurricane. Although Allied losses were light in the air fighting, damage on the ground and repair problems resulted in only ten Allied fighters being serviceable on the 27th. However, on this day, the Japanese air fleet returned to Thailand leaving the Allied air force still alive and kicking.

Both sides could claim some success in this operation but in the short term the advantage lay with the British. In retrospect it is amazing that not a single ship was lost either entering, unloading or leaving Rangoon. No doubt the main reason for this was that the Japanese wished to capture the port and its facilities intact and a steamer sunk in the narrow river approaches would have been a grave disadvantage. Nevertheless, ships could have been sunk at sea and there was to be a situation when a heavy attack on the army would have had a devastating effect. That it did not happen was a direct result of this RAF defence. Many of the soldiers on the ground did not appreciate this for, by the nature of air warfare, RAF successes were usually out of their sight whereas enemy air attacks were only too obvious.

There was another side to this success, however. Allied air strength had been weakened and General Iida was to write later in his diary:

"We now saw little of British aircraft. The constant air attacks that we had suffered up to the battle of the Sittang were drastically reduced as the Japanese gained control in the air. Until then even a single soldier was conscious of danger in walking along a road in daytime but now worry about enemy aircraft became unnecessary."

Wavell Reassumes Command

GHQ India was doing its utmost to provide reinforcements and, having scraped the barrel, had managed to assemble at Madras a brigade group of units who had had the minimum of training and had never met each other before. This was 63 Indian Infantry Brigade (63 Brigade) and their vehicles and heavy equipment had been sent to Calcutta. General Hartley, who had been Commander-in-Chief in India in Wavell's absence, was doing his best, but on the 19th of February had warned General Hutton not to be too optimistic:

"I have accelerated dispatch of 63 Brigade but point out that it requires a lot more training. It will be a good brigade but be under no illusion about its present position".[8]

Also in the Calcutta convoy was a trained but inexperienced artillery unit, the 1st Indian Field Regiment, armed with 25-pdrs and now of vital importance in view of the weakness in artillery in Burma. The brigade sailed from Madras on 26 February and the convoy from Calcutta on the 27th. General Hutton was now receiving reports of Japanese patrols and parties of armed Burmese at various places to the west of the Sittang. He therefore judged that if Rangoon were to be successfully evacuated, it would have to be done before these convoys were due to arrive on 3 and 5 March. Besides, having lately been Chief of the General Staff in India, he was well aware that 63 Brigade was largely composed of semi-trained raw recruits. On the 28th, therefore, he asked India to divert both convoys to Calcutta, which they did. On this day he also ordered the second stage of the evacuation, codeword JULIUS, to be put into operation. At this stage all personnel not essential to the final demolition of the main installations of the port were to leave. This included the withdrawal of the civil administration in the Rangoon area. Hutton also informed India that, unless he received orders to the contrary, he was proposing to issue the final order for the demolitions and evacuation of Rangoon on 1 March.

8. *Armindia VVV/3330/G of 19 February 1942.*

General Wavell now re-entered the picture. The Combined Chiefs of Staff had agreed that ABDACOM should be closed down and on the 26th he flew from Java to Ceylon, where he left General Pownall in charge, and on the 28th reassumed the post of Commander-in-Chief in India. His first action was to order Hutton to hold up the final evacuation order until his arrival in Burma, and the second to order the two convoys back on to their original courses to Rangoon. He then flew to Calcutta where he received a signal from the CGS in GHQ India saying that the demolitions in Rangoon were being blown early the next morning, so he turned the two convoys back towards Calcutta again and flew on to Magwe to meet Hutton, Stevenson and the Governor.

A curious scene now took place on the airfield. Wavell, normally the coolest and most reserved of men, stormed at Hutton in front of the other two in the most uncontrolled way. Hutton was totally taken aback and made no reply. He was particularly humiliated as he had been Wavell's friend and number two in India, and he had up till now been much respected by the Governor and Stevenson. The probable explanation was that not only did Wavell not yet appreciate the gravity of the situation, but that he was still in considerable pain. It was only a fortnight since his accident and only a week since he had left hospital. Broken vertebrae are not painless, nor are they helped by long flights in Service aircraft. The outcome of this meeting, when things quietened down, was that Wavell was informed that the demolitions had been postponed, so he turned the two convoys round towards Rangoon once again and directed that Rangoon was to be held at least until they arrived.

Wavell and Hutton now flew down to Mingaladon, where their arrival coincided with a small Japanese air raid, and Wavell drove up to HQ 17 Division at Hlegu. Here he interviewed and sacked General Smyth. No-one except these two knows what was said but hearsay at the time was that, after the interview, Smyth said "my career is finished," and added, "that man wouldn't forgive his own son." Brigadier Cowan was now appointed to command 17 Division. He had not yet commanded a brigade and so the appointment was unusual but he was widely respected and had been recommended for accelerated promotion. The choice was a good one and he was to command 17 Division with great distinction until the end of the Burma war.

On 2 March, Wavell paid a visit to the troops in Pegu and then flew up to Lashio in a Blenheim, with Smyth accompanying him in the bomb-rack, and met Chiang Kai-shek. The Generalissimo, pleased that Rangoon was being held, promised to speed up the movement of Chinese forces into Burma. On 3 March, still accompanied by Smyth, to whom he didn't speak, Wavell flew to Calcutta where he met General Alexander. He instructed him to hold Rangoon if at all possible but not to get trapped there. If withdrawal was unavoidable he was to hold north Burma to cover the construction of a road from India. Leaving Smyth behind, he then flew on to Delhi where he arranged that Smyth should be retired from the Army forthwith, medically boarded and sent on retirement leave. In his first four days of reassuming command of the operations in Burma, General Wavell had acted with exceptional speed and decision to do all that was possible to save the situation. Whether his judgement had been right now remained to be seen.

CHAPTER ELEVEN

The Battle at Pegu

Reorganisation of 17 Division

While 7th Armoured Brigade, supported by the newly-arrived 1st West Yorks and 1st Cameronians, held a screen covering the road approaches to Pegu from the north and north-east, what was left of 17 Division after the Sittang disaster was desperately trying to re-organise and re-equip itself. There were only enough men left to form two weak brigades, so 46 Brigade was disbanded. The two British battalions which had been on the wrong side of the Sittang, the 2nd KOYLI and the 2nd Duke's, had each lost more than half their strength and were temporarily amalgamated. Shortly afterwards they were separated again, Major Tynte from the Cameronians becoming CO of the 2nd KOYLI, and Major Faithfull becoming CO of the 2nd Duke's. The latter, their strength now 420, remained in Hlegu while the 2nd KOYLI, supported by one troop of the 2nd Royal Tanks, were ordered back to Tharrawaddy to guard the Prome road against any threat from the east.

48 Brigade, commanded by Brigadier Hugh-Jones, was holding the forward position at Pegu. In this brigade Colonel Lentaigne's 1st/4th Gurkhas were the only unit which had not had to swim the Sittang and were still virtually at full strength. The 1st/3rd Gurkhas and the 2nd/5th R Gurkhas, who had borne the brunt of the fighting at the Sittang bridge, were much weakened and had been temporaraily amalgamated to form the 5th/3rd under Colonel Cameron. The 1st/7th and the 3rd/7th Gurkhas, both battalions of the same regiment, had been amalgamated as the 1st/7th under Colonel White.

HQ 17 Division and 16 Brigade were at Hlegu (see Map 13). 16 Brigade, commanded by Brigadier 'Jonah' Jones, now consisted of the 1st/9th R Jats, the 4th/12th FFR and the 8th Burif. The latter had been on the wrong side of the Sittang and was only of one company strength while the Jats, who had been ordered to send a company to protect the demolitions taking place at the Syriam oil refinery, were very weak.

1 Burdiv, who were covering the advance of the Chinese from the north, were astride the Mandalay-Pegu road at Nyaunglebin about 15 miles north of Daik-u. However their only strong brigade, 13 Indian Brigade, was still deployed in the

north guarding the Salween crossing on the most likely route from Chiang Mai to Toungoo. They were in no position to intervene effectively with the Japanese thrust for Rangoon.

Equipment Problems

The units which had been caught on the eastern bank of the Sittang had lost all their equiment and were in a sorry state. The combined war diary of the 2nd KOYLI-2nd Duke's describes the problem at Pegu where they first assembled:

"There was very little shade from the hot sun and the varied headgear of the men, consisting of bush hats, native palm-leaf hats, steel helmets, civilian felt hats, puttees wrapped round the head and handkerchiefs, caused some headaches... Arms were very scarce.. apart from a few rifles the remainder were armed with grenades or pistols from the local police station."

The new 5th/3rd Gurkhas described similar problems. Although the 1st/4th shared out some of their weapons there were not nearly enough to go round and 100 men, for whom no arms could be provided, had to be sent back to Tharrawaddy. The message to India from the Western Desert had been that "any fool can be uncomfortable." It was strongly recommended that units should go to war with well-equipped officers' messes. Burma, however, was to be a tougher and less comfortable sort of war. Although the 2nd/5th had duly equipped themselves well, they had dumped nearly all of it when they went forward to the Bilin and all had now been lost. At Pegu, "the CO, Colonel Cameron, came to the fore and devised knives and forks from bamboo and plates from banana leaves. He also turned his hand to the kitchen and produced some excellent meals".[1] In due course crockery was acquired from deserted houses and officers picked up and kept their own cutlery. Though cooking pots for the Gurkhas had also been lost these were readily available locally.

While rearmament and domestic arrangements were being sorted out in every unit, it was clear that active operations would soon start again. Hutton had considered that no advantage would be gained by fighting at Pegu, which could easily be by-passed, and he intended that 17 Division should cover the withdrawal from Rangoon and then proceed up the Prome road before the Japanese were in the position to mount an attack. Wavell's decision to hold Rangoon until the last two convoys arrived changed all this. It was now essential to hold Pegu until the last convoy arrived on the 5th. However, if Rangoon were to be evacuated on the

1. War Diary, 2nd/5th RGR.

6th, it might still just be possible to slip away from Pegu before it was attacked and to cover the withdrawal up the Prome road before the enemy could interfere. So this was Hutton's new plan, but the timing was desperately tight.

The Japanese Plan

The Japanese halted for a full week at the Sittang. While this gave time for their troops to recover from the exhaustion of their hard cross-country marches, the main reason was to replenish supplies. This was not easy. The track across the hills from Thailand, though open to vehicles from 20 February, was still very rough. There were many vehicle casualties and continual engineer maintenance was necessary. The ferries from Moulmein to Martaban were of limited capacity and the British demolitions on the road and railway from Martaban to the Sittang were difficult to repair quickly. A company of railway engineers had reached Moulmein in February and managed to get the Martaban-Bilin sector into operation with the aid of two locomotives brought over from Moulmein. But the two bridges which had been blown proved difficult to repair and the line was not open until 5 March. They had not the capacity to tackle the demolished Bilin, Kyaikto and Sittang rail bridges and this sector was not repaired until much later.

There was also a difficulty over air support. RAF and AVG fighters made movement by day hazardous and it was essential to reduce their threat, both to reduce casualties and to avoid detection. However, RAF bombing of Moulmein airfield had caused damage which the Japanese, who had no earth-moving equipment, were unable to repair quickly.[2] Work started on 16 February but was not finished until the 24th, in time for the Japanese Air Force to fly in the next day.

General Iida therefore had a problem. It was essential to press on quickly to capture Rangoon before the British regained their balance or were reinforced, but on the other hand his troops needed food and ammunition. His mountain guns had started off with 120 rounds per gun and in some cases were now down to only 15. He told his gunners that they would have to manage with what they had. There were rumours that British tanks had landed at Rangoon and so he felt that it was worth waiting for a company of anti-tank guns, for a platoon of light tanks which were struggling up the road, and for a specialist bridging company to help with the Sittang crossings. On 27 February he gave out his orders. The advance of the main body would start on the night of 3 March. *33 Division* was given the task of capturing Rangoon. They were to make a wide right hook, hopefully not encountering the British until they suddenly attacked Rangoon. *215 Regiment* would cross the Sittang at Kunzeik, about 18 miles north of the bridge (see Map 13). *214 Regiment* would cross at the bridge, covered by *143 Regiment*, and break north-west from the road at Abya.[3] *Both 214 and 215 Regiments* would then take parallel courses, crossing the Pegu-Mandalay road north of Pyinbongyi, and then march over the forested hills to cross the Rangoon-Prome road near Hmawbi. *215 Regiment* would then advance on Rangoon through Insein and *214 Regiment* through Mingaladon. As for the air, 4th Dan would support *55 Division* when needed and 10 Dan would support *33 Division.*.

55 Division was given the task of covering the start of these moves and then of making a direct advance on Rangoon through Pegu. It was anticipated that they would engage the main British forces and thus ease *33 Division's* task. They were to send a battalion group[4] north-west via Kunzeik to Daik-u on the Mandalay road to block any advance by British or Chinese from the north. Another battalion group[5] was to go south-west from Sittang and go across country to Syriam with the aim of capturing the oil refineries there before they could be demolished. *143 Regiment* (less one battalion) was to cross the Sittang on the night of 2 March and advance on Waw, followed by *112 Regiment* (also less one battalion) on the next night. Both regiments would then cross the Mandalay road; *143 Regiment* would attack Pegu from the north-west while *112 Regiment* blocked the road south of Pegu (see Map 14).

The Japanese Advance on Pegu

On 1 March, HQ 17 Division was at Hlegu with 16 Brigade while 48 Brigade were holding Pegu. The 2nd Royal Tanks, with the 1st Cameronians under command, were covering the Mandalay road approach from north of Payagyi and the Sittang road approach from west of the Waw canal. 60 Field Company had demolished the road bridge at Abya on 24 February and on the 25th, at Waw, they demolished the railway bridge and the pontoon bridge which they had just built. They also burnt down most of Waw east of the canal.

The arrival of the British tanks was to introduce a new dimension into the fighting. At last the British had some battle-experienced and fully trained units. Brigadier J.H. Anstice's 7th Armoured Brigade came with a high reputation from their fighting in the Western Desert and they were to enhance that reputation in the very different conditions of fighting in Burma. The brigade consisted of two regiments, the 7th Hussars and the 2nd Royal Tanks (2nd R Tanks). They were supported by the 25-pdrs of 414 Battery, RHA, and had their own workshop and supply vehicles. Each regiment had 52 'Stuart' tanks.[6] In battle trim these

---

2. Nor did the British in Burma have any earth-moving equipment. However the Thai engineers had some angledozers and these were a great help in constructing the road from Raheng.

3. *33 Engineer Regiment* had built a wooden footbridge across the fallen girders.

4. A squadron of mounted infantry, *2/143 Battalion* and *8 Coy Mountain Artillery*.

5. *1/112 Battalion* and *5 Coy Mountain Artillery*.

6. These tanks were called 'Honeys' in the Western Desert.

***The demolished
railway bridge
over the Waw
canal.*** Yarrow.

American-made light tanks weighed about 13 tons and were powered by an extremely reliable aircraft engine.[7] Their main gun was a 37mm, firing solid shot only and with a telescopic sight. They also had two Browning machine guns, one co-axially mounted. Unfortunately the Stuart tanks did not have the cross-country mobility that had been expected. The clay ridges ('bunds') and banks which enclosed the rice fields were baked brick hard by the sun at this time of year and provided obstacles which the tanks were often unable to surmount. Consequently, except where there was tree-less and uncultivated land, the tanks were largely confined to roads or tracks. Another weakness of this tank was that its engine was air-cooled, and the turret hatch had to be left open while the engine was running, in close country this could be hazardous.

The 1st Cameronians had established a section standing patrol near Waw and rather unwisely kept it in the same place, relieving it morning and evening. When the relief section, carried on three tanks, arrived on the morning of 26 February they found their eight predecessors all dead with their throats cut. Their weapons and equipment were missing and they appeared to have been surprised while asleep. No-one knows quite what occurred. The officer who found them thought it the work of dacoits, but more likely the BIA were the culprits. The latter had been sent ahead of the Japanese advance and had been engaged in 'softening up' village headmen and murdering any stragglers from the Sittang that they came across.[8]

Apart from this, the first contact was not made until 2 March when a troop of the 2nd R Tanks, patrolling on the west bank of the Waw canal, were shelled at point-blank range by 75mm mountain guns on the other bank. Two tanks were knocked out and a third damaged. The latter managed to withdraw and only one man was lost. It soon became clear, however, that the Japanese had crossed the

3/112 Battalion crossing Waw canal with men and horses over an improvised footbridge on 3 March.

canal, so an infantry and tank attack, preceded by a bombardment by a troop of 414 Battery RHA, was launched that afternoon. However it was beaten off by *143 Regiment* who were now across the canal in strength, so an air strike was asked for on west Waw. A single Blenheim duly appeared and dropped its bombs on the target with great accuracy but not very much effect.

The Japanese now advanced to Kyaikhla (see Map 14), and an attack on 3 March by the 1st Cameronians, supported by the 2nd R Tanks and a troop of 414 Battery RHA, was unable to dislodge them. That night the 7th Hussars relieved the 2nd R Tanks who returned to Hlegu. The enemy were now reported to be in Naungpattaya on the Sittang railway with a light screen forward of the village. The 1st Cameronians were ordered to stop any further advance down the railway so two companies dug in at Shanywagy.

Meanwhile, activity was increasing on the Mandalay road. A road-block had been encountered at Pyinbongyi by a West Yorks carrier patrol and two carriers were ditched while trying to turn round. This road-block had been established by *3/214 Battalion* as a flank guard to cover the crossing of the road by *214 Regiment*, who were marching west on the north edge of the Moyingyi reservoir. A troop of tanks successfully recovered the carriers but two tanks were damaged by 75mm fire. On the 4th, the 7th Hussars, together with one company each of the 1st W Yorks and the 1st Cameronians, and supported by a troop of 414 Battery, attacked Payagyi village, setting it alight and causing great alarm to *112 Regiment* (less a battalion) who had just reached there. This attack was much

7. The engine was a radial, air-cooled, 220 H.P. Wright 'Whirlwind', running on high octane petrol. This was the engine which powered Lindbergh's 'Spirit of St Louis' in its trans-Atlantic flight. Account by Major A.J. Fearnley MC in the R Tank Museum library.

8. Fearnley, Major A. J., *Personal Account*.

more successful than the British realised and the Japanese were greatly relieved when the tanks withdrew at dusk.

That night a patrol of the 1st W Yorks was ambushed south of Payagyi, a number of men being wounded. On the next day, 'A' Squadron of the 7th Hussars, supported by a company of the 1st W Yorks, encountered *112/8* and *9 Companies* south of Payagyi and after a brisk encounter forced them to "advance back" to the east,[9] where they joined up with *143 Regiment*. *112/9 Company* was then ordered to march south-west along the Pegu-Sittang railway line and make a feint attack on Pegu from the north-east to disguise the main attack from the west.

On the 5th, Hutton and Cowan conferred, and orders were then given to 48 Brigade to thin out that evening and for the rearguard to withdraw to Hlegu that night. However, before these orders could be implemented, they were cancelled by General Alexander.

General Alexander had been ordered to proceed from the UK to Burma at once on 21 February but bad weather delayed his flight. He finally took off in a Flying Fortress on the 28th, landing in Egypt on 1 March. Here he changed planes and arrived at Calcutta, where he met Wavell on the 3rd. Wavell briefed him that Rangoon was vitally important and, if at all possible should be held but, if not, the British force must not be allowed to be cut off and destroyed but must be withdrawn for the defence of upper Burma.[10] Alexander then flew on to Rangoon arriving at noon and taking over command. In the afternoon he met Hutton and Cowan at Hlegu and, presumably judging after his very brief acquaintance with the problem that it was possible to do so, against their advice ordered that Rangoon was to be held. To effect this, Pegu would be defended and 63 Brigade, which had landed two days before, was to be put in a counter-attack against *55 Division*. This plan was strictly in line with his instructions from Wavell but ignored both the complete lack of training of 63 Brigade and, much worse, the major threat developing from *33 Division*. It was a fatal and unrealistic decision which cost many lives and very nearly led to a major disaster but, as Hutton observed later, "I think any fresh commander with his instructions would have done the same".[11]

The Armoured Encounter at Pegu

The 6th of March started well. Early in the morning, the 7th Hussars advanced in the heavy morning mist from their night leaguer, south of Pegu, to their day positions up the Mandalay road. Suddenly their headquarters was ambushed by a battery of Japanese 37mm anti-tank guns. A couple of tanks were hit and lost their tracks. Fortunately the mist soon lifted, and a quick attack by a company of the 1st W Yorks, supported by the tanks, overran the Japanese battery killing many of the gunners and capturing four guns.[12] There followed a report, not at first believed, of Japanese tanks nearby. But a reconnaissance proved it true and all three tanks were located and knocked out by the Hussars. They turned out to be seven-ton tanks which had been brought with great difficulty along the road from Thailand. They were quite out-classed by the Stuarts, and their 37mm guns, like those of the anti-tank battery, could not penetrate the armour of the British tanks.[13]

Meanwhile *143 Regiment* and *3/112 Battalion*, chary of meeting the tanks, had crossed the Pegu river further north and circled round through the wooded hills to the west of Pegu, which they were preparing to attack on the 6th.

63 Brigade is Decapitated

Further south, the British now suffered a most unfortunate reverse. On the evening of the 5th, Brigadier John Wickham of the newly-arrived 63 Brigade, his brigade major George Forteath, and his three battalion commanders and their adjutants, had driven up to Pegu to discuss their proposed attack the next day. They stayed the night and then set off back on the 6th. They went in an armoured convoy as some sniping had been reported on the road between Pegu and Hlegu. Two tanks led, followed by two wheeled carriers and another tank at the rear. After three miles they met a lorry blocking the road at a place where there were trees on both sides. The first tank by-passed the lorry via the left-hand ditch[14] but the second tank met concentrated machine-gun fire and the driver was killed by an unlucky bullet which penetrated his small glass visor. The engine stopped and the tank came to a halt blocking this route. The leading carrier, driven by Lieutenant Hawkins of the 1st/4th Gurkhas, therefore chose the other side of the road. As they passed under the branches of a large tree, an LMG-gunner in the tree fired two bursts from above into the open-top carrier. This carrier contained the Brigadier, his brigade major and Colonel Leonard of the 1st/10th Gurkhas, as well as three Gurkha riflemen. All, including the driver, were wounded, some very badly. The only person not hit was a Gurkha with a Bren gun sitting on the

9. *Memoir of 112 Regiment*, p.57. The Japanese, like Winston Churchill, did not believe in using the word 'retreat'.

10. Kirby, S.W., *The War Against Japan, Vol.2*, p.86.

11. Note by Lt-Gen. T.J. Hutton on the Burma Campaign up to the fall of Rangoon.

12. This was the *11th Anti-Tank Gun Company*.

13. Their armament of one 37mm gun and two machine guns was fine for supporting the infantry but quite ineffective against the British tanks. They were a platoon from the *2nd Tank Regiment* which had invaded Malaya. The light tank company of this regiment had been left in Thailand and this platoon had made its way into Burma on its tracks via Raheng. Originally there had been four tanks but one had slipped into the Sittang when the ferry had not been properly secured.

14. Ditches designed for the monsoon rains were wide and shallow.

outside of the carrier and he quickly disposed of the sniper. Although wounded, Hawkins appreciated that he must get medical help for his passengers, who were bleeding profusely, and so he succeeded in turning the carrier round and raced back to Pegu.

After an agonising struggle, Lieutenant Fearnley managed to worm his way into the driving seat of the second tank and to get it going again.[15] The remaining carrier and third tank followed him but they ran into another ambush two miles further on. A grenade landed in the carrier which was carrying the other two battalion commanders and their adjutants. All were killed. Thus, before it had even gone into action, the new and untried 63 Brigade had lost all its four senior commanders, its senior staff officer and two of its three adjutants. This was a grave set-back for the British and partly at the hands of the BIA, for it was this force, led by Japanese officers, who had laid the first ambush. The second ambush, which was to prove much more formidable, was at the south end of Payathonzu and was manned by *112 Regiment* (less the battalion which had gone towards Syriam and the two companies which had joined *143 Regiment*) supported by a troop of mountain guns.

The Fighting at Pegu

Early on the 6th, *55 Division*, having blocked the road to Hlegu and Rangoon, ordered *143 Regiment* to attack Pegu from the west. Achieving surprise, for 48 Brigade was still anticipating an attack from the north and north-east, the Japanese succeeded in penetrating a gap in the defences and occupying part of west Pegu including the railway station. This was a grave situation as the railway station was close to the Hlegu road. Accordingly, a three-company counter-attack to drive them out was launched at mid-day by one company each from the West Yorks, the Cameronians and the 1st/7th Gurkhas, supported by 414 Battery. After several hours of hard fighting, in which the Gurkhas particularly distinguished themselves in a bayonet counter-attack, the railway station was recaptured and the Japanese were driven away from the road.[16]

During the day, Pegu was heavily bombed, causing casualties and extensive fires. The fires spread to the forest beside the road to Hlegu and made problems for the 7th Hussars who, in the evening, had been ordered to clear the road to the south. However, they found a diversion round the blaze and reached the main road-block at Payathonzu in the dark. Too late to attack the strongly defended block that night, they leaguered in the open paddy fields to the east of the road and prepared for an attack the next day.

On the 6th, General Alexander had begun to realise the gravity of the situation and that there was no time to be lost. Finally, at midnight, he gave the order that

Rangoon was to be abandoned the next day, the 7th, and the final demolitions would take place that afternoon. The garrison was to march north towards Prome and 17 Division would form the rear-guard.

Most of 48 Brigade, including its headquarters and its 190 vehicles, were in the town of Pegu east of the river. In the evening of the 6th the brigade had closed into a tighter all-round defensive position and the night was relatively undisturbed. About 2000 hours Brigadier Hugh-Jones received orders to withdraw to Hlegu. 48 Brigade now faced a hard march and a hard fight. They were 21 miles from Hlegu and it was another seven miles to Taukkyan (pronounced Towkcharn) where the road from Pegu joined the Rangoon to Prome road. At all costs they must shake off the force attacking them in Pegu and break quickly through the road-block on the Hlegu road.

Hugh-Jones's first plan was to attempt a diversion round the road-block by using a track which went south-east to Thanatpin and then rejoined the main road near Tawa. However a reconnaissance patrol discovered that the bridge over the river at Tawa was only a flimsy one and too weak for the brigade's vehicles. This left only two courses. The first was to force a way back through the road block, and the second was to abandon the vehicles and guns and march round it. There could be no doubt which was correct and the decision was taken to fight back through the block.

This uncertainty created some problems for Lieutenant Frank Knowles, the Sapper officer responsible for blowing the big road bridge over the Pegu river. At first he laid out his cable from the explosives on the bridge to an exploder on the west bank, anticipating a withdrawal from east to west. When west to east became the plan during the early part of the night he had to lay out his cables on the other side of the river. At 0400 hours, east to west was decided on again, so he changed everything back to its original position. But his troubles were not yet over. The withdrawal took place in the early hours and at 0620 hours he was given the order to fire the charges. He went forward to make sure the demolition had succeeded (which it had) and saw a platoon of the enemy crossing the road ahead of him, so returned towards his truck to find it also a centre of Japanese attention. Wisely he rejoined the rearguard and summoned help to complete his task. A carrier crew from the Cameronians obliged and took him to the riverside to check the demolition but by this time there seemed to be Japanese everywhere and his truck had to be abandoned.

15. Fearnley, Major A.J., *Personal Account,* p.54.
16. An eye-witness account by a Japanese soldier, Mr Toshiaki Tadokoro, who later helped to cremate the Japanese bodies, states that in this action the company commander and 53 men of *112/8 Company* were killed.

Before first light the withdrawal started. The three Gurkha battalions were in the lead and the 1st Cameronians and the 1st West Yorks brought up the rear. The latter had a company of the 1st/4th Gurkhas under command. A platoon of the leading company of the Cameronians, moving down the railway as flank guard, encountered a Japanese platoon coming the other way. A Cameronian officer went across to identify them and had just shouted "Its alright, they're Gurkhas" when he was shot dead.[17] In the close-quarter fight which followed both sides suffered casualties and were dispersed. Apart from this the brigade withdrew from the town successfully, aided by the heavy morning mist, but the head of the column was held up and the going over the diversion was very rough. The vehicles could only move slowly and a queue developed. This prevented the rearguard from making a clean break. Alerted by the bridge demolition, the Japanese attacked the rearguard and there was some severe fighting. As the vehicles moved on a little, the 1st West Yorks were able to withdraw along the road but the company of the 1st/4th Gurkhas, who were between the road and the river and with an awkward stream to cross, became heavily involved and lost touch. They had many casualties before deciding to withdraw along the railway, which they did successfully, rejoining their battalion at Taukkyan on the 8th.

The Road-block on the Hlegu Road

The 7th Hussars, who were in Payathonzu about three-quarters of a mile short of the actual road-block, had intended to attack the block at first light but the morning mist was unfavourable for the tanks so they were forced to wait until it cleared. Finally at about 0830 hours, after a five-minute bombardment from the 25-pdrs of 414 Battery RHA, the 7th Hussars attacked down the road. The road-block was found to consist of two lorries nose-to-tail across the road. The leading tank rammed the block at full speed but was halted and attacked with petrol bombs. The crew bailed out under a hail of fire and miraculously managed to escape. They had succeeded in making a gap through which the following tanks forced their way, followed by 414 Battery, their own 'B' Echelon vehicles and a few of 48 Brigade's trucks. They all went straight on to Hlegu. Unfortunately the co-ordination between the 7th Hussars and 48 Brigade was far from perfect. After the 7th Hussars had passed through, the Japanese closed in again behind them and a number of soft vehicles which tried to follow were destroyed.

Meanwhile, at the head of the column, the three Gurkha battalions had closed up on the 7th Hussars before their advance. At the sound of the demolition in Pegu, the Japanese in woods and gardens on the west side of the road in the straggling village of Payathonzu, and a few on the east side, opened up on the column with guns, mortars and LMGs. Many vehicles were hit and some caught fire.

Groups of Japanese reached the road and there was some hard fighting. At Brigade HQ, which was between the 1st/4th and the 5th/3rd, the staff captain was killed and Colonel Cameron of the 5th/3rd was hit in both legs. The only Japanese to the east of the road, where the land was mostly paddy fields, were in an orchard opposite the 1st/4th Gurkhas, who soon cleared them out.[18] A Japanese infantry gun which had been established in the roadside ditch was captured in a bayonet attack, much to the relief of Colonel Leonard who was lying wounded in an ambulance close by. However, both the 1st/4th and 5th/3rd Gurkhas now attacked across the road into the woods and gardens on the west side, Cameron commanding his battalion from a carrier. Severe opposition was met but the Gurkhas pressed home their attack. Japanese losses were mounting and their pressure began to weaken.

Meanwhile, at the head of the column, the 1st/7th Gurkhas had been held up after the tanks had gone through. They put in an immediate attack but it was held, and their CO, Lieutenant-Colonel B.J.White, was killed. However, it was discovered that at the block the Japanese were only holding a narrow strip on each side of the road so the two leading companies by-passed the block on either side. Another company and the headquarter company adopted the same tactics and also got through unscathed, leaving only one rifle company from the 1st/7th north of the block. Unknown to the British, only *112/7 Company* now held the block. *2/112 Battalion* had been driven back into the forest by the fierce British attack.

Brigadier Hugh-Jones, although now without artillery, organised another attack on the road-block with the 5th/3rd on the left and the 1st/4th Gurkhas on the right. The 5th/3rd Gurkhas moved through the block on the east of the road without trouble but, still finding blazing vehicles and dead bodies on the road,[19] decided that there must be another block and continued down the road and, as it turned out, out of the fight. Two companies of the 1st/4th on the west of the road, however, met some stiff opposition and, having cleared it, decided to make a deeper sweep into the forest. To their surprise they encountered only small isolated parties of the enemy because the commander of *112 Regiment* had now withdrawn his force from the block into the forest to the north.[20] Lieutenant-Colonel Lentaigne, however, unaware of this, decided to attack the block directly with the reserve of his one company, and the one remaining company of the

17. Leggate, G., *Personal Account*.
18. It was this platoon, retreating up the railway, which encountered the Cameronians and were mistaken for Gurkhas.
19. These were the result of an abortive attack on the block by units of 63 Brigade and 2 R Tanks from Hlegu.
20. The commanders of both *112 Regiment* and *2/112 Battalion* were sacked shortly afterwards.

1st/7th. They skilfully picqueted the road right through the block so that the route was clear.

The Cameronians and the West Yorks, considerably reduced in numbers, had now arrived. A "stout-hearted officer from the Cameronians", Captain Mahoney, drove a carrier down to Hlegu and back to see if there were any further blocks. He reported that there were some snipers but no blocks, so Brigadier Hugh-Jones loaded the wounded into carriers and despatched down the road every vehicle that was still a runner. There being nothing further to protect on the road, he decided to avoid further casualties by marching across country. He therefore formed the brigade into a rough square and struck south-east across the paddy fields, before circling round and rejoining the road at Intagaw.[21] After a long and tiring march, they reached Hlegu at 1300 hours on the 8th to find lorries waiting for them on the west bank, the road bridge having been demolished at dawn by 24 Field Company. After some delay in crossing the river, they drove on to Taukkyan just in time to join the rearguard of 17 Division moving north up the Prome road.

The two companies of the 1st/4th Gurkhas north of the road were now on their own. They marched west along tracks through the forested hills without meeting anyone. Suddenly they entered a long open valley with a hamlet in the middle. As they drew close, they saw that this hamlet contained a Japanese cavalry unit, which was in fact *214 Regiment's* mounted infantry platoon, acting as a flank guard. Having instructed their men what to do if attacked, that is lie down and shoot the riders not the horses, they skirted the village and continued. However, before they reached the end of the valley, the 'cavalry' charged after them. Following their instructions, they spread out and shot several of the riders while the horses, as predicted, jumped over them and disappeared into the forest. Having thus faced, successfully and without loss, the last 'cavalry' charge encountered by British forces, they continued on their way, eventually reaching the abandoned Hlegu and rejoining their battalion at Taukkyi.[22]

The fight at Pegu had been a tough and savage one, and the Gurkhas had distinguished themselves by defeating a Japanese battalion and breaking a road-block. Although each of *55 Division's* four battalions had only three rifle companies and an MMG company, their total strength was greater than that of the five depleted British and Gurkha battalions of 48 Brigade. Moreover the British were very short of automatic weapons and mortars. The great British advantage of the tanks was offset by the Japanese advantage in the air. The strength of 48 Brigade's resistance had surprised and alarmed the Japanese. General Iida had been far from certain what the outcome of this battle would be and had feared a reverse which would ruin his plan. He ordered *33 Division* to delay its advance until the result was known. The British tanks had made a powerful impression and, if the British

The Japanese improvise a road bridge over the river at Hlegu on 8 March, the day after the previous bridge was demolished.

strength in Burma had not been so woefully weak, the tables might have been turned even at this late stage.

Both sides had suffered more losses than they had bargained for. No complete tally of Japanese casualties in the fighting around Pegu appears to exist, but *3/112 Battalion* alone records three officers and 79 soldiers killed there. There is no record of *2/112 Battalion's* losses but General Iida, on his way to Rangoon, recorded seeing Japanese soldiers (presumably, to be worth mentioning, more than a few) being cremated at Payathonzu. The casualties in the 1st West Yorks were 4 officers and 18 soldiers killed, and in the 1st Cameronians, one officer and nine soldiers.[23] The British battalions also record 45 and 75 respectively as missing but these were parties that were cut off and some found their way back later.[24] Gurkha casualties are not recorded but they were not heavy. 48 Brigade was already beginning to make its mark.

55 Division had shot its bolt as far as 17 Division was concerned and *143 Regiment* was now ordered by General Iida to turn round and prepare to advance up the Mandalay road. *112 Regiment* followed the British to Hlegu but without making contact. Only one of their companies was detailed to go into Rangoon and represent *55 Division* there, the remainder of the *Regiment* being turned back to go north. 17 Division and *55 Division* would not meet again for another seven weeks.

---

21. Padre Metcalfe of the 1st Cameronians had been prominent in helping the wounded in Pegu hospital and helping them into ambulances. He left with the last of the rear-guard and in the confusion came across a leaderless party of stragglers, whom he led across country after dark to Hlegu.
22. Both company commanders were 2nd Lieutenants, one aged 19. They were probably the only junior officers who had ever been instructed how to meet a cavalry charge. The instruction had been given by their Colonel in the Mess in India one night and at the time they had thought him quite dotty. Major D.S. Day, *1/4 GR Officers' Association Newsletter No.40*, and personal account to author.
23. From War Diaries.
24. The 'missing' had some extraordinary adventures. A few managed to rejoin their unit in the north, while some managed to reach India via Akyab and some via Assam. The majority headed for Rangoon, not realising that it was being abandoned, and were eventually captured. Twenty-nine soldiers of the Cameronians, some wounded, were taken prisoner and spent three-and-a-half years in Rangoon jail. All survived except one who was killed in an Allied air raid. Rifleman George Leggate, *Personal Account*.

CHAPTER TWELVE

The Last Days of Rangoon

The Evacuation of Civilians

The Chiefs of Staff had advised General Wavell at ABDACOM on 21 February that he should not try to hold Rangoon after its usefulness as a supply line to China had passed. Rather, he should block the port and "establish all forces on a port to the north." Which port was wisely unspecified as there were none in Burma. Presumably Calcutta was meant. The conference with his commanders on 23 February, together with the information that night that the Australians would not be coming, provided the vital information that General Hutton needed. He knew that Rangoon itself was indefensible with the small forces available to him. A sprawling city twenty miles up a narrow river, it could easily be cut off from the sea and isolated. Now that Singapore had fallen, command of the sea was in any case doubtful. Any attempt to hold Rangoon would achieve nothing and sooner or later would result in the loss of the garrison and all the British citizens who had not been evacuated. He therefore ordered 1 Burdiv to hold a position at Nyaunglebin on the road north to Mandalay and to patrol the main road and railway between that place and Pegu. He ordered 17 Division to reform in Pegu and hold it. They would be covered and supported by 7 Armoured Brigade and the two new British battalions. Meanwhile, the evacuation of Rangoon would be speeded up, and demolitions prepared both there and at the big oil refineries at Syriam.

As already mentioned, General Hutton's position in Burma was a complex one. As commander of the Burmese army he had responsibilities to the Burmese Government, and Defence was a subject reserved to the Governor, but his operational instructions and administrative support came from elsewhere. Although the Governor, Sir Reginald Dorman-Smith, was the civil head of the country, he was not, as in some British possessions, the commander-in-chief. There might well have been friction between him and Hutton but fortunately they got on very well together. Co-ordination was achieved by daily conferences, or war cabinet meetings, presided over by the Governor. The Burmese Prime Minister, Minister of Home Affairs and Minister of Finance attended, together with the three British Service Chiefs. Every day the Governor sent a telegram describing the situation to his minister in Whitehall, and Winston Churchill of course saw the important ones.

The Burma Civil Service, with its tiny British and Burmese content, was only large enough to run a small country in times of peace. It was totally inadequate to deal with the crisis of an enemy invasion, aggravated by the active disloyalty of a small part of the population and some members of the Burmese parliament, including the Speaker and, indeed, the previous Prime Minister. The Army was responsible, with the co-operation of the other two Services, for the defence of Burma, and this task clearly included, in conjunction with the civil power, planning the evacuation and denial of Rangoon, should it be necessary. This was a considerable extra burden for Hutton and his staff, already fully stretched dealing with the military situation.

Colonel F.J. Biddulph had been brought in from India as Director of Transportation on 27 January. After three days he recommended that the railways and the Irrawaddy Flotilla Company should be militarised. Desirable as this move was, it had been left too late to be practicable. Biddulph then proposed that the Burma Railway Battalion should be embodied, thus bringing many of the staff under military discipline, and this was agreed. The morale of the European, Anglo-Indian and Anglo-Burman staff remained high, but desertions by junior staff increased so much that, after the disaster at the Sittang, the Chief Railway Commissioner declared that no more trains could be run. This was an impossible situation because supplies still needed to go to Pegu and it was essential to run trains both for evacuees and stores to Prome. The Governor promptly stepped in and put the railways between Rangoon, Prome and Toungoo under military control. The Chief Railway Commissioner and his three Commissioners were despatched to Mandalay to control the railways in upper Burma. Fortunately, similar difficulties with the Irrawaddy Flotilla Company, an integral part of the transport system in Burma, were settled amicably.

Rangoon, by far the largest city in Burma, had a population of about 500,000, of whom some 200,000 were expatriates, the great majority Indian. There were about 12,000 Europeans, mostly British. The hard-working Indians provided the labour for the docks, the railways, the roads, the airfields, the hospitals and for conservancy, tasks which the easy-going Burmese preferred to avoid. They were an essential part of the fabric of the city. The British had encouraged them to come to Burma and were responsible for their protection. The Indians, however, were not popular with the Burmese population. Their religion and culture were different. Their commercial acumen was envied and their money-lending activities in rural areas much disliked. Without British protection many of them and their families faced a very uncertain future.

For the small British element the problems were different. Many of them intended to spend their working lives in Burma. Most of the younger Britons had joined the forces and, with their local knowledge, were to prove invaluable. For older people not in essential jobs it was more difficult. They were suddenly faced with losing their jobs, their houses and all their possessions. Many countries have had to face this problem but it was not one that the British had been used to, and it is hardly surprising if a few are said to have reacted badly.

One of the great difficulties of a retreat (and it would be a much more difficult problem nowadays) is what official information should be disseminated. The Governor did his best with a small and inexperienced staff but he did not avoid plenty of criticism. In particular, an unwise broadcast comparing Rangoon with Tobruk and Moscow (both currently being successfully defended) was much derided when Rangoon was evacuated. But in fact it is almost impossible to strike the right note when the enemy calls the tune. A realistic statement assists the enemy and encourages gloom and defeatism. An optimistic view raises morale temporarily but draws much abuse about ignorance and complacency when things go badly. However, in February, a Rangoon lawyer and author, Lieutenant-Colonel A.E. Foucar, was placed in charge of Public Relations. He was a success, and a far from uncritical Australian reporter[1] recorded after his appointment that PR "worked more smoothly in Burma under great difficulties than in most theatres."

Based on his appreciation of 18 February, General Hutton and his staff had produced a plan for the evacuation of Rangoon in three phases, code-named ANTONY, JULIUS and CAESAR. The first phase, ANTONY, was ordered on 20 February. This included the closing down of the three oil refineries at Syriam and preparations, necessarily elaborate, being made for their demolition. Patients from the hospital were sent by train to Mandalay. All women not in vital jobs

Indian refugees from Rangoon trekking up the road to Prome.
7th Hussars Museum.

were evacuated by sea or to north Burma. The big British trading companies in Rangoon closed their books, disposed of their assets as best they could, paid off their local staffs and arranged for the evacuation of their British and expatriate Indian employees. By an unfortunate error, a civil servant[2] who had misread the plan, ordered the convicts to be released from prison, and the lepers and the inmates of the mental home to be turned loose. Arson and looting spread quickly and stern steps had to be taken to stop the chaos.

Many thousands of Indian workers and their families had been leaving Rangoon ever since the air raids in December. Now this movement accelerated. Some went north towards Mandalay, hoping that either north Burma would be held or there would be a route to India via Assam. Others went to Prome hoping to make their way over the Arakan Yomas to Akyab and thence to Chittagong. Most went on foot as the numbers were far too great for the railways to handle. For the railways were now faced with the task of moving sufficient ammunition and supplies from the base at Rangoon to north Burma, to enable the Army and RAF in Burma to continue to fight there until it was possible to build a road to supply them from India. In addition to the military vehicles and supplies which the Americans were sending from Rangoon through Mandalay and Lashio to Chungking, supplies had also to be arranged for the Chinese armies now entering Burma, as this was one of the conditions for their coming. Nevertheless there was, until the railway was blocked, a daily passenger train to Mandalay and a continuous shuttle to Prome.

This Indian migration was to continue for the next three months, and providing food and medical facilities for the migrants was to strain the civil resources to the limit. In the end about 100,000 would reach Akyab via Prome. An outbreak of cholera in Prome was prevented from becoming an epidemic by the heroic efforts of a handful of doctors. Nevertheless many Indians died of dysentery, most were robbed, and many were murdered by Burmese on the arduous march over the Arakan hills, while in Akyab the civil organisation broke down and many refugees died of starvation.

The best route for the refugees was the one from Mandalay to the north-west entering India at Tamu. At first there was a hold-up in Mandalay, partly because it was thought that north Burma would be held, partly because there was talk of a road being completed to India, and partly because the Indian authorities restricted the immigrants to the 750 per day which was all that they could initially handle. By the end of March there were over 100,000 refugees in Mandalay and cholera broke out. Again heroic efforts to provide widespread inoculation

---

1. Burchett, W.G., *Bombs Over Burma*.
2. Overcome with remorse he committed suicide.

prevented the disease from spreading. Meanwhile, India was doing its best to help and increased the quota to 3000 per day. A 150-mile cart track from the Assam railway at Dimapur to Imphal and Palel was being improved to take vehicles and a new 60-mile road was being constructed at breakneck speed by the Sappers through the hills to Tamu, the frontier town on the Burmese plain. The Indian Tea Association not only provided and administered many thousands of men to help with this road-work but also assisted greatly in arranging staging posts and food for the refugees. Further north, a jeep road was constructed from Ledo over the Changsau Pass towards Shingbwiyang in Burma whence a track, much of it jeepable, led to Myitkyina.

Equally important, once India became responsible for operations in Burma a structure was set up to organise and administer the evacuation of refugees. Major General E. Wood, CIE, MC, was given the post of Administrator of Eastern Frontier Communications and had three senior administrators under him, one for each of the main routes, that is via Akyab, via Tamu and via Myitkyina.

In the end about 191,000 refugees passed through Tamu and reached Assam through Dimapur and Silchar. Another 28,000, including about 5000 sick or wounded soldiers, passed along the northern routes. Recorded deaths on these routes were 4300, but the real figure was certainly much higher as many refugees who died of dysentery, malaria, exhaustion or starvation simply disappeared in the forest.

Summing up after a later enquiry, the Honourable Mr Justice Braund was to say:

"That this forlorn army passed over into the land of their inheritance with casualties which, in the face of the conditions and difficulties, were no greater than they were, is a matter of deep gratitude. It was an achievement for the accomplishment of which those who gave their services, and some their lives, have reason to be satisfied."[3]

Nearly all Europeans were either among the 25,000 civilians, mostly Indians, evacuated by ship from Rangoon or among those who went by train or car to Mandalay and Maymyo in the belief that north Burma would be held. Most of those with important jobs stayed at their posts as long as was feasible. Many who went to the north were caught up in the bombing of the northern towns. Many wounded were evacuated by air from Shwebo. Most of the women and children who went north got to Myitkyina by train and were flown out from there. But the speed of the Japanese advance through the Shan States obliged many parties to walk out to India through the hills and forests of the north-west. Their hardships

The deserted main streets of Rangoon on 6 March 1942.

and adventures were heart-rending. They have been the subject of several books but are outside the scope of this one.

The Capital City

In the first week of March, the centre of Rangoon was as deserted as if some fearful natural catastrophe had overtaken it. Most of the major buildings were still standing though there were occasional gaps caused by bomb damage or arson. Bar the lunatics, very few people were to be seen as the convicts and other looters kept out of sight as much as possible by day. General Hutton had established a skeleton organisation under Major-General A.V.T. Wakely to control the line of communication units. Under him, Brigadier R.D. Leslie was made 'Rangoon Fortress' commander and responsible for the evacuation and necessary demolitions. Colonel Bagot of the 1st Glosters was appointed *de facto* military commandant and his battalion patrolled the streets and used stern methods to maintain law and order. Looters caught in the act were shot.

In spite of these firm measures there was a good deal of chaos. A vehicle park of several hundred brand new American trucks destined for China had been burnt by the Americans and all the trucks destroyed. It was claimed that about 100,000 tons of American lease-lend material was lying in the docks and awaiting onward transmission to China. Several large warehouses by the main docks were crammed with packing cases containing every sort of item of American military equipment. Larger boxes, mostly containing jeeps and trucks, were stacked high on the quays outside. At this stage, groups of British servicemen were helping themselves to make up unit shortages but making little impact on the mass of material.

The dock labourers had long since fled and the last troop convoys had to

3. *Hutton Papers*, 3/19-22.

unload their stores using the ship's derricks and their own soldiers. A late arrival was surprised to see men of a British unit doing coolie work in the docks under a tropical sun. Despite the arduous nature of the task they were working with remarkable good humour, for it was already becoming clear to everyone that the war in Burma was one requiring adaptability and initiative at every level.[4]

It was also clear to everyone that, bar a miracle, Rangoon's days were numbered. Nevertheless, the essential facilities, such as water and electricity, were kept going to the very last minute. The Chief Engineer at AHQ was Brigadier Charles Swift, MC. He had been CRE in Burma from 1939 dealing with the construction of barracks and hospitals for the Burma Army, a task which was more to his taste than the operational side of military engineering. Until late in 1941 no-one dreamed of any invasion of Burma and he was resigned to spending the war there. When war came he was promoted to Chief Engineer at AHQ. He had only a handful of engineer units under his command including the remnants of the Burma Sappers. He therefore had to do what he could with local contractors and the Public Works Department, who were very co-operative. With their help he had managed to keep Mingaladon airfield operational (for the RAF had no airfield engineers of their own) and to build various satellite airstrips between Rangoon and Magwe. On this last day in Rangoon, his main interest was, having made arrangements for certain key demolitions, to keep the electricity and water supply going until the end, which he did.

The Demolitions on 7 March

General Alexander had taken over command from Hutton at 1300 hours on the 5th. It was a desperate moment for a stranger to try and appreciate the situation and he can scarcely be blamed for delaying the withdrawal. He soon realised, however, that his initial reaction had been wrong, and codeword CAESAR, for the final evacuation of Rangoon and the destruction of all the facilities of use to an enemy, was issued at midnight on 6 March. The Governor had already left with the government for Maymyo. Evacuation would take place during the morning of the 7th and the demolitions during the afternoon.

The various demolition tasks had been delegated by Brigadier Leslie to the most suitable authorities still left in Rangoon. The biggest and most important task, to which General Hutton had given his personal attention, was the destruction of the three oil refineries at Seikgyi, Thilawa and Syriam, and the oil stocks in Rangoon. For this, a Shell-Mex Oil Engineer, Mr Leslie Forster, had been flown in. He was an acknowledged expert in this field and had already destroyed the Dutch oil installations at Palembang. He was assisted by Captain Scott RE and twenty Burma Sappers, and protection was provided by a company each

The warehouses ablaze on the waterfront at Rangoon on 7 March 1942.

from the 1st Glosters and the 1st Royal Jats. This protection was deemed necessary as several parties of the BIA had arrived in the Rangoon area by sea from Martaban. One boat, containing a Japanese officer and 35 armed Burmese, had been successfully intercepted by a sloop[5] of the Royal Indian Navy and several other boats had been found abandoned. Fortunately the Japanese battalion group which had set out for Syriam from the Sittang had found innumerable creeks barring their way and did not reach Syriam until the morning of the 9th.

The demolition was technically difficult as the essential features of the refinery had to be destroyed before the ignition of the oil stocks made access impossible. This was successfully done and the final demolitions were fired around 1400 hours. A huge cloud of dense black smoke then rose more than twenty thousand feet into the air and hung over Rangoon for the next few days.

The next biggest task was the destruction, as far as was possible, of the port facilities and this was the responsibility of the Port Commissioners. Rangoon was a large port and a total destruction was impossible. Spread over a wide area, there were many quays and wharves where ships could be unloaded in an emergency. Nevertheless, much could be done. Dredgers and other vessels were sunk alongside the main wharves and jetties. Workshops and cranes were destroyed, and some of the latter toppled into the river. The warehouses full of stores were set on fire and the smoke that arose from them rivalled that of the refineries. Mooring and channel buoys were sunk, as were most, but inevitably not all, of the motor launches in the harbour. What would have been most effective would have been the sinking of one or two large vessels in the narrow river between the

4. When a newly-arrived young 2nd Lieutenant innocently enquired from a corporal with a sense of humour why they had got this coolie task, he was told: "It's General Wavell, sir. He's very angry with us. We've all got VD. Why our officers they pays a hundred chips and even they gets a dose."
5. HMIS *Hindustan*.

port of Rangoon and the sea. This was suggested by Wavell, but the Navy, who were not under his command, did not attempt it, possibly because there was still a hope that Rangoon might be recaptured.

The Post and Telegraph Department successfully destroyed the wireless and telegraph installations and wrecked the telephone exchanges.

The Burma Railways were responsible for destroying the railway facilities of which the most important were any remaining locomotives and the big railway workshop at Insein. The Japanese only captured eight locomotives in Rangoon, all of which had been sabotaged and were unusable. A grave failure, however, was made with the railway workshop which does not seem to have been adequately destroyed. Many machines had been packaged for removal but had not been taken away. The Japanese soon got the workshop going again and staffed by its original work force. With its help they managed to repair some of the damaged locomotives. The workshop was also to prove a great help in the repair of damaged bridges.

Of the demolitions delegated to the Sappers, Lieut-Colonel Wilson,[6] CRE Rangoon, successfully destroyed the power station and waterworks, and the newly-arrived 70 Field Company (who had arrived with 63 Brigade) destroyed the important oxygen and acetylene factory.[7] A party from the Burma Sappers was detailed to demolish the two big bridges over the Pazundaung Creek. These bridges had been prepared for demolition for some time but, for security reasons, it had not been possible to fill the wooden boxes attached to the girders with explosives. The road bridge was successfully blown but on the rail bridge the obsolete detonating fuse malfunctioned. The bridge was only damaged and did not fall. There was no spare explosive and so this very important demolition was a failure. It was a big double-rack bridge on the main line between Rangoon docks and Mandalay. It could not be by-passed and the failure to ensure that it was properly destroyed was a grave error. It only took the Japanese railway engineers a few days to repair it.

Finally, the Rangoon Battalion of the BAF destroyed the antiquated guns guarding the mouth of Rangoon river while the Field Security police and the Rangoon Fire Brigade did their best to destroy any vehicles still remaining in the city before departing in the late afternoon.

Evacuation of the 'Last-Ditchers'

A chartered Danish steamer, the *SS Henrich Jessen*,[8] was moored in the river ten miles downstream from Rangoon and was used for the evacuation of those no longer required in Burma after Rangoon had been abandoned. Tickets had been issued to these people and only those in posession of a ticket were taken on the launches when the first wave left at 8am on the 7th. On completion of their work, the demolition parties from the refineries withdrew to Rangoon and embarked on launches which took them down river to the waiting ship. The escort company of the Glosters at Syriam were allotted vehicles and drove up to Taukkyan to rejoin their battalion which had left Rangoon at 11am and was now in Army reserve. Through an unfortunate error, the escort company of the 1 R Jats, with its two British officers, was ordered to embark on the *'Henrich Jessen'* and so took no further part in the campaign. Up until about midnight there was still a trickle of individuals arriving at the docks to be taken to the ship which finally sailed at 0300 hours on the 8th, reaching Calcutta a few days later without incident.

The main part of the military garrison marched out of Rangoon in the morning and harboured in the big rubber plantations north of Mingaladon airfield and around Taukkyan. They were followed in the afternoon by the remaining units and demolition parties. The Burma Military Police left mostly by train but not before there had been some unseemly scenes at the station as the Field Security police insisted on their relinquishing various looted stores. The last vehicle column left about 1700 and the last train about 1930. This train was to run into trouble as will be described later. There were no civil or military casualties during this last phase of the evacuation and on the whole the evacuation of the capital city had gone remarkably smoothly, an achievement for which General Hutton and his staff deserve much credit.

Now the long retreat began, but, as we shall see, within the next twenty-four hours it very nearly ended.

6. Wilson was recovering from dengue fever but refused to go sick and died later in the campaign.
7. They were advised by Mr Penderell Davies, the Principal of the engineering college at Rangoon University. This was the only plant of its type in Burma, and meant that all these industrial gases, essential for heavy repair work, would have to be imported.
8. Or *'Heinrich Jensen'* in some accounts.

CHAPTER THIRTEEN

The Drama of Taukkyan

General Alexander and Advanced AHQ left Rangoon on the morning of the 7th of March, followed by the remainder of the Rangoon garrison, with the intention of motoring through to Prome. When they reached the road fork at Taukkyan, 21 miles north of Rangoon, where the road to Prome bears left and the road to Pegu goes right, they were informed that the road to Prome was blocked by the Japanese a few miles ahead so they dispersed in the scrub about half a mile north of the fork.

Now one of the most extraordinary events of the whole campaign was to occur. This Japanese road-block had trapped not only AHQ and the Rangoon garrison, but 17 Division and 7th Armoured Brigade as well. Rangoon had been destroyed and evacuated. There were only two roads to the north, to Pegu and to Prome, and these joined at Taukkyan. *55 Division* was on the Pegu one and apparently *33 Division* was across the Prome one. Unless the British could break out of the trap a humiliating disaster loomed ahead.

Now General Hutton, suspicious that the Japanese might move across the Pegu hills towards the Prome road, had been well aware of the potential danger of such a move and this was why he had wished to evacuate Rangoon a few days earlier. He had already sent the 2nd KOYLI (only two companies strong) and a troop of the 2nd R Tanks to Tharrawaddy, 60 miles north of Taukkyan, to patrol the road. On 6 March this group was recalled and, reinforced by a battery of the newly-landed 1st Indian Field Regiment, was made the advanced guard to lead the Rangoon garrison to the north. Its commander was Lieutenant-Colonel Tynte, the new CO of the 2nd KOYLI. At first light on the 7th this force passed up the road without incident, leaving a company at Wanetchaung as a flank guard (see Map 15). It had not, however, been unobserved.

The advanced guard had reached Tharrawaddy when Colonel Tynte heard rumours about a block on the road behind him. He decided to return and, if feasible, mount an attack to clear the obstruction. Ordering his force to move to a rendezvous near Hmawbi, he drove south in a truck with a detachment of the 2nd KOYLI on a reconnaissance to locate the block. Half an hour later the truck returned carrying the mortally wounded Colonel, the rest of the patrol coming in

176

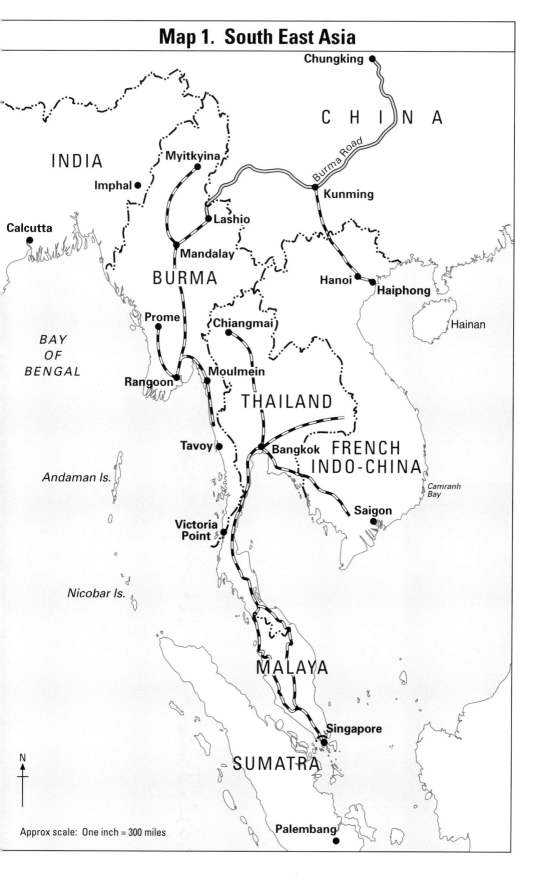

Map 1. South East Asia

Chungking

C H I N A

INDIA

Myitkyina

Imphal

Burma Road

Kunming

Calcutta

Lashio

Mandalay

BURMA

Hanoi

Haiphong

Hainan

Prome

Chiangmai

BAY
OF
BENGAL

Moulmein

Rangoon

THAILAND

Andaman Is.

Tavoy

Bangkok

FRENCH
INDO-CHINA

Camranh
Bay

Saigon

Victoria
Point

Nicobar Is.

MALAYA

N

Singapore

SUMATRA

Approx scale: One inch = 300 miles

Palembang

Map 2. The Initial Attack

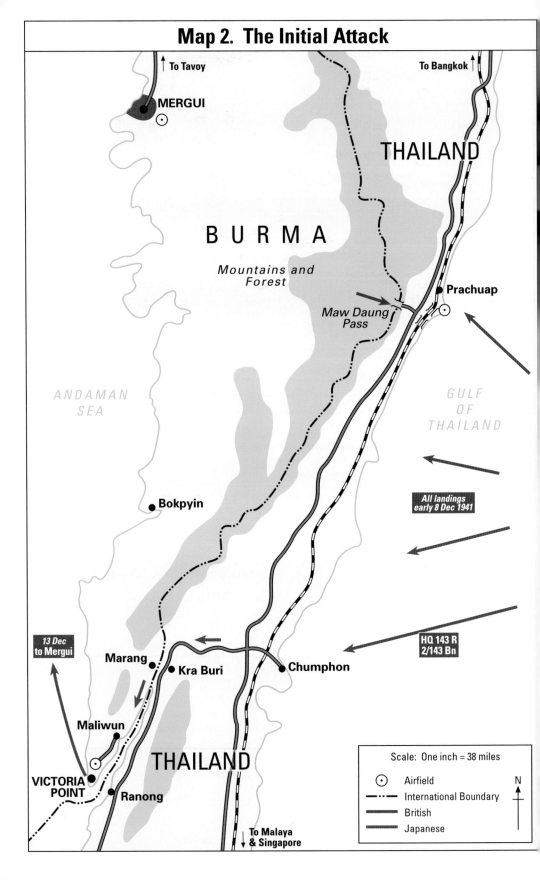

To Tavoy ↑

⊙ **MERGUI**

To Bangkok ↑

THAILAND

B U R M A

Mountains and Forest

Maw Daung Pass

● **Prachuap** ⊙

ANDAMAN SEA

GULF OF THAILAND

● **Bokpyin**

All landings early 8 Dec 1941

13 Dec to Mergui

Marang ● ● **Kra Buri**

● **Chumphon**

HQ 143 R 2/143 Bn

Maliwun ●

⊙

THAILAND

VICTORIA POINT ●

● **Ranong**

To Malaya & Singapore ↓

Scale: One inch = 38 miles

⊙ Airfield

N

–··–··– International Boundary

━━━ British

▓▓▓ Japanese

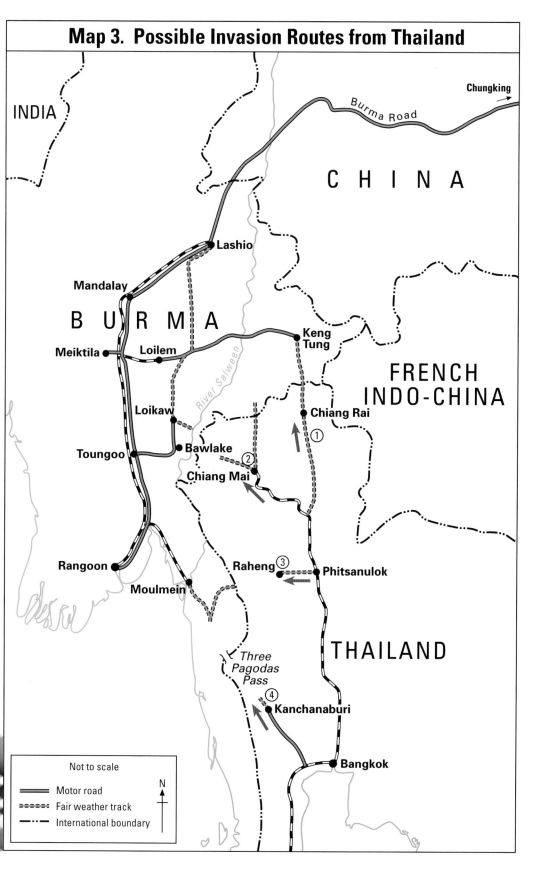

Map 3. Possible Invasion Routes from Thailand

INDIA

Burma Road

Chungking

C H I N A

Lashio

Mandalay

B U R M A

Meiktila

Loilem

Keng Tung

FRENCH INDO-CHINA

Loikaw

River Salween

Chiang Rai

①

Toungoo

Bawlake

②

Chiang Mai

Rangoon

Raheng

③

Phitsanulok

Moulmein

THAILAND

Three Pagodas Pass

④

Kanchanaburi

Bangkok

Not to scale

N

—— Motor road
▪▪▪▪ Fair weather track
–··– International boundary

Map 4. The Japanese Invasion Starts

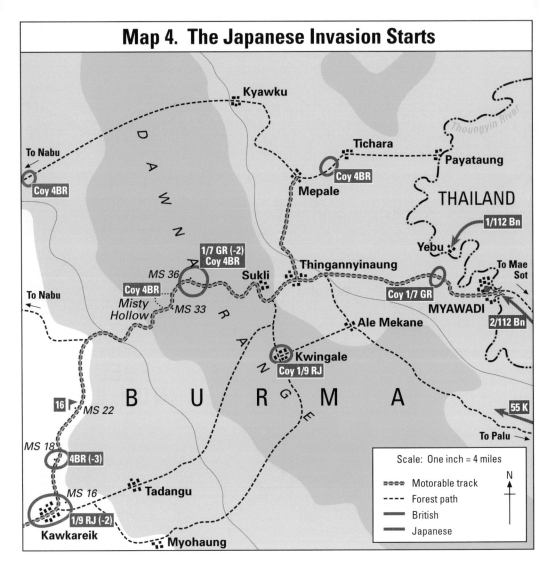

Kyawku

To Nabu

Coy 4BR

Tichara

Payataung

Thoungyin River

Mepale

Coy 4BR

THAILAND

1/112 Bn

Yebu

DAWNA

To Mae Sot

1/7 GR (-2)
Coy 4BR

MS 36

Sukli

Thingannyinaung

Coy 1/7 GR

MYAWADI

Coy 4BR

To Nabu

Misty Hollow

MS 33

RANGE

Ale Mekane

2/112 Bn

Kwingale

Coy 1/9 RJ

B   U   R   G   M   A

16   MS 22

55 K

MS 18

To Palu

4BR (-3)

MS 16

Tadangu

Scale: One inch = 4 miles

N

1/9 RJ (-2)

Motorable track

Forest path

British

Japanese

Kawkareik

Myohaung

Map 5. The Japanese Advance to the Salween

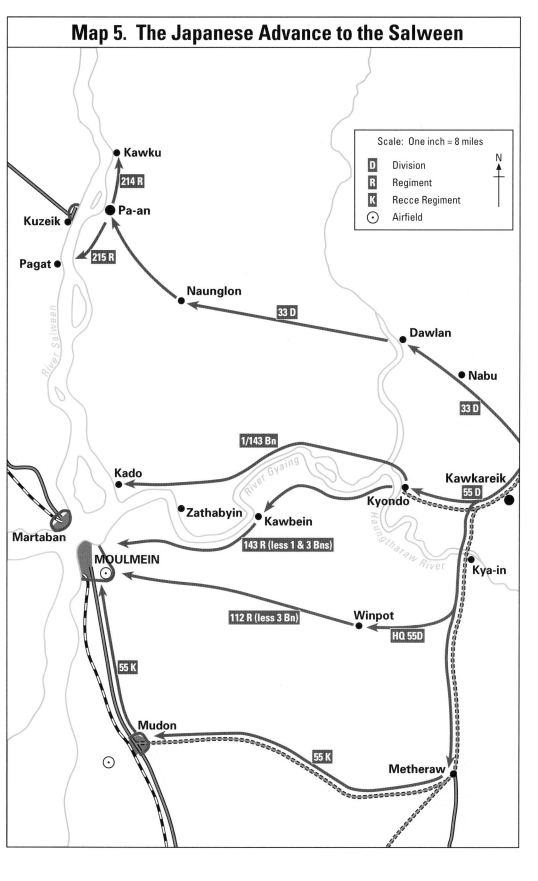

Scale: One inch = 8 miles

D Division
R Regiment
K Recce Regiment
⊙ Airfield

N

Kawku
214 R
Pa-an
Kuzeik
215 R
Pagat
Naunglon
33 D
Dawlan
Nabu
33 D
1/143 Bn
Kado
Kawkareik
55 D
Zathabyin
Kyondo
Kawbein
Martaban
143 R (less 1 & 3 Bns)
MOULMEIN
Kya-in
Winpot
112 R (less 3 Bn)
HQ 55D
55 K
Mudon
Metheraw
55 K

River Salween
River Gyaing
Haungtharaw River

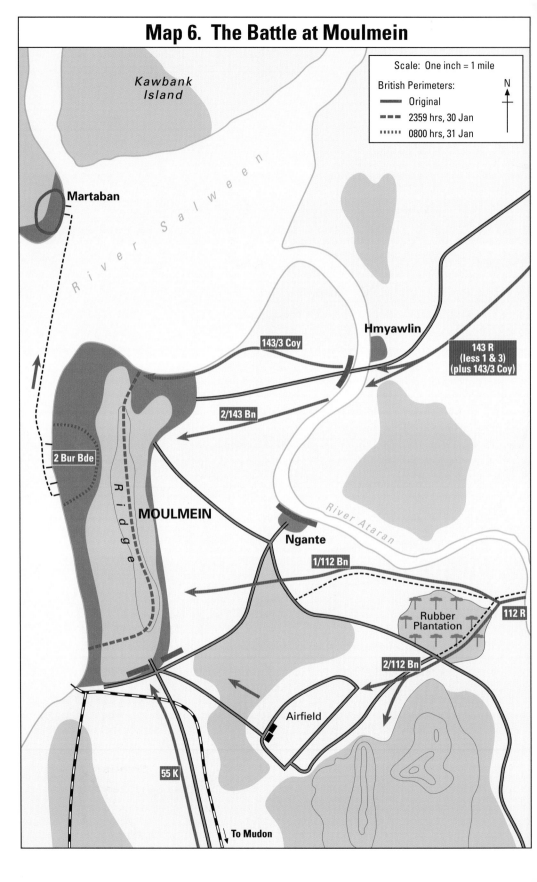

Map 6. The Battle at Moulmein

Scale: One inch = 1 mile

British Perimeters:
——— Original
- - - 2359 hrs, 30 Jan
······ 0800 hrs, 31 Jan

N

Kawbank Island

Martaban

River Salween

Hmyawlin

143/3 Coy

143 R
(less 1 & 3)
(plus 143/3 Coy)

2/143 Bn

2 Bur Bde

R i d g e

MOULMEIN

River Ataran

Ngante

1/112 Bn

Rubber Plantation

112 R

2/112 Bn

Airfield

55 K

To Mudon

Map 7. The Salween Actions

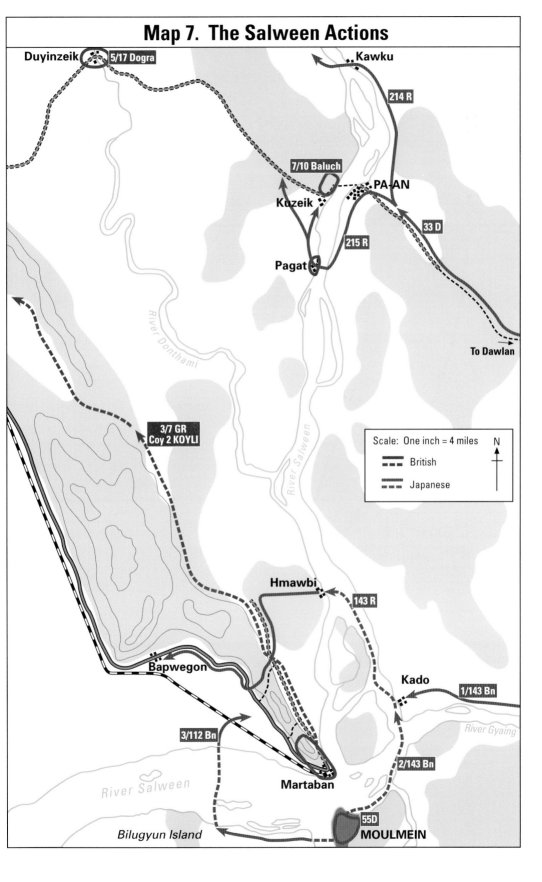

Duyinzeik 5/17 Dogra

Kawku

214 R

7/10 Baluch

PA-AN

Kuzeik

33 D

215 R

Pagat

To Dawlan

River Donthami

River Salween

3/7 GR
Coy 2 KOYLI

Scale: One inch = 4 miles   N

British

Japanese

Hmawbi

143 R

Bapwegon

Kado

1/143 Bn

3/112 Bn

River Gyaing

2/143 Bn

River Salween

Martaban

Bilugyun Island

55 D

MOULMEIN

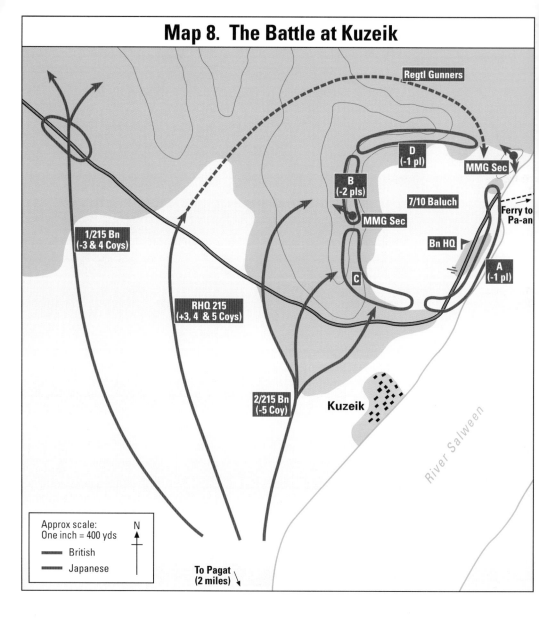

Map 8. The Battle at Kuzeik

Regtl Gunners

D
(-1 pl)

MMG Sec

B
(-2 pls)

7/10 Baluch

MMG Sec

Ferry to
Pa-an

1/215 Bn
(-3 & 4 Coys)

Bn HQ

A
(-1 pl)

C

RHQ 215
(+3, 4 & 5 Coys)

2/215 Bn
(-5 Coy)

Kuzeik

River Salween

Approx scale:
One inch = 400 yds

N

British

Japanese

To Pagat
(2 miles)

Map 9. Withdrawal to the Bilin

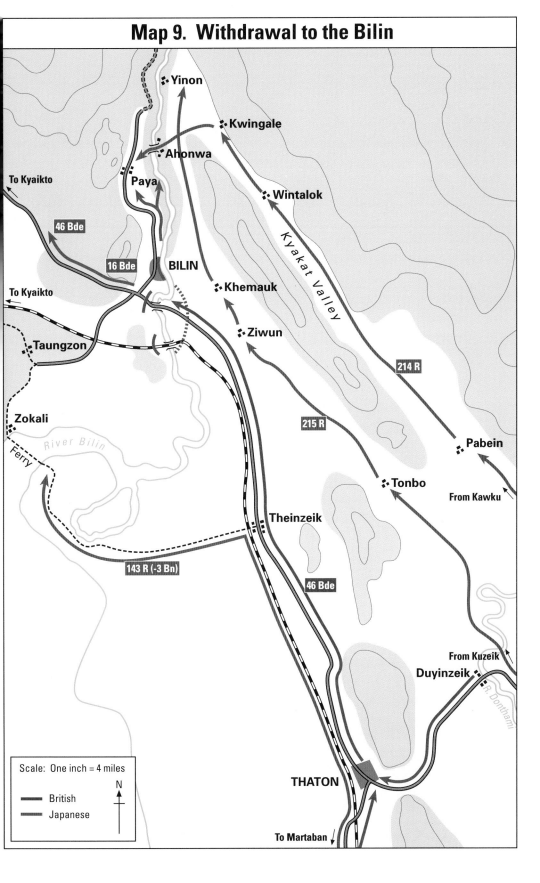

:• Yinon

:• Kwingale

:• Ahonwa

Paya

To Kyaikto

46 Bde

16 Bde

BILIN

To Kyaikto

:• Khemauk

:• Wintalok

Kyakat Valley

:• Ziwun

Taungzon

214 R

Zokali

215 R

River Bilin

Ferry

:• Pabein

:• Tonbo

From Kawku

Theinzeik

143 R (-3 Bn)

46 Bde

From Kuzeik

Duyinzeik :•

R. Donthami

THATON

To Martaban ↓

Scale: One inch = 4 miles

N

British
Japanese

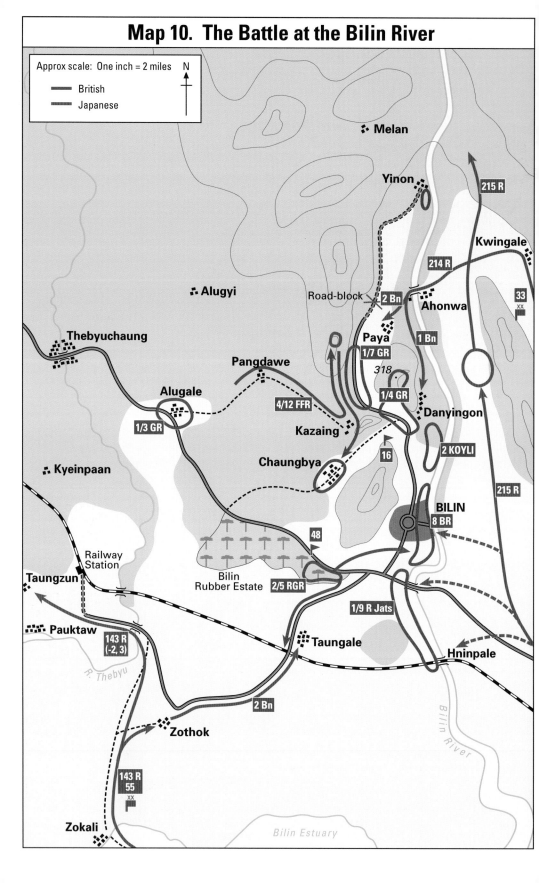

Map 10. The Battle at the Bilin River

Approx scale: One inch = 2 miles

N

British
Japanese

Melan

Yinon

215 R

Kwingale

214 R

Alugyi

Road-block

2 Bn

Ahonwa

33
XX

1 Bn

Paya

1/7 GR

318

Pangdawe

4/12 FFR

1/4 GR

Danyingon

Alugale

1/3 GR

Kazaing

2 KOYLI

Kyeinpaan

Chaungbya

16

215 R

BILIN

8 BR

48

Bilin
Rubber Estate

2/5 RGR

Railway
Station

Taungzun

1/9 R Jats

Pauktaw

143 R
(-2, 3)

Taungale

Hninpale

R. Thebyu

2 Bn

Zothok

143 R
55
XX

Zokali

Bilin Estuary

Bilin River

Map 11. Japanese Routes to the Sittang Bridge

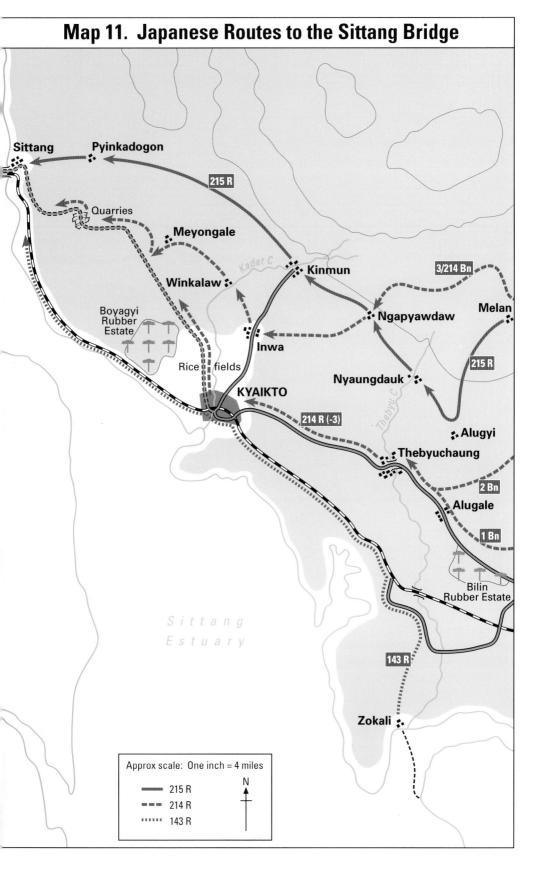

Sittang

Pyinkadogon

215 R

Quarries

Meyongale

Kadat C

Kinmun

3/214 Bn

Winkalaw

Melan

Boyagyi
Rubber
Estate

Ngapyawdaw

Inwa

215 R

Rice fields

Nyaungdauk

Thebyu C

KYAIKTO

214 R (-3)

Alugyi

Thebyuchaung

2 Bn

Alugale

1 Bn

Bilin
Rubber Estate

S i t t a n g
E s t u a r y

143 R

Zokali

Approx scale: One inch = 4 miles

N

——— 215 R

- - - 214 R

······· 143 R

Map 12. The Battle for the Sittang Bridge

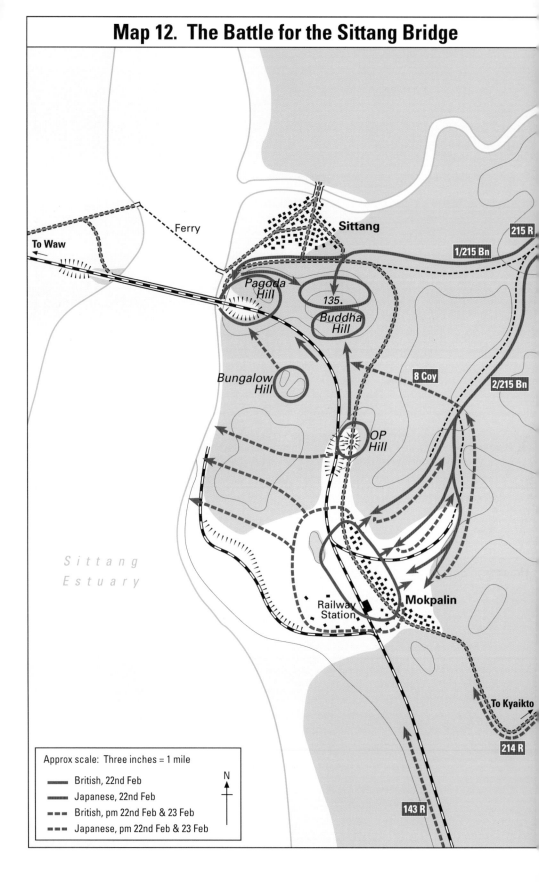

Ferry

To Waw

Sittang

215 R

1/215 Bn

Pagoda Hill

135.

Buddha Hill

8 Coy

2/215 Bn

Bungalow Hill

OP Hill

Sittang Estuary

Mokpalin

Railway Station

To Kyaikto

214 R

143 R

Approx scale: Three inches = 1 mile

N

British, 22nd Feb
Japanese, 22nd Feb
British, pm 22nd Feb & 23 Feb
Japanese, pm 22nd Feb & 23 Feb

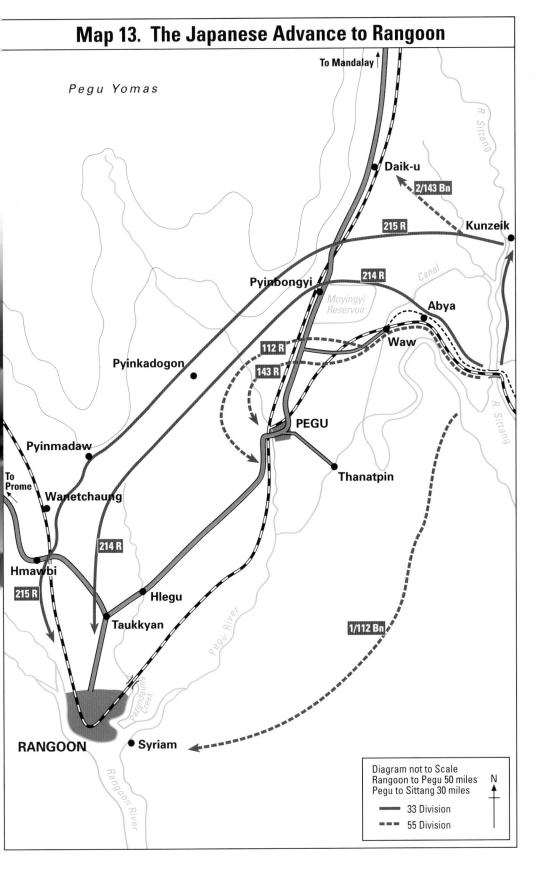

Map 13. The Japanese Advance to Rangoon

Pegu Yomas

To Mandalay

Daik-u

2/143 Bn

215 R

Kunzeik

Pyinbongyi

214 R

Moyingyi Reservoir

Canal

Abya

112 R

Waw

143 R

Pyinkadogon

PEGU

Thanatpin

Pyinmadaw

To Prome

Wanetchaung

214 R

Hmawbi

215 R

Hlegu

Taukkyan

Pegu River

Pazundaung Creek

1/112 Bn

R. Sittang

R. Sittang

RANGOON

Syriam

Rangoon River

Diagram not to Scale
Rangoon to Pegu 50 miles
Pegu to Sittang 30 miles

N

———— 33 Division

- - - - 55 Division

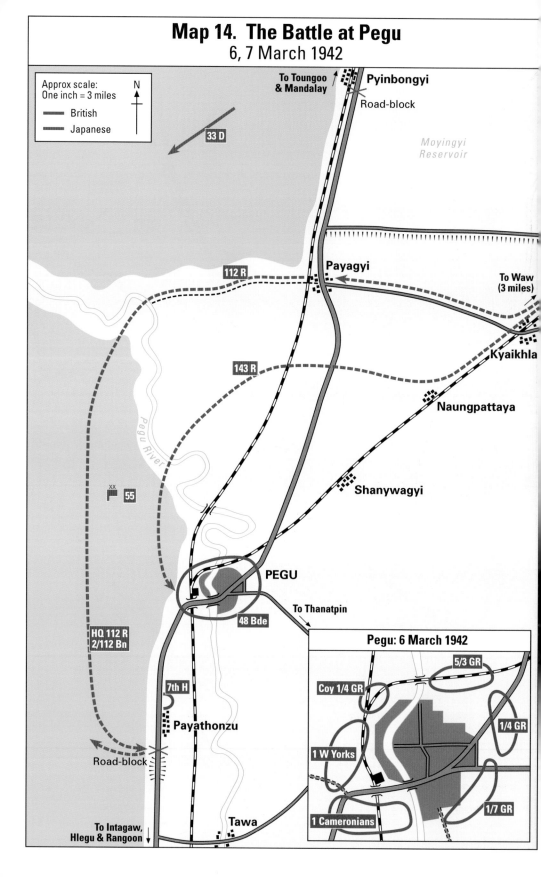

Map 14. The Battle at Pegu
6, 7 March 1942

Approx scale:
One inch = 3 miles

N

British
Japanese

33 D

To Toungoo
& Mandalay

Pyinbongyi

Road-block

Moyingyi
Reservoir

112 R

Payagyi

To Waw
(3 miles)

Kyaikhla

143 R

Naungpattaya

Pegu River

XX 55

Shanywagyi

PEGU

HQ 112 R
2/112 Bn

To Thanatpin

48 Bde

7th H

Payathonzu

Road-block

Tawa

To Intagaw,
Hlegu & Rangoon

Pegu: 6 March 1942

5/3 GR

Coy 1/4 GR

1/4 GR

1 W Yorks

1/7 GR

1 Cameronians

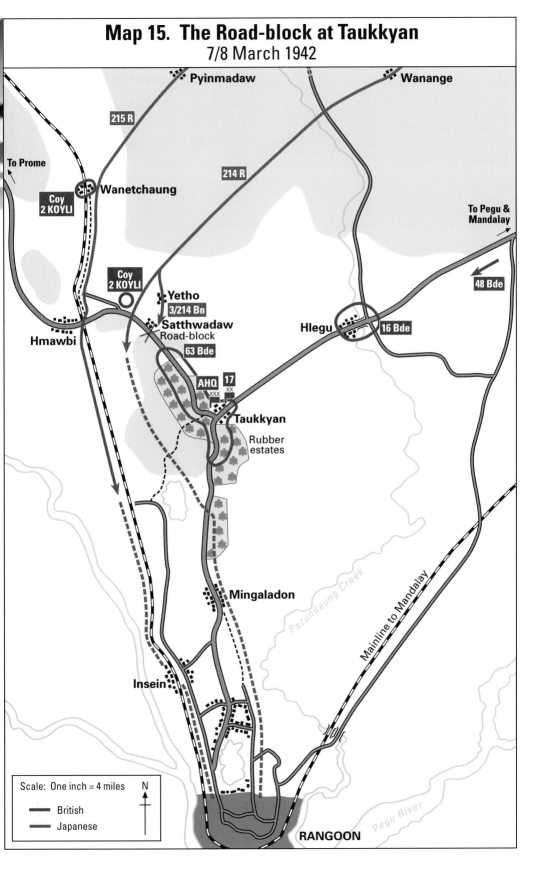

Map 15. The Road-block at Taukkyan
7/8 March 1942

Pyinmadaw

Wanange

215 R

To Prome

214 R

Wanetchaung

Coy
2 KOYLI

To Pegu &
Mandalay

48 Bde

Coy
2 KOYLI

Yetho
3/214 Bn

Satthwadaw
Road-block

Hlegu

16 Bde

Hmawbi

63 Bde

AHQ   17
xxx   xx

Taukkyan

Rubber
estates

Mingaladon

Pazundaung Creek

Mainline to Mandalay

Insein

Pegu River

Scale: One inch = 4 miles   N

—— British

▪▪▪▪ Japanese

RANGOON

Map 16. Detail of the Taukkyan Road-block
7 March 1942

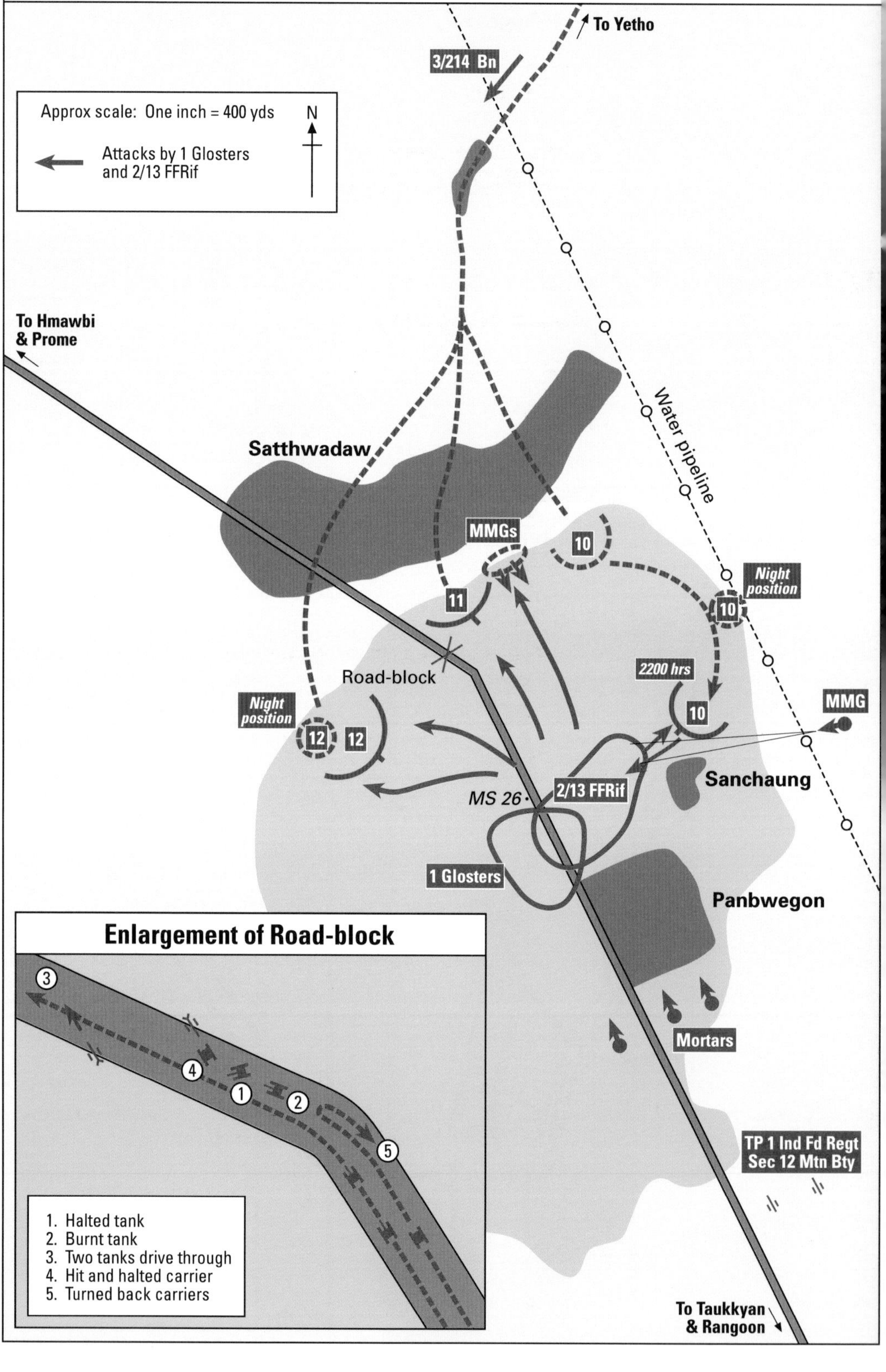

To Yetho

3/214 Bn

Approx scale: One inch = 400 yds

N

Attacks by 1 Glosters
and 2/13 FFRif

To Hmawbi & Prome

Water pipeline

Satthwadaw

MMGs

10

Night position

11

10

Road-block

2200 hrs

Night position

10

MMG

12 12

MS 26

2/13 FFRif

Sanchaung

1 Glosters

Panbwegon

Enlargement of Road-block

③

④ ① ②

⑤

Mortars

TP 1 Ind Fd Regt
Sec 12 Mtn Bty

1. Halted tank
2. Burnt tank
3. Two tanks drive through
4. Hit and halted carrier
5. Turned back carriers

To Taukkyan & Rangoon

about an hour and a half later. They had found the block but lost their colonel. Major Martin of the Gunners now took command of the advance guard. He sent the battery back north to Tharrawaddy and harboured for the night about 150 yards from where a track leading to Wanetchaung crossed the main road. During the night a large force of Japanese was observed passing along the track close to his position.[1] They were clearly too strong to be tackled, so after discussion with the tank troop commander, he withdrew the Infantry under cover of darkness leaving the tanks to move at first light.

On the way north, one company of the 2nd KOYLI, marching up the railway line, unexpectedly encountered a large force of armed Burmese. This was the main force of the BIA, commanded by Colonel Suzuki and with Aung San as his deputy, moving from east to west. Both sides had some men killed before the British continued on their way north.

The Japanese Account of the Taukkyan Road-block

3/214 Battalion, which was leading its regiment, had arrived after a forced march at Yetho village, about two miles east of the Prome road, on the morning of the 6th. It was ordered to lie low and await further orders. Lieutenant Tatumi Shiotubo made a reconnaissance in the evening and on the other side of a big village on the Prome road, Sattwadaw, found an unguarded dump of two hundred 40-gallon drums of petrol.[2] As this was a valuable find, Major Takanobe, the CO of *3 Battalion*, ordered Lieutenant Shiotubo to go off with his platoon at first light on the 7th and guard the area. No sooner had Shiotubo arrived back in the village than "a large column of tanks, armoured cars, guns and trucks fully loaded with soldiers holding rifles and looking out both sides, passed by the village. It was really impressive to see them from so close." This was the British advance guard on its way to Tharrawaddy. Shiotubo had 40 men, two LMGs and four grenade launchers. He now placed his two LMGs covering the road, one facing in each direction, and waited to see who would come next. For some time nothing happened, then a truck came at high speed from the north. It was duly shot up and the soldiers in it jumped out and after some shooting disappeared into the bush to the west. Meanwhile the truck managed to turn and disappeared up the road to the north. This was Colonel Tynte's reconnaissance party. The next arrival, a black saloon car, came from the same direction. When fired on, it stopped just in front of the platoon and several men jumped out and, taking cover under the car, started firing back. They had no chance and all were killed. The Japanese say one was wearing civilian clothes and the others were senior offi-

---

1. This was *215 Regiment*.
2. There was a satellite airstrip close by.

cers. The Japanese pushed the vehicle off the road and concealed it. Then an officer on a motor-cycle came along and he too was shot. There was now a lull until a column was seen approaching from the direction of Rangoon. A runner was sent off to *3/214 Battalion HQ* with the news. Meanwhile British mortars started firing accurately and Lieutenant Shiotubo was wondering whether it wouldn't be wise to "advance back" when the whole of the rest of his battalion appeared, together with the *Regimental Gun Company*.[3]

Major Takanobe quickly chose a site for the road-block just south of the village and about 60 yards north of a bend in the road. To the west of the road was a jungle "impassable even for men"; to the east was a forest with a mixture of tall and short trees. He placed one gun on each side of the road in the shallow ditches, facing in opposite directions, and deployed a company on either flank. Everyone was ordered to dig in.

Now General Iida, who was at Kyaikto, had ordered *33 Division* to pause in its advance on Rangoon until Pegu was captured as he feared a reverse there. It was not until 1100 hours on 7 March, Pegu having been cleared, that he gave the order for the advance to continue.[4] Major Takanobe's battalion had in fact put in this road-block before this order reached *HQ 33 Division*. General Sakurai now altered his plan. His original idea had been for *215 Regiment* to block the road at Wanetchaung and attack the British from the west while *214 Regiment* went for Rangoon. He now switched this round, ordering *214 Regiment* to attack at Taukkyan while *215 Regiment* went to Rangoon west of the railway, avoiding the British if possible.[5] Colonel Sakuma at *HQ 214 Regiment* appears to have regarded Sakurai's order as *post facto* confirmation of what he was already doing and kept his other battalion in reserve, perhaps hoping still to take part in the capture of Rangoon.

The Fighting at the Taukkyan Road-block on 7 March (Maps 15 and 16)

At the road-block, Takanobe and his battalion were now on their own. Sporadic rifle and machine-gun fire had started, and only part of the sandbag protection for the guns had been completed when the first British contact from the south materialised. This was a probe by 'B'Squadron of the 7th Hussars. The Japanese version of this skirmish describes how one tank came cautiously round the bend in the road, sweeping each side with its machine-guns. Their 75mm gun opened fire and, after several misses, hit the front of the tank which immediately caught fire, its ammunition continuing to explode for the next 20 minutes. After a pause, a second tank appeared and was hit and immobilised. A soldier of 'the tank-destroying unit' threw a hand grenade into this tank. The third tank didn't stop and drove at high speed straight through the position; a fourth tank did the same. The 75mm gun facing north failed to hit either of these as, unlike an anti-tank gun, it couldn't traverse quickly enough to hit a fast-moving target.[6]

The strength of the block was not yet realised and Colonel Bagot was ordered to put in an attack at about 1500 hours with the only Infantry available at that moment. His force consisted of a troop of the 2nd R Tanks, one company of the 1st Glosters, and a company of the 7th/10th Baluch Regiment in wheeled carriers. They were supported by a troop of 1 Indian Field Regiment (four guns) and a section of 12 Mountain Battery (two guns). Bagot sent a platoon up each side of the road and, when they were held up, committed the reserve platoon round the west flank. The latter ran into a strong enemy company position and suffered severely. No progress could be made. The Glosters lost three officers and 17 other ranks in this engagement.

63 Brigade, however, had now been recalled from Hlegu and a second and heavier attack was organised under Colonel Edward who was temporarily in command of the brigade. The 1st Glosters were reinforced by the newly-arrived 2nd/13th Frontier Force Rifles (2nd/13th FFRif), less two companies, and supported by a squadron of the 2nd R Tanks. After more artillery bombardment one Frontier Force company tried to work its way round each flank of the block. They met both dense forest and Japanese to the west, and open country covered by MMGs to the east, where they suffered many casualties. So they pulled back and tried again astride the road, assisted by the tanks, but on reaching the block could make no progress. It was now getting dark, so they established a perimeter (they had no digging tools) about 500 yards to the south and east of the block for the night and were joined there by their other two companies. Among those killed on this day was Captain Christison.[7]

The Japanese Version

This is the Japanese version of what happened in these attacks. A wheeled carrier first appeared round the corner. It was hit in the right front wheel and slid down sideways into the ditch a few feet in front of the gun. A hatch opened and an Indian soldier threw a hand grenade at the gunners and "started shooting a pistol bravely." He was killed by a captured LMG which had been allotted to the

3. Each Regiment had a company with two old-pattern 75mm mountain guns.

4. Japanese *Official History*, Vol.5, pp.172-177.

5. *Memoir of 215 Regiment*, p.159 *et al*.

6. There is no record of a British tank being lost on this day so possibly those hit and damaged were recovered.

7. Captain Christison was the only son of Lieutenant-General Sir Philip Christison who, in 1944-45, was to lead XV Corps with outstanding success down the west coast of Burma.

gunners. Two more carriers appeared firing their weapons but were hit and turned back. Tanks and infantry continued the attack supported by heavy shelling. Two Japanese MMGs were in a hollow east of the road to avoid the shelling. "A group of tall British soldiers with an LMG" got within 40 yards before they were noticed. The platoon of the 1st Glosters (for it was they) fired at one MMG section and four Japanese were killed and four wounded. The other MMG then opened fire and the British were driven back with a claimed loss of ten killed. Major Takanobe now took advantage of the lull to set up a barrier on the road with ten petrol drums with their caps off and a petrol-soaked rope dipped into one of them, the other end being led to a foxhole 50 yards away. When the tanks came again two hours later this was ignited and the drums exploded and "the area was flooded with fire." Spectacular though this must have been, there is no evidence that it was particularly successful. More importantly, he briefed *214/10 Company* to prepare for a night attack.

A Desperate Plan

After dark on the 7th it seemed to the British that the block was still solidly held. The mood of the units concentrated round the fork at Taukkyan was sombre. Repeated attacks on the block had been repulsed. It was known that some or all of *33 Division* were ahead[8] and it certainly looked as though Hutton's worst fears were about to be realised. Most of the Army in Burma, its tanks and guns, more than a thousand vehicles and several hundred mules were crammed into the woods and the rubber estates around the Taukkyan fork. General Cowan's 17 Division was fighting on two fronts. There was no news of HQ 48 Brigade and the three battalions still with them who, when last heard of, were on the other side of the road-block at Payathonzu. 16 Brigade was in Hlegu, still guarding against a follow-up by *55 Division* down the Pegu road. The only strike force left was the newly arrived 63 Brigade which had just lost all its senior commanders.

That evening Colonels Edward and Bagot and Major Elsmie, who was in temporary command of the 2nd/13th FFRif, were summoned to a meeting at Advanced AHQ which was close to the road about half a mile north of the road fork at Taukkyan. Here a plan was made by General Alexander for an all-out attack the next day. 17 Division was to attack the block at dawn on the 8th, so General Cowan ordered 63 Brigade, supported by 7 Armoured Brigade and all the available artillery, to prepare for this attack. The 1st/10th Gurkhas would attack on the left of the road and the 1st/11th Sikhs on the right. They were to move that night to their assembly positions respectively 1500 yards south-west and south-east of the block. The plan was for a heavy bombardment to start at 0845 on the 8th while the Infantry closed on the block; there would then be a concerted attack with the tanks and part of the 2nd/13th FFRif assaulting up the road.

After this meeting an extraordinary order, issued by General Alexander himself,[9] was circulated to all units. It said that "the attack on the road-block today has failed. Another attack will be made tomorrow morning. If that fails units are to split up into small parties of twelve men who are to make their own way to India independently."[10] Clearly this was influenced by the determination to avoid a mass surrender and issued in the belief that the whole of *33 Division* would attempt to block any move to the north. But General Alexander had been less than three days in Burma and did not realise that his plan was a recipe for disaster. India was 700 miles away somewhere to the north, the BIA would find many supporters among the dacoits and politically unruly elements of central Burma. Mapless and leaderless, hungry and thirsty, small units of a defeated army would have been very lucky if they had survived to reach India.

The Wheel of Fortune Turns

Elsmie, who had left Captain Rahim Khan in temporary command, was delayed at AHQ and in the dark was unable to get back to his battalion that night. About 10 pm the right hand company of the 2nd/13th FFRif near Sanchaung village was heavily attacked by *214/10 Company*, who succeeded in penetrating the perimeter. A Japanese officer even reached Battalion HQ and attacked the chief clerk before being shot dead by Rahim Khan.[11] It was a savage close-quarter fight in the dark and the 2nd/13th FFRif lost four officers killed[12] and three wounded, while 17 soldiers were killed and 51 wounded. According to the Japanese, "both soldiers were intermingled, a lot of hand grenades exploded and automatics were fired recklessly. *214/10 Company* was forced to pull back due to high casualties." The 2nd/13th FFRif held their position and the Japanese left their dead behind, a most unusual occurrence. It was a very good effort by a 'green' battalion in meeting their first night attack, and this sharp rebuff was to prove the final straw for the enemy.

3/214 Battalion was now completely exhausted and their casualties were well over a hundred with a high proportion of killed. *215 Regiment* and the remainder of *214 Regiment* having crossed the Prome road during the night, Major Takanobe, who was himself wounded, judged his task completed. He had been

8. *215 Regiment* had spent the day of the 7th resting in the woods around Pyinmadaw village. After dark they started to march as fast as they could for Rangoon, crossing the Prome road near Hmawbi. (From the account of Mr Tokutaro Mizushima.)
9. *Hutton Papers*, Personal Record, p.65.
10. The author was one of the recipients of this message.
11. According to the chief clerk his greatest fear was being shot by Captain Rahim Khan, who only hit the Japanese with the sixth shot from his revolver.
12. One of those killed was 2nd Lieutenant Khattack, heir to the Nawab of Teri.

authorised by Colonel Sakuma to withdraw when appropriate and so, much to the relief of his company commanders, he pulled back his battered battalion to Yetho in the early hours of the morning.[13] *1/214 Battalion* (less *3 Company*) and two companies of *3/33 Mountain Artillery Battalion* had halted their advance in case it should be necessary to go to the assistance of *3/214 Battalion*. There was a fear that if the British were to attack *3/214 Battalion* in strength, it might be annihilated. As the British made no attempt to do so, however, *1/214 Battalion* marched on down to Mingaladon later in the morning.

The Attack on the 8th of March

In three months' time 63 Brigade would be veterans, but at this moment the majority of its officers were very inexperienced and, of course, three-quarters of the soldiers were scarcely more than raw recruits. The 1st/10th Gurkhas, trying to march up to their assembly position in the dark, got dreadfully lost.[14] At first all went well. They marched west along a track to the railway and then moved north along it. At one point, hearing the sounds of movement about 200 yards away, they sent a patrol to investigate. The patrol reported horses and carts moving south towards Rangoon and they were assumed to be Burmese villagers going to market. Later they were to realise that it was part of *215 Regiment* advancing on Rangoon. Having reached a position opposite the block, the 1st/10th Gurkhas then turned west and tried to make their way through the dense forest between the railway and the road. This was the jungle which Japanese accounts were to describe as impassable. They got split up into several groups. Eventually realising that they were too late for the battle and completely cut off, one party returned to the railway and made its way north, but about half the battalion aimed west and after much difficulty reached the Irrawaddy at Yandoon. Here they marched north until picked up by boats opposite Henzada. The battalion was finally re-assembled at Okpo in mid-March.

The 1st/11th Sikhs got into equal trouble. They reached their assembly position correctly, but at 0800 hours, seeing two Japanese horsemen crossing their front, unwisely opened fire on them (unsuccessfully), thus giving away their position. The horsemen were in fact scouts from *HQ 214 Regiment* sent to find out what was going on in the road-block. About half an hour later, 18 Japanese planes appeared and the Sikhs, who were not dug in, were shortly afterwards heavily bombed and machine-gunned and some young soldiers fled.[15] The tanks and guns were also bombed and one tank, a petrol bowser, an ammunition truck and a big Scammel lorry were destroyed. Although practically all the AA artillery in Burma was in the block and, to the great alarm of the mules, all of it opened up, only one plane was hit. In the midst of this hubbub one company of the Sikhs and a troop

A Stuart tank and its crew beside the Rangoon-Prome road, near Taukkyan. Tank Museum.

of the 7th Hussars reached their objective and found that the block had been abandoned.

The Withdrawal to the North

The Sikhs, having rallied most of their men, were now ordered north to Hmawbi with a squadron of tanks to cover the track which led in from Wanetchaung, while AHQ, the Rangoon garrison and 17 Division headed for Tharrawaddy astride the main road. At Wanetchaung the Sikhs had a successful small action against a rear party of *33 Division* and captured some codes and documents. Another incident had taken place in this area the previous evening (7th) when *1 Company* of *33 Divisional Engineers* had ambushed the last train out of Rangoon. Supported by a platoon of infantry they had used half their explosive in an attempt to demolish the rail bridge just north of Wanetchaung.[16] The bridge, 45 feet long, consisted of two heavy plate girders and they had only enough explosive to attack one. This girder was not completely cut and the bridge did not fall. Soon a train was heard. It stopped at Wanetchaung station and then moved slowly on to the bridge. The train had two locomotives in front. The

13. *Memoir of 214 Regiment*, p.145.

14. The 1st/10th Gurkhas were particularly weak as they had been milked of many of their best NCOs and men to form a Gurkha parachute battalion.

15. The Japanese had a standard method of indicating enemy positions to their air force by means of strips of white cloth laid on the ground.

16. They were keeping the other half to demolish the water pipeline in case the British decided to make a stand in Rangoon. This was a lesson from Singapore. *Memoir of 33 Div Engineers.*

first passed over the bridge but the second tilted sideways and fell into the river. This train, the last to leave Rangoon, contained railway personnel and a company of armed Burma Military Police. The latter dismounted and drove the Japanese off before withdrawing to the main Prome road. The Japanese had eight men killed in this skirmish and when they returned at dawn found the train abandoned.

While the preparations for the attack on the road-block were proceeding, plans had been prepared for a rapid move to Tharrawaddy. Directly it was known that the road was clear, the congestion of transport and troops around the Taukkyan fork was unravelled in a tightly-controlled order, and the force made its way north. The road was picqueted and patrolled by the 7th Armoured Brigade. News at last being received that 48 Brigade and its three battalions had reached Hlegu, vehicles were provided for them and they joined the tail of the column without incident, although the Japanese were already in Mingaladon and Rangoon. The retreating troops marched initially across country and then, as the congestion cleared, on either side of the road with the vehicles passing down the centre. The first stop was around Taikkyi, 28 miles. It was very hot and this was a formidable march for troops already tired, so vehicles, having reached their harbour areas for the night, unloaded their stores and returned to pick up units, thus shortening the march. The next day's march was even further, 35 miles, and the system was repeated, although some help was given by a train sent down from Letpadan.

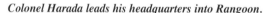

Colonel Harada leads his headquarters into Rangoon.

Japanese troops enter Rangoon past the Shwe Dagon pagoda. The leading soldier carries a white bag round his neck containing pieces of bone from those soldiers who have been killed, so that their spirits can share in the victory. IWM.

Movement on the road was continuous, units fitting in rest where they could. On the 10th, the last troops reached the Tharrawaddy area and it was possible to pause and re-organise. The Japanese did not follow up and it was a clean break.

Rangoon Falls

Wavell's gamble to wait for the arrival of 63 Brigade had succeeded, although Hutton can be excused for judging the delay too great a risk. All would still have been well but for the final 36-hour delay caused by the change of Army Commander. This was a very unwise move at such a moment and nearly led to a major military and political disaster.

On the Japanese side, Generals Iida and Sakurai had won a notable victory, but if Sakurai had continued to block the road he might have both destroyed the British and captured Rangoon. However, Iida had given the capture of Rangoon as the primary aim and destruction of the British forces as a subsidiary one. He was well aware that Rangoon was the key to Burma and he did not know what reinforcements might be about to arrive. Japanese ammunition was almost exhausted and the British with their tanks might yet inflict a severe reverse if cornered. Maintenance of the aim is a fundamental military principle and it seemed wisest to stick to the primary aim. Who will say he was wrong?[17]

During the night of the 7th/8th, *215 Regiment* and *214/3 Company* marched south towards Rangoon. *215 Regiment*, which had come down through the woods on the west of the railway, were the first to reach the city and at 10am on the 8th raised the Japanese flag over the Governor's Residence. *1/214 Battalion* marched down via Mingaladon during the morning and made its way to the docks where it was met by a party of Japanese Marines coming up the river in a Japanese naval vessel. Rangoon had fallen, and with it Burma.

---

17. After the war General Sakurai was to say in an interview with British commanders that "the road-block ... was removed prematurely and in error." However, he was then, of course, speaking with hindsight. *Burma Command Intelligence Summary No.7.*

PART TWO

The Long Retreat

Chapters 14 - 26, Maps 17- 32

CHAPTER FOURTEEN

The Chinese Enter the Struggle

The *Imperial General Headquarters* in Tokyo had, on 22 January, only autho-rised[1] *HQ Southern Area* to capture the essential parts of Burma, that is Tenasserim, with its threat to the forces invading Malaya, and Rangoon, the ter-minus of the Burma Road.and the key to the supply and reinforcement of any army in Burma. Orders about any further advance would be issued later.

There were good reasons for this. It was anticipated that considerable Chinese forces would come into Burma, and another two divisions would be needed to deal with them. For this task *18 Division* in Malaya and the reserve *56 Division* in Japan had been earmarked. If resistance increased at Singapore it might not be possible to transfer to Burma either *18 Division* or, indeed, *56 Division*. There was a shipping problem, too. Until Sumatra and Java had been captured, there would be no ships available for transport and heavy shipping losses in Indonesia would affect the plan for Burma. On a higher level, the outcome of Gemany's invasion of Russia was still uncertain and an increased threat on the Japanese north-west frontier might affect the southern operations.

The campaign in Malaya and Java proved successful, however, and on 4 March *Imperial GHQ* issued the order[2] for Mandalay to be captured and the whole of Burma to be occupied. In this order, the primary aim was given as the capture of Mandalay and the destruction of the Chinese forces, with the capture of the Yenangyaung oilfield being a secondary aim[3]. Accordingly, *HQ Southern Area* gave the order to advance north on 7 March and *15 Army* issued its opera-tion and administrative orders on the 15th. The aim was to trap and destroy the allied forces in the plain south of Mandalay and then to drive the remnants out of Burma. But it was appreciated that unless the British and Chinese were defeated while they were separated by the jungle-covered hills of the Pegu Yomas, which reach from Pegu to Meiktila, they might, when combined and supported by the effective British armour, prove a tough proposition. It was therefore particularly important to destroy the British armour south of Yenangyaung. Since the opera-tions which took place on the two routes to Mandalay were quite separate, we will first consider that on the eastern route, the main road and railway up the Sittang valley through Toungoo.

The Japanese Advance on Toungoo

While *33 Division* was establishing law and order in Rangoon and reorganising after its long march, *55 Division* was preparing for its advance up the main
Rangoon-Mandalay road towards Toungoo. The road-block which *2/143
Battalion Group* had put in at Daik-u, to cover from the north *33 Division's* crossing of the Mandalay road, was still in position.[4] Although specific orders had not
yet been received, General Iida was aware that a further advance had been
approved and, on 10 March, ordered *55 Division* to start moving towards the
north. He was anxious to capture the airfields at Toungoo[5] to cover a further
advance which would be beyond the effective range of fighters currently based
on airfields at Moulmein and Mudon. On 13 March, General Takeuchi held a
commanders' conference at Daik-u and outlined future moves. The aim was to
capture Toungoo, about 85 miles to the north.

So far the only formation of 1 Burdiv which had been in action was 2 Bur
Brigade, very briefly, at Moulmein. General Bruce Scott had had the task of
guarding the approaches from Thailand through the Shan states. Although
General Hutton had correctly appreciated that the main thrust would come in the
south, there was no knowing whether a second thrust would not be made along
the two roads which led into Burma from north Thailand. Bruce Scott's headquarters had been at Taunggyi where he was remote from the fighting in the
south.[6] Now, however, two Chinese 'armies',[7] were moving down the Burma
road. The Sixth Chinese Army (6 Chinese A/Division) was moving into the Shan
states and the Fifth Chinese Army (5 Chinese A/Division) was on its way to take
over from the British at Toungoo in the Sittang valley.[8] Bruce Scott was given
the task of covering the Chinese concentration at Toungoo so on 4 March he
moved his headquarters into that town.

1 Burdiv had three brigades, 1 Bur Brigade, 2 Bur Brigade and 13 Indian
Brigade (13 Brigade). There had been many desertions among the Burmese sol-
diers, mainly inspired by fears for the safety of their families, and the two
Burmese brigades were much under strength. Most of the riflemen in the

1. *IGH*, Order No.590.
2. *IGH*, Order No.603.
3. Official History, *Imperial General Headquarters, Army*, Vol.3, p.436.
4. This group consisted of *55 Division's Reconnaissance Regiment, 2/143 Battalion* and *1 Mountain
Gun Company.*
5. This was the AVG's main base in Burma.
6. General Bruce Scott did not hear of the Sittang disaster on 23 February until 1 March. Lunt.
7.Chinese 'armies' were equivalent to British divisions, and Chinese 'divisions' to British brigades.
They are referred to in this narrative as a/divisions and d/brigades. See Appendix 5.
8. These two 'armies' were said to have been trained by the Germans and to be the best that the
Chinese had.

Burmese units had lived all their lives among forested hills and they were fine woodsmen, with skills not unlike those of the North American Indians in the 19th century. Their talent for warfare lay in guerrilla actions, in which they were later to prove very useful. But they were not a success in set-piece fighting and their unsteadiness was a danger to others. Hence 1 Burdiv had been reorganised and each brigade now had one Indian and two Burmese battalions.

2 Bur Brigade was the leading brigade. Its HQ was at Nyaunglebin about 60 miles north of Pegu. The Japanese advance guard, which was from the units which had manned the block at Daik-u, had reached Pyuntaza, about eight miles to the south, and it was decided to attack them on 11 March. Accordingly, 1 Bur Brigade, supported by 2 Mountain Battery, and with the 2nd/7th Rajputs in the lead, attacked and seized the town against light opposition. However, they came up against a much stronger position about a mile to the south against which they could make no progress. A strong Japanese counter-attack over-ran the leading company of the Rajputs, the company commander, his VCO and the Gunner FOO being killed. The 5th Burif were also heavily attacked, so the force withdrew to a position about a mile north of Pyuntaza, having lost 25 killed and 79 missing. 2 Bur Brigade was more successful. Their task was to protect 1 Bur Brigade's flank by driving the enemy out of two large villages about eight miles away to the east and astride the Sittang. With the aid of the Malerkotla Sappers, the 5th/1st Punjabis crossed the river into a bridgehead established by 7 Burif. The Punjabis then captured Shwegyin which was held by the BIA, inflicting many casualties. Punjabi losses were four killed and 15 wounded. The 7th Burif then occupied the neighbouring village of Madauk. Later in the day both brigades were ordered to withdraw through a covering position held by 13 Brigade at Kyauktaga. With only minor incidents, 1 Burdiv then withdrew through the Chinese outpost line at Pyu, about 30 miles south of Toungoo, and entrained for Taungdwingyi. They were now to join up with 17 Division to form the newly-organised 1 Burcorps. The Chinese took over the defence of this main axis to Mandalay with Toungoo as their first strongpoint.

The Battle of Toungoo

Toungoo was to be held by General Tai's 200th D/Brigade. General Tai was an experienced and resolute commander and his d/brigade was one of the best in Chiang's army. Toungoo, astride the main road and railway, covering one of the two main routes into the Shan states and within artillery range of two vital airfields, was a town that the Japanese could not ignore. General Tai was ordered to hold it, and hold it he would. He created an all-round defensive position, pulling down and burning houses ruthlessly wherever it was necessary to improve fields

Chinese formations had few vehicles.
Tank Museum.

of fire. He had bunkers constructed and a circular communication trench dug so that all the positions were linked up.

Meanwhile, he sent a force south to delay the Japanese. Their first covering position was at Nyaungchidauk, about 20 miles south of Toungoo. It was attacked by *143 Regiment* on the night of 20/21 March and captured after a stiff fight. The Chinese then fell back on their main covering position at Oktwin and this was attacked by *112 Regiment* on 22 March. The Chinese were well dug in and supported by mortars, and the position was not captured until 2100 hours on the 24th. Casualties in *112 Regiment* are recorded as being "high". While this battle was going on, *143 Regiment*, by-passing to the west both Oktwin and Toungoo, captured the two airfields to the north of the latter on the afternoon and evening of the 24th.

55 Division was not a strong division, it still only had two regiments, but it had been brought up to strength, was now supported by powerful artillery, and ammunition no longer had to be so strictly rationed. It was gaining experience, and three weak commanders had been replaced. On the 26th, *55 Division* attacked Toungoo. *112 Regiment* assaulted and penetrated the south-west corner before being held up, while *143 Regiment's* attack on the north-west perimeter was beaten off. Realising that Toungoo was not going to be easily captured, General Takeuchi sent *2/143 Battalion* to block the road ten miles to the north. This battalion managed to prevent, with some difficulty, attempts to reinforce the beleaguered garrison.

While this battle was in progress, *56 Division* landed in Rangoon on the 26th. Like *55 Division* it had only recently been mobilised and was on a lower establishment than the pre-war divisions. Like *18 Division* it was raised from the north-west district of Kyushu, the southernmost of the four main Japanese islands. It had been held in reserve in Japan in case reinforcement had been needed in Malaya. Wasting no time, its motorised *Reconnaissance Regiment* drove up towards Toungoo on the 27th. This unit had been reinforced to make a powerful battalion group with six armoured cars, a company of mountain guns, an MMG company, an engineer platoon and a truck company. Leaving their trucks behind, they crossed at Wagyi to the east bank of the Sittang that night. On the 28th they attacked the Chinese flank guard east of the river and by mid-day on the 29th had overrun it. They then seized the vital bridge over the Sittang before it could be destroyed and at 7am on the 30th attacked Toungoo from the east.

Until this day, the Chinese had been holding out stubbornly in Toungoo. On the 27th they counter-attacked *112 Regiment* and regained some of the positions lost. On the 28th, the Japanese planned an attack supported by bombing and the newly-arrived 150mm medium guns. Due to mist at Mudon airfield, the six bombers did not arrive until 1500 hours and, in spite of the heavy guns, the attack failed. However, on the 30th, the Japanese engineers succeeded in blasting a gap in the thick brick wall which had been holding up the attackers from the south, and at the same time the reconnaissance regiment broke in from the east. The position could no longer be defended and the Chinese withdrew behind a stubborn rearguard.

General Tai's 200 Chinese D/Brigade had fought very well and their fighting spirit is highly commended in Japanese accounts of the battle. However, they had suffered heavy casualties, lost all their heavy equipment, and the failure to destroy the Sittang bridge at Toungoo,[9] which had been fully prepared for demolition by 1 Burdiv's Sappers, was to cost them dearly. General Iida's plan was for *56 Division* to cross here into the Shan States. The Japanese now had plenty of vehicles and there was a useful network of roads to the east of the Sittang. They intended to make good use of them. *Not* demolishing this bridge over the Sittang was to prove almost as great a disaster for the Chinese as demolishing the other one had been for the British.

Reorganization of the Allied High Command

In March, two new Allied commanders were brought into Burma. The first was the American Lieutenant-General Joseph W. Stilwell, aged 58. He was to remain in the Burma theatre for another three years and exert a deep influence on the course of the Burma War. His original posting was as Chief of Staff to the Generalissimo and commander of all US Army forces in the China-Burma-India theatre. He arrived in Chungking on 4 March, the day before Alexander reached Rangoon. As the Chinese forces entered Burma there was some confusion, largely caused by contradictory statements from the Generalissimo, about who was commanding whom. By 24 March this had been amicably settled. Alexander, with the temporary rank of General, would command all the Allied forces in

Above: General Joseph W. Stilwell commanded the Chinese Expeditionary Force in Burma. IWM. *Right: Generals Wavell and Alexander visit a Chinese headquarters.* IWM.

Burma with Stilwell responsible to him and commanding, so he believed, all the Chinese forces. Alexander in his turn was responsible to Wavell.

Stilwell was to become a controversial character. No-one could doubt his personal toughness and courage, or his ability as a fighting soldier, but he had a very critical nature which was applied indiscriminately to his superiors, his staff, his troops and, of course, his allies. However, in this campaign he was to prove a positive and co-operative commander and as effective as the lack of support from Chiang Kai-shek permitted.

It had long been apparent that a corps commander was required for the British forces to deal with the day-to-day conduct of operations, thus allowing the army commander to look further ahead and deal with the many political and civilian problems. Indeed, had one been provided when General Hutton first requested it, the Sittang disaster might well have been avoided. Wavell now saw that the post was essential and picked the best man he could find to fill it, no doubt making sure that he was absolutely fit. On 16 March the newly-promoted Lieutenant-General W.J. Slim arrived in Burma, having been plucked three days before from his command of 10th Indian Division in Iraq. He was ordered to form a Corps HQ as best he could and take command of 17 Division, 1 Burdiv and 7 Armoured Brigade.

Slim was 50 years old with an outstanding record and at the peak of his powers. From an early age he had shown an interest in military affairs and a talent

9. There were only two road bridges over the Sittang, this one at Toungoo and the converted rail-bridge over the estuary at Mokpalin.

Lieutenant-General 'Bill' Slim, Commander of 1 Burcorps.

for writing and speaking. After a distinguished career in the Royal Warwickshire Regiment in World War I, he had switched to the 6th Gurkhas in the Indian Army.[10] Between the wars, his reputation among his contempories continued to grow. He passed out top from the Quetta Staff College and was later selected as the sole Indian Army instructor at the Camberley Staff College.[11] A robust, intelligent man with a strong character and a friendly personality, he was a natural commander. More significantly, he was also a thinking man with an original and receptive mind. Earlier in World War II he had commanded a brigade in action in Eritrea and a division in minor operations in Iraq, Syria and Iran. He was, however, still unknown to the British public. Now his hour of destiny had come. He was not to let the opportunity pass.

Reorganization of 17 Division

The Japanese halted for a week while they sorted out Rangoon, and 17 Division, who were holding a position at Tharrawaddy, took advantage of this lull to reorganize. The 1st W Yorks were motorised and were put under command of 7th Armoured Brigade as their supporting infantry battalion. The 1st Glosters, who had become motorised by picking up many trucks during their spell in Rangoon, were made the divisional reconnaissance battalion. The 2nd KOYLI was sent back to guard the vital oilfields at Yenangyaung, now the only source of petrol.[12] A Royal Marine group of about company strength had been provided by the Royal Navy to help in the defence of Rangoon. When Rangoon was abandoned, they had established a patrol in motor launches on the Irrawaddy and now came under command of 17 Division.

There were also some significant changes in command. Brigadier A.E. Barlow, who had just finished three years in command of a Garhwali battalion in 1 Burdiv, took over command of 63 Brigade to fill the vacancy caused by the Pegu ambush. Brigadier Hugh-Jones of 48 Brigade fell sick with dysentery and was evacuated, his place being taken by Brigadier Ronnie Cameron, the doughty CO of the 2nd/5th R Gurkhas. Cameron was a tall, wiry, hard, tough bachelor and a man of high physical and moral courage. A red face, a sharp temper and a fondness for whisky concealed a naturally sympathetic nature. Essentially a regimental officer, he had an acute understanding of the capabilities of his soldiers and pushed them (and his senior officers) to the limit but never beyond. He was to command 48 Brigade with great distinction for the next two and a half years.

Many adjustments were required in Infantry battalions to deal with reduced strengths and with officer casualties. The latter had not been light. From the sixteen British, Indian and Gurkha battalions which had come under command of 17 Division since the start of operations, eight commanding officers had been killed, five more had been wounded and one had been taken prisoner.

Denial

During this period the divisional Sappers discarded their non-essential equipment and, with the help of some liberated vehicles, also became motorised on a very light scale. As became routine during the withdrawal, they assisted with defences and took over the running of the electrical and water supplies which in Burma were individual to each town. These installations were duly demolished on withdrawal, together with the railway station and any large rice-mills or sawmills. More importantly, between the 9th and 14th of March they also demolished some bridges of tactical and strategic importance. 70 Field Company blew a railway bridge south of Taikkyi on the 9th, and the substantial road and rail bridges south of Okkan on the 10th March, followed by the big rail bridge at Thonze, and an even bigger one at Kamonzeik on the branch line to Henzada, on the 13th.

Meanwhile 60 Field Company carried out an adventurous exploit on the west bank of the Irrawaddy. Henzada on the west bank was important, as it was the largest of the two river ports connected by rail with Bassein. Bassein was a small port in the Irrawaddy delta where coastal steamers could berth and through which all the coal for the Burma railways had been imported from India. The civil administration there had decamped, the BIA had taken over the town and there were rumours of Japanese having landed as well.[13] So two demolition parties from 60 Field Company, escorted by a company of the 4th/12th FFR and some Burma Military Police, were dispatched to demolish two west bank rail bridges, one north and one south of Henzada. They went by train to Tharrawaw and, by a chance meeting with two police launches, crossed the river to Henzada. The District Commissioner there, still at his post, helpfully provided a train. Second-Lieutenant Eric Yarrow took one party south towards Bassein (with the reluctant driver encouraged by a revolver in his ribs) and demolished the rail

---

10. Both his divisional commanders, Cowan and Bruce Scott, were personal friends from the same battalion of the same regiment.
11. He followed Lieutenant-Colonel Jackie Smyth who had recommended him as his successor.
12. A small amount of refined petroleum could be produced at the oilfields.
13. *215/4 Company* landed at Bassein on 14 March.

The railway bridge at Myagwin after demolition on 13 March. Yarrow.

bridge at Zayathla on the 12th, returning that night. The next day, he and Second-Lieutenant Trevor Parks commandeered some trucks and went north and demolished the big railway bridge at Myagwin. Crossing back to Tharrawaw they met a party of some 250 men from the 1st/10th Gurkhas who had gone astray at Taukkyan and had been making their way up the east bank of the river. Unfortunately, 17 Division had now moved further north and that day the Kamonzeik bridge had been blown. It was no longer possible to return to the main road by train. However, by joining the two big police launches together and improvising some decking, they were able to get the whole party, including the Gurkhas, on board and on the 14th started moving slowly up the river to Prome, which they reached on the 17th.

Henzada had not seen the last of the British. Major Michael Calvert RE had been the commandant of a School at Maymyo training guerrillas to support the Chinese in their war against the Japanese in China. Now that the Japanese were in Burma, he brought his trainees down to the new front. Slim ordered him to join up with the Royal Marines and cover the west bank of the Irrawaddy. He decided to make an offensive sortie with this detachment down the river. Using an old steamer, they chugged down the river, sank some river steamers and destroyed some locomotives at Myanaung, the terminus of the west bank railway. On the 17th they made a daring raid on Henzada, all wearing bush hats and attempting to convince the Burmese that they were an advance party of Australians. They landed, and Mike Calvert harangued a large crowd in the main square from the balcony of a house. Unfortunately a party of the BIA under Japanese control had come up the river and entered the town that morning. Surrounded and summoned to lay down their arms, the raiding party opened fire and fought their way back to their launch, which was luckily concealed behind a high bank of the river. After a brief skirmish they managed to get away with only four killed and seven wounded.

While this was going, on a young brigadier, a protégé of Wavell's, had been visiting Prome where he met the newly-arrived Corps Commander, General Slim. The young brigadier was Orde Wingate, already a guerilla leader of some fame. Slim listened to his ideas and advised him to contact Mike Calvert. Accordingly, Calvert was ordered to leave his raiding force and return at once to his school at Maymyo. There he met Orde Wingate. The two men, after an initial clash, found that they shared similar original ideas and talked long into the night. Their views coincided on many matters including General Slim, Wingate saying "Slim is the best man east of Suez, bar Wavell." A day or two later Wingate flew back to India but this meeting was to be the seed of a remarkable endeavour in the following two years.

The Japanese Advance from Rangoon

33 Division, after a week in Rangoon, started its advance up the Prome road on 16 March. They still had only two brigades but their third brigade, *213 Regiment*, would join them before the end of the month. They had received reinforcements to replace their casualties and they would shortly be supported both by a battery of 105mm heavy field artillery and by a battery of 150mm medium guns.

17 Division, conforming to the movement in the Sittang valley, had withdrawn to the area of Okpo. Colonel C.E.K. Bagot MC, the redoubtable CO of the 1st Glosters, hearing that the Japanese had, during the night, entered Letpadan, a small town on the road 20 miles to the south, decided on a surprise company raid at first light. Captain Richard Johnson's company was chosen for the task. Now Letpadan had road approaches from all four points of the compass. Captain Johnson split his company into two groups and sent one platoon, under Lieutenant Sibley, down the main road to simulate a frontal attack from the north. This platoon blazed away with LMGs and mortared the eastern and southern exits from the town. The Japanese were *214/9 Company*, leading the advance. They had put out a sentry on each road, were alerted to the British approach and moved out of the town to attack this platoon. A tough fight developed. Meanwhile the rest of the Gloster company, together with four carriers and two mortars, drove straight down a road to the west which ran parallel to the main road. Then, while the mortars and LMGs in the carriers gave covering fire,

'D' Company (less a platoon) drove straight into the town from the west. Driving round the streets they shot up everything they could see, threw grenades into the school which was thought to be the Japanese headquarters and seemed to be full of people, removed some Japanese baggage and, in spite of some scattered firing from houses, drove out unscathed by the way they had come in. The whole company then withdrew, leaving behind three damaged trucks and taking with them two captured 'Japanese'[14]. British casualties were nine missing and one wounded, mostly from a section of Sibley's platoon which the Japanese had managed to surround. The Japanese claim of capturing three trucks, some dead and wounded soldiers and five prisoners, is roughly identical.

However, there is a big discrepancy when it comes to Japanese casualties. The company commander reported that the Japanese must have suffered at least 30 casualties, a not unreasonable estimate from the two separate skirmishes. Everyone was anxious for a piece of good news and by the time the story reached HQ 17 Division the number of casualties had increased to 40; when it got to General Alexander it was 50.[15] Alexander passed the tale on to Wavell, adding that he suspected that the figures were exaggerated but, as it was good for morale, he proposed to publicise the story and he did so. The Japanese, however, claim to have lost only one man killed and two wounded, but admit their mortification at losing some of their baggage which these three soldiers had been guarding. They say that *214/9 Company* had doubled out of the town to oppose Lieutenant Sibley's platoon and the few men left took cover in the houses when the British came in, hence the low casualties. The probable answer is that the school contained a number of members of the BIA and their casualties are unrecorded. Nevertheless, although it may not have been quite as effective as was thought at the time, it was a well planned and executed raid and a welcome piece of aggression to lighten the gloom of the retreat. But the myth it created may have been one of the main causes of a serious misjudgement before the month was out.

Nemesis for the RAF

At the end of February it was clear that, with the Japanese closing in on Rangoon, the RAF needed to be re-deployed. The AOC-in-C in India (Air Chief Marshal Sir Richard Peirse) ordered Air Vice-Marshal Stevenson to reform his 221 Group Headquarters in Calcutta. Some 3000 airmen were withdrawn by air and sea to India and two mixed wings were organised to remain in Burma. One of these, Akwing, was at Akyab and the other, Burwing, was initially at Zigon, south of Prome, but was then moved to an old civil airfield at Magwe. The only radar set in Burma, which had done sterling work first at Moulmein and then at Mingaladon, was now moved to Magwe. This airfield only had an earth strip but it had good telephonic connections (the Burmese Observer Corps communicated by telephone). However, it lacked such military requirements as bomb stores and dispersal pens. From Magwe, Burwing would continue its support to the Army in Burma.

Unfortunately, the airfield at Magwe had been detected by a Japanese photo-reconnaissance plane on 27 February. Further reconnaissance of the area was then deliberately restricted until an attack in sufficient strength could be mounted. When the fighting in Java ended, the Japanese switched many aircraft to Burma with the aim of dealing a final knock-out blow to the RAF and AVG. However, the British struck first. On 20 March, an RAF reconnaissance over Mingaladon airfield showed a build-up of Japanese aircraft there. At dawn on the 21st, nine Blenheims and ten Hurricanes attacked the concentration at Mingaladon. The Blenheims bombed the airstrip and the planes assembled round it, while the Hurricanes shot up the aircraft on the ground and fought with the fighters who were attacking the bombers. The Japanese lost 11 aircraft damaged and two burnt out, but although most of the British planes were hit only two were lost.

A second raid in the afternoon was planned but the Japanese were not to be caught out twice. An adequate early-warning system had not yet been set up for Magwe nor had proper dispersal pens been constructed. At 1330 hours, the Japanese attacked Magwe with 25 bombers supported by 40 fighters. Catching nearly all the aircraft on the ground, they inflicted heavy damage. However, ten fighters which managed to get airborne shot down four Japanese bombers. Two more heavy Japanese raids, with a total of 57 bombers and 52 fighters, followed that afternoon. The next morning the Japanese deployed 77 bombers and 102 fighters in two devastating raids before 0900 hours. No warning had been received and the airfield was severely damaged. Nine Blenheims were destroyed on the ground and five were rendered unserviceable. The only three AVG aircraft still airworthy departed for their base airfield, now at Loiwing. Two more raids, of 26 and 27 bombers escorted by fighters, during the afternoon completed the destruction of Magwe. The only flyable RAF planes left were six Blenheims and 11 Hurricanes, nearly all unserviceable, and these were ordered to fly to Akyab. There they, and a small RAF wing already established there, were bombed on the 23rd, 24th and 27th, and the survivors were recalled to Chittagong. Wavell decided it was futile to send any more aircraft to Burma and the very few that were reaching India would be better employed in the defence of Calcutta and Ceylon. From now on, the Army in Burma would be on its own.

---

14. These turned out to be Gurkhas captured at the Sittang. They were being used as porters and presumably took the first opportunity to escape.
15. The war diary of the 2nd R Tanks records it as 70 killed.

The order to abandon Magwe and leave for Akyab came so suddenly that no proper plans had been made for the withdrawal of the ground personnel and such equipment as was transportable. A request to Air Vice-Marshal Stevenson in the evening of the 22nd for permission to withdraw the ground staff to Loiwing and Lashio was approved. The next morning a rather unseemly rush developed as RAF trucks full of airmen headed helter-skelter up the Burma road towards Lashio. After a hasty interview between AVM Stephenson and General Alexander it was decided that a team should return to Magwe so that it could be operated as a forward airstrip and the abandoned gear recovered. Arrangements were made for the remaining airmen to be evacuated by air to Calcutta. This incident was widely known and misconstrued and did nothing for inter-Service relations. It was a sad ending to a heroic, and often surprisingly successful, effort by the RAF to compete with a much larger and more experienced air force. The Air was to hold the key to success in Burma and the day would come when the British held that key.

However, the Japanese did not have it all entirely their own way. 5th Air Division had only one squadron of their most modern 'Oscar' fighters and this had taken part in the raids on Magwe and Akyab. The AVG at Loiwing had located the Oscars' base airfield which was at Chiang Mai in north Thailand. Just before dusk on 6 April they raided this airfield and took the Japanese by surprise. The Japanese claim to have shot down one P-40 with ground fire but they concede that three Oscars were burnt and four destroyed, a notable success for the AVG.[16]

The Royal Navy's Part in the Campaign

With the loss of Rangoon, the part played by the Royal Navy in this campaign came to an end and this is perhaps a suitable place to review what was achieved. The Royal Navy could take little direct action because of the major operations taking place elsewhere in the Far East. The Eastern Fleet had suffered a desperate blow within two days of the start of the Japanese war when HMS *Prince of Wales* and HMS *Repulse* were sunk off the east coast of Malaya. Thereafter they were engaged in a hopeless battle against superior forces, first to defend Singapore and then to defend the Dutch East Indies, and this battle continued until Rangoon was beyond saving. Apart from a brief period when a Royal Indian Navy sloop appeared, the only naval forces available to give direct support to the Army in Burma were five improvised armed motor launches manned by the Burma Royal Naval Volunteer Reserve. They did good work assisting the evacuations from Victoria Point, Mergui and Tavoy, and were then withdrawn to Rangoon to help in its coastal defence. The lack of naval support in the Salween estuary made a prolonged defence of Moulmein an impossible task.

However, until the very last minute, the Eastern Fleet very successfully organised and escorted a number of vital convoys into Rangoon from Ceylon, Madras and Calcutta. As there were seven Japanese submarines in the Indian Ocean and, once Singapore had fallen, the danger of a large Japanese fleet appearing at any moment, this was not a task to be undertaken lightly. No ships were lost, and the army could be very grateful for the efficiency and safety of the arrival of their much-needed reinforcements.

If the Eastern Fleet had been strong enough to match the Japanese it would have been difficult for the Japanese to send reinforcements into Rangoon. However, the Japanese had planned ahead for this eventuality. They knew that their naval forces in the south-west Pacific were much stronger than the British ones in the Indian Ocean. They planned to strike at the British Eastern Fleet, which they expected to be in harbour at Trincomalee on Easter Sunday, thus removing the British naval threat and encouraging anti-British feeling in India. At the same time they would strike at shipping in the Bay of Bengal, thus spreading alarm and despondency in India's east coast cities . These two moves in the first week of April were timed to cover the Japanese convoys moving from Singapore to Rangoon.

Vice-Admiral Nagumo's *First Air Fleet*, fresh from its success at Pearl Harbour and in the battle for Java[17], sailed south of Indonesia into the Indian Ocean on 1 April. Its aircraft attacked Colombo and Trincomalee, damaged the ports and sank a number of ships.[18] Admiral Somerville's much weaker Eastern Fleet was forced to withdraw to the west to cover the vital sea lanes from the Cape to Suez, Basra and Bombay. Meanwhile, a Japanese cruiser task force under Vice-Admiral Ozawa sank a large number of merchant ships in the Bay of Bengal and caused much alarm. However, the Japanese incursion was in essence a major raid. Having caused as much damage as possible, the two fleets withdrew through the Malacca Strait on 12 April. Their basic aim, which was to allow the reinforcements from Singapore to reach Rangoon unscathed, had been achieved. The Japanese Navy never returned to the Indian Ocean in force and, after the First Air Fleet was defeated at the Battle of Midway in June 1942, were never again strong enough to do so.

Wavell correctly assessed this incursion as a raid and continued to believe that

---

16. Account of Mr Yoshita Yasuda who had shot down a Hurricane at Akyab on 24 March. On 6 April he was on stand-by but correctly decided not to take off during the raid.

17. It had also made successful strikes on Rabaul and Darwin in Australia.

18. The two heavy eight-inch gun cruisers, HMS *Dorsetshire* and HMS *Cornwall*, which had done most of the escorting of convoys into Rangoon, were both sunk by Japanese naval aircraft in a few minutes.

the main Japanese threat lay to north-east India. But the vulnerability of the East African sea lanes, which the Japanese raid had exposed, alarmed the War Cabinet and Chiefs of Staff; aircraft which might have gone to Burma were switched to Ceylon and Madagascar. What would have happened if the British had been reinforced on land and in the air and had succeeded in holding Rangoon until the monsoon can only be speculation. It seems likely, however, that once the Japanese fleet had returned to the Pacific it would have been possible, if RAF strength had been adequate, to resume supplies to Rangoon.

CHAPTER FIFTEEN

The Defeat at Shwedaung

Wavell Calls for an Offensive

There were to be two battles at Prome and, although 17 Division was to be directed by three future Field Marshals, both were to fail. The first of these was the battle of Shwedaung, and some at least of the responsibility for its failure rests on the inexperience in Burma of the higher commanders. General Alexander had taken steps to move 1 Burdiv from the Sittang valley and set up a scratch Corps Headquarters (1 Burcorps) at Allanmyo under General Slim. Alexander's initial plan, probably inspired by General Wavell, was that Prome would be held by one brigade group and Allanmyo, thirty miles to the north, by another. There would be no withdrawals, and the rest of the British forces would operate in a mobile offensive role to deal with enemy by-passing these strongpoints. This, perhaps fortunately, was never tried. At this time there was much talk among the higher commanders (not including General Hutton) of inflicting a severe defeat on the Japanese and driving them out of Rangoon. It was an illusion. Without substantial reinforcement, and greater air and artillery support, the troops were not yet well-trained enough to achieve it.

The optimists were encouraged in their views by the defiant defence of Toungoo by the Chinese 200th D/Brigade. However, towards the end of March, pressure on this Chinese formation was increasing and, if they were not to be overwhelmed, help was needed urgently. The obvious solution was for the two Chinese d/brigades, one in Mandalay and one moving down towards Toungoo, to go to their assistance. Stilwell saw this clearly and ordered their advance, only to find his order ignored. It turned out that the Generalissimo had not bestowed on him the final authority of command which was necessary if the Chinese commanders were to obey him. All major decisions had to be referred to the Generalissimo. Stilwell still thought, however, that the Chinese from the north would attack the Japanese at Toungoo on the 26th and asked the British to engage the enemy in the Irrawaddy valley at the same time. This request was repeated by the Generalissimo when he met Alexander in Chungking on the 28th and Alexander passed it on to Slim as an order.

Now, military operations need specific military aims. Requests of the "for

God's sake do something" variety seldom inspire successful battles. Slim and
Cowan had been planning to make a firm defensive stand at Prome. Now they
had been ordered to take offensive action. They had only a scanty knowledge of
what their opponents were doing. In this part of Burma the BIA had many supporters and information was difficult to obtain. Such knowledge as they had came
from Burma FF units and the motorised 1st Glosters who, from Tharrawaddy on,
had been fighting a skilful rearguard action along the main road and covering the
denial activities of the Sappers. The latter[1] had demolished the road and rail
bridges, the railway stations, the power stations, the pumping plants and assorted
saw-mills and rice-mills in Gobingauk, Zigon and Nattalin. The rail bridge south
of Paungde was blown on 28 March and the Glosters, leaving a Burma FF column to cover it, bivouacked just north of the town.

The British Plan to Relieve Pressure on the Chinese

It was known at HQ 17 Division that the enemy were advancing up the main
road and that another force was advancing up the west bank of the Irrawaddy. So,
in answer to General Alexander's request, a plan, perhaps inspired by the earlier
raid on Letpadan, was made to strike at the Japanese down the main road. Its aim
was to seize Paungde in Phase One on 29 March. Then, in Phase Two on 30
March, a stronger force, which would include the whole of the 7th Armoured
Brigade and more infantry, would drive through Paungde and capture Okpo, 30
miles further down the road (see Map 17). Brigadier Anstice, commander of 7th
Armoured Brigade, was to command the 'Strike Force'. Except for 24 Field
Company[2] of the Bombay Sappers, the entire force in the first phase would be
British and comprised:

HQ 7th Armoured Brigade
7th Hussars
414 Battery RHA
One coy West Yorks
2nd Duke of Wellington's Regt
1st Glosters
1st Cameronians
24 Field Company

Unfortunately, due to battle casualties and sickness, the strength of the Infantry
units was hardly that of two weak battalions.

To give support and cover the flanks of the road back to Prome, one company
of the newly flown in 1st Royal Inniskilling Fusiliers was to hold the pass on the
road four miles north of Inma, and one company of BMP were to go to
Shwedaung, another to Inma and a third to Nyaungzaye.

The Japanese Plan

The Japanese were, of course, quite unaware of the proposed British offensive, but *33 Division* were preparing to advance in their favourite 'scorpion' formation. In this mode, one regiment advanced along paths and tracks on either side of the main axis. The third brigade, the artillery and the divisional troops followed on the main route, taking care to ensure that the flanking regiments were well ahead. This was an ideal posture both for attacking a strong enemy position and for confounding an enemy frontal attack. *33 Division* had not only been brought up to strength but it had now been reinforced by a company from *213 Regiment*,[3] and was supported by 105mm heavy field artillery and 150mm medium howitzers. The British 'Strike Force' was therefore aiming a blow at the strongest and most experienced enemy division in Burma.

214 Regiment had been leading up the main road, with *215 Regiment* advancing up the west bank of the Irrawaddy. On both routes the BIA had arranged for the villagers to welcome the Japanese, a new experience for the veterans of the war in China. Another pleasant feature was that they could now march and drive along the roads in daylight instead of marching through the forests at night as the RAF had previously obliged them to do.

On reaching Paungde, Major-General Araki, who was commanding *214 Regimental Group*, started to march up the railway with the aim of blocking the road north of Prome and attacking the town from the rear. *213/3 Company* and *33 Divisional Troops* who were following, continued to march up the main road but letting the other two brigades keep well ahead. The ideal 'scorpion' formation had now been achieved, but in the weak centre a calculated risk was being taken (see Map 17).

Anticipating some British action between Paungde and Prome, *2/215 Battalion* had been ordered to cross the Irrawaddy by ferry and country boats at Tayokhmaw on the evening of the 28th and to seize Shwedaung. Shwedaung village was an excellent site either for a rearguard action or for a road-block. It was the cork in a natural bottleneck formed by the Irrawaddy to the west and forest-covered hills to the east. The Kala Chaung, a dry river-bed 50 yards wide with steep sides, ran through the northern part of the village. At Tayokhmaw, some two hundred bullock-carts had been assembled by the BIA and, using these to

---

1. 60 Field Company.

2. An error in Kirby's *The War Against Japan*, Vol.2, gives this as 14 Field Company RE but there were no Royal Engineer field companies in this campaign.

3. *213 Regiment* had come by ship from China to Bangkok. From Raheng *3 Company* made the whole journey to Paungde in trucks. *1* and *3 Battalions* marched from Raheng to Waw and then were transported to Prome, arriving 3 April. *2 Battalion* marched to Moulmein and then went by sea to Rangoon, where they became Army Reserve.

transport both soldiers and ammunition, they marched through the night to Shwedaung. They were extremely lucky in their timing for HQ 7th Armoured Brigade and the last of the motorised British Strike Force had just cleared Shwedaung moving south. Japanese scouts had seen many vehicles and some tanks moving south and so they knew what to expect. On arrival in the village the Japanese quickly decided to make the Kala Chaung their northern perimeter, the bridge being covered with one of their two anti-tank guns, the other being sited to cover the road at the south of the village. Then, having put out a platoon road-block backed by two MMGs about a mile south of the town, *2/215 Battalion* dug themselves in.

The Actions at Paungde and Padigon

The BFF column in Paungde was heavily attacked on the morning of 28 March, so Colonel Bagot mounted a two-company attack on Paungde to relieve them. This achieved some success and there was some hard fighting in the town. However, it was clear that the enemy was in considerable strength, so the attack was called off and the Glosters withdrew up the road, a party from 60 Field Company destroying the road bridge behind them at Wetpok and then retiring to Prome. In this brisk action at Paungde, the Glosters lost two officers and 15 men killed and three officers[4] and nine men wounded. Meanwhile, Colonel Bagot ordered 'D' company to occupy Padigon, four miles to the east, and to stop any Japanese advance up the railway.

In the late afternoon of the 28th, the 7th Hussars arrived at Inma and shortly afterwards Lieutenant-Colonel Guy Burton, the GSO1 of 17 Division, arrived at Colonel Bagot's HQ there and broke the news about the plan for the 'Strike Force' the next day. A squadron of tanks from the 7th Hussars, the 2nd Duke's and 24 Field Company were put under Bagot's command for the night and he was ordered to hold his positions until Brigadier Anstice and the rest of the 'Strike Force' arrived at 0700 the next morning. During the night, while the Sappers prepared a diversion round the demolished Wetpok bridge, the Duke's sent one company patrol round through the forest to probe Paungde from the south, while another circled round to the north and probed the town from the north-west.

Just before first light on the 29th, the sound of heavy mortar and automatic fire was heard from Padigon where 'D' Company of the Glosters, commanded by the Captain Johnson who had distinguished himself at Letpadan, were entrenched. They were being heavily attacked by part of *214 Regiment* but it was reported an hour later that they were still holding all their positions. A troop of tanks was sent out along the lateral road to support them but a mile short of Padigon it ran into a road-block. The leading tank was knocked out by a 75mm mountain gun and the rest were held up.

At 7am on the 29th, Brigadier Anstice arrived and took command and, at about the same time, a wounded runner came in with a message from 'D' Company. This said that, although they had been surrounded, their mortars had inflicted many casualties and a large force of enemy was now bypassing their position to the west and moving on north. An attack supported by 414 Battery RHA was therefore launched on the road-block near Padigon and it was successfully cleared. However, the tanks, which were confined to the road, were again held up short of Padigon village, and a further tank was lost to an attack by petrol bombs.

To the south, '1' Company of the Duke's had engaged the enemy and called for more ammunition, so it was reinforced by two more platoons and 'C' Squadron of the 7th Hussars. Supported by 414 Battery RHA, they fought a sharp battle against *213/3 Company*, but enemy strength increased and they could make no further progress. Two tanks were hit by shells but, though slowed, they were able to continue to operate. Infantry casualties began to mount. Fortunately, soon after mid-day, the 2nd Royal Tanks had provided General Cowan with a direct radio link to HQ 'Strike Force'.[5] News about the road-block in Shwedaung had now reached HQ 17 Division and in the afternoon Cowan ordered Anstice to withdraw the 'Strike Force' to Prome, either through Shwedaung or through Padigon, whichever seemed the easiest. Anstice chose Shwedaung.

General Cowan's Problem

General Cowan had a difficult problem. The main task he had been given was to hold Prome and cover the route to the north, and his division had been deployed to do this. A strong force was now known to be advancing up the railway towards 48 Brigade at Hmawza. It was vital that this flank should be held, as a successful enemy advance here would cut off the whole division. He therefore ordered 48 Brigade, supported by most of the 2nd Royal Tanks, the 1st Inniskillings and one battery of the 1st Indian Field Regiment, to advance to Sinmizwe on the evening of 29 March with the aim of attacking the Japanese in the area of Thegon the next day. They were not to attack until the block at Shwedaung had been cleared.

Meanwhile he ordered both 16 and 63 Brigades to provide one battalion each to attack Shwedaung from the north. The 4th/12th FFR marched down towards Shwedaung on the afternoon of the 29th. They were met by a BIA force about 1200 strong, commanded by Japanese and armed with automatic weapons, in a

---

4. These included Colonel Bagot, but he stayed with his battalion until the battle ended.
5. Voice by day and morse by night.

small village about a mile north of Shwedaung. After a severe fight, 4/12 FFR overran the village, capturing an MMG, several LMGs and many rifles. The BIA suffered a severe defeat and never again attempted to intervene in a formal battle. They lost 60 killed, 70 taken prisoner and 300 wounded, while 350 deserted.[6] Their two Japanese commanders, Lieutenant Haruyama and Sergeant Ikebe, were both killed. The 4th/12th continued to Shwedaung but met stiff resistance on the outskirts. They could make no progress so formed a 'box' for the night.

The 'Strike Force' Approaches Shwedaung from the South on 29 March

Brigadier Anstice ordered the 1st Glosters and 'B' Squadron 7th Hussars to lead the way north, to clear the block and to picquet the road. 'D' Company of the Glosters in Padigon had to be left to extricate themselves as best they could. The whole column consisted of some 270 vehicles. Unfortunately the 1st Glosters at this stage only had three companies and the effective strength of 'A' and 'B' Companies was only about 90 officers and men. The first obstacle they met was a deserted ambulance which had been sent back that morning full of Gloster wounded. It had met the road-block just south of Shwedaung and all the wounded except two had been killed. These two were Captain Thorpe of the Glosters, who had been wounded that morning, and a wounded Inniskilling Fusilier who had helped him to a nearby copse, where a patrol now found him and brought him back to the road. The first block was fairly easily cleared, the Japanese platoon retreating when the tanks started to close up after a short artillery bombardment, and the advance now reached the second block at the edge of the village, which was much more strongly held (see Map 18).

After 15 minutes, bombardment, the first attack went in soon after dark but it was a bright moonlit night and the 1st Glosters, advancing across the open paddy fields, were soon pinned down by mortar and MMG fire and could make no progress. Two troops of the 7th Hussars were then ordered to try to burst through. The first troop, under Lieutenant Palmer, got through the first block, crashed through another near the bridge, and then drove on to Prome and reported to HQ 17 Division.[7] After the first troop had passed, the Japanese moved a bul-

This rice-mill at the south end of Shwedaung was a Japanese strongpoint.

Right: The main Shwedaung road-block, looking north along the bridge.

Below: A Japanese petrol bomb attack on the mined tank at the north end of the bridge. Presumably a re-enactment for the Press.

lock-cart onto the road[8] in the middle of the village. The second troop, under Lieutenant Patteson, slowed down on meeting this obstacle, and a party waiting with petrol bottles scored a hit on the front of his tank which caught fire, forcing the crew to bail out. His tank was also hit by several anti-tank shells but they did not penetrate the hull. Patteson was captured, beaten up and tied to the cart. The remainder of his troop called for covering fire from the 25-pdrs and under cover of this fire, which fell all around him, he managed to loosen his bonds and escape. With his hands still tied, he succeeded in making a detour to the east and re-joined the column. The remainder of his troop now attacked this central block. One got through, but the other two were hit by petrol bottles, and the crews were forced to bail out. The tank which had got through slowed down

6. Allen, Louis, *Burma: The Longest War*, p.63.

7. His impression was that HQ 17 Division did not yet realise the seriousness of the situation but it may be that they realised it only too well.

8. Like all roads in Burma this road was raised two or three feet above the general level and had wide shallow ditches on either side.

to pass a burnt-out truck which was blocking the road on the embankment on the far side of the bridge. Here it was attacked by a Japanese soldier with an anti-tank mine. The soldier was badly wounded[9] but the mine broke a track of the tank which slewed across the road, fatally blocking it. The tank was then attacked with petrol bombs. The crew bailed out and two were killed.

Colonel Bagot now spoke to Brigadier Anstice and said it was futile to continue attacking with too few and exhausted infantry; a full-scale attack was necessary. However, Anstice decided to try again at 0200 hours on the 30th with the Glosters, supported by the company of the 1st West Yorks and the mortars of the Cameronians. Although the Glosters tried a left hook through the forest, this attack was no more successful than the first and only succeeded in exhausting the Infantry even more. It was therefore decided to put in a full-scale attack with the whole force soon after dawn.

Meanwhile, *HQ 215 Regiment* across the river had received a message from Shwedaung at mid-day on the 29th explaining the situation. Colonel Harada therefore decided to leave *3/215 Battalion* (less two companies) and *7 Mountain Gun Company* on the west side of the Irrawaddy and take three companies and his regimental gun company to reinforce Shwedaung. Accordingly he crossed the river on the night of the 29th by the same route as *2/215 Battalion* had taken.

The Battle of Shwedaung, 30 March

Shwedaung was a large village mostly consisting of two-storey wood and bamboo houses with thatched or corrugated-iron roofs but with a few brick and plaster buildings. As day broke on 30 March, the British column was spread along about a mile of the road south of Shwedaung. The vehicles were mostly nose-to-tail and sometimes double-banked. 'B' Squadron of the 7th Hussars was in the lead. Not far behind them were the tanks of HQ 7th Armoured Brigade and

'A' Squadron. 'C' Squadron was at the rear of the column. On either side of the road were open paddy fields stretching up to the forest about 800 yards away, though isolated copses were closer. 414

Having crossed the Irrawaddy, HQ 215 Regiment march towards Shwedaung.

Field Battery RHA was deployed in the paddy fields west of the road. A welcome arrival during the day was 'D' Company of the 1st Glosters who, well led by Captain Johnson, had held their position at Padigon successfully against repeated attacks, and '2' Company of the Duke's, who had had the better of some minor clashes with Japanese patrols. Their attackers having moved away, the two companies marched across country and rejoined their battalions.

The Japanese made various attacks on the column during the day but none were very effective. During the night, Colonel Harada, marching up from Tayokhmaw with *215 Regiment,* heard the British guns, which he thought must be in the woods east of the road. He therefore ordered *215/11 Company* to cross the road and attack them. It duly crossed behind the rearguard but failed to find any guns. This was not surprising as they weren't there. At first light on the 30th, Harada sent two platoons of *215/10 Company* to attack the main column from the west under cover of the morning mist. However, they reached the edge of the forest west of the road just as the mist lifted and at the very moment that '2' Company of the 2nd Duke's under Major Robinson entered it as flank guard. A sharp close-quarter fight followed. One Japanese platoon was almost wiped out and the other retreated into the forest.[10] The British also suffered. Five NCOs were killed in the leading platoon alone and 30 men in the company were wounded. A few men who had retired were positioned by the CO as an inner flank guard in the paddy fields under the company 2nd-in-Command. Robinson, however, stayed in the forest and led the rest of his company north through the woods to join up with the column in the south of Shwedaung. He and his company had achieved their aim of shielding the column from the west.

Later in the morning, six Japanese fighter aircraft attacked the column and several vehicles were hit. Damage was not serious, however, and the Japanese record that two planes were shot down. Rather more damage, but again not much, was caused by *7 Mountain Gun Company* firing on the column from the west bank of the Irrawaddy. In the afternoon, General Sakurai ordered some of his heavy guns from *21st Heavy Artillery Unit* to advance from Paungde to a position from which they could shell the British. However, as they were deploying off the road, they were suddenly attacked by a tank from 'C' Squadron. The concentrated MMG fire from about 200 yards' range, although it only lasted a short time, caused many casualties and much consternation among the gunners, so the guns never got into action.[11]

Thus, although the column managed to protect itself during March 30th, the

---

9. He was decorated with the medal of the Golden Eagle, an unusual distinction for a soldier.
10. *Memoir of 215 Regiment.*
11. *Memoir of 33 Division.*

vital problem remained of how to get through Shwedaung. The British tanks could only fire solid shot from their 37mm guns and their main anti-personnel weapons were their two MMGs. However, they were immune from the front to the Japanese 37mm anti-tank gun and the only guns (apart from the heavier artillery) that could knock them out were the Japanese 75mm guns fired at short range[12] and these had difficulty in hitting a fast-moving target. They were, however, vulnerable to anti-tank mines and petrol bombs, so infantry protection was essential where there was cover close to the road, as in a village. Experienced as they were, this type of close co-operation with the Infantry was new to 7th Armoured Brigade. Brigadier Anstice wisely decided that he could only deal with one Infantry commander and so he appointed Lieutenant-Colonel Marindin of the West Yorks as temporary commander of all the Infantry units.

The three under-strength British Infantry battalions scarcely knew each other and were equally inexperienced at working with tanks. They had, until a few weeks previously, been employed on internal security duties in India and Burma, a task where the skills required were very different from those required in a forest war against a first-class enemy. In particular, the art of picqueting a route was unknown to many of the junior officers and soldiers. This was unfortunate as the Achilles, heel of the 'Strike Force' were the unarmoured 'soft' vehicles. The only way to get them through Shwedaung was either to capture the whole village, or to picquet each side of the road through it while the 'B' vehicles drove through. The truth was that the Infantry in the Strike Force were neither strong nor experienced enough for either role, but clearly the attempt had to be made.

The main British attack on Shwedaung was put in at 0730 hours on the 30th under cover of a bombardment on the southern end of the village by 414 Battery RHA. 'B' Squadron advanced up the road with the 1st Glosters and the company of the 1st West Yorks (total strength about 100 all ranks) on the left of the road and the 1st Cameronians (also strength about 100) on the right. The 2nd Duke's (strength about 150)[13] were in reserve, but 90 men ('2' Company) had already been deployed as a flank guard. The tanks blasted each side of the road and burst through the block at the edge of the village. The Japanese anti-tank gun at this end of the village was destroyed and nearly all the gunners killed. The Infantry following the tanks managed to penetrate the village as well on a narrow front on either side of the road. The head of the vehicle column moved forward into the village. The leading vehicle of 'B' Squadron was a scout car which, supported by two tanks, attempted to race across the bridge. It hit an anti-tank mine on the concrete bridge, slewed round and charged backwards through the parapet, stopping half on and half off the bridge. The following tanks swerved off the steep embankment to avoid the mines and toppled over on to their sides, one on each

Top: The main road-block centred on this bridge over the Kala Chaung at the north end of Shwedaung.

Below: One of the tanks that toppled off the steep embankment forming the southern approach to the bridge.

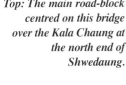

side of the approach. The other tanks could neither move forwards nor backwards because of the congestion of vehicles and the column came to a halt.

The Japanese, who had pulled back during the night to avoid the shelling, now started closing in again on each side of the road and there were not enough Infantry to stop them. They shot up at short range those 'B' vehicles which had followed into the town and some caught fire and enhanced the blockage. The enemy showed their usual skill in concealment and it was difficult to locate their machine guns. Inside the village the position became chaotic; units became fragmented and control was lost. Some officers and senior NCOs were prominent in organising a defence; they kept the enemy at bay but progress by the double-banked vehicles was impossible. 414 Field Battery had now joined the column. They had been attacked in their gun position before leaving but their attackers had been successfully beaten off by 'C' Squadron's tanks and a scratch force from the 2nd Duke's at the rear of the column.

Meanwhile, north of Shwedaung, the 4th/12th FFR, reinforced by the 2nd/13th FFRif, a squadron from the 2nd Royal Tanks and a battery of the 1st

---

12. In this campaign the Japanese 75mm guns only had explosive shells and no solid shot.
13. These figures for strengths come from the War Diary of the 1st Glosters. They appear low but refer only to those making the attack and do not include Battalion HQ, the mortar crews, the vehicle drivers, etc. Units had got mixed up in the vehicles and there was some difficulty in mustering full strengths.

Indian Field Regiment, had attacked Shwedaung itself that morning. The 2nd/13th penetrated the northern end of the village but were driven out after an hour. At 3pm the 4th/12th attacked again astride the road on a narrow front, reached the northern roadblock and picqueted the road. A number of vehicles and troops then managed to break out of the village. At 4pm the northern units were ordered by HQ 17 Division to withdraw and marched back, the 2nd/13th to Prome and the 4th/12th sixteen miles to Pauktaw. British casualties in these actions were not light. The 4th/12th lost 18 killed, including three officers, and 45 wounded including the CO, Lieutenant-Colonel W.D. Edward. The 2nd/13th lost one killed and 25 wounded.

The 'Strike Force' were out of touch with the troops to the north. About mid-day it was decided that the position in Shwedaung was desperate and the only solution was for the tanks to try and bypass the northern block. The remaining tanks of 'B' Squadron, led by Major Llewellyn-Palmer, MC, succeeded with great skill in forcing a way across the chaung and they were followed by Brigadier Anstice and his headquarter tanks and some of their 'B' vehicles. Close behind them, the tanks of 'A' Squadron led more small groups of 'B' vehicles through the gauntlet of fire and across the Kala Chaung. The Japanese resisted fiercely and many soldiers were killed or wounded in the trucks. 'A' Squadron lost four tanks and both squadrons lost a number of 'B' vehicles. Without the dash and leadership shown by the tank commanders, British casualties would have been far higher.

Once across the chaung, the 7th Hussar tanks which had got through, having used up all their ammunition, were sent back to Tamagauk, north of Prome, to replenish, while HQ 'Strike Force' halted a few miles south of Prome.

'C' Squadron of the 7th Hussars, the Gunners, the Sappers, the Infantry and most of the trucks were still held up in Shwedaung where the bridge was still blocked by disabled vehicles. The four COs, Lieutenant-Colonels Bagot, Faithfull, Marindin and Thomas were still in the block and it was decided to try and find another way out. A possible route was found, and 'C' Squadron tanks smashed through village houses and shepherded the guns and as many vehicles as they could over this route. Three gun tractors had been destroyed but only two guns were lost as one, although it turned on its side, was dragged away by a tank across the chaung. Many vehicles were still left, most of them burnt out or too damaged to move. With the tanks gone, Japanese pressure increasing and everyone getting more and more exhausted, Colonel Marindin now gave the order for those remaining in the block to split up into small parties and make their way out on foot.

Colonel Faithfull, commanding the reserve battalion, had been at the rear of the column. Having established a small rear party with two MMGs to cover the tail, he went forward to the head of the column and found that there was a lull at the north road block. With the help of Captain Scott of the Cameronians and Lieutenant Smele of the Glosters, he managed to get several more vehicles, some full of wounded and all full of men, across the chaung. It being impossible to get any further vehicles up to the crossing, he recalled his rear party, who had been firing at any sign of enemy activity, and took the decision to leave.

Captain P. Collister of the 1st Glosters has described this moment. He had been wounded twice during the day and was in an ambulance whose driver had been shot. He heard a voice calling out: "This is Colonel Faithfull of the Duke of Wellington's. I am ordering all men who can do so to make their own way out of this and rejoin their units which will try to reform on the other side of the village if possible." The Colonel then lifted the flap at the back of the ambulance and said "Sorry chaps, but if any of you can manage to walk, do your best to save yourselves." Collister and one or two others managed to clamber out and, together with a few other men, made an arduous but successful escape via the river to Prome.[14] Faithfull and two or three other officers then split up into groups with such men as they could collect. Having crossed the chaung, many by the bridge, they made their way north through the village and scrub west of the road. It was the end of the battle.

The majority of those who retreated on foot managed to dodge the Japanese and find their way back through the forest, either to the east or west of the road. The two Indian battalions attacking north of Shwedaung had been recalled soon after 4pm but they had cleared the northern end of the village and they had defeated and scattered the BIA who otherwise would have been a serious hazard to the small parties making their way north. The redoubtable Colonel Bagot, although wounded, led a party of thirty into the forest to the east whence they marched back the next day to Prome. But others were not so lucky. The Japanese claim to have taken 113 British prisoners. They also claim that their two doctors treated British as well as Japanese wounded. But many seriously wounded men, who had had to be abandoned, were not seen again. It was the Japanese custom to kill seriously wounded men in ambulances and they may have done so here.[15]

The British had just over 400 casualties and but for the heroic efforts of the 7th Hussars would have had many more. Ten tanks were lost, as well as two 25-pdr field guns, the four Breda guns acquired by the 1st Glosters at Mingaladon

---

14. Collister, Captain P. From his autobiography *Then a Soldier*. IWM Documents, 83/46/1
15. The Japanese claim that 40 seriously wounded British in two trucks were killed when British guns shelled the column. Certainly 1 Indian Field Battery fired a number of shells as harassing fire into Shwedaung at 8am the next day, the 31st, and several shells were seen, by a British escaper, to score direct hits on some of the vehicles..

Some of the abandoned transport in Shwedaung village.

and more than two hundred vehicles. Some of these from 7th Armoured Brigade were specialist vehicles, including a workshop lorry, and could not be replaced. Japanese figures for what was captured are unfortunately fanciful, for instance 62 guns! Figures for total Japanese losses are uncertain but they record 47 infantrymen and eight gunners killed at Shwedaung and 20 infantrymen killed at Padigon. So ended what the 7th Hussars War Diary aptly describes as "this useless venture". It was of no possible help to the Chinese who anyway abandoned Toungoo on this day. It sadly weakened the strength, and in some cases the morale, of the Infantry units involved, and it disrupted the plans for the defence of Prome.[16]

There is no doubt that the inspiration for this attack came from General Wavell, who had long been advocating offensive action. He saw it as a last chance to turn the tide of invasion, as he knew, from decoded Japanese signals, that enemy reinforcements would shortly arrive in Burma from Singapore. Militarily and psychologically correct as Wavell's wish for aggressive action was, he had misjudged the relative strength of the two sides.

---

16. As an example, the 1st Glosters had left Rangoon on 7 March with a strength of 640 all ranks and 87 Indian followers. On 1 April their strength was 240 all ranks. They had had 48 battle casualties at Taukkyan, ten at Letpadan, 64 at Paungde and Shwedaung and a few in minor skirmishes. Sickness losses had been heavy and there had been no reinforcements.

CHAPTER SIXTEEN

Confusion at Prome

If one of the factors leading to the disaster at the Sittang bridge had been the absence of senior commanders, it would not be unfair to say that at Prome the problem was the presence of rather too many. General Wavell was now firmly in the chair as theatre commander and taking a close interest in the operations. General Alexander, with Lieutenant-General Hutton as his chief of staff, was at AHQ. Lieutenant-General Slim was at Corps HQ. All these able commanders were directing their attention to Major-General Cowan and his 17th Division. Perhaps inevitably some confusion resulted.

It was clear that Prome needed to be held for as long as possible both to support the Chinese, who were successfully holding Toungoo, and to cover the withdrawal of the large amount of stores which had been evacuated from Rangoon to Prome by rail and boat and now needed to be moved to Mandalay. The railway ended at Prome and so, since the withdrawal of the RAF, this movement was now virtually only possible by road and at night. AHQ had informed HQ Burcorps that it was essential for the continuance of operations in Burma that no stores should be abandoned in Prome, so from 26 March as much as possible was sent back. Meanwhile, strenuous efforts were made to develop a strong defensive position around Prome.

However, as explained in the last chapter, late on the 28th Slim was ordered to stage an attack to the south to relieve pressure on the Chinese. Consequently, at 0215 on 29 March, HQ 17 Indian Division issued Operation Order No 7 for the attack to the south and

A Chinthe, later the symbol of the Chindits, guards the burnt-out town of Prome.

for a new-style defence of Prome. The new plan required a new deployment with fresh digging and, with its stress on mobile counter-attack forces, clearly bears the stamp of Wavell's and Alexander's views of how the defence should be conducted. The town of Prome, for instance, was to be held by two battalions under Lieutenant-Colonel Cox with a mobile counter-attack force of the 1st Royal Inniskilling Fusiliers (1st Inniskillings, who had just arrived in Burma by air), while Brigadier Barlow and the rest of 63 Brigade were to operate in a mobile role on the west bank of the Irrawaddy. This, however theoretically sound, was a method quite beyond the capability of the troops at this time. The Chinese had been more realistic at Toungoo. Fortunately, perhaps, Operation Order No 7 was overtaken by events almost as soon as it was issued.

The Reverse at Padaung

The growing crisis at Shwedaung and the threat to the east flank from *214 Regiment's* advance up the railway had obliged General Cowan to alter the plan. As we have seen, he sent a scratch force down the main road to attack Shwedaung from the north and ordered 48 Brigade to move forward and prepare to attack Thegon on the railway. In the early morning of the 30th there was another setback. Lieutenant-Colonel Musgrave and his Royal Marines had been operating as a screen on the west bank of the Irrawaddy. On the evening of the 29th they withdrew into Padaung village where they were hospitably received and had an evening meal. Offered accommodation for the night in village houses, they decided to stay. In the circumstances it was a grave misjudgement. The BIA were active and someone slipped off to tell *3/215 Battalion* who, less two companies, were only about five miles away in Magyiton village. At 0300 hours, the Japanese attacked the wooden buildings in which the British were sleeping. The buildings were raised on stilts and there were sentries with LMGs dug in below the houses. Surprise was not achieved and the fire fight lasted nearly an hour before the Marines, who had many casualties, were forced to withdraw. According to the Japanese they did this skilfully and most of the force managed to seize boats and go up-river to Prome. The Japanese had two officers and seven men killed and a number wounded. Seventeen Marines were left behind and they were captured on the river bank the next morning. They were then lined up in the village square and bayoneted to death in front of the villagers. It was *3/215 Battalion's* first battle in Burma[1] and presumably they were trying to demonstrate, both to their own soldiers and to the Burmese, Asian superiority over decadent Europeans. To the British this was a revolting and despicable atrocity, the worst (by the Japanese) recorded in this campaign.

The Defence of Prome

The battle at Shwedaung had over-shadowed the arrangements for the establishment of a proper defensive position at Prome. On 30 March and the morning of the 31st the 'Strike Force', and the units which had moved forward to support it, returned to Prome to take up new positions. It cannot be denied that some of the young and inexperienced British soldiers who had been involved at Shwedaung felt that they had been let down and were in an unhappy and demoralised state. However, it was clear that another battle was impending and there was no possibility of rest at this stage. New positions needed to be allotted and dug in.

The idea of a mobile force on the west bank of the Irrawaddy was now impracticable. General Cowan, therefore, ordered Brigadier Cameron and 48 Brigade to hold the left flank with a position covering Hmawza and patrols up the Paungdale road to the east. He was also to try and ambush the Japanese column advancing up the railway. To the west, Brigadier Barlow and 63 Brigade were to hold Prome with the river on their right flank. Brigadier Jones and 16 Brigade were to hold the centre and cover the road junction where the Paungdale road joined the Mandalay road. 7th Armoured Brigade, less a regiment under command of 48 Brigade, would be in reserve at Tamagauk (see Map 19).

Meanwhile the Sappers had been busy. On the 26th, diversions had been built round the bridges on the track beside the railway so that tanks and vehicles could reach Thegon. Army engineers had built a boom across the river just south of Prome and above this the local boats on both sides of the river were sunk. 60 Field Company denied the airfield and worked in shifts throughout the night, backloading to Allanmyo some of the stores stocked in Prome. Tracks were cut across the paddy fields to assist the deployment of tanks and a diversion was built round the main road bridge over the Nawin Chaung in case the bridge was hit by a bomb. To provide another alternative to this bridge, 70 Field Company strengthened the only other one, a rickety wooden bridge for bullock-carts north of the town, to Class 9 (sufficient for all vehicles in the division except tanks) by adding additional trestle piers. On the 30th, Captain Lubett and a party from 70 Field Company blew up an underground tank of 33,000 gallons of petrol five miles south of Prome beside the track to the river at Namayan. They were lucky to escape incineration when a Japanese fighter bombed and machine-gunned the party after the charges had been laid on the exposed surface of the tank.[2] Finally, the power station in Prome was demolished and two large trees were felled across the main road to form a block at the entrance to the town.

---

1. This battalion had been in Army reserve and had taken no part in the fighting in Phase One.
2. The demolition produced a gigantic ball of flame about a hundred yards wide.

Top British commanders, and the Governor's senior official, meet at Allanmyo on 1 April. Left to right: Maj-Gen. Bruce Scott, Sir John Wise, Gen. Alexander, Gen. Wavell, Lt-Gen. Slim, Brig. Davies.

On the 31st, all units in 17 Division were ordered to send back 95% of their vehicles and equipment to Allanmyo. To replace them, they were allotted a few bullock-carts and mules. The idea, of course, was to avoid being tied to the roads and thus losing more trucks and equipment at road-blocks. Where this idea originated is not clear, but it had a fatal flaw. Bullock-carts are very slow. They were useful to an advancing force, who could leave them behind when necessary, but to a force which might have to withdraw rapidly to avoid encirclement they were a fatal brake. However, orders are orders and, in spite of the misgivings in many units, on 1 April this reorganisation was carried out.

The previous night Japanese patrols had been encountered south of both Hmawza and Prome. In the morning some mountain guns on the far bank of the Irrawaddy fired a few shells. 1 Field Regiment returned the fire and one mountain gun was destroyed. In Prome occasional unexplained shots were fired in the ruined town during the day. It was clear to all that an attack was imminent.

That afternoon Generals Wavell and Alexander visited General Slim at his Corps HQ at Allanmyo. At this meeting it was decided that, in view of the Chinese withdrawal from Toungoo, there was now no point in holding Prome, but as much as possible of the stores and ammunition collected there should be back-loaded before withdrawing. The next defensive line would be based on Allanmyo-Thayetmo. A warning order conveying this decision was sent to 17

Division that evening. It arrived after the battle had started and was not passed on. It was too late to make any more changes.

The Attack along the River Flank

The centre of Prome had been pattern-bombed[3] and the main brick and stucco buildings were in ruins while most of the wooden buildings had burnt to the ground. Nearly all the trees in the centre were blackened skeletons, but round the fringes the trees and houses were untouched. Dominating the southern part of the town, which included the railway station, the jetty and the store dumps, was the northern end of a tree-covered ridge running parallel to the Shwedaung road. Its uneven top and its slopes, which were covered in trees and thick vegetation, were much indented with gullies. To the north of the sprawling town was the meandering Nawin Chaung and beyond that a forest stretching for many miles further north. It was not an easy place to defend (see Map 19).

Until the 30th, Brigadier Barlow had been under orders to split his brigade into two halves, one on each side of the Irrawaddy. For this he had been allotted five battalions. Now he was ordered to hold the town of Prome itself. One battalion, the 1st Inniskillings, was taken away and allotted to 48 Brigade. Another, the 2nd/13th FFRif, plus a field gunner battery, had been sent down the road on the 29th to attack Shwedaung from the north. They did not return until after dark on the 30th. He decided to hold the high ground to the south with two battalions, the 1st/10th Gurkhas on the left and the 5th/17th Dogras on the right covering the road. The 1st/11th Sikhs were to hold the eastern flank north of the railway and on return the 2nd/13th FFRif were put into reserve in the centre of the position. Brigade HQ was on the river bank. 12 Mountain Battery (less a Section)[4] was deployed behind the Dogras. 70 Field Company, less a platoon, were on the river bank near Brigade HQ.

This was to be Barlow's first battle in World War II. In World War I he had won an MC and he had just finished commanding the 18th Garhwal Rifles in 1 Burdiv. He had been promoted and brought across a fortnight earlier to replace Brigadier Wickham, seriously wounded in the road-block near Pegu. He did not know his units well, and the many changes of the previous few days had not helped the making of a sound tactical plan. No written record of his new orders appears to exist and probably he was only given verbal ones. He may well have been ordered to protect the stores still dumped round the railway station and this obliged him to hold the high ground to the south which overlooked it. The deci-

---

3. It was the Japanese practice for all the aircraft in a formation of bombers, often 27, to drop their bombs at the same moment.

4. One section had been on the wrong side of the Sittang so 12 Mountain Battery still had only two guns.

sion to hold a front over two miles long, most of it in broken and wooded ground and dotted with houses, meant that penetration at night was easy and fatal if all-round defensive positions of at least battalion size had not been established. The main position covering the road approach from the south had originally been allotted to the 2nd/13th FFRif. However, they had been sent off to ease the pressure on the 'Strike Force' at Shwedaung. Barlow's decision to replace them with the 5th/17th Dogras was an unfortunate one. The Dogras were only 350 strong and known to be a weak battalion.[5] Perhaps uneasy about this, he allotted them the Dogra company from the 2nd/13th FFRif to provide a reserve. At 1800 hours that evening Barlow held an 'O' group and gave out his orders for the night. He by no means gave the impression of being as resolute and determined to defeat the enemy as the occasion demanded.[6] He was to command 63 Brigade for the rest of the campaign but he made an unimpressive start.

About 1900 hours the Japanese opened the battle by firing bursts of MMG fire against the position blocking the main road. The brigade was still reorganising and it was another hour before the final vehicle convoys left the town. There was a full moon and in the bright moonlight visibility was unusually good. Barlow decided to deploy his reserve. Elsmie was ordered to send one company ('D') to take up a lay-back position at the southern end of the town and thus prevent infiltration along the river bank, and a second ('B') to give local protection to Brigade HQ. Barlow thus reduced his reserve to one company and split up one of his strongest battalions so that it could take little part in the battle.

The Japanese attackers were *215 Regiment* with *2/215 Battalion* (less a company), *215/11 Company* and an anti-tank platoon. *215/8 Company* and *215/10 Company* had suffered severely at Shwedaung and were in reserve. The main body of the Japanese left Shwedaung in trucks at dusk. Patrols the previous night had located the British forward positions. After a few miles they de-bussed and climbed up on to the high ground west of the road with *11 Company* nearest to the river and *2/215 Battalion* to the east of them. Around 1930 hours, *11 Company* overran a platoon from 'B' Company of the Dogras, which was all that was holding the block on the main road, and turned the British right flank. For the next hour a heavy attack was put in on the main Dogra position on the ridge but was beaten off. However, *11 Company* now penetrated further, overran the rest of 'B' Company and threatened the position of 12 Mountain Battery, which was to the north of it. The Gunners were ordered by Brigade HQ to withdraw and got their guns away in the nick of time, covered by a counter attack by 'C' Company of the 2nd/13th.[7] *11 Company* had 24 casualties and its commander was mortally wounded.

The country was very broken and thickly covered with scrub, and *2/215*

Battalion now infiltrated through the Dogra position and attacked battalion headquarters and the main position from the rear. About 2145 hours, the Dogras
decided to pull back to the cemetery area and cover the track leading down into
Prome. *2/215 Battalion*, which had occupied the vacated Dogra position, then
began to suffer increasing casualties from shelling by 1 Field Battery, which had
this position registered. They therefore decided to exploit *11 Company's* success.
Returning to the main road, they entered Prome near the river, unopposed, at
about 0300 hours. Shortly afterwards they were joined by *3/215 Battalion* from
across the river. This battalion (less two companies) had marched up the west
bank of the Irrawaddy to Magyiz, opposite Prome. Finding that the ferry and
local boats had been destroyed, they marched back to Sinde and crossed the river
there.

Meanwhile, Brigadier Barlow, at about 2045 hours[8,] informed General Cowan
that the enemy had broken through beside the river. Cowan was a man of few
words. After a few minutes thought, he said to the staff officer who brought the
message: "Tell him to deny his right flank and secure the line of the road".[9]
Nothing more. It is not easy now to determine quite what was meant by this cryp-
tic order, which may have referred to previous verbal instructions and therefore
was clear enough at the time. However, rightly or wrongly, Barlow decided to
pull out of Prome and cover the main road at the eastern exit to the town. This
left the good route through Prome to the north completely open.

By about 2130 this new deployment had been achieved. Brigade HQ and the
2nd/13th FFRif (less two companies) moved back east along the main road to the
vicinity of the level crossing. 70 Field Company followed. In the bright moonlight, Prome appeared to be deserted and there was no sign of friend or foe. A
new front facing west was established about a mile short (west) of the level
crossing. On the right, the Sikhs held north of the railway to the paddy fields bor-
dering the Nawin Chaung, 70 Field Company held between the railway and the
road, and south of the road were the 1st/10th Gurkhas. The 2nd/13th and the now
disorganised Dogras, together with HQ 63 Brigade, were in the 16 Brigade area
between the level crossing and the Paungdale road fork. Apart from some mortaring which caused a few casualties to the covering force while its position was
being established, there was no further action, and shortly after midnight 63

5. The Dogras were good fighters who also provided companies in the 13th FFRif. But they had
over-expanded. The 5th Battalion had not done well at Kuzeik or the Bilin. It was disbanded at the
end of this campaign.
6. I attended this 'O' group. *Author.*
7. The Battery Commander personally thanked Elsmie for 'C' Company's support. One section of
'C' Company apparently held its position to the end and none of them were ever seen again.
8. This is the record but it seems likely that it was earlier.
9. Note by Brigadier W.H.H. Wilberforce, then acting GSO2 (Ops) at HQ 17 Division.

Brigade was ordered to fall back through 16 Brigade and to establish a lay-back position astride the main road at Tamagauk. Prome had been lost with only one battalion having been in contact with the enemy.

The Japanese state that in this action *215 Regiment* had 12 men killed and about 30 wounded, while they captured 20 prisoners. They also claim to have captured 14 locomotives at Prome station, but all of these had been partially destroyed.[10]

The Attack on the British Left Flank at Hmawza

16 Brigade had only a few skirmishes that night, but to the west 48 Brigade had a rather different story to tell. 48 Brigade were holding a position at Hmawza (see Map 19) with a company of the 1st/7th Gurkhas four miles out to the east. Tank and carrier patrols had been sent another ten miles along the Paungdale road to get early news of any attempt at encirclement. *Araki Force*, basically *214 Regiment* supported by a company each of heavy field and medium artillery, were advancing from the south up a track near the railway. Brigadier Cameron saw a chance for an ambush. A company of the 1st/4th Gurkhas, led by Captain Bromhead, left in the evening and, avoiding all contact with Burmese, moved into a wood some seven miles to the south-east. They lay up all day on 1 April and that night moved into an ambush position covering the track to Paungdale near Ainggyaung. Sure enough a large Japanese force came straight into the ambush in close column and was thrown into confusion by the sudden attack. The devastating automatic fire caused many casualties before the company withdrew quite unscathed.[11]

Meanwhile an advance unit of *214 Regiment* had bumped the main position at 0130 hours. Cameron had emphasised concealment, partly because of the frequent appearance of enemy aircraft, and the Japanese, advancing from the east in column, seemed quite unaware of their danger. The 1st/4th Gurkhas, who had two MMGs, could hardly have been offered a better target in the bright moonlight and they took full advantage of it at short range. After the initial shock, the Japanese deployed into the paddy fields and a fire fight developed, the 1st/4th maintaining their position without difficulty. The Japanese unit appears to have been the leading company of *1/214 Battalion*. The company commander and three soldiers were killed and eight were wounded.

Brigadier Cameron had the 2nd Royal Tanks and the 1st Inniskillings under command and planned a powerful counter-attack when the enemy made contact, as he was sure they would do, that night. Later that evening the Inniskillings were withdrawn and ordered back to join 1 Burdiv. However, his three Gurkha battalions were well concealed and had splendid fields of fire across the open paddy fields. For once the area was one in which the tanks could operate. Then at 0400 hours came an order from Division for an immediate withdrawal. Command of the 2nd Royal Tanks reverted to 7th Armoured Brigade. 48 Brigade was ordered to fall back west of the road with 16 Brigade deployed to the east of it. More than half of 48 Brigade was on the move when a large body of the enemy appeared in close formation moving across the front of the 1st/7th Gurkhas. This was the chance for which all the plans had been made but it was too late to exploit it. Cameron never forgot this lost opportunity and often referred to it in subsequent years.

The withdrawal was skilfully conducted, the 2nd/5th R Gurkhas holding a lay-back position between Tanbauk and the Nawin Chaung through which the other two battalions passed in succession. The 1st/4th, who were in contact with the enemy, were well handled by Colonel Lentaigne and slipped away with only four casualties. Before first light 63 Brigade passed through and took up a lay-back position covering the road junction at Tititut. After dawn the Japanese tractor-drawn medium artillery, no doubt grateful for the improvements to the track from Thegon, moved forward and fired on targets near the road. The two brigades were well dispersed, however. 48 Brigade had eight casualties and 16 Brigade about the same. Meanwhile, the 1st Indian Field Regiment, which had pulled back to a position just north of the Nawin Chaung, covered the withdrawal by firing on likely targets and succeeded in silencing the enemy guns.

The Decision to Abandon Prome

General Cowan, whose headquarters was north of the Nawin Chaung, had decided in the early hours of 2 April that it was impracticable to recapture Prome. This meant that no more stores could be back-loaded. He was, of course, unaware of the opportunity awaiting 48 Brigade, nor did he know what *215 Regiment* were up to in Prome. He was uneasy that the latter, who had not followed up 63 Brigade, might be moving north using the bridge at Prome which he had ordered the Sappers to strengthen. He therefore decided to withdraw his division and establish a position astride the main road on the line of the Nawin Chaung. To block the northern exit from Prome, he ordered the 1st Field Regiment to fire on the Prome bridge in an attempt to destroy it.[12]

At 1000 hours on 2 April, having got his division north of the Nawin Chaung,

---

10. They were steam locomotives and on each the left-hand cylinder is said to have been destroyed.

11. This was probably a column of medium artillery but this incident has not been traced in Japanese records.

12. A very optimistic manoeuvre as hardwood bridges in Burma could withstand several direct hits from 25-pdrs.

Cowan received a critical report from a major[13] in the BMP. This officer claimed to have seen a large body of Japanese crossing the Prome bridge that morning and moving north into the forest up the track to Dayindabo. This report was discredited later in the official histories, but it was true. *215 Regiment* had indeed moved out of Prome at 0500 hours and marched north up the forest track. This was alarming news as the main road to the north passed through ten miles of forest in which road-blocks would be only too easy to establish. Cowan therefore contacted General Slim at Allanmyo and said that in view of this report he thought he should withdraw at once. Slim was faced with an immediate decision. He decided that the report was probably true and agreed to the withdrawal. Japanese patrols were now probing 17 Division's forward positions and shelling was increasing. Cowan wasted no time. The rearguard withdrew across the Nawin Chaung and started their march north, 2nd/Lieutenant Higgins of 70 Field Company demolishing the main road bridge behind them at 1138 hours.

Withdrawal from Prome

From Prome to Allanmyo was two day's march and they were to be two days that few would forget. To begin with it was now very hot, over 100 degrees in the shade and much more in the sun. For the first day water was non-existent except in contaminated village wells. The troops, who had had little or no sleep the previous night, were already very tired and Japanese aircraft were a continual threat.

63 Brigade was in the lead, then came divisional troops, with 48 Brigade to the west of the road and 16 Brigade to the east as rearguards. A squadron of the 7th Hussars led the division, and a squadron of the 2nd Royal Tanks brought up the rear. The rest of 7th Armoured Brigade moved in bounds, covering the guns, vehicles and carts on the road. The two rearguard brigades were initially deployed off the road in the paddy fields and it was just as well that they were, for there was a concentrated bombing attack soon after the start. It caused a handful of casualties in each brigade. After a few miles, however, the forest closed in and the two brigades were forced onto the road and into piqueting the forest on either side.

Progress, conditioned by the speed of the bullock-carts, many of which broke down, was very slow. The air was full of fine dust and the lack of water became a severe problem. There being none available locally, the Sappers arranged to fetch two water tankers from Allanmyo, and these gave some relief to the exhausted troops, who were beginning to suffer badly from thirst. In the evening, Japanese fighters and bombers came over again and struck repeatedly at the marching column. 63 Brigade was the main target. The 2nd/13th FFRif lost 25 killed and many wounded, the 1st/10th Gurkhas 20 killed and 40 wounded. Other battalions also had casualties but less than these two.

That night 17 Division halted for two or three hours, rest in the vicinity of Dayindabo before being ordered on again to Allanmyo. At Dayindabo, and to the north of it, 1 Bur Brigade held a covering position, while 2 Bur Brigade crossed the river to the west bank and covered the destruction of a small oilfield at Thayetmo.

During the night of the 2/3 April, 17 Division continued its forced march to the Allanmyo area, being assisted towards the end by ferrying in vehicles, the unwise use of bullock-carts having been abandoned. All but the minimum of equipment was sent back to Taungdwingyi and dumped, the vehicles thus freed being pooled and used for ferrying. General Slim had been ordered by General Alexander to hold Taungdwingyi as a strongpoint to support the Chinese on the main axis. He now judged that it was not possible to do both this and to block *33 Division* at Allanmyo. He therefore got permission to withdraw to the next defensive position. He issued an Operation Instruction saying that the new aim for the Corps would be to cover the Yenanyaung and Chauk oilfields by holding a position on the line of the Yin Chaung stretching from Minhla to Taungdwingyi (see Map 20). 1 Bur Div would hold the line of the Bwetkyi Chaung until the stores in Allanmyo, dumped there for the original plan, had been evacuated. 17 Division would pass through them and hold the line of the Linban Chaung while 1 Bur Div in their turn passed through and proceeded to their new position at the western end of the Yin Chaung line. Slim was tocomment later:

"I did not like the idea of another withdrawal; we were fast approaching the dangerous state when our solution to all problems threatened to be retreat, but I hoped this would be the last."[14]

On 3 April, 17 Division was again attacked from the air while on the march. Casualties from air attack on these two days were over 200. On 4 April, 17 Division, now very tired, reached the area of Nyaungbintha, where the Sappers managed to provide adequate water-points for men and mules and it was possible to rest.

After 17 Division had passed Dayindabo, 1 Bur Brigade became rearguard and marched back to Allanmyo, the Malerkotla Sappers demolishing five small bridges on the road. By the night of the 5th/6th the stores had been cleared from Allanmyo and the main installations had been set on fire by the sappers. So, the

13. Believed to be Major Chappell. His BMP force had been in Prome in the area of the jail and 63 Brigade had failed to tell him that they were withdrawing.
14. Slim, Field-Marshal Sir W., *Defeat into Victory*, p.50.

large bridge just north of the town having been demolished, 1 Birdiv started its withdrawal. While 2 Bur Brigade marched up the road on the west bank of the Irrawaddy towards Minhla, 1 Bur Brigade changed on to a pack (mule transport) basis and marched along a footpath on the east bank. Its destination was Migyaungyi, a few miles south of Minhla. 13 Brigade and the rest of 1 Burdiv moved up along the road through Taungdwingyi to their new positions. Meanwhile General Slim had withdrawn 7th Armoured Brigade (less one regiment) and 48 Brigade into Corps reserve at Taungdwingyi to guard against any unexpected enemy action. 16 Brigade and the 2nd Royal Tanks covered the rear at the Linban Chaung, and the large bridge there was blown by Second-Lieutenant Eric Yarrow of 60 Field Company on the 7th, both piers being destroyed. By the 8th, all units were in their positions on the new line, a 40-mile front stretching from the Irrawaddy to Taungdwingyi.

With Hindsight

Prome was a very unsatisfactory first divisional battle for Major-General 'Punch' Cowan. Shwedaung had been a defeat, and the British had been levered out of Prome with scarcely a fight. Undoubtedly the attempt at offensive action, and the subsequent reverse at Shwedaung, had inhibited the defence of the town, as had some of the impracticable ideas for mobile defence[15] with which he had been force-fed.[16] Moreover the sprawling town of Prome was a very difficult place to defend. However, 63 Brigade, or more accurately its commander, had not done very well. Cowan had had no need to supervise the tactical plans of 16 and 48 Brigades, whose commanders were rapidly becoming experienced, but perhaps he should have given more guidance to the 'new boy', Brigadier Barlow. Was the aim still to ensure that the remaining stores around the railway station could be evacuated, or was it to cover the track to the north on which the bridge over the Nawin Chaung had been strengthened only the day before? Barlow may well have been confused. It may not have been his fault but, in this thick cover, his brigade was far too dispersed. When his right flank battalion, known to be weak, was overrun, he really lost control and there was nothing to stop the Japanese from occupying Prome and turning the flank of the whole division.

17 Division had been gaining in confidence before Prome. Shwedaung and Prome were a set-back. Nevertheless it might have been much worse. Cowan had correctly foreseen the trap that was being laid for the division by an encirclement on each flank and his prompt and decisive action had prevented a potential disaster.

Not everyone agreed at the time. General Slim's chief of staff, Brigadier 'Taffy' Davies, was later to write:

"I have personally always doubted the accuracy of the report by the BMP officer concerning the advance of a Japanese regiment up the river bank. This force never appeared subsequently and it certainly never made any attempt to secure the road behind 17 Division... As the whole series of decisions taken depended on this report, it is obviously most important to know whether it was, or was not, true. If not true, then Prome was evacuated prematurely and without reason, and a strong position from which we had an excellent chance of dealing the Japanese a bad rebuff, possibly of stopping him altogether, was abandoned on a false report... A successful action at Prome ... might have exercised a decisive effect [*on the campaign*]."

Here is the true story. General Sakurai had originally planned a double encirclement aimed at Tamagauk but, when it became clear that the British were retreating from Prome too fast to be caught, he changed the encirclement to a deep right hook. Meanwhile he called for the maximum air effort to harass and delay the retreating British columns. He expected that the British would attempt a stand at Allanmyo, as indeed they had originally intended. *215 Regiment*, who had rested and had a meal at Zayitchaung, had already started for Tamagauk but were now ordered to turn back, march north and after dark cross the main road secretly from west to east at Ngamegan (see Map 20). Marching by night and resting in the shade of villages by day, they spent 3 April in Yengangyi and the 4th in Mahazin on the Bwetgyi Chaung (see Map 20). Here there was water and they were ordered to rest and await orders. The Japanese follow-up on the main road was slow, partly due to the activities of the British tanks and partly due to the demolitions. On the 5th, *215 Regiment* were ordered to advance after dark to a position in the hills overlooking Allanmyo, and to be prepared to attack the town from the north-east while the main forces attacked from the south. When the encircling force reached their position about 0400 on the 6th, they saw that the town was in flames. It was clear that the British had left, so they marched down and entered the town from the north as the leading unit of the main force entered from the south.

General Slim's judgement on the veracity of Major Chappell's report had been sound. He took the right decision and thus avoided General Sakurai's trap.

---

15. A famous General was to remark at a staff conference after the war when mobile defence was being discussed: "In my experience mobile defences are mobile in one direction only."

16. Hutton Papers, Personal Record, p.66: "At the time I [Hutton] blamed Alex for these suicidal orders and it was only later that I realised he was carrying out Wavell's orders."

CHAPTER SEVENTEEN

The Japanese Reverse at Kokkogwa

General Sakurai's trap at Allanmyo had been avoided by the British and contact was now broken. *33 Division* halted for three days in the area of Allanmyo to rest and reorganise for the attack on the oilfields. The British did not always appreciate that the Japanese troops were often as exhausted as they were. *33 Division* was now nearly at full strength with two regiments each having three battalions. *213 Regiment*, however, still had only two battalions as its third one was in Army reserve.[1]

Some new units had now arrived. There was a light armoured car unit equipped with 'tankettes', a form of turreted Bren carrier, useful in a scouting role. For some days[2] they had had the support of *21 Independent Mixed Field Gun Unit* with its eight tractor-drawn guns (four x 150mm howitzers and four x 105mm heavy field guns) to back up their 24 mountain guns. In addition, there was *51 Independent Field Anti-aircraft Unit*. Although this unit was not much use in its primary role, as there were now no British aircraft left to shoot at, it was useful both against infantry and as an anti-tank weapon. But most useful of all was the allotment to *33 Division* of *26 Independent Engineer Regiment*. This unit had a large selection of boats, four fast, three armoured,[3] ten landing craft large enough to carry a Japanese medium tank, and some 40 large steel motor boats, each capable of carrying 70 men. It was a unit which had proved of great use in China and here, with a river flank, it was again to prove invaluable.

There was also a new weapon. The threat of the British tanks was a continual worry to the Japanese and they were glad to receive 11 of the new Chibi anti-tank grenades. These were glass globes about four inches in diameter and filled with a toxic liquid.[4] When thrown at a tank they broke and filled the tank with poisonous fumes forcing the crew to bale out; at least this was their purpose and they did occasionally, although rarely, work.

The British Defensive Line West Of Taungdwingyi

General Slim was also reorganising his force, although his problem was the opposite of Sakurai's in that his force was diminishing rather than increasing. As most of the Burmese had vanished, 1 Burdiv had become very weak and so Slim transferred three British battalions from 17 Division to 1 Burdiv. These were the 1st Glosters, the 1st Inniskillings and the 1st Cameronians. Unfortunately these battalions were now much under strength as a result of the battle of Shwedaung and the rigours of the campaign. For instance, the 1st Cameronians could only muster 215 men for, in addition to battle casualties, they had had 220 men evacuated sick. The only British battalion left with 17 Division was the 2nd Duke of Wellington's Regiment, while the 1st West Yorks remained as a lorried Infantry battalion supporting 7th Armoured Brigade.

The Chinese forces in the Sittang valley were holding Pyinmana, so General Alexander instructed Slim to hold Taungdwingyi as a strongpoint to keep contact with them. Now, to hold Taungdwingyi, and also to stop an advance against the oilfields, entailed holding a front nearly 40 miles long. It was a very long front to hold against a powerful thrust from the south. General Slim felt it essential to have a reserve. He therefore asked General Alexander to arrange for the Chinese to take over Taungdwingyi and thus release at least one of 17 Division's brigades as a strike force. Although General Stilwell and General Tu Yu Ming of 5 A/Division agreed, in fact no Chinese troops ever appeared, so the final positions were as follows (see Map 20). 2 Bur Brigade held Minhla on the west bank of the Irrawaddy, while 1 Bur Brigade held Migyaungye, a little further south on the east bank. Further east, 13 Brigade held the important road junction where the main road turned north for Magwe and the oilfields. Still further east, 48 Brigade held a position astride the road at Kokkogwa, while, at the eastern end of the line, Taungdwingyi was firmly held by the rest of 17 Division. Unavoidably, the layout was an awkward one, for the main road turned sharply west at Taungdwingyi and ran parallel to the front for the next 25 miles. Hence it was very vulnerable to enemy infiltration.

This was the dry zone of Burma and there was little forest. Trees were mostly only found in villages or along the line of chaungs. The country was open and undulating, with patches of scrub and deeply etched with dry nullas. This suited the 7th Armoured Brigade which was very much the British trump card. Slim now allotted HQ 7th Armoured Brigade and the 7th Hussars to support the 1 Burdiv sector and 2 Royal Tanks to support 17 Division.

Slim's Corps Headquarters had been in Taungdwingyi, where it had been pattern-bombed in a 20-bomber raid, but on 17 Division's arrival on the 7th he

1. *2/213 Battalion* was in Army reserve and one of its companies was sent from Prome to capture Akyab. One mountain gun company was also in Army reserve.
2. This unit had been used against the British retreating from Prome.
3. The armoured boats had a turret similar to that on a Japanese medium tank, with a 57mm gun and two MMGs.
4. Believed to be hydrogen cyanide, incapacitating but not normally lethal under these circumstances.

moved to Magwe, which was more centrally placed. 17 Division set about making Taungdwingyi, a small market town, into a strongpoint. As it was surrounded by open paddy fields this was not difficult in spite of the total lack of barbed wire. Rather imperfectly controlled fires were started by the Sappers in the town as a fire precaution, thatched roofs being a considerable hazard in the latter respect. Positions were dug in, bunkers and command posts were constructed and Defensive Fire targets were registered by the Gunners.

A day or two later, Generals Alexander and Slim paid the garrison a visit. General Alexander, cool as ever, arrived in a shiny black saloon car with a flag on the front. As the road was regularly patrolled by Japanese aircraft, and likely at any moment to be the target for Japanese patrols, this display of courage by the Army Commander was much admired. But otherwise his visit made little impact. In contrast, General Slim went round the garrison talking to all the officers in small groups. It was the first time most had seen him. He gathered the officers round him informally and spoke easily and well. He said the usual things about the importance of holding Taungdwingyi firmly and of his confidence in 'Punch' Cowan. Then he added "General Cowan and I were at Staff College together - but I'm bound to say that some of the things that we learnt there don't seem to work too well out here!" This was encouraging. Many felt that they now had a leader who realised that new methods were required to counter Japanese tactics and was prepared to think them out.

The Japanese Plan

The main Japanese aim was to destroy the British forces and the secondary aim was to seize the oilfields before they could be destroyed. General Sakurai's plan was as follows:

a. *213 Regiment* (less *2/213 Battalion*), *33 Mountain Artillery Regiment* (less *3 Battalion*), most of the divisional engineers and a company of anti-tank guns, all under the command of Major-General Araki, were to advance along the east bank of the Irrawaddy and capture Magwe.

b. *215 Regiment* (less *3/215 Battalion* and *4 Company*), the light armoured car unit, a company of anti-tank guns, a company of three mountain guns, *21 Independent Mixed Field Gun Unit*, a company of *51 Field Anti-aircraft Battalion* and a company of engineers (less a platoon), were to form the right flank guard. Their task was to contain the British in the area of Taungdwingyi and prevent them from interfering with the main thrust.

c. *214 Regiment* (less *1/214 Battalion*), *3 Mountain Artillery Battalion* (less one company), a platoon of engineers and a section of the specialised water-supply unit, was to advance across-country as secretly as possible and at the appropriate time attack Yenanyaung from the north-east and cut off the British retreat.

d. *HQ 33 Division*, with *1/214* and *3/215 Battalions* under command, would follow *213 Regiment* along the east bank. *26 Independent Engineer Battalion* were to have 50 motor boats ready to carry troops up the river when required.

The orders to implement this plan having been given, at sunset on 9 April the advance from Allanmyo began.

The Battle of Kokkogwa

General Slim was hoping to fight a Corps battle to stem the Japanese advance, but that was not how it turned out. The Army Commander had insisted that Taungdwingyi must be firmly held at all costs to support the Chinese in the Sittang valley. Slim therefore had no spare troops to strike at the flank of the Japanese advance. As a result, 17 Division and 1 Burdiv were to engage in two separate battles. Here we consider the struggle which took place between *215 Regiment* and 48 Brigade at the villages of Kokkogwa and Thadodan.

The Japanese Advance

214 and *215 Regiments* moved in trucks up the Allanmyo-Taungdwingyi road on the night of 9/10 April as far as the demolished bridge at Nyaungbintha, where a small British patrol was brushed aside. Here they parted. The river being dry at this time of year, the demolition was no obstacle and *214 Regiment* drove off west along the cart track before debussing and marching north to Didokpin. From there they went north to Ngasaung (see Map 21). *215 Regiment*, having placed a temporary block across the main road about six miles to the north to cover the move, debussed at Lettet and marched across country to Yagyidaw. The troops in the temporary block having rejoined *215 Regiment*, there were now no Japanese fighting troops on the road between Taungdwingyi and Prome, or indeed Rangoon, but General Sakurai had rightly calculated that the British would not try again an adventure on the lines of their thrust south of Prome. In any case, his line of communication was now up the river, so the road to the south had lost its importance.

What happened to *214 Regiment* is considered in the next chapter. Here we are concerned with the fate of *215 Regiment*.

The British Position

48 Brigade was holding a rather featureless position, which included the hamlet of Kokkogwa, covering the main road from Taungdwingyi to Magwe. A dry river-bed ran through the position from east to west and much of the area was covered with scrubby thorn bushes. Brigadier Cameron had already impressed

on his brigade that the first rule of jungle warfare was to adopt a position of all round defence. Consequently he had deployed the 1st/4th Gurkhas to hold the northern perimeter, the 2nd/5th R Gurkhas to hold the east and south, and the 1st/7th Gurkhas to hold the western perimeter, which included part of Thadodan village. 'D' company of the 1st/3rd Gurkhas, detached from Taungdwingyi, was holding an outpost position in the village of Sonzu, about a mile to the south, and 'D' company of the 1st/7th Gurkhas was holding a similar position about a mile and a half to the west. Inside the perimeter he had a half squadron of the 2nd R Tanks and 2 Battery (less E Troop) of the 1st Indian Field Regiment. The remainder of 2 R Tanks (less one squadron which had gone west to support 13 Brigade), supported by a company of the 1st W Yorks, were in a leaguer astride the road near milestone 290.[5]

Both British divisions had deployed patrols some ten miles south of their positions and the Japanese likewise advanced behind a screen of scouts and Burmese dissidents. This was confusing for the British as not only were there many Burmese refugees on the move but they had been alerted to keep a look-out for Chinese troops. On 10 April, Captain Grieve took his company of the 2nd/5th R Gurkhas on a reconnaissance towards Yagyidaw, some seven miles to the south. He advanced with three widely separated platoons, leading the centre column himself. He found Yagyidaw occupied, apparently with Chinese troops, and, being hailed in English and Urdu by an officer, advanced with his orderly to make contact. After a short and apparently amicable conversation, he suddenly realised that his contact was Japanese and beat a very hasty retreat to his platoon, pulling them back without a shot being fired. He was lucky, for he had bumped into *1/215 Battalion*. His platoon to the west were also taken in at first, but they were engaged by the enemy, realised their mistake, and succeeded with some difficulty in withdrawing. About eight men were lost. To the east the third platoon under Subedar Dhirbahadur was also deceived and the whole platoon were taken prisoner, although some later escaped.

On Captain Grieve's return it was realised that a considerable force was now approaching from the south and steps were taken to improve the defences. This was not easy. There was no wire or other defence stores, and very few picks and shovels. Men had to make do with the mamooties,[6] and other village tools, which they had acquired *en route*. There was also a serious lack of the means of communication. Battalions had only one telephone and this was connected to Brigade HQ. Using runners was the only other means of passing messages. Of any one area there was only one map (black and white) per battalion. Nevertheless fields of fire were cleared and in some areas thorn bushes made a useful zariba.

The night of 10/11 April was quiet but very dark as the sky was overcast.

However, there was plenty of evidence of the enemy to the south and the south-west the next day. In fact *215 Regiment* were closing in and preparing for their attack on Kokkogwa and Thadodan that night. They were planning one of their silent bayonet attacks and the significant order had been given for all rifles (but not LMGs) to be unloaded. *1/215 Battalion* (less two companies) were to assemble in Songon and attack Kokkogwa up the Yaume Chaung from the east. *2/215 Battalion* (less one company) were to assemble in Yewe, cross the road and attack Thadodan village from the west. The regimental gun company, a company of mountain artillery and two infantry companies were to remain with *HQ 215 Regiment*. at Yewe, while the mixed medium artillery battery was deployed at Ywatha (see Map 21).

The Japanese Attack on Kokkogwa

1/215 Battalion left Songon at midnight and followed the Yaume Chaung down towards Kokkogwa. About 0130 on the 12th they were detected by a listening post and the 2nd/5th R Gurkhas unexpectedly opened fire on their leading platoon at short range. The Japanese attempted an immediate charge but the company commander, Lieutenant Hashimoto, and several men were killed at once and the attack fizzled out. For the rest of the night the Japanese probed the 2nd/5th perimeter in an attempt to find weak spots but the defence was well-sited and they were always repulsed. The three Japanese mountain guns shelled the garrison intermittently but in the dark they were relatively ineffective. The eight British 25-pdrs (2 Indian Field Battery less a troop)[7] could not put down defensive fire on the perimeter as the range was too short but they engaged and silenced the enemy mountain guns. Meanwhile the battalion's mortars fired at suitable moments on pre-arranged targets. At dawn the British tanks, supported by a company of the 2nd/5th, started a sweep round the perimeter and Major Mugita of *1/215 Battalion* hastily withdrew his men up the chaung, which had steep sides and gave good cover. Unlike the British he had a signal section with a man-pack radio.[8] Deciding to dispense with code[9] he sent a signal to regimental HQ saying "Kokkogwa has not been occupied. Request shelling on

---

5. They had little Infantry protection and were relying for protection on a tight formation and complete absence of lights. They were therefore rather disconcerted when a 7th Armoured Brigade replenishment convoy, unaware of the situation, came along the road at 10pm on the 11th with full headlights on.

6. A kind of draw-hoe widely used for digging in the East.

7. The 1st Indian Field Regiment had two batteries, each of three troops of four guns.

8. Normally carried on pack horses, this radio could be split into three man-pack loads of transmitter, receiver and generator. *Mr Yoshiro Tsukagoshi.*

9. The Japanese normally encoded their messages but it was unnecessary as no-one in 1 Burdiv or 17 Division could speak Japanese.

Kokkogwa". On receipt of this message, Colonel Harada ordered the battalion to rendezvous at Songon at 1300 hours. The Japanese attack had failed and, significantly, they retreated leaving their dead behind. The British claimed to have found ten corpses and assumed that the rest had been removed. According to Japanese accounts they only had 23 casualties of whom seven were killed. The 2nd/5th R Gurkhas had lost four killed and three wounded.

The Japanese Attack on Thadodan

The attack by *2/215 Battalion* on the same night was altogether a more serious affair. They started from Yewe also at midnight of 11/12 April but took some time to reach their objective because of the need to avoid the 1st/3rd Gurkha company at Sonzu. After some shelling, they started their attack at 0430 on the 12th. As it happened, the British perimeter in Thadodan was only lightly held as 'D' company of the 1st/7th Gurkhas, who had originally held that sector, had been sent out to the west. A runner had been sent to recall them at 0315 but meanwhile an MMG and two weak platoons did their best to stem the attack. A hand grenade battle took place but the Gurkhas were forced back across the road. Soon after 0400 'D' Company had come in over the bridge and they were now ordered to attack Thadodan from the south. In the dark, and in spite of some accurate shelling, they put in a hastily-organised and gallantly-led counter-attack They were met with showers of grenades and were finally held up at the village cactus hedge by concentrated LMG fire. The situation was now extremely serious as there was little between the Japanese and Battalion HQ and the guns. At Brigade HQ, Brigadier Cameron organised an officers' bombing team and ordered the guns to engage the enemy at point-blank range. The War Diary of the 1st/7th Gurkhas describes the scene:

"At this critical time the 25-pounders' crews with the utmost coolness and gallantry dragged their guns from their pits, slewed them round and opened up a devastating fire over open sights into the south[10] edge of the village. This undoubtedly saved the situation and when dawn broke gave the Battalion the opportunity to reorganise and re-establish their positions."

This is a handsome tribute to 2 Field Battery of the 1st Indian Field Regiment. However, the battle was far from over. There were still Japanese among the houses in Thadodan. When the tanks returned from their sweep of the southern perimeter, Captain Macpherson led a platoon of the 1st/7th, with powerful tank support, into Thadodan and after some sharp fighting succeeded in driving the Japanese out of most of the village. In doing this, Macpherson's platoon ran out

of grenades and ammunition. So Cameron ordered the 1st/4th Gurkhas to provide a company to continue the attack.

Colonel Lentaigne detailed 'B' Company under Captain Brodrick-Pittard for
the task. It was now discovered that most of the enemy had taken cover in a narrow and deep, dry nullah just west of the village. This nullah was more like a
trench, being between two and five yards wide and about six feet deep. The tanks
could neither get into it nor depress their guns sufficiently to deal with the enemy
sheltering under its walls. Supported by a fresh squadron of the 2nd Royal Tanks,
two platoons of 'B' Company completed the clearance of the village and were
then posted to cover the open ground at the southern head of the deep nullah (see
inset in Map 21) . Meanwhile Brodrick-Pittard led the third platoon round to the
mouth of the nullah and, little realising that nearly all *2/215 Battalion* was inside,
started to bomb and shoot his way up the narrow cleft. Several tanks circled
round each end and waited for the Japanese to emerge. This the Japanese were
very reluctant to do, knowing that either in the main chaung or in the open on
either side of the nullah, they would have little chance. The Japanese anti-tank
gun platoon attempted to get into action on the edge of the nullah and claimed to
have cut the track of one tank. However, it was soon knocked out, and a second
gun was crushed by a tank, the gunners suffering severe losses. It was very hot,
only a little sandy liquid could be obtained by digging in the bed of the nullah
and *2/215 Battalion* were soon in a desperate state. They were beginning to have
heavy casualties when, at about 1600 hours, the Japanese medium artillery came
to their rescue.[11]

Up to this point the Japanese artillery had not intervened due to the confusion
of the fighting. The Japanese had a radio but because of the depth of the nullah
they were unable to make contact. However, a signaller escaped from the nullah
and alerted the Japanese to their predicament. A daring Japanese gunner OP officer, with a field telephone and cable, then succeeded in infiltrating through the
scrub and right inside the British position.[12] He proceeded to direct the fire of the
105mm (33lb shells) and 150mm (80lb shells) guns on to the British tanks and
infantry. A tank was hit and set on fire and Captain Mountford, the adjutant of
the 1st/4th, who went to the assistance of the crew, was mortally wounded by the
next salvo. 'B' Company lost five killed (including two Gurkha officers) and 14
wounded. The shelling continued relentlessly and, before the OP was located and
the officer eliminated, there was some confusion during which some of the
Japanese managed to escape.

---

10. The war diary says 'south' but from the attached sketch it is clear that 'south-east' is meant.
11. Account of Mr Umeo Tokita.
12. Lieutenant-Colonel Lentaigne told me this story (which is confirmed by the Japanese) on the
14th, adding that the enemy OP was set up in the scrub 30 yards from his own HQ. *Author.*

Japanese from 33 Division driving a tank captured at Shwedaung. Note Japanese flag at side and rear, and white cloth wound round the turret.

By 1630 hours it seemed to Brigadier Cameron that, except for a few stragglers, the enemy had been driven off and it was time to prepare for another night. He therefore ordered a shortening of the perimeter to exclude Thadodan while 2 R Tanks (less a squadron) were brought inside the perimeter. He did not realise *2/215 Battalion's* desperate predicament. After dark, the remaining Japanese managed to retreat carrying their wounded and dead, the latter being cremated in a nearby village. They had had a very lucky escape.

The British, however, had suffered one reverse that night. 'D' Company of the 1st/3rd Gurkhas, commanded by Second-Lieutenant McGilchrist, had been attacked throughout the night in their isolated position at Sonzu, apparently by the two companies under command of *HQ 215 Regiment*. At dawn the attack was joined not only by the Japanese 'tankettes' but also by two captured Stuart tanks. The company broke out but were caught by the tanks in the open paddy fields before they reached cover and lost 37 men.

The Second Night

The night of 12/13 April was mainly quiet but at 0300 hours an attack developed up the Yaume Chaung, as on the previous night, and spread to the southern perimeter. It was fiercely resisted, however, and by 0400 hours had petered out. At dawn Captain Grieve took a fighting patrol, supported by a troop of tanks, to Yewe. Three Japanese planes appeared and strafed both the British position and the patrol. As they reached the village HQ, *215 Regiment* and two companies of infantry were streaming out on the other side. They were engaged at long range by the patrol and the tanks from their covering position. Three gunners of the *215 Regimental Gun Unit* were killed. The Japanese claim (but there is no mention of this in British war diaries) that at 1130 a Japanese sapper knocked out one British tank with a flame bottle, and killed three of the escaping crew before being killed by the fourth.[13] The Japanese also claimed, and there is no reason to doubt it, that Lieutenant Seinosuke Adachi, who spoke excellent English and was Intelligence Officer at *HQ 215 Regiment*, used the wireless in one of the tanks captured at Shwedaung to listen in on the 7th Armoured Brigade wireless net. He thus kept his HQ well-informed about the British moves.

During the afternoon there were more air raids and the bombers attacked Kokkogwa village, setting it alight. Two ammunition lorries caught fire and a number of mules were killed. The 7th Hussars relieved the 2nd Royal Tanks who moved west to support I Burdiv. In anticipation of another noisy night, the 1st/10th Gurkhas arrived from Taungdwingyi as reinforcements and one company was allotted to each battalion, the remainder going into brigade reserve.

Contrary to British expectations, the night of the 13th/14th was quiet. The Japanese had had enough. They did not renew their attack, and *33 Division* were to regard Kokkogwa as their one defeat of the 1942 campaign. Both Japanese battalions had been shaken by their experience. *1/215 Battalion* had failed to recover its dead, always shameful to the Japanese.[14] *2/215 Battalion* had been shattered by their near disaster and took some time to recover. However, the Japanese only record 42 officers and men killed and this figure includes 15 gunners. General Sakurai was not displeased for, as we shall see, the divisional aim of preventing British interference from the east had been achieved.

The British, on the other hand, had been much encouraged by their success at Kokkogwa. True, it was mostly a defensive success and easier to achieve than an offensive one, but 48 Brigade had fought as a team and Brigadier Cameron always regarded this battle as the day his brigade "found its soul". Certainly over the next three years 48 Brigade was to win many battles and lose very few.

Taungdwingyi

1 Burdiv to the west was in trouble, and on the 14th General Slim decided that Taungdwingyi would have to be maintained from the north. He therefore ordered General Cowan to send 16 Brigade back to Natmauk and to pull 48 Brigade back into Taungdwingyi to replace them. 70 Field Company were ordered to send a party to destroy the bridge at Thadodan. One span was destroyed and a pier damaged, but it was a strong wooden bridge, difficult to destroy and easy to repair. An attempt to burn the bridge failed, teak being fire-resistant. There was, in any

13. Possibly this tank was abandoned when the Japanese retreated and so was recovered and repaired.
14. In fact most of *1/215 Battalion* came back to Kokkogwa from Nyaungbingyi, seven miles to the south-west, on the 15th. Finding the British had left, they disinterred the bodies of their dead from shallow graves and, after collecting a relic for the next-of-kin, cremated them.

case, an easy diversion at this time of year so the demolition was of little value.

The noise of battle at Kokkogwa had been clearly audible to the garrison of Taungdwingyi and was in sharp contrast to the quiet time they were having. The Japanese Air Force was busy making major raids on the towns, including Mandalay, to the north and, surely rather unwisely, ignored the tempting target presented by the concentrated 17 Division. However, on 12 April four bombers appeared flying in diamond formation and flew slowly over the centre of the town at about 6000 feet. The LAA Gunners duly opened up and hit the rearmost plane which caught fire and crashed with a loud explosion about a mile away. The three remaining planes then circled round and came in again at the same height but much faster. This time they dropped all their bombs on the Gunner lines. Everyone was dug in and casualties were surprisingly few but two ammunition lorries were hit and their shells, which continued to explode for about an hour, caused some confusion.

As the main road was no longer a practicable line of supply to 17 Division it was clear that another route was required. Foreseeing this, efforts had been made by the Chief Engineer at Corps HQ to get contractors to remove the rails fom the railway running north out of Taungdwingyi and this had been done for about ten miles. As far as Natmauk, some 40 miles to the north, this appeared to be the only withdrawal route for vehicles. On the 16th, the divisional engineers were given the task of completing the work. There were a number of big railway bridges over wide chaungs, however, and it became apparent that a cross-country bullock-cart track, which had already been used by a few vehicles, would be as effective as the railway embankment and easier to drive over at night, so this was developed instead.

Attempts to Attack the Rear of 33 Division

As 1 Burdiv to the west was being forced back, General Slim saw a good opportunity for a Corps battle. If 16 Brigade held Natmauk, 17 Division, less a brigade but supported by the 7th Hussars, could strike along the road at the rear of *33 Division*. General Alexander, however, would not agree to this bold suggestion. He was determined to hold Taungdwingyi as long as possible in order to give firm support to the Chinese right flank. Consequently, the only help that 17 Division gave to 1 Burdiv, who were now getting into serious trouble, was to make some raids to the west from Taungdwingyi and Natmauk respectively. The first, from Taungdwinggi, consisted of one squadron of the 7th Hussars and the 1st/10th Gurkhas. On the 17th they reached milestone 304, just past the fork to Magwe and stayed in this area for the next two nights. Although they shot up a lorry-load of troops and two staff cars, burnt three villages and cut telephone wires, there was no major action as the Japanese had now moved further north and were being supplied up the river. A troop of the 7th Hussars had already made a raid from Natmauk on the 16th. In an encounter with the enemy, one tank had been hit with a Chibi grenade and the driver incapacitated. However Sergeant Campbell, the tank commander, succeeded in taking over and driving the tank back. On the 20th 'B' Squadron, supported by the 2nd Duke's, went out again from Natmauk to raid Magwe airfield. About nine miles from Magwe they met a block supported by artillery. In a brisk engagement two tanks were badly damaged by fire from 75mm anti-aircraft guns. 'B' Squadron now had only four 'runners' left and returned to Natmauk.

Withdrawal from Taungdwingyi

On 20 April, the Chinese 5th A/Division was forced out of Pyinmana and, further west, the Japanese made rapid progress in the Shan States and were threatening Taunggyi. This in turn posed a serious threat to the main British line of communication back to Mandalay and the Ava bridge. Thoughts of a possible counter-offensive were therefore abandoned and 17 Division was ordered, on the nights of the 21st and 22nd, to withdraw first to Natmauk and then to Mahlaing, about 30 miles north-west of Meiktila. The convoys drove with their lights on, but the clouds of dust made visibility poor and there were many delays as vehicles got stuck and needed help from the Sappers at the nullah crossings. The average time taken at the back of the convoy for the 40-mile journey was nine hours. The move continued on the nights of the 22nd and 23rd. The first 35 miles on this night was over a poor track but then the road improved, the 90-mile journey to Mahlaing taking an average of ten hours. Here new orders were issued, but before this phase is considered the misfortunes which had befallen 1 Burdiv to the west, and the 6th Chinese A/Division to the east, must be described.

CHAPTER EIGHTEEN

The Disaster at Yenangyaung

1 Burdiv, numerically weak and with a number of Burmese units of doubtful value, had scarcely been in action before and was now faced with the problem of defending the Burma oilfields against the best and most experienced Japanese division in Burma. It was a formidable task.

General Slim had, of course, intended to use his whole Corps for this purpose, but General Alexander had decided that it was essential to hold Taungdwingyi firmly. No doubt he felt that to abandon Taungdwingyi would inevitably lead to allegations that a premature British withdrawal had forced the Chinese to do the same. This made it difficult for Slim as he was obliged to keep one brigade on the west bank of the Irrawaddy to counter any Japanese advance on that flank. His solution was to keep this brigade, 2 Bur Brigade, under his own command, and transfer 48 Brigade and the 2nd Royal Tanks to 1 Burdiv. This gave 1 Burdiv three brigades, but 1 Bur Brigade and 13 Brigade, which each had two Burma Rifle battalions and only one Indian battalion, were far from strong. General Slim's headquarters were in Magwe and the headquarters of General Bruce Scott, who commanded 1 Burdiv, were at Sainggya at milestone 312 on the road to Yenangyaung (see Map 22).

The British suffered from two grave disadvantages at this period. Firstly, having no air support at all, they were not only exposed to continual harassing attacks from enemy aircraft but, an even worse handicap, could neither attack the enemy supply lines nor obtain news of enemy moves. The enemy, on the other hand, were free to move as they liked by day or night, on land or on the river, without fear of detection. Moreover, to the rather sparse local population it was only too clear which side was winning; few were willing to risk helping the British, so local 'intelligence' was scanty. Thus the British had little idea of how the Japanese were planning their attack. Nor did they fully realise that, for this phase, General Sakurai had abandoned the idea of a road or cross-country line of communication and had decided to rely entirely on water transport up the Irrawaddy. A second grave disadvantage was the lack of any reliable form of intercommunication. Apart from the radios in every tank, there were no radio links below brigade headquarters. Even those between brigade and divisional headquarters, and between divisional and corps headquarters, had often to be provided by 7th Armoured Brigade. Links between units and brigade HQ, and between units, had to be by telephone, runner or liaison officer. Vital messages sometimes never arrived, or arrived too late for action to be taken. This was in contrast to the Japanese who had sufficient radios and were well trained in their use.

The Japanese Plan

33 Division's plan was, as usual, a daring one. *213 Regimental Group* (less one battalion) would advance up the riverside track with the initial aim of capturing Magwe. They would be followed by *HQ 33 Division* with two reserve battalions under command. This time it was the turn of *214 Regimental Group* (known as the 'White Tigers'),[1] also less one battalion, to do the encirclement. They were to move secretly north and be prepared at the appropriate moment to attack Yenangyaung from the north-east. *215 Regimental Group*, as described in Chapter 16, was to provide the right flank protection by capturing Kokkogwa. When that task was completed, it would rejoin the division as a reserve for the battle at Yenangyaung.

The British Reactions

The result of these moves was that 48 Brigade, attacked by *215 Regiment*, became virtually cut off from 1 Burdiv and on 14 April was transferred back to 17 Division. This left 1 Burdiv with two brigades east of the river, but supported by 7th Armoured Brigade (less the 7th Hussars), to deal with *33 Division*. 1 Burdiv's two brigades had been deployed on 9 April with 1 Bur Brigade by the river at Migyaungye, and 13 Brigade between the road fork to Magwe and Thityagauk at milestone 300 (see Map 20). A patrol screen had been established on both sides of the Irrawaddy some 15 miles to the south. On the east bank, its limit was the Linban Chaung which crossed the Allanmyo-Taungdwigyi road at Nyaungbintha and ran roughly east-west. This patrol screen was provided by Burma Frontier Force units, part of which were mounted infantry. In addition to this screen, both brigades organised company patrols to the south of their areas. It wasn't long before contact was established.

Late on the 9th, news came in that the Japanese (*213 Regiment*) had occupied Sinbaungwe on the river. Then, on the 10th, 48 Brigade had made contact at Yagyidaw and a Burma FF mounted patrol had been ambushed north of Didokpin, five men being captured. The patrol had been followed to the north, and later that day the Japanese contacted 13 Brigade at Alebo, about five miles south of the road-fork at milestone 302.

---

1. The name stemmed from a heroic legend in the district from which they were recruited. Every soldier wore a cap-badge depicting the head of a white tiger.

There was still a belief at the higher levels of command that aggressive action would neutralise the apparent Japanese superiority. 1 Burdiv was therefore directed to strike at this Japanese force advancing from the south. This was distinctly unrealistic. 1 Burdiv was only partially trained, was numerically weaker and was far less experienced than its opponent. Although their grouping varied at times, each brigade had normally only one Indian battalion and two Burma rifle battalions.[2] The location and strength of the Japanese force in this area, and the location of other Japanese forces, was unknown. Nevertheless, 1 Bur Brigade moved six miles out of Migyaungye to the south-east on the 11th, leaving only a light detachment by the river, and the 2nd/7th Rajputs closed in on Alebo from the west. Similarly, the 1st/18th Royal Garhwalis of 13 Brigade approached Alebo from the north.

The Garhwalis were supported by 2 Mountain Battery. On the 11th their patrols located a large enemy force in Ngasaung (see Map 21). Further west, near milestone 300, were the 1st Inniskillings, supported by 'C' Squadron of the 2nd Royal Tanks. One of their patrols had also contacted a large enemy force north of Alebo and had suffered some casualties. Both of these contacts were with *214 Regiment*, who were preparing for their clandestine crossing of the road by doing what they could to silence the creaking of wheels and rattle of gun equipment

The 1st/18th R Garhwalis had asked permission to attack Ngasaung on the 11th but it had been refused. That evening, the 5th Burma Rifles entered Alebo after dark and found it empty. The Garhwalis, however, were shot up or 'jittered' as it came to be known, at Powe, three miles to the north and two miles south of the road. This was by a patrol of *214 Regiment* aiming to distract their attention while the main force moved forward to the road. For it was on this night that they made their critical crossing of the main road. They advanced along a dry nullah which passed under a road-bridge at milestone 296. Just before they started moving under the road, a 7th Armoured Brigade replenishment convoy, coming from west to east with full headlights on, drove along the road but was allowed to pass and saw nothing amiss. The Japanese then put out a platoon block about half a mile away on either side and *214 Regimental Group* successfully passed under the road without being detected.

In the early morning, Kokkogwa was attacked and it was clear that the enemy were also advancing up the east bank of the Irrawaddy. Urgent adjustments to 1 Burdiv's deployment were now required. With these distractions, the riddle of the disappearance of the enemy force in the centre of the front seems to have been temporarily disregarded, although the probability that it had gone north was duly reported. *33 Division's* failed right hook to Allanmyo had not been detected, otherwise alarm bells would surely have been ringing in HQ Burcorps. Since the

Japanese were using the same maps as the British it would have required no great discernment to see that the bottleneck of the Pin Chaung crossing was a possible target. Perhaps the bells did ring. But Slim was desperately short of troops and his repeated requests for the Chinese to take over defence of Taungdwingyi, and thus release 17 Division or part of it, bore no fruit. Both Generals Alexander and Stilwell had agreed, but no action resulted from the Chinese.

Because of the threat on the British right flank, 1 Bur Brigade was ordered to put a battalion into Migyaungye and withdraw north to cover the road leading to it. There was some delay in getting the order through and, by the time 1 Burif arrived, the Japanese had already captured the town by a ruse. They had gained entry by pretending to be a Burma Rifles unit and had soon overrun the BFF 2 police screen. 1 Burif, who arrived at first light on the 13th, were nearly taken in as well and the CO was captured but managed to escape. A fight ensued outside the town and 1 Burif were scattered.

The Withdrawal to the Yin Chaung

These reverses exposed the right flank of 1 Burdiv and General Slim decided to reorganise the defence. 1 Burdiv was to withdraw to the line of the Yin Chaung. There was some water in this chaung and the position was to be held as long as possible. There was no further water to be found in any side stream of the Irrawaddy until the Pin Chaung was reached some 40 miles to the north. 7 Burif were to cross back over the Irrawaddy and to join the Cameronians in Magwe. The 2nd KOYLI, who had been in reserve protecting the oilfields at Yenangyaung since mid-March, were relieved by the 1st Glosters on 12 April. They moved south to join 13 Brigade at Thityagauk, near milestone 300.

On the 14th, the 2nd KOYLI were ordered to send a company to Thazi, a village on the Yin Chaung four miles to the north of milestone 300, to see if there were any signs of Japanese there or on the other side. 'D' Company was duly despatched but there is no record of what they found. *214 Regiment* had indeed passed along the far bank there on the 12th and were now lying up in Polelon, awaiting orders by radio to cross the Natmauk-Magwe road and move further north (see Map 22).

Before 'D' Company returned, the 2nd KOYLI, whose total strength was about 330 all ranks, was ordered to move to Shabinhla in 7th Armoured Brigade vehicles. 'D' Company, the mortar platoon and the animal transport were to follow by march route. However, before they reached Shabinhla, the 2nd KOYLI were ordered to go to Myingun, on the edge of the Irrawaddy, where they would be joined by 1 Bur Brigade. They were ferried on tanks to the high ground near

---

2. The Inniskillings, woefully under strength, had been attached to 13 Brigade.

Toksan, a neighbouring village. A truck with a wireless set and operator was sent from HQ 1 Burdiv to accompany them but it was not of much use as it never managed to contact anybody.

There was no sign of 1 Bur Brigade, and the next morning, 14 April, the 2nd KOYLI sent out a patrol to Myingun. Before it returned there was firing from the village of Toksan. It transpired that 'D' Company, returning from its patrol to Thazi, had missed its guides and had spent the night with the mules and seven trucks containing the battalion's heavy weapons in Toksan. There they had been attacked at first light and dispersed by *213/10 Company*, who were the Japanese advance guard coming up the river bank. This was serious, and the CO decided on an immediate counter-attack, with 'A' Company from the north and 'C' Company from the west, to recover the weapons. This attack, pressed home with vigour, was successful and the enemy was driven out of Toksan. However, only one truck had an ignition key left in it[3] and this and two mule-carts were all that could be removed before a strong counter-attack by the Japanese, who had been reinforced by *213/12 Company*, obliged the two companies to withdraw. The 2nd KOYLI then pulled back to a new position and the Japanese, who had lost 13 men killed in *10 Company* and 20 killed in *12 Company*, did not follow up.

The battalion IO, Second-Lieutenant Watts, was now sent off to try and find HQ 1 Bur Brigade. He met a mounted Gunner subaltern who had volunteered to carry a message to the 2nd KOYLI, telling them to withdraw to the Yin Chaung. Having persuaded the Gunner subaltern to lend him his horse, Watts started back but fell off and broke his collar-bone. He survived but the message didn't get through. The CO made another attempt to contact Brigade and sent off a three-man patrol under Second-Lieutenant Cranfield. They were ambushed and only one private was ever seen again. There seemed to be Japanese everywhere. Lieutenant-Colonel Chadwick rightly deduced that he was behind the Japanese lines and that his orders to withdraw to the Yin Chaung, which he knew to be the next bound, must have gone astray. So after dark he ordered companies to slip out and make their way to the Yin Chaung, using the Pole Star as a guide. After various adventures this was successfully achieved. The battalion passed through the 2nd/7th Rajput Rifles, who were holding the north bank of the Yin Chaung, and were lifted in vehicles to Magwe, where they spent the night of the 15th/16th. The battalion strength was now down to about 200.

The Action at the Yin Chaung

1 Bur Div was holding the stretch of the Yin Chaung between the Irrawaddy and the road with 1 Bur Brigade on the right and 13 Brigade on the left (see Map 22). The chaung still had a shallow flow of water. Headquarters 1 Burdiv was at

Magwe. The 7th Armoured Brigade (less the 7th Hussars) was in support at Kantha, six miles north-east of Magwe, with 'B' Squadron of the 2nd R Tanks at milestone 322 and under command of 1 Bur Brigade. On the extreme right, the 5th Burma Rifles were in the area of Pado. Then came the 2nd/7th Rajputs around Zigyun. They were supported by 23 Mountain Battery and 1 Burif were in reserve. 13 Brigade covered from the left of the Rajputs to the main road.

On the 15th, certain preliminary action was taken. General Slim moved his Corps Headquarters back from Magwe to the Pin Chaung, and the next day to Gwegyo at milestone 380. As there was no water between the Yin and Pin Chaungs it was clear that no position could be held south of Yenangyaung if 1 Burdiv was forced to retreat further. On his way he visited the oilfields where the complex work required to prepare for the demolitions had been completed. Mr Forster, the oil engineer who had organised the destruction of the refineries at Rangoon, was in charge, assisted again by Captain Scott RE. Slim, who had been authorised by General Alexander to use his discretion about the timing, now decided that the demolitions must start. The power station, however, the largest in Burma, was to be kept in operation for as long as possible as it also supplied electricity to the oilfield at Chauk, 20 miles further north. Unfortunately the situation changed so fast that, 36 hours later, the order was given to destroy the power station, too, and this had the effect of stopping Yenangyaung's water supply.

Further south, the 5th/1st Punjab Battalion was also ordered to leave 2 Bur Brigade and cross the Irrawaddy to Magwe. They were allotted to 13 Brigade. The intention had been to bring all of 2 Bur Brigade across but time did not permit, so the remainder were ordered to march north on the west bank to Seikpyu, opposite Chauk. They took no further part in this battle. The 1 Burdiv Sappers denied Magwe airfield and its satellite, and established water points for men and animals behind the two brigade positions. 7th Armoured Brigade decided to replenish the 7th Hussars by sending a convoy, escorted by a troop of tanks, along the rough track to Natmauk early in the morning. It arrived safely.

At mid-day, 7th Armoured Brigade was told by Burcorps that a Japanese force, about 2000 strong, had crossed the Yin Chaung on their east flank and was moving north-east. They were to carry out a sweep the next day to see if they could locate it. The information was correct but too late. *214 Regimental Group* had already crossed the Natmauk track the previous night and were now holed up in Tanbinzu, well to the north of 1 Burdiv and about 12 miles south-east of Yenangyaung.

---

3. In 17 Division the second line transport was mostly provided by Indian transport companies and in 1 Burdiv by Burmese companies. The drivers were unarmed and naturally made themselves scarce if directly attacked and not protected. The trouble was that they often took with them the ignition keys of their vehicles.

The Japanese attack by *213 Regiment* on the Yin Chaung position was aimed at the 1 Bur Brigade sector and started as usual with probing fire, the purpose being to get the British to disclose their defences. At about 0100 hours on the 16th, the enemy charged across the white sand of the chaung in a bayonet attack and were driven back with casualties by the automatics of the two infantry battalions and the accurate defensive fire of 23 Mountain Battery. However, they renewed the attack and succeeded in breaking into the right-hand company of the 5th Burma Rifles and exploiting this with the bayonet so that the whole battalion position crumbled. Shortly afterwards they broke into the left-hand company of the Rajputs and a confused fight followed. The right-hand Rajput company under Captain Robert Grant continued to hold its ground firmly but battalion headquarters was overrun. The situation became critical and 23 Mountain Battery, there being no order to retreat, prepared their guns for destruction. At first light, however, the tanks of 'B' Squadron of the 2nd R Tanks came into action and checked the Japanese attack.

General Bruce Scott had ordered the 2nd KOYLI to march up from Magwe to support 1 Bur Brigade but, before they arrived, decided that the time had come to withdraw. Both brigades then withdrew successfully past Magwe, covered by two squadrons of the 2nd R Tanks who were supported by the 25-pdrs of 414 Battery RHA. The tanks came under some pressure and one tank and its crew were knocked out by one of the newly-arrived 75mm Japanese anti-aircraft guns. But the tanks were skilfully handled and a potentially dangerous situation was defused.

1 Burdiv left Magwe at mid-day and the Sappers completed the final demolitions there. On orders from Burcorps, now clearly uneasy about the 'missing' Japanese force to the east, rear Divisional HQ and all transport that could be spared was sent back to positions north of the Pin Chaung. General Slim also ordered the 7th Armoured Brigade back over this river, leaving one squadron of 2 R Tanks to support the rearguard. These were wise moves. Half the Malerkotla Field Company under Major Orgill went north to Yenanyaung and started loading lorries with 40-gallon drums of water pumped out of a Burma Oil Company swimming pool. These were sent back down the road, returning to be filled up again and repeat the trip. The other half of the company added to this with water from a few rare village wells, established water-points and did their best with improvised methods to dispense water to the marching troops and animals.

Throughout this period, the Japanese Air Force had continuously harried all movement on the road and had bombed any troop concentrations that they could see. Though casualties from this source had not been heavy, they included a number of officers, one of whom was Lieutenant-Colonel R.C. Cox, the CO of the

Inniskillings, who was killed while riding in a jeep driven by Brigadier Curtis of 13 Brigade. These attacks were to continue during the march to Yenangyaung and forced the troops to march in extended order off the road wherever possible.

The Withdrawal to Yenangyaung

The withdrawal to Yenangyaung was a severe ordeal for the exhausted 1 Burdiv. It was very hot, over 110 degrees (43 C) in the shade in the middle of the day and about 85 degrees at night. For the first time since leaving Rangoon three journalists appeared.[4] One, the American David Berrigan, described the scene colourfully:

"Men, mules and horses were strung out across the dusty hills under a white blazing sun. They were collapsing dog-tired in the sand for a brief rest, then heaving themselves to their feet and again marching forward. Bearded, dust-caked men, with the sweat-salt dried white across their shirts, their water-bottles clacking dry against their hips, fell into position as the sun sank behind the smoke from the burning city of Yenangyaung."

North of the Kadaung Chaung, the scrub and occasional palm trees ceased and the country was bare and shadeless. Moreover, it was very broken with small hills and deep nullahs, and marching off the road became impracticable. Matters were not helped by the sight of the huge flames and dense clouds of black smoke which rose high into the air from the burning oilfields to the north. Nor was morale improved by a rumour on the morning of the 17th that the Japanese were already in Yenangyaung. Unfortunately it was true. Early that morning the 'missing' *214 Regiment* had blocked the road astride the Pin Chaung ford.

Although the Sappers had managed to provide a minimum of water on the march to the Kadaung Chaung, where the two brigades bivouacked for the night of 16/17 April, there was little to be had the next day except what each man could carry. Unfortunately there were very few chaguls, the excellent canvas water-carrying bags much used in India, and so each man had to rely on his water-bottle, whose capacity was much too small for these conditions. The reason for the acute water shortage was that, after some early deliveries, those Malerkotla Sappers who had been filling the water drums in Yenangyaung had been attacked and cut off from the south by a part of *2/214 Battalion*, who were establishing a road-block at the south end of Yenangyaung town. Unable to deliver any more drums, the Sapper party decided to break out to the north and, having fortunately

---

4. They shared a jeep. One was the *Daily Mail* correspondent Jack Belden and his report of the next three days' action duly made the front page, a rare occasion for the Burma campaign.

acquired 17 abandoned BMP ponies for their gear, waded the Pin Chaung near its mouth and joined the forces on the north bank.

It is very difficult for those who have not experienced such conditions to realise how important water becomes when it is very hot and men are obliged to march or work without it. Mouths become parched, tongues swell and speech becomes difficult. Some men collapse from dehydration; others collapse from heat stroke. It is not long before even the best disciplined men become desperate, lose all restraint and ignore their orders. Several men collapsed on this day and could not be revived. Much worse was to come.

Headquarters 1 Burdiv reached the southern end of Yenangyaung in the early morning. At first light they were met by Lieutenant-Colonel Sharpe[5] of the Glosters, who confirmed that there was a road-block north of the town at the crossroads in the village of Twingon (see Map 23). There were also Japanese patrols in the town, so a block was put in across the road south of the town by the divisional Sappers, who were relieved in due course by Magforce[6]. As the two brigades arrived, they were allotted areas around the road junction at milestone 360, with all the animals by the river. The last units of 1 Bur Brigade did not get in until after midnight. It was a blessed relief for men and animals to get to the water, tainted though it was with petrol.

The Japanese Advance to Yenangyaung

33 Division was now planning to devote its full strength to the annihilation of the British force and to capturing the oilfield and what remained of its installations. *215 Regiment*, after its action at Kokkogwa, had been brought across to Migyaungye on 16 April. They moved by boat to Minbu on the night of the 17th/18th. On the evening of the 19th,[7] *1/215 Battalion*, with 550 men, two 75mm guns and three MMGs, embarked in nine large and ten small boats of *26 Engineer Regiment*. Just before midnight they landed without opposition at Nyaunghla. Later that night the rest of the regiment arrived with 268 horses.

Large Japanese engineer boats move troops up to Yenangyaung.

*214 Regiment in action
at Yenangyaung.*

214 Regimental Group, who had arrived in Tanbinzu early on 15 April, were relatively fresh. They had avoided the worst of the heat by marching by night and resting in the shade of villages by day. They also had with them a detachment of the specialist water-supply unit[8] with its purification filters carried on horseback. So they had been able to get water not only by digging in some of the chaungs but also by purifying the water from village wells. After a 36-hour rest in Tanbinzu they were ordered to leave the village and advance on Yenangyaung on the night of 16/17 April. They halted on high ground about three miles east of Yenangyaung and learnt there from some Burmese that a number of British tanks had already crossed north of the Pin Chaung. Major Sakuma thereupon decided to modify his plan and, rather than just attack the north of Yenangyaung, to put in a road-block both north and south of the river. *3/214 Battalion*, with the two regimental guns and a party of engineers with five anti-tank mines, would go north. *2/214 Battalion*, with the six guns of *3 Mountain Gun Battalion*, would seize the crossroads south of the river at Twingon and also set up a small block south of Yenangyaung town.

213 Regiment's follow-up along the main road was delayed. They had had a hard fight at the Yin Chaung and had been highly impressed by the British tanks. They moved into Magwe on the morning of the 17th. The activities of the 7th Hussars now caused them some alarm. On the 17th and 18th, a 7th Hussar sortie with infantry from Taungdwingyi caused casualties at Taunglebin near milestone 302, so, on the 18th, *1/213 Battalion* was detailed to put a block on the road at milestone 324 to protect Magwe. On the 20th, British tanks from Natmauk

---

5. The wounded Lt-Col. Bagot had been ordered into hospital by General Cowan after Shwedaung.
6. Magforce was the erstwhile garrison of Magwe and comprised the 1st Cameronians and the 7th and 12th Burma Rifles. Its Commander was Lt-Col. Thomas of the Cameronians.
7. It should have been the 18th but for some poor staff work which caused a delay.
8. The full name of this unit was Disease Prevention and Water Supply Unit. It had 200 men and included seven doctors and one pharmacist. As well as small filters which could be carried on horses it had four big motor-driven filters. It was liberally supplied with man-pack canvas containers and also had big canvas tanks which could be fitted into trucks.

attacked Nyaungbinywa, only nine miles from Magwe, and although hit by shells from a 75mm anti-aircraft gun escaped apparently unscathed. Nevertheless the main part of *213 Regiment* advanced on the night of the 17th/18th and, after another night march, reached Yenangyaung on the morning of the 19th and contacted *1/215 Battalion*.

The Action at Yenangyaung North of the Pin Chaung

After dark on the 16th, HQ 7th Armoured Brigade and the 2nd R Tanks, less 'A' Squadron, had been ordered to drive back from the Yin Chaung and harbour about five miles north of the Pin Chaung. Brigade HQ, 'E' Troop RHA and about half a squadron of tanks had crossed the Pin Chaung and had just passed through a cutting when there was a burst of fire and a staff car behind them was set alight. A tank attempting to pass this struck a mine and was immobilised, the crew managing to escape under covering fire from other tanks. Two hours later this tank was set on fire.

This was a most unexpected turn of events far behind the 'front'. The road was now firmly blocked and it was deemed unwise for the tanks to attempt to force a way through the block in the dark. Patrols from some nearby Burma FF units, under Lieutenant-Colonel Price, were sent out to locate the enemy. Meanwhile a long queue of tanks and soft vehicles built up north of the Pin Chaung. Useful news being received at dawn from the Burma FF, an attack along the ridge from the west was put in at 0800 hours on the 17th, supported by a detachment of the West Yorks and the 25-pdrs of 'E' Troop from the north. This was successful in driving the enemy away from the cutting, and a troop of tanks and about 30 soft vehicles were able to drive through. However, the Japanese then moved south and started mortaring and machine-gunning the queue of vehicles and many of the unarmed drivers fled. Some vehicles were able to be moved, however, and finally all the rest of the armour passed through.

The Japanese, confident that the broken country east of the road would protect them from the tanks, were eager to wait for the dark and then attack the road again. Colonel Sakuma did not agree. He saw that his main task now was to hold the block south of the Pin Chaung. He therefore ordered *3/214 Battalion* to leave *214/9 Company* close to the river on the north side and bring the rest of the battalion back across the Pin Chaung to Twingon, to reinforce the block there.

It was now clear that the Japanese were making a powerful thrust up the east bank of the Irrawaddy and, if it were not countered, their move might pose a serious threat to the withdrawal of the Chinese forces on Mandalay. Slim therefore requested reinforcement. Stilwell concurred and offered the newly-arrived 38th Chinese D/Brigade from the 66th Chinese A/Division, which was on its way to

Burma. Genral Alexander agreed, and so 38 Chinese D/Brigade[9] concentrated at Kyaukpadaung, about 35 miles to the north of Yenangyaung. A plan was agreed with 1 Burcorps by which the Chinese would clear the north bank of the Pin Chaung on the morning of the 18th, while 1 Burdiv cleared the southern block.

The Chinese Commander, Lieutenant-General Sun Li Jen, was one of the bright young officers whom Chiang Kai-shek had sent to get their military education abroad. He had been educated at the Virginia Military Academy in America and spoke English well. General Slim was much impressed by his personality and character. As the Chinese had no tanks or artillery, Slim offered to put one squadron of tanks and 'E' Troop RHA under his command for a proposed attack the next day. This offer, which was accepted, alarmed Brigadier Anstice but greatly enhanced General Sun's prestige with his d/brigade.[10]

The Chinese asked for sporadic harassing fire on the Japanese throughout the night and, at 0800 hours on the 18th, duly attacked south towards the chaung. Although communication was difficult, the attack seemed to go well and by the afternoon they had reached the chaung. *215/9 Company*, however, still held a small enclave covering the road crossing.

The Battle of Yenangyaung south of the Pin Chaung[11]

Headquarters of 1 Burdiv were in the grounds of a pagoda at Sadaing, about four miles south of Yenangyaung. At 2100 hours on the 17th, General Bruce Scott gave out his orders for the next day (see Map 23). Magforce, supported by 5 Mountain Battery[12], would advance up the road, capture Nyaunghla and exploit north, the main purpose being to guard the Division's left flank. 1 Bur Brigade would be in reserve with the primary task of guarding the Division from the south. 13 Brigade, supported by 'A' Squadron of the 2nd Royal Tanks, 'E' Troop of the 1st Indian Field Regiment and 23 Mountain Battery, would advance up the first Yenangyaung by-pass road and capture first Point 510 and then Point 501. Point 501 was about three miles further north and was the highest point of the ridge that dominated Twingon village.

The advance started at 0630 hours on the 18th. Magforce advanced through Nyaunghla against slight opposition and secured the end of the second by-pass

9. Chinese 'divisions' were of about brigade strength. They are described in this book as 'd/brigades'. Similarly, Chinese 'armies' are described as 'a/divisions'. See Appendix 5.

10. This is believed to be the first time in history that British forces were placed under direct Chinese command.

11. The American journalist David Berridge translated 'Yenangyaung' as 'Smelly Water Creek' but this seems rather too flippant a name to use for this desperate battle.

12. 5 Mountain Battery, which had lost its guns at the Sittang, had been re-equipped but as there were no mules available the guns had to be carried in trucks. The Battery had just arrived at Yenangyaung from the north.

to the north of it. However, they then encountered much stronger opposition and could make no further progress. By 0800 hours, 13 Brigade had secured the ridge at Point 510 without meeting any opposition and continued their advance. Lieutenant Pat Carmichael of 23 Mountain Battery has described vividly the view ahead from Point 510:

"The road now fell away on our right, steeply at first, before it levelled out and ran due north, rising and vanishing over a long series of small crests for two miles to the next feature, which was a long ridge across our front. At its left extremity were trees and some houses, more trees on the right and a long open space between. That was Point 501 and Twingon. The wave-like crests continued out into the country on the right of the road. These were less pronounced on the left for a short distance until submerged by a clutter of shacks, black pipework and derricks along the eastern edge of the town. The only structure on the right of the road was a whitewashed shack with a red tin roof, perched on a small plateau about half-way to the Twingon ridge."[13]

At 1100 hours, General Bruce Scott ordered 'A' Squadron of the 2nd Royal Tanks to join Magforce via Obozu from the north. This they did, drawing only sniper fire. However, when Magforce resumed its attack there was again heavy opposition and the attack stalled. The tanks were recalled at 1415 hours and ordered to rejoin 13 Brigade via the second by-pass.

Meanwhile, 13 Brigade had advanced with the Royal Garhwal Rifles on the right and the 5th/1st Punjabis on the left. The Garhwalis came under fire from a well-concealed and well-entrenched Japanese platoon near the red-roofed shack. They had a number of men killed but, with support from the mountain guns and MMGs, they succeeded in driving the Japanese out of their position. On the left of the road the Punjabis had also met opposition as they neared the Twingon ridge. Japanese mountain guns, mortars and MMGs caused heavy casualties but the Punjabis were well led and succeeded in securing a foothold on the top of the ridge.

General Bruce Scott was now faced with a difficult decision. It was extremely hot, 113 degrees (45 C), in the shade in Yenangyaung that day. On the by-pass there was no shade and the only water was being hand-pumped out of the Irrawaddy by the Sappers with a single pump and sent forward in drums. His Division, however, was getting very spread out and was becoming vulnerable to Japanese closing in from the south or attacking from the west. 13 Brigade was making good progress and a Chinese force seemed to have cleared the north bank. He therefore decided to leave the Irrawaddy and its water and try and break through to the Pin Chaung that night. The transport was ordered up the by-pass to the Point 510 ridge and Magforce was ordered to join the force via the second by-pass. Together with 1 Bur Brigade they were deployed protecting the transport from all sides. During this move there was some pressure on the rearguard from enemy who had come up the river.

At the sharp end, the 5th/1st Punjabis had been driven off the Twingon ridge by a Japanese counter-attack in the afternoon and had suffered severe casualties, the CO being among those wounded. However, 13 Brigade organised a counter-attack with the Garhwalis and the Inniskillings, the ridge was recaptured after a hard fight and the leading platoons penetrated the eastern part of Twingon village before being held up by concentrated fire from the enemy mountain guns. Unfortunately, in this action, the popular acting CO of the Inniskillings, Major S.B. McConnell, was mortally wounded.

Although Twingon village had not been cleared, patrols were able to get down to the river. One company of the Inniskillings, about 90 strong, after skirting Twingon village reached the Pin Chaung where they saw some Chinese on the north bank who answered correctly the agreed recognition signal of a rifle held aloft vertically with a cap on top. Both parties then moved out into the broad sandy chaung. Lieutenant Brian Petherick, who was with a small rear party, described how he saw the two sides meet and cigarettes being exchanged. He was moving to join them when suddenly he saw the Chinese surrounding the British and taking their rifles. Some fights broke out and men were being bayoneted. It was clear that the 'Chinese' were Japanese, so he beat a hasty retreat followed by a hail of bullets.[14] The company commander is said to have been shot and the rest of the Inniskilling company were taken prisoner and incarcerated in a village house. Here they spent the night together with some HAA Gunners and some Indian drivers captured by *214/9 Company* in the road-block north of the Chaung. However, all managed to escape during the next day's fighting.

There were a number of curious incidents on this day, with soldiers on both sides near the end of their tether from the heat. A party of Japanese from Twingon village under an officer approached a Punjabi platoon, apparently offering to surrender. Seeing reinforcements arriving, Captain Dayal Singh attempted to disarm them. The Japanese resisted, a fight broke out and many were shot. A similar attempt was made shortly afterwards by another large party from the village. This party claimed they were Chinese and called for a senior officer to liaise with. Major Hallifax of the Garhwalis went to a tank to check with HQ 13

13. Carmichael, Pat, *Mountain Battery*, p.144.
14. With acknowledgements to the Inniskilling regimental magazine, *The Sprig of Shillelagh*.

Brigade, while both sides took up defensive positions. Assured that there were no Chinese in the area, Hallifax resumed his attack.[15] The Japanese recount a similar incident. They say that a young Sergeant in a tank raised a white flag, climbed out, walked forward with his flag and was met by Japanese soldiers. He asked if anyone spoke English and two Lieutenants, Uchida and Yuzawa, together with interpreter Ishibashi, came forward. He then tried to persuade them that it was silly to continue fighting and it would be better if they pulled out of the village and further bloodshed was avoided. They replied that their division had just arrived and they had no intention of stopping fighting, wherupon the Sergeant retired to his tank and battle was resumed.[16]

General Bruce Scott spoke to General Slim at 1630 hours, using the 2nd R Tank radio van. He said his men were exhausted and could not break through the block that night. Some men were on the point of collapse through lack of water, and he suggested abandoning the transport and guns and breaking out across the chaung on foot. General Slim told him to hold on. He was arranging for the Chinese 38 D/Brigade to attack Twingon early the next morning and was confident they would clear the block. It was agreed that, at first light, the Chinese would attack west of the road and 13 Brigade and their 2nd R Tank squadron would attack east of the road. The two generals were in the same regiment, the 6th Gurkhas, and they and their families had been close friends for many years. It was a hard decision but neither man would have dreamed of letting personal considerations interfere with his duty.[17]

HQ 1 Burdiv, therefore, moved north and, with 1 Bur Brigade, established an all-round defensive position, a 'box' as they were to be called later, about a mile south of Twingon village. The box had a diameter of about 800 yards with the vehicles, guns and mules packed in wherever they could find space. 13 Brigade held a smaller box centred on the Point 501 ridge. The night of the 18th/19th passed relatively quietly, apart from what seemed at Divisional Headquarters to be a mild panic and unnecessary firing on the western perimeter. In fact *1/214 Battalion*, who had been in divisional reserve, had arrived by boat at Nyaunghla and, escorted by some mountain guns, were marching along the road from Yenangyaung, which approached the British position, to rejoin the rest of their regiment. The Japanese troops in Twingon were strengthened that night and the new battalion was given the task of attacking the British from the west and south.[18]

That evening a message came from General Alexander at Army HQ. A serious crisis was developing for the Allied armies. Slim was ordered to attend a conference with Generals Alexander and Stilwell at Pyawbwe the next day, the 19th. Now Slim's Corps HQ was at Gwegyo, but he had spent the night with his tactical HQ at the headquarters of 7th Armoured Brigade at milestone 376, nine miles north of the Pin Chaung. Pyawbwe was on the main road to Mandalay and central for the Allied command but over 100 miles away. Slim left his HQ in the early morning and did not return until the evening and so was away from the battle on most of this very critical day.

About 0800 hours on the morning of the 19th, there still being no sign of the Chinese attack promised for 0630, 13 Brigade and 'A' Squadron attacked and made a final all-out effort to clear the block. According to the Japanese[19] some tanks actually reached the vital crossroads where Japanese were concealed among the rubble of steel sheets, pipes and tanks which littered the area, but they were driven off by accurate fire from the 75mm mountain guns of *3 Mountain Artillery Battalion*. The Infantry were also shelled heavily and were held up by *214 Regiment* who had been reinforced during the night.

HQ 1 Burdiv then put the 2nd KOYLI and the 2nd/7th Rajputs under command of Lieut-Colonel Rea of the Rajputs and ordered them to march to the Pin Chaung, drink their fill and attack the road-block from the north-east. Owing to a confusion of orders following a bombing attack, most of the Rajputs failed to arrive, but Colonel Rea and the 2nd KOYLI reached the chaung. They were preparing their attack when an order came from Burcorps to cancel it. Their fear was that it would interfere with the Chinese attack, now scheduled for 1230.

There was another attack that morning, this time from the north bank. HQ Burcorps, aghast at the tardiness of the Chinese, who believed in very careful briefing and preparation, launched a small attack on the ford with a squadron of tanks and a company of the 1st West Yorks. It succeeded in crossing the ford and this success might well have been expanded but for an unfortunate muddle. A report reached HQ 7th Armoured Brigade, allegedly from HQ Burcorps at Gwegyo, saying that a force of Japanese were approaching Kyaukpadaung, some 25 miles further back, along a road from the south. This was possible and serious. Some tanks were sent north to Gwegyo to keep the road open and the tanks and West Yorks were recalled. Unfortunately the report was false, the troops seen approaching Kyaukpadaung were Chinese. In the absence of General Slim, someone at Burcorps HQ, not realising the position at the front, had overreacted.[20]

---

15. Both these stories are from WO 172/951.

16. Account of Mr Mitsuru Ishida.

17. According to Major Brian Montgomery (the Field Marshal's brother) who was on Slim's staff and heard the conversation, Slim spoke gently and courteously but firmly. He appears to have spoken in clear. Lewin, Ronald, *Slim*, p.94.

18. *Memoir of 214 Regiment*.

19. *ibid*.

20. Slim, Field-Marshal Sir W., *Defeat into Victory*.

It was now becoming clear that time meant little to the Chinese. Their advance did not materialise at 1230 and was now promised for 1600 hours. This was the last straw for the beleaguered 1 Burdiv. A number of men had already died of heat stroke and many, including officers, were verging on collapse through lack of water. The oven-like heat, the suffocating smell of crude oil and the insiduous effects of extreme thirst were making themselves felt. Men were beginning to trickle away to the chaung without orders. When a bullet fired into a pipe leaked a small amount of water there was an ugly scene as men fought each other to get a drink. In some cases rusty water was drained from radiators to fill water-bottles. Both Brigade Commanders reported that their troops were becoming unreliable. The problem was that the Pin Chaung was only knee-deep and could be forded by men anywhere, but the only place where vehicles could get over the rugged ground to the river was at the ford itself. However, 'A' Squadron now reported that there was a very rough track leading to the chaung upstream of the main crossing. It might just be negotiable by vehicles. Accordingly, those vehicles whose drivers could be found were organised in the order: tanks, guns, ambulances, remainder. The vehicles left behind were to be destroyed but in fact not many were as the force was too exhausted.

There still being no sign of any Chinese attack, General Bruce Scott gave the order at 1400 hours for the withdrawal to begin. Men made their way to the chaung and flung themselves into the blessed water. A few were so exhausted that they drowned, but the majority, refreshed by the water, were able to make their way to a collecting point a few miles up the road to the north. Once the mules of 23 Mountain Battery smelt the water they became uncontrollable and galloped frantically towards it. Their drivers pursued them, however, and they duly carried out all four guns.

The vehicle column was not so fortunate. They were shelled and mortared where the track crossed a ridge and several vehicles were hit, blocking the track. Those that got through this gauntlet came to a stretch of soft sand that only the tanks could cross. The tanks succeeded in dragging two lorry loads of wounded through this and across the river, but after this there was nothing to be done except get out as many wounded on the tanks as possible. The Divisional Commander was near collapse and he and Brigadier Roughton, the sub-area commander in Yenangyaung, were taken through in a carrier. The Gunners whose guns were towed by, or carried in, trucks were forced to abandon them, having first removed the sights and done what damage they could. By no means all the wounded could be got onto the tanks and many of the more serious cases had to be left behind. A gunner officer, who volunteered to return across the chaung that night and see if anything could be done for them, found that they had all been killed.

Aftermath

The exhausted troops of 1 Burdiv were lifted back through Kyaukpadaung and out of the dry belt to the pleasantly green area of the sacred Mount Popa to rest and reorganise. General Bruce Scott, after a good night's rest at Divisional Rear HQ, made a full recovery but his fellow passenger, Brigadier Roughton, collapsed on arrival and died. In 13 Brigade, Brigadier Farwell was evacuated with beri-beri and Lieutenant-Colonel Rea took over the brigade. In turn he was replaced as CO of the Rajputs by Robert Grant, a regular officer with three years' service, and aged 22. He was to command the headquarters and two companies remaining in his battalion for the rest of the campaign. Among those killed in divisional headquarters was the DAQMG. He was replaced by the highly regarded Major Thapar who was another Indian officer serving in this campaign who was later to become Commander-in-Chief of the Indian Army.

Altogether about a fifth of the division, which at this time was about four thousand strong, were killed or missing in this fierce struggle in conditions of extreme hardship which none would ever forget. Material losses included four tanks, four 25-pdrs, four mountain guns, two Bofors, many three-inch mortars, and about 200 vehicles. It was not so great a disaster as the Sittang, but it was a serious defeat, and 1 Burdiv would now be of little use until it was rested and re-equipped. Japanese casualties are recorded as 30 killed in *214 Regiment* plus five mountain gunners and four engineers, the relatively small numbers being due to their fighting a defensive battle.

The attack by the Chinese 38th D/Brigade, with a squadron of British tanks and a troop of British 25-pdrs under command, had been finally started at 1500 hours on the 19th. Under cover of a barrage from 'E' Troop of 414 Battery, RHA, the Chinese crossed the Pin Chaung and captured a village west of Twingon, where they dug in, but without attacking Twingon or clearing the road-block.[21] On the 20th, the Chinese attacked again to the south and advanced into the northern outskirts of Yenangyaung where they spent the first part of the night, having repulsed a Japanese counter-attack by the leading company of *215 Regiment*. However, as the whole of *33 Division* had now reached Yenangyaung and were clearly preparing a major riposte on the 21st, General Slim agreed with General Sun that they should be withdrawn to the north bank of the Pin Chaung later that night. For the next few days the Chinese and the 7th Armoured Brigade (less the 7th Hussars) covered the battered and exhausted 1 Burdiv while, in Slim's words, "it lay gasping but not dying". The battle of Yenangyaung was over.

---

21. Some accounts say that the Chinese cleared the road-block. Japanese records deny this and they are supported by the war diaries of 7th Armoured Brigade and 2 R Tanks. The British prisoners who escaped were held on the north bank of the Pin Chaung.

Hindsight

With hindsight, Alexander's recall of Slim to his HQ one hundred miles away at a critical stage of the Yenangyaung battle was the final move which sealed the fate of 1 Burdiv.[22] If Slim had been present at the battle on the 19th, he might have been able to persuade General Sun to attack earlier, although this is perhaps doubtful as Chinese preparations were maddeningly slow. Certainly, however, he would have reinforced the successful tank crossing of the Pin Chaung in the morning. The Japanese in Twingon were also near breaking point and either move might have enabled 1 Burdiv to burst out of their trap.

Slim might, of course, have refused to go to the meeting with his Army Commander on the grounds that the situation at the Pin Chaung was critical. No doubt as the commander of the British forces, however, he felt it was a vital duty to attend when the future course of the campaign was being decided. He clearly thought that, with the Chinese scheduled to attack early in the morning of the 19th, all that was possible would be done satisfactorily in his absence. At the conference at Army HQ he suggested that there was now a splendid opportunity for a decisive counter-attack against *33 Division*. If Stilwell would allot him another Chinese d/brigade he could hold the Japanese frontally while 17 Division struck at their rear from Taungdwingyi and Natmauk. Stilwell, always in favour of aggressive action, agreed, but Alexander, although he consented to the allotment of another Chinese d/brigade to Burcorps, did not agree to 17 Division moving west as he still considered that the Chinese would feel abandoned. This removed most of the point from Slim's plan. As it turned out, events on the eastern and central fronts were now moving far too fast for this bold counter-stroke, a last attempt to turn the tables on *33 Division*, to be practicable.

---

22. Neither Generals Alexander nor Slim refer to this critical incident directly in their published memoirs.

CHAPTER NINETEEN

The Loss of Central Burma

The Chinese are Out-Manoeuvred

While the British were licking their wounds at the western end of the Allied front, the Chinese 5th A/Division was being pushed steadily back up the main road to Mandalay in the centre and a severe crisis was developing with the Chinese 6th A/Division in the Shan States to the east.

Two new Japanese divisions had now come into action. *18 Division*, which had taken a leading part in the capture of Malaya and Singapore, reached Rangoon on 8 April. It had three regiments, numbered *55, 56* and *114 Regiment*[1]. Shipping was desperately tight for the Japanese and *18 Division* were without most of their horses and trucks. They reached Toungoo on 16 April and were ordered to advance by rail behind *55 Division*. *18 Division* was an old and experienced division which had been raised in 1937 and had fought in China for three years. As in *33 Division*, each battalion had four rifle companies, as well as an MMG company and an infantry gun platoon. This division also had a mounted infantry reconnaissance 'regiment', two mountain gun battalions and a 75mm field gun battalion. Its commander was Lieutenant-General Renya Mutaguchi who was later to command the *15th Army* for the fateful 'Imphal Operation' in 1944.

The other new division was *56 Division*. Like *55 Division*, which had led the advance into Burma, it was one of the new divisions raised in 1941, but it was equipped with more vehicles and fewer horses. About one-third of its men were 'first selection' conscripts[2] and two-thirds were reservists called up again after their two years' conscript service. Many had seen service in China. It had initially only two regiments, *113 Regiment* and *148 Regiment*. Like *55 Division* it only had three, and not four, rifle companies in each battalion. For artillery it had two battalions of 75mm mountain guns and one battalion of 105mm heavy field artillery. It had been held in reserve in Japan for the campaign in Malaya. Not being required there, it went directly to Rangoon from Japan. The Commander was Lieutenant-General Masao Watanabe and his chief of staff, who was very

---

1. *55* and *56 Regiments* of 18 Division must not be confused with *55* and *56 Divisions*.
2. The fittest recruits were known as 'first selection'.

highly regarded,[3] was Colonel Takeshi Fujiwara.

Powerful support to these two divisions was given by two tank regiments. The *1st Tank Regiment*, which had fought in Malaya, supported *18 Division,* and the *14th Tank Regiment* supported *56 Division.* Most of the tanks were the type 97 medium tanks weighing 15 tons (the British Stuarts weighed 13 tons) with a 57 mm gun (firing only explosive shells) and two machine guns.

The Japanese Advance up the Main Axis to Mandalay

While *55 Division* was attacking Toungoo, the Chinese from the north had attacked *143 Regiment*, who were north of the town, to relieve the pressure. When the town fell, the Chinese withdrew through Yedashe which was held by 22 Chinese D/Brigade. With the help of the medium artillery, this town was captured by *143 Regiment* on 7 April. Continuing its advance against a series of small Chinese rearguard actions, the Japanese reached Thawatti on the 15th. Their next major objective was Pyinmana and *55 Division* resumed the advance on 16 April. After breaking through two Chinese rearguard positions, they entered Pyinmana against only slight opposition on the 19th, the same day that Yenangyaung was captured. It was extremely hot, and water supply was a constant problem. (See Map 24.)

General Iida had moved his Advanced HQ to Thawatti on the 18th and he now ordered *18 Division* to take over the advance. Almost at once they came up against two strong Chinese positions. The first was Kyidaunggan, a village on the railway ten miles north of Pyinmana. The Japanese attacked this early on the 20th but the Chinese held a well-entrenched position there and it proved a tough nut to crack. *56 Regiment* had many casualties and ran short of ammunition while the forward troops suffered severely from thirst. Having received ammunition and water during the night, the Japanese resumed their attack on the 21st and in the afternoon were supported by a battery of 150mm medium guns. Nevertheless the Chinese still held out. However, that night the Japanese charged into the village in a bayonet attack and the Chinese were overrun, leaving about 400 dead.

Meanwhile, the other two regiments of *18 Division* had been in action. *55 Regiment* and *3/114 Battalion* surrounded Point 642, four miles north-east of Pyinmana. They also had a stiff fight but captured the position on the afternoon of the 20th. They claimed that the Chinese left 300 dead. In these two actions *18 Division* themselves lost 70 killed.

General Iida now felt that the key battles with the Chinese were already over and it was time to pursue them rapidly and annihilate them. Although he knew that more Chinese forces were moving into Burma, he judged that they were unlikely to be able to form an organised resistance. He therefore ordered all his divisions to advance 'fiercely and bravely' and to trap the enemy with their backs to the river near Mandalay and destroy them.[4]

There was only one road for the advance of both divisions so responsibility for operations to the west of the road was allotted to *55 Division* and to the east to *18 Division*. In spite of the single road the advance now gathered momentum. *2/114 Battalion*, motorised with trucks 'squeezed' from the field gunners and an engineer bridging-material unit, captured Yamethin against only slight resistance on the 24th. A tank squadron of the *1st Tank Regiment* took over the lead and at mid-day on the 25th occupied Pyawbwe without a fight. *2/114 Battalion* then drove through Pyawbwe to Ywathit, about half way to Meiktila. Here it rested for the night of the 25th and the next morning drove east along the track to the railway at Nyaungyan, where it debussed. Marching north up the railway, after a fight of several hours it captured Thazi. Meanwhile the leading unit of *55 Division, 2/112 Battalion*, also motorised, had reached a village about six miles south-east of Meiktila by the 25th.

HQ 5th Chinese A/Division was at Kyaukse and it was becoming clear that two of its brigades, 96 Chinese D/Brigade, holding Yamethin, and 22 Chinese D/Brigade, holding Pyawbwe, had been dispersed and were in full retreat. This is not surprising as these two Chinese brigades were opposed by two Japanese divisions and a tank regiment. Nevertheless, the imminence of the fall of Meiktila posed a severe problem for the British, with whom the Japanese on the central axis were about to clash. But before discussing this, the dramatic advance of the Japanese in the Shan States needs to be considered.

The Japanese Advance in the Shan States

The Chinese failure to destroy the road bridge over the Sittang at Toungoo was to cost them dearly. The British had realised the importance of this bridge and had prepared it for demolition before handing it over to the Chinese when 5 Chinese A/Division took over this front. But the Chinese force holding the bridge was surprised by the rapid advance of the Japanese. *56 Division's Reconnaissance Regiment*, which was motorised, arrived in Rangoon on 26 March, left on the 27th and by mid-day on the 29th, after a brisk fight in which they lost 13 killed, had overrun the bridge garrison on the east bank of the Sittang and captured the bridge intact.

Although the country was hilly and mostly covered in forest, there were some fair roads in the country between the Sittang and Salween rivers. Shortly after crosssing the Sittang, the road forked (see Map 24). *56 Division*, which had been

---

3. Unlike the chief of staff of *55 Division*, who was replaced.
4. Japanese Official History, *The Assault on Burma*, p.363

allotted a transport company of 250 vehicles and was supported by *14 Tank Regiment*, sent *2/113 Battalion* along the north road as a flank guard and headed west with the tanks and the rest of the division. By the evening of 13 April, they had seized Mawchi, with its valuable wolfram mine, the Chinese regiment there having withdrawn, contrary to its orders, to Bawlake. The next obstacle was the Htu Chaung where a Chinese regiment was holding a position in a village on the north bank covering the suspension bridge. General Watanabe attacked this both frontally and from the west while sending *2/148 Battalion* and an engineer platoon to cross the river further west and put in a road-block on the Bawlake road at Zayat and a company even further west to cut the road north of Bawlake. The suspension bridge was duly captured, the Chinese falling back on Bawlake. 55 Chinese D/Brigade had rushed up its third battalion from near Meiktila to Namhpe, about 12 miles north of Bawlake. On the night of the 17th/18th the Japanese attacked Bawlake and the next morning the battalion in Namhpe attempted a counter-attack but was unable to break through the road-block. That night the Chinese were overrun and dispersed.

At first light the tanks continued the advance and on the 19th joined up with the flank guard, *2/113 Battalion*. At Ngwedaung there was a fork in the road, the left fork going to Meiktila and the other going north to Loikaw and, eventually, Hopong. Watanabe sent *148 Regiment* up the left fork from which they were able to circle round and attack Loikaw from the north. On the 20th the Japanese seized Loikaw with its bridge intact and pressed on north.

The speed of this advance was now causing alarm at Allied HQ and forcing a change of plans. General Stilwell ordered 49 and 93 Chinese D/Brigades to concentrate at once at Loilem but, after a token attack, both brigades withdrew to the east to Takaw. When the Japanese reached Hopong on the 22nd, *2/113 Battalion* was sent west to Taunggyi to hold a flank guard position while the rest of the division turned to the east and seized Loilem on the 23rd. At Taunggyi the Japanese captured a large dump of supplies, including some badly-needed petrol.

From Loilem, Watanabe sent his mechanised reconnaissance regiment east along the road to Takaw as a flank guard. He had been strictly enjoined not to cross the River Salween as, under the Japanese-Thai agreement of 13 December 1941, the 'golden triangle' east of the Salween was reserved for the Thais. Before they got to Takaw, therefore, the cavalry regiment turned north along a cart-track and rejoined the division at Ke-Hsi Monsam.

The *56th Division* continued its rapid advance north and, at the next fork, *113 Regiment* took the left prong towards Namlan and cut the Mandalay-Lashio road at Hsipaw. *Divisional Headquarters* and *148 Regiment* took the right fork to Mong Yai. Here General Watanabe decided to leave the road and take a lesser

Japanese medium tanks advancing on 29 April towards Lashio.

track which led to the main road a few miles west of Lashio. There were two weak bridges to cross but the tanks found practicable diversions. On 29 April, *56 Division* and its tanks seized Lashio, the Chinese garrison putting up only a token resistance. Large amounts of fuel and supplies were captured.[5]

This brilliant advance had, in two weeks, dispersed the Chinese 6th A/Division, cut the main route to China, and totally disrupted the Allied plans. Its speed had surprised not only the Allies but the Japanese as well. *The 1st Japanese Parachute Regiment* had actually taken off for the attack on Lashio but had turned back because of low cloud on the hills. Now it was stood down and was not involved again in this campaign.

One result of the rapid Japanese advance in the Shan States was to upset the bold plan proposed by General Slim at General Alexander's conference on the 19th. At that conference General Stilwell had volunteered to send the 200th Chinese D/Brigade to join the 38th Chinese D/Brigade under Burcorps at Kyaukpadaung. The next day, however, the news that Loikaw had fallen caused this very bold plan to be abandoned. The 200th Chinese D/Brigade from 5 A/Division was re-directed to Taunggyi and ordered to take it, but they were held up by the Japanese flank guard. Stilwell arrived in person and offered 200 D/Brigade 50,000 rupees if they captured Taunggyi that evening. They did. Further progress, however, was slow and they did not reach the burnt-out Loilem until the 29th. They then followed the brigades of the 6th A/Division to Takaw, where they too crossed the Salween.

The Withdrawal Across the Irrawaddy

After the loss of Rangoon it had always been evident that it was very unlikely that Burma could be held. In mid-March Wavell had told Churchill that, if the British were driven out of Burma, there were two options. They could either withdraw north-west to Assam or north-east to China. He favoured the Chinese option because of the importance of maintaining contact with China and because

---

5. The capture of fuel was considered particularly important as many of the roads were one-way and returning trucks would cause traffic problems.

it would remain a threat on the flank of any Japanese advance to India. On this, General Alan Brooke, the new and very shrewd CIGS, asked Wavell "if his desire to maintain touch with the Chinese were based on political or military reasons; what role he intended for Burcorps in China; how he proposed to maintain it; if it would include an air detachment; and, finally, whether he could ensure the security of the Assam frontier if Burcorps retreated into China."[6] These were penetrating and pertinent comments. In his reply, Wavell said that he was influenced by the very poor tracks leading to Assam and the lack of supplies along that route. After discussion with Alexander at that time it was agreed that planning should be based on 7th Armoured Brigade and a brigade from 17 Division retiring towards China while the rest retired towards Assam. Slim was horrified. He could not see how such a force could ever be maintained in China.

However, events were now moving so fast that plans were changed daily. General Alexander sought a meeting on the 21st with General Lin Wei, the Generalissimo's representative in Burma. It was then agreed between them that it would be best if the 7th Armoured Brigade were to be retained in the Shwebo plain, where it could menace any Japanese force threatening Chinese withdrawal routes to the north-west. It would also be best if all British forces withdrew to Assam. This sensible decision having been made, Alexander issued an operation instruction on the 23rd. In this, Burcorps was to hold a line from Chauk to Kyaukpadaung to Meiktila, while 5 Chinese A/Division, supported by the 7th Armoured Brigade, held the Pyawbwe-Thazi-Meiktila area. If these positions could not be held, the Army in Burma would fall back across the Irrawaddy. There would be no question of fighting a major battle south of the river.

While these important decisions were being made, 1 Burdiv, covered by 38 Chinese D/Brigade, had sorted itself out near Mount Popa and was now operational again, though woefully weak in strength and short of equipment. 17 Division in Taungdwingyi were beginning to get very isolated with the Japanese far to the north on their west flank and rapidly moving north on the east. On the 20th they were ordered to withdraw to Mahlaing, north-west of Meiktila, through a lay-back position at Natmauk. On the nights of the 20/21 and 21/22 April, 63 Brigade made its way north through the deep dust of a very rough track to milestone 16 on the Meiktila-Kyaukpadaung road where a lay-back position was established. 48 Brigade followed on the next two nights going through to Mahlaing where they were joined by 16 Brigade from Natmauk. Although the vehicles of both brigades used headlights where necessary, the dust and the soft sand in the many nullahs made the move desperately slow in spite of the detachments of Sappers stationed at all the major crossings to give assistance. Some marching troops went along the railway line until their turn came to be ferried.

A Stuart tank crew resting near Meiktila.

7th Armoured Brigade now had a problem with its tanks. Remarkably reliable though they had been, a track change was much overdue if they were to continue to operate. On 22 April, it was arranged for one squadron from each regiment to harbour ten miles north of Meiktila for track-changing. On the 24th, 7th Armoured Brigade leaguered five miles south of them and the squadron of the 7th Hussars and 'E' Troop of the RHA, who had been supporting 38 Chinese D/Brigade, rejoined them there. However, one squadron of the 2nd R Tanks remained with the Chinese. On this day, too, orders were received that 7th Armoured Brigade was to come under command of 5 Chinese A/Division, so Brigadier Anstice went to Kyaukse to meet General Stilwell. It was arranged that 7th Armoured Brigade would come directly under Stilwell's command. It was also learnt that the 96th Chinese D/Brigade had disintegrated and that it was not thought that the 22nd Chinese D/Brigade would be able to hold Pyawbwe for long.

On the 25th, the 2nd R Tanks sent a scout car patrol down the road towards Pyawbwe. They found Chinese streaming north and about a mile from the village contacted three Japanese medium tanks so beat a hasty retreat. A 7th Hussar patrol on the Toungoo road 12 miles south of Meiktila met a column of enemy lorries and engaged them at point blank range, knocking out several trucks, but disengaged as it was getting dark. The Japanese lost several men killed including three newspaper reporters.

On this day also, General Alexander held a critical meeting with Generals Stilwell and Slim at Kyaukse (pronounced Chowk-see). Major Brian

6. Kirby, S.W., *The War Against Japan*, Vol.2, p.152.

Montgomery, a staff officer at Burcorps, attended this meeting. He was to write in 1975:

"I so well remember that conference on 25 April, for Slim clearly dominated the scene, and made certain once and for all that no British or Indian troops would retreat into China. Alexander gave me, at any rate, the impression of being rattled. I think he needed Slim to help him compete with Stilwell."[7]

If General Alexander was not his usual cool self, it may well have been because he was loyally trying to carry out his instructions from Wavell. These were far from easy to translate into practical terms. He was directed to maintain close touch with the Chinese; to cover the Kalewa-Tamu route to India; to keep a force in being; and to retain as many 'cards of re-entry' as possible to facilitate future offensive operations into Burma. Contact with the Chinese was the paramount consideration. They must be given no grounds for accusing the British of running away to India.

At this vital meeting all were now agreed that the Allies were unable to stem the Japanese advance. It was therefore decided that the time had come to start the withdrawal, not only across the Irrawaddy but out of Burma. In the first phase, 7th Armoured Brigade having reverted to its command, Burcorps would cover the withdrawal of the shattered 5th Chinese A/Division to Mandalay. Burcorps' vehicles, tanks and guns would cross the great river via the Ava bridge. 1 Burdiv, with its bullock-carts but less its motor transport, would cross the Irrawaddy by ferry at Sameikkon, as would 38 Chinese D/Brigade at Sagaing. If the second phase proved necessary, all British forces would withdraw to Assam via the track to Kalewa. 2 Bur Brigade, already on the west bank of the Irrawaddy, would move west from Pakokku and withdraw up the Myittha valley to Kalemyo, a few miles from Kalewa to which 1 Bur Brigade would withdraw by river up the Chindwin. A brigade from 17 Division would join 1 Burdiv, thus giving each division two brigades. General Stilwell, if the Burma road was blocked, was hoping to withdraw his troops to China via Katha, Bhamo and possibly Myitkyina (pronounced Mich-in-ar). Alexander supported the request by 38 Chinese D/Brigade that they should withdraw to India.

These firm decisions, and the speed with which they were implemented, were to deceive General Iida and rob him of the decisive battle south of Mandalay for which he had hoped.

Last Days in Mandalay and Maymyo

When it was clear that Rangoon might be lost, General Hutton's chief admin-istrative officer, Major-General E.N. Goddard, had back-loaded as many stores as possible to Mandalay and established an *ad hoc* base there. Carefully planned dumps on the roads to the north had kept the Army in Burma, and the Chinese Expeditionary Force supplied with the essentials for their fighting retreat. Now it was necessary to disperse the *ad hoc* base as well. Stores were sent back by all possible means to establish dumps on the main route to India via Ye-U, and also to Bhamo and Myitkyina for the Chinese and British taking the northern route. As a first move, all troops were put on 'half rations', that is the ration scale was reduced. Goddard was one of the unsung heroes of the campaign. He and his staff performed miracles. Although there was no supply from outside for the last two and a half months of the campaign, somehow the Army in Burma, and the Chinese, were kept supplied and, although always short, never starved nor ran out of ammunition and petrol.

However, it would be untrue to suggest that all went smoothly in the last days of the British and Chinese occupation of Mandalay and Maymyo, its attractive satellite in the hills 40 miles to the east. Both towns had been bombed, Mandalay repeatedly and heavily and much of it had been burnt out. In Mandalay the bulk of the local population fled, bringing most of the essential services to a halt. In one of the final air raids, the fire spread to the railway station and a train-load of bombs was detonated, destroying the station. It was never used again by the Allies in this campaign.

The evacuation of Rangoon had been relatively well-planned and executed but, owing to the lack of communications to India and the general uncertainty, this was not the case in the north. The Civil Government and AHQ had both moved from Rangoon to Maymyo, which was full of European refugees and their families. The harsh realities of being overwhelmed by an enemy, a rare experience for British citizens, now faced everyone. Homes and possessions were lost for ever and even survival was problematic. The lack of information lowered morale. As in Mandalay, hospitals were full and overflowing. The civil service and the police had by this time largely disintegrated and the Governor was widely and wrongly blamed for the chaos which he was powerless to pre-vent. AHQ was at full stretch running the war but did what it could to help. Transport was the bottle-neck. Every effort was made to fly out as many as pos-sible of the hospital patients from Shwebo with the handful of transport aircraft which was all that India possessed. Other casualties were evacuated by railway or river steamer towards Kalewa or Myitkyina. The women and children fol-

7. Lewin, Ronald, *Slim*, p.98.

lowed and then, finally, the men as it became impossible for them to continue their jobs. There was much chaos, and some regrettable scenes, but there were also many cases of extreme heroism, especially among the nurses and staff caring selflessly for the wounded and sick in appalling conditions.

Inevitably there were many personal tragedies. Most European, Indian, Anglo-Indian and Anglo-Burmese civilians, in essential jobs or domiciled in North Burma and hoping for a change of fortune, had been reluctant to leave the country until the last minute and now had to choose how they would get out. All would suffer hardship, some would suffer great hardship, and some would lose their lives.

CHAPTER TWENTY

The Rearguard Action at Kyaukse

With a Japanese division racing through the Shan States and two Japanese divisions and an armoured regiment closing in on Meiktila, there was clearly no time to be lost. Immediately after the meeting at Kyaukse on 25 April, 63 Brigade were ordered to march at once to Meiktila, arriving at dawn on the 26th. They were placed under the command of Brigadier Anstice. 16 Brigade and the rear echelons of 7th Armoured Brigade, together with 414 Battery less a troop, started on their journey back across the Ava bridge to Ondaw. 48 Brigade moved to a lay-back position at the little market town of Kyaukse.

Meiktila was to be held until that evening to cover units of the Chinese 5th A/Division who were withdrawing and planning to pick up a train at Wundwin (see Map 24). When 63 Brigade arrived at Meiktila it was agreed that, having rested, they would march and ferry in trucks to Wundwin, where they would provide a lay-back position to which the tanks would withdraw. Meanwhile, the 7th Hussars moved forward at first light and surprised a Japanese column of infantry advancing in trucks up the road, seven miles south of Meiktila. This was *2/112 Battalion* who were the leading element of *55 Division*. The British inflicted considerable damage on the column but the Japanese rapidly dismounted and went to ground in a village. A company of the 1st West Yorks was called up from Meiktila but due to a series of mishaps, including being bombed, the attack did not start until 5pm. It was far too late; all surprise had been lost and the enemy were well-prepared. The attack failed, there was some difficulty in extracting one of the West Yorks' platoons and two tanks were lost. In the initial attack the 7th Hussars claimed to have destroyed 12 vehicles and at least one gun and to have killed about 150 men. The Japanese say that 11 trucks were lost and one mountain gun was damaged. They claim one British tank destroyed and one damaged. There is silence about Japanese casualties but private accounts say there were not many. 7th Armoured Brigade moved to Wundwin at dusk and were joined later by the 7th Hussars. The 1st West Yorks were the last to arrive, having finally left Meiktila at midnight.

On the 27th, 17 Division took over command of the rearguard and Brigadier Anstice was ordered to hold Wundwin until 1800 hours. The 2nd Royal Tanks advanced to contact the enemy at first light. In view of the blow delivered by the 7th Hussars to the leading element of *55 Division* the previous day, they were not expecting much trouble. Unfortunately they met the powerful leading unit of a different formation, *18 Division*. This was *2/114 Battalion*, supported by an anti-tank battery and a squadron of tanks. There was some severe fighting and two tanks were lost. The Japanese claim that these were knocked out by the Japanese tanks and not by the anti-tank guns. Although the 57mm guns of the Japanese tanks were relatively low velocity and fired explosive and not armour-piercing shells, Lieutenant Kubota, the troop leader concerned, had been taught what proved to be an effective technique of several tanks firing simultaneously at one enemy tank.[1] The 2nd Royal Tanks continued to have a very difficult day. There was a lot of low scrub which concealed the enemy infantry. Japanese fighters made many sorties over the battlefield and its approaches, and bombed and machine-gunned anything they could see. Constant shelling, to which the British guns responded, and threats of outflanking forced several short withdrawals, but the tanks resisted stubbornly and the enemy never reached the 63 Brigade position at Wundwin.

An awkward hitch now occurred. 17 Division were unable to provide the transport for 63 Brigade's withdrawal until midnight. Anstice decided that a withdrawal in the dark would be risky. He therefore arranged to withdraw as ordered at 6pm, using a shuttle of the tanks and every possible vehicle to ferry 63 Brigade to the bridge at Kume, about half-way to Kyaukse. This plan worked well. The force disengaged without trouble, and 63 Brigade were duly picked up in trucks at midnight from Kume and transported through Kyaukse to a position covering the two big bridges over the Myitnge (pronounced Min-gee) river, another 16 miles further north. The steel girder bridge at Kume over the Panlaung river was duly blown behind the rearguard by 70 Field Company.

7th Armoured Brigade, having completed its task, drove back over the Irrawaddy by the Ava bridge to a harbour near Ondaw, leaving behind the 7th Hussars and a troop of 414 Battery to support 48 Brigade.

The Action at Kyaukse

When 48 Brigade reached Kyaukse on the 26th, the headquarters of the 96th Chinese D/Brigade were still in the village, busy collecting some of their units which were making their way north to Mandalay across country. Brigadier Ronnie Cameron knew, however, that there was no time to waste and quickly set about organising a defensive position. He had under his command four Gurkha battalions, his own 1st/4th, 2nd/5th and 1st/7th and also the much under-strength 1st/3rd, allotted for the occasion. Their total Infantry strength was about 1700 all ranks. He also had the 7th Hussars, a troop of 414 Field Battery RHA (three guns), one troop 95 Anti-Tank Battery RA, 1 Field Battery of the 1st Indian Field Regiment (twelve guns) and 70 Field Company of the Bengal Sappers. His task was to hold Kyaukse until 1800 hours on the 29th against the two Japanese divisions and an armoured regiment advancing up the road from the south.

Kyaukse was tactically important because the main road and rail from Rangoon to Mandalay and to the Ava bridge ran close to each other through its centre (see Map 25). The Zawgyi river, which ran through the town from south-east to north-west, had plenty of water in it even at this time of year but it was easily fordable. Kyaukse was the headworks of a number of canals feeding water to the surrounding countryside. Tactically it was dominated by a three-mile long ridge, about 600 feet high, whose western end overlooked the eastern edge of the town.

On the 27th, 70 Field Company, under orders from 17 Division, demolished the road and rail bridges over the Panlaung river at Myittha. This caused some alarm at first to General Yu Shao, commanding 96 D/Brigade, whose troops had been passing through all the morning, as he still had a battalion, as he thought, on its way from Wundwin by train. However, this battalion arrived along the line on foot and the Sappers helped them to cross the river without trouble. The Chinese still had another battalion to come somewhere to the west but, assured that the British would look out for it, General Yu Shao and his troops left for Mandalay. Meanwhile the Gurkhas worked hard at the defences, digging slit trenches, clearing fields of fire and erecting a road-block. The 7th Hussars, who arrived during the night, leaguered three miles north at Taungnauk, close to the position of the guns.

On the 28th, while work continued on the defences and the Sappers prepared three bridges in the town for demolition, patrols were sent out for some miles east, south and west. Brigadier Cameron took all the COs on a reconnaissance back to the Myitnge river. On his return he outlined plans for the withdrawal. If the attack was from the south, the withdrawal would be up the main road with lay-backs at milestones 404 and 408. If the enemy succeeded in putting in a road-block to the north of Kyaukse, the tanks, guns and transport would break through and the rest of the brigade would march through the forests to the north-east and cross the Myitnge river by the ferries at Ebya and Mandaw (see Map 25).

At 1730 hours, a 7th Hussar patrol down the road reported that it had met enemy tanks and lorries ten miles to the south. There had been an exchange of fire and both sides retreated but one tank was lost on the way back from a low-

---

1. Major-General Ushiyama was an instructor at the Japanese Tank Academy and remembers that he taught Lieutenant Kubota this technique. (Contribution in 1997.)

level bombing attack. On receipt of this news a tank-trap was set up about two miles south of Kyaukse. Two lorry-borne anti-tank guns, with an escort of Gurkhas from the 1st/7th in each truck, took up position there. Almost at once they encountered five tanks coming up the road with infantry on either side. The guns succeeded in knocking out the leading tank but were then forced to withdraw by the enemy infantry, which they did, unfortunately forgetting their escort. However, after a brisk exchange of fire, the escort made its way back successfully after dark.

Soon after 9pm, small enemy patrols contacted the forward positions of the 1st/7th Gurkhas on either side of the road and, being easily visible in the bright moonlight, were driven back with some loss (see Map 26). Shortly afterwards a two-company attack came in on 'D' Company's front on the east side of the road and was engaged at about 150 yards, retiring in confusion. For the next two hours the front was comparatively quiet except for small parties of the enemy creeping forward to recover dead and wounded.

Half-an-hour after midnight, a second frontal attack, very similar to the first, advanced on 'D' Company, now strengthened by another platoon. This time the enemy were allowed to come closer before fire was opened and then every weapon was used, including three-inch mortars firing on the rear areas and defensive fire from the guns. The attack broke up with an estimated loss of 40 killed, a higher figure than for the previous one.

The final attack came just before dawn when the moon had gone down and it was darker. This attack made better use of cover and was made on the extreme right and left of 'D' Company's position, but it met the same fate as the other two. On 'C' Company's front west of the road some patrols had been repelled during the night but there had been no serious attack.

Very little action had taken place during the night on the rest of the perimeter. The 2nd/5th R Gurkhas on the east flank had not been attacked, although one or two small patrols had probed their position and they had used their mortars to assist the 1st/7th. The 1st/4th Gurkhas to the west had a similar experience. The Gunners, however, had had a very busy time supporting the 1st/7th, who paid a glowing tribute in their war diary to their FOO, Captain Ranbir Bakshi, and the "exceptionally fine work" of the guns from the 1st Field Battery.[2]

There was another incident during the night when the big road bridge at Dwehla, seven miles out to the west on the road to Myingyan, was blown. As the British were responsible for covering the Chinese withdrawal, and there were believed to be Chinese troops still to come, the Brigadier had given specific orders that this bridge was not to be blown except on his personal order. Unfortunately the 7th Hussars were unaware of this. When a convoy of Chinese infantry in trucks came over the big bridge and announced that there was no-one behind them, the Hussars ordered the detachment of 70 Field Company to demolish the bridge, which they did successfully. Fortunately, no harm was done; it really was the last convoy.

The enemy remaining passive at dawn, Cameron decided on a counter-attack. Accordingly, at 0800 hours on the 29th, Lieutenant-Colonel Williams of the 1st/7th Gurkhas mounted an attack with Captain O.R. Gribble's 'B' Company, which had been in reserve during the night. The aim of the attack was to clear a village with the awkward name of Htanaungbinhla which straggled along the west side of the road. The north end of this village had been burnt to improve the field of fire but Japanese had been seen in the south end, and also sheltering in a large culvert under the main road about 150 yards ahead of the road-block. The attack duly went in supported by a troop of 25-pdrs and the battalion's mortars, the Gurkhas firing bursts of automatic fire and throwing grenades into any place likely to conceal an enemy. Well led by Gribble, the Gurkhas were in fine form. A Tommy gun and grenade attack dealt with the enemy sheltering in the culvert, a few who ran out of the other side were shot by 'D' Company. The village was completely cleared, the survivors retiring to the south.

This very successful little action was estimated at the time to have killed at least 70 Japanese, 38 being counted under the culvert alone. According to the Japanese the latter was being used as an advanced dressing station for the wounded and among the killed was Lieutenant Katayama, a doctor. However there were no markings to indicate this and there seem to have been some fit men sheltering there as well.[3] Three mortars, five LMGs and many rifles and pistols were captured. There was a general opinion among the British that the Japanese who had been attacking were nothing like so good as those in *33 Division*.

Now the Japanese were following up on this axis with two divisions and a tank regiment, and should have been able to run circles round 48 Brigade. Some explanation is required. *18 Division* had deployed *114 Regiment* out to the east and *3/114 Battalion* had established itself on the east end of the Kyaukse ridge. It was a battalion of its *55 Regiment* of *18 Division* which had been engaged all night on the east of the main road by the 1st/7th Gurkhas. To the west of the road, it was *112 Regiment* of *55 Division* who had made a rather tentative advance. They had been caught by the guns and mortars while forming up and retreated to a wood further back. Most of the wounded under the bridge belonged to this regiment. The absence of any tanks surprised the British. The reason was that General Iida had ordered the *1st Tank Regiment* to make a big left hook and seize

2. 1 Indian Field Battery fired 900 rounds at Kyaukse.
3. Memoir, Mr Kagawa, p.72.

the Myitnge bridges. Fortunately for the British, the going was very difficult and they arrived too late.

Faulty 'intelligence' from his staff also led General Iida to make a curious mistake. According to his diary, he was unaware that the great Ava bridge could take vehicles.[4] He was also unaware of the rapid move eastwards, to cover the Chinese withdrawal to Mandalay, made by 17 Division, 38 Chinese D/Brigade and 7th Armoured Brigade. He therefore judged that the British would cross the Irrawaddy somewhere in the area of Myingyan. As *33 Division* was temporarily exhausted by the fighting at Yenanyaung, he decided on the 29th to send the whole of *55 Division* to Myingyan via Myittha.[5] Thus at mid-day on the 29th, *55 Division* was withdrawn and *18 Division* took over the attack on Kyaukse.

While this readjustment was going on, the Japanese started to make full use of their medium artillery. Air reconnaissance (or the spy mentioned below) had located in which pagoda on the ridge (there were many) the OP of the RHA troop was located and it received a heavy plastering from the 150mm guns. Lieutenant Mason, the FOO, stayed put, however, and continued to direct fire on to the enemy positions. Shelling of Kyaukse town continued during the morning and many of the remaining wooden buildings were set on fire. The Japanese had now located the British gun position which was also heavily shelled. The 7th Hussars and the Brigade's rear echelon, who were nearby, also received attention. About 1300 hours, shelling switched to the forward infantry positions but no attack developed.

A battery of 150mm medium guns firing on 48 brigade at Kyaukse on 29 April.

During the day, battalions sent out patrols in front of their positions and the 1st/4th Gurkhas reported an enemy battalion moving into a large village four miles west of Kyaukse. A troop of the 7th Hussars with an FOO went out to investigate. The village was shelled by the 12 guns of 1 Field Battery and the dispersing enemy machine-gunned by the tanks. Meanwhile, 'C' Company of the 1st/7th reported enemy moving up east of the road. About two companies had moved into a banana grove and there were more in the village. There was a good deal of firing and two tanks from the 7th Hussars joined in from the road with their MMGs. Eventually it was decided to move 'C' Company, who had gone forward into the village, back to their old position. Covered by the tanks, this was achieved with only three men slightly wounded. Both these contacts were with *1/55 Battalion* of *18 Division*.

The Withdrawal from Kyaukse

Final orders for the withdrawal were to be given out at the well-concealed brigade headquarters at 2pm. But no sooner had the commanding officers assembled there than the position received 15 minutes' concentrated shelling. Fortunately, everyone jumped into slit trenches and there were no casualties, but the meagre contents of the headquarters were smashed to pieces. Directly the shelling stopped a move was made to a new position on the river bank. At the time no-one knew how the Japanese achieved this coup. But about an hour before, a saffron-robed Buddhist priest had appeared in Kyaukse and passed close behind brigade headquarters on his way up towards the pagodas on the ridge. Of course he should have been detained but he wasn't, and there is little doubt that he was a spy and delivered his information about the whereabouts of the headquarters to the Japanese FOO on the far end of the ridge.[6] That the shelling coincided with the meeting was just chance.

The plan of withdrawal was the straightforward one discussed the previous day. Zero hour was to be 1800 hours, at which time the main road bridge would be blown.[7] The forward battalions would start thinning out half-an-hour before zero and the forward positions would be abandoned at zero hour. Ten minutes after zero, British guns would fire on the vacated FDLs. Troops would make their way to the lay-back position, manned by the 1st/3rd Gurkhas, at milestone 404.

4. The Ava bridge had a single-track road on either side of the rail bridge, as could be easily seen from the air.

5. The road bridge demolition at Myittha was no obstacle at this time of year.

6. He was probably a member of the BIA. I am ashamed to admit that I was one of those who saw him and, naively supposing him to be genuine, took no action. *Author*.

7. The railway bridges being of strategic but not tactical importance, 70 Company had blown the one in Kyaukse at 0730 on the 29th, and shortly afterwards the one at Kyetsein, ten miles to the north.

An unusual feature, however, was that two tanks would remain at the road junction on the south (wrong) side of the river when the main bridge was blown. They would use their MMGs freely to cover the withdrawal from the FDLs, and would then circle the town and come in over the canal bridge to the west which would be blown behind them.

In spite of some steady shelling of Kyaukse, which set several houses on fire in the main street, the withdrawal proceeded smoothly. It was nearly marred by a tragic accident, however, when a lorry packed with Gurkhas, delayed by some mishap, came slowly along the river bank towards the main road bridge while the demolition fuses were burning. Oblivious of the danger, the driver stopped at the end of the bridge, carefully changed gear and then trundled slowly up the road. He had gone less than a hundred yards when the bridge, packed with 600 pounds of gelignite, went up with a tremendous flash and roar. In the hot, humid atmosphere the effect was stunning. Brigadier Cameron who had watched the demolition from close behind the firing party was clearly delighted by this dramatic finale to the battle. For a full minute all firing stopped and the only sounds were the thuds as large lumps of steel fell from the sky. Then normality returned and the tanks on the south bank started up again with their MMGs.

The FDLs were now vacated and the units south of the river crossed by wading or by a narrow causeway. Under cover of the 25-pdrs they marched north up the road to their check-point at milestone 404 and then on to waiting trucks. Once the Infantry were over the river, the two tanks on the south bank drove round the village and came in by the western bridge over the Zawgyi canal and this bridge was blown behind them at 1822 hours.

The action at Kyaukse was over. Amazingly, British casualties were only three killed and seven wounded. Japanese casualties are unknown and do not seem to be recorded anywhere. The British believed at the time that the Japanese had suffered at least 200 killed. A more likely figure is about 60. Clearly the British had been lucky, for if *18 Division* had put in a properly co-ordinated frontal attack, or inserted a road-block behind them, they would have had a much harder time. Nevertheless, 48 Brigade's operation was well planned and skilfully and stoutly executed. Slim's well-publicised tribute was justified:

"The action at Kyaukse was a really brilliant example of rearguard work. It not only enabled the last of the Chinese to cross the Ava bridge without molestation and gave us all a breathing space, but it inflicted heavy casualties on the enemy at extremely small cost to ourselves."

From Kyaukse, 48 Brigade drove back over the Myitnge and Ava bridges to

A road bridge north of Kyaukse twisted by the demolition to make repair more difficult.

Myinmu. 70 Company blew the road bridge at Ywatha (milestone 410) behind them and then followed to Ondaw.

The Demolition of the Bridges at Myitnge

63 Brigade, who were holding the lay-back position at the Myitnge river, were ordered to fall back and hold a bridgehead at the Ava Bridge. Accordingly, Major Darley and 24 Field Company of the Bombay Sappers blew successfully the two big road and rail bridges over the river at Myitnge. The two big bridges were very close together and so were demolished simultaneously, two spans on each bridge being cut and dropping into the deep river. Now these two big bridges, particularly the rail one, were very important, as all the supplies for Mandalay and the Burma Road to China had to pass over them. The demolitions had been designed and prepared months before. Darley's job was to execute these plans, which he did very well. However, more sophisticated methods[8] had been developed during the campaign which would have made these big bridges harder to repair. As it was, the Japanese engineers, who were well prepared for this particular task and started work at once, succeeded in jacking up on crib piers the major parts of the demolished girders of the rail bridge, and the first train passed over it on 30 May.

The Japanese Follow-up

18 Division entered Kyaukse close behind 48 Brigade and reached the Myitnge River on 30 April. On the morning of 1 May, *55 Regiment* crossed the river at Myitnge village and *114 Regiment* crossed by the ferry at Kinpet (Ebya).

---

8. The "one-and-a-half cut" method by which the girder is cut completely at one end and half-cut at the other. When the girder falls, the steelwork is distorted and repair made much more difficult.

18 Division crossing the Myitnge River on 1 May on a raft made from three folding boats.

55 Regiment reached Mandalay unopposed around 5pm and secured the north of the city. They were followed by the whole division, although *56 Regiment* did not arrive until after midnight. General Iida drove into Mandalay behind the leading elements and was said to have been welcomed by many inhabitants.[9] However he did not give *18 Division* much rest. On the next day they were ordered to destroy a Chinese d/brigade in the Shan States which had recrossed the Salween at Takaw and was threatening Loilem. On 3 May, *55 Regiment* went north to Lashio and turned south, while *56 Regiment* went back over the Myitnge river crossing (now very congested with units and supplies moving north) and drove west via Meiktila-Thazi to Loilem. After a stiff fight, a pincer movement between the two regiments was successful and, on the 9th, the Chinese were driven back across the Salween. On 4 May, *55 Division* returned after its fruitless excursion to Myingyan and assembled at Ava and Mandalay.

The Thai Army Enters Burma

In accordance with the agreement made on 13 December 1941, the leading elements of the Thai Northern Army crossed the border into Burma on 10 May. The Japanese had restrained them from entering Burma earlier mainly because they were uncertain of the strength of the Thai Army and were afraid that they might be defeated. The Thai aim was to occupy that part of the northern Shan States, secretly promised to them by the Japanese before the war started, and specifically to capture Keng Tung, its main town. At one time in the past the area had been part of Thailand. The boundary between the Japanese and Thai operations was generally the river Salween. However, that area south of the Shan States known as Karenni, the homeland of the Karens, was specifically retained under Japanese control as it was recognised as a possible source of resistance.

The Thais started their advance on 5 May with three infantry divisions and a cavalry division. *4 Thai Division*, followed by *3 Thai Division*, went north from Lampang by the Chiang Rai road to Keng Tung, while *2 Thai Division* took the road leading north from Chiang Mai to Wan Hsa-La. They soon captured Keng Tung from the retreating 93 Chinese D/Brigade without much difficulty. However, while most Chinese troops withdrew into China, desultory fighting continued with 93 Chinese D/Brigade throughout World War Two. In July 1943, General Tojo visited Bangkok and two Shan States in this area and four Malay States in northern Malaya were formally ceded to Thailand.

The Thais found much difficulty in supplying their Northern Army and it had many sickness casualties, mostly malaria. At the end of World War Two, the Thais disbanded the Northern Army *in situ* and it straggled back home in some disorder. 93 Chinese D/Brigade, by now largely a force of bandits under a war-lord, reoccupied the area and for some years after the war even maintained a presence on the Thai side of the border.

1 Burdiv's Crossing at Sameikkon

While the main part of Burcorps was crossing the Irrawaddy by the Ava bridge, 1 Burdiv was aiming to cross by ferry at Sameikkon. They had been re-organising in Myingyan for four days and collecting bullock-carts with the help of the District Commissioner, Mr D.C. Thomas, "who held on and maintained order splendidly." They had only a few vehicles left and these were sent round by the Ava bridge to meet them on the other side. By crossing at Sameikkon (instead of Kyauktalon, the original Burcorps proposal) they would greatly short-en their march to Monywa, whence 1 Brigade was due to go up the Chindwin by boat. Lieutenant-Colonel Dennis Swan, the very able CRE, organised the cross-ing and assembled every possible form of boat. On 27 and 28 April, 1 Burdiv, 500 oxen and 250 bullock-carts were successfully taken across the river by the Sappers and Royal Marines, and the boats were then destroyed. Meanwhile, 2 Bur Brigade had been instructed to protect the west flank by marching up the Myittha valley to Kalemyo. On the 28th they left Pakokku and headed west towards Pauk, so there were now no British forces on the west bank of the Irrawaddy. From the north bank, General Bruce Scott issued a warning order for 1 Burdiv to march on towards Monywa on the night of the 29th/30th. At Brigadier Curtis's request, however, on the grounds of the exhaustion of the

---

9. Rather surprisingly in view of the heavy Japanese air raid on Mandalay by 36 bombers on 3 April. This raid was estimated to have killed more than 2000 people and it burnt out the main part of the city.

The great Ava road and rail bridge, the only bridge across the Irrawaddy, demolished on 30 April.

troops in 13 Brigade, he postponed the march for 24 hours. It was a decision which he was to regret.[10]

The Ava Bridge

On 30 April the only British forces remaining on the south bank of the Irrawaddy were in the 63 Brigade bridgehead at the Ava bridge. This great bridge was the only one across the Irrawaddy. Nearly three-quarters of a mile long, it had 11 main girders each spanning 375 feet and, at this time of year, about 70 feet above the water. A double rail track ran down the centre and a one-way road was cantileverd out on either side. It was the only direct road and rail link to north Burma. As at the Myitnge bridges, the demolition had been designed some months before and wooden boxes to take the explosive had been fitted to the steel girders of two of the big spans. It fell to Major Darley and 24 Field Company to fit the explosive and prepare the firing circuits. All was ready by mid-day on the 30th when a flight of 27 bombers, in a tight formation of three Vs of nine, was seen heading straight for the bridge from the south-west at about 8,000 feet. It seemed most unlikely that they would attack the bridge but while they were over the river the leader rocked from side to side and all the bombers released their bombs together.[11] Their target was the village of Sagaing at the north end of the bridge. This village had been occupied by HQ Burcorps, and several other units, until earlier that morning but, when the raid came, was almost deserted. No more troops crossed during the afternoon and between 9 and 10pm the bridgehead troops were withdrawn. At 2320 hours on 30 April General Cowan gave the order and two great spans fell into the deepest channel in the river. It was the largest bridge that the Sappers had ever demolished and it would not be repaired for another 13 years.

---

10. The CO of 5 Burif was to comment in his war diary on 1 May: "Our two [sic] days unnecessary wait in Sameikkon let the Japanese get into Monywa and wait for us. Will they never learn how dangerous it is to give him time to move?"

11. This was the standard technique which the Japanese used in bombing many towns.

CHAPTER TWENTY-ONE

The Battle at Monywa

In the last week of April both Allied and Japanese Army commanders were forced to reassess the situation. Wavell, as Theatre Commander, had originally directed that, if northern Burma could not be held, part of the British forces should withdraw to China. The aim was basically the political one of ensuring that the Chinese would not blame the British for deserting them and thus causing their defeat. Accepting this instruction, General Alexander earmarked 7th Armoured Brigade and 48 Brigade for this role. General Slim was horrified. He thought that it would be impossible to get any supplies to them and the scarcity of food in Yunnan, where there was a famine, was such that they might starve. However, the Japanese capture of Lashio and the cutting of the Burma Road knocked this plan on the head. It was clear now that the only sensible solution was for the Chinese to withdraw to China, and the British to India, by such routes as were still available to them. Slim, however, at General Sun's request, made a plea for 38 Chinese D/Brigade also to withdraw to India and this was agreed.

General Iida was disappointed that he had been unable to prevent the rapid Allied withdrawal across the Irrawaddy and his plan to trap the Allied forces with their backs to the river had failed. He now proposed to encircle them and annihilate them in the plains of North Burma. *33 Division* would form the left claw of the pincer. They would send a force up the Chindwin to cut off any retreat to India, while their main body would capture Monywa and Ye-U and cut the road and railway to the north. They would be fighting the British. *55 Division* would form the right claw. They would advance north up the road and railway with one regiment while the rest advanced east of the Irrawaddy on Mogok, Bhamo and Myitkyina. *56 Division* would advance up the Burma road to the bridge over the river Salween in China. Both *55* and *56 Divisions* would be fighting the Chinese. *18 Division*, after repulsing in the Shan States an abortive Chinese counter-attack from Keng Tung, would be in reserve.

The Japanese Advance on the East Flank against the Chinese
56 Division had advanced with unexpected speed and captured the important railhead of Lashio on 29 April, the Emperor's birthday and a very significant date

to the Japanese. Although about one hundred miles from the Chinese frontier, Lashio was the railhead for the route to China and had all the air of a frontier town. Large stocks of American supplies awaited trans-shipment by truck to Chungking, and shady wheeler-dealers proliferated. Its capture not only cut the main Chinese line of communication but also provided the Japanese with some welcome food, petrol and trucks.

56 Division now saw an opportunity to take advantage of this rapid success. Near the Chinese border there was a fork in the Burma Road. The right fork went to China and the left to Bhamo about 80 miles away. Now *56 Division* was just about to be strongly reinforced. Their third regimental group, *146*, which was motorised, had arrived in Rangoon on 22 April and was on its way to join them. So *56 Division* requested, and was granted, permission not only to advance up the Burma Road to the Salween crossing but also to capture Bhamo and Myitkyina. They thus assumed the task of being the right claw of General Iida's pincer movement to encircle the Allied forces in North Burma.

56 Division's Reconnaissance Regiment (56 K), supported by some tanks, four 105mm field guns and two 75mm mountain guns, left Lashio on 30 April. Overcoming two Chinese rearguard positions held by 29th Chinese D/Brigade at Hsenwi and Kutkai, they reached the road fork at Mong Yu late on 2 May (see Map 27). Here they overran a Chinese force in trucks and captured a British Colonel, who seemed to be a supply adviser to the Chinese.[1] Racing on, in the early hours of the 3rd they reached the big suspension bridge over the 300-foot wide Shweli river near Namkham. This was an important bridge and inadequate attention appears to have been given to its demolition, which was entrusted to the Lashio battalion of the BFF. The Japanese approached in eight trucks led by an officer in a jeep wearing Chinese uniform. What happened next is unclear but Lieutenant-Colonel Jim Wallace, MC, commanding the battalion, was killed and a British account says the demolition failed because the fuses were defective.[2] According to the Japanese account some 900 Indians on the far bank surrendered, having killed their British commander. Whatever happened, the bridge was not blown, and pressing on, *56 Recce Regiment* captured Bhamo after a brisk fight with 200 Chinese, at 11pm on 3 May. Here they captured 13 boats loaded with weapons and stores. Since they left Toungoo on 1 April, their rate of advance, including a number of stiff fights, had averaged 26 miles a day.[3]

Meanwhile *148 Regiment* and the remainder of *14 Tank Regiment* entered China along the Burma Road and defeated the Chinese who were holding a position in the hills near Longling. They then turned back, handing over the advance to the newly arrived *146 Regimental Group*. This group defeated the 29th Chinese D/Brigade and reached the Salween, nearly a hundred miles inside

China, at mid-day on the 5th. However, the Chinese successfully demolished the bridge there before they could capture it.

Having turned back, *148 Regiment* took the Bhamo road, reached there on the 5th and pressed on to Myitkyina. The Chinese on this route were now becoming demoralised and many trucks, and much ammunition and equipment, were abandoned where bottlenecks had caused traffic jams on the road. *148 Regiment* reached the bank of the Irrawaddy opposite Myitkyina to find that it had been the headquarters of the 5th Chinese A/Division and there were many papers scattered around. They started crossing the Irrawaddy in the early hours of 8 May and by 9am had captured Myitkina without loss.[4] The Chinese had departed to the east on the previous two days. They spent the next two weeks, until the monsoon arrived, pursuing the Chinese and trying to block off their escape routes to the north and east.

General Iida's original plan had been that *55 Division* would be the right claw of his pincer movement. However, *56 Division* had now usurped that role so *55 Division*, not being motorised and having been sent on a wild goose chase to Myingyan, followed north more slowly. *112 Regiment* (less a battalion) advanced up the railway towards Shwebo, and *143 Regiment* (less a battalion) advanced up the west of the Irrawaddy towards Katha. Two battalions, one from each regiment, advanced up the Burma Road to Maymyo and secured the Gokteik viaduct. They then turned north off the Burma road and captured Mogok, one battalion marching on to Bhamo. Some elements of the division then went further north to help *56 Division* in their mopping-up operations.

The Gokteik viaduct on the railway between Mandalay and Lashio was a most spectacular railway bridge spanning in one arch a deep gorge which the road crossed at a lower level. At the centre it was 825 feet above the river below and it was the only other bridge in Burma besides the Ava which, if blown, would be impracticable to repair during the war. In late April Major Michael Calvert and an *ad hoc* group of 'commandos' had been sent up to protect it against a possi-

1. This was probably Brigadier Hobson who ended up in Rangoon jail. The British had supplied a liaison officer to each Chinese formation. These were mostly officers from the Burma Civil Service or businessmen. In fact the Chinese were not easy to liaise with and the LO's main task became buying rice and other supplies which the British had promised to provide, the Chinese having no administrative services of their own. It is said that 300 British trucks were employed in supplying rice and petrol to the Chinese *(Davy, George)*. Sadly Hobson, who set a fine example in jail, was killed in 1945, just after he had been released, during an RAF attack on the retreating Japanese.
2. Cooke, Major E.H., *Personal Diary of Events in Burma ... May and June 1942*, NAM, 1973-02-44-2.
3. *56 Recce Regiment (56 K)* claimed to have travelled 870 miles since 1 April. The figure seems exaggerated but they had unquestionably made a very fast advance.
4. As *148 Regiment* did not leave the Mawchi area until 15 April they had actually travelled further and faster than *56 Recce Regiment* but they had not had so much fighting.

ble Japanese advance from Lashio. When, at the end of the month, they were recalled, Calvert asked if he could demolish the bridge before leaving, but permission was firmly refused. On his return to Mandalay, General Alexander called him in and, to Calvert's chagrin, expressed surprise that he had not blown the bridge. Alexander explained that he had been unable to give a direct order because of the political implications. This was one of the many odd occurrences in which this campaign abounded. However, the fact is that although the bridge was useful to the Japanese in the following years, its demolition would have had little effect on the 1942 campaign.

The Japanese Advance on Monywa

While attention had been focussed on the eastern end of the Irrawaddy line, *33 Division* was on the move in the west (see Map 28). After a brief rest the division started its advance on 25 April. *215 Regimental Group*, which had crossed the river, was in the lead, marching up the west bank of the Irrawaddy. It was very hot and although they met no opposition, since 2 Bur Brigade had already marched off west to Pauk, it was not until the 29th that they reached Pakokku. Here some trucks were sent up for them and they drove on 45 miles over a very bad track to a position opposite Monywa, arriving at sunset. Second-Lieutenant Katayama and some men of the BIA crossed the river in the dark and took a look around. The British seemed to be quite unaware of any danger. When they reported back with this news, Colonel Harada decided to occupy the town without delay. *1/215 Battalion*, supported by two regimental guns, was ordered to make a surprise crossing of the river that very night and attack Monywa from the south (see Map 29). Accordingly, in the early hours of 1 May, the battalion marched back about two miles to Letpadaung and crossed the river to Linkwe. At first light they advanced to the nearby road at Magyigon village where they surprised and overran a detachment of 50 Field Park Company. The main part of the company was in Monywa but they had left a party under a British NCO to guard a dump of engineer stores in Magyigon. The Japanese made a silent bayonet attack and many of the group were bayoneted while still asleep. A Japanese detachment, aiming to block the road to the south at the nearby hamlet of Ma-U, scattered another group there, but more noisily.[5] Unknown to them this latter group was HQ 1 Burdiv. The battalion then advanced north and, just after mid-day, established themselves in the southern part of Monywa.

On the west bank of the river, the commander of *215 Regiment* had his remaining troops well-dispersed, his guns[6] and MMGs deployed and an excellent gunner OP established on the Letpadaung Taung, an extinct volcano covered in open forest which overlooked Monywa and its approaches. To mask the night crossing he had shelled, mortared and machine-gunned Monywa and its waterfront during the night. In the morning he could see no activity in Monywa and a low-level air reconnaissance reported nothing. So, three large *26 Engineer Regiment* boats having arrived, he decided on a daylight crossing of the river, here about 600 yards wide. Accordingly *2/215 Battalion* sent its first company over in the morning in armoured launches. They got across, but suffered a few casualties when they were shot up by MMGs in mid-stream. Covering fire proved effective, however, and the following waves crossed without loss. In the afternoon, *Regimental HQ* and the *3rd Mountain Gun Battalion* followed. *1/215 Battalion* guarded the south of the town, *215/5 Company* was allotted the northern sector and *215/7 Company* covered the roads to the east and was centred on the railway station. *Regimental HQ* and *6 Company* were further back in the town between *5* and *7 Companies*. One company of mountain guns (three guns) was allotted to each of the northern, eastern and southern sectors.

The British Reaction to the Japanese Seizure of Monywa

According to a plan made by General Alexander on 28 April, Burcorps and 38 Chinese D/Brigade were to hold the north bank of the Irrawaddy. 38 Chinese D/Brigade, which had reverted to General Stilwell's command, would cover the withdrawal of the 5 Chinese A/Division in the Irrawaddy bend east of Sagaing. General Alexander had allotted the 7th Armoured Brigade to Stilwell to back them up. 48 Brigade would cover the area from Myinmu to Ondaw (see Map 28). 1 Burdiv was to march to Monywa whence 1 Bur Brigade would go by boat up the Chindwin to secure Kalewa and Kalemyo. 13 Brigade would cross the Chindwin at Monywa and cover the routes to the south-west, while 63 Brigade would come under command of 1 Burdiv and cover the approach from the south-east. Monywa would thus be the hub for the British withdrawal.

On the 30th, General Slim, now much concerned about the hazardous withdrawal to India which clearly loomed ahead, moved his HQ from Sagaing to Songon, 16 miles north of Monywa. The best route to India for the many civilians still to be evacuated, and for some administrative units no longer required, would be by steamer up the Chindwin. Preparations had been made for them to embark at Monywa or Alon, a little further north. Late that evening he had an unpleasant shock. The ominous and unexpected sound of gunfire[7] was heard from the south and an officer driving through reported that Monywa had fallen.

5. Until the shelling on Monywa started, the British had no idea that there were any Japanese troops within 30 miles.

6. A mountain artillery battalion of nine guns, a battery of four 105mm heavy field guns and six 75mm AA guns. *Namba*.

7. This was the Japanese covering fire on Monywa to divert attention from the night crossing to the south.

This was a bombshell. If true (at that moment it wasn't), it completely destroyed the Army plan. A glance at Map 28 will show why. The Japanese possession of Monywa not only outflanked the British defensive position on the Irrawaddy but threatened to block the British line of withdrawal to India.

Immediate action was required. 1 Burdiv was marching that night towards Chaung-U, 15 miles south of Monywa. General Slim ordered 63 Brigade to move at once by train to join them at Chaung-U, and 48 Brigade to send one battalion there and follow as quickly as possible with the rest of the brigade. HQ 17 Division and 16 Brigade were ordered to Ye-U. General Alexander was alerted and he allotted two squadrons of tanks to Burcorps, one to go to Chaung-U and the other to Ye-U. With these reinforcements, General Bruce Scott was ordered to recapture Monywa.

Slim then advised General Winterton, the Chief of Staff at Army HQ who had driven down to Burcorps HQ on hearing the news, to collect every possible vehicle, dumping all but vital stores, and despatch to Kalewa without delay the sick and wounded and all those waiting to go by steamer. Winterton was to say afterwards that this quick and firm advice was a major factor in avoiding serious losses.[8]

General Bruce Scott had moved his HQ to Ma-U, where it was joined by the HQ of 27 Mountain Regiment (see Map 28). Nearby were 1 Burdiv's few remaining vehicles which had made their way round via the Ava bridge. With them, it so happened, was Lieutenant-Colonel Thomas of the Cameronians who, having a septic throat, had moved back to his 'B' Echelon for 24 hours' rest. At HQ 1 Burdiv, the night of 30 April-1 May was a disturbed one. First there was the unexpected shelling of Monywa from the far bank. Then the orders from General Slim started coming in and plans had to be made. General Bruce Scott had at that moment no fighting troops at his disposal, but at 4am he summoned Colonel Thomas and ordered him to collect any support he could find and go into Monywa and take command of the scratch garrison there. Accordingly Thomas, in a staff car and accompanied by two carriers full of Cameronians, drove into Monywa in the dark.

An hour later, as already mentioned, Burdiv headquarters at Ma-U was attacked and overrun. Fortunately for the British, the Japanese attack was a noisy one and this gave just enough time for men to seize their weapons and pull on their boots. The Burmese defence platoon soon vanished but the clerks and batmen held up the attack for some vital minutes. They were also dispersed, however, and nearly all the equipment of the headquarters was lost. General Bruce Scott and his GSO1 had initially helped to man an old-fashioned firing line. Realising, however, that the position was hopeless, they loaded a jeep with the ciphers and secret papers and withdrew, on foot initially, successfully to

Chaung-U.[9] Here they were joined in due course by the AQMG and other members of the staff. Surprisingly soon they had the headquarters in action again, but without its wireless sets. It was not, however, an ideal start for an operational headquarters aiming to control a vital battle.

When Colonel Thomas arrived in Monywa he found it apparently quiet. However, the shelling and mortaring from the far bank had persuaded the captains of the river steamers that it would be wiser to move further upstream to Alon. The only British forces there were two companies of the 1st Glosters with a total strength of about 100, a platoon of the 1st Inniskillings, 50 Field Park Company (less a section) and about 100 BFF police. Their purpose was to protect the civilians[10] in the town and assist their evacuation. Shortly after his arrival Thomas found that the road had been cut behind him and, an hour or two later, the Japanese, under cover of shelling and mortaring, started a direct crossing of the river in armoured launches. Parts of his small force began to give way and, it being clear that the port was no longer useable, Colonel Thomas ordered the town to be evacuated, using his remaining resources to cover the withdrawal towards Alon.

General Alexander was acutely aware of the dangerous situation that had arisen. On 1 May he moved his HQ to Ye-U and met General Stilwell there. It was their last meeting. It was agreed to abandon the Irrawaddy line and start the final withdrawal. 7th Armoured Brigade was transferred back to Burcorps. Stilwell proposed to use the 38th Chinese D/Brigade to cover the retreat of the remnants of the 5th A/Division to Katha, and then let them make for India. On 2 May General Alexander sent a personal message to General Wavell:

> "Owing collapse Chinese forces below Mandalay I was obliged extend front Imperial force to take over rearguard on axis Meiktila-Mandalay. Owing to inadequate Imperial force my disposal this caused delay in regrouping of force astride Chindwin and Japanese secured Monywa while moves were in progress. Sit [situation] now is that 1 Bur Bde, 13 Inf Bde, 48 Bde, 63 Bde all under Burdiv are SE Monywa with Japanese astride road that place... Am apprehensive that Japanese may reach Kalewa and Kalemyo via Chindwin and Myittha valleys before my fighting forces." [*This was followed by an urgent request for air reconnaissance and air attacks on river craft*].

The Battle at Monywa

63 Brigade were the first reinforcements to arrive at Chaung-U. They had come by train straight from covering the demolitions at Myitnge and Ava, the lat-

8. Lunt, James, *A Hell of a Licking*, p.242.
9. From *Indian Years* by Colonel B.J. Amies who was AQMG of 1 Burdiv.
10. The civil administration was still functioning.

ter just before midnight that night. They were ordered to continue in the train to Kyehmon station about four miles south of Ma-U, detrain there and, supported by a newly-arrived squadron of the 7th Hussars, to make an immediate attack on Monywa from the south. Accordingly, 63 Brigade advanced on the town with the 2nd/13th FFRif on the left of the road and the 1st/10th Gurkhas on the right. The 7th Hussars were on the road and the right flank. The 1st/11th Sikhs were to follow when they arrived. Nothing was known about the strength or dispositions of the enemy. Overcoming some sharp opposition at Ma-U and Magyigon, where many mangled corpses provided melancholy evidence of the previous night's encounter, the two battalions reached a bottle-neck where the road and railway were forced by a marsh to run close to the river. The formidable assembly of enemy artillery and mortars (see Note 6) from across the river, who had excellent observation of this approach, took full advantage of this. The 2nd/13th FFRif suffered severely[11] and in the first ten minutes had 75 casualties. Two 7th Hussar tanks were knocked out, one by a well-concealed 75mm regimental gun firing at point-blank range.[12] Exhaustion of the troops now decided Brigadier Barlow to call the attack off, and leaving the 1st/11th Sikhs, who had now arrived, to hold an outpost line, he withdrew the other two battalions to Ma-U.

That evening, General Bruce Scott held a conference and ordered a two-brigade, attack for early the next morning. The Burma Rifle battalions, very low in strength after Yenanyaung, would be in reserve with Divisional HQ. 63 Brigade would renew its attack from the south. 13 Brigade, now consisting of the 1st Inniskillings, the 5th/1st Punjab Regiment and the 1st/18th R Garhwalis, would march across country to Zalok during the night and attack south-west astride the Monywa-Shwebo road. Each brigade would be supported by a troop of 25-pdrs from the 1st Indian Field Regiment and a mountain battery. 1 Bur Brigade, now consisting of the 2nd KOYLI (only 150 strong), the 2nd/7th Rajputs (only two companies) and the 1st/4th Gurkhas, who had not yet arrived, would be in reserve behind 63 Brigade. This hastily conceived plan had the weakness that the attacks were converging and care would be needed to avoid accidents.

The next day, 2 May, 63 Brigade renewed their attack with the Gurkhas on the right, the Sikhs on the left and 2 Mountain Battery in support. The Sikhs advanced into the southern suburb of the town, called E-ywa, and after some stubborn fighting, cleared it. During the action they attacked successfully some boats on the river. Resistance then stiffened and they were held up by a strongly-defended road-block. Shelling and mortaring began to cause many casualties and they could make no further progress. A bold attempt by tanks of the 7th Hussars to force the road-block was met with short-range fire from both regimental and mountain guns and they were driven back. On the right flank, the 1st/10th

Gurkhas were delayed by the marsh and were unable to keep up with the Sikhs. While negotiating this marsh they sustained some mortar casualties and eventually made a wide detour and joined up with 13 Brigade.

At the same time, 13 Brigade advanced from the east and quickly secured the village of Shaukka. They had a very difficult task because the advance was across open paddy fields while the enemy were concealed amongst the trees and vegetation of the town. They continued the advance with the Garhwalis on the left of the road, the Punjabis on the right and 23 Mountain Battery plus a troop of 25-pdrs in support. The 1st Inniskillings were in reserve.[13] The Garhwalis advanced across the open with great courage and, despite casualties, succeeded in seizing a few houses only 50 yards from the railway line. Here they were pinned down by intense machine-gun and mortar fire. The Punjabis on the right were also pinned down by machine-gun fire from the line of the railway. After mortaring and shelling the objective, however, one company renewed the attack and pressing forward with great determination succeeded in capturing the railway station, a fine feat of arms. They could make no further progress and an hour later a Japanese counter-attack drove them out again. There was now a lull, but at 11.30am the attack was resumed. On the right, the Punjabis recaptured the railway station but again lost it to a heavy counter-attack two hours later. Further to the right, another company cleared some Japanese outposts on the Ettaw road but were held up by the Japanese position in the town. On the left flank, the Garhwalis captured a grove of palm trees close to the level crossing in spite of accurate shelling from the Japanese medium guns on the other side of the river. A reserve company tried to work its way into the town round the left flank but was engaged by the Rajputs coming up from the south who were unaware of this move. Both units had casualties. In spite of this confusion, morale in 13 Brigade was still high and there was a feeling that success was in the air.

On the southern front, General Bruce Scott had decided about 3pm to put in his reserve, 1 Bur Brigade. They were to pass through 63 Brigade and advance to the road running past the railway station and into the town. The 1st/4th Gurkhas were to advance between the road and the railway, with the Rajputs on their right and the 2nd KOYLI in reserve. The Rajputs soon had trouble with the marsh and the scrub, changed direction to their right and engaged what they believed to be enemy but were in fact the Garhwalis, of whose presence they had no knowledge. The Gurkhas were confined by the road and railway and could

11. NAM, 1977-09-64, *Second Bn 13 FFRifles War Diary (unofficial) Jan 1942-Nov 1946*, compiled by Brigadier J.C. Weld, 1951.
12. Account of Mr Yoshiyuki Kobayashi.
13. All the British battalions were now very weak in strength due to battle casualties, sickness and the lack of reinforcements. For instance, the strength of the Cameronians at this date was 80.

only attack at first on a one-company front. They worked round the road-block and reached a large and well-defended pagoda close to the railway station. The Sikh and Gurkha mortars plastered this, and the Gurkhas thought they saw a way of getting behind this position. Before a new company could be moved up, however, they were ordered to stand fast.

At about 4pm, the British thought that they were getting on top (although, according to Sergeant Namba, the Japanese did not think so).[14] However, at this point a message was received from an officer of the Armoured Corps that the Army Commander had ordered 1 Burdiv to abandon the attack and pull back to Alon on the Ye-U road. As many orders came through the Armoured Brigade net, for they had the only reliable radios, this was believed and passed on to 1 Burdiv. General Bruce Scott was surprised but accepted it. The attack was halted, and the division was ordered to skirt Monywa to the east after dark, and march north up the Ye-U road to Alon. General Slim at Corps HQ had no knowledge of this order. He believed at the time that this was another example of the Japanese disseminating a deceptive message through the Armoured Brigade wireless net. However, he is more guarded in his book.[15] It seems probable that the order did come from General Alexander but, by a failure in staff work, was not passed to General Slim but issued direct. Whatever the source, it was a sensible order for, even if Monywa had now been captured, the cost would have been heavy and not justified at this stage.

The plan for the withdrawal was for 1 Burdiv to circle round via Zalok and Ettaw and to strike the Alon road about five miles north of Monywa. In the dark, they moved in three parallel columns with the brigades on the left, the vehicles in the centre and the bullock-carts on the right. The Sappers had made a track for the vehicles across the paddy fields by cutting gaps in the bunds that divided the fields. After a time the MT column used their lights and this and the various burning villages helped navigation. It was hard going for the exhausted troops and the experience of the 1st/4th Gurkhas is typical of many:

"At 9pm that evening the battalion withdrew and, skirting the swamp, moved off in the dark across country to the north-east. The withdrawal was not followed up. Of about 50 casualties, five could not be evacuated because the advanced dressing station had closed down. Four of them could sit a horse and were given ponies from the battery; the fifth had to be carried over 20 miles, by the regimental stretcher-bearers. It was a very trying march. The men had not fed since half-past four on the morning of the battle; they had been under arms continuously ever since. The day had been blazing hot and there was little water."

Once they reached the road, 63 Brigade took up a covering position and the other two brigades marched through. The division rested during the day of the 3rd but that evening resumed the march, every possible vehicle being sent forward to ferry the troops to the area of Ye-U, which some did not reach until the evening of the 4th.

So ended the battle at Monywa. The Japanese comment on the severity of the fighting and the bravery of the 'Indo-Gurkha' soldiers who still kept attacking "although many fell under our bullets" and in face of the point-blank fire from the mountain guns. British shellfire, though heavy, was not as effective as it might have been as most of the shells exploded in the branches of the trees.[16] The Japanese claim to have lost (from the infantry) only one officer and 20 men killed and to have captured 403 prisoners, mostly Gurkhas.[17] They rightly claimed a victory and to have been attacked by three brigades plus armour, but the odds against them were by no means so large as they supposed as the brigades were now greatly under strength.

Withdrawal to Ye-U

After this battle, the Japanese were as exhausted as the British. They did not start their advance until sunset on the 3rd. *2/215 Battalion* was in the lead, but ahead of them was their tank company which consisted of six British tanks, mostly captured at Shwedaung. After passing Alon there was a clash with British tanks and one of the Japanese tanks was knocked out. The Japanese tanks continued their advance and came on two British tanks blocking the road. In the dark the 2nd R Tanks mistook the enemy for a returning flank guard. The Japanese fired first at short range and knocked out one of the British tanks, the other withdrawing. The Japanese were cock-a-hoop at having knocked out one of the dreaded British tanks with a captured one. In fact they also captured another British tank this night but this was one from the flank guard which had fallen into a nullah in the dark and had to be abandoned.

The redoubtable Colonel Bagot, though not fully fit, returned on the 27th to command the 1st Glosters in Shwebo. That day they received a draft of three offi-

---

14. Namba, Shukou, *Burning Earth*. Namba was Chief Clerk at *HQ 215 Regiment* which had moved into Monywa in the afternoon of 1 May and his story of the campaign is in general an objective one.

15. Slim, Field-Marshal Sir W., *Defeat into Victory*, p.96.

16. *Memoir 215 Infantry Regiment*.

17. The Japanese tended to regard anyone wearing a bush hat as a Gurkha. Because there were so many prisoners they were temporarily held in a steamer on the river. A photograph of the prisoners indicates that they were of many races and not all were soldiers. The 1st/18th Royal Garhwal Rifles record their casualties here as seven killed, 32 wounded and 25 missing of whom 11 were 'followers'.

cers and 120 men who had come out from England and been flown in to Myitkyina. The first order they received on joining their regiment was to burn all their kit except what they could carry on their backs. The next was to set off with the battalion that night on the 20-mile march to Ye-U. Unfortunately they could not keep up with the rest of the battalion and dawn, and some passing Japanese bombers, found them in the open where they lost six killed and 14 wounded. Another but smaller party of Glosters were flown in a day or two later and had an equally traumatic time. Their train south from Myitkyina reached Naba station to find the line blocked by a horrendous rail crash two days before. Dead and dying were still lying all over the station. Very fortunately they met up with Colonel Abernethy and 4 Burif who had been covering the despatch of hospital trains to Myitkyina. Under his command they marched west to Homalin on the Chindwin and on to India.[18]

On 2 May, Colonel Bagot was ordered to take over command from Colonel Thomas, who was ill, of the scratch force which had been assembled to protect the proposed embarkation at Monywa. With the aid of a squadron of 2 R Tanks, he was to hold a delaying position at Budalin for the rearguard to pass through. Early in the morning of the 4th, they beat off a substantial Japanese patrol attack and shortly afterwards were ordered back to Ye-U.[19]

There were now rumours of boat-loads of Japanese moving up the Chindwin and it was clear that if these were not true, they soon would be. As well as HQ 17 Division, 16 and 48 Brigades had been recalled to Ye-U and had reached there via Shwebo by 3 May. The Japanese were doing their best to slow up the withdrawal with numerous air attacks and it was obvious that there was no time to be lost if the Burma Army were to withdraw to India successfully. There were two hazards. If the Japanese reached Kalewa before the British, the trap would be closed. But it would be just as big a hazard if the monsoon, due any day after 15 May, arrived while the British were still retreating over forest tracks and crossing innumerable river-beds, now dry but due to become raging torrents once the rains came. A dramatic race lay ahead.

---

18. Colonel Abernethy reported that they were greatly helped at the river crossings by a party of Burmese Sappers from their depot at Maymyo led by Major Stack. In spite of their reputation for unreliability, these Burmans from central Burma accompanied the party loyally up to the Chindwin. 19. As a regular battalion with an internal security role, the 1st Glosters, like the 2nd KOYLI, had brought out to Burma their Regimental Colours and regimental silver. Bagot had sent the former back to India when things looked bad, but the regimental silver had been stored in Maymyo. While in hospital there he had managed to have it packed and brought to Ye-U. He and some others now carried the smaller items in their packs but the main part was put on a truck for Kalewa. Unfortunately the truck was commandeered for some emergency before it got there and the silver had to be buried in the forest. In 1945 a party visited the spot only to find that the silver had been found and looted by Burmese. One candelabra was later recovered from an antique shop in Singapore.

CHAPTER TWENTY-TWO

Last Stand at Shwegyin

The collapse of the Chinese forces on the east flank, in the face of the very rapid advance of the Japanese *56 Division*, made it clear that there was no chance, as had at one time been hoped, of holding a position in North Burma. There was no other course than to withdraw to China and to India.

When Rangoon was about to fall, the Governor, Sir Reginald Dorman-Smith, his staff and the senior Burmese members of the Government had moved to Maymyo (May-Mew) in the hope that North Burma would be held. When it became clear that this could not be done and Burma would be lost, they moved further north to Myitkyina. Evacuation of the remaining European civilians from Burma was now imperative. It was a large group, comprising those who either lived and worked in the north or had moved there earlier from Rangoon, and included many wives and children. It also included those Army wounded and sick who were still in the hospitals in Maymyo and Mandalay. The latter were being flown out from the airfield at Shwebo, but only a few aircraft were available and there was a big backlog.

Some of these evacuees travelled over the track to Tamu in their own cars and many went further north to Myitkyina by car, train or river. Mandalay was being repeatedly bombed and in one raid a train loaded with RAF bombs was hit and the gigantic explosion wrecked the station which was not used again. At Myitkyina, the RAF made heroic efforts to fly out the wounded, and the women and children, in Dakota aircraft acquired from the Americans, and many were evacuated in this way. However, the Japanese advance on Myitkyina was swift. Lady Dorman-Smith flew out on 2 May but the Governor was determined not to leave until all the refugees had been successfully evacuated. On 4 May, however, he received a direct order from Winston Churchill to fly out, and left the next morning. On the 6th, two RAF transport planes were destroyed on the airstrip by Japanese fighters while refugees were embarking. On the 7th, Myitkyina was evacuated, and on the 8th, the Japanese seized the town and airfield.

Some ten thousand men, of whom five hundred were Europeans, were now forced to attempt the difficult march through the forests of the Hukawng valley and over the hills to Assam. On the Burmese side there was only a bridle path but this had been improved into a jeep track on the Indian side of the frontier. They were not pursued but there was little food to be had until the frontier was reached and many suffered extreme hardship. Every effort was made to locate refugees and drop food to them from the air, but malaria, dysentery and starvation took its toll. The monsoon striking in the middle of May washed out tracks and made the crossing of streams hazardous and most parties took several weeks, and some took several months, to reach Assam. There were many stories of heroic determination and leadership, and some of disgraceful behaviour by ill-disciplined military stragglers. These are the two faces of all retreats. By the end of July, including the wounded, 1800 children, 925 Europeans, 17,000 Indians, 365 Anglo-Indians and 265 Chinese had reached India by air from Myitkyina or by marching out through the Hukawng valley. Once across the frontier, the Indian Tea Association[1] did a wonderful job in feeding the refugees and helping them on their way to India where many had to spend a spell in hospital.

Some of the 5th Chinese A/Division, mostly from the 96th D/Brigade, finding their retreat blocked, skirted the area of Myitkyina and made their way back to China by various tracks and foot-paths over the hills to the north-east. Most of the remnants of the 22nd Chinese D/Brigade, together with Lieutenant-General Tu and the headquarters of the 5th A/Division, straggled up the Hukawng valley to Ledo in Assam.

General Stilwell and his headquarters joined up at Indaw with the American Dr Seagrave and a party of nurses. Seagrave had been running a mission hospital in the Shan States before the war and had been invited by General Hutton to help cope with the problem of the Chinese sick and wounded.[2] He and his team did a wonderful job under the most difficult conditions. The whole party of Americans and Chinese was nearly one hundred strong. Stilwell decided to make for India by the track which led to Homalin on the Chindwin. They went as far as they could in trucks and then marched for four days to the Uyu River. Although he was 58 years old, Stilwell was a tough man and out-marched most of his staff. At the Uyu river they assembled some rafts and floated down the river for three days to Homalin. From here they marched up the east bank for two days to Kawya where they were met by a British relief party, which included a doctor, from Imphal. This party provided food and some animal transport and guided them across the Chindwin and back over the hills to Imphal which they reached on 22 May (see Map 31).[3]

Lieutenant-General Sun's 38th Chinese D/Brigade, which had done well at Yenangyaung and was still an effective fighting force, had asked if they could make for India and this had been agreed. From Indaw, which they reached by train, they took a more southerly route to the Chindwin than General Stilwell and their flank guard had a clash with the advancing Japanese at Wuntho. They reached the Chindwin at Paungbyin on 13 May where they encountered a small Japanese force which had come up the river. However, the 113th Chinese R/Battalion held off the Japanese while the other two R/Battalions crossed safely and reached Imphal on 24 May. 113 Chinese R/Battalion succeeded in crossing the Chindwin a week later.

On 24 May, under orders from the Generalissimo, the Chinese staged a counterattack down the Burma Road with the newly arrived 71st A/Division to take the pressure off their retreating formations. Part of this A/Division crossed the Salween south of the bridge, captured the village on the west bank and advanced west along the road. This was a serious threat, and General Iida ordered *113 Regiment* back from Katha and Bhamo to deal with it. By 10 June they had restored the situation and the Chinese were driven back over the Salween.

The Withdrawal of the Army in Burma to the Chindwin

AHQ Burma had moved to Shwebo together with many Army administrative units. These had now to be evacuated, and no less than 2300 wounded and sick men would also have to pass over the track to India. There were grave doubts whether vehicles would get through, particularly over the last stretch between Pyingaing and Shwegyin. Some clearly would not, and orders were given for the destruction of the remaining heavy anti-aircraft guns and also the solid-wheeled 77mm Italian field guns issued as a stop-gap after the Sittang disaster.

Shwebo had been bombed several times and mostly burnt to the ground and with it perished most of the records of the campaign. So General Alexander had moved his HQ to Ye-U and had held a conference there with Generals Slim and Stilwell at which the final moves in the retreat were discussed. He had already arranged for dumps of supplies and petrol to be deposited at 25-mile intervals on the track to Shwegyin on the east bank of the Chindwin, and had asked General Wavell to provide similar dumps on the road from Kalewa on the west bank to Tamu. The administrative problems were far from easy as supplies, and particularly petrol, were now very short. As a precaution, rations were again reduced. From Ye-U, it was 107 miles to Kalewa, 225 miles to road-head at Tamu and 425 miles to rail-head at Dimapur (see map 31).

The few Army engineers that there were had been working on the worst places on the track to Shwegyin. It was just a dusty track winding through about one

1. There were many big tea estates in Assam.
2. The Chinese had no medical services of their own. The British supplied them with a General Hospital, some minor medical units and some medical supplies from their own limited stocks. Chinese wounded were, wherever possible, treated in British hospitals. (See Appendix 5, para 5).
3. Rooney, D.D., *Stilwell*.

hundred miles of uninhabited forest and dipping down to cross, or sometimes follow, the soft sandy beds of innumerable chaungs or nullahs. At about half-way, at a place called Pyingaing,[4] it crossed a large nullah nearly half a mile wide called the Maukkadaw Chaung. A few miles further on there was a steep and winding hill section, with some roughly improvised bridges, and finally the track reached the Chindwin at Shwegyin, about six miles downstream from Kalewa. Many private cars (including the Governor's black Rolls-Royce) had already got stuck in the earlier sandy nullahs and had been abandoned, but it was hoped that the army trucks, though very few were four-wheel-drive, would be able to get through provided the rains held off. When the rains came the track would be impassable to all wheeled vehicles.

On 3 May it was rumoured that Japanese troops in boats had been seen moving up the Chindwin from the direction of Monywa. In fact they were probably Indian refugees but no-one could be sure of this. General Slim ordered 17 Division to picquet the 'India Road' as far as Pyingaing. 1 Burdiv would then pass through. At Pyingaing, 1 Bur Brigade would break away from the 'road' and march north on a path which led to the river north of Kalewa at Pantha. The rest of 1 Burdiv would cross the river at Kalewa and 13 Brigade would hold the area of Kalewa-Kalemyo. 7th Armoured Brigade would support the rearguard. Accordingly, 17 Division ordered 63 Brigade to set up a lay-back position at Tawgyin and patrol south. 48

Brigade would then pass through and set up a similar lay-back at Pyingaing. All the remaining British units would then pass through to Shwegyin and cross the river. Finally, 48 Brigade, supported by the 7th Hussars, would withdraw as rearguard to Shwegyin. Early on 4 May, all but the barest necessities having been destroyed, these moves started. The track was deteriorating and it was still uncertain whether it would be possible to get any vehicles beyond Pyingaing.

Officers of the 7th Rajputs take a rest on 1 Bur Bde's long march from Pyingaing to the Chindwin.

Before the bulk of the units left Ye-U there was another event of some interest. An RAF Blenheim aircraft appeared and dropped by parachute a quantity of 'goodies', mostly NAAFI cigarettes. This is worth recording for two reasons. One is that it was only the third British aircraft that the forward troops had seen since leaving Rangoon, although they had seen Japanese aircraft nearly every day. The other is that it occurred to several people that here was the answer to the Japanese road-block tactics. If air supply could be developed, encircled forces could hold out and this was discussed seriously at this time in HQ 17 Division. Several people were later to lay claim to this idea which in those days was quite novel (although General Slim had advocated it years before on the North-West Frontier) but in Burma this is where it originated.

As far as possible all units, except those with mules, were lifted in vehicles a part, if not all, of the way. Trucks were packed full and the twisting, bumpy track made the ride very uncomfortable. Movement was dreadfully slow. There was no possibility of passing and every time a truck stuck in a nullah, which was often, the column halted while everyone in the vicinity helped to either get it moving or get it pushed clear of the track. Meanwhile, some of the drivers, who like everyone else were absolutely exhausted, fell asleep and officers had to move up the column to wake up the drivers and get their vehicles moving again. Those who left Ye-U at mid-day on the 4th did not reach Pyingaing until dawn on the 5th, an 18-hour convoy for a 57-mile trip.

At Pyingaing, a force was improvised and jeeped down the Maukkadaw Chaung to its confluence with the Chindwin. Their task was to attack any Japanese coming up the river and to provide a guard on the western flank. The force, commanded by Major Eric Holdaway and with Major Mike Calvert as 'adviser', consisted of 120 hastily-collected British soldiers and two composite companies of Gurkhas made up from units of 48 Brigade. On arrival at the river many of the British soldiers, who belonged to a miscellany of units, were found to be unfit for this type of operation and were sent back to Pyingaing. Twenty-six, including five officers, volunteered to stay and these were mainly staff from Calvert's Bush Warfare School. This small force watched the river for three days, checking the many hundreds of civilian refugees who were making their way up the river in sampans. On the 8th they were ordered to withdraw towards Shwegyin the next morning. Hearing that a Japanese force had landed five miles to the south, Holdaway decided to concentrate his force at Moktha, about three miles inland, for the night. The next morning, accompanied by 60 Burmese porters, they set out on a tortuous and difficult march through the forest to Kywe, about nine miles south of Shwegyin.

---

4. Soon labelled 'Pink Gin', a favourite drink in the East.

Meanwhile, 48 Brigade had arrived at Pyingaing on 5 May and established a firm position through which the rest of the Army in Burma duly passed during the next three days. The Army was now overtaking the tail of the mass civilian exodus along this route and there were some pathetic sights of familes struggling to make their way to India. Where possible these were helped with lifts in trucks but cholera and dysentery were a constant worry.

At Pyingaing, the Sappers dug a large pit, revetted with bamboo matting, in the sand of the Maukkadaw Chaung and this produced ample water, two canvas tanks being kept full with a mechanical pump. Two other smaller water points were also established, one for refugees and one beside the path to the north which 1 Bur Brigade was to take. The sandy crossing of the Maukkadaw Chaung was deteriorating fast, but 200 Gurkhas were allotted to cut brushwood and help the Sappers to keep the track open. The Sappers had also been ordered to patrol for seven miles on either side of Pyingaing and instantly to clear from the track any vehicle which broke down 'by whatever means you think fit'. On the morning of the 8th all abandoned but serviceable vehicles were blown up. By the afternoon of the 8th the whole army, less the rearguard, had passed through.

The 7th Hussars, who were the last of the armour, left Pyingaing at 1630 hours on the 8th, followed in trucks by 70 Field Company. The latter left a marching platoon with 48 Brigade, who were the marching rearguard. The Sappers destroyed all vehicles abandoned in Pyingaing and along the track to Shwegyin, and demolished the track at an awkward bend in the hill section. It was a hard march for those on foot and although the rearguard was picked up in MT after marching 22 miles they did not reach Shwegyin until the evening of the 9th. They were not to get much rest.

The Scene at Shwegyin

At Shwegyin the British faced a severe problem but one which is easy to explain. The point where the track reached the Chindwin at Shwegyin was six miles downstream of Kalewa on the west bank, where the track started again for India. In between was the deep river, about 600 yards wide, and flowing south with a three-to four-knot current. Both banks were hilly and covered with forest and many escarped cliffs. The only means of moving vehicles or guns across this obstacle was by loading them on to one of the five surviving river steamers. Each steamer could take about 600 men and three or four vehicles, but loading over an improvised jetty was a slow process, as was unloading at Kalewa. In spite of all efforts, not more than a maximum of 24 vehicles a day were getting across. It was no help that the Chittagonian crews, for fear of air attack, would only work at night. Only one crew would work by day. One tank, loaded on a raft improvised from two country boats and towed by a steamer, had successfully crossed, as had most of the surviving 25-pdr and mountain guns. The great majority of vehicles, however, were still awaiting their turn and being held wherever space was available along the last five miles of the track to Shwegyin. On the 8th, the original jetty at Shwegyin had been submerged by a four-foot rise in the river-level, due to rain in the hills upstream, and a few planks onto a barge were doing duty as a landing stage. Many vehicles were getting stuck on these planks. One did not need to be a mathematical genius to see that, with the monsoon expected within the next week, much equipment would have to be abandoned whether the Japanese interfered or not .

Such a tempting target did not escape the notice of the Japanese Air Force. The parked transport was bombed on the 7th, and the approach to the jetty was bombed on the 9th, but apart from a few vehicles set on fire there was little damage. On the second occasion, the 3rd Indian LAA Battery, who had somehow managed to get four of their unwieldy Bofors guns to Shwegyin, shot down one of the attackers.[5]

About a mile-and-a-half south of Shwegyin, a boom consisting of sampans roped together, had been prepared by the small Royal Marine detachment and stretched across the Chindwin with the aim of obstructing boats coming up the river. It was, of course, useless unless covered by fire and the 5th/17th Dogras, now only two companies strong but reinforced by the 17 Royal Marines with five Breda MMGs, had been deployed on the west bank to cover it. Its efficacy was never tested as it was bombed and broken in the second air raid. To back them up, a company of the 1st R Jats had been positioned on the west bank of the river opposite Shwegyin. These west bank forces dug defensive positions but they were not attacked and were eventually ordered back to Kalewa.

70 Field Company, less one platoon, reached Shwegyin early on the 9th and were given the task of improving the jetty, now scarcely useable due to the rise in the level of the river. The jetty was just to the north of the mouth of the Shwedaung Chaung (see Map 30). Surrounding it was a small grove of palm and banana trees. Inland from this copse was a flat area of paddy fields some 300 yards wide and 600 yards long. This area was surrounded by steep forest-covered hills and became known as the 'Basin'. By cutting down some of the palm trees and using them to make crib piers on top of the old jetty, a serviceable landing stage with a half-floating bay onto a barge was completed by dusk that evening. Loading became much easier and several successful steamer trips were made that night.

---

5. They had started from Ye-U with six guns but two had got bogged down on the way and had to be destroyed.

When HQ 17 Division reached Shwegyin on the evening of the 8th they found Brigadier Ekin (the erstwhile commander of the disbanded 46 Brigade) in charge there. He had been appointed as L of C sub-area commander responsible for the vital crossing to Kalewa. He had deployed the troops to cover the boom and also stationed two anti-tank guns at Shwegyin where they could fire down and across the river. This left him with the Jats, less two companies, to protect the Basin and jetty.[6] General Cowan now took over command although Ekin remained to help with the embarkation.

At this stage the crossing was going well and large numbers of men were moving each night onto the steamers. Army and Corps troops had all crossed.[7] HQ 7th Armoured Brigade and 2nd R Tanks had already gone. The latter had started from Ye-U with 35 tanks. Three had broken down and two had fallen off the road at the hill section. During the 9th, all 30 remaining tanks had been methodically destroyed. By early morning of the 10th, the only troops left were Divisional HQ, the 7th Hussars and their company of the 1st West Yorks, 48 Brigade and the 1 R Jats, 1 Indian Field Battery,[8] 12 Mountain Battery (two guns on mules and two carried in trucks), a troop of 3 Indian LAA Battery (four guns), 60 and 70 Field Companies and some medical and supply units.

It was too good to last. Hardly had the sky begun to lighten on the 10th when there were some ominous rifle shots from the south side of the Basin. These were quickly followed by some sustained bursts of MMG fire, the typical signature of a Japanese attack. Something had gone wrong with the force covering the approach up the river from the south.

The Story of the Flank Guard

Major Holdaway's force, marching through the forest and out of sight of the river, had reached Kywe at dusk on the 9th. They were about to enter the village when they heard that 700 Japanese, who had come up the river during the day and thus by-passed them, had just left and were aiming for Shwegyin. This information was correct; it was *2/213 Battalion* (less a company) who were leading the advance. At the same time Major Calvert and a few men, who had gone on a reconnaissance, reported by runner that 1500 Japanese and stores were being landed on the other (west) bank from motor-boats and barges manned by Japanese marines[9] at Ingonyi, about a mile downstream. This was only partially correct. It was a feint by *2/214 Battalion* who deliberately made a lot of noise to give the impression that they were establishing themselves on the west bank. After dark they re-embarked and landed on the east bank between Kywe and Shwegyin. Although unaware of the deception, Holdaway realised that there were large parties of Japanese closing in on Shwegyin. Unfortunately, his heavy wireless sets were at the back of the column. His task was to warn 17 Division at Shwegyin of the impending attack. So he left orders for the column on arrival to abandon its heavy equpment, discharge the 60 coolies and march across country to Shwegyin that night. Meanwhile he went on ahead with his small all-British advance party hoping to avoid the Japanese, reach Shwegyin and give the alarm before the attack started.

Behind him, the back of the column had been delayed. Some of the coolies had dumped their loads and tried to desert and, while this was being sorted out, Holdaway and his advance party, conscious of the urgency of their information, moved off and lost contact. A few of the Gurkhas escorting the coolies with the heavy wireless sets had still not turned up. While Captains Gribble and Willis with the main Gurkha party searched unsuccessfully at Kywe for Holdaway's party, large numbers of boats were observed passing up the river in the dark and showing the minimum of lights. Finding no sign of Holdaway, Willis and Gribble took their Gurkha party, now about 190 strong, into the forest to the north-east and rested for a few hours. Before dawn on 10 May they continued their march and shortly after heard the sounds of heavy firing at Shwegyin. Realising that their information was no longer useful and considering that 48 Brigade would probably have withdrawn before they could reach them, they decided to give Shwegyin a wide berth. They marched east for Kado and then north for Kanni before reaching the Chindwin at Singaung, about six miles north of Kalewa. Here they crossed the river in sampans and marched for several days through the forested hills, buying food in villages where they could, and eventually joining 17 Division's rearguard at Yazagyo.

What happened to Holdaway's advance party is only partially known. They seem to have been surprised that night while resting in the forest by *2/214 Battalion* which had landed further north. As planned if such an eventuality should occur, they broke up into small groups. Holdaway, who had done so well in the first clash with the Japanese on the Thai border, led a party of seven. Unfortunately they ran into the Japanese again. Corporal Howson of the 2 KOYLI found a raft and got across the river. Sergeant Hirst, also a Yorkshireman, was captured and died later as a prisoner. Holdaway apparently tried to swim the river and was drowned.

When Major Mike Calvert returned from his reconnaissance he found that the rest of the party had disappeared. So with his two soldier companions he swam the river and the trio, having perforce abandoned all their kit, joined a party of

---

6. One company had been ordered to withdraw by ship from Rangoon.

7. General Alexander and Army HQ crossed the Chindwin on the 7th.

8. 1 Indian Field Regiment, less 1 Field Battery, had already crossed.

9. Not marines but engineers of *26 Independent Engineer Regiment*.

Indian refugees making their way up the west bank. This Indian party, at considerable risk to themselves, befriended them but insisted on their adopting women's dress so that they could conceal their faces if Japanese appeared. Thus, surely rather imperfectly disguised, they successfully reached Kalewa.

The rear party of Gurkhas escorting the coolies had been held up about two miles short of Kywe when the coolies deserted. However they managed to collect eight of them, just sufficient for the wireless sets, and marched on to Kywe in the dark, finding it deserted. This party consisted of Captains MacPherson and McRea and 24 Gurkhas of the 1st/3rd and 1st/ 7th, plus an Indian Signals wireless operator. They withdrew into the forest for the night and attempted unsuccessfully to make wireless contact with 17 Division. At first light they tried again to get through but again failed. The coolies were now in a state of collapse so MacPherson ordered the wireless sets to be destroyed and discharged the porters.

Hearing the firing to the north, the two Captains and their party determined to rejoin 48 Brigade. After several hours of marching in the confusing maze of wooded hills, they reached the Shwedaung Chaung and were able to get some water. A little further on they surprised a large party of Japanese resting at a water point and attacked them before retiring into the forest. Crossing the chaung further up, they came on another Japanese party, who fled at their approach leaving behind their meal of tinned fish. Macpherson's party then climbed a nearby hill, where they consumed the tinned fish, and coming down found their way to HQ 17 Division, which was only about 400 yards away. They had done well and were rightly congratulated by General Cowan.

The Japanese Advance on Shwegyin

At this stage it is helpful to know what the Japanese moves were. Lieutenant-General Sakurai had given to Major-General Araki, his Infantry Commander, the task of cutting off and annihilating the forces attempting to escape to India. To achieve this, Araki, who had his own small staff, was allotted *213 Regiment* (less *5 Company*), *1/215 Battalion, 2 Mountain Artillery Battalion*, one engineer company and *26 Independent Engineer Regiment* with 40 boats. However, because of an outbreak of cholera in *1/214* and *3/214 Battalions*, who were due to advance north from Monywa towards Katha, these two battalions had to be halted for ten days and *1/215 Battalion* took their place. Araki was allotted *2/214 Battalion* to replace *1/215* and this joined him by boat up the Chindwin.

The force left Monywa on the evening of 4 May. *1/213 Battalion* was directed to follow up along the track the British had used from Ye-U. Araki's headquarters, *3/213 Battalion* and most of the gunners marched up the east bank of the Chindwin. However there was no proper path, the country was broken and there were many chaungs to cross, so they made slow progress.

Two battalions, together with several day supplies, went up the Chindwin by boat. *2/213 Battalion* (less *5 Company*) was in the lead. On the night of the 8th/9th it passed Holdaway's flank guard without seeing it, or being seen, and landed at Kywe on the east bank, about nine miles south of Shwegyin. On the night of the 9th it set off for Shwegyin along the path beside the river as far as Kyauktan and then made its way across country to the Shwegyin Chaung near its mouth. Two mountain guns of *2 Company* of *33 Mountain Artillery Regiment* accompanied them.

2/214 Battalion also went up the river in the boats of *26 Engineer Regiment*. It landed first at Ingongyi on the west bank about a mile downstream of Kywe and tried to give the impression that the main force had landed there by making a lot of noise and lighting fires. Later in the night they embarked again and moved quietly up the river, landing on the east bank north of Kywe. There were cliffs along the river bank for several miles south of Shwegyin and they were only able to land about three miles north of Kywe. Somewhere here they claim to have surprised and dispersed Holdaway's British party and to have captured a box of silver rupees, very useful as the locals had little use for Japanese military currency notes. They then marched inland along a path to Thanbaya and from there took a path north-west to the Shwegyin Chaung which they struck around mid-day on the 10th to the east of *2/213 Battalion*.

The British Defence of Shwegyin

General Cowan, now in command at Shwegyin, had received no information of the imminence of the Japanese attack. Holdaway had known late on the 9th but he had been unable to pass the news on. However, although Cowan still believed there was an outpost screen to the south who would give some warning, he took no chances. When 48 Brigade arrived from Pyingaing after dark, very tired after a 22-mile march and a bumpy 30-mile ride in vehicles, the 1st/7th Gurkhas were ordered to march at once into the Basin and prepare to take over from the 1st/9th R Jats at dawn the next day. They worked their way through the mass of tanks and vehicles and arrived in the Basin at 2030 hours, arranged a meal and lay down to sleep in the ricefields. At first light on the 10th, shooting started from the hills to the south, so the Gurkhas were ordered under cover while the two commanding officers conferred. As Lieutenant-Colonel Godley of the Jats had been defending the Basin for three days and knew the ground well, and as HQ 48 Brigade was harboured some three miles further back, Lieutenant-Colonel Williams of the 7th Gurkhas very sensibly agreed that, to ensure co-ordination, Godley should for the moment command this part of the battle.

The Basin was a difficult area to defend as it was overlooked from the south and east by a series of forested hills, most of whose faces on the Basin side were vertical precipices, around 200 feet high (see Map 30). The ground to the south of the hills which rimmed the Basin was a mass of small jungle-covered hills. In 1942 the only map of this area available was a quarter-inch one in which the cartographer had made only a vague attempt to define the confusion of hill features. One obvious line of enemy advance from the south was down the dry bed of the Shwegyin Chaung which curved in through a gap in the hills and reached the Chindwin about 50 yards south of the jetty. Godley had only two companies of the 1st R Jats at Shwegyin. He had deployed 'B' Company astride the chaung where it entered the Basin, and used 'D' Company, when not employed cutting wood for the steamers, to picquet the main hill features of 'East Ridge' and 'Knoll' by day. The main artillery support for his battalion at this stage were 3 Indian LAA Battery's last four Bofors guns, which Major Charles MacFetridge had somehow managed to tow to Shwegyin. Three of these had been posted on the north side of the Basin, primarily in a ground role, and one on the south side for anti-aircraft defence.

South of the mouth of the chaung a high ridge ('South Ridge') formed the river bank and dominated both the jetty and the river, so Godley posted 'A' company of the 1st/7th Gurkhas on this to secure the river flank. Meanwhile he attempted to establish one of his platoons on Knoll, a hill overlooking the Basin from the south. It now transpired that the Japanese were not only advancing down the chaung where the initial clashes had taken place, but were also spreading into the hills overlooking the Basin from the east and his platoon was repulsed. Now the 1st/7th Gurkhas only had three companies as 'B' Company was with Holdaway's flanking force. They had improvised a fourth company, called 'X' Company, from sick and recently joined reinforcements, and this was posted on 'North Ridge'. 'C' Company was detailed to reinforce the Jat company covering the approach down the chaung while 'D' Company was given the difficult task of capturing East Ridge. The problem here was that East Ridge presented a high precipice to the Basin which even the Gurkhas couldn't climb. The only way up was from the south end and this, being only lightly covered with scrub until the trees at the top were reached, was fully exposed to the Japanese on Knoll. However Captain Joy led his company with skill and determination and, helped by the Bofors keeping heads down on Knoll and Saddle Hill, successfully seized the south end of East Ridge against light opposition. This company had taken with them some improvised orange piqueting screens,[10] as used on the North-West Frontier, and these were very useful in indicating their positions to the watching Gunners.

A platoon from 'C' Company of the Gurkhas joined with a Jat platoon in a second effort to capture Knoll but they were unsuccessful. Resistance, supported by mortars from Saddle Hill, was stubborn and both platoons had casualties and were forced back. A party of Japanese caused a minor crisis by working their way through the scrub at the foot of Knoll and approaching the HQ of the 1st R Jats, but a hastily organised counter-attack drove them back with heavy loss. Henceforward the Japanese on Knoll and Saddle Hill were neutralised as far as possible by MMG and Bofors fire, while 'A' Company snipers from South Ridge took a steady toll of unwary soldiers on these two features.

By 0900 hours, the position in the Basin was stable. Meanwhile, General Cowan had ordered 48 Brigade to march forward and take control. Cameron ordered the 1st/3rd Gurkhas to hold 'Long Ridge' and two squadrons of tanks of the 7th Hussars were deployed to give some protection from the north in the Shwegyin Chaung. The 1st/4th Gurkhas were ordered to secure the 'Col' and capture 'Stop Hill' which dominated the approach of an enemy up the Shwegyin Chaung from the south. They were nearly too late. The leading troops of *2/214 Battalion* had got there first and it required a bombardment with mortars and a quick and determined attack to drive them off.

There had been some mortar and LMG fire on the jetty but it was largely screened by palm and banana trees and the Sappers, who worked there throughout the day, only had one casualty. During the night, several steamers had come in and the last units of 63 Brigade had been successfully loaded, together with 414 Battery RHA and its guns, and all but two guns of 'A' Battery, 95 Anti-Tank Regiment RA. At about 0530, the final steamer had come into the jetty and some more troops were being put aboard when a launch appeared carrying the Corps Commander, General Slim, and tied up alongside the steamer. Slim came ashore and met Brigadier Ekin, who was in administrative control of the troops embarking, and with two or three staff officers stood in the paddy fields surveying the scene. They were soon spotted and a Japanese MMG gunner fired a long burst at them from Saddle Hill. The bullets, easily discernible from the admixture of red tracer, fell short and some ricocheted into the party off the hard paddy field. To the amusement of the onlookers, General Slim and party then skipped smartly into the scrub on the west side of the Basin, which is where they should have been all along. It was all good for morale. It is not often that troops see their Corps Commander come under aimed small arms fire.

Slim watched the fighting for a time and then accosted one of the three tanks which had been moved into the Basin to cover the approach down the Chaung. Failing to contact General Cowan (who was on his way to the Basin), he left a

10. Made from the saffron robes of a Buddhist priest.

message saying, firstly, that he would try and get another steamer to evacuate the wounded, and secondly, that Cowan had authority to withdraw his force that night if he judged that the position could be held no longer. Slim then left in his launch, followed by the fully-loaded steamer. No-one knew at the time that this would be the last steamer to reach the jetty and the Sappers spent the rest of the day building a second landing bay so that loading would be speeded up the next night.

Meanwhile, the battle hotted up as *2/213 Battalion* renewed their efforts to enter the Basin down the chaung. Because there was little room for horses on the boats only two Japanese mountain guns had been landed. On land the going was so difficult that only one gun with the strongest horses was taken forward. This gun accompanied the battalion and was dragged up onto the top of the cliff on Saddle and fired several rounds into the Basin, claiming to hit one tank. It did not last long. One of the Bofors gun teams spotted it and fired a clip of five shells, three of which hit the gun destroying it and many of its crew.[11] In the Basin, the direct fire of the Bofors was most effective and they were kept busy. The artillery support had been augmented both by a section of 12 Mountain Battery who were in action from near Col (at the head of the Basin) and by 'B' Troop of 1 Indian Field Battery, who had now moved to a position near HQ 17 Division. Captain Bakshi, who as FOO contacted Godley, found it difficult to use his 25-pdrs in close support as the only map made no pretence to show the broken ground accurately. However, the guns fired effectively on known and probable enemy positions, and one stonk on a pagoda compound to the south landed on the headquarters of *2/214 Battalion*.

At about 1530 hours, *2/214 Battalion* launched a two-company attack on Stop

The Sikh section of 12 Mountain Battery in action at Shwegyin.

Hill but, well supported by their mortars, the 1st/4th Gurkhas beat them off. Meanwhile, 48 Brigade had considered an encirclement to attack *2/213 Battalion* in the Basin from the rear. It became clear, however, that the country was far too broken for this to be feasible. 17 Division then planned, if more steamers could be persuaded to come to the jetty, to secure the Basin firmly and move the whole force into it. As a preliminary move, the 2nd/5th R Gurkhas were moved into the Basin with the aim of capturing Knoll and Saddle Hill while two groups of the Burma Frontier Force (mostly Chins) were moved to secure Col at the head of the Basin. The 2nd/5th R Gurkhas were only two companies strong, their third (they now only had three) being with the flank guard. They put in a company attack on 'Knoll' but were unsuccessful. Knoll, however, was vital so Cameron ordered a two company attack at 1650 hours. This would almost certainly have succeeded. The Japanese on Knoll had had very heavy casualties and their ammunition was exhausted, but at 1630 the proposed attack was cancelled.

The Withdrawal to Kalewa

A new situation had now arisen. At about 4pm, a message was received from Corps HQ that only one steamer crew could be persuaded to come down the river and they would make one trip only, after dark. This completely altered the situation. The Japanese were clearly going to be reinforced, and there was now no point in holding Shwegyin after the last steamer had left. This vessel duly arrived at a quarter to six and tied up to the steep wooded river bank about 250 yards north of the jetty. There was a track along the bank about 50 feet above the water and the Sappers cut a path from this down to the steamer. There were rather more than a hundred wounded men in the Basin and these were all embarked, together with some sick men, a few valuable pieces of equipment, some stores and a few civilian refugees.

It was now clear that all the remaining tanks, vehicles and guns would have to be abandoned and the force would have to march north until they were opposite Kalewa where the steamer crews, although flatly refusing to go downstream, were prepared to operate a ferry service across the river. The first problem was to decide on the route. A rough footpath leading north across the hills from opposite Long Ridge had been discovered and was said to have been reconnoitred. A good footpath, almost a bridlepath, went along the hillside of the river bank.[12] Unfortunately, this withdrawal path had not been reconnoitred, although it should have been and easily could have been. In fact several small parties of men had passed along it that day. At first the plan was to use both routes with those in

---

11. Source: Maj-Gen. Renichi Misawa.
12. It was later developed into a road by the Japanese.

Top right: Major R.K. Kochhar, 60 Field Company, holds an 'O' Group at Shwegyin. He later became QMG of the Indian Army.

Below: A battery of the 1st Indian Field Regiment destroys its guns before the final withdrawal.

the Basin retiring along the river and those in the area of Long Ridge retiring by the footpath, now called the 'Getaway Path'. Unfortunately this was rejected on the grounds that firstly, the river-side route had not been reconnoitred, and secondly, to split the force was unsound.[13] It was therefore decided that the whole force would retire over the Getaway Path. It was a grave mistake and only good luck prevented a disaster.[14]

The next problem was to destroy as much as possible of the equipment being left behind. Units did what they could with their own vehicles, the 7th Hussars successfully destroying the remaining tanks. The Japanese only managed to make three runners out of the 60-70 tanks which were abandoned. The favourite method for vehicles was to drain the sump and run the engine at full throttle until it seized up.[15] In the Basin, where many vehicles were parked, the Sappers' request to use explosives or fire was disallowed for fear of giving away the withdrawal. However, without such drastic action there was not the time to destroy more than a proportion of the many vehicles.

Apart from the mules which carried one section of the guns of 12 Mountain Battery, there were 72 mules to be distributed among the other units. One day's rations was to be carried and the rest of the lift was for ammunition. A minimum scale of mortars and their bombs were to be man-handled. Every bit of kit that an officer or man could not carry on his back was to be destroyed. Except for the two mountain guns, all remaining guns would eventually be destroyed. Zero hour was to be at 1955 hours. For the last hour before this the mountain guns would fire steadily on the area of Saddle Hill and behind Knoll. By Zero, the 2nd/5th R Gurkhas (less two companies) would hold a lay-back position on Col at the head of the Basin and, at Zero, the 1st/9th R Jats and the 1st/7th Gurkhas would withdraw simultaneously and pass through this lay-back. At ten minutes after Zero, the Bofors and mountain guns would fire as fast as they could at the Japanese positions for ten minutes and if possible use up all their ammunition. Finally, at twenty minutes past Zero, all units were to be clear of the first lay-back, and the 2nd/5th Gurkhas in turn would pass back through a lay-back formed by the 1st/4th Gurkhas across the Chaung further north.

All seemed to go like clockwork. It was a very dark night, but the darkness was relieved by the flames of blazing lorries and equipment. The rapid fire of the guns, and particularly the automatic Bofors, made a most dramatic display as the shells crashed into the hills, and into the ground and trees at the top of the precipices. The Japanese appeared to be stunned and did not react. Everyone passed through the second lay-back on time. Lieutenant-Colonel Lentaigne was about to call in his last company from 'Stop Hill' when he turned a corner of the Chaung and saw an amazing sight. Virtually the whole of 48 Brigade, now augmented by the 1st/9th R Jats and the 1st W Yorks as well as the Gunners and the transport personnel with their mules, was stationary in a short stretch of the Chaung, which was here quite wide. There seemed to be some blockage on the Getaway Path. If the Japanese were now to follow up, there was all the makings of a disaster. The war diary of the 2nd/5th R Gurkhas describes the scene:

"So there we were - a sitting target if the Japanese cared to follow up. We were surrounded by cliffs 300 feet high on two sides, difficult enough to climb by day, imposssible to take against opposition by night. The 1st/3rd Gurkhas held the third side (Long Ridge) and on the fourth, to the east, ran the road back into Burma. On this road were several ammunition

13. *War Diary HQ 48 Brigade*. WO 172/584.
14. Brigadier Ekin, and others who had been several days in Shwegyin, must have known all about this track but were presumably not consulted.
15. In those days the trucks all had additional hand throttles which could be jammed at full throttle.

lorries burning furiously and lighting us up as we sat there. Small arms and mortar ammunition was exploding continuously..."

It was not until 0400 hours the next morning that the last man left the Chaung. Two hours later the advance guard of *1/213 Battalion*, *213/4 Company*, arrived along the track from Ye-U to find that the bird had flown.

The reason for this debacle was that the Getaway Path was more suitable for goats than men or mules. It was often necessary to slither down steep hillsides into nullahs and clamber out as best one could on the far side. There were frequent unscheduled halts at which some men usually fell asleep. The 'paths' along the hillsides were sometimes too narrow for the mules who missed their footing in the dark and rolled down the hill. Under the trees it was very dark and the path twisted and turned as it crossed chaungs and climbed over ridges until all sense of direction was lost. How long the route was is difficult to estimate but, not including a two-hour halt for sleep, the bulk of the column marched for over 12 hours before they reached the village of Kaing, opposite Kalewa. Here steamers were waiting and the river was quickly crossed. From war diaries it appears that some units at the rear of the column, who were soon marching in daylight, broke away from the goat track and made their way to the much better track along the river bank, being picked up by steamer from Paunggyaung, some three miles downstream from Kalewa. These included the 1st W Yorks and the 1st/4th

Gurkhas who were the last to leave Shwegyin. They were lucky, and their march only lasted eight hours. The

Exhausted troops emerge from the forest in the early morning of 11 May and board the ferry across the Chindwin to Kalewa. Tank Museum.

312

A mixed load on one of the last ferries crossing to Kalewa.

enemy did not follow up and by mid-afternoon on the 11th the whole of 17 Division, except 1 Bur Brigade to the north, were across the Chindwin.

Shwegyin had been another Japanese victory, but not a complete one. Certainly they had forced the British to withdraw, abandoning nearly all their heavy equipment. However, British casualties were not high and seem to have been rather less than 150 killed and wounded. On the other hand, Araki Force had been dealt a severe jolt and *33 Division* appear to have suffered more casualties in this battle than in any other action of the campaign. There are no recorded figures, but their losses have been estimated in Japan at about 80 killed and 160 wounded. A Japanese soldier of *213/8 Company*, which spearheaded the attack, records that "after the severe fight of a whole day our company almost perished; only 12 men headed by Sergeant Sasaki survived on the hill."[16] Another soldier in *213/6 Company*, which reinforced *8 Company*, records the severe fighting and many killed, not least from the shelling.[17]

The Japanese aim of annihilating the enemy had not been achieved and, although the British did not yet know it, the last battle of the 1942 campaign had been fought.

16. Account, Mr Hiroshi Ishikawa.
17. Account, Mr Masaichi Nagai.

CHAPTER TWENTY-THREE

Withdrawal to India

Akyab is Captured

While the main battle proceeded in the north, the Japanese had tidied up their conquest of central Burma by occupying Akyab. This place was militarily important as it comprised a useful small port and naval base as well as an airfield. It also lay astride a possible route to India. Repeated bombing of the airfield had forced the RAF to withdraw and had unsettled the local inhabitants. The district was an unruly one at the best of times, and the situation was not improved when the District Commissioner and his staff left prematurely on 30 March, and his loyal Burmese deputy, who had stayed behind, was murdered. The police became ineffective and many joined the unruly elements in what was fast becoming an insurrection. Meanwhile, a large BIA force was making its way up the coast from Taungup and a company from *2/213 Battalion*, strengthened by an MMG platoon, was advancing along the track from Prome. After some skirmishes with the BIA, the small garrison, as ordered, completed the demolitions and withdrew by sea on the night of 4 May. Shortly afterwards the Japanese entered the town unopposed and in June were joined by the rest of *2/213 Battalion*.

General Iida was to write in his book that at that time Akyab was considered to be important as it would be useful for a possible invasion of India. Later he concluded that it should have been left alone, as in 1943 it tied up a division which could have been used better elsewhere. General Wavell, and Iida's successor General Kawabe, did not agree with this view and Akyab was to be the focus of much fighting over the next three years.

The Allies Cross the Chindwin

By the evening of 11 May, 17 Division were all across the Chindwin, the main part of the two Gurkha companies who had formed the flank guard having crossed after dark at Singaung, about six miles north of Kalewa. 1 Bur Brigade, who had marched across country from Pyingaing and were the last formation of the Army in Burma to reach the Chindwin, crossed the river at Pantha, about 60 miles north of Kalewa, on the 13th. The previous day General Stilwell's party had reached Homalin and they crossed the river near there on the 14th. The bulk of the 38th Chinese D/Brigade crossed the river at Paungbyin, 45 miles south of Homalin, on the 13th after a clash with a small Japanese party coming up the river.

There were still several problems for General Slim. It was known that the Japanese had enough boats to make themselves mobile on the river and so they might attempt to cut off the British retreat, for instance at Tamu. Kalewa was about 100 miles from the Indian border and there was some doubt whether adequate food was available on the track for the whole force. The monsoon might arrive any time after the middle of May and movement up the valley to Tamu would then become a nightmare. So General Cowan was ordered to send part of his force by river to Sittaung (see Map 31) whence a track led to Tamu. Accordingly he sent 48 Brigade, together with the 2nd Duke's and the 1st R Jats, up the Chindwin on the five river steamers. They left early on the 12th and reached Sittaung, about 20 miles from Tamu, on the 14th. There the five steamers were scuttled by the small detachment of Royal Marines. Major Jim Robertson remembers one incident on this voyage well. He was Brigade Major of 1 Bur Brigade who had just reached the Chindwin after their exhausting cross-country march from Pyingaing. They were having great trouble trying to persuade the Brigade's mules to swim the wide river. Just as they had at last got them started in the right direction, what should come round the corner but a steamer with Brigadier Ronnie Cameron and HQ 48 Brigade on board. Robertson took off in a sampan and shouted to them to keep away. As the steamer came relentlessly on, he redoubled his efforts but unfortunately overbalanced and fell into the river, from which he was rescued by the steamer's crew. However, all went well. The mules got across and Jim Robertson got a drink before returning to his Brigade.[1]

63 Brigade now took over the rearguard and, on the morning of the 12th, the last British troops left Kalewa and marched inland towards Kalemyo. The Japanese moved into Kalewa that evening but then seem to have paused, presumably because they were using their boats to assemble supplies. According to their records, they reached Mawlaik on 16 May, Pantha on 18 May, Sittaung on 19 May and Homalin on 24 May. They had been ordered to go as far as Tamanthi and this was reached on 30 May. These timings do not explain the alleged Chinese clash with the Japanese near Paungbyin on 13 May; possibly a small advance party had been sent up the river in a motor launch.

The Imphal-Kalewa Road

The Indian State of Manipur, which abutted on Burma where the road from

---

1. Later Major-General J.A.R. Robertson, CB, DSO. I am indebted to him for this story. *Author*.

Kalewa entered India, was one of the six hundred or so Indian States which comprised one third of British India. In return for some loss of independence they
were guaranteed protection from external, and sometimes internal, enemies.
Provided the Maharajah of Manipur ran his State with reasonable care for his
people, there was little interference from the Government in Delhi. Manipur, or
at any rate the main part round the capital, was prosperous and up until now the
only real outside threat had been from an expansionist Burma. This threat disappeared when the British annexed Burma in 1886. One result of this happy state
of affairs was that the Maharajah was quite content for only one road to reach his
capital from India. This was the pony-cart track from Dimapur, a station on the
metre-gauge railway which served the tea estates in the Brahmaputra valley. It
was 136 miles from Imphal.

The bulk of the population of Manipur lived in a large oval valley which had
once been a huge lake, the central part of which still remained (see Map 31). The
valley was about 2,500 feet above sea level, and lay between the eastern two
ranges of the range upon range of steep hills dividing India from Burma. In this
valley was the capital, Imphal, and from Imphal a pony-cart track ran south for
30 miles to Palel whence a bridle-path wound for 34 miles over the hills to the
village of Tamu, just inside Burma. Except for footpaths through the hills, this
route was the only connection with Burma.

When, several days after the Japanese war had started, GHQ India was at last
(but only for twelve days) put in charge of the Army in Burma, General Wavell
saw at once that it was advisable to have a land route to Burma from India if possible. The first suggestion was for a road through Manipur to Tamu and Sittaung
and thence to the railway at Wuntho. A reconnaissance showed, however, that the
route via Kalewa to Ye-U, though longer, was easier to construct. Accordingly,
the Indian Government was made responsible for building the stretch through

Manipur and the Burmese Government was made responsible for the
Burmese portion. The small Public
Works Department in Burma, however, was already swamped with war
requirements in Burma and had no
effort to spare for road-work. Much
the same applied to the PWD in
Assam, but India was able to supply

*A new road, cut at maximum speed over
the Shenam Pass from Palel, greatly
assists the withdrawal.*

some Sapper units and the Indian Tea Association was able to provide and administer large numbers of coolies for road-work. Somehow, by early May, a fair weather motor road was driven from Palel over the Shenam Pass and down through the forests to the Burmese plain at Tamu. It was a remarkable feat for which the irascible but highly competent Brigadier Mike Gilpin, who was in charge, deserved much credit. Without it the Army (and many of the civilian refugees) would have been in grave trouble, for only with vehicles was it possible to provide the essential dumps of food on the Kalewa road.

Civilian Assistance

One remarkable character made his entrance at this time. This was Mr J.H.W. Williams, widely known as 'Elephant Bill'. He worked for the Bombay Burma Trading Corporation, one of the handful of big trading companies in Burma. His task was the extraction of teak from remote parts of the Burmese forest, using elephants to drag the great logs to a river down which they could float to a saw-mill. This was a task requiring both a knowledge of forestry, so that regeneration matched extraction, and a deep understanding and affection for the elephants and their drivers. In February 1942, the Bombay Burma Coporation decided to move the wives and families of all its European employees to Mawlaik on the Chindwin. Williams was sent to collect elephants to move their baggage over the hills to Tamu should it prove necessary, as it did. Indeed, he went one better and took his elephants over the Shenam Pass to Palel, a remarkable feat as the road had not yet been completed. He then brought them back and they were used in April to build bridges over the worst of the nullahs on the Tamu-Kalewa road. In May they helped 48 Brigade climb over the hills between Sittaung and Tamu. Williams and his elephants were to give a lot of help to the 14th Army over the next few years but that is another story.

Another notable character who enters the story at this stage is Mr Norman Kelly, who was the Assistant Superintendent in the Burma Frontier Service at Tiddim. His sub-divison covered the homeland of those Chins who lived in the mountainous area to the west of the Kalemyo-Tamu road. Kelly was very energetic and widely respected among the Chins. As those Chins who had enlisted in the Burma Rifles returned to their homes, many disillusioned and disheartened, he organised those still willing to fight, and other stout-hearted villagers, into the nucleus of an invaluable guerrilla force which later developed into the Chin Levies.

The March from Kalewa to Imphal

General Alexander had decreed that the civilian refugees, by now entirely Indian, were to be given priority for transport and that the soldiers should march.

Indian refugees, carrying all their possessions, head through the forest towards Tamu.

No-one objected to this policy. It was obviously correct as most of the refugees were women and children and many of them were sick. In fact there were enough vehicles to help the marching troops as well for part of each march, as long as the rains held off. The only soldiers who really suffered were those from 7th Armoured Brigade who were unused to such a basic method of travel and, valuable specialists that they were, were given special help.

Some lurid accounts of this march, well seasoned with leeches and other jungle horrors, have been published but the truth is rather different. It was two days' march along a dusty track to Yazagyo, 44 miles from Kalewa, but most people got a lift for the last ten miles or so of each march. By this time everyone was used to squashing at least 40 people into the back of a truck. Indeed the Gurkhas once achieved 58 and there was a rumour that they were loaded in two layers. There had been an ominously heavy shower on the 12th but for the next week it remained fine and sleeping on the ground under the stars was no hardship for tired men.

The marching was along the flat and would have been no problem for fit soldiers, but of course the men of the Burma Army were under-nourished amd mentally and physically exhausted. All had lost weight, many having lost two stones or more. Although everyone carried the minimum on their backs, usually only one groundsheet or one cut-down mosquito net, all the units of 17 Division carried their arms and some carried extra weapons or tools as well. It was a severe test of endurance.

From Yazagyo to Tamu was 58 miles, again achieved in two days with the help of ferrying. Shortly after Yazagyo a gentle watershed was crossed into the Kabaw valley. This valley, although the slope remained gentle, had a fearsome reputation for disease, a reputation which was unfortunately to prove well-founded. Two or three times a day during the march from Kalewa an aeroplane would be seen, usually flying low. Sometimes they were British and sometimes Japanese but all were trying on the nerves for troops marching in the open, as was necessary to cross the occasional clearings. The Japanese two-engined bombers and the British Blenheims looked very similar, and it was hard to be sure which was which until they actually flew overhead and the markings could be seen. The Japanese planes, however, were apparently bent only on reconnaissance and the columns were never attacked.

At Tamu the character of the country changed. There were several streams in the area but there were also hundreds of dead refugees. Not a few had died in the streams. One had to climb up into the hills to get clean water. The transit area was in thick forest and there were many, many mosquitoes. Gecko lizards abounded and their nightly refrain of 'Uk-yew' was easily translated and depressing. More interesting were the rarer flying lizards which flew, or more accurately glided, from one tree to another. At Tamu everyone was inoculated against cholera, a very wise precaution, as there were several fatal cases in the next few days, mainly among high-caste Hindu Brahmins who had dodged the inoculations, fearing contamination of their caste.

Tamu was at the foot of the hills which had to be crossed to reach Palel, the first town in Manipur. The fair-weather motor road over the hills was only completed in early May and there were many abandoned cars belonging to earlier arrivals. In deference to the climb from the Burmese plain at an altitude of 500 feet to the top of the Shenam pass at over 5000 feet, three days were allotted for crossing this stretch. There would be no vehicle lifts. The first day was 11 miles to Lokchao where the road crossed a gorge with a substantial mountain stream. Here the Sappers had erected an Inglis bridge, unique as the only military bridge in India at this time.[2] The transit area was on a steep hillside, every tiny perch of which was covered by the droppings of refugees. It was a very unpleasant place to spend the night. The next day was 14 miles to Tengnoupal. Some units chose to try the old bridle path but soon found that marching along this was far more tiring than marching up the steady gradient of the road. The final stage was nine-miles over the top of the Shenam Pass and down to Palel. The Pass was held by the 1st Indian Brigade of 23 Indian Division. They were the only troops from India which had so far reached Manipur. At Palel most units were picked up in transport and taken to accommodation in village houses in Imphal or, more often, to transit areas of scrub jungle north of Imphal.

During the march up to the Pass, General Slim, riding in a jeep, had been

2. This particular bridge had been used in Iraq in World War I. Between the wars it was used for Sapper training at Roorkee in northern India and went from there to Lokchao in 1942. After the Burma Army had passed over it, it was taken down and eventually erected again on the road to Tiddim, where it was blown up when our forces withdrew from that town in 1944.

much in evidence. He watched his troops intently, asking the name of each unit as it passed and making some encouraging remark. General Alexander did not appear. On the 20th he handed over command of the Burma Army to General Irwin of 4 Corps in Imphal and then left to report to Wavell and return to England.

48 Brigade had marched over the hills from Sittaung and reached Tamu on 17 May and Palel on the 21st, having been held up one day at Lokchao to cover dismantling of the invaluable bridge there. 63 Brigade provided the rear-guard from Kalewa to Palel and passed through Tamu on the 19th, reaching Palel on the 22nd. Along the way a Sapper party with them destroyed all abandoned vehicles. The monsoon had broken on the evening of the 18th and for both brigades the last three nights of bivouacking in the open in the drenching monsoon rain and the days of marching up over the hills were a very testing time. Sickness rates had been surprisingly low among Indian units in Burma, now they would escalate. The Army in Burma had reached India only just in time.

Reception in Manipur

Many of the Army and Corps administrative troops, mostly unarmed and untrained, had lost their cohesion during the final stages of the retreat and, together with the leaderless soldiers from reinforcement camps and the convalescents from the hospitals in Mandalay, appeared to onlookers as an ill-disciplined and disorganised rabble as they entered India. But the same was not true of the fighting troops. They may have looked a bit scruffy, for they had long had to make do with the clothes they stood up in, but they marched out as formed units and carrying their full scale, and in some cases more than their full scale, of personal arms. The strength of 17 Division[3] as it reached Imphal was as follows:

    HQ 17 Division and divisional troops 3566
    16 Brigade 1504
    48 Brigade . . . . 3142[4]
    63 Brigade 1696
    Total 17 Division 9908

1 Burdiv, two-thirds of whose troops had been Burmese and had nearly all faded away to their homes,[5] had a total strength of about two thousand and, like 17 Division, their British and Indian fighting units had marched out in good order and carrying their personal weapons. This exhausted army, some of whose units had been fighting without relief for four months and most of whom had marched for many hundreds of miles in the tropical heat, looked forward to some relief on arrival in India.

Unfortunately the reception for the Army in Manipur was not well-managed, either practically or psychologically. General Irwin began by being rude to

Map 17. The Battle at Shwedaung, Phase 1

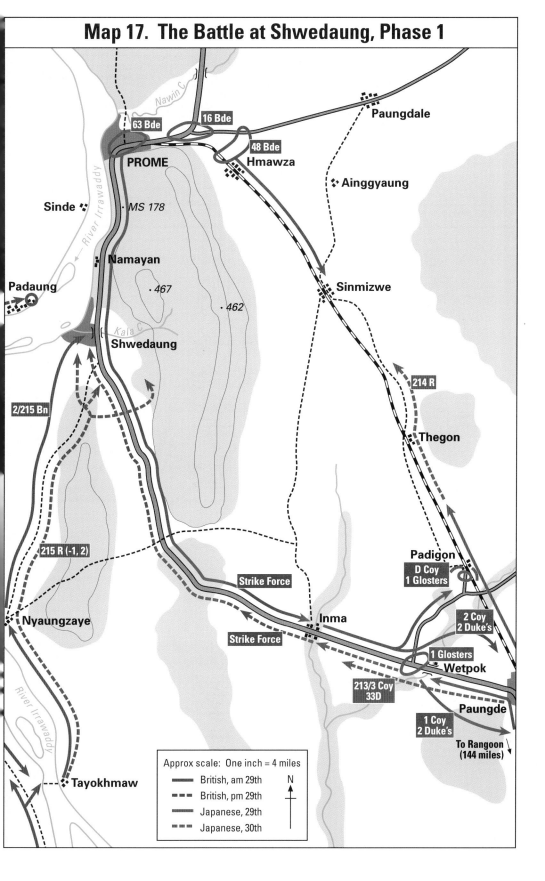

Approx scale: One inch = 4 miles

N

British, am 29th
British, pm 29th
Japanese, 29th
Japanese, 30th

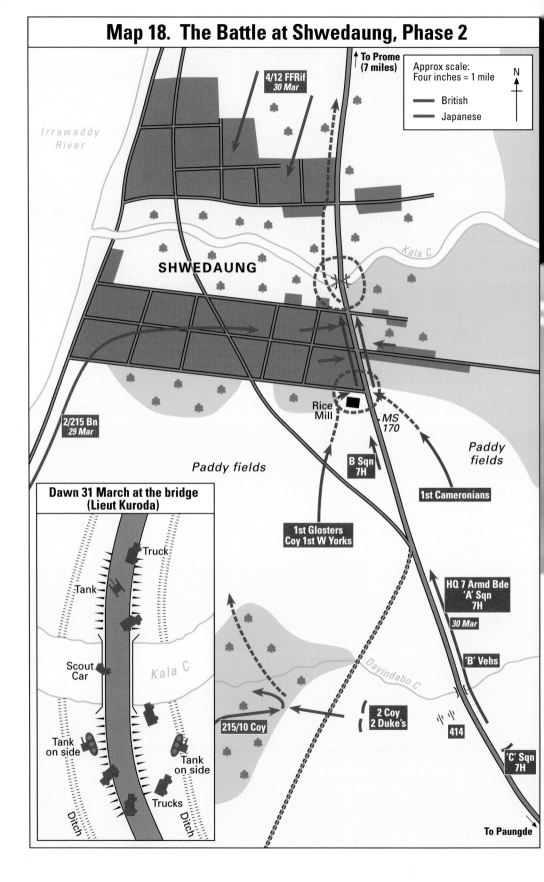

Map 18. The Battle at Shwedaung, Phase 2

To Prome
(7 miles)

Approx scale:
Four inches = 1 mile

N

British
Japanese

Irrawaddy River

4/12 FFRif
30 Mar

SHWEDAUNG

Kala C

2/215 Bn
29 Mar

Paddy fields

Rice Mill

MS 170

B Sqn
7H

Paddy fields

1st Glosters
Coy 1st W Yorks

1st Cameronians

HQ 7 Armd Bde
'A' Sqn
7H
30 Mar

'B' Vehs

Dawn 31 March at the bridge
(Lieut Kuroda)

Truck

Tank

Scout Car

Kala C

Tank on side

Tank on side

Trucks

Ditch

Ditch

215/10 Coy

Davindabo C.

2 Coy
2 Duke's

414

'C' Sqn
7H

To Paungde

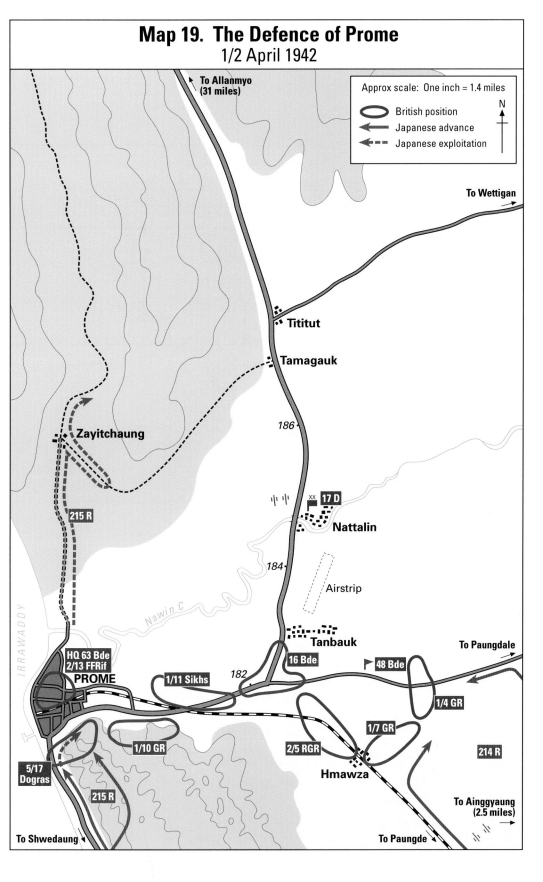

Map 19. The Defence of Prome
1/2 April 1942

Approx scale: One inch = 1.4 miles

N

⬭ British position

◀ Japanese advance

◀ Japanese exploitation

To Allanmyo
(31 miles)

To Wettigan

Tititut

Tamagauk

186

Zayitchaung

XX 17 D

Nattalin

184

215 R

Airstrip

Nawin C

Tanbauk

To Paungdale

HQ 63 Bde
2/13 FFRif

16 Bde

48 Bde

PROME

1/11 Sikhs

182

1/4 GR

1/10 GR

2/5 RGR

1/7 GR

214 R

5/17
Dogras

Hmawza

215 R

To Ainggyaung
(2.5 miles)

To Shwedaung

To Paungde

I R R A W A D D Y

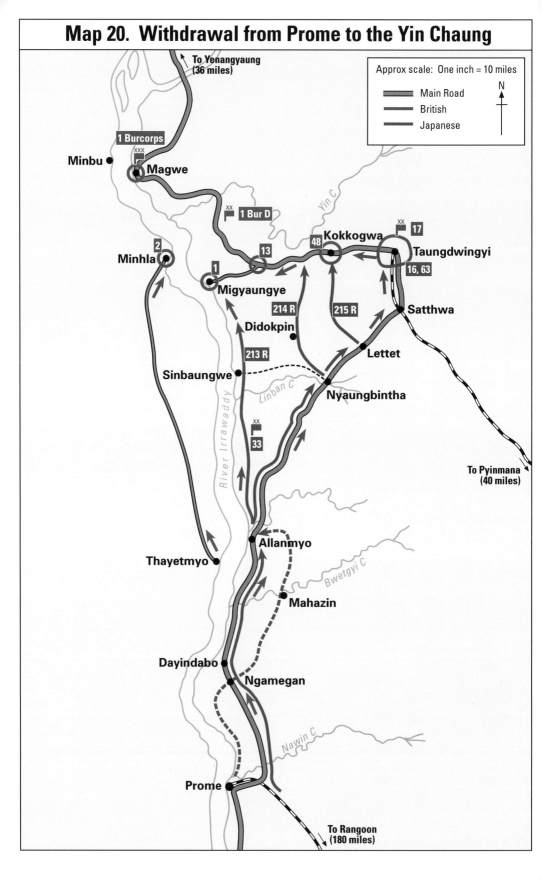

Map 20. Withdrawal from Prome to the Yin Chaung

To Yenangyaung
(36 miles)

Approx scale: One inch = 10 miles

Main Road
British
Japanese

N

1 Burcorps
xxx

Minbu

Magwe

xx
1 Bur D

Minhla
2

1

Migyaungye

13

48

Kokkogwa

Taungdwingyi
xx
17

16, 63

Didokpin

214 R

215 R

Satthwa

Sinbaungwe

213 R

Lettet

Linban C

Nyaungbintha

xx
33

River Irrawaddy

To Pyinmana
(40 miles)

Allanmyo

Bwetgyi C

Thayetmyo

Mahazin

Dayindabo

Ngamegan

Nawin C

Prome

To Rangoon
(180 miles)

Map 21. The Battle at Kokkogwa
12 April 1942

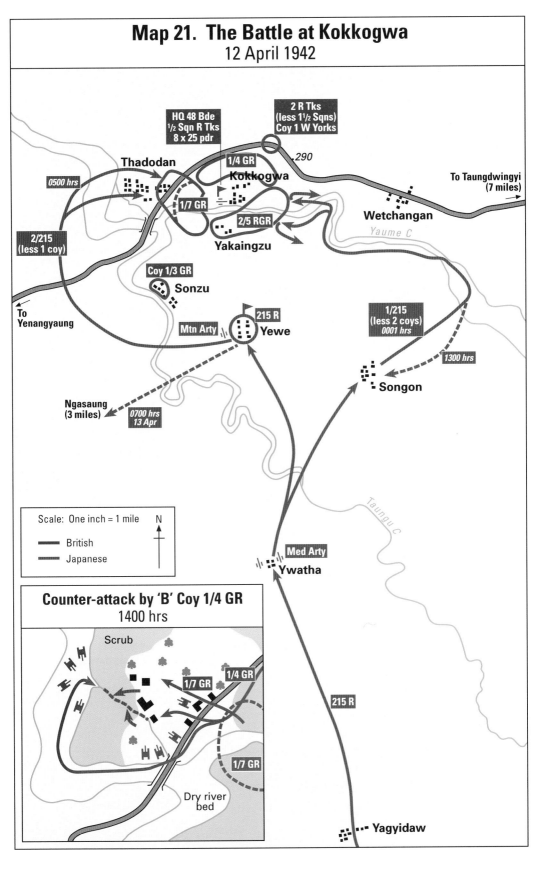

2 R Tks
(less 1½ Sqns)
Coy 1 W Yorks

HQ 48 Bde
½ Sqn R Tks
8 x 25 pdr

.290

Thadodan

1/4 GR

Kokkogwa

To Taungdwingyi
(7 miles)

0500 hrs

1/7 GR

Wetchangan

2/5 RGR

2/215
(less 1 coy)

Yakaingzu

Yaume C

To
Yenangyaung

Coy 1/3 GR

Sonzu

1/215
(less 2 coys)
0001 hrs

Mtn Arty

215 R
Yewe

1300 hrs

Songon

Ngasaung
(3 miles)

0700 hrs
13 Apr

Scale: One inch = 1 mile   N

British
Japanese

Taungu C

Med Arty

Ywatha

215 R

Counter-attack by 'B' Coy 1/4 GR
1400 hrs

Scrub

1/4 GR

1/7 GR

1/7 GR

Dry river
bed

Yagyidaw

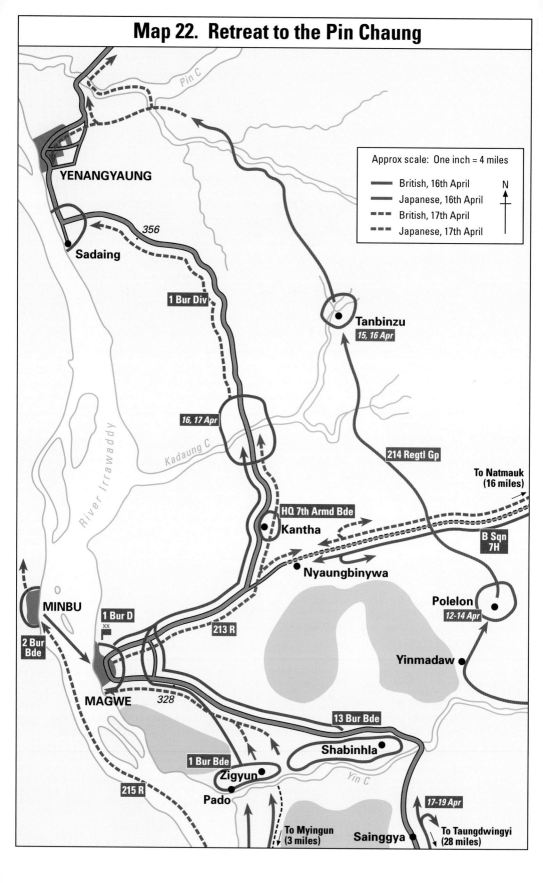

Map 22. Retreat to the Pin Chaung

Approx scale: One inch = 4 miles

— British, 16th April
— Japanese, 16th April
--- British, 17th April
--- Japanese, 17th April

N

Pin C

YENANGYAUNG

Sadaing

356

1 Bur Div

River Irrawaddy

Kadaung C

16, 17 Apr

Tanbinzu
15, 16 Apr

214 Regtl Gp

To Natmauk
(16 miles)

HQ 7th Armd Bde

Kantha

Nyaungbinywa

B Sqn
7H

Polelon
12-14 Apr

Yinmadaw

MINBU

1 Bur D
XX

2 Bur
Bde

213 R

MAGWE

328

13 Bur Bde

Shabinhla

1 Bur Bde

Zigyun

Yin C

215 R

Pado

To Myingun
(3 miles)

Sainggya

17-19 Apr

To Taungdwingyi
(28 miles)

Map 23. The Battle at Yenangyaung

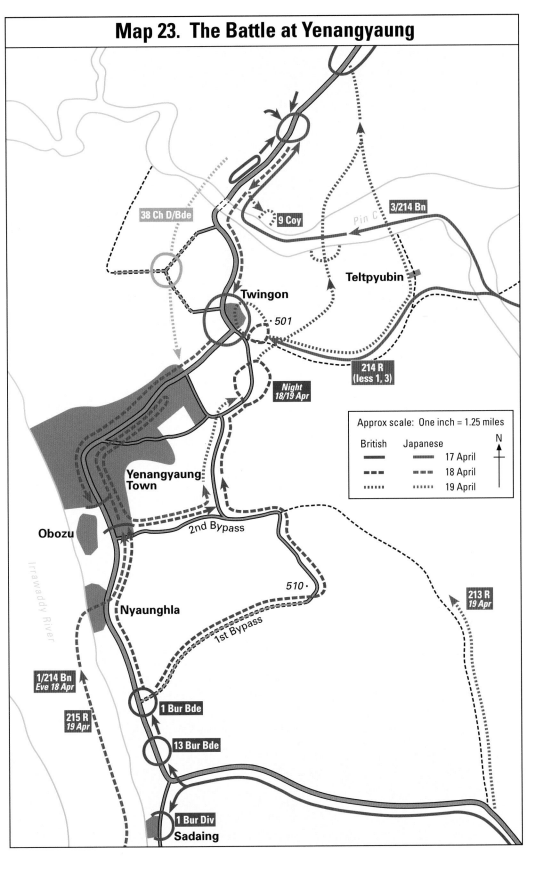

38 Ch D/Bde

9 Coy

3/214 Bn

Pin C

Teltpyubin

Twingon

501

214 R
(less 1, 3)

*Night
18/19 Apr*

Approx scale: One inch = 1.25 miles

British   Japanese

17 April

18 April

19 April

N

Yenangyaung
Town

Obozu

2nd Bypass

510

213 R
19 Apr

Nyaunghla

1st Bypass

Irrawaddy River

1/214 Bn
Eve 18 Apr

215 R
19 Apr

1 Bur Bde

13 Bur Bde

1 Bur Div

Sadaing

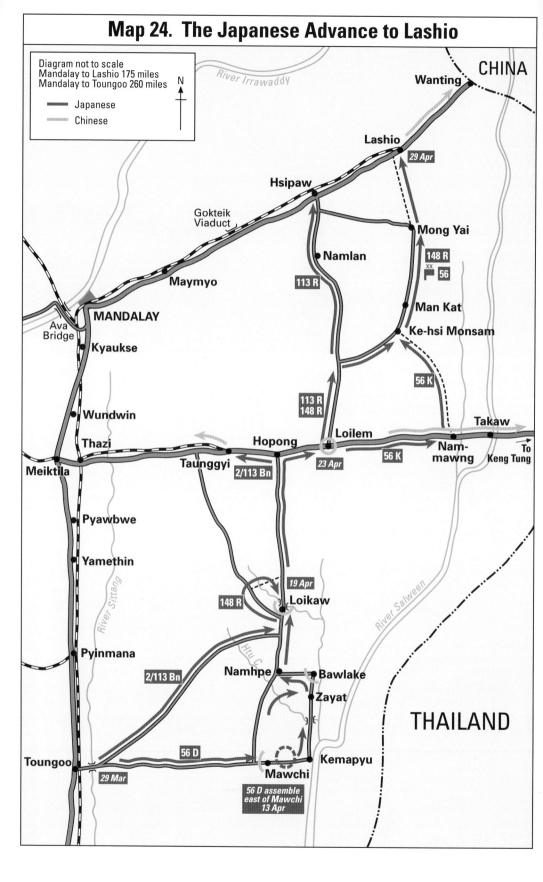

Map 24. The Japanese Advance to Lashio

Diagram not to scale
Mandalay to Lashio 175 miles
Mandalay to Toungoo 260 miles

— Japanese
— Chinese

N

CHINA

River Irrawaddy

Wanting

Lashio
29 Apr

Hsipaw

Gokteik Viaduct

Mong Yai

Namlan

148 R
xx 56

113 R

Maymyo

Man Kat

Ava Bridge

MANDALAY

Kyaukse

Ke-hsi Monsam

56 K

113 R
148 R

Takaw

Wundwin

Loilem

Thazi

Hopong

Nam-mawng

To Keng Tung

Meiktila

Taunggyi

2/113 Bn

23 Apr

56 K

Pyawbwe

Yamethin

River Sittang

19 Apr

148 R

Loikaw

River Salween

Pyinmana

2/113 Bn

Htu C.

Namhpe

Bawlake

Zayat

THAILAND

Toungoo

56 D

Kemapyu

29 Mar

Mawchi

56 D assemble
east of Mawchi
13 Apr

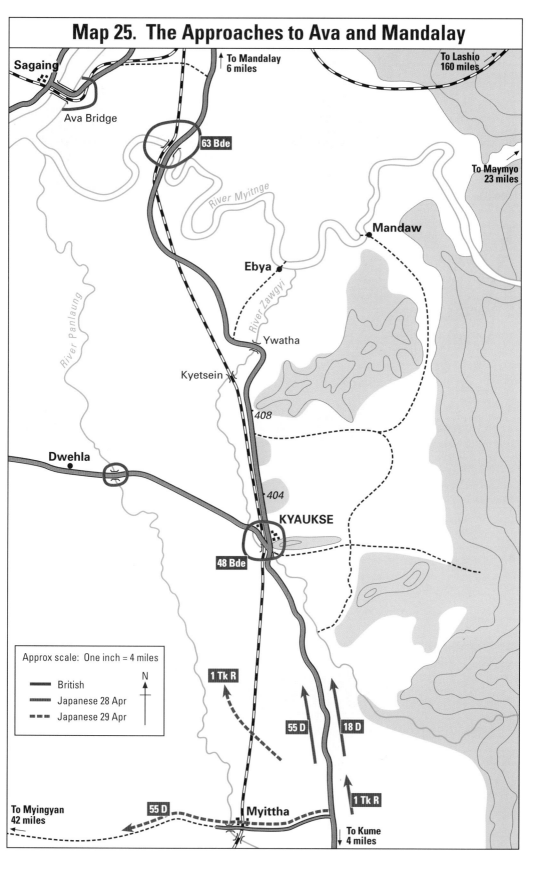

Map 25. The Approaches to Ava and Mandalay

Sagaing

Ava Bridge

To Mandalay
6 miles

To Lashio
160 miles

63 Bde

River Myitnge

To Maymyo
23 miles

Mandaw

Ebya

River Zawgyi

River Panlaung

Ywatha

Kyetsein

408

Dwehla

404

KYAUKSE

48 Bde

Approx scale: One inch = 4 miles

N

British
Japanese 28 Apr
Japanese 29 Apr

1 Tk R

55 D

18 D

55 D

1 Tk R

To Myingyan
42 miles

55 D

Myittha

To Kume
4 miles

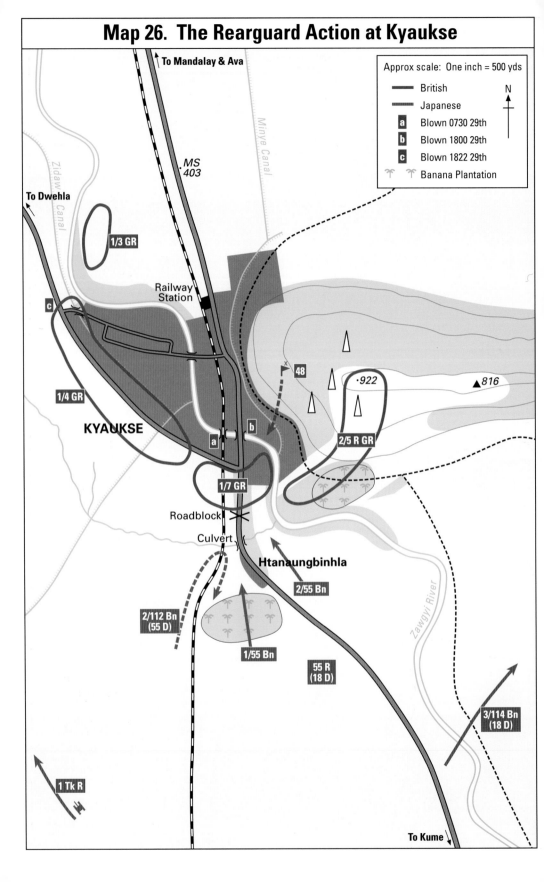

Map 26. The Rearguard Action at Kyaukse

To Mandalay & Ava

Approx scale: One inch = 500 yds

▬▬▬	British
▥▥▥	Japanese
a	Blown 0730 29th
b	Blown 1800 29th
c	Blown 1822 29th
🌴 🌴	Banana Plantation

N

Minye Canal

MS ·403

Zidaw Canal

To Dwehla

1/3 GR

Railway Station

c

1/4 GR

KYAUKSE

× 48

·922

▲816

2/5 R GR

b

a

1/7 GR

Roadblock

Culvert

Htanaungbinhla

Zawgyi River

2/55 Bn

2/112 Bn (55 D)

1/55 Bn

55 R (18 D)

3/114 Bn (18 D)

1 Tk R

To Kume

Map 27. The Japanese Advance to Myitkyina

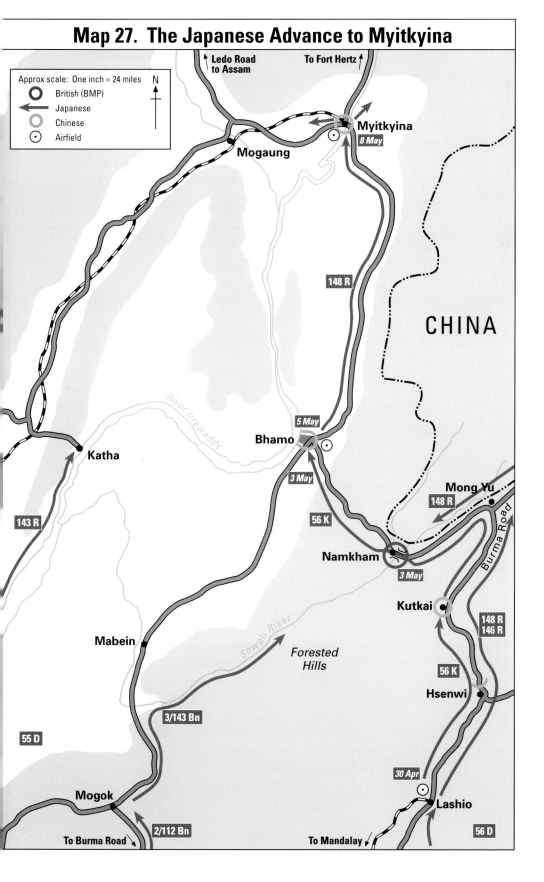

Approx scale: One inch = 24 miles   N

- British (BMP)
- ← Japanese
- Chinese
- ⊙ Airfield

↑ Ledo Road to Assam

To Fort Hertz ↑

Myitkyina
8 May

Mogaung

CHINA

148 R

River Irrawaddy

Katha

5 May

Bhamo

3 May

56 K

143 R

Mong Yu

148 R

Namkham

3 May

Kutkai

148 R
146 R

Mabein

Shweli River

Forested Hills

Burma Road

56 K

Hsenwi

3/143 Bn

55 D

30 Apr

Mogok

2/112 Bn

Lashio

56 D

To Burma Road ↓

To Mandalay ↓

Map 28. The British Cross the Irrawaddy
Situation at dusk 30 April

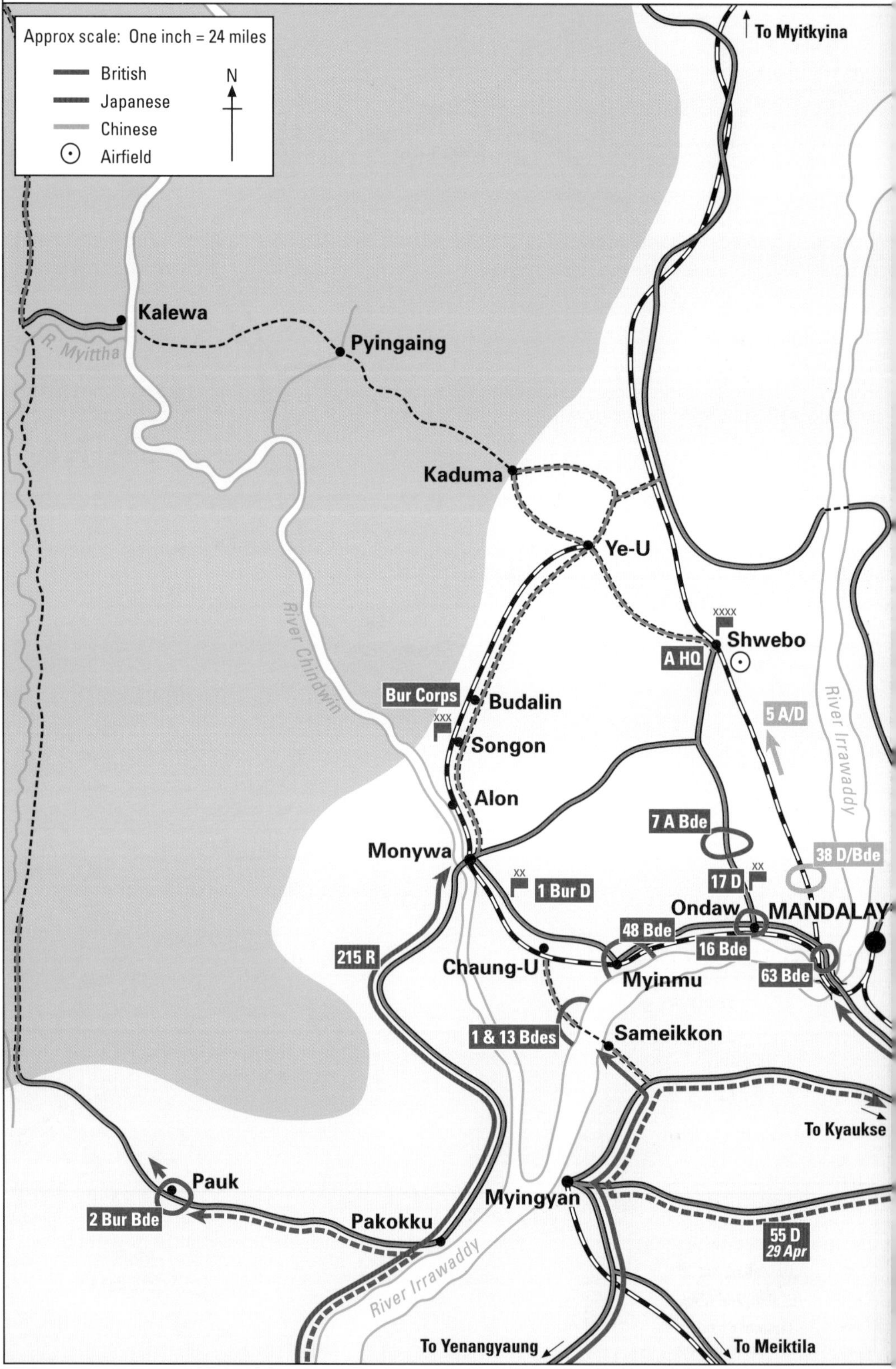

Approx scale: One inch = 24 miles

British
Japanese
Chinese
⊙ Airfield

N

To Myitkyina

R. Myittha

Kalewa

Pyingaing

Kaduma

Ye-U

River Chindwin

XXXX
Shwebo ⊙
A HQ

5 A/D

River Irrawaddy

Bur Corps
XXX
Budalin

Songon

Alon

7 A Bde

38 D/Bde

Monywa

XX
1 Bur D

17 D
XX

Ondaw
MANDALAY

48 Bde

16 Bde

215 R

Chaung-U
Myinmu

63 Bde

1 & 13 Bdes
Sameikkon

To Kyaukse

Pauk

2 Bur Bde
Pakokku

Myingyan

55 D
29 Apr

River Irrawaddy

To Yenangyaung

To Meiktila

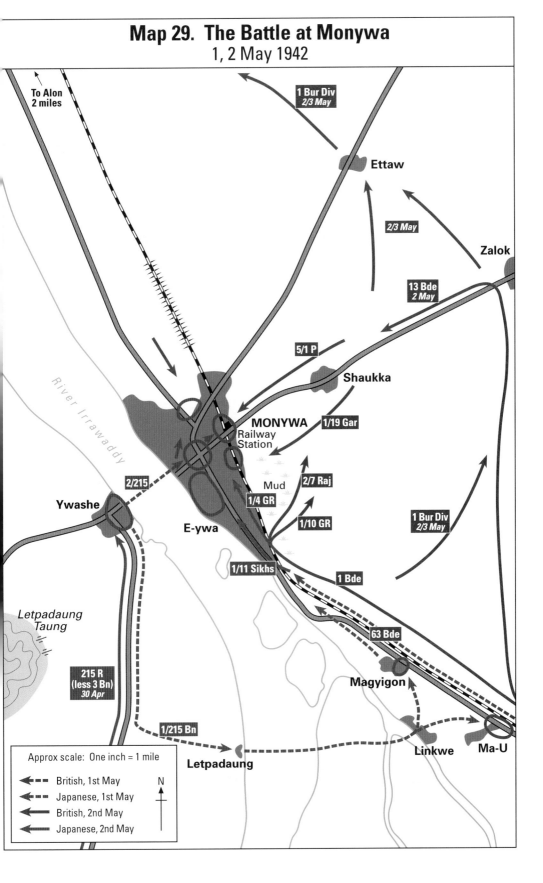

Map 29. The Battle at Monywa
1, 2 May 1942

To Alon
2 miles

1 Bur Div
2/3 May

Ettaw

2/3 May

Zalok

13 Bde
2 May

5/1 P

Shaukka

MONYWA
Railway
Station

1/19 Gar

Mud

2/7 Raj

2/215

1/4 GR

1 Bur Div
2/3 May

Ywashe

1/10 GR

E-ywa

1/11 Sikhs

1 Bde

River Irrawaddy

*Letpadaung
Taung*

63 Bde

215 R
(less 3 Bn)
30 Apr

Magyigon

1/215 Bn

Linkwe

Ma-U

Letpadaung

Approx scale: One inch = 1 mile

⬅--- British, 1st May   N
⬅--- Japanese, 1st May   ⊢
⬅ British, 2nd May
⬅ Japanese, 2nd May

Map 30. The Battle at Shwegyin
10 May 1942

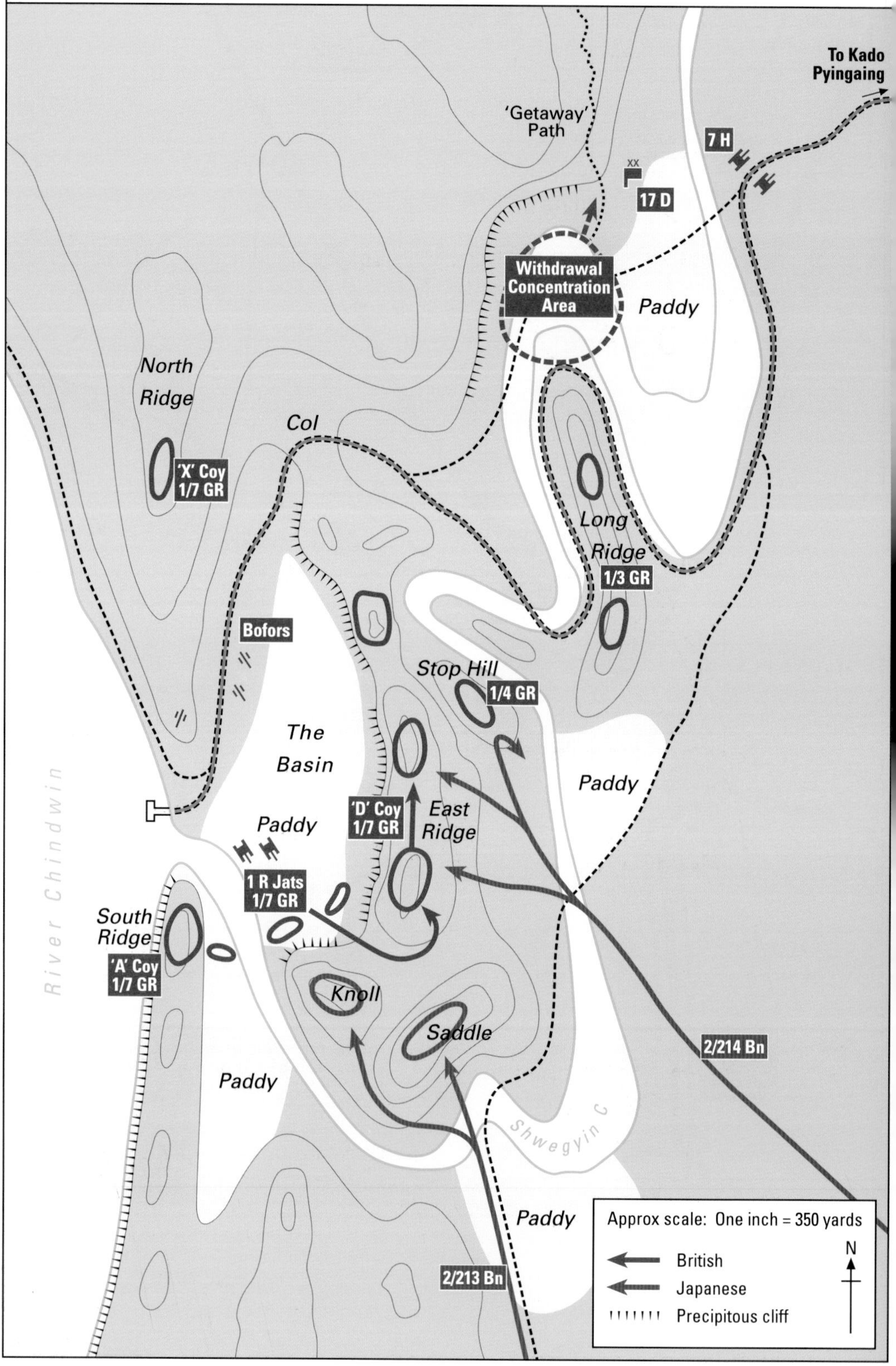

To Kado
Pyingaing

'Getaway'
Path

7 H

XX
17 D

Withdrawal
Concentration
Area

Paddy

North
Ridge

Col

'X' Coy
1/7 GR

Long
Ridge
1/3 GR

Bofors

Stop Hill
1/4 GR

The
Basin

Paddy

'D' Coy
1/7 GR

East
Ridge

Paddy

River Chindwin

Paddy

1 R Jats
1/7 GR

South
Ridge

'A' Coy
1/7 GR

Knoll

Saddle

2/214 Bn

Paddy

Shwegyin C

Paddy

Approx scale: One inch = 350 yards

N

British

Japanese

Precipitous cliff

2/213 Bn

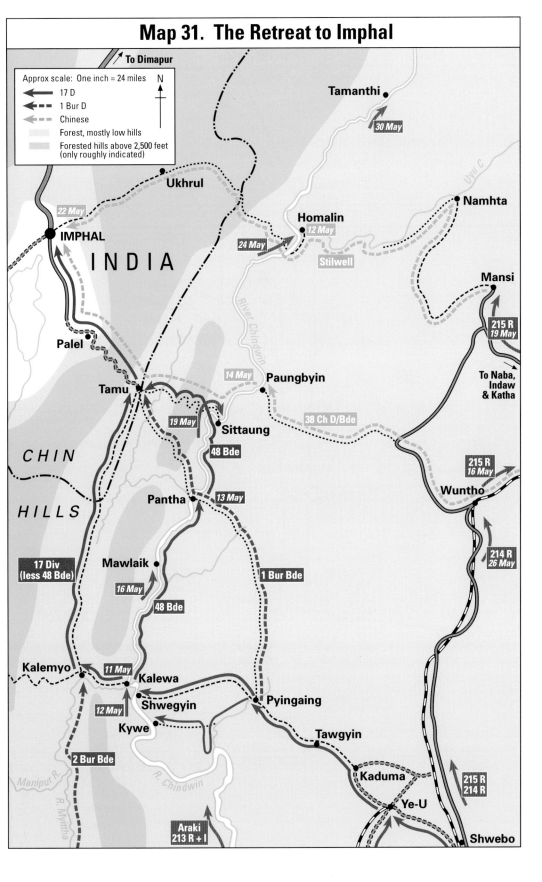

Map 31. The Retreat to Imphal

To Dimapur

Approx scale: One inch = 24 miles

N

— 17 D
--- 1 Bur D
--- Chinese
Forest, mostly low hills
Forested hills above 2,500 feet
(only roughly indicated)

Tamanthi

30 May

Ukhrul

22 May

IMPHAL

Namhta

I N D I A

Homalin

12 May

24 May

Mansi

Stilwell

Palel

215 R
19 May

14 May

Paungbyin

To Naba,
Indaw
& Katha

Tamu

19 May

C H I N

Sittaung

48 Bde

38 Ch D/Bde

215 R
16 May

H I L L S

Pantha

13 May

Wuntho

214 R
26 May

17 Div
(less 48 Bde)

Mawlaik

1 Bur Bde

16 May

48 Bde

Kalemyo

11 May

Kalewa

12 May

Shwegyin

Pyingaing

Kywe

Tawgyin

215 R
214 R

2 Bur Bde

Manipur R.

R. Chindwin

Kaduma

Ye-U

R. Myittha

Araki
213 R + I

Shwebo

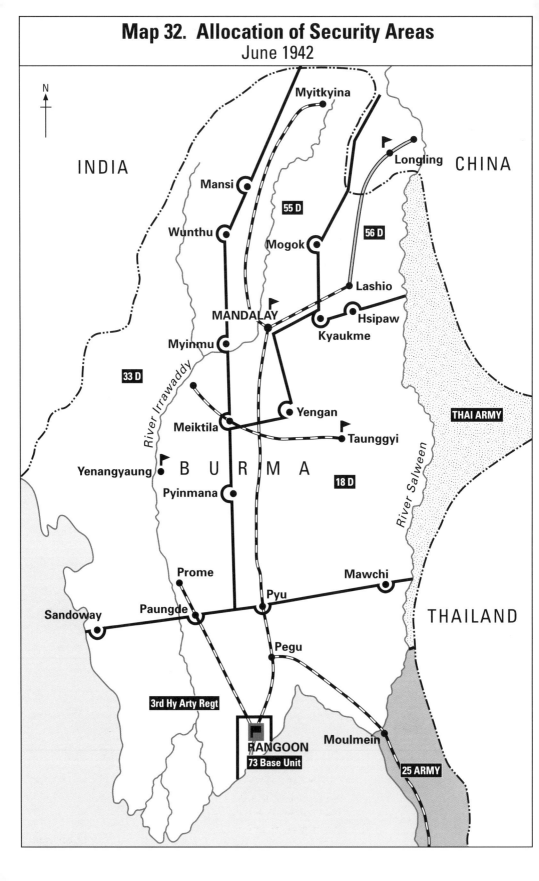

Map 32. Allocation of Security Areas
June 1942

N

INDIA

CHINA

Myitkyina

Longling

Mansi

55 D

56 D

Wunthu

Mogok

Lashio

MANDALAY

Hsipaw

Myinmu

Kyaukme

33 D

River Irrawaddy

Meiktila

Yengan

Taunggyi

THAI ARMY

Yenangyaung

B U R M A

18 D

River Salween

Pyinmana

Prome

Mawchi

Pyu

THAILAND

Sandoway

Paungde

Pegu

3rd Hy Arty Regt

RANGOON

Moulmein

73 Base Unit

25 ARMY

General Slim concerning the withdrawal and this soon became generally known. Now Slim had won the hearts of his troops and such an attitude was resented by soldiers who knew that he and they had done their best in an impossible situation. General Irwin, however competent in other respects, was clearly an unimaginative man. Instead of encouraging the troops and taking an interest in the valuable lessons so painfully learnt, he seemed scornful that the Army in Burma had not done better. This attitude rubbed off on his staff and caused much ill-feeling. As a British battalion recorded:

"Unfortunately, many of those responsible for receiving the survivors at Imphal behaved as though a contemptuous sense of superiority was the right reaction. For the lack of consideration shown to the men who had endured a retreat of 900 miles in burning heat, often short of water and food, and pressed by a relentless and superior enemy, there can be no excuse."[6]

If the reception arrangements had been efficient this attitude might have been tolerated. But they weren't. A large part of 17 Division and 1 Burdiv was deposited on virgin scrub-covered hillsides in the Kanglatongbi area. The monsoon had broken on the evening of 18 May but no cover or cooking arrangements had been made. At 2500 feet it was cold at night but there was no issue of hot food, blankets or groundsheets for the destitute troops, most of whom were carrying only a cut-down mosquito net. For three miserable days the drenching monsoon rain continued while the exhausted troops did what they could to build shelters out of brushwood or tarpaulins purloined from lorries and to survive on cold tinned meals.

Now Imphal had been bombed twice, the last time by a large force of bombers on 16 May. Many inhabitants had fled to the surrounding villages and their thatched houses were empty. Some troops had been lucky and moved straight into these. But many more houses were still empty as were the Assam Rifle barracks, a neatly laid out camp of wooden huts with corrugated iron roofs near the centre of Imphal. It had apparently been the target of the last air raid. After a show-down between Generals Cowan and Irwin, it was arranged that the troops

3. From *History of Indian Armed Services, Medical Services, Campaigns in the Eastern Theatre*.
4. This figure seems rather high and presumably includes all infantry units grouped under 48 Brigade's command in the last stages of the withdrawal.
5. Only 2 Burif, under Lt-Col. O'Callaghan, retained its cohesion but Lt-Col. Abernethy of 4 Burif brought out a mixed force of Burma Rifles about 350 strong. An officer records that five Burif colonels reached the Chindwin at Tonhe without any troops. Several Burif COs, however, were awarded DSOs for their part in the campaign. Enriques, Major C.M., *The Story of the Burma Rifles*.
6. Barclay, C.N., *The History of The Duke of Wellington's Regiment, 1919-1952*.

of 17 Division still out in the open would move into this vacant accommodation where, of course, they should have gone in the first place.

It is only fair to point out that 4 British Corps had been rushed up to Manipur and only arrived a fortnight before the first troops. They had had very little time to find their feet and get things organised. Moreover the line of communication to the base in Calcutta was long and fragile and inadequately staffed. Nevertheless, the provision of shelter, food and medical supplies were obvious priorities. Malaria and dysentery, picked up in the notorious Kabaw valley and aggravated by the cold, wet nights after the monsoon had broken, soon caused heavy casualties among the troops already weakened by the harsh conditions of the retreat. In 17 Division more than a quarter of the Division reported sick in their first ten days in India and about half of these were hospital cases. Unfortunately there were practically no medical supplies or medical facilities in Imphal and the one small civilian hospital and the one Field Hospital were unable to cope. There was no airfield on the Imphal Plain at that time. The only hope of survival, for the many who were seriously sick, was somehow to get down to the base hospitals in India. This was far from easy as, now that the monsoon had come, the road to Dimapur was blocked by landslides for days at a time. It was only through the devotion and untiring efforts of a handful of doctors that fatal casualties from sickness were not greater than they were.

General Wavell paid a visit to many units on 25 May, congratulating them on doing their best and making two points. Firstly, he didn't want any cribbing about the Civil Administration in Burma. They had done their best in a unique and impossible situation. This comment passed over most people's heads. The Japanese bombing of towns had caused the desertion of some public servants in the rear areas and the public services had consequently largely disintegrated towards the end. However, the few civil servants that 17 Division and 1 Burdiv had come across seemed to be staying at their posts far too long, rather than the reverse.[7] Secondly, he didn't want any cribbing about the RAF. He had himself recalled them from Burma because they were required for the more urgent defence of Ceylon and he had reckoned that the Army in Burma could stand up to Japanese air attacks. Most people admired him for these straight-from-the-shoulder remarks. But there were still some who groused about the lack of air support.

Resurgence

Once established in Imphal, 17 Division showed that they had far from lost their spirit. By 3 June the divisional Sappers had restored the electricity and water supplies to the heavily bombed town. The next day Divisional Headquarters issued Training Instruction No 1 incorporating the lessons of the campaign. General Cowan was determined to be ready for the next encounter with the Japanese and training started almost at once.[8] At the same time he gave Brigadier R.T. Cameron the task of writing a report identifying the new organisations, battle techniques and equipment needed to fight successfully in Burmese conditions. Based on this report, HQ 17 Division devised a new divisional organisation. The aim was to produce an equally powerful division but one more mobile, less unwieldy and less dependent on vehicles. This proposal was duly agreed at GHQ in Delhi and 17 Indian Light Division was born. It was to prove a very successful organisation for the fighting in the Chin Hills in 1944, but was abandoned in 1945 when the division became mechanised for its thrust into Central Burma.

In parallel to this official action each unit sent back its own views on the lessons of the campaign. British Army reports went to GHQ in Delhi and Indian Army reports both to GHQ and to regimental centres all over India. In this way the training policy in India began to swing away from its position of being one hundred per cent aimed at desert fighting, and moved towards teaching the different technique required for fighting a forest war. The virtues of strict discipline, a high standard of physical fitness, night movement and cunning fieldcraft were emphasised. It was generally realised that tougher and more advanced training was essential and two training divisions were established for this purpose in the forests of India.

General Cowan also decided that the organisation of his division was not the only thing that needed changing. For a division which had just retreated a thousand miles in four months the divisional sign, a 'Streak of Lightning', might be misconstrued. Perhaps he was not amused by a sly announcement by 'Tokyo Rose', the English-language propagandist of Tokyo Radio, that 'the division whose sign is a yellow streak' had been driven out of Burma. So a new sign of a 'Black Cat' was adopted. This sign became famous and is still used in the modern Indian Army.

What was left of 1 Burdiv went back to India to form the nucleus of one of the new training divisions while 17 Division remained in Imphal in support of 23 Indian Division. The latter were gradually building up on the frontier as fast as movement up the line of communication permitted. HQ Eastern Army, based in Calcutta, started a huge programme to develop this route from the base at Calcutta to Dimapur and thence to Imphal. The many installations required included hospitals, airfields, transit camps, stores depots, ferries across the huge

---

7. There had, no doubt inevitably, been friction and criticism during the final stages of the civilian evacuation.

8. At that time few people realised how precarious was the line of communication and everyone expected operations to restart when the rains ended in October.

This rock-slide, at milestone 42 from Dimapur, completely blocked the road to Imphal for a week in June 1942.

unbridged (and never to be bridged) Brahmaputra, and not least a two-way all-weather motor road from railhead at Dimapur to Imphal. The latter was to prove much harder to construct than expected as the hills in Manipur were unstable and the rains brought continual major rock-slides. Meanwhile, HQ 4 Corps started a programme to improve communications in the Naga Hills (which are north of Imphal) by developing the most important paths into jeep tracks. They also started an ambitious project to build a military motor road south to Tiddim through the Chin Hills and thus provide a second route into Burma on this front.

All this activity was slowed down by the bottle-neck of the single-line metre-gauge railway east of the Brahmaputra, the torrential rainfall and the high incidence of malaria, there being in those days no anti-malarial prophylactic pills. Soldiers taking two weeks' leave at their homes in India were away from their units for two months, sometimes three, and often contracted malaria on the journey. 17 Division remained on reduced rations throughout the summer. Towards the end of the year, a civil disobedience campaign by the Congress Party in Eastern India further hampered the efforts of the administrators. Nevertheless, GHQ India was already considering what offensive action could be taken to recapture Burma as soon as the rains ceased.

The Next Campaign

The British were not alone in having aggressive ambitions. In July, *Imperial GHQ* in Tokyo ordered *HQ Southern Area* to research and prepare for an invasion of Assam. They considered that the best way of dealing with any attempt to supply China by air was to take the initiative and capture the important airfields in Eastern India. The aim would be to seize the area from Akyab to Imphal and then advance to the line of the Brahmaputra. A larger rear organisation would be necessary. On 22 August the order came from Tokyo for preparations to start.[9] General Iida's plan to implement this directive featured *33* and *18 Divisions* and was much on the lines of what was to be attempted in 1944.[10]

The higher HQ on both sides were being thoroughly unrealistic. It would be 20 months before communications were sufficiently improved on each side for serious operations to start again on this stretch of the Indo-Burmese frontier. By then the British would have accepted and put into practice the lessons painfully learnt in this campaign. When operations restarted on this main front, the British-Indian army would be properly trained and Allied air superiority would have been achieved. The balance of power would have changed decisively.

---

9. Japanese Official History, *The Assault on Burma*, p.546 *et al*.

10. *ibid*, p.564. Both Generals Sakurai and Mutaguchi strongly opposed the plan on administrative grounds. On 5 September the order came from Tokyo to suspend the preparations.

CHAPTER TWENTY-FOUR

The View from the Other Side

Completion of the Conquest of Burma

General Terauchi, at *HQ Southern Area* in Singapore, reported completion of the Burma Operation to Imperial GHQ in Tokyo on 19 May, 1942. From the Japanese viewpoint it had been a highly successful campaign. The plan to capture Rangoon with two lightly equipped divisions, each with only two infantry regiments, advancing on foot along forest tracks and for four weeks without a road line of communication, was a very daring one. They had been supported by only 21 mountain guns with a very limited supply of ammunition, and the Japanese Air Force could only partly compensate for this lack of fire-power. Their judgement that the Allies would be unable to build up their strength in time to stop them had proved to be correct.

The timing of the whole operation had been immaculate. The advance into Burma had not been started until it was clear that the Malayan campaign was being successful, that additional reinforcements would not be needed there and that the Thais were being co-operative. This gave time for the engineers, greatly assisted by the Thais, to make the footpath up to the Burmese frontier passable for horses and to start the construction of a motor road. Rangoon was the target for the first phase and this had to be captured before the Chinese were able to move down in strength from the north. After the capture of Rangoon a pause was

The first Japanese train crosses the repaired Myitnge bridge on 31 May.

anticipated until Singapore fell and the port could be used, but in fact Singapore fell three weeks before Rangoon. Java fell soon afterwards and a major part of Admiral Kondo's *2nd Fleet*, fresh from their success at Pearl Harbour, were able to move into the Indian Ocean and force the weaker British fleet to withdraw towards Africa. This move covered the transports bringing into Rangoon *18 Division*, two tank regiments and medium and field artillery, all from Singapore, and the motorised *56 Division* from Japan. It also enabled the Andaman and Nicobar islands to be occupied and this gave additional protection against any British naval or air intervention from India or Ceylon.

Speed had been the key to the success of the operation, both to forestall the British and Chinese build-up and to complete the campaign before the monsoon. The Japanese troops were given no rest and no sooner was Rangoon captured than phase two was started. The speed of their advance was greatly helped by the meticulous planning and the provision of specialist engineer and water-supply units at an early stage.

For logistics, the Japanese had put their trust in railways, a form of transport in which they had long been expert and which required less manpower than trucks and roads. One battalion of the *5th Railway Engineer Regiment* was brought in at Moulmein. It was unable in the short term to repair either the Bilin or Sittang bridges but did get the railway operating from Ye to Bilin. The other two battalions, followed by the *9th Railway Engineer Regiment*,[1] were more successful. Owing to the British failure to destroy the big mainline rail bridge over the Pazundaung Creek near Rangoon, and their failure to remove or destroy the machinery in the main railway workshops at Insein, the Japanese were able to get the mainline to Toungoo quickly into operation. Although they record that 85% of the locomotives in Burma had been destroyed or disabled, for *56 Division's* advance to the north they were able to provide initially two trains a day and eventually three. They were able to repair quite quickly most of the demolished railway bridges on the main-line to the north. River levels were low, timber was plentiful and their engineers were skilled in its use.[2] However, the big Myitnge bridge was a problem as the river was deep and the repair took three weeks. Fortunately the Gokteik viaduct had not been demolished and so by 30 May the railway was open for the 610 miles from Rangoon to Lashio via Mandalay. The railway network north of the Irrawaddy was captured largely intact. However, the Ava bridge demolition was a serious obsta-cle. The bridge was too big to repair during the war and so there was no direct rail (or road) link with the main network south of the river. This, and the destruction of

---

1. This Regiment was later transferred to Thailand, and placed under command of *25 Army*, for the construction of the notorious Thailand-Burma railway.
2. General Iida commented that the railways would have been harder to repair if the Allies had removed some of the railway embankments, as the Chinese often did in China

the bulk of the Irrawaddy Flotilla Company's fleet, was to make the build-up of supplies for any invasion of India a slow business.

Aftermath

With the campaign completed, a military government was set up under General Iida in Rangoon and the four divisions were made responsible for defence and law and order in the four quarters of the country. The allocation of areas is shown in Map 32.

Meanwhile a ceremony was held at Maymyo at the end of May to commemorate those who had been killed or died during the campaign. The numbers of dead then recorded, and the figures may be taken as accurate, were:

18 Division 123
33 Division 730
55 Division 702
56 Division 286
Other units 590
Total 2431   (161 were officers)

After this ceremony, General Iida, the *15th Army* commander, awarded letters of citation to the formations which had done particularly well. They were:

33 Division . . . . .Lieutenant-General Sakurai
214 Infantry Regiment . . . . .Colonel Sakuma
215 Infantry Regiment . . . . .Colonel Harada
56 Division . . . . .Lieutenant-General Watanabe
56 Recce Regiment . . . . . . .Colonel Hirai

Lessons of the Campaign

Like the British, the Japanese were quick to publish their views on the lessons of the campaign. These, though not always flattering to their enemies, are of some interest and so this is a summary of the points in the report "Lessons Learnt from the Burma Operation" published in August 1942 by *HQ 15 Army*.

"The British forces were superior in weapons, tanks, artillery and vehicles but their fighting spirit was inferior. They did not carry out aggressive actions and were lazy in digging trenches and positions. They were excellent at concentrating artillery, mortar and machine-gun fire on the front line but were not good at jungle fighting. Commanders did not control their units well and co-ordination between units was poor. However they were persistent, and British officers believed in the superiority of the British Empire and were convinced of the final victory of Britain.

The Chinese forces in Burma showed remarkable fighting strength in the early stages, notably at Toungoo and Pyinmana which were comparable to the battles at Shanghai. Co-operation between the Chinese and British was loose.

The aim in phase one was the capture of Rangoon, key base for the British and Chinese forces. However, some of the leading Japanese troops were too eager to capture the city and did not pay sufficient attention to attacking the enemy.[3] In phase two, front line troops, in spite of specific orders from Army HQ, continued to prefer to capture key areas, or to obtain resources, rather than concentrate on destroying the enemy.

In phase one, the greatest worry was whether the Chinese would come south from Toungoo while *15 Army* was advancing on Rangoon. In order to slow them up rumours were spread that a Japanese force would advance into the Shan States from north Thailand via Keng Tung. Some deceptive Japanese moves were carried out in north Thailand to support these rumours. Captured Chinese papers show that this ruse succeeded.

15 Army had expected that the key battles in phase two would be fought on the line Taunggyi-Pyawbwe-Yenanyaung, followed by a decisive battle in the Shan States. But things went better than expected as the main Allied strength was destroyed in battles at Loikaw and Yamethin against the Chinese and at Yenangyaung against the British. The rapid advance by *56 Division* to capture Lashio was then decisive.

It was found to be essential to hold in readiness tanks and motorised units to pursue the enemy as soon as the main front positions were broken through. In this way advantage could be taken of the 'vacuum' behind the enemy positions, as was done in *56 Division's* advance to the Salween."

Air Operations

The Japanese Air Force, as in the United States at that time, was not a separate Service and was split between the Army and the Navy. However, the Japanese Army understood that, in order to take advantage of its flexibility, its Air Force should be controlled centrally.[4] Accordingly, command of the air forces used in the operations in Burma, Malaya and Indonesia, the bulk of which had been moved south from Manchuria, was centralised under Lieutenant-

---

3. This would seem to be a reference to the abandonment of the road-blocks at Pegu and Taukkyan.
4. The relatively long range of all the Japanese aircraft made their air forces particularly flexible.

General Sakaguchi at HQ Southern Army.[5] There were two air divisions. It was mainly the *5th Air Division* which was used in Burma, although it was reinforced by the *3rd Air Division* for heavy raids.

The *5th Air Division* had initially two groups, the *10th Dan* having fighters, light bombers, scout and transport planes, and the *4th Dan*, which was transferred from the Philippines by 22 January, having fighters and light and heavy bombers. Later, when the operations in the Dutch East Indies were completed, they were reinforced by two more groups from the *3rd Air Division*. They were careful not to bomb facilities which would be useful to their own forces and concentrated on bombing all the major towns, apparently to impress and terrorise the inhabitants (in which they succeeded). As a result, although the retreating British forces were frequently attacked from the air and suffered many casualties, they were not attacked as much as they might have been.

The Allied successes in the early air battles over Rangoon had been an unexpected shock. In the first three months, almost 100% of the fighters were lost and this used up nearly all the Japanese reserves.[6] Most of these losses were in combat or from air attack when on the ground. An appreciable number, however, were also due to damage caused by the rough surfaces of hurriedly-prepared airstrips. Once Rangoon had been captured, therefore, they brought in bombers from the *3rd Air Division* and made a series of heavy attacks on the RAF and AVG at Magwe and Akyab and in three days destroyed them. For the next two months, the Japanese in Burma enjoyed complete air supremacy.

A serious weakness of the Japanese aircraft was the lack of armour for the pilots and the lack of self-sealing petrol tanks. Far too often their aircraft caught fire when attacked. Interestingly, the Japanese, like the British, concluded that they needed more transport planes.

Comments on the British air operations by a staff officer in *5th Air Division* are recorded in their Official History. He thought that RAF pilots had high morale and an excellent aggressive spirit. They were not, however, as well trained as the Japanese. They were brave and persistent in their attacks both on ground targets and on Japanese aircraft but single planes were careful to avoid dog-fights at which the Japanese were better. The main reasons for the Japanese success were more aircraft and early capture of the airfields at Mudon and Moulmein, and then at Rangoon. He thought that the British were on the defensive from the beginning. Their aggressive actions were more like small scale guerrilla raids and these inevitably led to defeat in detail.[7]

Political Infiltration

The efforts made by Colonel Suzuki and his M-Kikan in 1940 and 1941 to create a Burma Independence Army proved well worthwhile. The main help that the BIA gave the invaders was in gathering information and in administrative support. Indistinguishable from the local population, members of the BIA moved ahead of the Japanese forces and marked paths and tracks through the forests for them. A notable example of this was the route taken by *215 Regiment* from the Bilin to the Sittang bridge. They arranged with village headmen for the Japanese to be welcomed and for rice and bullock-carts to be collected, and they picked up intelligence from the villagers about the British whereabouts.[8] They spread propaganda about independence and as a result the Japanese were usually warmly welcomed by the locals, a reception very different from that experienced in China. Moreover-the hostility that the BIA showed to anyone with British sympathies caused anxiety for the safety of their families among those soldiers who were domiciled in Burma. It was the chief cause of their many desertions. By the time the Japanese reached Rangoon the BIA strength had risen to about 12,000.

Militarily their one great success was the ambush south of Pegu in which the commander of the newly-arrived 63 Brigade, his brigade major and one battalion commander were seriously wounded. In minor skirmishes with the British they usually came off worse. In the one battle, Shwedaung, where a large BIA force was involved in an ancillary fighting role, they suffered a severe defeat at the hands of an Indian battalion and were never used again in a formal battle. The lure of a rifle and loot had attracted many dacoits to their ranks and they soon gained a shocking reputation for atrocities. There is no doubt that many Army stragglers, Indian refugees and Burmese sympathisers with the British were murdered by the BIA. At the end of the campaign they committed a series of major racially-motivated atrocities in the Delta area, wiping out all the inhabitants of several Karen villages. *15 Army* then intervened. The BIA, which had reached a strength of over 20,000, was weeded out and reorganised to become the Burma Defence Army (BDA) with a strength of about 10,000. Suzuki, who was felt to have become more pro-Burmese than pro-Japanese, was sent home.

In October 1941, a Japanese team (F-Kikan) under Major Fujiwara had been

---

5. As an exception, a small independent wing of 18 scout planes and nine ground-attack fighters was allotted to *25 Army* in Malaya.

6. According to Lieutenant-Colonel Kato, a distinguished fighter pilot, only one squadron was equipped with the latest Type 1 fighters (Oscars). He thought their performance was about the same as the Hurricanes but the Oscars were better in a dog-fight. This view was echoed by a very experienced British fighter pilot, Group-Captain Dennis David. He thought that "the Oscar was a good fighter and [*because of its range*] more fitted for the role in Burma than our dear old and tried Hurricane." *The RAF and the Far East War*.

7. He probably did not realise how slender the British resources were.

8. Resistance was unwise. A loyal headman who refused to co-operate was tied up and is alleged to have been personally bayoneted to death by Aung San.

secretly assembled in Thailand. Its aim was to persuade Indian soldiers to change sides and to join a pro-Japanese Indian National Army (INA) dedicated to the liberation of India. There was already a civilian Indian Independence League (IIL) with this aim and this was planned to be the controlling political organisation of which the INA would be the military arm. The INA, which was formed on 31 December 1941 at Taipin in Malaya, was mainly recruited from prisoners captured in Malaya and in Singapore. In early February 1942, Captain Tsuchimochi, second-in-command of F-Kikan, three Japanese officers and 60 INA members were sent from Kuala Lumpur to Burma. However, there is no record of the INA taking part in any battle in the first Burma campaign. Nor is there any record of prisoners being recruited, though some probably were. The Japanese were well aware of the antipathy of the Burmese to Indians, and General Iida was unenthusiatic about the use of the INA. Captured Indian soldiers, however, were frequently given the choice of either helping the Japanese as porters or labourers, or being executed. It was not a difficult decision to make. Not a few escaped and found their way back to India. The IIL had requested from the military government that the income from properties abandoned by Indian refugees should be allotted to them but they were rebuffed. Both INA and IIL languished in Japanese disfavour until the end of 1942.

The Japanese Commanders

Most of the Japanese commanders were highly professional and had up-to-date battle experience. General Shojiro Iida was a dedicated soldier who had had a brilliant career. He made few mistakes in this campaign and kept the momentum of the advance going with scarcely a pause in spite of formidable administrative problems. Apart from being a first-class soldier (like his father) and renowned for his strong will, he was also, unlike his successor General Kawabe, a broad-minded and cultivated man. When a Japanese Military Government was set up in June 1942, with the aid of 300 officials sent out from Tokyo, he proved to be an able administrator of the country and was admired and respected by the Burmese politicians. In March 1943 he returned to GHQ in Tokyo and in March 1945 he was posted to command the *30th Army* in Manchuria. He was taken prisoner there by the Russians in the last week of the war and spent five years in a labour camp in Siberia. Unlike many others he survived the terrible conditions and died in Japan in 1980, aged 92.

Lieutenant-General Seizo Sakurai, aged 52, the commander of *33 Division*, was also outstanding. He had had a distinguished career, passing high out of the staff college and later specialising in combined operations. He was credited with the design of the original landing craft, first used in the invasion of China in

1937.[9] He spoke French and spent two years as military attaché in Paris. After a series of command appointments, he took over *33 Division* in January 1941 in China, where his best-known feat was the rescue of another Japanese division which was surrounded. His division was considered by many to be the best in Burma, until it was destroyed in 1944 in the battle of Imphal. In this campaign his aggressive encircling tactics, and the speed of his division across country, posed a problem for the road-bound British which they were unable to solve. In March 1943, Sakurai returned to Tokyo as Director of the Armoured Corps. In January 1944, he was posted back to Burma to command the *28th Army* on the west coast. His army was destroyed in the fighting in 1944/45 and he was a prisoner in Rangoon until 1947. After the war he lived very simply and devoted his life to the welfare of old soldiers by whom he was very highly regarded. He died in 1985 at the age of 95.[10]

Sakurai was well-served. All his four subordinate commanders were later promoted. His second-in-command, Major-General Araki, became a Lieutenant-General and Colonels Harada, Sakuma and Miawaki became Major-Generals.

The other division which did very well in Burma was *56 Division*. Its commander was Lieutenant-General Masao Watanabe, a Gunner. Although a 'new' division, it was motorised and in this campaign supported by *14 Tank Regiment*. The speed of its advance through the Shan States to Lashio, and then to Myitkyina, disrupted the Chinese forces and forced them to retreat out of Burma. General Iida thought that both Watanabe and his chief-of-staff, Colonel Takeshi Fujiwara, were exceptionally good.

Lieutenant-General Renya Mutaguchi, who commanded *18 Division*, had taken part in the campaign in Malaya and the capture of Singapore, but *18 Division* was mainly in reserve and only played a minor part in this campaign. He was well-known in army circles as a thruster, and was widely believed to have instigated the 'incident' at the Marco Polo Bridge outside Peking which led to the war with China. He was later to be given command of *15 Army* and in 1943 became a passionate advocate of seizing Imphal and Kohima, with a view to advancing into India. It was a disastrous misjudgement. However, in 1942 he opposed any advance across the Chindwin.

55 Division was considered to have done only moderately well in Burma.

---

9. An idea later copied by the Allies.

10. General Sakurai was a notably modest and humane man. A little-known fact is that in August 1942 he ordered a victory memorial for the Japanese dead to be built at Yenangyaung and alongside it a smaller memorial, much to the amazement of his staff, for the British and Indian dead. He held a memorial service there for the dead of both sides. In recognition of this he is said to have had preferential treatment as a British prisoner at the end of the war. (Account of Mr Eiichi Sugimoto and others.)

Lieutenant-General Yiroshi Takeuchi's performance was considered only average and he was retired in 1943. His chief-of-staff and one regimental commander were sacked during the campaign for inefficiency. Although *55 Division* had fought from the beginning to the end, it received no commendation from General Iida. In the first phase it had fought against the British and, after some cheap early victories while the British tried to find their feet, it had been roughly handled at Pegu by 48 Brigade. In the second phase it had had a very hard fight at Toungoo against the Chinese. Its casualties were second only to those of *33 Division*, but General Iida felt that its commanders had lacked aggressive spirit.

The Japanese Soldiers

In 1904 and 1905, Lieutenant-General Sir Ian Hamilton headed a British team of observers who, for ten months, accompanied the Japanese in the field during their war with the Russians. He had a wide experience of war himself and his comments were penetrating. He compared the Japanese with the Gurkhas:

> "The same ready smile; the same jolly good humour; the same independent manner, evincing clearly but not offensively, the soldier's pride and his conscious superiority to any civilian... these were surely Gurkhas, better educated, more civilised: on the other hand not quite so powerful or hardy."

Later in the campaign he was to say, watching a group of soldiers after making a night attack:

> "Many of them are wounded, but none the less happy on that account unless they suspect that the doctor may take too serious a view of such a trifle as a bayonet wound in the eye or a bullet through the foot, and put them temporarily on the shelf. For the tenth time at least I must write down that the Japanese infantry consist of superb material. Guileless as children, brave as lions, their constant ruling thought is to do their duty by their ancestors and by the Emperor."

Thirty-seven years later the Japanese had changed a little but there was still much truth in his comments. Unlike the British, the Japanese had not suffered the dreadful trauma of the trenches in World War I. They still had a deep pride in their expanding empire and a simple and uncomplicated attitude to the glory of war.

Japanese soldiers before World War II were mainly recruited from the rural population. These small farmers lived a very hard and frugal life in conditions of poverty. Tough physical standards in the Army were no great problem to them.

They were, however, by no means uneducated; there were many schools, and education in Japan was highly esteemed. Although many of the reservists who were called up for the 'new' divisions in 1940 and 1941 were married, and therefore perhaps not as single-minded as the younger recruits, they had, like all Japanese, been indoctrinated at school with the belief that nothing was more honourable than to give one's life for one's country as symbolised by the Emperor. In all High Schools, drill and simple military training were part of the curriculum. On going overseas it was customary for a soldier to write his will and to leave something personal, like a lock of hair, to be buried in his place if his body was not recovered. His life was dedicated to the Emperor and death was something not to fear but to expect. This attitude, combined with the innate belief that the Japanese were the toughest race on earth, provided a very strong motivation. It was this motivation which was their greatest asset.

Discipline in the Army was strict. Any order had to be obeyed implicitly and no excuse was tolerated. Whether at home or overseas, soldiers had to recite morning and evening towards the Emperor the five basic rules for a soldier's behaviour. Briefly these were loyalty to the Emperor and Japan, courtesy, courage, honesty and indifference to material things. Punishments for infringements of orders were physical and given on the spot. They could be given at all levels by seniors to juniors. Soldiers were slapped or beaten and often knocked down.[11] Such treatment, which would have been deeply resented in most countries, was accepted in the Japanese Army as an admirable way of punishing a man without removing him from duty.[12]

Although the Japanese armoured units, gunners and engineers were competent and professional, it was the infantry who were regarded as the cream of the Army. In a predominantly infantry war, as it was in 1942, they were very effective. Fieldcraft, concealment, digging and night movement were much practised and they were very good at them. Their particular speciality, on which much emphasis was laid, was silent night attacks with the bayonet. This emphasis on close-quarter fighting, however, seems to have resulted in a skimping on musketry training for their shooting was often very poor.

They lived in a heavily-forested country and they had found the forests of Burma to be friendly places, excellent for concealment and full of snacks to

11. Lt-Col. Henry Power, who was the senior combatant officer taken prisoner, kept a personal diary in which he records an incident he witnessed while in Rangoon jail. Two Indians passing the jail entrance and suspected of being looters were set upon and beaten up by the guard. "The Commandant apparently witnessed the incident from his bungalow, came across and played merry hell with the guard, beating up each man in turn. Steel helmets and other equipment went flying all over the place. A good example of the Japanese method of awarding summary punishment; it is very effective, though primitive."
12. It was not so well understood by British POWs.

enliven a diet of plain rice. But, particularly in the early stages when the Allied fighter aircraft were around, there was much forced marching along forest tracks carrying heavy loads. They were often much more exhausted than the British realised but their weakness was concealed by their aggressive tactics. Above all, their determination literally to fight to the last man and the last round made them a very difficult enemy to beat. To be taken prisoner was utterly shameful and in this campaign not more than a handful of Japanese were captured.[13]

The Rules of War

The Japanese fought a total war and did not agree with some Western ideas. They thought that the killing of seriously wounded enemy soldiers was a perfectly reasonable act. Such soldiers would be a drain on the limited Japanese resources and could be of no further use as labour. It was what they hoped would happen to themselves if they were ever in a similar position. When later their turn came to retreat, they often killed their own wounded rather than let them fall into enemy hands. But apart from this there were, in this campaign, as the narrative shows, very few recorded atrocities actually carried out by the Japanese, although they must take the responsibility for some of those carried out by the BIA, who were under their control.

The Japanese claim to have taken nearly 5000 prisoners in this campaign, British, Indian and Chinese (see Appendix 8). Partly for political reasons and partly because the Japanese believed that it was utterly shameful to be taken prisoner, their treatment of prisoners in 1942 in the first few months after their capture, was disgraceful. Officers were beaten up and publicly humiliated, before spending two or three months in solitary confinement during which they were forbidden to speak to each other. All prisoners were considered junior to any Japanese soldier and were therefore liable to be punched, slapped, kicked or beaten by any of their captors for alleged breaches of jail discipline. However, in September 1942 the original brutal Camp Commandant of Rangoon jail (where all the prisoners were held once Rangoon was captured) was replaced. Although Japan had not signed the Geneva Convention, the new Commandant made some effort to conform to it. Captured airmen continued to have the worst treatment, but solitary confinement became rarer and physical punishment, although it continued to the end, was reduced.

Living conditions were extremely primitive and, apart from some books, there were no amenities. Clothing and footwear soon wore out and replacements were few. No clothing or Red Cross parcels ever reached the prisoners in Burma.[14] The worst features, however, were the inadequate rations and the almost total lack of medicines and medical facilities. The rations issued were much the same as those issued to their own troops and the Japanese saw no reason to give better rations to prisoners while their front-line troops often went short. Unfortunately the metabolism of Europeans is different from that of Japanese. Most European prisoners were incapable of obtaining sufficient nourishment from the food they received and there were many cases of the deficiency disease beri-beri. Medical supplies were virtually non-existent and, although the handful of British and Indian doctors did their best, dysentery was common and many prisoners died of beri-beri unnecessarily. However, the sick were not forced to go on working parties and convalescents were permitted to do light duty. It was permitted to grow some vegetables and sometimes to buy small quantities of additional food. Imprisonment in Rangoon Jail was a dreadful experience[15] but there was no comparison with the horrors suffered by those who worked on the infamous Thailand-Burma railway.[16]

Summary

For the Japanese the campaign had been an outstanding success. In the four months available before the monsoon arrived, they had achieved their aim of closing the Burma Road and driving out of Burma such British and Chinese forces as they had been unable to destroy.

The careful research and planning during the previous twelve months had paid a handsome dividend. They had appreciated that speed was the key to the problem. In the first phase it was essential to capture Rangoon before the British could substantially reinforce Burma's tiny garrison or the Chinese could reach southern Burma. In the second phase the Allied forces had to be destroyed or driven out of Burma before the monsoon arrived.

In the first phase, their hardy infantry, advancing rapidly with BIA help along village paths, had generally out-fought and always out-manoeuvred the British. It had been a sort of infantry blitzkrieg. In the second phase they had used tanks and motorised infantry, advancing with remarkable speed, to outflank and disperse the main Chinese forces. This had been a more orthodox but equally successful blitzkrieg.

13. Winston Churchill commented in September 1943, "The Japanese breed like vermin and die like heroes." Eade, Charles, article in *The Sunday Telegraph*, 15 January 1998.
14. Kirby, S.W., *The War Against Japan*, Vol.5, p.533.
15. Mackenzie, Colonel K., in *Operation Rangoon Jail*, no doubt strongly influenced by the disgraceful lack of medical care, takes an extreme anti-Japanese stance. Lieutenant-Colonel Henry Power in his diary shows a much more balanced view. In spite of having been beaten unconscious in the early days, he continued to lodge complaints with the commandant when necessary, sometimes with success. (His views are confirmed by other survivors.)
16. No prisoners from Burma worked on the Thailand-Burma railway, all action in Tenasserim being the responsibility of *HQ 25 Army* in Singapore. (See Map 32.)

Their forces had been well co-ordinated. General Iida had been fully conscious of the importance of capturing the British airfields. As soon as it was possible, the two air divisions in Southern Area were concentrated to knock out the RAF and AVG. Similarly, as soon as it was required to move troop convoys into Rangoon, the Japanese Navy made a major raid into the Indian Ocean and the Bay of Bengal to cover the move.

The political angle was also handled skilfully. The liaison cultivated with the Burmese nationalist party, the Thakins, lead to the formation of the BIA whose activities both helped the advance directly in many ways and projected the image of the Japanese as liberators. As a result, the Military Government set up by the Japanese initially received ready co-operation from the Burmese and this solved many problems.

In the face of this brilliant achievement two things surprised the Japanese. The first was why the Indian Army units had continued to fight against them so well. As they were fellow Asians, the Japanese had supposed that they would welcome those who ostensibly had come to liberate them from their 'brutal masters'. Disconcertingly, that had not proved to be the case. The second curious fact was that virtually all British prisoners continued to maintain that in the end the British were bound to win the war. This seemed inexplicable to the Japanese in view of their rapid successes. It was all very puzzling.

CHAPTER TWENTY-FIVE

Reflections on the Campaign

The Lack of Training

With hindsight it is clear that the failure to recognise the importance of Burma, and to make adequate preparations for its defence, was a major strategical error. It posed a grave risk to China and caused a major diversion of Allied effort over the next three years. The reason for this fatal mistake lay in London and is discussed in the next chapter. Here the purely military aspects of the campaign are discussed.

Unquestionably the main factor which influenced the fighting was the lack of training and the lack of war experience of the bulk of the British units. It was like entering a team of amateur footballers, who had never seen each other before and were uncertain both of the rules of the game and how to play it, into the field against a well-experienced and highly-motivated team of professionals.

No-one, and this applied as much to officers as to men, had trained for jungle warfare. Since GHQ India was specifically excluded from the chain of command in the Far East until after the Japanese invasion had started, all training instructions and training in India had been for desert warfare, GHQ India being responsible for operations in Iraq and Iran and for the administrative support of Indian Army units in North Africa. As a result of Churchill's directive in May,[1] the War Office seems to have given little attention to the special problems of a Far Eastern war. The paradox thus arose that the British forces, who throughout their history had fought many jungle wars, entered Burma poorly clothed and equipped and blissfully ignorant of the special problems they would face.[2] The Japanese on the other hand, who had never fought a jungle war, were provided both with suitable clothing and equipment and with an excellent training pamphlet. With the help of the latter they were able quickly to adapt to Burmese conditions (see Appendix 9).

---

1. See Chapter 2. pp.31,32.
2. As long ago as 1756 in North America the Governor of Virginia had warned a newly-arrived General that he had "come into a Country covered with woods ... the European Method of Warring is not practised here." In this savage war against the American Indians a successful commander recorded that to be successful in this type of war a soldier needed "several years' intensive training." Ward, Matthew C., *War in History*, Vol.4, No.3

Moreover, no troops in India or Burma were given any information about the Japanese and their traditional fighting methods. It was not that it was not available. General Sir Ian Hamilton, an official observer of the Russo-Japanese war in 1904, had written an excellent and informative book on Japanese strengths and weaknesses. A team from the Indian Staff College had in 1907 toured the battlefields of that war and no doubt its records survived. More recently, the Military Attaché in Tokyo had reported to London on the fighting in China and warned that the Japanese forces, although they might look scruffy, were stronger and more efficient than commonly supposed. All was inhibited by the negative attitude towards the Far East taken by the War Cabinet.

The Higher Commanders

Unlike in Singapore, the higher commanders in Burma were about as good as Britain could provide. There was no Theatre Commander more experienced than General Wavell and no-one with a greater ability for clear thinking and decisive action.[3] In his despatch he was to criticise his own judgement in the early days[4] but it was a misjudgement which he would not have made if he had been placed in command of Burma earlier. He was also sometimes criticised by the Army in Burma for appearing to underestimate the Japanese. It is likely, however, that his statements to this effect were designed to counter the tendency after a number of defeats for soldiers to regard the enemy as 'supermen'.

Lieutenant-General Hutton was an exceptionally able man, his only failing was that he lacked charisma and didn't look the part. Nevertheless he deserves much credit for creating a credible Army in Burma and for doing all that was possible to hold the ring until reinforcements arrived. When it was clear that Rangoon could not be held he made a successful plan for its evacuation and for continuing the fighting further north. The removal of his Theatre Commander, General Wavell, to a headquarters two thousand miles away and quite out of touch, made his task impossibly difficult. His replacement by General Alexander was largely a political move by Churchill so that he could be seen to be doing something. There is no evidence, however, that Hutton would not have conducted the retreat as well as his successor.

There were mixed opinions at the time about General Alexander, although his courage and coolness were admired by all. He controlled a very difficult situation competently, but his great reputation does not rest on the brief period he spent in Burma, to which, significantly, he allots only three pages in his memoirs.[5]

It is doubtful if Britain could have found a Corps Commander more suitable than Lieutenant-General Slim for the task in Burma. His honesty, intelligence and toughness were manifest and he soon won the hearts of the soldiers in his polyglot Corps. In 1945 he would reconquer Burma as quickly as he was now forced to retreat from it.

Wavell, Alexander and Slim were all to reach the very peak of their profession and become Field Marshals.

Three officers commanded a division in this campaign. Major-General Bruce Scott entered Burma before the war started and did his best to instil some reality into the scene. He was unlucky in that the Burmese units, who formed the bulk of his division, were not battle-worthy. His division was no match for the Japanese *33 Division*; it suffered a severe defeat at Yenangyaung and was out-manoeuvred at Monywa. He was an able and popular commander but never fully recovered from his experiences in this campaign and did not get another active command. Major-General 'Jackie' Smyth VC, literate and articulate and with an extrovert personality, was considered to be an outstanding star of the Indian Army. He would almost certainly have justified his reputation if he had been fit, but he wasn't. His successor, Major-General 'Punch' Cowan, an able commander and a man of remarkable resilience and moral strength, was to have the unique distinction of commanding 17 Division very successfully and mostly in action for the next three-and-a-half years.

Nor were the senior staff officers any less able. Major-General Winterton and Brigadier 'Taffy' Davies were both very able chief operations officers while Major-General Goddard was a brilliant logistics staff officer. The higher staffs were as competent as they reasonably could be in the conditions of Burma at that time.

With most of the troops totally 'green' and untrained, much depended on the Brigadiers and Commanding Officers. The Indian Army had sent seven divisions to the Middle East and three to Malaya. Its corps of regular professional officers was a very small one.[6] It would be too much to expect that all the Brigadiers and COs in Burma were of the highest standard. Some were very good, most were competent, but there were one or two duds. This was a situation which was constantly changing as there were many casualties among senior officers.

---

3. General Cowan was not alone in rating him Britain's finest General. *Smyth Papers*, private letter. IWM Archives.

4. "I admit that I did not at this time consider the threat to Burma serious; I over-estimated the natural difficulties of the wooded hills on the Burmese frontier. Nor did I realise the unreliable quality of the Burmese units nor the lack of training of the British and Indian troops."

5. North, John, *'The Alexander Memoirs'*.

6. Small but select. Promotion was quicker, responsibilities for young men greater and pay much better than in the British Army. It was necessary to pass out of Sandhurst in the top thirty to get a vacancy. Field Marshal Montgomery, who tried for the Indian Army, just failed to make it. Montgomery, Brian, *A Field Marshal in the Family*.

The Army in Burma

The British 7th Armoured Brigade was the only fully-trained formation in Burma and more than half of its officers and men were battle experienced. They went into battle within two days of landing in Rangoon and made an instant impact on the fighting. Although ignorant of forest warfare, and starting with the 'private army' complex beloved of the armour in the Western Desert, they quickly adapted to the new conditions and fought with tremendous spirit and determination in close co-operation with the Infantry. Their radio communications were the only efficient ones in the army and provided a vital link in many battles. Their confident presence was always a great boost to morale. They greatly impressed the Japanese as well, and it is doubtful if the Army in Burma would have succeeded in making an orderly withdrawal, or indeed any other form of withdrawal, to India without them.

The two British Infantry battalions already in Burma, and three of the four brought in during the campaign, came, with one exception, from duties in an internal security role. They had not had the opportunity to train for war nor to learn how to fight in forest country. Many of the conscript soldiers were not physically fit enough for the very tough conditions and sickness rates were high. Although they impressed the Japanese and fought with great courage, their lack of training and experience led to many casualties and, without reinforcements, unit strengths soon dwindled.

The volunteer Indian Army was composed of two nationalities, Indian (and now Pakistani) and Nepali. The Indian part was at this stage at its weakest because of its recent six-fold expansion. Some 80-90% of the Indian soldiers in the units that came to Burma were recruits with only a few months' service. The majority of the British officers were straight out of OCTU. In the Infantry much depended in the early battles on the quality of the three or four regular officers in each battalion. Some units did very well, most did well, one or two not so well. All needed more training. The Gurkhas from Nepal were different. Nepal has a small population and although units were doubled, a larger expansion could not be sustained. Consequently, Gurkha standards, always high, did not fall so far as in some of the Indian units. Most did very well and fought with undiminished courage throughout the campaign. It was clear that with more training and better equipment they would be more than a match for even the best of the Japanese.

The Gunners had a very difficult time in this campaign. There were far too few of them.[7] The only British Army Gunners were 414 Field Battery RHA and a battery from 95 Anti-Tank Regiment RA, both with 7th Armoured Brigade. The former in particular did well in the strange conditions. With the exception of two Burmese Auxiliary Force units in the first phase, all the other Gunners, field, mountain, HAA and LAA, were Indian, although the anti-aircraft Gunners had some British NCOs. The mountain and LAA Gunners had a very difficult time in the early part of the campaign. As was the custom in those days many of their men carried no personal arms, a very undesirable situation in close-quarter fighting.[8] The mountain guns, designed for action in steep hills, were greatly outranged by all the Japanese artillery. In close country, however, they were often very effective and they took part with great spirit in nearly every battle. It was a tragedy that, for lack of mules, many guns had to be carried in trucks and thus fell victim to road-blocks. Notable in the second half of the campaign was the 1st Indian Field Regiment, new to battle but taking part in many actions and doing exceptionally well at Prome, Kokkogwa and Kyaukse.

With the exception of the 1st Burma Field Company, which distinguished itself at the frontier and at Moulmein but then quickly dwindled in strength, all the divisional engineers in Burma were Indian Sappers and Miners. One or more of these five divisional field companies took part in nearly every battle. Their many demolitions hampered the Japanese logistic follow-up and would have done so much more if the British retreat had been up the main axis to Mandalay, rather than up a subsidiary one. As it was, the demolitions slowed up the flow of supplies to northern Burma and were an important factor in the Japanese decision not to advance into Manipur in the winter of 1942-43, when they would have had a good chance of success. Behind the divisions, the Sappers were very thin on the ground but with the willing assistance of the Burma Public Works Department they managed to provide satellite airstrips for the RAF, emergency hospitals, water supply for the refugees and improvements to essential roads and tracks.

It is not possible in an operational account like this to cover all army activities but certainly two others must be mentioned. Firstly, the Medical Services. The doctors did amazingly well in the face of appalling difficulties. Apart from the battle casualties, there were many sick and there was the constant threat that a cholera epidemic among the flood of Indian refugees would spread more widely to the troops. Altogether, eight Burmese and three Indian General Hospitals were established as well as many minor specialist units. In the final stages all the hospitals had to be emptied and it was a remarkable achievement that nearly all the patients, both military and civilian, were successfully evacuated to India by

7. The Army in Burma was supported by the equivalent of half a field regiment and two mountain regiments in Phase One and by never more than one-and-a-half field regiments and one mountain regiment in Phase Two. This may be compared with the 70 artillery regiments which supported the 14th Army in its advance to Rangoon in 1945. HQ ALFSEA, *Some Facts about the Burma Campaign, 1944-45.*

8. It was the same in the Japanese army, but every soldier carried a bayonet.

air from Shwebo or Myitkyina, or by truck via Kalewa. Secondly, the supply and transport services deserve mention. Apart from the one British RASC company supporting 7th Armoured Brigade, there were several Indian RIASC companies and many more Burmese BASC companies. Although some disintegrated towards the end, they gave much invaluable support both by helping to move the fighting troops and by establishing the dumps of food, petrol and ammunition on which the army was totally reliant in its long retreat. The fighting troops owed a deep debt of gratitude to both these Services for coping so well in the difficult conditions.

The Burma Army

The Burma Rifles units, with one or two exceptions, were a disappointment. It was soon discovered that, although by no means lacking in courage, they were not sufficiently motivated or trained to stand up to a formal attack. Therefore, if included in a defence layout, they were not only of little use but they endangered everyone else. There were several reasons for this. One was the shortage of British officers. Another was that the traditional Burmese method of fighting was guerrilla action from the security of the forests, a practice at which they were adept.[9] Although this was quickly realised after the war started, it was then both politically and militarily too late to effect a change in their role and organisation. Another main reason was the political climate. Japanese support for the Burma Independence movement made those supporting the British fearful for the safety of their families and increasing numbers deserted with their weapons for this reason. The Burmese Army battalions made up of Indians and Gurkhas domiciled in Burma were steadier in battle but equally affected by the threat to their families.

Only about eight hundred Burmese riflemen reached Imphal. They were given the option of staying or returning and about half of them opted to return home. The other half were employed on various intelligence tasks, notably with the Chindits to whom they were invaluable. Only the 2nd Battalion, under Lieutenant-Colonel O'Callaghan, who were mostly Karens, reached India as a formed unit although Lieutenant-Colonel Abernethy, of the 4th Battalion, brought out a composite unit of about the same strength.

The Burma Military Police were highly regarded in peace-time but were too short of men to deal with the widespread disruption of war. The Burma Frontier Force units formed from them often did good work on patrol, providing information and protecting dumps. However, they were subject to the same stresses as the Burma Rifles and towards the end one or two units are alleged to have mutinied and gone over to the enemy.

The Royal Air Force

Like the Army, the Royal Air Force in Burma was a casualty of Whitehall policy. When the war broke out their operational strength consisted of one squadron of sub-standard Buffalo fighters. Fortunately the AVG contributed a squadron of more modern Curtiss Tomahawks and agreed to fight under RAF control. Between the two of them they succeeded, with the help of the one radar equipment and the efficient Burma Observer Corps[10], in seizing air superiority over Rangoon. During January 1942, the RAF was reinforced with some old Hurricanes and a handful of Blenheims from the Middle East. With these they managed to fight successfully against superior numbers while harassing very successfully the Japanese ground forces. It is a fact that reflects great credit on the two Allied air forces that, out of the vital reinforcement convoys sailing into Rangoon, not a single ship was sunk.

The pilots, from all parts of the Empire, were young, daring and brave and it was remarkable that they stood up so well to the much superior numbers of the Japanese Air Force. Unlike in the UK, their problem was that they had more pilots than aircraft. This was not the fault of the ground staff, who, desperately short of spares, performed prodigies of improvisation to keep damaged aircraft serviceable. However, when Rangoon was lost and the enemy approach forced a move to Magwe, the RAF lacked adequate early warning. The urgency of taking suitable measures to counteract this weakness was perhaps not fully realised. The enemy, however, realised it only too well and once their much superior air force was in a position to eliminate them, it quickly did so.

Control of the air, or at least air equality, was essential to success on the ground in Burma as everywhere else and the great battles of 1944. and the reconquest of Burma in 1945, were to be truly joint Army/RAF operations. But in 1941-2 Whitehall had let the RAF down badly in Burma by failing to provide even the minimum requirements for air defence.

The Tactical Policy

The British were quite unprepared for the type of warfare they were to encounter. In some respects it was a more sophisticated version of the 'wilderness warfare' that had initially so confounded the 'redcoats' fighting against the North American Indians in the mid-18th century. Wavell summed it up:[11]

---

9. As Kipling had noted. "A Snider squibbed in the jungle, somebody laughed and fled and the men of the First Shikaris picked up their Subaltern, dead, with a big blue mark in his forehead and the back blown out of his head."

10. Organised by the civilian Post and Telegraph department.

11. Supplement to *The London Gazette* dated 11 March 1948, para.28.

"We found ourselves up against a new feature in warfare - an enemy fully armed, disciplined, and trained on the continental model using the mobility, independence of communications and unorthodox tactics of the savage in thick jungle. It was perhaps little wonder that our troops were out-manoeuvred and became bewildered."

During the campaign there were two main tactical controversies. The first was about the policy in Phase 1. Wavell ordered, and Hutton loyally obeyed him, that the Japanese should be fought as far forward as possible, that is at Kawkareik and Moulmein and then on the line of the Salween. His reason was the excellent one that, if only sufficient delay could be imposed, the reinforcements that he had been promised could be got in through Rangoon and Burma might be saved. The forward policy would also enable the RAF to have adequate early warning and give air cover to the convoys.

To General Smyth, already aware of the formidable Japanese strength, such a policy was unwise. The distances were great and his troops were few. The Japanese could concentrate superior force wherever they chose so that his units would inevitably get defeated in detail. He therefore wished to withdraw to the Bilin River for his first check and then fight the main battle for Rangoon on the line of the Sittang.

Although Wavell was right in theory, in practice, due to the inexperience of the troops, the forward policy was not very successful. It provided little extra delay and there were many losses, which did not help to build up morale. It would, of course, have been more successful if the Burma Rifles had been trained to operate in a guerrilla role. If Wavell had been in closer touch with the realities, instead of being exiled in Java, he might well have taken a different view.

The second controversy was at Prome. Wavell believed strongly that an offensive policy would prove effective against the Japanese and might even yet turn the scales before they were reinforced through Rangoon. Again he was right in theory, but he had not yet realised either the relative strengths of the two sides, or what an effective riposte the enemy could mount to a road-bound force. This led to the defeat at Shwedaung which, together with the Chinese defeat at Toungoo, sealed the fate of central Burma.

The Strategic Policy

Both sides knew that Rangoon was the key to Burma. The largest city, the only major port, the centre of industry, the home of many skilled workers, a huge depot of military stores, close to a good airfield complex, it was clear that who-ever held it and its sea approaches could, with adequate reinforcement, dominate

Burma. British policy was to hold it as long as possible but not to get surrounded there. Japanese policy was to travel across-country with lightly equipped forces at maximum speed and capture Rangoon before either the British could be sufficiently reinforced to stop them, or the Chinese could assemble to attack their northern flank.

In the event, the scandalous lack of preparation for war, the crippling command set-up and the fatal shortage of aircraft and experienced troops, played into Japanese hands. The Chinese were encouraged by the Japanese to believe that a thrust against the Burma Road would come through the northern Shan States (as it well might have done) and so were reluctant to advance south of Mandalay. But it was a close-run thing. Certainly before, and probably even after, the Sittang disaster, 17 Division, reinforced with 63 Brigade, could have defeated the not very strong *55 Division*. If, as well as the 7th Armoured Brigade, one good battle-experienced division such as the 7th Australian, together with a modest accretion of aircraft, had also been available, both Japanese divisions, short of ammunition as they were, might well have been defeated and driven back. With Chinese intervention they might then have been routed. What would have happened next can only be speculation but certainly such a reverse for the Japanese would have had a profound effect on the war in South-East Asia and on British prestige.

However it proved impossible to get a good division there in time,[12] and after the last despairing throw at Shwedaung and the withdrawal of the RAF from Burma, it was clear that, as the Japanese strength was rapidly increasing, the chances of holding any part of Burma were slim. When the Chinese were rapidly defeated and Lashio was lost, there was no chance at all. The problem then became to protect the many civilians trying to reach India and to withdraw after them before the monsoon arrived. Under steady pressure from the Japanese, and in very difficult circumstances, this withdrawal was achieved with considerable skill.

Casualties

The Japanese lost 2401 men killed in this campaign in all the fighting against both British and Chinese. At least half of these were killed in fighting against the British (see Appendix 8), and this figure was about the same as the official total for British killed. The figures for Chinese losses are not available and it is doubtful whether any such records were kept. British losses, as is inevitable in such a

---

12. Consideration was given by the War Cabinet to diverting the 18th British Division to Burma, rather than to Singapore. It was not battle-experienced and had been trained for war in the Middle East. A terrible decision had to be taken and it was allowed, largely for political and not military reasons, to continue on its fateful voyage.

long retreat, were complicated by the large number of "missing" and it is probable that the full number of British (including Indian) soldiers who were killed or
who died was about double the official figure. This is not a high figure when one
considers the heat and the length of the withdrawal through a lawless and sometimes ill-intentioned population. It might have been far worse. In addition,
between four and five thousand British (of whom about 350 were from the UK)
were taken prisoner.

The combined strength of the two British formations as they marched back
into India was 12,751. Sadly 26 per cent of this number went sick within ten days
of reaching Imphal, nearly all with malaria and dysentery contracted in the last
stages of the retreat in the Kabaw valley.[13]

A Harsh Lesson Learned Well

Although to superficial observers the British had once again suffered a humiliating reverse, the Army in Burma had in fact done rather better than was generally realised. True, it had been defeated, had lost all its heavy equipment and had
been driven out of Burma; but as Kirby's official history observed, "the British
army in Burma was called upon to carry out a task beyond its powers." In his sim-
ming-up of the campaign General Wavell wrote:[14]

> "The troops who fought in the Burma Campaign were subjected to a
> very severe strain. They were opposed by a well-trained, vigorous and
> determined enemy, usually superior in numbers; they had to fight in a type
> of country and under conditions quite unfamiliar to the majority; they had
> no relief and very little rest during more than five months; in the later stages
> they were almost entirely deprived of air support... In the circumstances the
> troops put up a remarkable performance and showed a fine fighting spirit."

As ever in severe conditions, the units with high discipline fared best. They
had both fewer battle and fewer sickness casualties. Although some of the hastily raised Indian line of communication troops disintegrated, as did all but two of
the Burmese Rifle battalions, nearly all the British and Indian fighting units of the
two divisions marched into India as formed (although depleted) units and with all
their personal weapons. To the surprise of many observers, the morale of these
fighting units was high, and it remained so in spite of the lack of medical facilities, the shortage of food and the lack of any form of amenity. The main reason
was their knowledge that the fighting had been much less one-sided than was
apparent from the result and their conviction that, with proper equipment and
with adequate air support, they knew how to beat their formidable enemy.

With one or two exceptions the British and Indian troops had been totally inexperienced when they started the campaign. In the early stages they made all the beginners' mistakes, but by the end of the five-month campaign, sickness and the Japanese had weeded out the weak, and those that remained, both officers and men, were veterans. Of course, they were lucky. The geography of Singapore had led inexorably to disaster, but the Army in Burma had the good fortune to have a sanctuary within reach. Thanks to the skill of their leaders, and the resilience and fortitude of their soldiers, the British managed to reach that sanctuary.

There is no doubt that a forced retreat clears the mind wonderfully. Weaknesses and unrealistic theories are mercilessly exposed. General Slim saw very clearly what was required; basically tougher and more highly-trained Infantry, air superiority and air supply. The units in 17 Division had discovered that war against the Japanese was savage and total, kill or be killed. There was much to learn, and they knew that only hard training could produce the high standards needed for success. But they had also learnt that the Japanese were not supermen, and their performance against them had been steadily improving. Reports at all levels were sent back to training establishments in India describing the many lessons that needed to be learnt to fight a forest war successfully in Burma. The seeds of eventual victory were sown and 18 months later their fruit would ripen.

---

13. A number contracted the very dangerous 'cerebral' malaria, for which the Kabaw valley was notorious and this often proved fatal.

14. Despatch, 14 July 1942.

CHAPTER TWENTY-SIX

Why Burma's Defence Was Neglected

The Background

In May 1940, Winston Churchill was elected Prime Minister as Britain faced defeat. His courage and energy and his magnificently defiant speeches inspired the country. When the RAF defeated the Luftwaffe in the Battle of Britain, the threat of invasion was temporarily removed until the following Spring. Uniquely experienced and supremely self-confident, Churchill then re-organised the higher direction of the war, appointing himself Minister of Defence. He formed a tiny War Cabinet consisting of himself and four others (initially Chamberlain, Attlee, Halifax and Greenwood) but not including any Service ministers. Through this structure, democratically achieved with the full support of Parliament, he controlled every aspect of the nation's affairs and not least the military operations.

In early 1941 it was difficult, in spite of Wavell's brilliant victories over the Italians in the Middle East, to see how Britain could possibly win the war. Most of the Army's equipment had been lost at Dunkirk and had not yet been fully replaced. Britain's lifelines across the Atlantic were seriously threatened. The loss of the French Navy made the naval position in the Mediterranean precarious. The RAF bombing of Germany was ineffective.[1] Britain was virtually bankrupt. A better-planned German attempt to invade Britain, when the Winter storms had abated, seemed likely. The Prime Minister saw clearly that victory was impossible without American help and he set about trying to obtain it.

Churchill Alters the Strategic Priorities

Britain's pre-war strategy had been based, firstly, on the defence of the United Kingdom and its sea communications, for without these the war was lost. Second priority was the defence of the naval base at Singapore from which the Royal Navy, in partnership with the US Navy, could defeat any aggression from the Pacific, that is from Japan, and thus protect Malaya and Australia. Only third priority was the defence of the Middle East. Churchill, however, was a devotee of the Middle East, about which he knew a great deal from World War I, and from where it was possible to attack the Germans and Italians. It was anathema to him to lock up forces in the Far East, about which he knew little, against a threat which seemed to him most unlikely to materialise, when there were Germans to fight in the Middle East.[2] The strategy thus changed to giving priority to the Middle East and putting the Far East at the bottom of the pile.

Churchill, however flawed his views on minor strategy may sometimes have been, was a master of grand strategy. He realised that only Germany was capable of conquering the British Isles, and that if Germany were defeated Japan would be unable to avoid a similar fate. This reinforced his predilection, not shared at this stage by the Americans, for fighting in the Middle East. It seems likely that, in April 1941, he already knew from secret sources that a German attack on Russia was probable. As long as Russia kept fighting, Germany would be unable to deploy sufficient forces in the west to invade Britain. It was therefore vital to do everything possible to help Russia. The only ways in which Britain could do this was at sea, by sending war supplies to Archangel, and, on land, by harassing the enemy in the Middle East. Hitler's invasion of Russia in June removed, for the time being, the possibility of an invasion of Britain but, during the second half of 1941, it was far from certain that Russia would not be defeated. If it were, Britain would again face invasion.

The General Staff of the Army Disagree

In the spring of 1941, the General Staff in the Army became uneasy with this strategy and suggested that the priorities of the Middle East and Far East should be reversed. This provoked a violent reaction from Churchill and, without discussion with the Chiefs of Staff, he issued on 28 April what can best be described as a firman. This 'Directive by the Prime Minister and Minister of Defence' has already been mentioned in Chapter Two. It stated that it was most unlikely that Japan would enter the war, that this was to be accepted as a guide for all plans and actions, and that there was no need to strengthen the existing garrisons of Malaya and Singapore. During the vital six months during which Japan edged forward into Indo-China and built airfields commanding the Gulf of Siam, Churchill adhered firmly to this clear directive. Discussion on the Far East was thus inhibited and one major result was that the growing strategic importance of Burma, as China's supply lines were progressively severed, was ignored.

The CIGS, General Sir John Dill, disagreed strongly with the priority given to the Middle East but was unable to convince the other two Chiefs of Staff. On 6 May, he sent a paper to Churchill which expressed doubt about the wisdom of

---

1. A.J.P. Taylor remarked that "the strategic air offensive of 1940-41 killed more members of the RAF than German civilians." Lewin, Ronald, *Churchill as Warlord*, p.96.
2. General Rommel and German forces started arriving in Libya in February 1941. Captain Basil Liddell-Hart was to comment that "Rommel indirectly produced the fall of Singapore." Stewart, Adrian, *The Underrated Enemy*, p.205.

sending armoured forces from Britain to the Middle East while the threat of invasion remained. He thought that the loss of Egypt would be a calamity but was unlikely and, if it did occur, it would not end the war. Singapore was more important and should have priority over Egypt.³ Churchill did not agree.

In his memoirs, he said:

"Many governments I have seen would have wilted before so grave a pronouncement by the highest professional authority, but I had no difficulty in convincing my political colleagues, and I was of course supported by the Chiefs of the Navy and the Air. My views therefore prevailed and the flow of reinforcements to the Middle East continued unabated."⁴

However, Dill continued to believe that the Far East should be given priority over the Middle East for reinforcement, and later in the year he is said to have been with difficulty dissuaded from resigning on the issue.⁵

Winston Churchill was a firm supporter of the British Empire and so his reluctance to provide adequately for its defence needs some explanation, particularly since the bulk of the troops on which he was relying for operations in the Middle East were Imperial ones.⁶ In his memoirs, he summed up this controversy as follows:

"The confidence which we felt about Home Defence did not extend to the Far East should Japan make war upon us. These anxieties also disturbed Sir John Dill. I retained the impression that Singapore had priority in his mind over Cairo... For my part I did not believe that anything that might happen in Malaya could amount to a fifth part of the loss of Egypt, the Suez Canal and the Middle East. I would not tolerate the idea of abandoning the struggle for Egypt, and was resigned to pay whatever forfeits were exacted in Malaya. This view was also shared by my colleagues [*in the War Cabinet*]."⁷

A point of interest in this statement is the lack of any mention of Burma. The 'Burma Road' to China would shortly become China's only supply route. Its closure threatened the collapse of Chinese resistance and the possible release of up to 20 Japanese divisions for other tasks. China's position in the East was therefore analogous to Russia's in the West, although not of the same magnitude, and its support was an essential Allied interest. Much too late the Prime Minister understood this, for in June 1942 he wrote in a minute to the Chiefs of Staff:

"I have repeatedly stated that the dangers of the collapse for Chiang

Kai-shek is one of the greatest that we have to face at the present time."[8]

There was also another major Allied interest in the Burma Road. Staff talks with the Americans had revealed that, should war come with Japan, the Americans planned to use bases in China to bomb Japan itself. Without an overland supply route, the build-up of such bases would be very difficult.

The Attitude of the United States

After Japan's conquest of Manchuria in 1931, Japan was condemned as an aggressor by the League of Nations. Japan's reaction was to withdraw from the League and little more happened. However, when in 1937 Japan started a further major aggression by launching a full-scale invasion of China, the United States became seriously alarmed. An expansionist Japan was a serious threat to American strategic interests in the Pacific area and also to her, and other nations', commercial interests. However, the United States was firmly isolationist and too weak militarily to do more than give moral and material support to China. The advent of the European war and the possibility, indeed likelihood, of a Europe dominated by Fascist Germany changed all this. President Roosevelt became convinced that Fascism must be defeated and therefore America must expand its military forces and in due course take part in the war. With difficulty, the US Congress was persuaded to authorise a massive expansion of the armed forces. Under the US Constitution, however, war could only be declared by the President with the support of Congress, and with the strong isolationist feeling in America this would be very difficult to obtain. It would, of course, be quite a different matter if the United States were to be attacked. In July 1941, with Germany embroiled with Russia, Roosevelt felt strong enough to risk a war with Japan by applying an oil and steel embargo. The aim was to discourage Japan from undertaking new military adventures and to give decisive help to China. Either Japan must climb down and withdraw from China or there would be war.

Churchill saw the Far East as primarily a naval problem and so, in the absence of a British fleet, he was content to leave the conduct of negotiations with the Japanese in American hands. However, although they were minor players in this great drama, the British had a major interest, for in Hong Kong, Malaya and

3. Churchill, Winston, *The Second World War*, Vol.3, p.373.
4. *ibid*, p.377.
5. Elphick, Peter, *Singapore, The Pregnable Fortress*, p.182.
6. Fourteen Imperial divisions; seven Indian, three Australian, two South African, one New Zealand and one East African. Churchill, Winston, *The Second World War*, Vol.3.
7. *ibid*.
8. Churchill, Winston, *The Second World War*, Vol.4, p.779.

Burma they held three certain targets for Japanese attack if war came. It is clear that Winston Churchill had a very good idea of Roosevelt's aims in the Pacific and where they were heading, but he could not believe, in August 1941, "that Japan would face the combination now forming against her of the US, Great Britain and Russia, while already preoccupied in China."[9]

British Apathy Concerning the Far East

After the Russians had entered the war, the Far East was pushed even further down the scale of priorities. In his memoirs, Churchill gives his views at that time:

> "I confess that in my mind the whole Japanese menace lay in a sinister twilight compared with our other needs. My feeling was that if Japan attacked us the United States would come in. If the United States did not come in we had no means of defending the Dutch East Indies or indeed our own Empire in the East. If, on the other hand, Japanese aggression drew in America I would be content to have it. On this I rested. Our priorities during 1941 stood: first, the defence of the Island, including the threat of invasion and the U-boat war; secondly the struggle in the Middle East and Mediterranean; thirdly, after June, supplies to Soviet Russia; and, last of all, resistance to a Japanese assault... I am sure that nothing we could have spared at this time, even at the cost of wrecking the Middle Eastern theatre, or cutting off supplies to the Soviet, would have changed the march of fate in Malaya. On the other hand, the entry of the United States into the war would overwhelm all evils put together."[10]

Again there is no mention of Burma in this statement. It is outside the scope of this book to speculate whether such reinforcements as could have been made available would have altered "the march of fate" in Malaya. But there is no doubt that relatively small air and ground forces would have tipped the balance in Burma without "wrecking the Middle Eastern Theatre" or "cutting off supplies to Russia" Churchill's fatal directive of 28 April seems to have continued in operation until the Japanese attack at the beginning of December. But for this blight, much could have been achieved in Burma in those six months. Wavell, now C-in-C in India, saw clearly the fatal weakness of the command set-up. In his despatch he said:

> "Except as a subsidiary air base, Burma hardly entered into the strategical plans of the Far East Command... Similarly in administration the War Office was too far away and too occupied with other matters to concern

itself with, or even to understand, the needs of Burma, to which India would have given sympathetic consideration as part of her own defence problem."[11]

As the Japanese edged nearer, Wavell flew to London in September 1941 and pointed out forcibly that the defence of Burma was of major strategic importance to the Allies and was also an essential part of the defence of India.[12] India was the only place from which reinforcements could be provided for Burma in an emergency and Burma's defence should certainly be made India's responsibility. This plea was refused by the Chiefs of Staff who considered, for some reason not now apparent, that the defence of Burma needed to be closely co-ordinated with that of Malaya. As a result, Wavell, although he perceived that to close the Burma Road was likely to be a Japanese aim second only in importance to the capture of the Indonesian oilfields, could do nothing to put Burma on to a war footing or to reinforce and prepare it for the coming war. This was extremely frustrating for him as he watched the stealthy Japanese approach. Having visited Burma and Singapore he repeated his request again in November. This time his plea was supported by the Chiefs but he got no answer from the War Cabinet.

As it was, only seven per cent of the total British and Imperial ground forces was allotted to what Churchill described as the "fortress garrisons" of the Far East, that is Hong Kong, Borneo, Malaya and Burma.[13] The naval base at Singapore had been designed to support a British fleet operating in the South China Sea. But since the fall of France it had been clear that Britain was quite unable to provide such a fleet. In 1941, Singapore was a bluff. As war with Japan became imminent, Churchill persuaded the Admiralty to raise the stakes by sending two modern capital ships to Singapore at the last moment, partly as a 'deterrent' and partly to honour Britain's repeated assurances to Australia that a British Fleet would go to Singapore if the Japanese were to launch an attack. But as the Japanese with their highly trained Naval Air Force well knew, without air support such ships, though dangerous, could be neutralised.

Was the Japanese War Unavoidable?

If priorities had been different and Malaya and Burma had been adequately

9. Churchill, Winston, *The Second World War*, Vol.3.

10. *ibid*, p.522.

11. *The London Gazettte*, 11 March 1948.

12. Three previous Commanders-in-Chief in India, Field-Marshal Sir Philip Chetwode, General Sir Robert Cassels and General Sir Claude Auchinleck had made the same plea. Kirby, S.W., *The War Against Japan*, Vol.2, p.6.

13. Churchill, Winston, *The Second World War*, Vol.3, p.453. *Directive dated 9 October 1941.*

reinforced in 1941, particularly in the air, Thailand, whose assistance, or at least acquiescence, was vital to the Japanese plans, might well have joined the Allies. For the Japanese, the odds against success would then have been much greater and it might have deterred them. As it was, the strength of the RAF in Malaya and Burma was so inadequate that no help could be offered to the Thais if they were to be attacked. This was a crucial factor in the Thai decision not to resist the Japanese incursion. The arrival of HMS *Prince of Wales* and *Repulse* made the Thai Prime Minister pause in reaching a decision, but the successful arrival of the Japanese convoys indicated to him that the Japanese were too strong to be resisted.[14]

The British Ambassador in Tokyo, Sir Robert Craigie, had advised that the war could be prevented in another way. To Churchill's annoyance, he insisted on repeating his views in his report on his return.[15] His view was that if an offer of small quantities of oil and steel had been made in return for Japanese withdrawal from South Indo-China, the hand of the still powerful peace faction in Japan would have been strengthened and the offer might well have been accepted. War would have been averted for the time being and before long it would have become clear that Germany was not going to defeat Russia. This would have deterred Japan from her southern gamble. In his view it was the combination of American determination to enforce a crippling blockade and British military weakness that made war in South-East Asia inevitable.

Britain Faces up At Last to the Far East Problem

Although the likelihood of a Japanese attack had been known for some months, and the certainty for at least a week before it took place, it was the shock of Pearl Harbour, followed swiftly by the sinking of HMS *Prince of Wales* and *Repulse* and the defeat of the RAF in north Malaya, that brought a change of attitude in London. There were promises of aircraft, tanks and brigades now miraculously available, but mostly it was far too late for them to reach their destinations. Burma was at last put under Wavell's command on 12 December and in the next two weeks he changed the Army Commander, boosted up the staff and did everything possible in the time to make this peaceful backwater ready for war. After 19 dynamic days he was suddenly ordered by the Chiefs of Staff to go to Java and assume Supreme Command of all American, British, Dutch and Australian forces fighting the Japanese in or around Burma, Malaya, Indonesia and the Philippines. In Washington, Churchill, backed by the War Cabinet and the COS, argued strongly against this arrangement, but the Americans were very keen on it, and so in the first flush of the vital alliance, he had no choice but to agree. For AHQ Burma this was a disaster. It put their Theatre Commander virtually out of touch two thousand miles away and his orders, relayed through India, were often out of date by the time they arrived.

As the swift Japanese advance in Malaya progressed, the strategic importance of Burma and the Burma Road was at last recognised. Churchill, having heard the American views, now felt that "Burma was more important than Singapore"[16] and even suggested that it might be best to cut losses in Singapore by "blowing the docks and naval base to pieces" and concentrating everything on the defence of Burma.[17] However militarily desirable, this was politically impossible, so frantic efforts were now made to reinforce Burma. Only three formations had any chance of reaching Rangoon before it fell. 18 British Division was on its way to the Middle East and, mainly for political reasons, was diverted to Singapore. The 7th Armoured Brigade was on its way to Singapore and was diverted to Rangoon. The 7th Australian Division was on its way back to Java from the Middle East. Churchill tried his hardest to get it diverted to Burma, where it might have turned the tide, but the Australian government felt it had been let down by the weakness of the Singapore garrison, in their view an "inexcusable betrayal" of trust, and refused permission in spite of a personal requests from Churchill and Roosevelt. With this refusal, the last chance of defending Burma had gone.

Conclusion

The loss of Malaya and Burma in less than six months was a lasting blow to Britain's prestige in the Far East and to the record of the British Empire. The main justification of the Empire to its subjects was that it provided good and fair government based on the preservation of internal law and order while guaranteeing protection from external attack. The failure to provide that protection in the Far East was a failure of Imperial duty which was to strain, for years to come, Britain's relationship with Malaya, Australia and New Zealand.

The loss of Burma in particular was a serious reverse to the Allied cause. It weakened China and seriously delayed the American plan for the strategic bombing of Japan.

In his history of the war, Winston Churchill makes no attempt to evade his

---

14. The sinking of these two great ships also sounded the death-knell of the British Far Eastern strategy of the inter-war years. The naval base at Singapore was revealed as the white elephant that it was.

15. Sir Robert Craigie's first despatch, written on his return in 1942, was openly critical of British policy and he was invited to revise it. He did so producing a sanitised version in February 1943 which, however, still contained his main argument which he refused to modify. It was given a very limited circulation. *Public Record Office, FO 371/35957*.

16. Butler, J.R.M., *Grand Strategy*, Vol.3, p.417.

17. Lewin, Ronald, *Churchill as Warlord*, p.134.

direct responsibility for the Far Eastern defeats. He could not believe that the Japanese would risk war with America but, if they did, he was sure that neither Australia nor New Zealand would be directly threatened and that Hong Kong and Borneo were indefensible. Britain had not the resources to be strong everywhere and, after allowing for the essential defence of the UK, it was his decision to allot the maximum strength to the Middle East and to risk the possible loss of Malaya and Singapore. No doubt he was influenced to some extent by the knowledge that if Japan did *not* attack, his decision would be proved right, while if it did attack, the Americans would enter the war and eventual victory would be ensured.

Two unfortunate decisions in Whitehall helped to seal the fate of Burma. The first was Churchill's directive of 28 April which seems to have anaesthetised discussion of Far Eastern problems. It also seems to have prevented Churchill himself, now deeply involved in the detail of over-ambitious Middle-Eastern operations, from discerning Burma's growing strategic importance and vulnerability. The second unfortunate decision was the failure of the Chiefs of Staff to agree to Wavell's powerful plea that GHQ India should be responsible for Burma's defence. Many vital months of preparation for meeting an attack were thereby lost. No outside resources were required to undertake such essential tasks as studying defence problems on the ground, setting up an Intelligence organisation, providing for civil defence, providing military control of the transport systems, preparing training pamphlets and maps, and improving communications. All that was required was time.

The tragedy of Burma was that the diversion of only a small amount of battle-experienced air and ground forces from the Middle East in 1941 would have been sufficient to prevent the Sittang disaster and, with Chinese help, to hold Rangoon and defeat the phase one Japanese attack.[18] Such a reverse for the Japanese at this early stage would have had a profound psychological effect and the war in the Far East would certainly have taken a very different turn.

Winston Churchill was to lead Britain with consummate skill on its march to eventual victory; but no man is infallible and, in 1941, over Burma, he stumbled.

---

18. In addition to the two divisions (1 Burdiv and 17 Division) and the armoured brigade which he already had, Hutton asked for one infantry division to hold the line of the Sittang and take the offensive, and another to be in reserve in case of a seaborne assault on Rangoon. Kirby, S.W., *The War Against Japan*, Vol.2, p.79.

The British Command Structure for the First Burma Campaign

1. **Up to 11 December 1941**

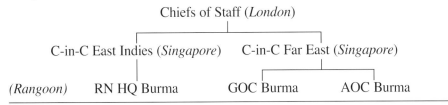

Chiefs of Staff (*London*)

C-in-C East Indies (*Singapore*)   C-in-C Far East (*Singapore*)

(*Rangoon*)   RN HQ Burma   GOC Burma   AOC Burma

2. **13 - 30 December 1941**

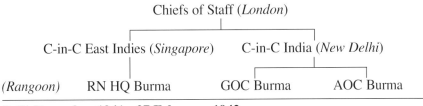

Chiefs of Staff (*London*)

C-in-C East Indies (*Singapore*)   C-in-C India (*New Delhi*)

(*Rangoon*)   RN HQ Burma   GOC Burma   AOC Burma

3. **31 December 1941 - 27 February 1942**

Combined UK/US Chiefs of Staff (*London, Washington*)

C-in-C ABDACOM (Wavell *at Bandoeng*)

(*Rangoon*)   RN HQ Burma   GOC Burma   AOC Burma

4. **28 February - 5 March 1942**

Reverts to the structure in 2 above but with the RN HQ coming under C-in-C Eastern Fleet at Colombo.

5. **6 March - 20 May 1942**

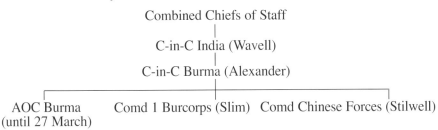

Combined Chiefs of Staff

C-in-C India (Wavell)

C-in-C Burma (Alexander)

AOC Burma   Comd 1 Burcorps (Slim)   Comd Chinese Forces (Stilwell)
(until 27 March)

APPENDIX TWO

The Order of Battle of the Army in Burma

By the end of December 1941 the composition of the Army in Burma was:[1]

Army Headquarters, (Rangoon) (*Hutton, Alexander*)
In Army Reserve
1st Armoured Car Company, BAF
1st HAA Regiment, RA, BAF

Rangoon Garrison
1st Gloucestershire Regiment (*Bagot, Sharpe, Bagot*)
3rd Burma Rifles (less two coys) (*Taylor*)

1st Burma Division (Southern Shan States) (*Maj-Gen J. Bruce Scott*)
27th Indian Mountain Regiment (*Constable*)
  2nd Indian Mountain Battery (*Hartley*)
  5th Indian Mountain Battery (*Wilberforce*)
  23rd Indian Mountain Battery (*Witherow*)
5th Field Battery, RA, BAF [2]
56 Field Company, Madras S&M(*Sloot, Eccles, Garthwaite*)
50th Field Park Company, Madras S&M (*Kent*)
Malerkotla Field Company, S&M (*Orgill*)
1st Burma Field Company, S&M (*Ward*)
BFF1, BFF3, BFF4, BFF5[3]

1st Burma Infantry Brigade (*Farwell*)
  2nd King's Own Yorkshire Light Infantry (*Keagan, Tynte, Chadwick*)
  1st Burma Rifles
  5th Burma Rifles (*Devenish-Meares*)

2nd Burma Brigade (*Bourke*)
  1st/7th Gurkha Rifles (*White, Williams*)
  Tenasserim Battalion, BAF

360

2nd Burma Brigade (cont'd)
    2nd Burma Rifles *(O'Callaghan)*
    4th Burma Rifles *(Abernethy)*
    6th Burma Rifles *(Cotton)*
    8th Burma Rifles *(Bowers)*
    Two companies 3rd Burma Rifles
    BFF2

<u>13th Indian Brigade</u> *(Curtis, Rae)*
    5th/1st Punjab Regiment *(Marsland, Bell)*
    2nd/7th Rajput Regiment *(Marsland, Rae, Grant)*
    1st/18th Royal Garwhal Rifles *(Barlow, Lyle)*

<u>16th Indian Brigade</u> *(Jones)*
    1st/9th Royal Jat Regiment *(Hey, Godley)*
    4th/12th Frontier Force Regiment *(Edward, Edwards-Stuart)*
    7th Burma Rifles *(McCarthy)*

This meagre force was gradually built up as described in the narrative and by the time Rangoon fell and no further reinforcements were possible except by air, the following units had arrived:

January 1942
Army Troops
    8th HAA Battery RA
    8th Indian HAA Battery
    3rd Indian LAA Battery *(MacFetridge)*

HQ 17 Division *(Maj-Gens Smyth, Cowan)*
    <u>46th Infantry Brigade</u> *(Ekin)*
        7th/10th Baluch Regiment *(Dyer, Lindsay)*
        5th/17th Dogra Regiment *(Power, McIntyre)*
        3rd/7th Gurkha Rifles *(Stevenson)*

1. Subsequent Commanders are also shown.
2. Service in the Burma Auxiliary Force (BAF) was in 1940 made obligatory for all European British subjects of military age.
3. BFF units were formed in 1941 from Indians and Gurkhas in the Burma Military Police and domiciled in Burma. They were controlled by the Army but continued to be administered by the civil authorities. They were organised into two troops of mounted Infantry and three Infantry columns, each about 100 strong. Their initial role was to harass and delay any enemy advance.

48th Infantry Brigade *(Hugh-Jones, Cameron)*
   1st/3rd Gurkha Rifles *(Ballinger, Thornton)*
   1st/4th Gurkha Rifles *(Lentaigne)*
   2nd/5th Royal Gurkha Rifles *(Cameron, Townsend)*

February 1942
Divisional Troops 17 Division
   28th Mountain Regiment *(Peskett)*
     12 Mountain Battery *(Hume)*
     15 Mountain Battery *(Lock)*
     28 Mountain Battery *(Chaplin)*
   2nd Indian A-Tk Regiment *(less most of its guns)*
   24th Field Company, Bombay S&M *(Smith, Darley)*
   60 Field Company, Madras S&M *(Kochhar)*
   17 Divisional Signals *(Allen)*

7th Armoured Brigade *(Anstice)*
   414 Field Battery, RHA *(Pereira)*
   'A' Battery, 95th A-Tk Regiment, RA
   7th Hussars *(Fosdick)*
   2nd Royal Tank Regiment *(Chute, Yule)*

Three British Infantry battalions arrived separately as reinforcements from India in the last days of January and early February. Two of them joined the fighting almost at once. Only one, the 1st West Yorkshire Regiment, which, after the loss of Rangoon provided the Infantry support for the 7th Armoured Brigade, was permanently attached to any one formation. The battalions were:
   1st West Yorkshire Regiment *(Marindin)*
   1st Cameronians *(Thomas)*
   2nd Duke of Wellington's Regiment *(Owen, Faithfull, Theyre)*

3 March 1942
   Divisional Troops 17 Division
     1st Indian Field Regiment *(Digges)*
     70th Field Company, Bengal S&M *(Lyall Grant)*
   63rd Infantry Brigade *(Wickham, Barlow)*
     1st/11th Sikh Regiment *(McLaren, Windsor-Aubrey)*
     2nd/13th Frontier Force Rifles *(Grey, Elsmie, Hofman)*
     1st/10th Gurkha Rifles *(Leonard, McCready)*

7th Armoured Brigade was under command of Army HQ. 46 and 48 Brigades came under command of 17 Division but after the heavy losses at the Sittang crossing, 46 Brigade was disbanded and on arrival 63 Brigade replaced it in 17 Division. The 1st/7th and 3rd/7th Gurkhas were amalgamated and joined 48 Brigade.

After the loss of Rangoon it became impossible to reinforce the Army in Burma except by air. At the end of March one more major unit was flown in. This was:

The 1st Royal Inniskilling Fusiliers *(Cox, McConnell, Clifford)*

There were no more, but a trickle of reinforcements were flown in by the handful of DC 2 and DC 3 aircraft held by 31 Bomber/Transport Squadron RAF based in India. This squadron also did the most valiant work in evacuating casualties and refugees.

APPENDIX THREE

Notes on the British Forces in Burma
in the 1942 Campaign

Abbreviations

1. The abbreviations used in this book are those most commonly used in conversation. The only exception is that the letter 'R' is inserted in certain cases where the units have the word 'Royal' in their title. They are not the official abbreviations used in military messages.

Numbering of Units in the British Army

2. In the Royal Armoured Corps, units of battalion size were called 'regiments' and the Cavalry used their historic names. In the Royal Tank Regiment, however, the 'regiments' (of battalion size) were numbered consecutively as they were formed.

3. In the Royal Artillery, field-gun units in armoured divisions were entitled to the suffix RHA (Royal Horse Artillery). This applied to the only British field-gun battery in this campaign, which was the one supporting 7th Armoured Brigade.

4. There were no Royal Engineer units in Burma at this time but the Indian and Burmese Engineers were trained by RE officers and NCOs and officered very largely by RE officers.

5. Infantry battalions were numbered consecutively within their parent Regiment. Thus the 2nd KOYLI was the second battalion of the King's Own Yorkshire Light Infantry Regiment.

Numbering of Units in the Indian Army

6. Gunner units were numbered consecutively, by type, as they were formed. In this campaign, the 1st Indian Field Regiment and the 3rd Indian Light Anti-Aircraft Battery took a prominent part.

7. Mountain Gun batteries had a long and distinguished history in the Indian Army. They were originally numbered consecutively and batteries raised before 1919 had a name, as in 5 (Bombay) Mountain Battery. Although organised into regiments in this campaign they retained much of the form of independent units.

8. The field engineer units in the Corps of Indian Engineers still kept the name of 'Sappers and Miners'. They were raised and trained at three different centres and the groups retained the names of the three original British Presidencies in India, that is Madras, Bengal and Bombay. Their field companies were indepen-

dent units. Blocks of numbers were issued to each centre and in these blocks the units were numbered consecutively.

9. Infantry Regiments in the Indian Army were organised into eighteen Regiments, each of which had a number and a name. In peace-time, each regiment had a training battalion and between two and five active battalions. When war came, the regiments in this volunteer army expanded to produce many more active battalions. So the 7th/10th Baluch battalion would be the seventh battalion of the 10th Baluch Regiment. Some confusion can be caused by the two Frontier Force Regiments, the 12th Frontier Force Regiment (12 FFR) and the 13th Frontier Force Rifles (13 FFRif).

10. The Gurkhas were part of the Indian Army but, being volunteers from the allied country of Nepal, were numbered separately. They were divided into ten regiments, each of which expanded from two to four battalions. Thus the 1st/4th was the first battalion of the 4th Prince of Wales' Own Gurkha Rifles. One regiment, the Fifth, had been awarded the title Royal and so is abbreviated as the 2nd/5th R Gurkhas.

Ranks in the Indian Army

11. Excluding the Indian Cavalry, who took no part in this campaign, the style of Indian private soldiers was in general similar to their British counterparts, *e.g.* Gunner, Sapper, Rifleman. Infantry regiments not styled as 'Rifles' called their private soldiers by the traditional name of Sepoys. Instead of Sergeant, Corporal and Lance Corporal, the equivalent NCO ranks were called Havildar, Naik and Lance Naik.

12. An unusual feature of the Indian Army were the Viceroy's Commissioned Officers. These Indian junior officers were experienced long-term soldiers and formed the backbone of the Indian Army. In general, each platoon had a Jemadar, each company a Subedar, and each battalion a Subedar-Major. In the Gurkhas, in deference to the independence of Nepal, VCOs were styled Gurkha Officers. As the number of British officers in an Indian Infantry battalion was only half that in a similar British battalion, it was common for some Jemadars to command platoons, and, after casualties in battle, for some companies to be commanded by Subedars.

13. The VCOs formed a vital link between the British officers and their Indian soldiers. They were able to help young British officers to understand factors, such as varieties of religion and caste, which influenced their men. The VCOs' job was to settle the minor grievances that worried the soldiers and to alert his officer to any that might become major ones and so needed to be quickly settled. This liaison was particularly important in war when many officers were new to India, could speak Urdu or Gurkhali only indifferently and so found direct com-

munication with their men difficult.

The Burma Army

14. At the outbreak of World War II, the Burma Army consisted of four battalions and these were doubled to eight in the next two years. Initially the soldiers were all recruited either from Indians and Gurkhas domiciled in Burma, or from the sturdy and trustworthy hill tribes, the Karens in the south and the Chins and Kachins in the north. Under political pressure, however, some battalions included a company of Burmans, considered less reliable, from the central plains. Battalions had very few British officers and resources for training were scanty. After the Japanese war had started it was suggested that the Burma Army should have been trained in a guerrilla role, but this would never have been politically acceptable. Dacoits, or brigands, living in the forests and preying on villagers, had long been a problem in Burma and the Government had no wish to train potential reinforcements for them.

15. A small voluntary force, recruited from Europeans, Anglo-Indians and Anglo-Burmese, was called the Burma Auxiliary Force. They had an armoured car unit, a field gun battery, a HAA battery and some other small units. Unfortunately the spirit and courage of these units was largely nullified by their obsolete equipment.

The Burma Military Police

16. Before the war, the internal and external security of Burma rested with the well-respected nine battalions of the Burma Military Police (BMP). In 1938, six of these battalions were converted into the Burma Frontier Force (BFF) and, on the outbreak of war, were given the additional task of protection of the airfields. A number of special units were now raised from the BFF, and styled FF1, FF2, *etc*. (In the narrative these units are styled BFF 1 etc. to avoid confusion with Frontier Force units in the Indian Army.) Their task was to harass and delay any enemy advance and they were organised into five companies, two of which were mounted infantry. A month before the Japanese war started, the BFF was transferred from civil to military control, but continued to be administered by the civil government.

Followers

17. It was the custom in India for units, British and Indian, to have an official scale of Indian civilian camp followers attached to them. These unarmed men comprised cooks, tailors, saddlery and boot repairers, and so on, and their value was recorded in Kipling's verses about Gunga Din. They made units self-contained for minor repairs, overcame certain religious scruples and relieved soldiers for their main task. In 1942 there were several thousand 'followers' with the Army in Burma. Later their numbers were much reduced and soldiers on active service became more self-sufficient.

The RAF Order of Battle

The Order of Battle

1. In December 1941 the handful of aircraft available for the defence of Rangoon was based on and around the airfield of Mingaladon about 15 miles north of Rangoon. Air HQ, commanded by a Group Captain, was housed in Rangoon University near Army HQ. The air force consisted of:

> 67 Squadron RAF (18 'Buffaloes', obsolescent fighters)
> Burma Volunteer Air Force (11 'Tiger Moths', communication tasks)
> 3 Squadron, American Volunteer Group (21 'Tomahawks' or P-40s)

This tiny force was all that was available to meet the two major air raids on Rangoon on 23 and 25 December. 60 Squadron (Blenheims) was also nominally on the strength but when the Japanese attacked it was training in Malaya and never returned to Burma.

2. On 1 January, Air Vice-Marshal Stevenson arrived to take over command and established 221 Group Headquarters. He estimated his requirement as fourteen Hurricane squadrons and eight Blenheim squadrons. On 7 January, 113 Squadron (Blenheims) arrived and it was possible to start limited offensive action. By the end of January there were only four Buffaloes left, but Hurricanes for three fighter squadrons were being flown in from Iraq in nine stages.

3. During January and February his force increased by:
HQ 221 Group
17 Squadron, RAF (Hurricanes)
135 Squadron, RAF (Hurricanes)
113 Squadron, RAF (Blenheims)
28 Squadron, RAF (Lysanders)
1 Squadron, IAF (Lysanders) *(These army co-operation planes were sometimes used as light bombers)*
and in early March:
45 Squadron, RAF (Blenheims)

4. The RAF ground organisation to support this force had been built up in an equally piecemeal way and was gravely lacking in spares and tools. This was unfortunate as the Hurricanes in particular were being intensely used on ground attack missions as well as in an air defence role and many pilots were flying three missions a day. Inevitably they suffered much damage. As a result, the maximum force that could be assembled during February and early March never exceeded six Blenheims, 12 Hurricanes and 12 Tomahawks.[1]

5. In late March the Japanese decided to eliminate the enemy air opposition and assembled a powerful strike force, using most of 3rd and 5th Air Divisions. The RAF and AVG were driven out of Burma to India and China repectively. RAF support to the Army in Burma was then confined to air transport based in India to evacuate casualties and evacuees and, in May, some bombing of Japanese river craft.

Siting of Airfields

6. A number of simple emergency airfields had been built in 1941 by the Burma Public Works Department, their sites having been chosen by the RAF under direction from Air HQ in Singapore. If Burma had been considered as an extension of the air defence of Eastern India, as it would have been if GHQ India had been in command, the siting would have been different. Most airfields were located in the Sittang valley or forward of it. Air Vice-Marshal Stevenson was to maintain that they were too far forward, and indefensible because they could not be given adequate radar protection. In his view they should have been in the Irrawaddy and Chindwin valleys where it was possible to give advanced warning of an enemy attack.

---

1. Cotton, S/Ldr 'Bush', *Hurricanes Over Burma*.

The Chinese Expeditionary Force

1. The Chinese Expeditionary Force began to arrive in Burma in mid-March and consisted of:

```
                    C-in-C (General Stilwell, US Army)
                                    |
                    Deputy C-in-C (Lt-Gen. Lo Cho Ying)
                                    |
        _____
        |                          |                           |
5th A/Division (Lt-Gen. Tu)  6th A/Division(Lt-Gen. Kan)  66th A/Division (Lt-Gen. Chang)
        |                          |                           |
22 D/Brigade (M-Gen. Liao)  49 D/Brigade (M-Gen. Peng)  28 D/Brigade (M-Gen. Liu)
96 D/Brigade (M-Gen. Yu)    55 D/Brigade (M-Gen. Ch'en)  38 D/Brigade (Lt-Gen. Sun)
200 D/Brigade (M-Gen. Tai)  93 D/Brigade (M-Gen. Lu)
```

2. These were said to be some of the best troops in the Chinese Army and certainly on several occasions they fought very well. Their indifference to time, however, and of course the language barrier, made co-operation difficult. A problem for British and Indian troops was to distinguish the Chinese from Japanese (and indeed from Gurkhas and Burmese) and some unfortunate mistakes were inevitable.

3. The move of the Chinese Expeditionary Force to Burma was an epic in itself, for it involved being transported for hundreds of miles through mountainous country before the railhead at Lashio could be reached. It would have been logistically impossible had it not been for the American war material, such as ammunition, trucks and petrol, which was coming up in the opposite direction from Rangoon.

4. The British guaranteed to supply all Chinese forces in Burma with rice, their staple diet, and with medical support. At its peak, the task of supplying rice, for which a Burmese-speaking British liaison officer had to be provided with each formation, required the use of three hundred lorries a day.

5. The Chinese had virtually no medical services. They had not before operated outside their own country where their custom was to leave wounded and

sick in the nearest village. The British were fully stretched trying to provide medical support for their own military and civilian sick and casualties. However a Burma General Hospital and one section of an Indian General Hospital, together with some minor units, were set aside for the Chinese, while General Hutton arranged for an American civil medical mission, led by Dr Seagrave, which happened to be in Burma, to do what it could to fill the gap.

6. In general, the Chinese troops were lightly armed and had few mortars, no artillery and no armour. In any formation, about one-third of the troops were not armed at all. The task of the unarmed personnel was to act as porters, to help collect supplies and to arm themselves as casualties occurred. General Slim has recorded that the size of a Chinese 'division' was around 8000 men. At full strength, however, there were rarely more than 3000 rifles, 200 LMGs and 30-40 MMGs. Their transport consisted of one or two staff cars, half-a-dozen trucks and a couple of hundred shaggy ponies. General Alexander noted that the power of a Chinese battalion was about the same as a that of a British company. It is therefore confusing to refer to Chinese 'armies' and 'divisions' when their effective strength was about the same as full-strength British or Japanese divisions and brigade groups. Hence in this narrative, Chinese 'armies' are referred to as 'a/divisions', Chinese divisions as 'd/brigades' and Chinese regiments as r/battalions.

7. Stilwell was originally Generalissimo Chiang Kai-shek's Chief of Staff but was also appointed by the Generalissimo as C-in-C of the Chinese Expeditionary Force in Burma. In this capacity he agreed to serve in Burma under General Alexander. It turned out, however, that the Generalissimo had not given him the vital seal of command and all his orders had to be transmitted through his deputy, Lieutenant-General Lo. The chain of command was further complicated, for there was also, at Lashio, a Chinese General Staff Mission whose chief was Lieutenant-General Lin Wei. He was Generalissimo Chiang Kai-shek's personal representative in Burma and his approval was required for all major orders. This ponderous system was, of course, a grave handicap in mobile operations.

APPENDIX SIX

Composition and Command Structure of the Japanese Forces Operating in Burma in the First Half of 1942

Composition and Command Structure

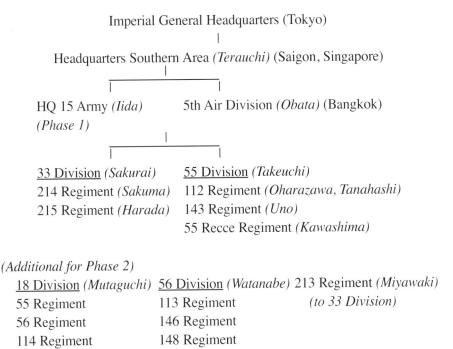

Imperial General Headquarters (Tokyo)

Headquarters Southern Area *(Terauchi)* (Saigon, Singapore)

HQ 15 Army *(Iida)*
(Phase 1)

5th Air Division *(Obata)* (Bangkok)

33 Division *(Sakurai)*
214 Regiment *(Sakuma)*
215 Regiment *(Harada)*

55 Division *(Takeuchi)*
112 Regiment *(Oharazawa, Tanahashi)*
143 Regiment *(Uno)*
55 Recce Regiment *(Kawashima)*

(Additional for Phase 2)

18 Division *(Mutaguchi)*
55 Regiment
56 Regiment
114 Regiment
1st Tank Regiment

56 Division *(Watanabe)*
113 Regiment
146 Regiment
148 Regiment
14th Tank Regiment
56 Recce Regiment

213 Regiment *(Miyawaki)*
(to 33 Division)

Each Division had a mountain or field gun regiment (or a mixture of mountain and field), an engineer battalion and a transport regiment.

Phase 1

2. In Phase 1, both *33* and *55 Divisions* advanced on a light scale. Each had only two infantry regiments. Because of their high consumption of ammunition, neither division took any mortars, but they did take grenade dischargers. However, they soon captured and used British three-inch mortars.

371

3. *33 Division* left behind their *Infantry Group Headquarters* (see Appendix 7) and only took one battalion of mountain guns (nine guns), one engineer company and two horse companies, each of about 400 men and 300 horses, from its transport regiment. The remainder of the division rejoined at Rangoon for Phase 2. They also took one anti-tank gun company which was destroyed at Pegu. A supporting platoon of light tanks, detached from *2 Tank Regiment* in Malaya, was destroyed at the same time.

4. *55 Division* had lost *144 Regimental Group*, which had gone to Guam under command of the division's *Infantry Group Headquarters*. The Division advanced into Burma without *2/143 Battalion Group*, which had gone to Victoria Point, and *3/112 Battalion Group* which had gone to Tavoy. Both battalions rejoined at Moulmein. Their two remaining mountain artillery battalions each had six guns.

5. Both divisions were backed up by troops under *15 Army*, which included two independent engineer battalions (*4th* and *20th*), two bridging material companies, a railway battalion and two base hospitals.

Phase 2

6. In Phase 2 the mountain gun regiments of both *33* and *55 Divisions* were made up to a full complement of 27 guns.

7. *33 Division* was reinforced with *21 Mixed Heavy Artillery Unit* (four x 105mm and four x 150mm), *26 Independent Engineer Regiment* (water transport) and one company each of anti-tank and 75mm AA guns.

8. *18 Division's* mountain gun regiment had two battalions of 12 guns each and one battalion of 12 x 75mm field guns. At Kyaukse it was reinforced by eight x 150mm guns of the *3rd Heavy Artillery Regiment* (less one battalion).

9. *56 Division* had a field gun regiment composed of two battalions of 75mm field guns and one battalion of 105mm guns, each battalion having 12 guns.

Notes on the Japanese Army

Japanese Divisions

1. Japanese divisions were commanded by a Lieutenant-General with a Colonel as Chief of Staff. An unusual feature of the divisional organisation was an Infantry Group HQ, commanded by a Major-General who had his own small staff. He was used when it was desirable to split off a substantial portion of the division away from the main body. This was often useful when operating with small forces in a large country.

2. The actual organisation of a standard Japanese division in Burma was otherwise basically similar to that of a British division but the infantry units were appreciably larger. There were three infantry regiments (= brigades) each of three infantry battalions. They had an artillery regiment of three battalions, each of three companies (=batteries), an engineer battalion of three companies and a transport regiment of three companies, usually two of horses and one of trucks. They also had the following units:

Signal company (190 men)
Medical unit (15 doctors and 500 men)
Disease Prevention and Water Supply unit
 (7 doctors/pharmacists and 200 men)
Ordnance troop (120 men)
Two field hospitals (each of 16 doctors and 240 men)
Veterinary hospital (50 men)

A notable feature is the strong medical support based on an appreciation of the high incidence of disease in the tropics and the Japanese philosophy of curing sick and wounded soldiers as far forward as possible, so that they could return quickly to duty.

3. There were two types of Japanese division. The 'old' divisions, formed before 1941, had four rifle companies and an MMG company in each infantry battalion, whereas the 'new' ones, raised in 1941 or later, had only three rifle companies and an MMG company. *18* and *33 Divisions* were 'old' divisions, *55* and *56* were 'new' ones.

Infantry Regiments

4. The standard infantry regiment was commanded by a Colonel and had the following units in addition to three Infantry battalions:

RHQ Command and Staff ...... 15 men
Medical section .... 12 (2 doctors)
Supply and Pay 80
Intelligence company .... 133(8 radios, 12 telephones)
Regimental artillery company ... 132 (2 or 4 x 75mm mountain guns)
Anti-tank gun company .... 72 (2 or 4 x 37mm guns)
Mounted infantry platoon ...... 40 (*33 Division* only)
Transport unit .... .Variable

5. There were more than 500 men in the regimental headquarters. The large Intelligence company is of interest and explains the good control achieved when the forces were widely dispersed. The regimental guns, like the battalion guns, were used in a direct fire role, notably in road-blocks.

6. The total infantry strength of a regiment was variable but was substantially more than that of a British brigade. *112 Regiment* of the 'new' *55 Division* is recorded as having an infantry strength of 2933 at the start of the campaign and *55 Regiment* of the 'old' *18 Division* is said to have been 4000 strong when they disembarked at Rangoon.

Infantry Battalions

7. Infantry battalions, normally commanded by a Major, consisted of:

Battalion HQ .... 103 men
Four (or three) rifle companies, each .. 180
MMG company (8 x MMG) 122
Infantry gun platoon .... 45 (2 x 70mm guns)
Total .... **990 (or 810)**

Infantry Companies

8. Infantry companies, normally commanded by a Captain or Lieutenant, consisted of:

Command unit

Staff Sergeant	....	1
Sergeants	Orders from battalion HQ	1
	Liaison with platoons ...	1
	Weapons and ammunition	1
	Supplies	1
Messengers	....	6

Trumpeters 4	
Medical orderlies 3	18
Three rifle platoons, each 53	159
Total	**177 (plus 3 officers)**

9. The platoons were divided into three rifle sections of 13, each with one LMG, and one section with three or four grenade launchers. In a section, all except the LMG gunner carried extra equipment. The section commander carried night binoculars (4x) the others either a shovel, pickaxe (2) or sickle (1).

10. A notable fact is that the companies were about half as large again as British companies. In practice, the number of men in a Japanese company varied and at the start of a campaign was often even higher than the figure given above. For instance *143 Regiment* of *55 Division* crossed the Thai frontier with company strengths of 200 men or more.

The Numbering of Japanese Units

11. In the narrative of this book, to avoid confusion with Allied units, Japanese formations and units are shown in italics. Japanese infantry regiments had three battalions numbered 1, 2 and 3. Here they are described with the number of the battalion first and then the number of the regiment. Thus *1/215 Battalion* is the *1st Battalion* in *215 Regiment*.

12. Companies, like battalions, were numbered consecutively throughout the Regiment. Thus the companies in *1/215 Battalion* would be numbered 1, 2, 3, 4. In *3/215 Battalion* they would be numbered 9, 10, 11, 12. In this narrative companies are described with their number after the regimental number, thus in an 'old' division *215/7 Company* would be one of those in *2/215 Battalion*.

13. In 'new' Divisions the numbering of companies followed the same system, but as there were only three infantry companies in each battalion the results were slightly different. *4 Company* would now be in *2 Battalion* and *7* and *8 Companies* in *3 Battalion*.

14. It was a very logical system and well suited to warfare in undeveloped countries where the large Japanese companies were commonly used in an independent role and needed a definite identity. Companies were proud of this identity and a number of company histories have been published.

Infantry Weapons

15. The basic infantry weapon was the rifle with a 15-inch bayonet. The bayonet was normally fixed to the rifle when in action. The rifle (like the British one) was of an antiquated pattern. Its calibre was .256 inches as opposed to the British .303. The lighter ammunition had logistic advantages but the bullet was less

effective. Two types of LMG were used, the earlier weighing 22 lbs and the later 20 lbs. They used the same ammunition as the rifles. However, captured British LMGs firing .303 ammunition were often used as well.

16. The MMGs used in this campaign were the Model 92 weapon which fired .303 ammunition. The gun weighed 60 lbs and the tripod another 60.

17. The grenade dischargers in every company were comparable to British two inch mortars but were a more sophisticated design. They had a spirit level so that the weapon could be held at a constant 45 degree angle and the range (up to 700 yards) was then set by a simple adjustment to the size of the combustion chamber. The barrels were rifled and there was a trigger mechanism so that the dischargers could be fired at short range at a low angle, and they often were. They weighed ten pounds and fired a shell weighing 1.75 pounds. No true mortars were used in this campaign except for British three-inch mortars captured in Burma or Singapore.[1]

18. The two infantry guns were known as the 'regimental gun' and the 'battalion gun'. The former was an early version of the 75mm mountain gun and, like it, could be carried on six pack ponies. Its range was 6600 yards but like the mountain gun it was often used at short range in an anti-tank role, although neither gun had armour-piercing shells in this campaign.

19. The battalion gun was a light (450 lb), low-velocity weapon firing an 8.36 lb shell. At a high angle it had a range of about 3000 yards, but it was normally used in a direct-fire role at a short range. Because of its low velocity, the shell could be heard coming and so it was often referred to by the British as a 'whizz-bang'. When broken down, it was designed to be carried on ponies but it was also man portable.

Artillery

20. There were four types of artillery field gun used in this campaign. They were:

	Weight of Shell	Range
75mm Mountain Gun (model 94)	13.4 lbs	9800 yds
75mm Field Gun (model 95	14.3 lbs	12000 yds
105mm Heavy Field Gun (type 92)	33 lbs	20100 yds
150mm Medium Howitzer (type 96)	80 lbs	13000 yds

Other artillery weapons deployed were:

	Weight of Shell	Muzzle Velocity
37mm Anti-Tank Gun (model 94)	1.54 lbs	2300 ft/sec
75mm Anti-Aircraft Gun (model 88)	14.6 lbs	2360 ft/sec

21. The mountain gun could be taken to pieces and was normally carried on six pack ponies. The 75mm field gun and the anti-tank gun were mostly towed by horses but sometimes by trucks. The two heavier field guns and the 75mm AA guns were towed by tractors. The 75mm AA gun could be, and was, used in an anti-tank role but it did not have armour-piercing ammunition.

22. The Japanese, for logistic reasons, used their artillery sparingly. They rarely fired except at specific targets. They did not believe in 'bracketing' and their first shot was fired for effect.

Armour

23. Japanese 8-ton light tanks with a 37mm gun and 15-ton medium tanks with a 57mm gun were used in this campaign, but Japanese armour was used almost entirely against the Chinese. Three of the light tanks were used against the British at Pegu but their gun could not penetrate the armour of the British Stuarts and they were quickly destroyed. Only for three days between Meiktila and Kyaukse was there an inconclusive clash between the Japanese medium tanks and British tanks. These Japanese tanks did not, in this campaign, have armour-piercing shells and only in exceptional circumstances could they knock out a Stuart.

Reconnaissance Regiments

24. The units used for reconnaissance varied between divisions. After a re-organisation in 1941, *33 Division* had a mounted infantry platoon and a light armoured vehicle company, both attached to divisional HQ, and a mounted infantry platoon attached to each regimental HQ.

25. *55 Division* had a reconnaissance 'regiment' with three mounted infantry companies, one MMG company, one armoured vehicle company and one anti-tank gun company. They referred to themselves as a 'cavalry' regiment (the 'last cavalry'). One mounted infantry company and part of the MMG and anti-tank gun companies went to Guam and were not present in this campaign.

26. Mounted infantry units were armed with a light rifle, a carbine, fitted with a folding bayonet. The light armoured vehicle companies of both divisions did not arrive until Rangoon was captured.

27. *56 Division's* reconnaissance regiment was basically similar to *55 Division's* but was motorised, the mounted infantry companies being replaced by two companies of lorried infantry.

---

1. General Slim in *Defeat into Victory* (p.104) writes that: "Their mortar, the equivalent of our three-inch, was their most effective weapon... A high proportion of our casualties came from it. Fortunately its shell was not as powerful or lethal as our own..." In fact the Japanese were using captured British three-inch mortars.

Analysis of British and Japanese Casualties in the First Burma Campaign

General

1. The conditions of the first Burma campaign were such that no accurate assessment of casualties can be made. Many papers referring to British and Indian casualties were lost in battle or destroyed in air raids, while a trickle of men who had been cut off, or otherwise left behind, continued to arrive at their depots long after official returns had been finalised. For Burmese Army casualties the figures are only rough estimates. Large numbers of the Burmese soldiers deserted as their home districts were over-run and nearly all the remainder were sent home when withdrawal to India became inevitable.

2. After the cease-fire order in August 1945 the Japanese, under orders from their Higher Command, destroyed all their records. The Japanese were, however, very conscious of their duty to those Japanese soldiers who were killed or died. It was important both that their family should have a memento of a member who had lost his life, and also that his death should be commemorated at the Yasakuni Shrine in Tokyo, dedicated to the spirits of dead warriors. As a result, while details of casualties in any particular battle were mainly compiled many years later, and so are necessarily inaccurate, the totals of those who died, as recorded at the end of the campaign, can be taken as correct.

British Casualties

3. The official British casualty figures are as follows:[1]

	Killed	Wounded	Missing & PW	Total
British & Indian Officers	133	126	115	374
British Other Ranks	348	605	647	1600
Indian and Gurkha OR	769	1738	5555	8062
Burma Army	249	126	3052	3427
Totals	**1499**	**2595**	**9369**	**13463**

4. In this campaign the Japanese claim to have captured 4918 prisoners and it is likely that this total is more or less correct. Unfortunately there is no break-

down of this figure and it is not known with any accuracy how many were British, how many were Indian, nor how many were Chinese. Nor among the Indians is it known how many were Gurkhas, how many were Indians of the Burma Rifles or Burma Military Police domiciled in Burma, and how many were 'followers'. Two British officers[2] captured early in the campaign have, however, given this rough breakdown: British about 350, of whom a dozen were RAF; Chinese only about 50; the rest Indian. As the different nationalities were kept in separate blocks of Rangoon Jail it was impossible to make an accurate estimate.

5. The small number of Chinese prisoners (which included a General[3]) was explained in this way by a Japanese officer, "we understand the Chinese… if they catch you, they cut off your heads and if you catch them, you cut off their heads… There was a certain understanding [*between us*]. But fighting the Allies was a different matter. The ground rules, you may say, are not so simple as fighting in China."[4] In fact the Chinese were sometimes taken prisoner and used as porters, and the small number taken in Burma was mainly because the mechanised forces which defeated them, being confined to the roads, provided plenty of opportunities for avoiding capture.

6. The difference between the British figure for missing, 9369, and the Japanese figure of prisoners, excluding Chinese, is 4501. It may be assumed that the 'followers', being civilians, were not taken prisoner but either taken into employment or turned loose. As a guess, it may be that at least half of the 4500 unaccounted for were Indians or Burmese domiciled in Burma, who disappeared to their homes. This would give a figure of some 2000 British and Indian Army soldiers unaccounted for. Some of these may have managed to make their way to India later, and some may have deserted, but the majority must have died, either killed in battle, dying of exhaustion or murdered by the BIA or Burmese dacoits.

Japanese Casualties

7. The Japanese do not seem to have any records of the numbers of soldiers wounded and, of course, as the advancing army, had virtually no missing. Although a handful of badly-wounded men were taken prisoner, it is believed that none survived. There is, however, a firm record of the number who were

---

1. From Kirby, S.W., *The War Against Japan*, Vol.5, Appendix 31.
2. Captain Bruce Toothill and Lieutenant Charles Coubrough.
3. Known to the British as General Chi. He spoke excellent English and was much respected. However he was later stabbed by one of the other Chinese prisoners (believed to be a communist) and died despite the efforts of Colonel Mackenzie (the captured ADMS of 17 Division) to save him. Mackenzie, Colonel K.P., *Operation Rangoon Jail*.
4. Mr Okada, *IWM 2866/02*.

killed or died of wounds or sickness during the campaign. They were commemorated at a special ceremony at the end of the campaign (see Chapter 23) and the
figures can be taken as correct. They were:

18 Division . . . 123
33 Division . . . 730
55 Division . . . 702
56 Division . . . 286
Other units 590
Total **2431**

8. *18 Division* scarcely fought against the British except at Kyaukse and just
before it. There they are thought to have had about ten men killed. *33 Division*,
on the other hand, scarcely fought against anyone else although at the very end
they lost four men in a skirmish with the Chinese. *55 Division* lost 79 men fighting against the Thais at the very start (see Chapter 3) and they fought throughout
Phase 1 against the British. They also fought again with the British at
Nyaunglebin, Meiktila and Kyaukse. An analysis of their losses in each encounter
shows that, in spite of their heavy fighting with the Chinese at Toungoo, at least
300 (and probably about 350) were killed in fighting the British.

9. Although it is probably true that a disproportionate number of the other unit
casualties were, because of the RAF, the AVG and the British artillery, incurred
against the British, a more objective view is to allot them according to the divisional casaualties. An estimate, therefore, of the Japanese who were killed in
fighting against the British is:

33 Division 726
55 Division 300
Other Units 249
Total **1275**

Conclusion

These total figures can only be taken as rough estimates but are probably as
good as can now be discerned. It appears true to say that the number of British
and Indians known by their comrades to have been killed in battle was about the
same as the number of Japanese but, when the overall figures are considered, the
total number of British and Indian soldiers who lost their lives in the campaign
was rather more than double that of their opponents.

APPENDIX NINE

'Read This and We Will Win'

Several hundred thousand copies of a Japanese Training Pamphlet called "Read This and We Will Win" were printed by Imperial Army Headquarters in Tokyo and issued to every officer and soldier as he embarked for the 'Southern War'. Japanese is not an easy language to read but the pamphlet was written in a clear and simple style and it was anticipated that nearly all soldiers would read it through.[1] This remarkable pamphlet, which had about 80 pages and was designed to fit into the breast-pocket of a shirt, was produced by a team of staff officers working throughout 1941 in Taiwan. Their leader was Lieutenant-Colonel Masanobu Tsuji.[2] They collected their information from every possible source, tourists, diplomats, businessmen, expatriates, spies and from under-cover visits by army officers. Training exercises were held to clear up certain points, particularly in regard to movement by sea, landing operations and movement in forests. The latter took place in the forests of southern Taiwan. Extracts from this pamphlets which give its flavour, or are particularly applicable to Burma, are given below.

PREFACE

This pamphlet has been prepared to give all officers and men a full understanding of the aim and special characteristics of the Southern Operation Area. In particular:

a. Military war, ideological war and economic war have been combined into one.

b. Only those principles from official manuals which apply to war in a tropical area are included.

c. The pamphlet has been written in simple language so that it can be understood by all and read quickly and easily in a cramped transport vessel.

The book is to be distributed to all officers and men soon after embarkation.

---

1. There was a high degree of literacy in the Japanese Army, probably higher than in the British Army and certainly much higher than in the Indian Army.
2. Masanobu Tsuji was an able man but a ruthless extremist. He is said to have 'disappeared' for several years after the war to avoid trial as a war criminal.

CHAPTER ONE
What is the Southern Operation Area Like?

1. *An Oriental Treasure-house seized by the British, the Americans, the French and the Dutch*

Overseas expansion by the Japanese was forbidden until after the Meiji Restoration. During this period the English, the French, the Americans, the Dutch, the Portugese and others sailed into the Orient as though they had the right, terrorised and subjugated the culturally backward natives and colonised their countries... These areas, the richest in resources in the Orient, were taken by a few white men, and ever since hundreds of millions of Asians have suffered continual exploitation and persecution. We Japanese were born in a blessed country and, by virtue of the holy influence of His Majesty the Emperor, our land has never been invaded and occupied by a foreign power. The Oriental people look on Japan with envy; they trust and respect us; they hope in their hearts that with Japanese help they will achieve independence and happiness.

2. *A Hundred Million Asians Tyrannised by Three Hundred Thousand Whites*

... In Indonesia, Indo-China, Malaya and the Philippines 450 million Orientals are under 300,000 invaders. Once you set foot in the enemy's lands you will see very clearly the oppression of the white men. Grand and splendid buildings look down from high on mountains or hills over the small thatched houses of the natives. Money squeezed out from the blood of Asian races are spent by these small number of whites in their luxurious living, or sent back to their respective home countries. These white people at birth are allocated a few hundred Oriental people as their personal slaves. Could this be God's will?...

3. *A World Source of Oil, Rubber and Tin*

Without oil neither planes, warships nor vehicles can move. Britain and America control more than half of the oil in the world and have more oil than they can use themselves. Yet they not only refuse to export oil to Japan, but prevent Japan from buying oil elsewhere. Rubber and tin are also indispensable to our military operations. The countries in South-East Asia are the richest source of these valuable commodities but the British and Americans have prevented us from buying them. These malicious actions are one of the reasons that we have had to start this campaign... Shortage of oil and iron is the weak point of Japan, but the weak point of America is the shortage of rubber, tin and tungsten. The latter are mostly found in South-East Asia and southern China. If Japan can occupy these areas she will get the oil and iron which she needs as well as striking at America's weakest point. This is the real reason that America dislikes and opposes Japan's southern expansion.

4. *Lands of Everlasting Summer*

The theatre of operations has no seasons; throughout the year it is as hot as Japan in mid-summer. So we call it 'the land of everlasting summer'. The heat comes up soon after sunrise, reaches its peak about noon and continues until sunset... Because of the high humidity, gun-powder becomes damp, rifles, guns and shells rust, spectacles and binoculars mist up and electric batteries run down more quickly. Fruit such as bananas and pineapples are available throughout the year but so, unfortunately, is the malarial mosquito. There are many undeveloped areas of dense forest and marsh where neither men nor horses are able to get through...

CHAPTER TWO
Why Do We Fight? How Should We Fight?

1. *Obey the Will of the Emperor for Peace in the Orient*

Japan's return, at the 1868 Restoration, to her ancient system of government by His Majesty the Emperor, saved Japan from grave peril when the black ships of the foreigners came to Nagasaki and Uraga hoping for the chance to occupy Japan. The Showa Restoration of the 1930s aims at the establishment of peace in the Orient under the will of the Emperor; the rescue of Asia from white aggression; the restoration of Asia to the Asians, and finally the establishment of peace throughout the world.

As they objected to the rise of Japan, the British and Americans tried by every means to obstruct our development. They forced Chiang Kai-shek to fight against us and urged the regimes in French Indo-China and the Dutch East Indies to regard us as an enemy. Their greatest hope is that the Asian people will be destroyed by fighting among themselves, and their greatest fear that the people of Asia will work together for independence under the leadership of Japan...

Already Japan has rescued Manchuria from the ambitions of the Soviets and freed China from exploitation by the British and Americans. Now we have the mission to assist the independence of the Thais, the Annamese and the Filipinos and give the blessing of happiness to the natives of the south and to the Indians.

The aim of the present war is to realise the Emperor's ideal that the people of the world, and first of all in the Orient, should each be granted possession of their rightful homeland. To effect this, the Oriental countries should plan an overall coalition, uniting their military resources and co-operating economically for the common good, while respecting each other's independence. Through such a combination of strength we shall liberate the Orient from white invasion and oppression.

The significance of the present war is really great and the national peril that Japan faces, as the central and leading force, is greater than anything she has ever faced since our country was created. The people of the South deeply respect the

Japanese and place high hopes upon our success. It is vital that we should not betray their respect and hopes.

2. *Treat the Natives with Friendliness, but Do Not Expect Too Much of Them*

These 100 million natives, who have been treated like slaves, look like ourselves in the colour of their eyes and skin. They should have received from the gods at birth the right to inherit their homelands, the treasure houses of the world. You may feel pity for them if you wonder for what past sins they have to suffer under the oppressive rule of the white men. To the natives, looking at it from a geographical or historical point of view, the British, the Americans, the French and the Dutch are mere armed robbers, while we Japanese are brothers, or at least relatives. However, there are many natives who have become the tools of the white men and spy for them, sell their fellow countrymen, and betray Asia. Such men are particularly numerous in the higher ranks of the civil and military services and should be eliminated as harmful to us. But we must have the magnanimity to pardon those who come to surrender.

However, the countries of great natural blessing, where it is possible for men to live naked and eat without working, breed large numbers of idle men who are almost emasculated after centuries of subjection to Europeans and exploitation by the Chinese. So we should not expect too much of them in the way of hard work in the short term.

3. *Respect Native Manners and Customs (Omitted)*

4. *Destroy Harmful Enemies, but Show Compassion to the Guiltless (Omitted)*

5. *Who Are the Overseas Chinese? (Omitted)*

6. *Be Strong, Behave Correctly and Control Yourself*

If you look at the history of past battles you will see that troops who are really strong in battle do not plunder or rob, chase after women or drink and quarrel. Those who flee and hide in the midst of bullets are the braggarts and the great tormentors of the weak. Bear in mind that the misbehaviour of one soldier reflects on the good name of the whole army; so discipline yourself. When a hero of many battles is court-martialled for plunder or rape and sentenced to several years of penal servitude, there is no excuse at all. Always remember the banzais and excited cheers on the day you set out for the war. Remember also that your parents, brothers and sisters are visiting the shrines every day on your behalf and laying a meal tray for you at the family altar as a prayer for your good fortune in the war. So if your family were to know of your misconduct on the battlefield and its punishment, what sort of triumphal return do you expect? How can you apologise to your brave comrades who have died? Particular attention to good behaviour is necessary in camp after a hard battle and in rear areas where there is little danger. For the rest of your life it may be impossible to atone for any failure.

As good warriors you must discipline yourselves to behave correctly so that your distinguished military services and tough endurance are not reduced to nothing through a moment of dissipation and debauchery. When living hard and undertaking hard tasks you must be patient and control yourself, reflecting on the spirit of your comrades who have already died.

7. *Preserve and Protect Resources and Installations.*

Due to the malicious acts of the Anglo-Americans, Japan has become unable to buy the vitally important oil from anywhere in the world. It is absolutely essential for our national survival to get the oil in the South but it is unlikely that the enemy will surrender it to us without making difficulties. We must expect them to try every means in their power to destroy the oil facilities by bombing or dynamiting. We must anticipate them, seize the installations and guard them against damage. Similarly we must capture as much as possible of every sort of supply and either use them on the spot or send them home to Japan. We must bear in mind that once oil installations, factories and railways, *etc*. are damaged, it is not easy to restore them. Captured vehicles and weapons are often ruined by being mucked about by those who don't know how to handle them properly. In the past it was the thoughtless custom to destroy or burn captured enemy supplies because of a lack of manpower to deal with them. In this war, however, it is imperative to seize the enemy's supplies intact and utilize them as much as possible. Similarly it is important to use most economically our own supplies, be it a single bullet, a scrap of bread or a drop of petrol. We must think of lessening the drain on our national resources.

8. *Is the Enemy Stronger than the Chinese Army?*

If we compare our enemy with the Chinese Army we see that while the officers are Europeans, the NCOs and soldiers are nearly all natives and the sense of unity between officers and men is virtually nil. Although they are better equipped than the Chinese Army and have aeroplanes, tanks, motor vehicles and artillery, most of these are of old and out-dated types. Moreover the soldiers who operate them are weak and ill-trained and as a result they are useless. Night attacks are what our enemy fears the most.

9. *You May be Killed in Battle but Do Not Die of Disease*

Your enemy will come in tanks on the land, planes in the air, warships on the sea and submarines beneath the surface. But there is another Great Enemy in this campaign and that is a variety of deadly diseases and a host of malarial mosquitoes lying in wait for you. It is an historical fact that in all tropical campaigns in the past far more men have died from disease than have been killed in battle. In the tropics, as in Japan, most diseases enter through the mouth but in the South you must also take precautions against mosquitoes and snakes. To die by bullets is to be a hero, but it is never an honour to die of disease or by an accident through inattention or carelessness. Furthermore you should consider well that almost all native women are infected with venereal disease. Moreover, if you tamper with them you will make all the native inhabitants your enemy.

CHAPTER THREE
By What Stages Will the War Progress?
(Omitted)

CHAPTER FOUR
What to Do on the Ship
(Omitted)

CHAPTER FIVE
The Landing Assault

1. *Water is Your Saviour*

To mention the importance of water in a tropical operation may appear ridiculously obvious. But those without experience cannot conceive how valuable water is and how difficult it is to obtain it. It will be an advantage to carry water with you, not only in your water-bottle but in beer bottles or any other containers you can find. The amount of water necessary for one day varies according to the heat but you must know that it is at least ten litres for a man and 60 litres for a horse. Moreover, water is not available everywhere and it is important to use it economically and to replenish it whenever good water is found. Do not drink it in large quantities even if you are very thirsty; it is always better to drink a little at a time. Coconuts, which contain a quarter to a half-litre of water, pineapples and sugarcanes are good for quenching thirst. In the hills cutting off a vine of wisteria and sucking at the cut end will prove helpful. In the tropics some wisterias grow to a very large size and contain plenty of water. To obtain this water you should cut the vine off at the base, insert a container and then cut the vine again two or three feet higher up and collect the water in the container. As the water from all varieties of wisteria is harmless you may drink it without worry. For horses it is necessary to add salt to the water from time to time.

2. *Sleep Well, Eat Well*

When the situation permits, it is best to march in the cool period between nightfall and morning and to rest in the hottest time of the day. But if night marches continue day after day there is a danger of soldiers becoming weak through lack of sleep. So it is necessary to sleep as much as possible. The main causes of sun-stroke (heat-stroke) are lack of sleep and an empty stomach. Though you may lose your appetite in the heat it is absolutely essential to avoid having an empty stomach and, by carrying snacks, to eat more often than usual. This is an example of how meals might be taken on the march:

a. Breakfast: eat half before departure, the remainingg half about two hours later.

b. Lunch: divide into two portions and take at around 10am and 1pm.

c. Supper: as usual but in the case of a night march preferably divided into two or more parts.

3. *Clothing on the March*

When marching during the day in strong sunshine it is not correct to wear thin clothing which allows the sunlight to reach your skin. As protection of your head is vital you must wear your military sun cap, and it is helpful to cover or line the cap with green grass or leaves or fix foliage into the knapsack so that it shades your head. Clothing should be worn as loose as possible to allow air to circulate and it is a good idea to carry a fan. For horses, too, it is necessary to attach foliage to their saddles and to cover their heads with a sun-hood or something similar.

4. *When You Rest*

Short breaks on the march should be increased to rest periods of twenty to 30 minutes every 30 to 40 minutes and a longer rest of two to three hours is desirable when it is possible. On falling out you should immediately take off your equipment and remove coat and shoes to feel the air, but watch out for poisonous snakes. These lie in thick grass or on the branches of trees and if you do not watch out and put your feet or hands on them, you may well be bitten. At night particular care is necessary, tiresome though it may be, to use the mosquito net provided and to make smoke by burning grass and tree branches, that is to take all measures to deter the deadly malarial mosquitoes.

5. *Tyres on Cars and Bicycles Swell in the Heat; Engines Overheat (Omitted)*

CHAPTER SEVEN

Camping in the Tropics

1. *Do Not Catch Cold Early in the Morning while Asleep*

Even in the tropics the temperature suddenly drops in the second half of the night. If you are sleeping in the clothes that you have been wearing during the day and which are damp with sweat or rain, you are likely to catch cold or suffer from diarrhoea. Always remember to change into dry clothes before going to sleep at night whenever it is possible.

2. *Native Settlements are Nests of Fleas, Bed-bugs and Infectious Diseases*

Since the standard of living of natives is extremely low and they have no idea of hygiene, native settlements are full of fleas, lice, bed-bugs and infectious diseases. If you are to use such a settlement it is advisable to occupy only the local government offices or public buildings and to avoid the ordinary houses. When you are obliged to use ordinary dwellings, you should make sure that there is no direct contact between soldiers and natives. Demarcate strictly an area for the troops, remove all natives from that area, clean it thoroughly and disinfect it. On most occasions you will find bivouacking in neighbouring rubber plantations or coconut groves both less troublesome and far more convenient and comfortable.

3. *Use of Temples and Mosques*

You must not do anything to offend the religious beliefs of the deeply super-stitious native people. Even the most distinguished local men do not enter a tem-ple or mosque without removing their shoes. You must remember to avoid com-pletely using any mosque or other Islamic place of worship.

4. *Precautions Against Mosquitoes, Dangerous Animals and Poisonous Snakes*

For dealing with mosquitoes, you should be strict in taking the necessary pre-cautions such as using mosquito nets, burning anti-mosquito incense sticks or powder, taking anti-malarial tablets and applying anti-mosquito ointment. For protection against dangerous animals, provided there is no worry about the enemy, light lamps and fires. If you find a dangerous snake, kill it. You should swallow its liver raw and cook the meat; they are an excellent medicine for strengthening the body.

5. *Fuel for Cooking*

The green wood of mangrove trees burns well. Other material useful as fuel are the husks of coconuts, dry sugar cane after pressing, and rice chaff.

6. *Do Not let Your Weapons be Stolen*

When you drop asleep exhausted, you may forget where you put your weapon and it may be stolen by the natives. For your own sake, and for the honour of the army, you should take the greatest care of your weapon.

CHAPTER EIGHT
Scouting and Guarding

1. *Inattention is the Great Enemy*

You reach the camp-site for the night, having scarcely avoided sun-stroke and exhausted by the boiling heat, with a feeling of relief and the chance to rest. Then you are ordered to take on the important task of sentry, patrol or scout. The enemy is waiting for us, well-prepared in country that they know, and capable of attack-ing or ambushing us. In order that the whole troop can rest, you must whip your tired body and carry out your duty of searching and watching, keeping your eyes and ears more alert than usual.

2. *On Sentry Duty*

Choose carefully a position where there is a cool breeze and protect yourself against direct sunshine. Take off your pack and other equipment if feasible and concentrate on your responsibility to guard the safety of the whole troop.

3. *Patrolling*

Use bicycles on patrol whenever possible and use only light equipment. There are advantages in employing natives as guides or to obtain information, but they often tell lies and the language barrier often causes misunderstanding. As natives readily believe, and are influenced by, unlikely rumours you should watch their movements carefully.

CHAPTER NINE
The Battle

1. *The Long Voyage and Sweltering March are Preliminaries for the Decisive Battle*

When you encounter the enemy after landing, regard yourself as an avenger who at last faces the murderer of your parents. Here before you is the enemy on whom you should vent your anger. If you fail to destroy him you will never be satisfied and the first battle is the most important one.

2. *Heavy Showers, Mist and the Night are our Allies*

Westerners are foppish, very effeminate and cowardly, so they dislike fighting in the rain, in mist or at night. In particular, they regard the night as a proper time for dancing and not for fighting. This gives us a great opportunity to exploit their weakness.

3. *Battle Tips in Extreme Heat*

a. To prevent sweat running into your eyes and upsetting your aim, bind a cloth round your head under the steel helmet to catch the sweat before it reaches your eyes.

b. Keep the sun at your back. Fighting towards the sun not only makes aiming difficult but enables the enemy to see us better than we can see him.

c. Bullets travel further through hot air and targets stand out more clearly in the sunlight. Hence you must guard against a tendency to judge targets as nearer than they actually are.

d. Because of the heat, gun barrels may expand and the efficiency of recoil systems may be impaired. Don't overdo your rate and duration of fire. Do thorough maintenance and, when resting, take care of your weapon and keep it out of the sun whenever possible.

4. *The Final Blow at a Retreating Enemy*

To trap a retreating enemy, one of your aims should be to outflank him and gain control of the wells and springs in his rear.

5. *Guarding Large Strategic Areas*

When guarding natural resources, railways and harbours, a small number of troops will be left to guard a large area. This requires much ingenuity. You must seek to tire the enemy without exhausting yourself by constructing road-blocks, by winning the natives over to our side or by utilising natural barriers such as cliffs, dense forest and marshland. Protect your own water-supply as well as denying water to the enemy. You must also take care to guard well at night, in rain or in mist, and force the enemy to launch his attack from some distance away and in the heat of the day.

CHAPTER TEN
Protection Against Poison Gas
(Omitted)

CHAPTER ELEVEN
For Signal Troops
(Omitted)

CHAPTER TWELVE
For Motor Transport

1. *Be Determined to Get Through*

If a man can get through, so can a motor vehicle. If a road is too narrow, cut a way through. If there is a cliff in the way let a group of 40 or 50 men haul the vehicle up it. Whether trucks get through or not depends on your determination. Go where you want to even if you have to carry the vehicle on your shoulders.

2. *Is the Maintenance Excellent? (Omitted)*

3. *A Drop of Petrol is a Drop of Blood. (Omitted)*

4. *Do Not Over Boost the Engines. (Omitted)*

5. *When the Engine Gets Wet. (Omitted)*

6. *Oil and Water. (Omitted)*

CHAPTER THIRTEEN
Take Care of Your Weapons
(Omitted)

CHAPTER FOURTEEN
Food and Drink

1. *Water Supply and Sterilisation*

You may get dirty water anywhere but clean water is not so easily found. As natives defecate and urinate freely in all lakes and streams, even the water used by natives for drinking is full of germs, so it is safest only to drink water which has been properly purified by filtering. Do not forget to carry creosote pills. If you do find a source of good drinking water, see that no-one defiles it and if necessary post sentries to watch it. When you are perspiring heavily, drink warm tea with about 0.8 % of salt dissolved in it. To sterilise wells, put some chloride of lime in an empty bottle, add water, shake until the mixture is clear and pour some of it into the well. The well is safely sterilised when the water you draw has a faint taste of chloride.

2. *How to Prevent Cooked Rice from Becoming Stale*

    a. Pure boiled rice is better than rice and wheat.

    b. Wash the rice well before boiling.

c. Cook the rice harder (*i.e.* with less water) and allow some time for the moisture to evaporate before packing the rice in your container.

d. It is better to cook in a mess-tin than in a large pot.

e. Place two or three salted plums in each meal.

f. It is best to add a little salt, a salted plum or a small quantity of vinegar when cooking.

g. It is effective to add one preservative tablet to each mess-tin of rice when cooking.

h. Wash mess-tins and rice baskets in boiling water and dry thoroughly before packing them with rice.

j. When carrying two meals, pack each meal separately.

k. You should pack rice lightly and if possible place a piece of cloth between the lid and the container to absorb moisture.

l. Attach mess-tin and rice baskets outside your pack, cover them thoroughly with leaves, *etc.*, and when you rest keep them out of the sun.

m. Dried or tinned goods are recommended as subsidiary foods, but do not open tins until immediately before the meal.

n. Keep biscuit rations in a moisture-proof bag.

o. Cooking rice in a cellophane bag is extremely effective.

3. *Which Fruits Should You Eat?*

Fruit is nutritive and excellent for your health. The following types of fruit are dangerous, but most others can be eaten:

a. Those of excessively vivid colour.

b. Those of excessively strong smell.

c. Those with excessively sweet saccharine-like taste.

d. Those with excessively beautiful flowers.

e. Those growing on low bushes with beautifully coloured or mottled leaves.

When eating mangoes do not drink goat's milk or alcoholic drinks at the same time.

CHAPTER FIFTEEN
Hygiene

As explained earlier, in the tropics we have to fight against a wide variety of diseases. You should be particularly careful to avoid malaria, sun-stroke, beri-beri and snake-bite. Besides these, there are throughout the year in the tropics bad diseases such as cholera, typhus, bubonic plague, smallpox, tuberculosis and leprosy. Moreover the enemy may in desperation spread around these terrible germs to infect us. You must be constantly on your guard and refrain from incautious use of food and wells abandoned by the enemy.

It is probably the heat which drives even the dogs mad. Rabies is not rare and if you are bitten by a dog you must report at once for medical attention.

1. *How Do You Contract Malaria?*

The first priority is to avoid malaria. Since the dawn of history the success or failure of tropical campaigns has depended on how much malaria can be checked. One new case of malaria in our own army is a far more dangerous source of infection than any number of cases among natives. Report for examination and treatment early, not only for your own sake but also for the sake of your comrades.

Malaria is spread by mosquitoes. Although the malarial mosquito hardly exists in Japan, it exists in large numbers throughout the tropics. There are many varieties but the easiest way to recognise them all is by their habit at rest of keeping their noses down and their hindquarters raised. You may think that since most mosquito larvae generally hatch in dirty stagnant water, so the malarial mosquitoes would develop in the same way. However, this is not the case. The malarial mosquito dislikes stagnant water and is commonly found in clear mountain streams or at places near the coast where fresh water and sea water mix. Since many mosquitoes in Japan live in thick woods, you might expect them to be plentiful in the jungle, but in fact the malarial mosquito is rarely found in the jungle away from the sea. In Java and Malaya there are even places where the clearing of forest has been restricted by law to control malaria. The malarial mosquito is most active from dusk to midnight but less so during the second half of the night.

There are also striped mosquitoes which, unlike the malarial mosquitoes, are active during the day. You should guard against these as well since a bite will cause a fever. It is important not to be bitten by day, as well as to use a mosquito net at night. Take your anti-malarial medicine as directed, use your anti-mosquito kit and apply anti-mosquito ointment.

2. *What is Sun-(Heat-)Stroke?*

Sun-stroke is a sickness caused by the heat of the sun. Men who are in a weak state after an illness, who have a poor appetite, who are suffering from insufficient sleep or who are chronic malaria cases should be particularly careful since they are most likely to suffer from it. The first symptoms of sun-stroke are heavy sweating, high temperature and a flushed face. Gradually the sweating ceases, the vitality weakens, the face turns pale and the patient stumbles and seems about to fall. At this stage if the patient rests immediately in the shade he will recover, but if nothing is done he will lapse into unconsciousness and collapse.

3. *How to Avoid Sun-(Heat-) Stroke*

The best way to prevent sun-stroke is to drink ample water, to have sufficient sleep and to avoid being too hungry.

4. *How to Deal with Someone who has Sun Stroke*

Take off his knapsack, remove his clothing, lay him down in the shade where there is a breeze, keep his head raised, fan him, give him water to drink and splash cold water all over his body. If his breathing is weak apply artificial respiration. Let him rest quietly and even when he has recovered do not allow him to move too soon.

5. *Do Not be Bitten by Snakes (Omitted)*

6. *Do Not Get Beri-beri (Omitted)*

CHAPTER SIXTEEN

Hygiene for Horses

(Omitted)

CHAPTER SEVENTEEN

Movement in Special Types of Terrain

There are many bamboo groves, jungles and sugar fields in the tropics. In general, movement in these is just the same as in the forest. Apart from taking the usual precautions against fire and gas, a towel should be wrapped round the face to cover the cheeks, and gloves should be worn, as protection from thorns and brambles. Particular care should be taken on the following points.

1. *Movement in Bamboo Groves*

The bamboo groves in the south differ from those in Japan in that many bamboo canes grow in a cluster from one trunk and are spiked with thorns, so it is impossible to step into their midst. When traversing such groves, move through the gap where the bamboo is less dense, lop off lower branches and make cuts in the stems so that the white interior will act as a route marker. In a frontal attack on a bamboo grove it is best to make a concentrated rush through a less dense gap. In defence, bamboo groves are useful both as an obstacle and for concealment but one must remember that the fearful noise of bullets crashing through the bamboo can affect soldiers' morale.

2. *Movement in Jungle*

Jungle is a dense forest with a large variety of trees, grasses and thorny plants entangled with each other and where many fierce animals, snakes and harmful insects live. As jungle is a very difficult sort of country for troops to pass through, it will be necessary to form special teams for the task. Such terrain is regarded by the feeble Westerners as impassable and for this reason, and to out-manoeuvre them, we must often force our way through it. With proper preparation and determination it can be done. Note that maintenance of direction and supply of water are very important.

3. *Movement in Sugar-cane Fields*

Movement through sugar-cane fields is similar to that through the kaolin fields of Manchuria and special care is necessary to maintain the correct direction. For this purpose scouts should be sent ahead to mark the trail either by observing from ladders and trees or by using compasses. These fields provide opportunities for local outflanking in an attack. In defence, an effective obstacle can be made by breaking off the sugar-canes at a height of about two feet, binding them with ropes and reinforcing them with steel wire criss-crossed at random.

4. *Movement in a Marsh or in Wet Ricefields*

French Indo-China and Thailand are second only to Japan in the production of rice and there are paddy fields everywhere. There are also many large marshes. In crossing such land it is often best for each man to wear snow-shoes and carry a pole while heavy equipment may be pulled on sledges or hurdles. When advancing on snow-shoes you should pause as little as possible between each step to avoid sinking into the mud. If you get stuck you should put the full weight of the body on the pole and pull up the shoes one at a time... Field and mountain guns can cross slightly wet ground if the wheels are fitted with wide tracks.

CHAPTER EIGHTEEN

Conclusion

This war will decide whether the Empire prospers or declines. America has been prohibiting the export of oil and steel to Japan, slowly strangling us with a soft, silken cord. The reason for such cautious action is the fear that Japan might be driven to invade the South if supplies were stopped at once, and this would hurt America even more than Japan's lack of oil and steel. American policy has been to weaken Japan without arousing her violent anger.

It may already be nearly too late. If we were to wait any more, Japan's aeroplanes, warships and vehicles would be unable to move. Five years have passed since the outbreak of the 'China Incident'. More than a hundred thousand of your comrades have perished on the mainland and the majority of the weapons with which Chiang Kai-shek killed our men were sold to him by the English and Americans. The desire of England and America is to keep the Orient as permanent colonies and they are afraid of any solidarity between the Asian peoples. Their firm policy has been to enlarge the war between Japan and China. Our Allies, Germany and Italy, are engaged in a life-and-death struggle with England, America and the Soviet Union in Europe. America is virtually participating in the war, fully supporting England. For the sake of our country's existence and because of our moral obligation as members of the Tripartite Alliance, it is impossible for us to endure the present situation any longer. We, representing all the races of the Orient, now face the great mission of putting an end to the aggression of past centuries. Our invincible Navy is fully prepared and ready to strike with its full strength. The ratio of fleet tonnage decided by an agreement between England, America and Japan is 5:5:3 but the true effective strength is 5:5:7. Moreover, half of the English fleet has been destroyed by Germany. Now is the best time for our Navy. The umbilical cord of the Chungking regime runs to the

Anglo-Saxons. Unless this is cut, the China Incident will never come to an end. The present war will be the final settlement of our holy crusade. The souls of more than a hundred thousand heroes are watching us. Victory in this war will be our offering to them. The Navy is dominating the wastes of the ocean, sweeping it clear of enemy possessions and obstacles and ceaselesly protecting us. We must express our thanks to them and win the victories to justify all that they have done. We must carry forward our glorious 2600-year-old history and, in accordance with the trust placed in us by His Majesty the Commander-in-Chief, embark upon the honourable duty of changing the course of world history on behalf of the people of Asia. Officers and men working together and inspired by one spirit must demonstrate to the whole world in this campaign the true value of men from Japan. The completion of the Showa Restoration's aim to free Asia, which is the desire of His Imperial Majesty, rests on our shoulders.

> *Corpses drifting in the water, when we go to sea*
> *Corpses rotting in the grasses, when we climb the hills*
> *We shall die by the side of our great lord*
> *We shall not look back.*

(Translation by Kazuo Tamayama)

BIBLIOGRAPHY

BRITISH SOURCES
The Official British Report on the Campaign
1. Wavell, General Sir Archibald, *Supplement to The London Gazette*, dated 5 March 1948, being General Sir Archibald Wavell's Despatch on the Operations in Burma from 15 December 1941 to 20 May 1942 and including the Reports of Lieutenant-General T.J. Hutton and General The Honourable Sir Harold R.L.G. Alexander.

British, Indian and Burma Army Formation War Diaries
1. WO 172 / 369, HQ Burma Army, 'G' Branch.
2. WO 172 / 371, HQ Burma Army, 'A' Branch.
3. WO 172 / 403, HQ 1 Burma Corps, 'G' Branch.
4. WO 172 / 404, HQ 1 Burma Corps, Chief Engineer.
4. WO 172 / 447, HQ 1 Burma Division.
5. WO 172 / 475, HQ 17 Indian Division.
6. WO 172 / 476, HQ 17 Indian Division, CRA.
6. WO 172 / 547, HQ 1 Burma Brigade.
7. WO 172 / 548, HQ 2 Burma Brigade.
8. WO 172 / 560, HQ 7th Armoured Brigade.
9. WO 172 / 563, HQ 13 Indian Brigade.
10. WO 172 / 570, HQ 16 Indian Brigade.
11. WO 172 / 583, HQ 46 Indian Brigade.
12. WO 172 / 589, HQ 48 Indian Brigade.
13. WO 172 / 601, HQ 63 Indian Brigade.

British Army Unit War Diaries
1. WO 172 / 694, The 7th Hussars.
2. WO 172 / 706, The 2nd Royal Tank Regiment.
3. WO 172 / 748, 414 Field Battery, RHA.
4. WO 172 / 855, 1st Battalion, The Cameronians.
5. WO 172 / 858, 2nd Battalion, The Duke of Wellington's Regiment.

6. WO 172 / 861, 1st Battalion, The Gloucestershire Regiment.
7. WO 172 / 863, 1st Battalion, The Royal Inniskilling Fusiliers.
8. WO 172 / 869, 2nd Battalion, The King's Own Yorkshire Light Infantry.
9. WO 172 / 898, 1st Battalion, The West Yorkshire Regiment.

Indian Army Unit War Diaries
1. WO 172 / 474, 17 Divisional Signals.
2. WO 172 / 476, CRA 17 Division.
3. WO 172 / 806, 1st Indian Field Regiment, IA.
4. WO 172 / 817, 5 Mountain Battery.
5. WO 172 / 822, 12 Mountain Battery.
6. WO 172 / 843, 3 Indian LAA Battery.
7. WO 172 / 904, 5/1st Punjab Regiment.
8 WO 172 / 923, 2/7th Rajputana Rifles.
9. WO 172 / 926, 1/9th Royal Jats.
10. WO 172 / 928, 7/10th Baluch Regiment.
11. WO 172 / 929, 1/11th Sikh Regiment.
12. WO 172 / 932, 4/12th Frontier Force Regiment.
13. WO 172 / 936, 2/13th Frontier Force Rifles.
14. WO 172 / 950, 5/17th Dogra Regiment.
15. WO 172 / 951, 1/18th Royal Garwhal Rifles.
16. WO 172 / 956, 1/3rd Gurkha Rifles.
17. WO 172 / 957, 1/4th Gurkha Rifles.
18. WO 172 / 960, 2/5th Royal Gurkha Rifles.
19. WO 172 / 964, 1/7th Gurkha Rifles.
20. WO 172 / 966, Combined 1/7th & 3/7th Gurkha Rifles.
21. WO 172 / 971, 1/10th Gurkha Rifles.
22. WO 172 / 1031, 17 Artisan Works Company, IE.
23. WO 172 / 1032, 18 Artisan Works Company, IE.
24. WO 172 / 1074, 24 Field Company, Bombay S&M.
25. WO 172 / 1078, 50 Field Park Company, Madras S&M.
26. WO 172 / 1081, 60 Field Company, Madras S&M.
27. WO 172 / 1085, 70 Field Company, Bengal S&M.

Burma Army Unit War Diaries
1. WO 172 / 975, 2nd Burma Rifles.
2. WO 172 / 976, 3rd Burma Rifles.
3. WO 172 / 977, 4th Burma Rifles.
4. WO 172 / 978, 5th Burma Rifles.

5. WO 172 / 980, 8th Burma Rifles.

Allied Campaign and General Histories
1. Allen, Louis, *Burma: The Longest War.*
2. Allen, Sydney, *Japan Among the Powers*.
3. Barker, A.J., *Japanese Army Handbook.*
4. Behr, Edward, *Hirohito: Behind the Myth.*
5. Bisheshwar, Prasad, *Indian Armed Forces in World War II—The Retreat from Burma.*
6. Bond, Brian, (ed), *The Diaries of Lt-General Sir Henry Pownall, Vol II.*
7. Callahan, Raymond, *Burma 1942-45.*
8. Calvert, Mike, *Fighting Mad.*
9. Carew, Tim, *The Longest Retreat.*
10. Carmichael, Pat, *Mountain Gunner.*
11. Chamberlin, W.H., *Japan Over Asia.*
12. Churchill, (1) The Rt Hon. Winston, *The Second World War, Vols 3 &4.*
13. Churchill, (2) The Rt Hon. Winston, *The End of the Beginning.*
14. Collister, Captain P., *Then a Soldier.*
15. Connell, John, *Wavell, Scholar and Soldier.*
16. Cotton, M. C., *Hurricanes Over Burma.*
17. Davies, Major-General H.L. *The Small Green Men.*
18. Davy, George, *The Seventh and Three Enemies.*
19. Dillon, Terence, *Rangoon to Kohima.*
20. Draper, Alfred, *Dawns Like Thunder.*
21. Elphick, Peter, *Far Eastern File.*
22. Elphick, Peter, *Singapore, The Pregnable Fortress.*
23. Fergusson, Bernard, *Portrait of a Soldier.*
24. Forteath, G.M., *Pipes, Kukris and Nips.*
25. Fraser, David, *Alanbrooke.*
26. Gallagher, O.D., *Retreat in the East.*
27. Ghosh, K.K., *The Indian National Army.*
28. Giffard, Sir Sydney, *Japan Among the Powers.*
29. Gilchrist, Sir Andrew, *Malaya 1941.*
30. Grenfell, Russell, *Main Fleet to Singapore.*
31. Hedley, John, *Jungle Fighter.*
32. Hickey, Colonel Michael, *The Unforgettable Army.*
33. Hodson, J.L., *War in the Sun.*
34. Horner, D.M., *High Command.*
35. Izumiya, Tatsuro, *The Minami Organ.*

36. James, Lawrence, *Mutiny.*

37. Kennedy, Sir John, *The Business of War.*

38. Kirby, S.W., *The War Against Japan,* Vols 1, 2, 3, & 5.

39. Lewin, (1) Ronald, *Churchill as Warlord.*

40. Lewin, (2) Ronald, *Slim: The Standard-bearer.*

41. Liddell Hart, B.H., *History of the Second World War.*

42. Lunt, James, *A Hell of a Licking.*

43. Mackenzie, Compton, *Eastern Epic.*

44. Mackenzie, Colonel K.P., *Operation Rangoon Jail.*

45. Mains, Anthony, *The Retreat from Burma.*

46. Mason, Philip, *A Matter of Honour.*

47. Masanobu, Tsuji, *Singapore, The Japanese Version.*

48. Maybury, Maurice, *Heaven-Born in Burma*

49. Morton, H.V. *Atlantic Meeting.*

50. North, John, *The Alexander Memoirs.*

51. Paull, Raymond, *Retreat from Kokoda.*

52. Perrett, Bryan, *Tank Tracks to Rangoon.*

53. Probert, Air Cdre Henry, *The Forgotten Air Force.*

54. Reynolds, E. Bruce, *Thailand and Japans Southern Advance.*

55. Rooney, D.D., *Stilwell.*

56. Rusbridger, James & Nave, Eric, *Betrayal at Pearl Harbour.*

57 Shores, Christopher & Cull, Brian, *Bloody Shambles,* Vols 1 & 2.

58. Slim, F.M. Sir William, *Defeat into Victory.*

59. Smyth, Brigadier Sir John, *Before the Dawn.*

60. Stewart, Adrian, *The Underrated Enemy.*

61. Toland, John, *The Rising Sun.*

62. Trench, Charles Chenevix, *The Indian Army.*

63. Ward, Ian, *Snaring The Other Tiger.*

64. Williams, Lt Col J.H., *Elephant Bill.*

65. Wilson, Theodore A., *The First Summit.*

66. Zich, Arthur, *The Rising Sun.*

British and Indian Army Regimental Histories

1. Anon (1), *British Army Signals in the Second World War.*

2. Anon (2), *The History of the 5th Royal Gurkha Rifles (FF)*, Vol. 2.

3. Barclay, C.N., *The History of The Duke of Wellingtons Regiment,1919-1952.*

4. Barclay, C.N., *The Regimental History of the 3rd Q.A.O. Gurkha Rifles*, Vol. 2.

5. Brereton, T.M. & Savory, A.C.S., *The History of the Duke of Wellingtons Regiment (West Riding), 1702-1992.*

6. Davy, George, *The Seventh and Three Enemies*.

7. Fox, Sir Frank, *The Royal Inniskilling Fusiliers in World War II*.

8. Graham, *The History of the Indian Mountain Artillery*.

9. Hingston, Lt-Col. Walter, *History of the Kings Own Yorkshire Light Infantry, 1919-42*.

10. McAlister, R.W.L., *Bugle and Kukri, the Story of The 10th P.M.O. Gurkha Rifles*, Vol. 2.

11. Mackay, Lt-Col. J.N., *A History of the 4th P.W.O. Gurkha Rifles*, Vol. 3.

12. Ross, J. & Hailes, W.L., *War Services of the 9th Jat Regiment*.

13. Routledge, N.W., *Anti-Aircraft Artillery, 1914-1955*.

14. Sandes, Lt-Col. E.C.W., *From Pyramid to Pagoda*.

15. Sandes, Lt-Col. E.C.W., *The Indian Engineers 1939-47*.

Personal Reports, Papers and Letters

1. Ahmad Khan, Lieutenant Bashir, *Personal Account of the Sittang Bridge Demolition*.

2. Amies, Colonel B.J., *Personal Account of Retreat with 1 Burdiv*.

3. Ashfield, Captain Vic, *Personal Account of the Sittang Battle*.

4. Cowan, Major-General D.T. Punch, *Private Letters*.

5. Coubrough, C.R.L., *Personal Account of Kuzeik, Capture and Rangoon Jail*.

6. Davies, Major-General H.L., *Some Notes on the Withdrawal from Prome*, (April 1942).

7. Day, Major D.S., *Personal Account of Bilin, Sittang Bridge and Pegu*.

8. Fearnley, Major A.J, *Personal Account of the Retreat with the 2nd Royal Tank Regiment*.

9. Foucar, Colonel E.C.V., *Draft of a Short History of the First Burma Campaign, (1943)*.

10. Hudson, Major Roy, *Papers Concerning Operations of the Malerkotla Sappers*.

11 Hutton, Lieutenant-General Sir Thomas, *The Hutton Papers*, (a major source of information about the first half of the campaign).

12. Kelly, Professor Desmond, *Papers Concerning Mr Norman Kelly in the Chin Hills*.

13. Kinloch, Major Bruce, *Personal Account of the Sittang Battle*, and other papers.

14. Leggate, Rifleman G., *Personal Account of Pegu, Capture and Rangoon Jail*.

15. MacFetridge, Lieutenant-Colonel C.H.T., *Personal Account of Shwegyin*.

16. Power, Lieutenant-Colonel Henry, *Diary of Life in Rangoon Jail and Final Relief*.

17. Randle, Brigadier J.P., *Personal Account of the Battle of Kuzeik*.

18. Stevenson, Lieutenant-Colonel H.R., *An Account of the Defence of Martaban*.

19. Toothill, Captain H.B., *Personal Account of Kuzeik*.

20. Tutt, Gunner L.E., *Personal Account of Retreat with 7 Armoured Brigade*.

JAPANESE SOURCES
Burma Campaign Histories
1. Official Histories, Research Centre for Defence Studies, Japanese MOD.
Vol. 1.The Assault on Malaya (1966, 650 pages).

2. *ibid*, Vol. 5, *The Assault on Burma* (1967, 638 pages).

3. *ibid*, Vol. 20, *Imperial General Headquarters Army 2, until December 41*,
(1965, 692 pages).

4. *ibid*, Vol. 34, *Army Air Operations in the Advance to the South*, (1970,
763 pages).

5. *ibid*, Vol. 35, *Imperial General Headquarters Army 3, until April 1942*,
(1970, 676 pages).

6. *ibid*, Vol. 61, *Operation of 3rd Air Army in Burma and Indonesia*, (1972,
712 pages).

7. *Prelude to the War, IGH Army*, Vol. 1 (1973, 525 pages).

8. Military Academy Histories of World War II, *The Invasion of Burma*, (1968,
251 pages).

9. Everymans History of Showa Japan, Series 7, *The Pacific War*, Vol. 1.
(Photographs}

10. Iida, Lt-General Shojiro, *From the Battlefields* (1967, 281 pages).

11. Hata, Ikuhiko, *Road to the Pacific War*, Vol. 6, 1940-41, (1963).

12. Reprints, Asahi Newspaper, 1941.

13. Reprints, Yomiuri Newspaper, 1941.

14. *Organisation of the Imperial Army*, Vol. 2, Rekishi Tokuhon War Series
No 29.

15. Monograph 57 (Army) Burma Operations Record, Phase 1.

Regimental Histories
The following Memoirs were written by editorial committees of veterans of the
respective regiments, units or areas.

1. *Memoir 213 Infantry Regiment* (1972, 1359 pages).

2. *Memoir 214 Infantry Regiment* (1974, 1426 pages).

3. *Memoir 215 Infantry Regiment* (1972, 1325 pages).

4. *Memoir 33 Mountain Artillery Regiment* (1977, 928 pages and 1986,
303 pages).

5.*Memoir 33 Engineer Regiment* (1982, 890 pages).
6. *Memoir Signal Unit of 33 Division* (1982, 172 pages).
7. *Memoir 213/4 Company* (1977, 325 pages).
8. *Memoir 215/3 Company* (1979, 596 pages).
9. *Memoir 112 Infantry Regiment* (1992, 123 pages).
10. *Memoir 143 Infantry Regiment* (1982, 765 pages).
11. *Memoir 55 Mountain Artillery Regiment* (1984, 678 pages).
12. *Memoir 55 Cavalry Regiment* (*The Last Cavalry*), (1984, 618 pages).
13. *Memoir 55 Transport Regiment* (1989, 884 pages).
14. *Evening Glow of Burma*, Memoir 55 Division Tokushima Prefecture Residents, Vols 1 & 2. (Vol. 1, 1972, 520 pages; Vol. 2, 1977. 359 pages).
15. *Ah! Burma*, (Memoir 55 Division Ehime Prefecture Residents) (1977 357 pages).
16. *Broken Army Shoes* (Memoir Ikeda Town Residents, 143 Regiment) (1990, 373 pages).
17. *Recollection of Regiments based in Wakamatsu*, (214 Regiment, *etc.*) (1967, 4 Vols).

Japanese Campaign and General Histories
1. Fujino, Hideo, *Singapore and Burma* (2/114 Bn) (1995).
2. Fujiwara, Iwaichi, *F-Kikan and the Independence of India.* (1966, 424 pages).
3. Iida, Shojiro, *Senjin Yawa, (Stories from the Battlefields).* (1990, 302 pages)
4. Ishii, Sadao, (1 MG Coy, 112R) *Fighting Spirit, Burma War Records.*
5. Izumiyama, Takuro, *Minami Kikan, Behind the Independence of Burma* (1967, 238 pages).
6. Kamijo, Akira, *General Seizo Sakurai* (1992, 386 pages)
7. Namba, Shukou, *Burning Earth* (Diary of HQ 215 Regiment from 10 Jan to 31 May 1942) (1985, 254 pages)
8. Ochi, Harumi, *Struggle in Burma* (1967, 247 pages).
9. Oyashiki, Hisao, *Boat Branch of Burma Independence Army* (1956, 64 pages).
10. Shigematsu, Sadayoshi, (112/7 Coy), *Fighting Around Burma.*
11. Sugita, Saiichi, *Burma Operation* (1942, 278 pages).

Personal Accounts by Japanese Soldiers
1. Abe, Yoshizo. (Private) *Account of the battle at the Sittang bridge.*
2. Aoyama, Seiichi. (Corporal) *Account of the advance into Rangoon.*
3. Kawamata, Koji. (L/Corporal) *Account of arrival, battle at the Bilin,*

advance to Rangoon.

4. Miura, Toshio. (Corporal) *Account of the advance into Rangoon.*

5. Mizushima, Tokutaro. (L/Corporal) *Account of the advance into Rangoon.*

6. Nakai, Buhachiro. (L/Corporal) *Account of the capture of Tavoy.*

7. Sugimoto, Eiichi. (Lieutenant) *Platoon Commander 215/5 Coy and later Adjutant to General Sakurai.*

7. Suzuki, Tadashi. (Captain) *Account of the battle at Kuzeik.*

8. Tadokoro, Toshiaki. *Account of the fighting at Pyagyi and Pegu.*

9. Tokita, Shiro. (L/Corporal) *Account of the battle at the Sittang Bridge.*

10. Yoshino, Shuichiro. (Lieutenant) *Account of water supply in the field.*

11. Yoshito, Yasuda. (Lieutenant) *Account of air fighting by the pilot of an 'Oscar'.*

BURMA 1942: THE JAPANESE INVASION

GLOSSARY OF MILITARY TERMS

AA	Anti-aircraft.
ABDACOM	The combined American-British-Dutch-Australian Command.
ADMS	Assistant Director of Medical Services, the chief doctor in a division.
ADS	Advanced Dressing Station, first stop for those badly wounded.
AHQ	Army Headquarters.
AQMG	The senior administrative staff officer in a division.
A tk	Anti-tank.
AVG	American Volunteer Group. These were American volunteers, mostly ex-USAAF pilots, flying American-built fighters for the Chinese.
Bde	Brigade.
BFF	Military police recruited from Indians and Gurkhas domiciled in Burma and organised for a defence and reconnaissance role.
BM	Brigade Major, the senior staff officer in a brigade.
BMP	Burma Military Police.
Bn	Battalion.
Burcorps	Burma Corps.
Burdiv	1st Burma Division.
Burif	The Burma Rifles.
Chaung	A river, in some areas dry for much of the year. (Nullah, Wadi).
CIGS	Chief of the Imperial General Staff (i.e. Head of the British Army).
CO	Commanding Officer of a major unit.
COS	Chiefs of Staff, the professional Chiefs of the Royal Navy, Army and RAF.
Coy	Company.
CRE	Commander, Royal Engineers
D	Abbreviation used on maps for 'Division'.
FDL	Forward Defended Locality ('front line').
FOO	Forward Observation Officer, the Gunner officer observing and controlling the fire of the guns.
GHQ	General Headquarters.
GSO1	General Staff Officer, Grade 1, the senior staff officer in a Division.
HQRE	In a division, the CRE's headquarters.
IO	Intelligence Officer.
K	Abbreviation used on maps for a Japanese Reconnaissance Regiment.
Lay-back position	A defensive position held in rear of the fighting through which the forward troops can retire for temporary relief.
L of C	Line of Communication.
LMG	Light Machine Gun (e.g. Bren).
MMG	Medium Machine Gun (e.g. Vickers).
MT	Motor Transport.
Nullah	See 'chaung'.
OC	Officer commanding a minor unit.
OCTU	Officer Cadet Training Unit.
R	Abbreviation used on maps for a Japanese Infantry Regiment.
RA	Royal Artillery.
RE	Royal Engineers.
Recce	Reconnaissance.
RHA	Royal Horse Artillery.
SDO	Sub-Divisional Officer, the officer in the Burma Civil Service in charge of a sub-division.
Staff Captain	The administrative staff officer in a brigade.
VCO	Viceroy's Commissioned Officer (see Appendix 3).

404

INDEX

The Index covers the Introduction, main text and Appendices. Page numbers in italics refer to illustrations. Numbers in brackets following place names give the maps showing them.

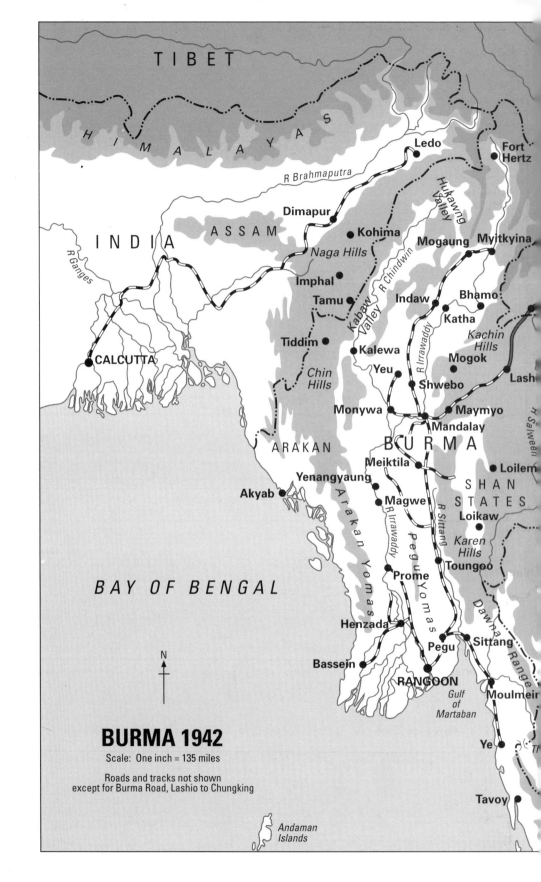

BURMA 1942

Scale: One inch = 135 miles

Roads and tracks not shown
except for Burma Road, Lashio to Chungking